# AMERICAN CHARITIES
# AND SOCIAL WORK

# AMERICAN CHARITIES AND SOCIAL WORK

BY

AMOS GRISWOLD WARNER, PH.D.
*Late Professor of Economics and Social Science in the Leland Stanford Junior University*

STUART ALFRED QUEEN, PH.D.
*Professor of Sociology in the University of Kansas*

AND

ERNEST BOULDIN HARPER, PH.D.
*Professor of Sociology in Kalamazoo College*

*Fourth Edition*

THOMAS Y. CROWELL COMPANY
PUBLISHERS :: :: :: NEW YORK

*Twenty-sixth printing*
*(First printing of the Fourth Edition)*



*Printed in the United States of America by*
J. J. LITTLE AND IVES COMPANY, NEW YORK

FIRST EDITION
1894
DEDICATED BY

AMOS G. WARNER

TO

JOHN M. GLENN

THEN CHAIRMAN OF THE EXECUTIVE COMMITTEE
OF THE CHARITY ORGANIZATION SOCIETY
OF BALTIMORE

# PREFACE TO THE FOURTH EDITION

The rising profession of social work is producing a rapidly increasing volume of "literature." Indeed, for years there have been appearing books, articles, and pamphlets dealing with human beings in trouble and the agencies for their relief. Most of these publications have been ephemeral in interest and value, but here and there one has stood out like a landmark, summing up the achievements of some period or pointing the way for new developments. Among these "philanthropic classics" may be named Juan Luis Vives' *De Subventione Pauperum,* published about 1525, the reports of the British Poor Law Commissions of 1832 and 1909, Amos G. Warner's *American Charities* which appeared in 1894, and Mary Richmond's *Social Diagnosis* of 1917. By examining these and similar documents one might get a very clear idea as to some of the important changes that have taken place in the development of social work. However, there would be many gaps to fill; the story as a whole would be quite disjointed.

An entirely different method of tracing the course of "charity," "philanthropy," "welfare work," or "social service," as it has been called at various times and places, is to examine a number of conventional histories and combine their accounts into a single narrative. In such a project one would turn to Lallemand's *Histoire de la Charité,* Uhlhorn's *Christliche Liebestätigkeit,* Ratzinger's *Kirchliche Armenpflege,* Nicholl's *History of the English Poor Law,* Breckinridge's *Public Welfare Administration in the United States,* Watson's *Charity Organization Movement in the United States,* and similar treatises. Such a review as this was attempted by Queen in *Social Work in the Light of History.*

But the historical approach does not appeal to everyone; many students and citizens want a bird's-eye view of contemporary social work without much reference to its origin and development. For their benefit a number of interesting books have been written. Among them are O'Grady's *Introduction to Social Work,* Halbert's *What Is Professional Social Work?* and Devine's *Social Work*. Each of these is a useful survey of the field of social work as it is today.

The present volume rests on a belief that the layman and the beginner in social work need both a graphic picture of the present situation and something of its background. But instead of a general historical review we shall present a detailed contrast between American social work of two different periods, the eighteen-nineties and the nineteen-twenties. During this third of a century most significant changes have taken place. The "charities" of 1893 and the "social work" of 1929 display striking differences, between which lies an interesting period of transition. In order that the changes in attitudes, interpretations, methods, and agencies may be most vivid we shall present the situation of the 'nineties in the words of Professor Warner, whose book more adequately than any other depicts the spirit and procedure of American charities in that period.

Thus, while we are in one sense "revising" *American Charities,* we are not trying to "bring it up to date"; neither are we trying to discredit it. Professor Warner did so good a piece of work in stating the assumptions and describing the machinery of social work in 1893 that his original contribution should be preserved as nearly intact as possible. To attempt to "work it over" into a description of contemporary social work or a running contrast, item by item, of the 'nineties with the present, would be to invite the twin disasters of spoiling Warner's clear picture of the earlier period and failing to give an adequate view of the later. Hence we are retaining most of Warner's original material just as he presented it. The only changes are certain omissions and consolidations which it has seemed legitimate to make in the interest of brevity. But in making these relatively unimportant changes we are preserving Warner's point of view and essential data, expressed in his own words. By adopting this plan we hope to avoid the inconsistencies which so often rise up to plague the reviser.

As a matter of general information, it should be stated that *American Charities* has already gone through three editions. The first was published in 1894; the second and third, both being revisions by Mrs. Mary Roberts Coolidge, appeared in 1908 and 1919 respectively. For reasons already given it has seemed wise in this present edition to make no use of the two revisions, in spite of their undoubted usefulness in years gone by.

The book as it now stands is divided into three parts. Part I, written by Mr. Queen, is an attempt to give the reader a perspective. Part II is Mr. Warner's description of American charities in the 'nineties. Part III, in which Mr. Harper and Mr. Queen have collaborated, is an account of American social work ten years after the War. While the entire book represents a coöperative effort, Chapters I, II, XVI, XVIII, XIX, XX, XXII, XXIII, XXV, XXXI, XXXII, and XXXIII were written by Mr. Queen; Chapters XVII, XXI, XXIV, XXVI, XXVII, XXVIII, XXIX, and XXX were written by Mr. Harper; Chapters III to XV inclusive represent about two-thirds of the first edition by Mr. Warner. Deletions can easily be identified by comparison with the original.

Acknowledgments are due many individuals and organizations whose coöperation has made the preparation of this book possible. We regret that it is impossible to present a complete list. But among those who have furnished us with information and advice or permitted the reprinting of published materials are the following— Miss Jane F. Culbert, Professor Seba Eldridge, Mr. David Holbrook, Dr. Samuel Langer, Miss Louise Odencrantz, Professor Jesse F. Steiner, Dr. Frankwood E. Williams; The Commonwealth Fund Division of Publications, Henry Holt and Company, Harper and Brothers, Alfred A. Knopf, Inc., The Macmillan Company, The New Republic, Inc., University of Chicago Press, Yale University Press; American Association of Social Workers, American Association for Organizing Family Social Work, American Hospital Association, American Red Cross, Association of Community Chests and Councils, Associated Out-Patient Clinics of the City of New York, Child Welfare League of America, Hebrew

Sheltering Guardian Society of New York, Kalamazoo Stationery Company, National Conference of Social Work, National Information Bureau, National Probation Association, National Social Work Council, New York School of Social Work, Russell Sage Foundation; *Better Times, The Family, Social Service Review,* and *The Survey*. To these and others who have contributed to the making of this book we express our hearty appreciation.

STUART ALFRED QUEEN
ERNEST BOULDIN HARPER

*January, 1930*

## CONTENTS

### PART I

*AN HISTORICAL PERSPECTIVE*



### PART II

*AMERICAN CHARITIES IN THE 'NINETIES*

## PART III

## *CONTEMPORARY SOCIAL WORK*

# PART I

# AN HISTORICAL PERSPECTIVE

# AMERICAN CHARITIES AND SOCIAL WORK

## CHAPTER I

### THE BEGINNINGS OF SOCIAL WORK

A new profession has made its appearance in the United States during the past third of a century. Social work as a specialized, skilled service, for which specific scientific and technical training is essential, has really come into being during the lifetime of persons not yet forty years old. It is, of course, not absolutely different from anything the world had seen before, nor is it without roots in the distant past. On the contrary, we shall presently note developments reaching back hundreds of years through which this new profession has come to be. Just as the automobile—new within the same period—was preceded by the wheel, the highway, and the internal combustion engine, so social work was preceded by mutual aid, pious almsgiving, public relief, and bourgeois benevolence. Both automobile and social work were new, yet both consisted largely in achievements of the past.

Because the term social work means different things to different people, it seems important at the very outset to offer a tentative definition and to distinguish between this and other terms with which it is often interchanged. Some would restrict the meaning of social work to "caring for derelicts," while others would make it include everything that promotes the public welfare. Many people make no distinction between social work, charity, philanthropy, uplift, reform, and public welfare. As we shall see in our historical review, this is perfectly natural, but it is none the less confusing to the student of contemporary social work.

The words charity, philanthropy, and benevolence represent a set of attitudes, a spirit of kindliness and generosity, which some call a virtue. They mean the offering of goods or services without expectation of the usual return. They may involve putting oneself in the place of another, seeing and feeling with him, then acting in his interests, as they are understood through this process of "sympathetic insight." But to many people charity is merely a collection of miscellaneous activities vaguely designated as "doing good"—carrying baskets to poor widows, gathering children into orphan asylums, feeding tramps in midnight missions, dispensing free medicines to the sick. Also the term charity has come to connote a measure of social distance. When we help our relatives, our friends, or our neighbors we do not call that charity. It is when we offer assistance to someone who "does not belong," at least not fully, that this word is used.

The words uplift and reform connote the existence of superior and inferior; they emphasize condescension rather than kindness, and pity rather than understanding. They mean "good deeds" as gratuities handed down, "out of the goodness of one's heart," to members of "the lower classes." They smack of smugness and self-righteousness. Reform in particular seems usually to be a matter of making other people do what we believe to be good for them. However, this latter term is also used at times to describe cooperative ventures in social reorganization.

The terms welfare work and public welfare naturally refer to anything and everything that is "good for us" collectively. But in current usage they have a much more restricted meaning. They are applied chiefly to such things as almshouses, orphan asylums, reformatories, pensions, and doles. In Massachusetts we call those officials who feed hungry men and send old ladies to the poor farm "overseers of the public welfare"! In several states we have in addition to departments of education, health, labor, public utilities, and the like, Departments of Public Welfare, as if the other departments had nothing to do with the common weal!

The term social work is itself used in two widely different senses. The first is very general and covers all sorts of civic activities, while the second refers to a rather specific vocation. One of the best statements of the first or "general" viewpoint has been made by Edward T. Devine.

Social work, then, is the sum of all the efforts made by society to "take up its own slack," to provide for individuals when its established institutions fail them, to supplement those established institutions and to modify them at those points at which they have proved to be badly adapted to social needs. It may have for its object the relief of individuals or the improvement of conditions. It may be carried on by the government or by an incorporated society or by an informal group or by an individual, or it may be a temporary excrescence on some older institution which exists primarily for some other function. It may be well done or badly. . . . It may be inspired by sympathy or expediency or fear of revolution or even of evolutionary change, or by a sense of justice and decency. It includes everything which is done by society for the benefit of those who are not in position to compete on fair terms with their fellows, from whatever motive it may be done, by whatever agency or whatever means, and with whatever result.[1]

For ourselves we have found it more helpful to use the term social work in a more restricted sense. We have called it the art of adjusting personal relationships and reorganizing social groups. Sometimes difficulties arise between husband and wife, parent and child, teacher and pupil, employer and employe, native and foreign born, black and white. Whenever such misunderstandings and conflicts occur the integrity of some social group is threatened: a family is becoming disorganized, a neighborhood is disintegrating, a community is going to pieces, a school or an industrial group is breaking up. Social work consists in the analysis of such a problem-situation, in the interpretation of it to the persons concerned, in the planning with them of an acceptable way out, and in the cooperative carrying through of such a plan. The client of the social worker may be a single person, a family, a neighborhood, a church, a trade union, a city, a state.

Now it is probable that such difficulties have always arisen among men and that there have been from time immemorial efforts to straighten them out. Our task is now to show by what stages friendly intervention has graduated into professional service. We shall attempt to trace the movement from (1) simple neighborliness in primary groups through (2) organized mutual aid, (3) assistance to detached outsiders, (4)

[1] Devine, Edw. T., *Social Work,* pp. 21-22. Copyright, 1922, by The Macmillan Company. Reprinted by permission.

repression of begging and other uses of the police power, (5) the poor law, (6) uplift and reform programs conducted by one social class in the interest (real or assumed) of another, at last to (7) a more or less skilled service available to any unadjusted person or disorganized group.

So long as people lived their whole lives in small isolated communities, social maladjustments were few and their correction was effected largely through group pressure and other collective action. With the complexity that comes from increasing numbers, things that worked themselves out "naturally" in the simpler situation had to be dealt with systematically. As means of transportation improved, more and more persons became separated from their friends and relatives; when they got into trouble special provision was required to help them out. When these outsiders took undue advantage of the assistance offered and demanded alms as a right repressive measures were instituted. When Europe became urban and industrial, instead of rural and agricultural, new social classes appeared, a bourgeoisie or middle class and a proletariat or laboring class. Out of the poverty of the latter and the surplus of the former arose some of the humanitarian movements of the nineteenth century. Finally the democratic movement and the development of the social sciences made possible a profession of social work.

**Simple Neighborliness.** An attempt has sometimes been made to account for social work by referring it directly and solely to the teachings of Jesus and practises of the early Christian Church. But it is now recognized that this explanation errs by being too simple and by ignoring social-work activities of much earlier times. The real significance of the early Church for the development of social work may be briefly described. In the beginning each Christian congregation was a small compact body of friends in the midst of a hostile community; they practised mutual aid as one of the natural functions of a primary group and also from hard necessity. When the congregation became larger and included heterogeneous elements this mutual aid had to be organized and promoted. As a stimulus to the service of needy fellow Christians the Church Fathers appealed to the ancient doctrine of the religious merit of almsgiving. For the moment, however, our concern is with the early Church as a primary group, whose members were bound together by the enthusiasm of a new-found faith and by persecution from without.

> The church thoroughly bore the character of the family, and was, even in its manner of life, only the continuation of the family-like circle by which our Lord was surrounded. In this circle community of goods had prevailed. Its members lived upon what was given not merely by those outside, but also by those within it. . . . Each contributed of that which was his own to what was necessary for the common maintenance, without thereby depriving himself of all property. Still less were any compelled to do this, or to persevere in it, by any decree of the church. The family feeling was, however, so strong, that none of them said "that aught of the things which he possessed was his own, but they had all things in common." . . .
>
> Great self-sacrifice was found in all the churches. Christians gave willingly, not merely according to their means, but beyond them. They gave not of their superfluity, but of their labour, and shunned no sacrifice. . . .
>
> Special tasks were imposed on Christian charity in times of persecution. Poverty and distress might easily become a strong temptation to apostasy. Persecution too inflicted material damage on many, their business suffered, they were entirely withdrawn from it, when they were either thrown into prison, exiled, or compelled to flee. Confiscations also took place, or the houses of Christians were plundered by the heathen populace. . . .
>
> The pestilence raged in Alexandria under the Emperor Gallienus. Eusebius has preserved a letter of Dionysius, then its bishop, in which he describes the conduct of the Christians during this visitation: "Most of our brethren, in the fulness of their brotherly love, did not spare themselves. They mutually took care of each other, and as instead of preserving themselves they attended on the sick, and willingly did them service for Christ's sake, they joyfully laid down their lives with them.[2]

This mutual helpfulness is properly described as simple neighborliness, for it was spontaneous, unorganized, and in the main restricted to members of the congregation.

The feudal estates of medieval Europe embraced similar primary groups. The inhabitants of these rural villages were more fixed and more isolated than were the early Christians, but both lived as compact social groups whose members prac-

[2] Uhlhorn, Gerhard, *Christian Charity in the Ancient Church*, pp. 73, 122, 195, 188.

ticed mutual aid after the fashion of real neighbors the world over. Most of the people on a medieval manor were blood kinsmen. Their families had lived in the same place for generations. They knew each other well and hardly knew anyone outside the village at all. They farmed their strips in the great fields, raising the same crops in the same way, pasturing their cattle and hogs on the commons, rendering the same customary services to the lord of the manor. They worshipped at the same parish church, attended the same manorial court and celebrated the same holidays. Traveling little and seeing few strangers, their lives were so bound together that they naturally shared each other's sorrows and misfortunes. It is significant that we can find no historical mention of charity within the manor, and that during the Middle Ages there was very little tithing or parochial relief. There seem to have been no committees, no collections, and no institutions of a charitable sort maintained by these little communities. When anyone suffered misfortune, he was among friends who took it for granted that he should receive their help.

The merchant and craft gilds of the Middle Ages were at the outset primary groups similar in many respects to the early Christian congregations and the villages on feudal estates. They were composed of persons engaged in the same trade; they were quite exclusive; they developed a considerable degree of self-government; they lived near together in the town; they attended the same parish church and celebrated the same holidays. Apprentices frequently lived with their masters; journeymen expected soon to become masters; all worked together in the intimate relations of the small shop. So long as these conditions lasted there was mutual aid, spontaneous and unorganized.

Similarly the pioneers of our own country shared the misfortunes of crop failure, forest fire, and hostile raid. In barn-raisings and corn-huskings their mutual aid took the form of festivals. In time of sickness, accident, or death the neighbors came in, doing whatever they could gladly and as a matter of course.

None of the instances cited involved what we today would call social work. They are examples rather of its absence.

Moreover, if we had continued to live in such small, localized, primary groups, with so few outside contacts, social work might never have appeared. It was the expansion and growing complexity of these communities or the dispersion and detachment of their members that started a chain of events out of which this new profession has developed.

**Mutual Aid Organized.** The early Church at Jerusalem affords a classic example of the type of social change which preceded and necessitated the formal organization of mutual aid. While the congregation started out "like one big family," its numbers increased rapidly and soon included members who spoke Greek as well as those whose tongue was Aramaic.

> Now in these days, when the number of the disciples was multiplying, there arose a murmuring of the Grecian Jews against the Hebrews, because their widows were neglected in the daily ministration. And the twelve called the multitude of the disciples unto them, and said, It is not fit that we should forsake the word of God and serve tables. Look ye out, therefore, brethren, from among you seven men of good report, full of the Spirit and of wisdom, whom we may appoint over this business.[3]

Other changes of a similar nature followed. The common meals of the members gave way to rather formal "love feasts," which became incidentally a means of providing for the poor. Homeless children were at first welcomed into the homes of relatives and neighbors, but before long they were referred to the bishop who was supposed to see that they were properly brought up. Visiting and ransoming of prisoners, which at first needed no urging, soon became the object of official exhortation. Hospitality to visiting brethren likewise became a burden and was gradually displaced by the establishment of institutions called *xenodochia*. Ere long these *xenodochia* were housing a miscellaneous assortment of wayfarers, lame, halt, blind, widows, orphans, aged, and sick persons. Plainly simple neighborliness no longed sufficed; it was being supplemented by organized and institutionalized care. But it should be noted that these new relief measures, like the more spontaneous helpfulness, were largely for the benefit of those who "belonged." Not often were they extended to the "heathen."

[3] Acts, 6: 1-3.

In the medieval gilds it was the raising of barriers between the various grades of workmen that occasioned the development of organized relief. Conditions of apprenticeship were made hard; journeymen were hindered from becoming masters; some of the masters set up an inner circle known as the "mystery." Hence simple neighborliness could not be counted upon to meet the needs of workmen in trouble. To deal with the new situation some gilds made contracts with hospitals or almshouses, others established institutions of their own, and some collected funds for helping needy members and their families in other ways. Thus the bakers of Strassburg made an arrangement with a hospital in their city according to which the superintendent was to receive any member of the gild who might be brought in by the proper official. This officer of the gild was to visit his sick brothers three times a week in order to supervise their conduct and see that they left the hospital as soon as they were well.[4]

In numerous ways the gilds prepared the way for municipal action. Activities at first carried on by separate organizations of merchants or artisans were gradually transferred to the city government. So the towns more and more assumed responsibility for citizens who lacked family, friends, or funds. In addition the municipalities dealt with problems which gilds acting separately could not possibly handle, such as famine, pestilence, and the influx of beggars.

Municipal charities in England, Germany, and France seem often to have begun with the provision of grain in time of famine.

> The general alms (l'aumône générale) of Romans owed its origin to a famine which occurred in the fourteenth century. Private charity having proved insufficient, leading men of the city formed a bureau to distribute relief to the needy. This relief was called "general" because of the great number of persons who shared in it. After the famine was over, the organization was continued because of its obvious advantages.[5]

All medieval towns had institutions for the care of the sick,

[4] Lallemand, Leon, *Histoire de la Charité*, vol. 3, p. 82.
[5] *Ibid.*, p. 323.

aged, infirm, and other needy persons. A good many abuses appear to have developed in their administration, whether they were in the hands of gilds, religious orders, or other groups. For this and other reasons the towns undertook first to regulate and then to administer these "hospitals." Thus we are told that at Bridport in the thirteenth century the provosts conducted a yearly investigation to see "whether the brethren and lepers were well treated." At Sandwich the mayor and jurats appointed the governors of St. Bartholomew's Hospital, audited the accounts and controlled admissions. The city of Venice in the fifteenth century established a municipal hospital. A citizen of Tournai and his wife founded the Asylum of St. John the Baptist in 1493, operating it themselves; their son was to succeed them, but after his death the management was to pass to the mayor and provost of the city.

In addition to disaster relief and institutional care there was developing in the fifteenth and sixteenth centuries more or less systematic aid to the poor in their own homes. As early as 1413 the city of Genoa appointed *officiales misericordiae* to gather and distribute alms to the indigent. French communes established relief funds which they frequently called *tables des pauvres*. As early as the fourteenth century in Southampton "forfeits and alms were awarded to the poor," and in the fifteenth century "the townys almys were settled on a plan."

About 1525 the city of Ypres developed a program which soon became famous. It appears to have been based on a book written by Juan Luis Vivès, in which these points were stressed. The public authorities were responsible for proper relief of the destitute. They should begin with a census of the needy, dividing them into three classes, (1) those sheltered in hospitals and almshouses, (2) homeless beggars, (3) the honest and shamefaced poor abiding in their own houses. The able-bodied should be put to work, begging should be forbidden, and those unable to work should be given institutional care. The city of Ypres undertook to put these principles into practise. It took a census of the poor, reformed the hospitals, forbade begging, sought to provide employment, and centralized the administration.

In the transition from simple neighborliness to organized

neighborliness several important changes occurred. Informality gave way to institutionalization; spontaneity was succeeded by planning and exhortation; the spirit of neighborliness was obscured by material relief; mutual aid was supplemented by use of the police power. But still we have primarily mutual aid among the members of local groups. In fact, the relief measures of parish, gild, and municipality were almost exclusively for the home folks.

**Assistance to Strangers.** But what happened to strangers? Throughout the Middle Ages the number of persons who wandered away from their home communities was fairly small. But there were at all times pilgrims on their way to holy shrines, traveling merchants or peddlers, knights errant, shipwrecked sailors, begging friars and ordinary mendicants. While medieval communities were not lacking in hospitality, they regarded these wayfarers for the most part with suspicion. If a man away from home fell ill, were robbed or suffered other misfortune, not only did he lack the friendly aid of kinsmen and neighbors; he could not take advantage of the institutions maintained by his gild or town, and he was usually regarded as ineligible for admission to those of the region in which he happened to be.

Hence, as the numbers of detached folk increased, there grew up a distinct set of agencies, usually under the auspices of the Church, but quite independent of the local parishes. The various monastic and hospital orders established institutions which serves as refuges for pilgrims, soldiers, peddlers, beggars, and other wayfarers. The monastery was the inn or hotel for all travelers in those days.

> Many of them (the monks) whose revenues were sufficient thereunto, made hospitals and lodgings within their own houses, wherein they kept a number of impotent persons with all necessaries for them, with persons to attend upon them, besides the great alms they gave daily at their gates to everyone that came for it. Yea, no wayfaring person could depart without a night's lodging, meat, drink, and money, it not being demanded from whence he or she came, and whither he would go.[6]

[6] Quoted from an anonymous writer of the 16th century by W. J. Ashley in *English Economic History,* Part 2, p. 315.

During the Crusades a number of hospital orders were established for the care of pilgrims and soldiers of the Cross. Typical of these was the Teutonic Order, founded about 1200 in Palestine. Its members were sworn to chastity, poverty and obedience. Their first duty was care of the sick, their second defense of the Holy Land. One of the rules of the Order specified that wherever the knights acquired land they must build a hospital.

A patient entering the hospital first confessed, then received the sacrament if the confessor advised it. Then he was put to bed. His clothes and property were taken by the hospital attendant and a mark placed upon them. The attendant also was to warn the patient that he should have care for the salvation of his soul. Possible wishes of the patient concerning disposal of his goods were so far as possible to be promptly carried out. The care was ample. The sick received the same bread the Brothers had, "the best which was baked," also mornings two dishes of milk or vegetables and at noon three dishes. If they could not eat these things the Spittler had such food and drink brought to them as he thought suitable for them. In the head House of the District there were always to be doctors. The District Commander decided whether there should be doctors in the other Houses. Sundays the Epistle and the Gospel were read to the sick and they were sprinkled with holy water. In the head House of the District this was accompanied by a procession, but not in the smaller ones.

Besides the care of the sick, these Hospitallers of the Teutonic Order, like all others of the Middle Ages, had general missions. They received the shelterless and impotent poor, gave alms freely to the poor of the district, sought out deserted, orphaned, and "exposed" children for care and rearing, and gave lodging to strangers and travelers. An account from Coblenz in 1318 says: "They dedicate themselves with pious zeal to the care and needs of the poor and sick, they feed the hungry, give water to the thirsty, they receive travelers with hospitality, clothe the naked, visit the sick, show sympathy and pity with their suffering, and send tokens of love to their burials." [7]

As indicated above, the monasteries and hospitals not only provided institutional care; they also distributed food and other alms from the gate. Prelates and nobles had "dealing days," and there were general distributions in connection with

[7] From an unpublished manuscript by Anna T. Gilchrist.

funerals and anniversaries. Some of these furnished food to hundreds of people, usually without any discrimination among the applicants. Frequently the only thing required of the beneficiaries was that "they pray God for me and for my said company."

While these institutions and these doles might also serve the needy of the immediate vicinity, their principal function was the care of strangers. Thus they differed from the agencies developed within the community for the benefit of its own people. Control was usually vested in some power outside the locality—e.g., in the head of a religious or hospital order—and the beneficiaries were dealt with as individuals rather than as members of a local group.

The basis on which this development took place was the doctrine of the religious merit of almsgiving. Countless statements of this teaching may be found in the writings of the Church Fathers. One example must suffice. Cyprian, Bishop of Carthage, wrote about the middle of the third century:

> An illustrious and divine thing, dearest brethren, is the saving labour of charity; a great comfort of believers; a wholesome guard of our security, a protection of hope, a safe-guard of faith, a remedy for sin, a thing placed in the power of the doer, a thing both great and easy, a crown of peace without the risk of persecution; the true and greatest gift of God, needful for the weak, glorious for the strong, assisted by which the Christian accomplishes spiritual grace, deserves well of Christ the Judge, accounts God his debtor.[8]

For the most part emphasis was laid on the virtue of giving; little attention was paid to the specific needs of the recipients and even less to the results of indiscriminate almsgiving. As a consequence idleness and begging were encouraged; at times gangs of vagrants went up and down the countryside demanding food and shelter and frightening "quiet folk." Eventually stern measures were adopted throughout Western Europe in the effort to repress mendicity.

**The Police Power.** Apparently all peoples have found it necessary to deprive individuals of liberty, property, or even life in order to achieve certain purposes deemed valuable by

[8] Quoted by Lilian Brandt in *How Much Shall I Give?* p. 85.

the group as a whole. Besides punishing criminals some communities isolate persons afflicted with communicable diseases. It is said that 19,000 lazar-houses were constructed for the lepers of Europe in the twelfth century. Even villages set aside places for these unfortunates, and required them to stay apart from healthy persons.

> After separation the fate of the outcast is irrevocably sealed. Remembering the exhortation, he must never frequent places of public resort, nor eat and drink within the sound of any; he must not speak to them unless they are on the windward side, nor may he touch infants or young folk. Henceforth his signal is the clapper, by which he gives warning of his approach and draws attention to his request. . . . Compelled to leave home and friends, many a leper thus haunted the highway—his only shelter a dilapidated hovel, his meager fare the scraps put into his dish.[9]

But the police power is related to social work chiefly through its application to the group of problems associated with vagrancy. In the fourteenth century, as in more recent times, this word denoted not only loafers, beggars, and petty thieves, but also unpropertied wage-earners whose conduct was displeasing to the ruling class. Hence it was not merely a desire to check mendicancy and indiscriminate almsgiving that produced the repressive measures of that period. It was also an effort to keep laborers in the state of servitude from which they were just emerging with the breakdown of feudalism. This is quite apparent in the famous Statute of Laborers passed shortly after the Black Death in England (1349).

> It begins by stating, that, "Because a great part of the people, and especially workmen and servants, late died of the pestilence, many, seeing the necessity of masters and great scarcity of servants, will not serve unless they may receive excessive wages, and some rather willing to beg in idleness than by labour to get their living"; and it then goes on to direct "that every man and woman, of whatsoever condition, free or bond, able in body, and within the age of threescore years, not living in merchandise, nor exercising any craft, nor having of his own whereof he may live, nor proper land about whose tillage he may himself occupy, and not serving any other, shall be bound to serve him which him shall require, and take only the wages, livery, meed, or salary

[9] Clay, Rotha Mary, *Medieval Hospitals of England*, p. 40.

which were accustomed to be given in the places where he oweth to serve. . . ."

. . . It is, among other things, enacted, "That, because many valiant beggars, as long as they may live of begging, do refuse to labour, giving themselves to idleness and vice, and sometimes to theft and other abomination, none, upon pain of imprisonment, shall, under colour of pity or alms, give anything to such which may labour, or presume to favour them in their sloth, so that thereby they may be compelled to labour for their necessary living." [10]

This was followed by a series of enactments of varying degrees of severity, but apparently with uniform failure to accomplish their expressed purpose. Laborers were ordered to stay in their home communities. Able-bodied persons were forbidden to beg. "Beggars impotent to serve" were attached to the place of their residence or birth, where they sometimes received licenses to ask for alms. Gypsies were deported. The penalties imposed included whipping, cutting off the ears, branding, compulsory labor amounting almost to slavery, and even death. But in England, as on the Continent, abundant evidence attests the failure of these repressive measures. The preamble of an Act of 1530 recites that,

In all places throughout this realm, vagabonds and beggars have of long time increased, and daily do increase in great and excessive numbers, by the occasion of idleness, mother and root of all vices, whereby hath insurged and sprung, and daily insurgeth and springeth, continual thefts, murders and other heinous offences and great enormities, to the high displeasure of God, the unquietation and damage of the king's people, and to the marvellous disturbance of the common weal.[11]

**The Poor Law.** By the beginning of the sixteenth century it was felt by many persons that the repressive legislation, the ecclesiastical charities and the other existing machinery for dealing with social problems were inadequate and ineffective. However, it was not primarily a rational consideration of these facts which produced the English Poor Law. It was rather the combination of a strong central government

[10] Nicholls, Sir Geo., *History of the English Poor Law,* vol. 1, pp. 36-37.
[11] *Ibid.,* vol. 1, p. 115.

and the Protestant Revolt with a more or less personal quarrel between Henry VIII and the Catholic Church. Of course there were other factors, too. Growth of the domestic system of industry, enclosures of farm land, dismissal and escape of retainers, and increasing mobility of the population were creating a difficult situation which was made very acute by the dissolution of the monasteries. The steps taken during the sixteenth century to meet this situation have been summarized by Sir George Nicholls.

> First the poor were restricted from begging, except within certain specified limits. Next the several towns, parishes, and hamlets were required to support their poor by charitable alms, so that none of necessity might be compelled "to go openly in begging," and collections were to be made for them on Sundays, and the parson was to stir up the people to be bountiful in giving. Then houses and materials for setting the poor on work were to be provided by the charitable devotion of good people, and the minister was every Sunday to exhort the parishioners to contribute liberally. Next the collectors for the poor, on a certain Sunday after divine service, were to set down in writing what each householder was willing to give weekly for the ensuing year; and if any should be obstinate and refuse to give, the minister was gently to exhort him, and, if he still refused, then to report him to the bishop, who was to send for and again gently exhort him; and if still refractory, the bishop was to certify the same to the justices in sessions, and bind him over to appear there, when the justices were once more gently to move and persuade him; and if he would not be persuaded, they were then to assess him in such a sum as they should think reasonable.[12]

In 1601 was passed the great Elizabethan poor law which required each parish to impose a definite tax for furnishing employment to the able-bodied, apprenticing children and maintaining the "impotent poor" in almshouses. This law also established the liability of relatives to support their needy kinsmen and threatened with jail or house of correction those who refused to work or failed to pay their poor rates.

After a time it appeared that poor people were crowding into parishes where relief was plentiful and easily secured. Hence the Settlement Act of Charles II restricted relief to those who

[12] *Ibid.*, vol. 1, pp. 197-8.

had a legal residence in the parish where help was asked. This legal residence or "settlement" was acquired by birth, apprenticeship or ownership of property. Persons who seemed likely to become a burden upon a parish to which they had recently come could be forcibly ejected any time within forty days.

Still the cost of administering the poor law continued to mount; so in 1723 provision was made for the establishment of workhouses and it was ordered "that no poor who refused to be lodged and kept in such houses should be entitled to ask for parochial relief." This became famous as the "workhouse test."

In the late eighteenth century there grew up what was known as the "allowance system." The workhouse test was abolished; only the aged and infirm, unmarried mothers and young children were sent to the poorhouse; the able-bodied poor were supposed to be given employment and their wages supplemented, if necessary, from the poor rates. These wage subsidies were carelessly administered and hence the law was taken advantage of by both employers and employes. However, those who hold the allowance system alone responsible for the quadrupling in thirty-five years of the bill for poor relief evidently forget that this was the period of the Industrial Revolution and the Napoleonic Wars.

In 1832 a special commission was appointed to make a study of the poor laws; two years later it reported to Parliament and important new legislation was enacted. In the Report of 1834 three principles were stressed—less eligibility, workhouse test, and national uniformity. Less eligibility meant that "the condition of paupers shall in no case be so eligible as the condition of persons of the lowest class subsisting on the fruits of their own industry." With the workhouse test we are already familiar; it meant the re-establishing of deterrent conditions. By national uniformity was intended the creation of precise rules of procedure which should be followed without deviation throughout the country, "removing from the distributors all discretionary powers, and thereby diminishing abusive administration." The new law followed in the main the recommendations of the commission, establishing a central authority with power to regulate the work of local officials in minute detail, enlarging the units of administration, providing unpaid boards of guardians and paid executives to carry on the actual work.

In 1905 another Royal Commission was appointed, whose conclusions were very different from those of 1834. However, the members of this second commission were unable to agree on many points; and, consequently, they presented two separate reports. The majority held the boards of guardians to be delinquent in the performance of their duties, and recommended numerous changes in administrative detail. The minority found fault with the whole system; they recommended the repeal of all the poor laws, providing instead specialized services—health, education, employment, and others—under distinct authorities. Furthermore they would make these services available to members of all social and economic classes. During the nineteenth century it had come to pass that persons of small means were handled by the poor law officials regardless of whether they were sick or well, feebleminded or superior, out of work or employed, homeless or living with their families. On the other hand, people with money looked to the education authority for schooling, to the health authority for hospital care and to still another office for care of the mentally defective. Obviously the two programs were in conflict. The minority report proposed also to abandon all three of the "principles of 1834," substituting for minimum relief (less eligibility) adequate relief and curative treatment, for deterrence (workhouse test) universal provision (e.g., schooling, health, and other services for all on the same terms), for a fixed routine (national uniformity) discretionary powers and individualization. The 1834 report urged in effect that the government do as little as possible for persons in need of special help. The 1909 minority report urged that the government do a great deal more than ever before for all the people. The issues raised by the British Commission of 1905-09 deserve special study, because they are the problems on whose solution depend the next steps in social work under public auspices.

On the whole the American poor laws have followed the English legislation and practise down to about a hundred years ago. Most of our states still cling to the settlement law, the liability of relatives, local autonomy and the principle of less eligibility. However, there has been since the Civil War a gradual increase of centralization and of curative treatment.

**Middle-Class Humanitarianism.** It must not be supposed that when a new type of social work or allied activity developed the older types ceased to exist. On the contrary, all of them tend to continue indefinitely. We have today neighborliness both simple and organized, ecclesiastical charities, repressive measures and public poor relief. But about a hundred years ago there appeared numerous private, non-sectarian agencies, sponsored by one social class and serving another. The explanation of this new development lies in certain aspects of the Industrial Revolution.

Toward the end of the eighteenth century in England a number of circumstances combined to produce the factory system of large-scale production through the use of power machinery. To man the factories it was necessary to bring together large numbers of workmen into towns and cities. This in turn was made possible by improved agriculture and transportation. In the factories division of labor made it possible to use children as well as adults with a limited amount of training. This system, with its massing of many employes in a single establishment, destroyed the personal relations of the gild and the family cooperation of the domestic workshop. Crowded houses and long hours of work away from home interfered further with family life. But most significant for the development of social work was the realignment of social classes.

Previously the great bulk of the people in England and Western Europe were agricultural tenants; by the end of the nineteenth century a large percentage were industrial wage-earners. Previously the ruling classes were the nobility and the clergy; after the Industrial Revolution control passed gradually to the manufacturers, merchants and bankers. Moreover, an intense conflict arose between the proletariat or laboring class and the bourgeoisie or middle class (middle in the sense of standing between the old nobility and the "common people").

In the course of their rise to power the middle class adopted the economic and political philosophy of *laissez faire*. They were anxious to be rid of old customary and legal restrictions on manufacturing, so they urged "less government in business and more business in government." Gradually the control of industry and ownership of the new wealth were concentrated in their hands. They came to dominate the political machinery and then aspired to a place in "society." In all these realms "welfare work" was a device for gaining recognition and power. Employers wanted to "keep the workers contented." Business men sought political preferment through conspicuous philanthropies. Their wives loved the sense of importance derived from having poor families "under their wing" and the publicity gained through sponsoring charity balls. Some of them found a thrill in the adventure of "slumming." Some were genuinely sympathetic with the unfortunate members of the working class. They hoped somehow to bridge the gap between social classes and to offset some of the hard things in the capitalistic system. But in general they guarded against "mixing philanthropy and business."

Among the forms which this middle-class humanitarianism took were employers' welfare work, housing betterment, prison reform, child-saving, charity organization and social settlements.

The nature of these uplift and reform movements appears rather clearly in the commonly accepted definition of employers' welfare work—"Anything for the comfort and improvement, intellectual or social, of the employees, over and above wages paid, which is not a necessity of the industry nor required by law." [13] In other words, this was neither a matter of business nor of justice; it was essentially a gratuity. The facilities and activities generally listed under this head include company houses, rest rooms, playgrounds, nurseries, schools, churches, hospitals, visiting nurses, pensions, group insurance, and other enterprises. That they are often used to exploit as well as to help working people is notorious.

In the course of their rapid growth modern cities have split up into areas occupied by people on different economic levels.

[13] *U. S. Bur. Lab. Stat.*, Bul. No. 250, p. 8.

When they went "slumming" it was quite natural that middle-class folk should first be impressed with the external aspect of streets and houses. Being "horrified" by the dilapidation, accumulation of filth, lack of sanitary facilities and overcrowding, they felt that they must "do something about it." So they organized limited dividend companies ("charity at five per-cent") to build "model tenements." They bought old tenement houses that they might improve both the buildings and their occupants through friendly visitors who served as rent collectors. Sometimes, seeing the limitations of such piecemeal measures, they brought about restrictive legislation. In Europe, but not in America except during the late War, they accepted the necessity of state or municipal housing.

Until about a hundred years ago prisons were places for detaining a miscellaneous lot of human beings, pending a decision as to whether they should be deported, whipped, executed or otherwise punished. Here the uplifter was almost overwhelmed with visions of filth, vice and utter wretchedness. But first the Quakers and then others started societies for "relieving distressed prisoners," through which they offered personal comforts and religious services. From these activities they went on to wrestle with the problems of prison construction and administration. Still other societies had as their purpose the removal of children from jails to "houses of refuge."

Writers of the nineteenth century often linked together prison reform and child saving. The reason apparently lay in a belief that to check "the rising tide of crime" it would be necessary to rescue the children of the poor from their sordid surroundings. So it is not surprising that a book devoted to the history of the New York Children's Aid Society should be called "The Dangerous Classes of New York and Twenty Years' Work Among Them." Of course, it is always easy to make an appeal for needy children; but in the nineteenth century there was a veritable epidemic of orphan asylums, home-finding societies, humane societies, societies for prevention of cruelty to children, and many others. Behind this group of agencies there was a curious mixture of motives, sentimental, religious and economic. These are interestingly set forth in a circular issued in 1853.

As Christian men, we cannot look upon this great multitude of unhappy, deserted, and degraded boys and girls without feeling our responsibility to God for them. The class increases: immigration is pouring in its multitudes of poor foreigners who leave these young outcasts everywhere in our midst. These boys and girls, it should be remembered, will soon form the great lower class of our city. They will influence elections; they may shape the policy of the city; they will assuredly, if unreclaimed, poison society all around them. They will help to form the great multitude of robbers, thieves, and vagrants, who are now such a burden upon the law-respecting community.[14]

Another expression of bourgeois benevolence, as Carlton Hayes has called it, was the host of petty relief societies bearing such titles as Society for Increasing the Comforts of the Poor, Mendicancy Society, Visiting and Relief Association, Society for the Prevention of Pauperism, Association for Improving the Condition of the Poor. Besides "overlapping and overlooking" they were accused of numerous other faults.

There were in many cities voluntary general relief societies professedly ready to undertake any sort of humane task within their ability. In some instances they laid claim to most approved maxims of work, such as raising the dependent poor into independence, the need of investigation as a basis of relief, the duty of repressing imposture. Rarely they employed the Friendly Visitor, and made employment the basis of relief. But, as they were invariably the distributors of material aid, this function submerged all others, and they sank into the sea of common almsgiving, appealing to their patrons for support on the ground that the money given to them would enable them to enlarge the number of their beneficiaries or increase the amount of their gifts, and attracting the needy to their doors with the hope of loaves and fishes.[15]

To overcome these difficulties there grew up in England and America Charity Organization Societies which sought to correlate the work of the many agencies in every city, to abolish public outdoor relief, and to mediate between the client and possible sources of help. Their methods included investigation, friendly visiting, registration, various "provident schemes" and cooperation with the police to stamp out begging.

[14] Quoted in Report on History of Child-Saving, National Conference of Charities and Correction, 1893, p. 3.

[15] Kellogg, Chas. D., in *Nat. Conf. Char. & Cor.*, 1893, p. 52-53.

Another important phase of the humanitarian movement was the rise of social settlements starting in the 'eighties. A German student has defined a settlement as follows:

> A settlement is a colony of members of the upper classes, formed in a poor neighbourhood, with the double purpose of getting to know the local conditions of life from personal observation, and of helping where help is needed. The settler gives up the comfort of a West End home, and becomes a friend of the poor. . . . The settler comes to the poor as man to man, in the conviction that it means a misfortune for all parties and a danger for the nation, if the different classes live in complete isolation of thought and environment. He comes to bridge the gulf between the classes.[16]

Settlement workers have insisted that they represented "a philosophy and not a technique," that they were being good neighbors rather than carrying on specific activities. Nevertheless, they have maintained many and varied "activities," including kindergartens, day nurseries, night schools for adults, social clubs, athletics, pageants and entertainments. They have conducted some important studies of their own districts and of larger social problems. They have sought to promote a revival of neighborhood life, making their houses the headquarters of communal activities.

Whatever motives may have guided any or all of these middle-class ventures in philanthropy, they have given us a wider knowledge of social problems and have contributed not a little to the development of techniques for dealing with them.

In the next chapter some of the influences helping to make social work a profession will be indicated, as we contrast the situation in the 'nineties with that in the 'twenties.

[16] Picht, Werner, *Toynbee Hall and the English Settlements,* p. 1.

# CHAPTER II

## SOCIAL WORK FROM 1893 TO 1928

**Changing Approaches.** By the 'nineties middle-class humanitarianism was at its height. But soon after that uplift and reform began to slip into the background, making way gradually for professional services available to an ever-widening clientele on a basis more in harmony with the spirit of democracy. The differences both in theory and in practise are akin to those over which the English Commission of 1905-09 fought. In the 'nineties American charities consisted of a variety of activities carried on by the charitably-minded members of the well-to-do class on behalf of the unfortunate members of the "lower classes." It was assumed that an "instinct of sympathy had prompted to kindly acts," wherein benevolent individuals made generous contributions to philanthropic organizations, and "charity agents" either without remuneration or for a paltry sum devoted their lives to alleviating the distress of the destitute. There was some concern lest there be an undue "sacrifice of capable people to the incapable," offset, however, by the assurance that "kindness is its own reward." So college students studied "economic aspects of altruism," while cultivating a "humanitarian interest" in convicts, insane, feebleminded, drunkards and "analogously degenerate classes."

In contrast with the humanitarian approach to social work in the 'nineties, we find more and more a professional approach in the 'twenties. By professional is meant skilled service in place of or in addition to good intentions and sympathy; making knowledge and skill available to persons who wish to use them rather than setting out to reform people regardless of their wishes in the matter; sporting interest in a difficult task rather than smug satisfaction with "doing good"; and expectation of reasonable compensation rather than a spirit of self-sacrifice. No one has stated this newer attitude more clearly than Miriam Van Waters.

> The social worker is not concerned primarily with reform, or with betterment of human beings. That is a confused and belittling definition of social work which has done much to bring about smugness in social workers and suspicion in the public generally. The human race could not bear the burden of an entire group, who unauthorized by divine sanction, conceived it their sole task to mold human lives into models designed by reformers. Social work is the task of those who aid mankind in the art of living together. Social work is neither a science seeking merely to know, nor a business seeking to profit. Social work is an art, a flowing and dynamic art. It uses tools of science and business to bring about adjustments which are necessary between the individual and his human world for successful living together. Its method of work is development of personality. Its goal is the fostering of adequate social relationships.[1]

The philanthropists of the 'nineties assumed an ideal state of society which "ought" to be brought about, and measured the needs of their beneficiaries by their deviation from the "normal." The social workers of the 'twenties approach their clients and their communities somewhat after this fashion: "What is the trouble here? How did all this come about? What would you like to do about it? But, don't you see that if you do so-and-so you will have to take the consequences, which are such-and-such? Is that what you really want, or would you rather have this? If this is it, here is the way to go about getting it. Do you want us to help you start?" See how inappropriate for this are such labels as charity, uplift, reform. Some of the older generation, sensing the changes that are taking place, yet failing to appreciate their significance, lament the "loss of idealism" among the younger workers. But while the quiet, objective social worker of today may not be so spectacular as the enthusiastic reformer of a generation ago, there is good reason to believe that he is doing a much more effective job.

**Changes in Specific Fields of Work.** The significance of these shifting approaches to social problems may be realized best through an examination of the changes taking place in certain specific fields of effort.

[1] Van Waters, Miriam, *Youth in Conflict*, p. 1.

Employers' welfare work formerly consisted, as we saw in the preceding chapter, of gratuities of employers to their employes in the form of health, education, recreation, insurance, pensions or personal guidance. Today many of these activities are being continued, but on a different basis. Some are still administered by the employer, but as "good business" rather than as charity. Some are being taken over by the employes organized for self-help. Still others are being prescribed by law. The State itself is establishing bureaus of vocational guidance, employment exchanges and insurance funds. The old employers' welfare work was in the nature of a bounty; the new social work in industry represents skilled service, regardless of the auspices under which it may be performed.

Prison reform represented the friendly intervention of philanthropic citizens to secure the improvement of sanitary conditions in penal institutions, better food for prisoners and more humane treatment generally. Social work with delinquents involves the study of each offender to discover the kind of a person he is and how he came to break the law. In many cases it includes his removal from the community for a time, in others the modification of his conduct through changed relationships within the community. More and more this work is being carried on by trained institutional workers, probation and parole officers on the public payroll. The old struggle between "sentimental reformers" and "hard-boiled" officials is gradually giving way to intelligent cooperation between citizens and public servants.

In the 'nineties charitable folk were interested in the "saving" of "juvenile paupers and criminals." Today these terms have disappeared from use; we hear instead much about "child welfare," meaning the well-rounded development of *all* children. To promote physical development we have "well baby stations" and school nurses. To foster recreation and wholesome use of leisure-time we have supervised playgrounds, summer camps, Boy Scouts and Campfire Girls. To make formal education more profitable we have child-study departments, special schools, "socialized" curricula and visiting teachers. To stabilize the emotional life and assist in various types of adjustments we have child guidance and habit clinics. Not all these efforts would be classified as social work in the limited sense; perhaps we would include therein only the work of playground and recreation directors, visiting teachers, and case workers attached to clinics, courts and other agencies. But the important thing is that in all three fields of work for children—education, health and social work—there has developed skilled service for practically all the children of the community.

Out of the field known in the 'nineties as charity organization have come two new developments, family welfare societies and councils of social agencies. The charity organization societies undertook the difficult task of correlating relief-giving and friendly visiting to "poor" families. The family welfare societies of today deal "with the social needs of individuals as parts of family groups, and the adjustment of their relation to these groups and to society." The function of correlation in any community is performed largely through a council to which the various social agencies belong. But perhaps the most important development in this field has been the gradual formulation of an "educationally communicable technique," known as social case work, which has been defined as "those processes which develop personality through adjustments consciously effected, individual by individual, between men and their social environment." [2] Of course, social workers from other fields have aided in the development of this technique. As the possibilities of the case-work approach have been grasped by workers with children, old people, unemployed, sick, mentally defective, delinquents, and others, each group has made its own contribution. But the principal credit belongs without doubt to people connected with family welfare societies.

In the 'nineties the social settlements were just getting started in the United States. Indeed, in 1893 the settlement workers had no place on the program of the National Conference of Charities and Correction. But gradually they came into their own and gained recognition, not only for their particular agencies, but also for the neighborhood as a significant grouping of people in urban areas. Then about the time of the Great War there sprang up a still wider interest in the promotion of neighborhood and community organization. In place of social

[2] Richmond, Mary, *What Is Social Case Work?* pp. 98-99.

settlements in "slum" districts this movement has come to emphasize more and more the self-organization of natural groupings of people. It has given us neighborhood improvement associations, social centers in schools, community churches and community clubs. A slowly increasing number of these organizations is making use of trained and salaried workers, but the majority still depend largely on "volunteer" service.

In these five representative fields we discern a tendency toward a more democratic spirit, both diversification and integration of activities, and especially the development of techniques which can be passed on systematically to the younger generation.

**The Changing Scope of Social Work.** But not only have there been changes within existing fields of work; new lines of effort have appeared, and the range of activities has widened greatly. One means of contrasting the scope of American charities in the 'nineties and social work in the 'twenties is to study the proceedings of the National Conference of Social Work (National Conference of Charities and Correction until 1917). As a sample of the first period we have selected the Proceedings of 1893, because that was the twentieth anniversary of the Conference and it was the year in which the first edition of this book was being written. To represent the second period we shall use the Proceedings of 1928, the latest available at this writing. Side by side we place the major items from the 1893 program and the divisions of the Conference in 1928.

The changed names of the Conference and of its Divisions indicate both a changed attitude and an enlarged scope. Only one title—Immigration—is substantially the same in the two lists. However, the content of Division IX in 1928 is fairly comparable to that of items 1 and 3 in 1893. The scope of Division II in 1928 is somewhat wider than that of items 6 and 7 in 1893, with more emphasis on causes of delinquency and less on problems of administration. A similar, though even greater, difference obtains between Division VII of 1928 and items 8 and 9 of 1893. The problems dealt with under the head of Charity Organization in 1893 were considered in Divisions IV and VIII in 1928, but in both the horizon had widened markedly. Between the two meetings Child-Saving had grown

| NATIONAL CONFERENCE OF CHARITIES AND CORRECTION 1893 | NATIONAL CONFERENCE OF SOCIAL WORK 1928 |
|---|---|
| 1. State Boards of Charities | I. Children |
| 2. Charity Organization | II. Delinquents and Correction |
| 3. Indoor and Outdoor Relief | III. Health |
| 4. Immigration | IV. The Family |
| 5. Child-Saving | V. Industrial and Economic Problems |
| 6. Reformatories | VI. Neighborhood and Community Life |
| 7. The Prison Question | VII. Mental Hygiene |
| 8. The Feebleminded | VIII. Organization of Social Forces |
| 9. The Insane | IX. Public Officials and Administration |
| | X. The Immigrant |
| | XI. Professional Standards and Education |
| | XII. Educational Publicity |

into a concern for the welfare of all children. Also in the intervening period the settlements had gained recognition and then merged into the broader concept of Neighborhood and Community Life. In creating Division V on Industrial and Economic Problems the Conference had demonstrated its desire to get down below the details of social work to the underlying causes of social maladjustment. The same spirit has grown apace throughout the organization. The newest divisions of the Conference are those on Professional Standards and Education and on Educational Publicity. The former is perhaps least like anything one might find in the papers of 1893.

Since 1893 many new types of social work have come into being. One of these is hospital social service which supplements medical treatment by "dealing with the patient's personality, and altering or adjusting his home conditions, occupation, habits and community relations." Another is psychiatric social work which deals with cases of social maladjustment in which a mental factor or a behavior problem is of primary importance. A third is carried on by visiting teachers who seek to correlate the efforts of teachers, parents and various agencies in untangling the personal difficulties of school children. A fourth type new since the 'nineties is vocational guidance "designed to help the individual to choose, to plan his preparation for, to enter upon, and to make progress in an occupation." A fifth, the playground and recreation movement, had really started in the 'eighties but it did not develop much until the opening of the new century. It has been concerned with directing leisure-time activities in the interests of self-expression and participation in group life. A sixth, community organization, involves the promotion of various specific programs, but its real function consists in adjusting difficulties between groups living in a local area so that they may work effectively together in the pursuit of common aims. Many other new phases of social work represent in part new functions and in part new machinery for the accomplishment of old purposes. Among these are juvenile courts, child guidance clinics, mothers' pension bureaus, courts of domestic relations, old age pensions, rehabilitation bureaus, industrial accident boards, community chests and councils.

The evidence considered so far indicates that social work of 1928 is a vastly larger field than American charities of 1893. Unquestionably we have a growing variety of activities carried on by an increasing number of workers in the service of an expanding clientele. But when the agencies and programs of both periods are tested by our definition of social work—the readjustment of personal relations and the reorganization of social groups—we see the need of a restatement of the situation. Social work as such has clearly undergone significant growth, but whether the charities of today are more or less extensive than those of the 'nineties is hard to say. In terms of actual volume and cost of work they have probably increased. But relatively—compared, that is, with professional services paid for by individuals and groups benefited—they appear to have decreased. Unfortunately we do not have reliable data from the earlier period nor adequate figures for the present.

**Changing Definitions of Problems.** In 1893 little distinction was made between social maladjustments, poverty, physical disease, and mental aberrations. The philanthropist of the 'nineties was interested in the miscellaneous array of "evils" that beset mankind and in the equally miscellaneous array of programs that promised relief from them. The social worker of the 'twenties regards all these as of vital importance and having social as well as individual significance. But he is coming to make certain distinctions which did not occur to his predecessor. Thus, while recognizing still the intimate relations between all phases of life, he distinguishes rather sharply between a physical disease and the disturbance of personal relationships which may accompany it. Control of the former he regards as a task for the medical profession; the latter he considers a function of social work.

In the 'nineties the feebleminded were considered proper objects of charity partly because they were "degenerate," but especially because often they did not earn their own living and had to be supported by others. Today we realize that many of the feebleminded are rather well adjusted socially and require neither economic assistance nor social service. When they do need the attention of a social worker it is not because they are mentally defective as such, and they may not be an immediate financial burden; it is primarily because they are not getting on well with other people. They may annoy in petty ways, they may be quarrelsome, they may absorb an excessive amount of other persons' time, they may destroy the morale of a group at school or work, they may be slovenly housekeepers or restless wanderers, they may be rearing a family of incompetents.

In discussing another problem the author of the 'nineties wrote, "It is only when non-employment results in destitution that its treatment is germane to our present purposes." But even if the unemployed man does not have to apply for material relief, we in the 'twenties are concerned about the possible damage to his morale, the strain and friction that may develop within his family, lost contact with industry, and identification with "the army of the unemployed."

Students and workers of the 'nineties stated their problems largely in the language of political economy, using such terms as paupers, indigents, dependents, causes of poverty, relief of destitution, and the like. Charities were defined as meaning "all those institutions and agencies which give direct material aid to the poor as such." Students and workers of the 'twenties are stating their problems more and more in the language of psychiatry and sociology, using such terms as personality, social relations, attitudes, maladjustment and disorganization. Social work is defined as meaning those processes whereby adjustments are deliberately effected between men and their social environment through direct personal influence, reorganization of groups or manipulation of the physical environment.

Philanthropists of the 'nineties thought largely in terms of a pauper class, a submerged tenth. Social workers of the 'twenties are interested in people on all economic levels whose social relations present difficulties to themselves or to those with whom they associate.

Charity workers of the 'nineties were still talking about the "worthy" and "upright" poor whom they contrasted with "willing paupers" and "voluntary dependents" on the ground that their destitution was caused by "misfortune" rather than by "character defects." They were like the lawyers who still impute "free will" and "responsibility" to some, while defending others as "unfortunate" and "irresponsible." Social workers of today are by no means consistent in this matter, though they tend to regard all conduct and all human relations as "natural processes" subject to causal interpretation and ultimately to control. Whereas the workers of the 'nineties were assessing moral values and passing judgment on their applicants, the workers of the 'twenties are simply seeking to understand their clients. The reactions of the former were more highly charged with emotion; they were more frequently shocked or disgusted. But if there has been a decline of "righteous indignation" and "moral enthusiasm," it does not necessarily imply callousness or indifference. It means rather an increase of flexibility and objectivity in line with the scientific spirit.

**Changing Interpretations of Causes.** Obviously if there is to be a successful treatment or effective prevention of anything, there must first be a search for causes. This has long been realized, but more often in the past than in the present the search has not been very persistent; it has frequently ended in guessing rather than verification. When students and workers undertook to classify causes under the captions of "misfortune" and "misconduct," they were not only guessing; fundamentally they were giving expression to their own feelings about the matter. Much of the "interpretation" of popular grievances, as well as of poverty, crime and disease, is little more than the rationalization of emotional reactions. Whether the general public has changed much in this respect during the last third of a century is hard to tell. But there is no doubt that social workers have gone far toward substituting intellectual analysis for emotional response.

Likewise the very concept of causation has undergone change. It is true that outstanding students of social problems even in the 'nineties recognized that causation is multiple rather than simple, and showed considerable skill in analyzing the complex of influences which converge upon the life of the individual. (See, e.g., Chapter IV.) But many, perhaps the majority, of "charity workers" were content to select some one striking feature of a situation and refer to it as *the* cause. While a few were attempting to classify causes as "chief" and "tributary," "exciting" and "predisposing," a larger number were making tables which purported to show that certain numbers or percentages of "cases" were due to specified, single causes. Not only that; they worked these ratios out to the hundredth of a per cent, thus presenting the appearance of accuracy which could not possibly be achieved. Very often the categories, with reference to which these meticulous mathematical calculations were made, represented subjective opinions or feelings of the workers rather than objectively measurable traits or conditions. The social worker of the 'twenties is much less likely than his predecessor of the 'nineties to say that specific percentages of his clients are in difficulty because of laziness, shiftlessness, immorality, intemperance or roving disposition.

Students and workers of the 'nineties used a simple statistical method in their search for causes of poverty, but they usually failed to compare data concerning "the poor" with similar data concerning persons on other economic levels. Since they made little use of control groups, their conclusions are of less value than they would otherwise have been. Moreover, the belief has been growing in recent years that in addition to enumeration, classification and correlation, there must be a description of processes before the interpretation of causation is adequate. The statistical methods alone leave us with a static conception, while the identification of processes makes the thing dynamic. The student of the 'twenties does not regard the two techniques as in conflict, but as complementary.

In Part II of this book are set down the results of the best studies made in this field down to 1893. To appreciate the advance in the social sciences since that time, let the reader contrast these results and the methods employed with those presented in *Suicide* by Mrs. Cavan, or *Family Disorganization* by Mowrer, or *The Gang* by Thrasher. In these later books he will find not only statistical analyses, but also case studies, examination of cultural settings and "ecological" studies. That is to say, contemporary students of social problems examine a mass of data, some of which seem incapable—for the present, at least—of statistical manipulation, and which present the issues in the form of processes instead of fixed conditions.

To elaborate further, the social worker of the 'twenties is not content to enumerate a few facts about a client or a city, such as place of birth, occupation, income, sickness, crime, and the like. He tries to get as complete a picture as possible of the situation before him and the process of which it is a cross-section. It is not enough to determine the proportion of foreigners among his clients; he wants to know how the cultures of these foreigners differ from his own and what particular difficulties confront persons who move from one social milieu to another. As a result he is likely to interpret juvenile delinquency among Italian youth in Chicago, let us say, not in terms of their Italian ancestry, but in terms of a process involving the conflicts, the accommodations and gradually the assimilation of two culture groups. Likewise, if he should find more drinking or more prostitution among persons of small incomes—which is very likely not to be the case—he would not hasten to attribute the poverty to the alcoholism or the alcoholism to the poverty. Instead, he would seek to discover how both these facts might be related to occupation, regularity of employment, educational opportunities, health, place of residence, cultural backgrounds, neighborhood life, and similar factors. All this he would treat statistically, so far as possible, and also descriptively. He would be on the lookout for typical combinations of factors recurring regularly in certain time or space relations. He would seek especially for typical sequences or processes.

In many discussions of the 'nineties we find confusion of biological and social heredity. That is, when a social worker found alcoholism or begging or stealing or prostitution appearing frequently in each of several generations of a given family, he was likely to infer that these traits were transmitted through the germ plasm. Apparently it did not occur to him that the recurrence of these types of behavior might be accounted for in terms of parental influence, neighborhood mores, lack of primary group controls, segregation of despised groups, or other social factors which would be likely to affect successive generations. This does not mean that social workers of the 'nineties ignored environmental influences or that social workers of the 'twenties are "pure" environmentalists. It simply means that the latter have learned to distinguish between physical and mental traits that may be transmitted through the germ plasm, and habits that may reappear as responses to similar situations or be "taught" as part of the group code.

The classic example of this confusion of social and biological inheritance is the comparison of the "Jukes" and the Edwards families. The former case was supposed to demonstrate the biological inheritance of pauperism, harlotry and crime or at least of "occult characteristics tending to inefficiency or absolute pauperism"; while the latter case was considered proof of the biological transmission of prosperity, success and good citizenship. The student of the 'twenties remembers, however, that the Edwards family was an economically prosperous group with a tradition of "culture" and education; while the "Jukes" family was an isolated and poverty-stricken group without education but with a tradition of lawlessness. He is still waiting for evidence to show him definitely that an exchange of environments would or would not have made a difference in the relative status of the two families.

In order not to overrate the difference between the thinking of the two periods, we must realize that many teachers still exploit the old Jukes-Edwards fallacy and that some contemporary social workers believe in the inheritance of shiftlessness by various racial, national, and other groups. Also it is well to recall the fact that the following was written in 1893: "The sons of the influential classes grow up under conditions which favor their education and advancement, while the children of the pauper, born in the poorhouse or the slums, are foredoomed by the conditions under which they grow up to pauperism." Also, "we cannot conclude that certain families are degenerate and essentially unfit to survive until we have given their offspring the very best opportunities for right development." [3]

**Professional Standards and Education.** Practically all the changes we have discussed in this chapter are related to the rise of professional standards and education for social work. The charity workers of the 'nineties included (a) persons in various professions, such as law and medicine, who offered their services free of charge, (b) kind-hearted, leisure-time folk who had no special skill, (c) paid workers who were genuinely interested in their work and had a background of training in economics, (d) paid workers who had no claim to a position except their own need of employment. None of these types has disappeared. But in addition to them we have in the 'twenties (a) college trained persons with a background of social and biological science, who learn the art of social work through an apprenticeship, and (b) persons who add to a general cultural and scientific education specific training in a school of social work.

Before 1898 there was no professional school in this field; in 1928 there were about forty in the United States and Canada, of which twenty-five belonged to a national association. Ten of these were strictly graduate schools. Most of them offered more or less technical courses in case work—including its various specialties—recreation, industrial work, research, and administration. They provided opportunities for practise work with cooperating agencies.

By 1921 this movement had gone far enough to make possible a professional organization, the American Association of Social Workers. In spite of relatively high membership requirements, this organization included in 1928 over 4,000 persons

[3] *American Charities,* first edition, pp. 87, 122.

who had at least part of a college course plus training and experience in "recognized" agencies. With *esprit de corps* and higher standards of work as major objectives, the Association is engaged in job analysis, and studies of personnel practices, professional ethics, recruiting and training of new workers.

One of the most significant evidences of change in this whole field is the growing interest and participation in research. The Federal Children's Bureau has made many studies of specially needy children and facilities for helping them. The Russell Sage Foundation has delved painstakingly into delinquency, unemployment, homelessness, recreation, family life and the techniques of social work. The National Federation of Settlements recently made an interesting study of prohibition. The Joint Committee on Methods of Preventing Delinquency has conducted a number of demonstrations of visiting teaching work and child guidance clinics from which are coming very significant results. Some of the local councils of social agencies, like the welfare Council of New York City, have established bureaus of research. Increasingly, however, social research is being carried on cooperatively by social agencies and academic departments or professional schools. One of the outstanding cases of such joint effort is the Local Community Research Committee in Chicago. This converging of social work and social science upon a common interest in research was signalized by the creation in 1927 by the American Sociological Society of a section on Sociology and Social Work.

Just what forces have produced the changes of the last thirty-five years is hard to tell. But, whatever the reasons may be, social workers of today are rapidly losing their resemblance to the kind-hearted uplifters of the nineteenth century. Instead, they are showing themselves more and more to be skilled workers with a "sporting" interest in their profession. Young men and women seem to be choosing this vocation on much the same basis as they might select law or medicine or teaching or engineering as a life work. They regard it as an interesting game which challenges them to give the best that is in them; they expect from it the recognition that comes from satisfactory performance of any important task; they hope to find in it security of tenure and adequate remuneration.

# PART II

# AMERICAN CHARITIES IN THE 'NINETIES

# CHAPTER III

## POVERTY AND ITS CAUSES

**Methods of Studying Poverty.** Three tolerably distinct methods have been employed by those students of the social sciences who have sought to ascertain the causes of poverty. First, there are those deductive or philosophical thinkers, who, from the well-known facts of social organization, have sought to deduce the causes tending to poverty, as a systematic writer on pathology seeks to set forth the inherent characteristics of the bodily organism which tend to make disease likely or inevitable. Secondly, there are those who study the classes not yet pauperized, to determine by induction what forces are tending to crowd individuals downward across the pauper line, as the health officer of a city might undertake, by an examination of the drainage system, or an analysis of the water or food supply, to ascertain the causes of disease in a given locality. Thirdly, there are those who make an inductive study of concrete masses of pauperism, usually separating the mass into its individual units, seeking to ascertain in a large number of particular cases what causes have operated to bring about destitution. This work resembles that of the practising physician, endeavoring to ascertain the causes of sickness by a careful diagnosis of the cases under his care.

Examples of the philosophical or deductive method are found in the writings of men like Malthus, or Karl Marx, or Henry George, who, while they describe actual conditions at great length, still make the philosophical reasoning which is the heart of their work antecedent to their facts. Their facts are given by way of illustration rather than of proof. Writers of this class are prone to think that they can find some single underlying cause of all the misery and destitution that exist. The three names just mentioned recall three explanations of poverty, each alleged to be universal, and the three mutually exclusive. Malthus was too wise a man to put forth his principle of population as an all-sufficient explanation of distress; but his followers have not been so wise. It has been a fundamental thought in the writings of many economists that poverty exists mainly, if not entirely, because population tends to increase faster than food supply. All other causes are held to contribute to this, or to be derived from this. The pressure of population against the means of subsistence is held to guarantee that there shall always be a vast number of persons who can just manage to live miserably. A rise of wages will promote early marriages and rapid increase among laborers, until population is again checked by over-crowding and consequent misery and death. So wise a man as John Stuart Mill allowed his economic philosophy to be overshadowed by this idea.

Mr. Henry George, as is well known, ridicules the Malthusian explanation of poverty, and offers an all-sufficient explanation of his own, which is, substantially, that poverty exists, on the one hand, because the landlord receives in rent so large a share of the annual product; on the other, because private property in land encourages the withholding of natural resources from use, the owners waiting to obtain an unearned increment. The owner of land receiving wealth without labor to an increasing extent with the development of society, there must be an increasing number of those who labor but receive little or nothing.

Opposed to both these explanations of the existence of poverty, is that of the socialists, who follow for the most part Karl Marx's analysis of capitalistic production. Reduced to a sentence by Dr. Aveling, this explanation of poverty may be stated by saying that labor is "paid for, but not paid." The consumer pays enough for the product to remunerate the laborer, but the capitalist retains all except what will barely suffice to keep the laborer alive.

No one who has studied carefully modern industrial society can doubt, I think, that each one of these explanations explains much; that each one of these causes is efficient in producing a very considerable amount of destitution. But neither can it be doubted that no one of them, nor all three of them together, can be taken as an all-sufficient explanation of the existence of poverty.

The second class of investigators, those who study inductively the operation of poverty-begetting causes among the relatively well-to-do, are more numerous at the present time than ever before. The best example of such work is probably that of Mr. Charles Booth in his "Labour and Life of the People." Almost all the reports of our labor statisticians, the works on occupational mortality and morbidity, and in fact everything of a descriptive nature that has been written about modern industrial society, can be used in this second method of seeking for the causes of poverty. We shall find that many causes can be studied best, and some only, by this method.

The third method of seeking for causes of poverty, that of case-counting, or the inductive study of concrete masses of poverty and pauperism, is the one with which we are specially concerned in this chapter. It is the one most likely to suggest itself to a student who is brought in contact with relief work, and many have expected from it much greater and more definite results than it is likely to yield. Its limitations suggest themselves, if we reflect on the analogy of the physician standing by the sick-bed, and trying to learn the cause of disease from an examination of the patient only. He may learn the immediate or exciting cause or causes of sickness; but back of these are the remoter causes, which can only be learned by other methods of investigation. This will become clear if we glance at the analysis on the following page of the causes of poverty. It is not intended to be complete, but only to give in general outline a map of the field upon which we are to enter.

**Statistical Summary of Case-Counting.** A statistical analysis of a concrete mass of poverty or pauperism will probably give more light concerning the subjective causes of poverty than the objective causes. In dealing with individuals, their character is apt to be more studied than their environment. Even when environment is the primary cause of poverty, the immediate cause or coordinate result, is often deterioration of character. Sickness is more obvious than bad sanitation; laziness than a malarial atmosphere; inefficiency than a defective

ANALYSIS OF THE CAUSES OF POVERTY.

**SUBJECTIVE.**

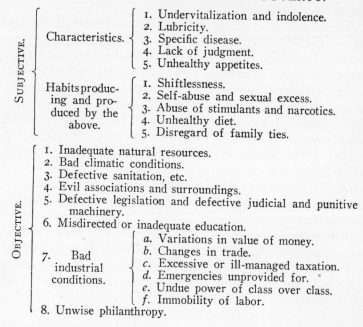

- Characteristics.
  - 1. Undervitalization and indolence.
  - 2. Lubricity.
  - 3. Specific disease.
  - 4. Lack of judgment.
  - 5. Unhealthy appetites.
- Habits producing and produced by the above.
  - 1. Shiftlessness.
  - 2. Self-abuse and sexual excess.
  - 3. Abuse of stimulants and narcotics.
  - 4. Unhealthy diet.
  - 5. Disregard of family ties.

**OBJECTIVE.**

- 1. Inadequate natural resources.
- 2. Bad climatic conditions.
- 3. Defective sanitation, etc.
- 4. Evil associations and surroundings.
- 5. Defective legislation and defective judicial and punitive machinery.
- 6. Misdirected or inadequate education.
- 7. Bad industrial conditions.
  - *a.* Variations in value of money.
  - *b.* Changes in trade.
  - *c.* Excessive or ill-managed taxation.
  - *d.* Emergencies unprovided for.
  - *e.* Undue power of class over class.
  - *f.* Immobility of labor.
- 8. Unwise philanthropy.

educational system. The one who attempts the analysis of cases is apt to be confused by the fact that under the operation of exactly similar general causes, some families are destitute and some are not. One man is able to secure an adequate income under the most adverse circumstances—bad climate, bad housing, bad taxing, no opportunities for education, etc. Another man, under exactly the same conditions, will become destitute, and the observer puts down as the final and determining cause something in the physique or character of the latter person. The ministers and charity agents who come most immediately in contact with the poor are very prone to take short-sighted views of the causes of poverty. On the other hand, as we have seen, those who study the question from a philosophical standpoint are apt to lay too much stress on the influence of institutions or environment. The questions of character are very far from insignificant; and until it is possible to trace character to its source more fully than anyone can pretend to do at present, we shall have need to study character as a cause of the failure of the individual.

The results to be obtained from an investigation conducted on the case-counting principle will manifestly vary much according to the particular class of destitute persons investigated. To count the cases of those who simply apply for relief will give different results from an investigation of the inmates of an almshouse. To study a group of distinctly pauper families having close interrelations will give different results from an inquiry about all the poor in a given locality. To study in a locality where all the deaf and dumb, the blind, the feeble-minded, and the insane have previously been taken to institutions, will, of course, give different results from those in a locality where these classes are still mingled with the population. If the cases be those of persons who have merely applied for relief, the first thing to be ascertained is how many of these applicants really ought to have material relief of any sort. The following table gives the returns in 27,961 cases of applicants for relief who were investigated by the Charity Organization Societies in 1887.

TABLE I.

| | |
|---|---|
| Worthy of continuous relief | 2,888, or 10.3 per cent. |
| Worthy of temporary relief | 7,451, or 26.6 per cent. |
| Need work rather than relief | 11,280, or 40.4 per cent. |
| Unworthy of relief | 6,342, or 22.7 per cent. |

It will be noticed that more than 22 per cent of the applicants were held to be "unworthy" [1] of relief. Commenting upon this table, Mr. Kellogg, who submitted the report containing it to the Conference, says that among all the societies of the country "there is a notable unity of opinion that only from thirty-one to thirty-seven per cent, or, say one-third, of the cases actually treated, were in need of that material assistance for which no offices of friendly counsel or restraint could compensate. The logical application of this generalization to the whole country is that two-thirds of its real or simulated destitution could be wiped out by a more perfect adjustment of the supply and

[1] The term "unworthy" was subsequently dropped, as it did not express what was meant. It carried an implication of ill desert, which was not intended, and which was frequently misleading.

demand for labor, and a more vigorous and enlightened police administration." An exacter view of the same thing may be obtained if we consider the statistics of some of the better organized charity organization societies in the large cities only, and especially the tables for recent years, when a fuller classification is used. For this purpose are given the returns from Baltimore, Boston, and New York, presenting percentages as well as absolute numbers.

TABLE II.

DECISIONS IN THE CASES OF 8,294 APPLICANTS FOR RELIEF BALTIMORE,[2] BOSTON AND NEW YORK, 1891-92.

| *Should Have* | *Number* | *Per Cent* |
|---|---|---|
| Continuous relief | 333 | 4.01 |
| Intermittent relief | 228 | 2.75 |
| Temporary relief | 1,710 | 20.63 |
| Work rather than relief | 2,915 | 35.06 |
| Indoor relief | 950 | 11.57 |
| Transportation | 305 | 3.68 |
| Visitation and advice only | 616 | 7.42 |
| Discipline | 482 | 5.81 |
| No relief | 755 | 9.10 |
| Total | 8,294 | |

The Charity Organization Societies of the United States, represented in the National Conference of Charities and Corrections held in Buffalo in 1888, agreed upon a schedule of causes of poverty to be used by all the societies. It was further agreed to give in these tables only the chief cause of destitution, and not the tributary causes. The schedule as drawn was based partly upon one already elaborated by the Buffalo Society, which that society had used in tabulating the results reached by an investigation of 6,197 cases that had come under its care during the ten years 1878-87. The table of the Buffalo Society is reproduced on the next page.

The question most commonly in the minds of those who undertake to investigate the causes of poverty by a system of case-counting is this: Is poverty a misfortune or a fault? No full answer to the question can probably be worked out by scientific methods, but the question is so frequently asked that

[2] Baltimore figures are for 1892-93.

TABLE III.

CAUSES OF POVERTY IN BUFFALO, 1878-87.

| | *Number* | *Per Cent* |
|---|---|---|
| Lack of employment | 1,873 | 30.2 |
| Sickness | 1,268 | 20.5 |
| Accident | 208 | 3.4 |
| Insanity of bread-winner | 51 | .8 |
| Insufficient earnings | 451 | 7.3 |
| No male support | 397 | 6.4 |
| Imprisonment of bread-winner | 108 | 1.7 |
| Intemperance | 700 | 11.3 |
| Shiftlessness | 440 | 7.1 |
| Physical defects | 525 | 8.4 |
| No cause | 176 | 2.9 |
| Total number of cases | 6,197 | 100 |

it seems worth while to ascertain what light a case-counting investigation of poverty can throw upon it. With this end in view, I have arranged a table giving a comparison of the results reached by German investigators, by Mr. Charles Booth, and by the American Charity Organization Societies, grouping the specified causes of poverty under three main heads: first, those indicating misconduct; second, those indicating misfortune; and third, those not classified, or unknown. (See Table IV.)

The first duty of one presenting such a table as this is to indicate clearly what it does not show. It deals, as already indicated, only with the exciting causes of poverty; and yet this fact is not kept clearly in mind, even by careful workers. Mr. Booth, for instance, includes "pauper association and heredity" in this list of causes; and the American societies include "nature and location of abode." Both of these are by their nature predisposing causes, rather than immediate or exciting causes; and it is confusing to mix the two. Secondly, many of the persons whose cases are here tabulated have been, as Mr. Booth says, the football of all the causes in the list. Under such circumstances to pick out one cause, and call it the most important, is a purely arbitrary proceeding. Any one of the causes might have been inadequate to produce pauperism had not others cooperated with it. A man is drunk and breaks his leg; is the cause "accident" or "drink"? When this question was submitted to a group of charity organization workers, it was very promptly answered by two of them; but their answers were different. A man has been shiftless all his life, and is now old; is the cause of poverty shiftlessness or old age? A man is out of work because he is lazy and inefficient. One has to know him quite well before they can be sure that laziness is the cause. Perhaps there is hardly a case in the whole seven thousand where destitution has resulted from a single cause.

The writer was so thoroughly convinced of this that, at the Conference of Charities at Buffalo, when the first of the cause schedules was adopted, he tried to have the societies directed to consider the influences resulting in destitution in each case as making up ten units, and indicate the relative force of each cause by a proportionate number of units. This would serve to show the grouping of the causes. The chief cause could be indicated in each case, and also the contributory causes. The system was rejected as too complicated; and after the writer tried to have the agents of a single society, that of Baltimore, use it in making their reports to the central office, he concluded that possibly the objection was valid. Yet if the requisite amount of skill and care were used, it would give valuable results.

The impossibility of giving an accurate statistical description of the facts is still clearer when we try to separate the causes indicating misconduct from those indicating misfortune. Back of disease may be either misconduct or misfortune. The imprisonment of the bread-winner indicates misconduct on his part, but may only indicate misfortune on the part of wife and children. The same is true in the case of abandoned children and neglect by relatives. This particular classification is made in deference to popular inquiry only. In the writer's opinion its chief value consists in showing how little it is worth.

But after all possible allowance has been made for the "personal equation" of the investigator, and for all the inevitable inconclusiveness of the figures, there is a residuum of information to be got from the tables. They give, as well as such statistics can, the conclusions reached by those who are studying pauperism at first hand. If the figures furnished by all the investigators were added together in one great total, and this only were put before him, the author would indeed hesitate to base any conclusions whatever upon it. But when it is found that different investigators, at different times, in different places, reach conclusions which, while varying in many and often inexplicable ways, are yet in agreement as regards certain important facts, we can but think that the figures to some extent reflect actual conditions. It will be noticed that these tables are not totalized, and that for many cities the figures for different years are not combined. They were left separate in order that their consistency might be tested by comparison.

So far as these tables show, the most constant cause of poverty everywhere, at all times, and according to all investigators, is "sickness." In both American and English experience, the percentage attributable to this cause sinks but once slightly below 15, and never quite reaches 30. The average is between 20 and 25. This is one of the most significant facts brought out by these tables. It was not one which the author anticipated when the collection of statistics began; and yet it has been confirmed and re-confirmed in so many ways, that the conclusion seems inevitable that the figures set forth real and important facts. Personal acquaintance with the destitute classes has further convinced him that most of the causes of poverty result from or result in a weakened physical and mental constitution, often merging into actual disease.[3]

Nearly all of the causes named might furthermore be grouped under the general heading "incapacity." Six of them avowedly belong there. The six which we have tabulated as indicating misconduct can be so classed if we are willing to include under the term infirmities of character as well as of body. The causes which indicate lack of normal support may also be said to show that the dependents are personally incapable of self-support, and that, through fault or misfortune on the part of their natural guardians, they have been left to themselves. The four causes grouped as "matters of employment" would seem at first to be of a different nature, and to indicate that capable persons may suffer from enforced idle-

[3] How this confirms conclusions previously reached by Dugdale will be noted later on.

ness to the extent of becoming paupers. There are, of course, such instances; but, as already noted, those who have undertaken the work of finding employment for the unemployed, and who are intimately acquainted with the people about whom information is given in these tables, know that most of those out of employment are not capable in any complete sense of the term. They may be able-bodied, but they are not able-minded. They may lack one thing or another, but they almost always lack something; it may be skill, or strength, or judgment, or reliability, or even temper. For the faithful and efficient there is work in all ordinary times. Often the incapacity seems to consist in nothing more than a lack of ingenuity, which prevents the person from fitting himself into the industries of the time. Give him a set task requiring little skill, and he will do it gladly. But such set tasks are very few in modern industry, and the result is that the individual is unemployed.

The English and German figures made a part of Table IV are not readily comparable with the American statistics, and yet there are enough points of similarity to make some comparison useful. The essential differences can for the most part be accounted for by the difference in the type of pauperism studied. The great majority of the German and all of the English cases are those of inmates of institutions. The cases at Stepney are examples of chronic pauperism to a greater extent than any group in the American Charity Organization Society tables. At St. Pancras the pauperism is still more definitely fixed and hopeless. The German figures are the only ones covering all the official relief work of a large number of cities. The writer knows so little of the methods of German relieving officers that it is perhaps dangerous to venture an opinion; but we might explain the very high percentage attributable to sickness, and the very low percentage attributable to drink, on the assumption that they are strict in their methods of granting relief, and disinclined to relieve those who because of drunkenness deserve punishment.

The American figures that can be most profitably compared with the German and English tables are those collected by the New York State Board of Charities, embodying the result of an investigation regarding the inmates of all the almshouses of that State in 1874 and 1875. The number of almshouse inmates was 12,614, embracing at that time a considerable number of children, lunatics, and others since removed to special institutions. The length of time that a large number of persons had been inmates of the almshouses made an inquiry into the remote causes of dependency impracticable. The table of immediate or existing causes is as follows:[4]

TABLE V.

EXISTING CAUSES OF DEPENDENCE, N. Y. ALMSHOUSE INMATES.

| | *Number* | *Per Cent* |
|---|---|---|
| Shiftlessness and inefficiency | 767 | 6.1 |
| Imprisonment of bread-winner | 74 | .6 |
| Orphans and abandoned children | 1,956 | 15.5 |
| No male support | 278 | 2.2 |
| Sickness | 1,580 | 12.5 |
| Physical defect | 589 | 4.7 |
| Insanity | 5,289 | 41.9 |
| Old age | 2,081 | 16.5 |
| Total | 12,614 | 100 |

Two facts are brought out prominently by the general character of this table; one is the tendency of statistics based on case-counting to degenerate into mere description of the personal characteristics or condition of dependents, and the other is the tendency of drink as a cause of pauperism to disappear when we study chiefly chronic cases of long standing. In this table of "existing causes" it is not mentioned at all, its results only being registered.

By the courtesy of the General Secretaries of the Charity Organization Societies of Baltimore, New Haven, and New York, and of the Associated Charities of Boston, original schedules regarding somewhat more than eight thousand cases of destitution investigated by these societies were furnished for the present work. With the separate cases at hand, it was possible to recombine the facts so as to get much information not obtainable from the published reports.

As the first question popularly asked regarding the causes of poverty would probably be whether poverty indicates mis-

[4] Tenth Annual Report State Board of Charities, New York, p. 109.

conduct or misfortune, so the second would probably be: What are the indications as to the tendency of different nationalities or races to become poor?

For the purpose of finding what answer could be obtained to this question, Table VI was prepared, giving the facts regarding 7,225 American cases. They are classified horizontally according to the causes of poverty, the causes being grouped as in Table IV, and vertically according to nationality.

A classification in Table VII of 4,176 Boston and New York cases according to the number of persons in a family, and by nationality, confirms the indication of Table IV, that large families are a relatively unimportant cause of destitution.

Unmarried persons with no one dependent upon them are not included in this table. The "families" of only one person are either widows or widowers. The largest single family is ✓ found among the colored people; but the largest proportion of relatively large families, say those numbering from five to nine persons each, is found among the Italians and the Poles ✓ and Russians. The families of paupers or semi-paupers usually average smaller than those of the population as a whole, partly because the number among classes degenerate enough to be dependent is not as large as is ordinarily supposed, partly because of a high infant mortality, and partly because the families of these classes tend to disintegrate rapidly, children drifting away from parents, and aged parents in their turn being shaken off by adult children. The "family," therefore, which applies for relief is often only the fragment of a family.

Table VIII gives classifications of applicants for relief by marital condition and nationality.

Of those applying to the charity organization societies, about half are married people living together, and about one-half the remainder, or one-quarter of the whole, are widows. Deserted wives make up about 7 per cent of the total. The difference in the work of different societies is the principal thing reflected by the fact that "single men" make up 20 per cent of the applicants in New York, or over 13 per cent in New Haven, while in other places this category is relatively unimportant. The classification of nationality does not seem to yield many results that are at once important and reliable. The

# TABLE VII

**Boston and New York.**

| Number in Family. | American. | | Colored. | | English. | | French. | | German. | | Italian. | | Irish. | | Polish and Russian. | | Scandinavian. | | Other Countries. | | Total. | |
|---|---|---|---|---|---|---|---|---|---|---|---|---|---|---|---|---|---|---|---|---|---|---|
| | No. | % | No. | % | No. | % | No. | % | No. | % | No. | % | No. | % | No. | % | No. | % | No. | % | No. | % |
| 1 | 202 | 14.81 | 31 | 16.14 | 87 | 17.54 | 8 | 10.38 | 45 | 12.06 | 8 | 7.33 | 203 | 15.77 | 6 | 4.68 | 4 | 18.18 | 16 | 12.40 | 610 | 14.60 |
| 2 | 285 | 20.90 | 52 | 27.08 | 95 | 19.15 | 17 | 22.07 | 65 | 17.42 | 12 | 11.00 | 247 | 19.19 | 11 | 8.59 | 3 | 13.63 | 19 | 14.72 | 806 | 19.30 |
| 3 | 240 | 17.61 | 44 | 22.91 | 87 | 17.54 | 18 | 23.36 | 66 | 17.69 | 15 | 13.76 | 233 | 18.10 | 25 | 19.53 | 6 | 27.26 | 28 | 21.70 | 762 | 18.24 |
| 4 | 243 | 17.82 | 26 | 13.54 | 93 | 18.75 | 14 | 18.18 | 57 | 15.28 | 20 | 18.34 | 199 | 15.46 | 16 | 12.50 | 5 | 22.72 | 23 | 17.82 | 696 | 16.66 |
| 5 | 158 | 11.59 | 15 | 7.81 | 64 | 12.90 | 10 | 13.00 | 65 | 17.42 | 21 | 19.26 | 165 | 12.82 | 23 | 17.96 | 3 | 13.63 | 18 | 13.95 | 542 | 12.97 |
| 6 | 108 | 7.90 | 15 | 7.81 | 30 | 6.06 | 2 | 2.59 | 31 | 8.31 | 11 | 10.09 | 103 | 8.00 | 12 | 9.37 | ... | ... | 13 | 10.07 | 325 | 7.78 |
| 7 | 77 | 5.64 | 6 | 3.12 | 19 | 3.83 | 6 | 7.78 | 20 | 5.36 | 17 | 15.59 | 73 | 5.67 | 14 | 10.93 | 1 | 4.54 | 8 | 6.20 | 241 | 5.77 |
| 8 | 33 | 2.34 | 1 | .52 | 12 | 2.45 | 1 | 1.29 | 9 | 2.41 | 3 | 2.75 | 39 | 3.03 | 13 | 10.15 | ... | ... | 3 | 2.32 | 114 | 2.72 |
| 9 | 11 | .80 | 1 | .52 | 3 | .60 | 1 | 1.29 | 7 | 1.87 | 2 | 1.83 | 18 | 1.39 | 4 | 3.12 | ... | ... | 1 | .77 | 48 | 1.14 |
| 10 | 5 | .46 | ... | ... | 3 | .60 | ... | ... | 3 | .80 | ... | ... | 6 | .46 | 3 | 2.34 | ... | ... | ... | ... | 20 | .47 |
| 11 | 1 | .08 | ... | ... | ... | ... | ... | ... | 3 | .80 | ... | ... | 1 | .07 | 1 | .78 | ... | ... | ... | ... | 6 | .14 |
| 12 | ... | ... | ... | ... | 3 | .60 | ... | ... | 2 | .53 | ... | ... | ... | ... | ... | ... | ... | ... | ... | ... | 5 | .11 |
| 13 | ... | ... | 1 | .52 | ... | ... | ... | ... | ... | ... | ... | ... | ... | ... | ... | ... | ... | ... | ... | ... | 1 | .02 |
| Total | 1,363 | | 192 | | 496 | | 77 | | 373 | | 109 | | 1,287 | | 128 | | 22 | | 129 | | 4,176 | |

proportion of "deserted wives" among the colored people might have been expected to exceed the average under that head more than it does. As a rule, the white Americans exceed the average more under this heading than the colored. The average of all nationalities and all cities is 6.91 per cent, which may be considered large by those unacquainted with the modern urban population, but it is lower than many of the charity organization workers expected to find it.

Table IX shows for the four cities the percentage of native white, colored, and foreign born among the population as a whole, and among those who applied to the charity organization societies in these cities. It will be noted that the proportion of applicants who are foreign born is considerably larger than of the population as a whole.

A matter which is not brought out by the tables thus far given, but which is well shown by the collateral investigations of the different agencies, is the large number of children either dragged into pauperism by the destitution of their parents or entirely abandoned by the latter. In the investigations of almshouse pauperism, of course, this is not brought out, as the children have been put in other institutions, and are beyond the view of the investigator. But in the American experience, where the cases are studied as they cross this pauper line, the large number of children is striking. Out of 4,310 persons dealt with by the New York C. O. S. in 1891, over 40 (40.8) per cent, or 1,762, were under 14. In Boston, out of 3,972 individuals dealt with, over 42 (42.5) per cent were under 14 years of age. In Buffalo, out of 2,515 individuals, over 48 (48.3) per cent were under 14 years of age. In Baltimore the percentage of those under 14 years of age drops to a little less than 16 (15.8); but, on the whole, it may be concluded that, while the leading cause of confirmed pauperism, as investigated by Mr. Booth in England, is the weakness of old age, the leading cause of incipient pauperism, as investigated by the American Charity Organization Societies, is the weakness of childhood.

Taking this in connection with the large percentage of pauperism which is constantly and everywhere attributed to sickness and physical defect, and we have a striking confirmation

TABLE IX.

| Locality | Native White: Population Number | Per Cent | Applicants Number | Per Cent of Total | Colored: Population Number | Per Cent | Applicants Number | Per Cent of Total |
|---|---|---|---|---|---|---|---|---|
| New York | 851,757 | 56.21 | 1,053 | 37.12 | 23,601 | 1.55 | 57 | 2.00 |
| Boston | 282,180 | 62.91 | 727 | 30.40 | 8,125 | 1.81 | 164 | 6.85 |
| Baltimore | 298,332 | 68.55 | 1,072 | 47.64 | 67,104 | 15.45 | 348 | 15.46 |
| New Haven | 55,871 | 68.70 | 105 | 19.05 | 2,433 | 3.00 | 45 | 8.16 |
| Total | 1,488,140 | | 2,957 | 36.83 | 101,263 | | 613 | 7.63 |

| Locality | Foreign: Population Number | Per Cent | Applicants Number | Per Cent of Total | Total: Population Number | Applicants Number | Per Cent of Population |
|---|---|---|---|---|---|---|---|
| New York | 639,943 | 42.23 | 1,726 | 60.86 | 1,515,301 | 2,836 | .18 |
| Boston | 158,172 | 35.25 | 1,500 | 62.73 | 448,477 | 2,391 | .53 |
| Baltimore | 69,003 | 15.86 | 830 | 36.88 | 434,439 | 2,250 | .51 |
| New Haven | 22,994 | 27.05 | 401 | 72.77 | 81,298 | 551 | .67 |
| | 890,112 | | 4,458 | 55.53 | 2,479,515 | 8,028 | .32 |

## TABLE VIII

| | American. | | German. | | Colored. | | Irish. | | English. | | French. | | Polish and Russian. | | Italian. | | Spanish. | | Scandinavian. | | Other Countries. | | Total. | |
|---|---|---|---|---|---|---|---|---|---|---|---|---|---|---|---|---|---|---|---|---|---|---|---|---|
| | No. | % | No. | % | No. | % | No. | % | No. | % | No. | % | No. | % | No. | % | No. | % | No. | % | No. | % | No. | % |
| Married . . . . | 1379 | 46.63 | 570 | 58.40 | 271 | 44.20 | 902 | 44.00 | 318 | 45.82 | 74 | 55.65 | 110 | 62.50 | 71 | 60.68 | 19 | 46.34 | 9 | 24.32 | 100 | 42.75 | 3823 | 47.62 |
| Widows . . . . | 654 | 22.11 | 176 | 18.03 | 187 | 30.50 | 610 | 29.75 | 153 | 22.04 | 29 | 21.80 | 17 | 9.65 | 26 | 22.22 | 12 | 29.26 | 3 | 8.10 | 36 | 15.38 | 1903 | 23.70 |
| Deserted Wives . | 207 | 7.00 | 54 | 5.53 | 52 | 8.48 | 123 | 6.00 | 54 | 7.78 | 9 | 6.76 | 27 | 15.34 | 7 | 5.98 | 3 | 7.31 | 5 | 13.51 | 14 | 5.98 | 555 | 6.91 |
| Single Women. . | 186 | 6.29 | 22 | 2.25 | 48 | 7.83 | 133 | 6.48 | 32 | 4.61 | 5 | 3.75 | 1 | .56 | 2 | 1.70 | 5 | 12.19 | . . | . . . | 12 | 5.12 | 446 | 5.55 |
| Deserted husbands and Widowers . | 145 | 4.90 | 50 | 5.12 | 24 | 3.91 | 98 | 4.78 | 33 | 4.75 | 6 | 4.51 | 4 | 2.27 | 5 | 4.27 | . . | . . . | 7 | 18.91 | 12 | 5.12 | 384 | 4.78 |
| Single men . . . | 353 | 11.93 | 99 | 10.15 | 31 | 5.05 | 170 | 8.29 | 93 | 13.40 | 10 | 7.51 | 16 | 9.09 | 6 | 5.12 | 2 | 4.87 | 12 | 32.45 | 59 | 25.21 | 851 | 10.60 |
| Orphans . . . . | 15 | .50 | . . | . . . | . . | . . . | 5 | .24 | 2 | .28 | . . | . . . | 1 | .56 | . . | . . . | . . | . . . | . . | . . . | . . | . . . | 23 | .28 |
| Divorced . . . . | 13 | .43 | 4 | .41 | . . | . . . | 5 | .24 | 5 | .72 | . . | . . . | . . | . . . | . . | . . . | . . | . . . | 1 | 2.70 | 1 | .42 | 29 | .36 |
| Miscellaneous . . | 5 | .16 | 1 | .10 | . . | . . . | 4 | .19 | 4 | .57 | . . | . . . | . . | . . . | . . | . . . | . . | . . . | . . | . . . | . . | . . . | 14 | .17 |
| Total . . . | 2957 | | 976 | | 613 | | 2050 | | 694 | | 133 | | 176 | | 117 | | 41 | | 37 | | 234 | | 8028 | |

of the conclusion reached by Dugdale in his study of the Jukes. He says:—

1. Pauperism is an indication of weakness of some kind, either youth, disease, old age, injury, or, for women, childbirth.
2. Hereditary pauperism rests chiefly upon disease in some form, tends to terminate in extinction, and may be called the sociological aspect of physical degeneration.

We find, phrasing our conclusions in medical terms, that the commonest exciting cause of the poverty that approaches pau-

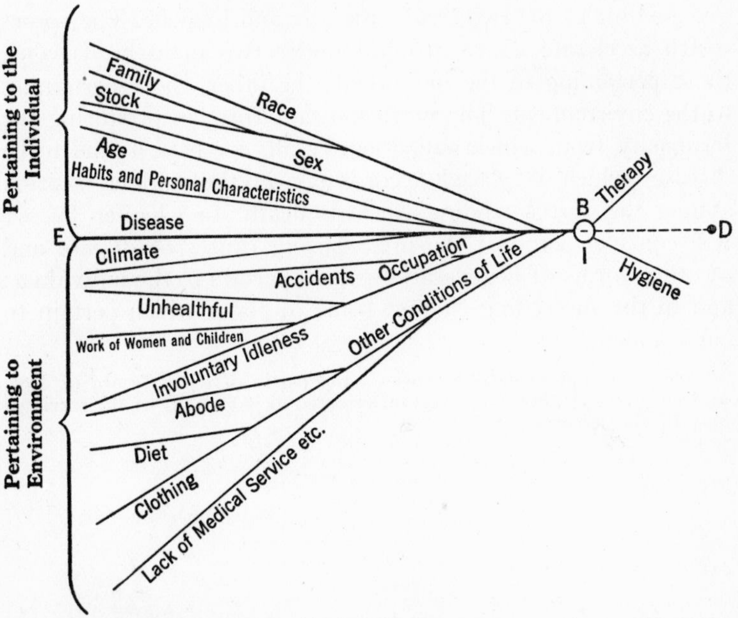


perism is incapacity, resulting in most chronic cases from sickness or other degenerate and degenerating conditions. Weakness of some sort is the most typical characteristic of the destitute classes. The predisposing causes of this degeneration and weakness are next to be sought for. A physician turns from diagnosing a case to inquire for predisposing causes, first in the habits and heredity of the individual, and secondly in the nature of his occupation, or other conditions of life. If we assume, as is roughly true, that the forces which tend to break down the physical man, and bring about the various forms of degeneration, are those which are pushing him towards death, we may present them graphically by a modification of a diagram used by Dr. J. S. Billings in the Cartwright lectures delivered before the Alumni Association of the College of Physicians and Surgeons of New York.[5]

Let the point *B* represent birth, and the point *D* represent death. The individual *I* passes to the right along the line *ED* at a rate proportionate to the progressive exhaustion of his vital energies. The forces which retard his movement are grouped under the two heads, therapy and hygiene. The forces which accelerate it are grouped under two main heads: one, those pertaining to the individual; the other, those pertaining to the environment. The most constant force in producing the incapacity from which pauperism results we have found to be disease, which is placed accordingly in the middle position among the forces tending towards death. In Chapter IV we will consider some of the predisposing causes of disease and of other forms of degeneration which pertain to the individual; and in the succeeding chapter some of those which pertain to environment.

[5] "On Vital and Medical Statistics." Printed in *Medical Record* of Nov. 30, Dec. 7 and 14, 1889. The diagram referred to is on p. 37 of the reprinted copy of the lectures.

# CHAPTER IV

## INDIVIDUAL DEGENERATION—PERSONAL CAUSES

Of the causes which pertain to the individual and tend to produce degeneration, we have said in the preceding chapter all that there is space to say regarding disease, age, sex, and race. There remain to be considered in the present chapter personal habits and characteristics, and the influence of stock and family through heredity; that is, the characteristics and habits of the individual himself which render him incapable or likely to become so; first, as to their nature, and, finally, as to their origin. In other words, having advanced from the effect, poverty, to the exciting cause, incapacity, we proceed from that to the predisposing causes.

It is to bad habits that the ordinary observer attributes a large part of the misery of the world; and, as immediate causes of degeneration, they undoubtedly have great influence.

**Intemperance,** meaning by this the abuse of alcoholic drinks, is commonly believed to be a very important cause of pauperism. It is held to be the predisposing cause back of sickness, back of insanity, back of crime. Probably nothing in the tables of the causes of poverty, as ascertained by case-counting, will more surprise the average reader than the fact that intemperance is held to be the chief cause in only from one-fifteenth to one-fifth of the cases, and that where an attempt is made to learn in how many cases it had a contributory influence, its presence cannot be traced at all in more than 28.1 per cent of the cases. It will be remembered that the Ishmaelites, as a rule, were temperate; and Mr. Dugdale did not consider intemperance the fundamental vice of the Jukes.

The scientific study of inebriety has only recently been entered upon, and this chiefly from the medical standpoint. In all the great mass of literature bearing upon the social influence of intemperance, very few conclusions are stated which are based upon inductions sufficiently wide to be final. An examination of the scattered material at hand, however, serves to explain the difference between popular impressions on the subject, and the conclusions reached by the statistical studies of pauperism. The ravages of intemperance are most plainly to be traced in classes distinctly above the pauper class. It is among artisans and those capable of earning good wages that the most money is spent for alcohol, and the most vitality burnt out by it. The man that has become a pauper does not find it easy, for one thing, to get liquor; and his vitality is apt to be so low that the exhilaration to be had from alcohol is not as much craved as by one with greater remaining strength. This does not correspond to the conclusion reached by Dugdale, who thought that drunkenness was usually the result of exhaustion rather than the cause of it, and that intemperance usually appeared in an individual subsequent to licentiousness and ill-health, and that its cause is antecedent hereditary or induced physical exhaustion. It is suggested, as an hypothesis which would reconcile the facts given by Mr. Dugdale [1] with others which have been observed, that intemperance is most likely to develop in persons of considerable natural strength who have become exhausted by vice, or overwork, or conditions of work or life that tend to undermine the health. This hypothesis would fit the cases detailed by Mr. Dugdale, though not that part of his conclusion which attributes drunkenness to hereditary exhaustion. By this hypothesis, intense work, irregular work, bad air, either in the home or workshop, inadequate or ill-prepared food, as well as the exhaustion resulting from vice, would tend to produce intemperance; while at the same time it would account for the fact that the most degenerate stock is not intemperate, and that frequently we cannot trace intemperance as a direct cause of pauperism in any considerable proportion of cases. In passing through the wards of an almshouse, the writer has frequently been surprised at the number of inmates who were said to have been temperate, and of whom the statement was apparently true. On the other hand, on learning the habits of laboring people, and especially those of skilled artisans, he has frequently been

[1] *Jukes*, pp. 40, 41, and 93.

surprised at the enormously heavy handicap of dissipation which many of the men were carrying.

W. Bevan Lewis, who writes in the *Fortnightly* for September, 1893, on "The Conditions of Crime," finds that, territorially, crime rather than pauperism seems to accompany drunkenness. He concludes, however, that drunkenness "makes itself felt in the development of epileptic offspring amongst the non-criminal community, in the moral obtuseness and degradation of such subjects, in the frequency of imbecile or idiot offspring, and peculiar *epileptoid* states of mind." This confirms the conclusion reached by Dr. S. G. Howe, in his well-known study of the causes of idiocy in Massachusetts.[2] The habits of one or both parents of 300 idiots having been learned, 145 of the children were found to be the progeny of habitual drunkards.

Irrespective of transmitted tendencies to degeneration, the children of drunken parents fare badly because of neglect and privation. Whether the mother herself drinks, or is merely linked to a drunken husband, her life during the period of gestation is almost inevitably such as endangers the well-being of the child. The fact that, when a large part of the family income goes for liquor, other branches of experience must be curtailed, is so obvious that it only needs to be mentioned. Moreover, the irrational and often brutal treatment received by children of the intemperate makes right development almost impossible for them. One fact brought out by the statistics of the Registrar General of England may be given as showing in an extreme instance the perils attending child life when parents drink: A much larger number of children are suffocated in bed on the nights of Saturday and holidays than on other nights of the week. This prompt extinguishing of infant life is hardly a greater misfortune than for the child to grow up with irrational guidance and the evil example of drunken parents.

"Typically the action induced in the brain [by alcohol] is of the nature of a progressive paralysis, beginning with the *highest level* and its most delicate functions, and spreading gradually downward through the lower. Moral qualities and

[2] Report to the Legislature, 1848, and subsequent reports and pamphlets.

the higher processes of intelligence are, therefore, first invaded." Children growing up under the influence of parents subject to such degeneration are not likely to develop the higher qualities at all, since the development of such qualities comes very largely from imitation. The utter lack of foresight, and the impossibility of postponing present gratification for the sake of future gain is one of the pronounced characteristics of the drunkard, and is also common among the distinctly pauper class.

It has been repeatedly pointed out that the latest social development, especially in the United States, tends to separate the community into two classes—the total abstainers and the hard drinkers. The tenser nervous organization of the modern man is in a state of less stable equilibrium than that of his progenitors, who lived largely out of doors, used their muscles in heavy work, ate large quantities of coarse food, and drank large quantities of mildly alcoholic liquor.[3] In America, climatic conditions intensify the tendency indicated. A dry atmosphere, and extremes of heat and cold, produce nervous diseases unknown to European medical practice, or, at least, known here in advance of their appearance in Europe.[4] It is a matter of common observation that the children of European immigrants usually drink either less or more than their parents, and those who drink resort to the stronger liquors.

The general conclusion regarding drink as a cause of poverty is sufficiently well formulated by Mr. Booth:[5] "Of drink in all its combinations, adding to every trouble, undermining every effort after good, destroying the home, and cursing the young lives of the children, the stories tell enough. It does not stand as apparent chief cause in as many cases as sickness and old age; but, if it were not for drink, sickness and old age could be better met." Mr. Booth's conclusions were reached by a study of concrete masses of pauperism, and yet they serve equally well to express the results reached by the study of

[3] See on this and following points, Simon N. Patten, "The Economic Basis of Prohibition," *Annals of Am. Acad. of Pol. and Soc. Science*, vol. 2, p. 59 *et seq.* An able article.

[4] See Beard, "Physical Future of the American People," *Atlantic Monthly Magazine*, vol. 43, p. 718.

[5] *Pauperism*, pp. 140-141.

inebriety as a disease. It is at once an effect and cause, a symptom and a source of degeneration.

**Immorality.** In the tables of the causes of poverty, the column next to the one giving the percentages for intemperance gives the number of cases in which poverty has been traced directly to "immorality." This term is here used to stand for sexual licentiousness, or other perversion of the sexual instinct. The small number of cases of poverty directly attributable to this factor in no wise reflects its importance as either a direct or a predisposing cause of destitution. Careful observers believe it to be a more constant and fundamental cause of degeneration than intemperance.[6] It certainly effects degeneration of a more or less pronounced type in a much larger number of persons. It persists almost to the end in the most degenerate stock, while at the same time it is operative among the healthier classes. A reference to the accounts quoted later on, describing the habits of the Rooneys, the Jukes, and the Ishmaels, will show that in these distinctly pauper families sexual vice plays a part in degradation more important than intemperance. The medical profession has given us even less of scientific exposition of the degeneration which results from perversion of the sexual instincts, than of that which comes from the abuse of stimulants and narcotics. The changes which must undoubtedly take place in the structure of the nervous and circulatory systems, as a consequence of self-abuse or sexual excess, have not been sufficiently studied. Venereal disease has been treated at length, but the effect upon the physical and mental man of vice as vice has been neglected. The great bulk of literature existing upon the subject is simply the output of advertising quacks.

And yet the effect of lubricity as such is appreciated to be an evil, and we condemn without hesitation such plans as those once put forward by Annie Besant for limiting population by mechanical appliances for preventing conception. It is felt at once that a sparse population which is vicious may be more miserable than a comparatively dense one which is moral. If,

[6] Mr. Booth speaks of intemperance as the most prolific of all the causes of poverty; but, so far as his publications show, he has not studied with much thoroughness the influence of sexual immorality as a cause of pauperism.

while limiting population, we promote sensuality, we do more harm than good. Anything which encourages sexual excess promotes misery. Mrs. Besant herself acknowledged this by withdrawing her book from publication. She said that the remedy proposed was materialistic, and she withdrew the book because she no longer accepted materialism. In this she was consistent; but even a well-reasoned materialism might surely have shown that her "remedy" for misery would probably produce more misery than it cured. ("If we consider man merely as a machine . . . let us not forget what a piece of mechanism he is.")

No boy among boys, or man among men, can have failed to have evidence thrust upon him showing that a very great amount of vitality is burnt out by the fires of lust. Among the rougher classes of day laborers upon railroads, in quarries, and even upon the farms, the whole undercurrent of thought, so far as conversation gives evidence of it, is thoroughly base and degrading. In several cases that the author investigated carefully, inefficiency certainly resulted from the constant preoccupation of the mind with sensual imaginings. At the present day, a given amount of such preoccupation will diminish a man's industrial efficiency more than ever before, because of the increasing importance of the mental element in all work. If a man has brute strength, he can shovel dirt quite passably, even though his thoughts are elsewhere. But most of the occupations of the present require alertness and sustained attention. Personal acquaintance with railroad day laborers, and others of a similar class, convinces the writer that they are very commonly kept from rising in the industrial scale by their sensuality, and that it is this and the resulting degeneration that finally convert many of them into lazy vagabonds. The inherent uncleanness of their minds prevents them from rising above the rank of day laborers, and finally incapacitates them even for that position. It may also be suggested that the modern man has a stronger imagination than the man of a few hundred years ago, and that sensuality destroys him the more rapidly. A highly developed nervous system makes him a more powerful man, if it is properly used, but it enables him to destroy himself more promptly if that be his tendency.

Mental Incapacity and Laziness. After drink-crave and sensuality, we might enumerate a large number of characteristics or habits which result from and result in a tendency to degenerate. On the side of appetites would be the craving for opium, and for various kinds of unwholesome food. On the side of defects, would be all those sufficiently pronounced to have been enumerated in the table of causes, and in addition the mental incapacity to judge wisely in the ordinary business affairs of life. This last is one of the most vexatious causes of poverty with which the ordinary friendly visitor for a charity organization society has to deal. It sometimes manifests itself in the form of extravagance, but oftener in pure blundering, which does not even bring the satisfaction of temporary indulgence. "Against stupidity the gods themselves are powerless." A proverbial saying, which has a very direct bearing on the subject, asserts that "Poor folks have poor ways." This cause is generally operative; yet writers upon social pathology seldom give it distinct treatment, apparently thinking that it is an individual and not a social phenomenon. The social results of it, however, are not to be ignored. The development of modern industries puts upon the judgment of individuals an ever increasing burden. The breaking down of the barriers of custom, the rapid changes in the methods of industry, the increasing amount of purchasing to be done to obtain family supplies, the increased need of wise bargaining in the selling of services, the extension of the borrowing habit both for good and evil, these and a hundred other features of modern industry tend to add to sobriety and industry as prerequisites of industrial success, a further requisite—that of good judgment, and a judgment that acts not only surely but promptly. From the proprietary farmer all the way down to the disease burdened man who decides whether or not he will go to a hospital, mistaken judgments are constantly pushing people towards and across the pauper line. One of the commonest mistakes is an utter failure to appreciate in advance the burden of a debt at compound interest. The chattel mortgage shark, the pawnbroker, and the "instalment plan" houses thrive because of this failure.

The only remaining characteristic to which special reference need here be made is that of laziness. Philosophers of the Benjamin Franklin type find in this the cause of nearly all destitution. Yet, in so far as it has a physical basis in under-vitalization, it is hardly to be cured by exhortation or even by hunger, any more than intemperance can under similar circumstances be so cured. Frequently what appears to the pushing citizen to be laziness is only the result of general incompetence, which the subject does not consciously recognize as existing, but which checks any ambition to do by a premonition of failure. The weightiest charge which many contented and discontented vagabonds might bring against the modern industrial organization is that they have become what they are through the effect of involuntary idleness; for idleness, voluntary or involuntary, tends to produce a degeneration, physical, mental, and moral, which perpetuates the condition that begets it.

The old economists sought to starve everybody back into habits of work and thrift; but starvation as a remedy for idleness is a medicine which the community is not willing to have administered in large doses, and even laziness is an evil which we must assail in its causes. The cause may be unwise coddling of the individual, but it may not.

**Hereditary Tendencies.** Thus far we have not needed to inquire whether the evil propensities and bad habits which result in degeneration have come through free choice on the part of the individual, or have been the result of foreordination in the theological or the scientific sense of the term. We have been concerned simply with their interactions and their effects. Ignoring all discussion as to the freedom of the will in any absolute sense of the term, it is our present business to trace causes just as far as they are found to be traceable. As an insurance company is justified in refusing to take a risk upon the life of a man who comes of a sickly family, or is engaged in some peculiarly dangerous occupation, so the student of social science is justified in concluding that certain influences of heredity and environment have an influence upon the character of the individual that is often manifest, and that is frequently to some extent measurable. In the one calculation relating to the longevity of an individual, and in the other relating to the character and career of an individual, there is always an uncertainty, but there is also a very constant element of probability.

From the time of birth, or even from the time of conception, the characteristics of race and of sex are fixed; and these are not without influence on the industrial history of the individual, as our tables show. In addition to this the transmission of a tendency to suffer from some specific disease such as gout, or consumption, or scrofula, or insanity, is very generally recognized. Observations more than ordinarily careful show that more varieties of bodily and mental weakness are transmitted from parent to child than is ordinarily supposed. Beyond this, occult characteristics tending to inefficiency or absolute pauperism are undoubtedly transmitted, although their exact nature, either in parent or child, cannot be ascertained and described. The proof is that the child follows by some secret but almost irresistible propulsion the history of the parent. The transmission of hereditary tendencies to degeneration can be most easily traced where some palpable defect is the result and evidence of degeneration. In his "Memoir upon the Formation of a Deaf Variety of the Human Race," Professor Alexander Graham Bell has collected with thoroughness and caution the facts available for this country, which show the transmissible character of deafness. It has been shown by three different investigators that where two persons born deaf marry, about one-third of the children are born deaf.[7]

On page 25 of the "Memoir" is given a much more detailed statement of the same facts, from which Professor Bell draws the conclusion that "A hereditary tendency towards deafness, as indicated by the possession of deaf relatives, is a most important element in determining the production of deaf offspring. . . . It may even be a more important element than the mere fact of congenital deafness in one or both of the parents." The following diagram of "The Brown Family of Henniker, New Hampshire," from page 28 of the "Memoir," is given, as showing at a glance the extent to which deafness prevails in certain families.

[7] *Marriage*, pp. 4 and 5; *Memoir*, Chap. iii, giving tables and detailed statements.

Professor Bell calls attention to the fact that lack of information leads to an under statement rather than an over statement in both the diagrams and the tables.

In his work on "Marriage and Disease," Dr. Strahan has given striking instances of the hereditary transmission of disease tendencies. He enumerates certain diseases which, in his opinion, spring from degeneration, and shows how a tendency to degenerate may result in one case in drunkenness; in another in deaf-mutism; in another in consumption; in another in insanity or imbecility. He quotes authorities to show that the ratio of blindness among deaf-mutes is fourteen and

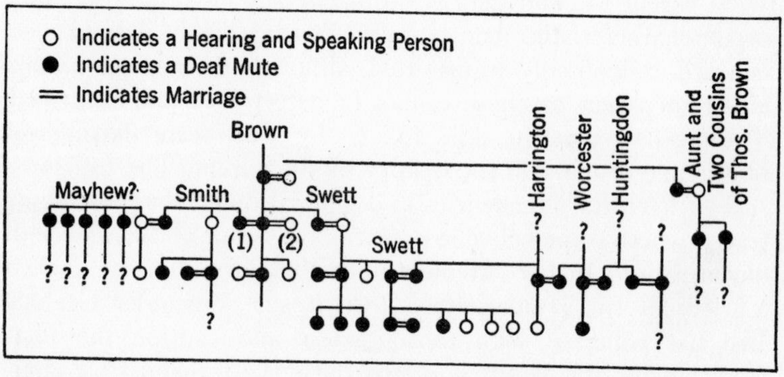


a half times as great as among the whole population; while idiocy, the deepest of all forms of degeneration, is forty-three times as great among these unfortunates as among the general population.[8] In his opinion the intermarriage of deaf-mutes or other defectives will not result in the formation of a deaf variety of the human race, but rather in the extinction of the degenerate stock.[9] The more important diseases transmissible by inheritance which he regards at once as results, evidences, and causes of degeneration, are insanity, imbecility, epilepsy, drunkenness, deaf-mutism, blindness, cancer, scrofula, tubercular disease, gout, rheumatism, and instinctive criminality. While he has not marshaled the statistics which might be given

[8] *Marriage and Disease,* p. 169.

[9] Congenital deafness is not the simple absence of one of the senses which is not absolutely necessary for life; it is a sign of a general decay, which, if deepened by intermarriage, must soon reach the necessarily fatal type and extinguish the family.—*Ibid.,* p. 171.

to show the common dependence of the diseases upon general degeneration, yet his diagrams and statements of family history abundantly prove the interdependence of these diseases, or of many of them, and establishes beyond question the fact that they are frequently transmitted by inheritance.[10]

In his investigation of the causes of idiocy in Massachusetts, Dr. S. G. Howe had careful inquiries made regarding the influence of heredity. The facts most pertinent at this stage of the inquiry are grouped in the following table.

TABLE X.

HEREDITARY TENDENCIES APPARENTLY AFFECTING IDIOCY IN MASSACHUSETTS.

| | *Congenital Idiocy* | *Idiocy Supervened* | *Total* |
|---|---|---|---|
| Idiotic persons who are known to be of decidedly scrofulous families | 355 | 64 | 419 |
| Idiotic persons whose parents were known to be habitual drunkards | 99 | 15 | 114 |
| Idiotic persons some of whose near relatives are idiotic or insane | 177 | 34 | 211 |
| Idiotic persons whose parents were known to be neither very scrofulous nor very intemperate | 5 | 5 | 10 |
| Idiotic persons who have 1 near relative idiotic | 44 | 5 | 49 |
| Idiotic persons who have 2 near relatives idiotic | 8 | 1 | 9 |
| Idiotic persons one or both of whose parents were idiotic or insane | .. | .. | 50 |
| Idiotic persons who are parents | .. | .. | 21 |
| Idiotic persons whose parents were advised to marry on account of ill-health | 12 | .. | 12 |
| Families where the parents of idiotic persons are near relatives | 17 | .. | 17 |
| Parents who have 2 idiotic children | 43 | 2 | 45 |
| Parents who have 3 idiotic children | 10 | 3 | 13 |
| Parents who have 4 idiotic children | 8 | .. | 8 |

Satisfactory experiments with infants of known descent not having been conducted with sufficient care, or in sufficient number, to warrant any final conclusions as to the force of heredity in pushing the individual away from pauperism or

[10] Boies, in his work on *Prisoners and Paupers,* pp. 281-2, has reproduced eight of Strahan's diagrams of families.

towards it, two other methods of observation, less conclusive but more practicable, have been resorted to. The first is to study the family relations of a large number of conspicuously successful or unsuccessful persons, and learn as far as possible what influence heredity has had in bringing about success or failure. The second method is to study the careers of all the children of a family whose members are in general conspicuous for success or failure, in order to see whether or not the manifest tendency can be accounted for by the influence of environment. This second method is, of course, for the most part only a way of checking the results obtained by the first. As examples of the first we may summarize the investigations of Galton regarding relationships of the English judges, (*b*) Booth's summary of the "Stories of Stepney Pauperism," (*c*) the investigation of the almshouse population of New York; and as illustrating the results to be got by the second method, some account is given of the study of the Jukes of New York, and the Ishmaelites of Indiana.

Mr. Galton undertook a study of the English judges between the accession of Charles II. and the year 1864. He found that a very large number of these men were related one to another, and an analysis of the facts showed that a very eminent man was more likely to have eminent relations than one who had attained a less degree of success. Out of the 286 judges, more than one in every nine had been either father, son, or brother to another judge, and the other high legal relationships had been even more numerous. "There cannot remain a doubt," he says, "but that the peculiar type of ability that is necessary to a judge is often transmitted by descent." [11]

As showing the possibilities of the persistence of capacity in certain families, the following is inserted from Galton's works:—

> The names of North and Montagu, among the judges, introduce us to a remarkable breed of eminent men, set forth at length in the genealogical tree of the Montagus, and again that of the Sydneys (see the chapter on "Literary Men"), to whose natural history—if the expression be permitted—a few pages may be profitably assigned. There is hardly a name in those pedigrees

[11] Page 69.

which is not more than ordinarily eminent: many are illustrious. They are closely tied together in their kinship, and they extend through ten generations. The main roots of this diffused ability lie in the families of Sydney and Montagu, and, in a lesser degree, in that of North.

The Sydney blood—I mean that of the descendants of Sir William Sydney and his wife—had extraordinary influence in two different combinations. First with the Dudleys, producing in the first generation, Sir Philip Sydney and his eminent brother and sister; in the second generation, at least one eminent man; and in the third generation, Algernon Sydney with his able brother and much-be-praised sister. The second combination of the Sydney blood was with the Harringtons, producing in the first generation a literary peer, and Elizabeth, the mother of the large and most remarkable family that forms the chief feature of my genealogical table.

The Montagu blood, as represented by Sir Edward, who died in the Tower, 1644, is derived from three distant sources. His great-grandfather (*g*F.) was Sir John Finnieux, Chief Justice of the King's Bench; his grandfather (g.) was John Roper, Attorney General to Henry VIII.; and his father—by far the most eminent of the three—was Sir Edward Montagu, Chief Justice of the King's Bench. Sir Edward Montagu, son of the Chief Justice, married Elizabeth Harrington, of whom I have just spoken, and had a large family, who in themselves and in their descendants became most remarkable. To mention only the titles they won: in the first generation they obtained two peerages, the earldom of Manchester and the barony of Montagu; in the second they obtained two more, the earldom of Sandwich and the barony of Capel; in the third five more, the dukedom of Montagu, earldoms of Halifax and of Essex, the barony of Guilford, and a new barony of Capel (second creation); in the fourth one more, the dukedom of Manchester (the Premier in 1701); in the fifth one more, the earldom of Guilford. The second Earl of Guilford, the Premier of George III. (best known as Lord North), was in the sixth generation. ("Hereditary Genius," pp. 70-72.)

In contrast with this, the following pages are reproduced from Mr. Booth's "Stories of Stepney Pauperism."

Martin Rooney, aged 85, now in Bromley Workhouse, married Eliza King, and this family has been prolific in paupers.

First there is Mary Rooney, the wife of Martin's brother James, who was deserted by him in 1867, and has had relief in various forms since, including residence in the sick asylum for several years. She also applied on behalf of her married daughter, Mrs. Wilson, and her son Michael appears on the books; but with this branch we do not go at present beyond the second generation.

The old man Martin, who is now blind, applied for admission in 1878. His wife was then in hospital, having broken her leg when intoxicated. He had been a dock laborer, and had received £21 from the company on breaking a leg in 1857. He was admitted to Poplar Workhouse. A month later his wife, who is twenty-four years his junior, came out of hospital, and was also admitted. The relieving officer makes a note that he does not know a more drunken, disreputable family than this one. He has seen the woman "beastly drunk" at all times of the day. From this time the old man remains in the house; but the woman goes out several times, and when out was more than once seen in the streets in a drunken condition. She works sometimes at the lead-works, sleeping occasionally with her sons, at other times in various places—water-closets, on stairs, etc. When her son Patrick was sent to prison for two months she went into the house. In 1888 she absconded, but in March, 1889, applied for re-admission; she had fallen down and cut her face on the Saturday night before.

This couple had three children, Patrick, James, and Bridget. Patrick, born in 1853, by trade a stevedore, is now in Poplar Workhouse. He was living with his mother in 1886, and she made application for medical attendance for him. He was suffering from rheumatism. He became worse, and was sent to the sick asylum; was discharged, and again admitted a month or two later. Next year he was sent to Bromley Workhouse. He bears a bad character, and was in prison two months in 1888, and had one month in 1889 for attempting to steal some ropes. On coming out of prison he again applied for admission to the workhouse, and was sent to Poplar. He had a bad leg. He got work on the day he was discharged from the sick asylum, injured his leg, and was re-admitted to workhouse. He served fourteen or fifteen years in the Royal Marines, and was discharged in 1885 for striking a petty officer. He was for this sentenced to six months' imprisonment by court-martial.

James, the second son, is a laborer, not married. He used to live with a woman named O'Reill, but left her, or she him, and is at present living with another woman.

Bridget, the eldest, born in 1847, married John Murdock, a bricklayer's laborer, eight years older than herself, and there are four children, all boys. Murdock deserted his wife several times, and has been sent to prison for it. She in turn left him in 1877, and has been living with another man since. After this he was in Bromley House with the children. The two eldest were emigrated to Canada in 1880. The man's sister married Richard

Bardsley, whose mother, a widow, is living at Bromley, and whose brother and brother's wife both had relief there.[12]

The study of the inmates of the almshouses of New York, made by representatives of the State Board of Charities in the early 'seventies, included an examination of 12,614 persons in those institutions. At that time many insane and many children and many of the defective classes were still in the local almshouses. In the rural communities it was found possible to get information as to the relationships of these persons with tolerable fulness, while in the cities little could be learned bearing upon the subject. Of course the classes under investigation are those where the ties of relationship are peculiarly loose and untraceable, and yet it was found possible to collect very conclusive facts as to the influence of heredity in perpetuating pauperism. Of the whole number of persons examined, it was ascertained that 397, or nearly 3.15 per cent, were the offspring of pauper fathers; 1,361, or 10.79 per cent, of pauper mothers. The dependence dated back to the third generation in 55 cases on the paternal, and 92 cases on the maternal side. 1,122 had (living or dead) pauper brothers; 951, pauper sisters; 143, pauper uncles; and 133, pauper aunts.

10,161 different families were represented. The total number of persons in these families, including three generations (living and dead) who were known to have been dependent upon public charity was 14,901. The total number of the insane in the same families (living and dead), 4,968; the total number of idiots in the same families (living and dead), 844; and the total number of inebriates in the same families (living and dead), 8,863. The number of heads of families in the poorhouses at the time of inquiry, consisting of both parents, was 2,746; these were said to have in all 7,040 living children. The condition of these children was stated to be as follows: in poorhouses, 1,010; in asylums, 149; in hospitals, 2; in refuges, 29; in prisons and penitentiaries, 9; bound out, 346; self-supporting, 4,586; condition unascertained, 909. Thus about 22 per cent of the children of poorhouse parents were

[12] *Pauperism,* pp. 14-15. There is about twice as much more description of individuals belonging to this stock, and pages 18-43 are filled with accounts of similar families.

found to be of the dependent or delinquent classes. Taking only those whose condition was ascertained, the percentage of those who were a charge upon the public rises to a little more than 25. It should also be noted that a considerable number of those self-dependent at the time would probably with advancing years become public charges; and while some of those in a condition of dependency would perhaps eventually become self-supporting, they would hardly become so as a permanent thing. It is doubtful if half these children would get through life without some taint of dependency.

The suggestion at once occurs to anyone who reviews these facts, that environment may have had as much to do as heredity with the success of the successful, and the failure of those who fail. The sons of the influential classes grow up under conditions which favor their education and advancement, while the children of the pauper, born in the poorhouse or the slums, are foredoomed by the conditions under which they grow up to pauperism. The only way of learning how much force should be given to these considerations is to make a careful analysis of the successful and the unsuccessful families, and to see whether individuals descended from these families, but placed under conditions different from those surrounding the family, nevertheless work out careers analogous to those of their relatives. Mr. Galton has pursued this second method of investigation with apparent care, and proves to his own satisfaction that individuals of successful families are successful by virtue of inherent capacity, and only secondarily by virtue of their opportunities. Mr. Booth has also analyzed the returns regarding Stepney pauperism, and puts pauper association and heredity together as a contributory cause in 106 cases out of 634. His uniting of the two causes in the table reflects the difficulty there is of disassociating the two. In the New York investigation no direct attempt was made to trace out the careers of individuals descended from pauper stock who had yet escaped from pauperism. But two elaborate investigations have been conducted in the United States regarding the life-histories of individuals descended from distinctly pauper families. The first of these included doubtless many of the same individuals, or their progenitors, that were found in the New York almshouses in 1870.

The investigation referred to is the well-known one conducted by Mr. Dugdale concerning the family of the Jukes.[13] The facts regarding this family were so thoroughly worked out that it has become a stock example of the influence of heredity as a factor in crime and pauperism, and exaggerated stories are current as to the number of criminals descended from the woman spoken of by Mr. Dugdale as Ada Juke, but better known as Margaret, the Mother of Criminals. Mr. Charles L. Brace has said that twenty-seven of her descendants were prosecuted by one attorney; one judge stated that he had sentenced sixty-nine of them, and six hundred are estimated to have been tried by law.[14] Mr. Dugdale's tables of ascertained facts, however, while not disproving these statements, do not contain a verification of them. The family has been traced back to a man whom Dugdale calls Max, a descendant of the early Dutch settlers, born between the years 1720 and 1740. He is described as a hunter and fisher, a hard drinker, jolly and companionable, averse to steady toil, working hard by spurts and idling by turns, becoming blind in his old age, and entailing his blindness upon his children and grandchildren. Two of his sons married two of the Juke sisters, of whom there were six in all. The progeny of five of them have been traced with more or less exactness through five generations. The number of descendants registered includes 540 individuals who were related by blood to the Jukes, and 169 connected with the family by marriage or cohabitation, in all 709 persons of all ages, alive and dead. The aggregate of this lineage reaches, says Mr. Dugdale, probably 1,200 persons, but the dispersions that have occurred at different times have prevented the following up and enumeration of many of the lateral branches. They grew up in the rural districts of New York, and out-door life probably aided the degenerate stock

[13] The report in which the results of this study are embodied has been published by Putnams in "Questions of the Day" series. The best summary for present purposes is Mr. Dugdale's paper on "Hereditary Pauperism," read at the National Conference of Charities in 1877, see pp. 81-95.

[14] Baltimore Conference on Charities, p. 107.

to resist the tendencies to extinction. The family, as indicated by the statement of its origin, may be considered distinctly American.

The genealogical tables given by Mr. Dugdale, together with a description of the family in his text, would make it possible to reproduce a description of the individuals and their degenerate condition, of still more hideous particularity than that employed in describing the Rooney family and its connections; but for present purposes a statistical summary of the facts will throw more light upon the problems of heredity.

In the subsidiary tables given by Mr. Dugdale, it is shown that, whether we consider pauperism, or crime, or harlotry, or prostitution, this family has produced a number of dependents and delinquents out of all proportion to the numbers of individuals it has contributed to the population. For instance, it is shown that pauperism is nearly seven times as common in this family as in the population of the State at large; but a closer analysis of the tables gives still more striking confirmation of the tendency of heredity as compared with environment. Mr. Dugdale classes under the head of X all families not related to the Jukes who married into the last-named family. It is found that if we take people of the Juke blood simply, pauperism is 7.37 times as common among them as in the population as a whole; while if we take X blood only, that is, those families that married into the Juke family, we find pauperism to be only 4.89 times as common as in the population as a whole. In the matter of harlotry, 52.40 per cent of the adult women of Juke blood are found to have been harlots, while but 41.76 per cent of the women of the X blood were found to be such. Turning to the matter of crime, it is found that within the family itself, there are some distinctly criminal, and some distinctly pauper strains. Intermarriage between people of the Juke blood, that is, breeding within the family, intensified the tendency to pauperism, while marriage with non-related stocks usually resulted in a larger proportion of criminals among the descendants. This last is probably to be accounted for by the greater constitutional vigor that resulted from marriage with non-related groups. As pauperism rests upon weakness of some sort, the tendency to degenerative diseases, as the result of in-and-in breeding, readily accounts for the access of pauperism in the consanguineous lines.

As to environment, it can be said that the family lived at a time and in a State when success was entirely possible, and when many of those with whom the Juke family came in contact were constantly succeeding. At the same time, the "tendency of heredity is to produce an environment which perpetuates that heredity." The child born on the roadside or in the poor-house comes up under conditions that make progressive degeneracy of the individual likely. The licentious parent is an example which greatly aids in fixing habits of debauchery in the child. Yet, this being true, it is still remarkable that, under environments substantially the same, we are able to trace distinctly different tendencies in those of Juke blood and of X blood, and even between the different strains of the family itself.

While the facts with which we must deal in studying the influence of heredity on pauperism are often elusive and ambiguous, yet from what has been said it is manifest that there are strong hereditary tendencies making for individual success or failure. Could there be, without encouraging pauperism, a business company to insure people against it, its representatives would inquire about an applicant's family as particularly as about his financial and physical condition, and scions of many stocks would be considered "very undesirable risks."

# CHAPTER V

## INDIVIDUAL DEGENERATION—SOCIAL CAUSES

If it were planned to give any complete view of the social and industrial influences which tend to push down the individual financially as well as physically, it would be necessary to review nearly the whole of political economy, descriptive and theoretical; but we are to concern ourselves at present merely with those extrinsic influences which tend to cause incapacity and degeneration in the individual. We must therefore pass by without consideration all the poverty begetting causes that reside in the fluctuation of the purchasing power of money, although many concrete examples could be given of families pushed from the propertied class even across the pauper line by this influence. Neither can we concern ourselves with those changes in industry which have displaced large numbers of individuals, although presumably benefiting the community as a whole, and even laborers as a class. Neither can we take up the undue power of class over class, either of employer over employed, or of organized over unorganized labor. Indirectly, of course, this power of class over class does result in conditions which tend to degenerate the individual, consequently, it will be touched upon; but our view for the most part is limited to the direct influence of occupation and conditions of life upon health, character, and capacity.

At the same time, we cannot but note in passing, that if the conditions and character of working-men have tended to depress many of them below the standard of efficiency which permits them to be useful, it is also true that the standard of efficiency has risen, or perhaps we should say changed, so that the man who would once have been useful can no longer find a place. In the development of modern industry, a vast amount of heavy work is accomplished by the free use of capital, machinery taking the place of men. Man as a source of mechanical energy at the present time is therefore a cumbrous and uneconomical tool, costing much to produce, much to keep in repair, and not nearly so adaptable in many lines as machinery.

Along with this tendency of machinery to take work away from the merely strong has come the formation of trades unions, so that now, as Hobson puts it, the laborers must either "organize or starve." [1] The development of modern industry has forced higher organization; and just as Franklin said to the thirteen colonies, so now the conditions of industry say to the laborer, "join or die." Those who in consequence of conditions or character cannot organize, and who for the most part belong to the ranks of low-skilled labor, find it constantly more and more difficult to maintain themselves. While at the start they may have possessed a degree of efficiency that formerly would have won them place and living, they are now unable to get work, and through involuntary idleness their incapacity is intensified and perpetuated.

**Industrial Accidents.** The most palpable means by which occupation lessens the capacity of the individual is accident. The industry in which this palpable thing is most obvious is that of transportation, and no country in the world offers more illustrations of such injury to railroad employees than the United States. There were killed on the railroads of the United States during the year ending June 30, 1892, 2,554 employees, and 28,268 were injured; that is, one employee for every 322 men at work in this industry was killed, and one injured for every 29 men in the employ of the railways. In the case of trainmen, the statistics for the same year show that there was one man killed for every 113 of this class of employees, and one was injured for every 10. The accidents were most numerous in the districts where the railroads are run most cheaply and are least expensively built. In the States of Virginia, North Carolina, and South Carolina, one trainman was killed for every 33 men in employment, and one injured for every 6 employees. In the Middle Southern States the proportion was

[1] *Problems of Poverty,* p. 225. This and the following pages contain a wonderfully clear and concise account of the status of low-skilled labor in modern industry.

equally high.[2] Many of these cases were probably provided for by benefit associations maintained by the men or by the relief work of the companies; but such relief is always partial and temporary, and of course makes no atonement to the industry of the country as a whole for the amount of personal capacity destroyed. It would not usually be easy to trace pauperism in a given case to an accident on a railroad, although the author has himself been called to deal with some cases of destitution resulting directly from such accidents; but frequently pauperism does not result until years afterwards, when a widowed mother has broken down in the attempt to support her family, or when some aged or incapable relative has been turned adrift from the incapacity of the family to maintain him longer.

The transportation industry is but the most conspicuous example of the destruction of personal capacity that comes from accidents, many of which are preventable; and the tendency of legislation to protect factory operatives, miners, and all engaged in exposed trades, from gratuitous harm due to preventable accidents, is one that should be wisely furthered.

**Industrial Diseases.** There is a destruction of personal capacity and a strong tendency to degeneration in a large number of occupations because of the disease-begetting conditions that surround the work. Much more has been done in England and European countries in searching out the source of diseases that have their origin in occupation than in this country.

In this country, curiously enough, very few of our labor bureaus have investigated this feature of the conditions of labor. The best work thus far done is probably that of the New Jersey Bureau of Labor Statistics, published in its Annual Reports for 1889, 1890, and 1891. The effect of occupation upon the health and duration of the trade life of workmen is traced in three industries—pottery, hat-making, and glass-blowing. As specimens of the facts brought to light by the investigation of these trades may be cited that of pot-makers, who prepare the pots in which the raw material for glass is melted. These pots are made of fine clay, which requires a great deal of care in its preparation, involving grinding, pulverizing

[2] Report of the Statistician of the Interstate Commerce Commission, 1892, pp. 68 and 78.

the dry clay, its mixture, and tempering. Little attention has been paid to the improvement of the machinery in use and the buildings in which these processes are conducted, so as to keep the workmen from inhaling the dust. As a consequence, from ten to fifteen years is about the length of time a man can work at the trade continuously in health. "The writer has witnessed the decline of three generations of pot-makers within the past forty years." [3]

The description of the conditions of work for the hatters, prepared by a physician for the New Jersey State Board of Health, is given in the Report of the Labor Bureau, and a table which shows that of 240 sizers or makers, 76 have catarrh; 44 have rheumatism; 41 have coughs; 17 have had "the shakes"; 13 now have "the shakes"; 12 constantly catch cold because of sudden changes of temperature; 7 complain of dyspepsia; 200 use stimulants and tobacco.[4]

In these three industries, as in others, it is found that the men themselves are recklessly indifferent to the healthfulness of the conditions under which they work. They will strike against a very small reduction of wages, but rarely or never for improved sanitation. It is this indifference that has made it necessary for the State to interfere and fix the plane of competition, below which employers are not allowed to go, nor workmen to permit themselves to be employed. The cheaper way to get a wise and capable generation of laborers is to educate the men to something better, rather than to allow the unwise stock to exterminate itself.

**Improper Employment of Women and Children.** Turning from the countless preventable causes of disease that exist in the various occupations from unsanitary surroundings, there is one force which tends constantly to individual degeneration and race deterioration. This is the improper employment of women and children. It has been more dwelt upon by writers on political economy, and the agitation for the factory acts has brought it more prominently before the public than many of

[3] Annual Report of the Bureau of Labor Statistics of New Jersey, 1889, p. 35.

[4] *Ibid.*, p. 36. The last item regarding the use of stimulants and tobacco indicates the interaction of occupational and personal influences in producing degeneration.

the others; but it is so fundamental and so entirely mischievous that it cannot be passed without mention. An English writer, Dr. Rentoul, gives the following sketch of women's work and its influence on their character and physique:

Suppose that a girl at the age of thirteen to sixteen is placed in one of the Lancashire mills, and is fed on stewed tea, bread, and occasionally badly cooked meat and fish. How can she, with such surroundings, develop into a healthy woman? Her pale, bloodless, colorless face shows she is bordering on the first stage of consumption. In a few years she is engaged. Married on a Saturday, she returns to work on the following Monday. After some time a baby is about to be born, and she leaves the mill just when labor compels her, but no sooner. She must return to the factory in a few days, else her place will be filled by some one else. Consequently, she has to forsake her infant. It is given out to some nurse or baby farmer, the mother paying from four to six shillings per week towards its support. It is "taken care of" by a girl eight or ten years of age, fed on unsuitable foods, drugged with "soothing syrups," and probably insured in a burial club. Now, what are the products of this system which demands such continuous labor? Only ruin—ruin to the health of the girl, woman, and mother; ruin to her babe denied the food nature intended for its use; ruin to all home comforts—for all the family beyond the children are in the mill—and ruin to the young husband. The human animal may be the cheapest in to-day's market, and have less attention than that given to the brute creation; still, if such a condition be allowed to continue, the country at large must soon feel the evil results which spring from so unnatural a condition. It may seem strange that during the siege of Paris, while the general mortality was doubled, the infant mortality was reduced by about forty per cent. This was owing to the fact that the mothers, having to stay at home, had sufficient time to nurse their infants. A similar experience was recorded during the cotton famine in Lancashire.[5]

The statements regarding experience in Paris and Lancashire, which are presumably correct, give the most striking evidence of the evils resulting from the employment of married women.[6]

[5] *The Dignity of Woman's Health,* pp. 122-124.

[6] The best and most accessible reference on child labor in the United States is to be found in the two articles by Willoughby and De Grafenried in Publications American Economic Association, vol. 5, pp. 229-271. Probably the best argument for the Factory Acts within brief compass is Macaulay's speech on the Ten Hours' Bill, *Speeches,* vol. 2, pp. 7-30. See also Jeans, *Factory Legislation.*

**Enforced Idleness.** A common cause of degeneration is enforced idleness, coming from the necessities of variable seasons, or from the spasmodic nature of modern industry, or from the inclination of employing companies, as in many of the bituminous coal regions, to keep a large number of men partially employed, rather than a small number occupied all the time. Every great industrial crisis like that through which we have been passing during the present year leaves behind it a legacy of individual degeneration and personal unthrift, which tends to sink more and more those who have not girded themselves to improve through adversity instead of being depressed by it.

**Occupational Mortality and Morbidity.** Another way of finding out the influence of occupation upon health is by a study of mortality statistics, especially of occupational mortality and morbidity. It is generally recognized that there is a higher death-rate among laboring classes than among the well-to-do, but a careful search among statistics collected by American bureaus of labor and for the Federal census shows that we have no vital statistics that are a safe guide in considering occupational mortality.

The only conclusive way to study occupational mortality is to secure the number dying during one year in a given occupation at a given age out of 1,000 engaged in that occupation of the same age. From certain statistics on this point given by Josef Körösi, the eminent statistician of Budapesth, the following table is derived.

TABLE XI.

Mortality and Morbidity in Five Occupations.[7]

| *Occupation* | *No. Living at 25* | *No. Living at 60* | *Years of Life, 25–60* | *Years of Health, 25–60* | *Years of Sickness 25–60* | *Ratio of Health to Sickness* |
|---|---|---|---|---|---|---|
| Merchants .... | 1,000 | 587.7 | 28,501.23 | 27,676.63 | 824.6 | 33.5 : 1 |
| Tailors ....... | 1,000 | 421.2 | 25,673.45 | 24,515.91 | 1,157.5 | 21.1 : 1 |
| Shoemakers ... | 1,000 | 376.2 | 23,872.38 | 22,624.78 | 1,247.6 | 18.2 : 1 |
| Servants ...... | 1,000 | 290.2 | 22,416.92 | 20,997.32 | 1,419.6 | 14.7 : 1 |
| Day Laborers.. | 1,000 | 253.3 | 22,317.04 | 20,823.64 | 1,493.4 | 13.9 : 1 |

[7] Josef Körösi, *Mitteilungen über Individuale Mortalitäts*—Beobachtungen, Budapesth, 1876, p. 26.

It is not improbable these figures exaggerate the difference between the occupations, and too much reliance should not be placed on them; but at the same time they have some value, and help us to understand how it is that sickness is held to be the cause of so much pauperism.

Dr. Farr, in his work on "Vital Statistics," gives the following table as to the mortality at six age-periods in certain occupations:

TABLE XII.

MORTALITY PER 1,000 LIVING AT SIX AGE-PERIODS.[8]

| AGES | | | | | | |
|---|---|---|---|---|---|---|
| *25* | *35–* | *Occupations* | *45–* | *55–* | *65–* | *75* |
| 10.15 | 8.64 | Farmer ......... | 11.09 | 24.90 | 55.30 | 148.02 |
| 9.12 | 10.59 | Shoemaker ...... | 15.03 | 28.69 | 65.05 | 164.46 |
| 7.97 | 10.56 | Weaver ........ | 15.37 | 32.99 | 74.59 | 173.08 |
| 7.63 | 10.46 | Grocer ......... | 15.79 | 22.65 | 49.72 | 124.57 |
| 8.12 | 12.40 | Blacksmith ..... | 16.51 | 37.24 | 74.43 | 167.10 |
| 9.45 | 10.32 | Carpenter ...... | 16.67 | 29.66 | 65.86 | 142.86 |
| 11.63 | 14.15 | Tailor .......... | 16.74 | 28.18 | 76.47 | 155.28 |
| 9.79 | 12.52 | Laborer ........ | 17.30 | 29.20 | 67.90 | 173.94 |
| 8.49 | 11.35 | Miner .......... | 20.15 | 34.50 | 80.51 | 178.67 |
| 7.59 | 14.75 | Baker .......... | 21.21 | 33.01 | 66.78 | 150.66 |
| 11.30 | 16.53 | Butcher ........ | 23.10 | 41.49 | 66.47 | 154.49 |
| 13.83 | 20.45 | Innkeeper ....... | 28.34 | 38.97 | 81.51 | 180.84 |
| 9.48 | 12.36 | All England ..... | 17.87 | 30.31 | 63.96 | 140.55 |

The death-rates based on the English experience are here lower than those given by Körösi, and the indicated relative healthfulness of the trades is not the same. According to this calculation, which is based upon very wide inductions, the most unhealthful business is that of an innkeeper, or, as we would say, of saloon-keeper. This illustrates again the interaction of personal and occupational causes of degeneration. Next to this comes the business of the butcher, and so on up, the most healthful occupation being that of the farmer. Dr. Farr makes an examination of the conditions in several occupations, the results of which are presumably reflected by the statistics given.

**Class Mortality.** But the entire story regarding the degenerative influences brought to bear upon the weaker classes of the community is not brought out by the study of occupa-

[8] William Farr, *Vital Statistics*, p. 397. The several classes are arranged in the order of the mortality at the age (45-55).

tional mortality. We must turn to the matter of class mortality in order to obtain this. In occupational mortality we deal only with the diseases and deaths of adults, whereas in class mortality we deal also with the diseases and deaths of minors and of incapable members of the families. In his work on "The Rate of Mortality, etc., in the Upper and Professional Classes," Mr. Charles Ansell, Jr., gives [9] the following figures:

TABLE XIII.

| *Out of 100,000 Born Alive There Will Be Living* | *End First Year* | *Age of 15* | *Age of 60* |
|---|---|---|---|
| Peerage families | 93,038 | 85,890 | 51,166 |
| "Upper class experience" | 91,955 | 83,392 | 53,398 |
| "Clergy children" | 91,667 | 79,536 | ..... |
| "English life tables" | 85,051 | 68,456 | 36,983 |
| "Carlisle table" | 84,610 | 63,000 | 36,430 |

That is, out of a hundred thousand children born in the upper classes, nearly ten thousand more will reach the age of fifteen than in the population at large. The influences which induce a higher rate of mortality among the lower classes are given by Ansell as follows:

PHYSICAL.

1. Food insufficient in quantity and improper as to kind.
2. Deficiency of warm clothing.
3. Want or delay of medical attendance in illness.
4. Crowded and unhealthy dwellings.
5. Neglect on the part of parents (especially when the mother is at work).

MORAL.

1. Illegitimacy.
2. Children being a burden upon or considered as such by their parents.
3. Parents having a direct pecuniary interest in the death of their children.

For our purpose perhaps the most convenient class-mortality statistics are those prepared by Dr. Grimshaw, Registrar-General of Ireland, giving the experience in Dublin for the four years 1883 to 1886.

Now, let us notice how heavy a burden the condition of

[9] Table II of work cited.

things here indicated imposes upon Classes III, IV, and V, as compared with Classes I and II. Pressure is brought to bear upon the poor, and especially upon Class III in a fourfold way. First, the number under fifteen years of age, and therefore of

TABLE XIV.[10]

ANNUAL RATE OF MORTALITY PER 1,000, DUBLIN, 1883–6.

| *Occupation or Social Position* | *All Ages* | AGE *0* | *5* | *20* | *40* | *60 and Upwards* |
|---|---|---|---|---|---|---|
| All Persons— | | | | | | |
| Years of life....... | 1,406,124 | | | | | |
| Deaths ........... | 39,476 | | | | | |
| Rate per 1,000...... | 28.07 | 81.43 | 8.84 | 13.30 | 29.38 | 90.85 |
| I.—Professional and Independent Classes— | | | | | | |
| Years of life....... | 122,198 | | | | | |
| Deaths ........... | 1,857 | | | | | |
| Rate per 1,000...... | 15.20 | 20.52 | 2.94 | 6.26 | 12.97 | 51.67 |
| II.—Middle Class— | | | | | | |
| Years of life....... | 230,212 | | | | | |
| Deaths ........... | 6,034 | | | | | |
| Rate per 1,000...... | 26.21 | 58.25 | 7.99 | 13.85 | 29.74 | 157.36 |
| III.—Artisans Class and Petty Shop-keepers— | | | | | | |
| Years of life....... | 430,493 | | | | | |
| Deaths ........... | 9,902 | | | | | |
| Rate per 1,000...... | 23.00 | 69.05 | 8.67 | 11.41 | 23.62 | 61.65 |
| IV.—General Service Class, incl. Work-House Inmates— | | | | | | |
| Years of life....... | 623,221 | | | | | |
| Deaths ........... | 21,683 | | | | | |
| Rate per 1,000...... | 34.79 | 108.73 | 10.38 | 15.45 | 36.93 | 108.37 |

non-producers, is relatively high; second, the expense of a disproportionately large number of deaths is imposed upon the poor; third, the amount of sickness is disproportionately large; and, fourth, the number of births is larger than in the upper classes. Let us see what effects these influences will have upon a population of 1,000 in each class.

[10] Reproduced by Billings, "Vital Statistics," p. 24.

TABLE XV.

BURDENS AND BURDEN-BEARING POWER OF 1,000 PERSONS IN VARIOUS CLASSES, POPULATION OF DUBLIN.

| *Class* | *No. of Persons Under 15* | *Persons Over 15* | *Deaths* | *Years of Sickness* | *Years of Health for Persons Over 15* | *Ratio of Sickness to Effective Health* |
|---|---|---|---|---|---|---|
| I ............ | 229 | 771 | 15.20 | 30.40 | 746.5 | 1 : 24.5 |
| II ........... | 300 | 700 | 26.21 | 52.42 | 663.3 | 1 : 12.6 |
| III .......... | 322 | 678 | 23.00 | 46.00 | 645.6 | 1 : 14 |
| IV and V..... | 277 | 723 | 37.79 | 75.58 | 665.5 | 1 : 08.8 |

"By effective health," as used in the table, is meant the health of persons fifteen years of age or over, that is, of persons capable of doing something for their own support, and possibly for the care of relatives. It will seem from the table regarding burdens and burden-bearing power, that in Class I there will be one year of sickness to 24.5 of effective health; in Class II one to 12.6; in Class III one to 14; and in Classes IV and V one to 8.8. Thus we have some explanation of how the high death-rate among the unfortunate classes operates to impose burdens that crush them.

There are too many assumptions involved in the derivative tables given to make it possible to consider the results reached entirely accurate, but in their general outline the figures doubtless reflect the actual situation. The fundamental and well-ascertained fact upon which all the conclusions are based is the high death-rate among the poorer classes; and, as just indicated, all that these derivative tables do is to show how and to what extent this high death-rate imposes disproportionally heavy burdens upon the poor.

**Charity as a Factor in Human Selection.** The influence of charity in the natural history of mankind has operated in such diverse ways that many have doubted whether its influence was for good or for evil.[11] We hear it spoken of as

[11] "I wish the art of benefiting men had kept pace with the art of destroying them; for, though war has become slow, philanthropy has remained hasty. The most melancholy of human reflections, perhaps, is that on the whole it is a question whether the benevolence of mankind does most good or harm. Great good, no doubt, philanthropy does, but then it also does great evil; it augments so much vice, it multiplies so much suffering, it brings to life such great populations to suffer and to be vicious, that it is

promoting the survival of the unfit, and frequent intimations are made that its interference with the struggle for existence is essentially pernicious. Spencer's dictum that the ultimate result of shielding people from the consequences of their folly is to fill the world with fools, appears to some to justify unmitigated hard-heartedness. Our analysis of the causes of poverty must, however, make it clear that there is a possibility of almost unmixed helpfulness in charity in the future, whatever have been the results in the past. The children of misfortune can be rescued from distress, without enabling the children of degradation to "be fruitful and multiply." [12] In fact, to prevent the one result is as much the work of charity as to promote the other. When charity is willing to canvass the remote results of its activity, it may be of use not only to individuals but to the race.

The most obvious result of charity as a selective force has been to lengthen the lives of the individuals cared for. There are many who believe it to be in and of itself a uniformly desirable result. They hold that no spark of human life can be extinguished without greater indirect loss than the direct gain which comes in freedom from the necessity of supporting the individual. They would care with all tenderness for the most misshapen physically and morally, until death could no longer be postponed. As the author has stood by the beds of consumptive or syphilitic children, he has wondered if it was a kindness to keep life in the gasping, pain-racked body. Cure was out of the question so far as medical science now knows, and one wonders why days of pain should be added to days of pain. The same questions recur as one passes through the incurable wards of an almshouse, especially as one studies the cases of the cancer-patients. The answer of religion to such questions is

open to argument whether it be, or be not, an evil to the world; and this is entirely because excellent people fancy that they can do much by rapid action, that they will most benefit the world when they most relieve their own feelings, that, as soon as an evil is seen, "something" ought to be done to stay and prevent it. One may incline to hope that the balance of good over evil is in favor of benevolence; one can hardly bear to think that it is not so; but, anyhow, it is certain that there is a most heavy debit of evil, and that this burden might almost all have been spared us if philanthropists, as well as others, had not inherited from their barbarous forefathers a wild passion for instant action." Bagehot's Works, vol. 4, p. 556.

[12] See McCulloch, *N. C. C.*, 1888, p. 154.

easy, and it seems very sure that without religious incentive we should not have entertained our present views regarding the sanctity of human life. But now that the feeling is developed, even science can explain in some sort how it is expedient that it should exist. We cannot extinguish or in any wise connive at the extinction of human life without injury to all the instincts and sensibilities that render it possible for us to live together with our fellows in civilized society.

Another reason why it is expedient to care for all that suffer is that eventually this policy compels us to search for causes of degeneration and suffering. By assuming the burden of protection we give bonds for our final interest in prevention. Could we cheaply rid ourselves of incapables, and close our hearts to the appeal of distress, we might never have the compulsion put upon us of seeking out the wiser plans, which may eventually give us a more uniformly healthy race. Some talk as though extermination would be a remedy for pauperism. Possibly, but it would be a costly remedy biologically; and if we allow our instincts to compel us to forego the use of it, we shall eventually find something better. In view of our present slowness in resorting to wise preventive measures this may seem almost like an unsubstantial refinement; but there are already indications that, as the burden gets heavier, the search for causes and the use of prophylactics will be pushed.

The influence of charity in diminishing the death-rate has probably had much to do with the increase in the proportion of insane and feeble-minded persons to the total proportion. The propagation of insanity by enabling the mentally diseased to become parents will be considered later. The mere lengthening of the lives of lunatics greatly increases their absolute and relative numbers. This is one of the most conspicuous, though possibly not one of the most important, effects that the death-delaying influence of charity has upon the average quality of population.

While the intended and usual effect of charity is to diminish the death-rate, mistaken or badly administered charities may have exactly the opposite result. An unclean hospital may result in the death of an undue number of the sick brought to it. In one maternity hospital the death-rate rose as high as two women for each five confinements. Previous to and during the 'sixties, European experience in maternity hospitals gave a mortality rate of about one death to twenty-nine confinements. In some large hospitals it was as high as one in seven. It is only recently that hospital service has become better than home service in this branch of medical practice. Undoubtedly the actual result of many foundling hospitals is to kill more infants than would meet death did such hospitals not exist. The death-rate is fearfully high; sometimes 97 per cent of the children fail to reach the age of three years; and in such circumstances the results ought to be pleasing to the most uncompromising advocate of the extermination of the "unfit." Few realize how almost impossible it is to raise babies by wholesale. Many who support charities designed to save infant life might conclude, if they studied all the facts, that they were contributing to its destruction.

The influence of charity upon the death-rate can be traced with comparative ease, though not with anything like exactness. Its influence on the birth-rate is much more obscure. Long before natural selection was discussed under that name, Chalmers called attention to the fact that the relief of the poor from public funds resulted in taking money from the thrifty and giving it to the thriftless. Apparently the last possibility in the way of contributing to the survival of the unfit was reached in the administration of the unreformed English poor-law which has been already referred to. The additional allowance per child was then so large as to make it pecuniarily profitable to have them. As the allowance for illegitimate children was somewhat larger than for those born in wedlock, a premium was put upon illegitimacy.

While the infant death-rate is known to be increased through institutions that receive without question all children brought to them, it is more of a question, or at least one that is more difficult to answer definitely, whether or not their influence tends to increase the number of illegitimate and abandoned infants. Lax morals and open foundling hospitals usually are found together; but it is not so easy to demonstrate the causal influence of the institutions in producing laxness of morals, though that they have such an influence is usually believed. The extreme facility and secrecy with which a child could be disposed of to French foundling hospitals of the older type is alleged to have had this result. The author's own observation leads him to think that foundling hospitals of the kind usual in America, because of the high death-rate already mentioned, tend to exterminate rather than to multiply the progeny of unfit stock.

Certain it is, that while charity may not cease to shield the children of misfortune, it must, to an ever increasing extent, reckon with the laws of heredity, and do what it can to check the spreading curse of race deterioration. The desire to prevent suffering must extend to the desire to prevent the suffering of unborn generations.

# CHAPTER VI

## THE ALMSHOUSE AND ITS INMATES

**The Almshouse as a "Catch-All."** The almshouse is the fundamental institution in American poor relief. It cares for all the abjectly destitute not otherwise provided for. Its shelter is the guarantee against starvation which the State offers to all, no matter how unfortunate or degraded. Consequently the inmates of the almshouses are often the most sodden driftwood from the social wreckage of the time. It is ordinarily a depressing experience to visit an almshouse, and accordingly we find it an institution that even the benevolent willingly forget. In many of the country almshouses no clergyman comes the year around; and no friendly visitor appears to encourage the superintendent to be faithful, or to bring to light abuses that may exist. Yet, since the institution is so fundamental, and since the number of its inmates is necessarily considerable, it may be doubted whether a more profitable work can easily be found than that for right organization and proper management of almshouses. The benevolent too frequently hurry away to make excellent provision for certain classes, while the maladministration of the local almshouse leaves a large assortment of destitute people under evil conditions.[1]

In New England, except New Hampshire, where there are both county and town institutions, the town (township) is the

[1] Many attempts have been made to avoid the stigma attaching to the almshouse by changing its name. "Almshouse" itself, although thought to be a better term than "poor-house" or the English "work-house," has in its turn degenerated, so that in many States the term "County Infirmary," or "County Home," is substituted. But an almshouse by any other name is much the same institution; and to call it a "home" or "retreat" will no more remove the disgrace of inmateship, than it will remove the "institution smell" from the suds-soaked floors of the building. The "stigma," whatever it may be, comes primarily from the average character of the inmates, and secondarily, from the character and want of skill of the officers in charge.

local political unit to which the care of the poor is entrusted, and the almshouse is accordingly managed by the town officers. In the other states the almshouse is usually a county institution. "It is not uncommon for several townships or counties to form themselves into an association, and establish what is called an 'association or district almshouse.'"[2] A low per capita expenditure for maintenance usually results from having a large institution with many inmates; but a small institution may also be economically managed if properly located on a farm, and under an efficient superintendent.

In 1880 there were 66,203 inmates of almshouses in the United States, or one almshouse pauper to 758 inhabitants; in 1890 there were 73,045 almshouse inmates, or one to 857 inhabitants.[3] The decrease in proportion to population does not indicate a general diminution of pauperism, but merely that a historical development, already in progress, has been continued. When the work of relief is first begun by the newly formed political units of an American settlement, it is usual to board out such dependents as must be supported entirely. Farmers or others are paid to care for old people, for imbeciles, and even for sick persons who have no homes of their own. Chiefly with a view to providing a place for the better care of the dependent sick, especially incurable cases, and also to economy, a public almshouse is established. During the first stage of its development, it acts as the charitable catch-all for the community. Idiots, epileptics, incurables, incompetents, the aged, abandoned children, foundlings, women for confinement, and a considerable number of the insane, the blind, and the deaf and dumb are all dumped together into some old farmhouse that has been bought by the authorities, and put to this use. The public then goes on its way, and thinks as little about the institution as possible, only grumbling annually at the expenses perhaps, when it happens to review public accounts.

In some populous cities the almshouses are hardly more than enlarged specimens of this same type. The different classes of dependents are still assembled in one great institution, and the public assumes it has discharged its whole duty by giving

[2] Census Bulletin, No. 90, p. 3.
[3] Bulletin, Eleventh Census, No. 90, p. 3.

enough food and fuel to keep the individuals that make up the incongruous mass from hunger and cold.

The defective classes of teachable age, the deaf, the dumb, and the blind, were the first to be drafted off to educational institutions, usually supported by the State. Next an effort was made to have the State take care of the insane. This is now usually done so far as the acute insane are concerned, but the great expense of providing for the increasing numbers of the chronic insane has led to a suspension of their transfer from the almshouses to specialized asylums. The movement for State educational institutions for the feeble-minded has only recently made much headway, and the custodial care of feeble-minded adults in special institutions is not yet attained in more than one or two States. The first special public institution for epileptics has recently been founded in Ohio.

It was early seen that a sure way to train up paupers was to rear children in almshouses. Their mimetic tendencies and the utter lack of education, or of anything to stimulate ambition or provoke energy, guaranteed their ruin. The placing them out by the local poor-law officers gave very unsatisfactory results, as they were spoiled by the time they were old enough to do anything, and the class of people applying for them at the almshouse seldom wanted them for purposes other than service. There was constantly much agitation and some legislation to get children out of the almshouses, either into special institutions, public or private, or into suitable homes.

**Differentiation of Charitable Work.** This differentiation of charitable work has left the old, the infirm, the decrepit, and the chronic invalids and paupers for the almshouse of the present time. A comparison of the figures of the Tenth Census with those of the Eleventh will show this change in progress, and indicate how far it has gone. The average age of almshouse paupers in 1880 was 45.1 years. In 1890 it was 51.03. The average age is lowest in the South Atlantic and the South Central divisions, where differentiation is least advanced, and highest in the Western division, where, as a rule, it is most advanced. In the far West one-half of all the almshouse paupers are between 60 and 80 years of age.

It appears that the largest proportion of children, relatively though not absolutely, at both dates, was found in the South Atlantic and South Central divisions, and the smallest in the Western. In all the divisions, however, there was a marked decrease in both the proportionate and absolute number of children in almshouses. Many who have been interested in the agitation for the removal of children from these institutions will be disappointed at finding that 4,338 are still so cared for —or rather so neglected. But it should be noted that of this number 793 are under one year of age, and 380 more are under two. The large number under one year of age indicates that many almshouses serve also the purpose of maternity hospitals, and that the children are not retained there after one or two years of age. On the whole, the showing of progress is satisfactory. In those communities where the burden of pauperism is light the proportion of almshouse inmates who are children is large, indicating that this is a condition of things that is tolerated in communities where relief work, because of its small volume, or for other reasons, has not drawn the interested attention of the community.

As to other classes of dependents in process of removal from almshouses, the figures are not given in a way to make results equally determinable, but in general it may be inferred that the decrease in the proportionate almshouse population comes not from a diminution of pauperism, but rather from the differentiation described. From other sources it is known that expenditures for relief work are in no wise falling off in the North Atlantic division, and yet this is the only section showing an important decrease in almshouse population, both absolutely and relatively to population. It is also the section where the differentiation of charitable functions has been most rapid.

**Inmates of Almshouses.** If we attempt to look past the statistics and get a completer view of these more than seventy thousand people in the almshouses of the United States, we can find much material in the reports of the State Boards of Charities. Probably the completest picture of an American almshouse population ever presented was that set forth, statistically and otherwise, by the New York State Board of Charities in response to a legislative resolution passed in May, 1873. It was the beginning of differentiation in that State, and gave the basis for the agitation which resulted in removing the children from New York almshouses, and has finally brought about the removal of the insane from those institutions. Of the 12,614 inmates, 422 were born in the almshouses, and of the remainder, 1,650 were admitted when less than ten years old. At the time of examination, nearly thirteen per cent were under ten years of age, and almost exactly the same proportion was over seventy. From the body of the Report,[4] it is learned that 3,085 of the inmates had been in the almshouses less than one year, while 38 persons had been inmates more than forty years. The average time of previous dependence for all inmates amounted to 4.88 years, not including time when they had been public charges in other institutions, or as out-door paupers.

This gives a total of 61,595 years of almshouse care for the benefit of the persons examined. Estimating the number of temperate and intemperate persons from those whose habits were ascertained, it was concluded that 84.36 per cent of the males, and 41.97 of the females, over sixteen years of age, were intemperate. Among the insane the percentages were 79.21 and 21.44 respectively. Of the parents of the insane, reckoning, however, from a much smaller basis of exact information, it was estimated that 45.59 per cent of the fathers and 17.72 per cent of the mothers were intemperate. As to the prospects of the inmates some day becoming independent, the following conclusions, based on a very careful study of each case, were reached; [5]

| | *Number* | *Percentage* |
|---|---|---|
| Permanently dependent | 8,145 | 64.57 |
| Will probably recover | 1,116 | 8.85 |
| May recover under proper training | 1,379 | 10.93 |
| Future doubtful | 1,974 | 15.65 |

In all the poor-houses were found, at the time of examination, more or less inmates whose ancestors were paupers, and who also had, living or dead, other near pauper relatives. The information upon this subject was obtained with considerable fulness in the rural counties, wher the history of pauper families was generally well known to the officers and others assisting in the examination. In the cities, however, but little could be learned bearing upon the subject.[6]

[4] Page 103. [5] Page 110. [6] Page 107.

The report farther says that the popular impression that the almshouses of the State give shelter to persons who, through misfortune in business or otherwise, have fallen from high estate, is not borne out by the facts. But few of the inmates had ever owned property to any considerable extent. While an exceptional case was found occasionally, the mass confessed to idle and shiftless habits in early life which kept them ever on the margin of destitution.[7]

The committee appointed by the town of Hartford, Conn., to report upon out-door relief in that place, made a careful examination of the almshouse and its inmates. They found that a considerable number of the insane and imbecile were kept there under very unsatisfactory conditions, also some children suffering from paralysis or other incurable disease. The committee were at first shocked to find that some wards of the building were used as a prison to which police-court cases were sent. It seemed distressing that the "worthy poor" should be put in the same building with criminals. Further inquiry, however, showed that of the two hundred and twenty-nine adult inmates of the almshouse proper, all but nine had probably been intemperate, and that a very large proportion of them had been sentenced for crimes or misdemeanors at some time in their career. It was also found that the most notorious police-court recidivists were most likely to be or to have been in the almshouse.[8] This was an unusually bad showing, but most communities would be surprised to learn how large a proportion of the inmates of their respective almshouses have been through a long experience in the police-court and jail. In San Francisco, the jail, the hospital, and the almshouse is each, in turn, the resort of the typical inmate. They come to the latter to recuperate so long as any vitality remains, and finally return there to die, when completely wrecked by dissipation and irregular living. The women are much completer wrecks than the men,

[7] Pages 106-07. On the other hand, the almshouses of California, and especially the San Francisco almshouse, have sheltered an unusually large number of persons of formerly high industrial and social standing and wealth. Though few in proportion to the total number of inmates, they are numerous as compared with Eastern institutions of the kind. Doubtless they were capable persons; but in a new country, and amidst a chaotic population, they risked all and lost. Some are no longer even respectable.

[8] Report of Committee, pp. 42-45.

because prostitution gives the idle and vicious an alternative career until the last.[9]

The disgrace that attaches to almshouse relief will not be lifted until differentiation has been carried a step farther, and there is some classification of inmates on the basis of character as disclosed in individual and family history. Reformatory institutions to which habitual drunkards, prostitutes, and other misdemeanants can be sent, and in which they must remain until reformation or death supervenes, would relieve the almshouse of many inmates, and the worthy poor of a very considerable portion of the disgrace which attaches to going there.

**Almshouse Abuses.** Of the almshouse abuses which result from the mistakes or wrong-doing of individual officials we shall say but little. Among them may be enumerated dishonest or wasteful management of the funds; culpable stinginess on the part of the appropriating power, resulting in inadequate or unhealthful food, lack of proper buildings, heating apparatus, clothing, and so forth; insanitary conditions, including dirt and vermin; and finally, actual cruelty, resulting from either brutality or neglect on the part of the officials in charge. Few understand how easy it is for an official in charge of the utterly helpless to do cruel things without intentional cruelty. In the rural districts especially, abuses are apt to arise because so few persons concern themselves with the institution. The superintendent has dreary work, small pay, and practically no general recognition of his services, whether they be good or bad. A sensitive, high-minded, ambitious man is not likely to apply for or accept such a place. The incumbent is, therefore, almost of necessity a tolerably stolid, unsympathetic person, and one who has not been very successful in other lines. The officials under whom he works send to him a miscellaneous assortment of the diseased, defective, and incapable, but do not give him the proper facilities for providing for these various classes. They cut his appropriations to the lowest possible point, and he fears that any vigorous protest would lose him the place. He therefore concludes that he may as well get along as

[9] Another factor is that women of good character are less likely than men to drift far away from all relatives, and relatives are also less likely to refuse to support them.

best he can, since to object would only bring some more docile man into his place. On the other hand, most of the inmates with whom he has to deal are bad-tempered, unreasonable, and inveterately querulous. They would complain no matter what might be done for them; and he gradually acts on the unrecognized impression that it does not matter what is done for them —that anything is good enough for them. He becomes brutal unconsciously, and almost in self-defence. After a few years he does, without question, things that would have seemed absolutely awful to him when he first entered on his duties. No influential person reviews and criticises his conduct, and he not unnaturally settles into the conviction that he is managing the almshouse as well as the community cares to have it managed. One can but sympathize with such an official, even when very grave abuses have grown up under his management.

There are, however, certain characteristics of our American almshouse administration which beget evil results, even when capable and conscientious officials are in charge. Among the evils of systemic origin for which the legislature or the community itself is responsible, one has just been indicated—the neglect of the almshouse and its management by the general public.

Probably a majority of the grave evils which could be charged at the present time to the American almshouse have their origin in a lack of proper classification of inmates. Classification is of two kinds, that which takes selected cases out of the almshouses altogether and puts them in specialized institutions, and that which groups properly those that remain in the almshouse. The former has already been discussed at length, and existing faults arise chiefly from the fact that many of the States have not kept pace with the march of opinion among specialists.

Classification inside the almshouse is easy in proportion as the drafting off of special cases to special institutions has been practiced; but it is always important, and in some of its branches calls for constant care and readjustment. 1. The separation of the sexes. In small institutions their constant and complete separation involves practical difficulties, and occasionally a hideous condition of affairs is brought to light. 2. Classification by color, resulting in almost duplicate institutions. 3. Isolation of defectives. It is partly because this separation is so frequently out of the question that they ought not to be here huddled together. 4. Special provision for the sick. From one-tenth to one-half the inmates are often practically bedridden. A special ward for syphilitics is often necessary, even in small institutions. Cancer patients must be isolated because of the offensive nature of their malady; and, in view of recent evidence as to the origin of consumption, those suffering with this disease ought also to be separated from the others.

Classification by age. This is especially necessary where there are children, but is usually not practiced. Young vagabonds and loafers drift into almshouses during the winter, and those who are virtually boys give themselves over for instruction in the arts of vice to the old and decaying devotees of sensuality. Classification according to character for reasons indicated in discussing classification on the basis of age. This is usually not attempted, and can only be carried out profitably where the matron or superintendent has great tact, patience, and ingenuity. In the San Francisco almshouse, instead of wards they have a large number of rooms—a form of construction which under the ordinary official would be very undesirable, but which has here been used to good purpose to give the self-respecting and improvable cases a semi-privacy which they value.

The second great evil which springs, not from the character of the officials, but from the nature of our almshouse organization, is laxness regarding admission and discharge of inmates. Since every person is entitled to be saved from starvation and death from exposure, and as that is nearly all that the almshouse does for its beneficiaries, anyone that wills to claim its shelter can have it. On the other hand, as it is not a penal institution, and as it is to the interest of no one to have persons stay there who can support themselves outside, an inmate wishing to discharge himself is allowed to do so. The average almshouse official regards the justification of our laxness indicated above as entirely conclusive. Whatever official or board may have the legal right of admitting or discharging inmates, the right of applicants to be admitted or discharged is regarded as inalienable. The door swings, accordingly, outward or inward with the greatest ease. Even the unduly lax rules regarding detention enforced in the English workhouse are unknown with us.

The results of this apparently defensible practice are thoroughly bad. Of the abuses to which it gives rise we may mention as first and least the support by the county of persons having pensions or property, or relatives able to support them. In some States, even where it is found after death that an almshouse inmate had considerable property, no attempt is made to recoup the county or town for the outlay.[10] A second and more serious abuse is the making of the almshouse a winter resort for tramps, and a place where the drunkard and the prostitute can recuperate between debauches. The Hartford Committee thus describes the life of drunken almshouse recidivists:

> They present themselves, or are brought, not infrequently ragged, filthy, shoeless, shivering with incipient delirium, at the office of the selectmen, receive a card, and are transported to the almshouse. There they are bathed, clad in a new suit, if necessary sent to the infirmary, carefully nursed out of their delirium, fed when convalescent upon whiskey and milk. A few days' work follow, prolonged into weeks, perhaps, if it be midwinter; only a few of those who can get away staying during the summer. The work, otherwise beyond their impaired forces, is made bearable, it may be, by occasional stimulants. Presently—and it is never long delayed—comes the drawing toward the old life; there is nothing to restrain them, and the bird has flown. Almost before his absence has been well noted, he is back again. The new suit has been pawned, or reduced to rags and filth by two or three days' debauch, and there follow bath, a second suit, more whiskey and milk, a feeble attempt at work, another flight, another debauch, a third application for ticket at the halls of record,—and so on in a vicious circle as unending as the patience of the first selectman and the indifference of the Hartford taxpayer.[11]

This description is in general terms, but particular instances are given. One woman came and went thirteen times in twenty-two and one-half months. A man who went and came at pleasure had allotted to him, in the course of two years and seventeen days, clothing which at wholesale prices amounted in value

[10] A number of San Francisco misers have had themselves supported at the almshouse.

[11] Report, pp. 14, 16.

to $85.28. Two pages of the Report are filled with an itemized account of this clothing. The man was receiving during all this time a pension of $8.00 per month from the Federal government. In some institutions inmates are given passes for ten days or more.

The final and worst result of permitting the destitute to admit and discharge themselves at will is that it enables the dissolute and degenerate to have offspring "after their kind." The results are most manifest in the cases of feeble-minded women. Mr. Charles Booth gives an instance of an English woman who in a little more than eight years presented the rural workhouse at Ashby-de-la-Zouch with five illegitimate children. In the workhouse this woman was capable and industrious, and a good nurse.[12]

A third very prevalent evil in the management of American almshouses is lack of a work-test, and a failure to enforce proper discipline among the inmates. This is placed among the evils of systemic origin because, while in some places an energetic and specially capable official may overcome all obstacles and enforce discipline and compel work, yet such an undertaking is usually discouraged, or at least not encouraged, by the authorities, and the sentiment of the community and the nature of legislation are usually such as to make this course difficult.

In small rural communities an almshouse is sometimes self-supporting. This usually means that the county or town owns a farm of moderate size, and that a thoroughly good farmer has been employed as superintendent. As a rule, not more than twenty per cent of the expenses of an almshouse can be defrayed by the work of the inmates. Often certain classes of the insane are the most efficient workers, and their presence in the almshouse contributes much towards making it self-supporting. But many of them are incapacitated by disease or old age for any work at all. Under the average superintendent, as a rule, it costs more to set the inmates of an almshouse to work than their work is worth. That is, a given number of inmates can be supported more cheaply in idleness than when they are put to work. It is for this reason that the labor in the

[12] *Pauperism*, etc., pp. 117-18.

English "workhouse" has degenerated so persistently into mere task-work.

The advantage to the management in obliging all inmates capable of doing anything to work consists in the deterrent influence of this policy upon would-be applicants. It is the surest and most commendable deterrent known. Its influence is especially valuable in preventing tramps from using the institution as a winter club-house.

From the side of the inmates, work for all is desirable because they are happier for having it. About the only happy persons one finds in an almshouse are those who are occupied. Idleness conduces to restlessness, sensuality, bad temper, and various forms of nervous disorder. In almshouses, as well as in prisons, insane asylums, and other kinds of institutions, discipline is doubly hard when the inmates are idle. That idleness in and of itself brings misery can be seen by anyone who passes through one of our Soldiers' Homes, especially the magnificent one for soldiers of the regular army at Washington. So well is this fact now ascertained that special societies are formed in the large cities for giving employment to the inmates of the great public institutions. There ought to be similar societies, or at least similar work done, in our rural communities; if it accomplished nothing else, it would at least interest some of the influential classes in the neglected institutions of the locality.

If there could be in American almshouses thorough investigation of all applicants for admission and all applications for dismissal, if within the institution there could be a thorough classification, thorough discipline, and an intelligent and kindly application of the work-test to all capable of doing anything at all, there would be no danger that almshouses would be overcrowded; while at the same time they would afford cleanly and honorable relief to the real children of misfortune. After some centuries of experiment, England has not realized this ideal, and we are very far from doing so; but it must be realized before the basis of our system of public and private charities can be considered sound.

**Substitutes for the Almshouse.** While the almshouse is, as a rule, the best place that public authorities yet consent to provide for the aged poor of good character, there have grown up in all centres of population a considerable number of private homes for the aged, usually managed by churches. Admission to these is generally obtained by the payment of a sum down which insures care during life. It is really a life annuity for somewhat less than its money value. One hundred to six hundred dollars is the sum charged, and persons are usually not admitted under sixty years of age. Sometimes the age limit is still higher. Frequently there is a provision that persons must be members of a particular denomination; sometimes the homes are established for a particular class, as for the wives of deceased ministers, and so on. Friends often contribute the admission fee for a deserving person, and obtain a place for him. Very frequently they are used as a means of providing a safe and comfortable place for the aged having a little property, or possibly a pension, who have no relatives with whom they can live, and who have not property enough to support them outside such an institution. When well managed, these homes furnish a very satisfactory way of providing for the aged of good character, and prevent the possibility of their degradation to the almshouse.

The Catholic Order of the Little Sisters of the Poor maintains in various large cities homes for the aged, to which persons are admitted without regard to creed or character, if only they are amenable to the rules of the house after admission. These homes are supported entirely by the Sisters, who beg from door to door, and from office to office, and go at the close of business to the markets and stores to collect the refuse or whatever may be given by the owners; and who further collect from hotels, restaurants, and private dwellings the broken victuals and other material that can be used. These homes are models of order. The Sisters, most of whom come from France, where is the other house of the order, have perfect control of the very querulous and often exacting inmates, whom they speak of as "the children."

There has lately developed a tendency for these institutions, including the homes of the Little Sisters of the Poor, to ask for public appropriations. This may possibly be the beginning of a new classification among those formerly sent to the almshouse—a tendency to support those of good character in special homes receiving public subsidies, and on the other hand, to leave those of degenerate character to be provided for in the almshouse. A wiser way would seem to be that heretofore suggested: Draft off those of bad character to special institutions, and leave the almshouse as a home for the unfortunate.[13]

[13] The very serious agitation in England for a system of relief for the aged more honorable than that afforded by the poor-law authorities has crystallized about the idea of old-age pensions. It seemed likely for a time to carry everything before it. Canon Blakesly of the church, Charles Booth the statistician, and Joseph Chamberlain the politician, each had plans to propose for the endowment of old age. The agitation at present seems to have lost some of its force, but will probably come up again in other forms until something results from it. No analogous agitation has taken place in the United States; but it is likely enough that if successful in England, it will be transferred to the United States. We already have in California what amounts to a pension for the aged. The State law provides that any institution maintaining persons over 60 years of age shall receive for each such person an annual allowance of $100 per year. (Institutions owning property worth $15,000 or more, and supporting at least ten inmates aged 60 years or over, are entitled to $100 per year for each inmate. Statutes and Amendments to Codes, 1883, pp. 380-382.) This applies to the county almshouses and public institutions as well as to private charities. It thus comes about that county officials can admit old people to the benefits of the institution and the bill will be paid by the State. There is sometimes even a profit. On the explanation of the county officials, it was shown to the State authorities that many old people might just as well be given their $100 in their homes as to be compelled to take up their residence in the alsmhouse. This was assented to; and it thus comes about that there is an old-age pension in California, which can be obtained from the county authorities, but is paid by the State. As soon as the law has brought about some of the results that must spring from its operation, it will no doubt be repealed.

# CHAPTER VII

## RELIEF OF THE POOR IN THEIR HOMES

**The Scope of Out-Door Relief.** There are absolutely no reliable statistics of out-door relief in the United States as a whole. The census figures of 1880 are avowedly incomplete, and those of 1890 cannot be expected to be much better. Out-door relief in the United States is given by county and township officials; and from its nature the bookkeeping is likely to be even more faulty, especially as to the number of persons aided, than is that of almshouses. In addition to this, out-door relief does not have the same meaning in different places and according to different laws. In England it usually means all relief that is given outside of the workhouse. The indigent insane, consequently, who are relieved in special institutions, are classed among those receiving out-door relief, though, as Mr. Sanborn suggests, if anybody is in-doors, it is apt to be the indigent insane. The same policy is followed in the United States, where English precedents have obtained. For instance, in Massachusetts what is called "State out-door relief" is given very largely to cases of the sick poor chargeable to the State, who are placed in hospitals, and their expenses defrayed from the funds at the disposal of the State Board of Lunacy and Charity. Cases of dangerous disease are also provided for under the same heading; and, finally, the administrative expenses of the department are reckoned in with the amount spent for out-door relief; consequently, only a small modicum of the expenditure really goes in temporary aid to the poor in their own homes.[1] Those who dispute about the advisability of out-door relief often confuse themselves and each other by sometimes including and sometimes excluding such relief when given from private funds. Unless otherwise specified, the term

[1] See Report of State Board of Lunacy and Charity, 1893, pp. 38-41.

out-door relief, as used in this chapter and volume, will mean the relief given from public funds to the poor in their homes, not including medical relief.

Mr. Sanborn and others would dissent from the statement made at the beginning of the preceding chapter that the almshouse is the fundamental institution in the relief of the poor. They would say that the system of relieving the poor should be founded upon family relief, or what is generally called out-door relief, that is, the relief of the poor in their own homes. They point to the fact that this is one of the kindliest, and may be one of the cheapest, forms of alleviating distress, especially incipient distress, and say that only after a case has been found to belong to some special class, requiring institutional care, should it be passed on to the limitations of institution life. On the other hand, there are those who believe it to the interests of the poor and of the whole community to demand the total abolition of out-door relief; who point again and again to the English experience under an unreformed poor-law before 1834, and to the many disastrous experiments in out-door relief in this country.

**Arguments for and Against Out-Door Relief.** The following may be mentioned as the principal reasons assigned by those who believe in the maintenance of out-door relief as a fundamental part of the relieving system:

1. It is believed to be kindly. The poor person is not separated from relatives and friends, families are not broken up, and the receipt of relief is not as conspicuous and consequently as disgraceful as it is where resort must be had to an institution.

2. It is apparently economical. Many families can almost support themselves, and it seems folly to dismember them and place the children in refuges or board them in private families, and compel the adults to resort to the poor-house, when a little relief given in the home would keep the family together and enable them to make part of their support by ordinary methods. Those who receive out-door relief receive usually less than it would cost to maintain the same number of persons in the almshouse.

3. There are not institutions enough. The demand for re-

lief always keeps considerably in advance of the supply; and it would be uneconomical, and in fact impossible, to have buildings enough to accommodate all who should be relieved from time to time. Especially in the winter months, a large number of persons need relieving for a short time; and if the almshouses were large enough to accommodate them during the winter, there would be great buildings vacant during the summer.

This gives certainly a good *prima facie* case for the retention of a certain amount of out-door relief. On the other side the following considerations are urged:

1. It increases the number of applicants, because it is less manifestly disgraceful than the in-door system, and is much more pleasant to receive for other obvious reasons. The saving in cost for a single person supported is more than made up by the additional number of persons that will claim to require relief. It is a sufficiently pleasant form of being relieved, so that if no requirement except indigency is made, a large number of persons will become duly indigent in order to qualify for the receipt of alms.

2. It is urged that out-door relief is undesirable, because it requires an amount of discrimination between cases that is practically impossible where the work is done by public officials. It has long been a principle that any work was suitable for a government to do in proportion as it could be reduced to a routine and done in a semi-mechanical way. As the work of giving out-door relief cannot be done in this semi-mechanical way, it is unsuitable for public officials to undertake.

3. It is urged that corruption of politics results from the system, and that, in fact, the whole tone of the population is lowered where this form of relief is given. In many cases, it is unworthy motives favoring the retention of the system that makes it difficult to secure its abolition.

4. Where out-door relief has been given lavishly, as in England at some times and places, it has simply resulted in reducing the rate of wages, the amount given in relief being reckoned on as a possible resource, so that the employee would accept lower wages than would otherwise have been possible.

Those who favor the system of out-door relief usually argue

upon theory, or draw their facts from rural communities where the problems are comparatively simple, and where abuses are readily checked.

**Experiments in the Abolition of Out-Door Relief.** On the other hand, the opposers of the system deal mainly with facts, and these facts very largely gleaned from the administration of out-door relief in large cities.

The most instructive experiments that have been made in this matter in the United States have consisted chiefly in cutting off peremptorily the supply of out-door relief. The two stock cases of this sort are Brooklyn and Philadelphia. The first was reported to the National Conference of Charities in 1879 by Seth Low, under whose administration as mayor the change had been accomplished. The account of this experiment is given in Mr. Low's own words.

Out-door relief, so-called, began in Brooklyn in 1851-52. For the year ending July 31, 1852, the number of people helped was 6,754, at a cost of $7,139.99. With some variations this had grown in 1864 to 20,743 persons helped, at a cost of $25,921.47. In 1865 the general demoralization which set in after the war placed a corrupt man in charge of the poor-funds, and the figures bear witness to the result. From that moment bad became worse uninterruptedly. In 1865, while only 1,500 more people were helped than in 1864, it cost the county $72,708.97, against $25,921.47 in 1864, an increase of $46,000 in a single year. In 1877 help was given to 46,350 persons, or nearly one-tenth of the population, at a cost of $141,207.35. For the six years from 1872 to 1877, an average of 35,109 were helped at an average cost of $114,943.72. The total outlay for this period of six years by Kings County for out-door relief alone was $689,662.35. To such an item at last had grown the kindly and apparently harmless thing. The population of Kings County is estimated in round numbers to have been in 1852, 150,000; in 1864, 320,000; in 1877, 550,000.

The system had become furthermore a sore on the body politic. The friends of politicians received help whether needy or not, and so the system was perpetuated. Families with voters were the first served. The "out-door relief" appropriations became a vast political corruption fund. Large numbers of the population were taught to rely on the county help, and sought it for no other reason than that the county gave it. One woman received help under nine different names. Many sold what they received. Men came from the country every autumn to live at the expense of the city during the winter, because the city was offering a premium to the idle to come there and live in idleness. The poor did not get the chief benefit of increased appropriations. Most of it went to underlings connected with the work of distribution. In every way, and in every direction, the effect was hopelessly bad.

In 1875 the Commissioners of Charity employed paid visitors to investigate the cases of applicants for relief; and it cost sixty cents to distribute every dollar's worth of food or fuel. This was so monstrous that public clamor compelled a change. In 1876 the visiting system was abandoned, and all applicants were compelled to take oath that they were paupers. As may be imagined, the result was horrible. Moreover, many who lived in New York availed themselves of such easy opportunity to be fed by Brooklyn.

. . . . . . . . .

In 1877 a committee of volunteer visitors was organized, who agreed to investigate the cases of all applicants for relief. Their services, fortunately, were accepted by the Charity Commissioners. These visitors were not given power to control the distribution of relief, but could only report. They did not directly accomplish much. But they saw thoroughly the working of the system, and came to the conclusion that "out-door relief" could not be administered by the county so as to be worth giving. The following year, 1878, the volunteer visitors so reported to the Charity Commissioners and to the Board of Supervisors. The visitors said, however, that as out-door relief had been given for so long, and many of the poor had been educated, in a sense, to depend upon such help, they would continue to visit for that year also, provided nothing should be distributed excepting coal. The visitors suggested that the year following even coal might properly be withheld. . . . Long attention to the subject had convinced some that "out-door relief," on the part of the county, was not legal under the laws of the State. At this crisis, through friends in the Board of Supervisors, the question of legality was referred to the counsel of the board.

The opinion of counsel was delivered at a meeting of the Board of Supervisors, held Jan. 31, 1878. It was to the effect that, in the absence of special laws authorizing it, the system of out-door relief was contrary to the general poor-law of the State of New York. This opinion prevented an appropriation for out-door relief in Kings County during the last winter, 1878-79. Many anticipated great and unusual suffering among the poor by consequence. The testimony of the private relief associations, and of many who give much time personally to visiting among the poor, is all to the same effect. The poor have suffered less this winter in Brooklyn than either last year or the winter before.

The saving in the interests of morality cannot be expressed in money.[2]

Philadelphia in 1879 had a similar experience. The amount distributed in out-door relief in 1875, also in 1876, was $82,-000, and in 1879, $66,000. The supply of relief was then cut off peremptorily; and while the secretary of the Society for Organizing Charity reports that there was for a time a somewhat greater pressure upon private relieving agencies, the pressure soon passed away, and the demand for relief was not greater than it had been, while the population of the almshouse decreased, even in the face of the increasing population of the city.

The only suggestion that has ever been made as to evil results from the experiment in Brooklyn, is that the number of dependent children increased after out-door relief had ceased to be given. But the number of dependent children also increased in other parts of New York, where no change in out-door relief administration had occurred, indicating that it was a change in the laws affecting dependency among children that produced the increase. I have never heard of any well-authenticated instance where out-door relief was stopped and where the population of the public charitable institutions subsequently increased. In other words, as administered in the United States, it is found apparently, that out-door relief educates more people for the almshouse than it keeps out of it, and that therefore it is neither economical nor kindly.[3]

It Wisconsin it has repeatedly been the case that, when an almshouse was built, the expense for poor relief decreased by half, and the moral tone of the community improved.[4]

Both Dugdale and McCulloch held out-door relief to be

[2] *National Conference of Charities*, 1879, pp. 202-204.

[3] Almost the only report that has been made in favor of out-door relief was that of the Committee of the Boston Overseers of the Poor in 1888; but a report by the committee in favor of the system was said to be a foregone conclusion, and certainly the facts adduced do not in any obvious degree support their conclusions. A correspondent of *The Boston Herald*, Aug. 14, 1888, apropos of their report, gives an analysis of 73 cases that have been relieved with more or less regularity by the Overseers of the Poor from 1883 to 1888; and the conclusion reached on the basis of the facts ascertained was that out-door relief as there administered was a bad thing for the community.

[4] Rep. of State Board of Control, 1892, p. 374.

largely responsible for the persistence of the pauper families they studied.[5]

It may be that the system of out-door relief is especially difficult to administer under the county system of local government. In the smaller townships the officials are measurably well acquainted with the people, at least until the population becomes dense, and the people scrutinize public expenditures quite carefully. Under the county system, until the population is large enough to compel the employment of special officials, the writing of orders for out-door relief is frequently left to the individual supervisors or commissioners. As a rule, each one attends to all applications from the district from which he is elected, and the approval of the entire board is a mere formality. The payments are sometimes made in money, sometimes in orders on stores, and sometimes relief is given in goods purchased by the authorities under contract. Obviously this latter method lends itself least readily to abuse. Where orders are given on stores, the goods selected by the beneficiary are often absurdly unsuitable to his condition,[6] and in the state of California such orders are frequently traded for liquor.

On the whole, it must be admitted that the advisability of giving out-door relief is a question of administration. Under the Elberfeld system in Germany, and with the great care exercised by the *Bureaux de Bienfaisance* of France, it has been successful. But it must be remembered that the people of the United States have a larger share of administrative awkwardness than any other civilized population. Nearly all the experiences in this country indicate that out-door relief is a source of corruption to politics, of expense to the community, and of degradation and increased pauperization to the poor. Whether at its worst or at its best, it has not been found a satisfactory method of relieving distress. In the new communities of the

[5] Dugdale comments as follows: "Lavish public charity becoming a custom, it is manifest that certain families receiving help generation after generation will display a persistence of dependence identical in form to that produced by hereditary pauperism from physical degeneration, but entirely different in nature, and as easy to suppress as true hereditary pauperism is difficult to control." (*N. C. C.*, 1877, p. 94.)

[6] See Hartford Report, pp. 19, 20, and Table VII. On 594 orders, 132 articles were drawn, among which were canned lobster, green pease, pie, pineapple, canned salmon, and tobacco. There was also some evidence that the orders were used in trade and payment of debts.

West it has seemed to be almost necessary; but it is always to be watched with care, to be kept at a minimum, and in large cities to be definitely prohibited.

Finally something must be said regarding private out-door relief.

**Superiority of Private Charity.** In all large centres of population, there are certain societies, which, together with the churches and private individuals, do a considerable amount of relief-work. These agencies dispense an amount which is not large, as compared with public expenditures for the relief of the poor, but which is sufficient to accomplish a great deal of good or a great deal of evil in the populations among which it is scattered. Those who, like Mrs. Lowell and others, insist that public out-door relief should be abolished, believe in this extension of private associations to care for the cases to whom the alternative of going to the almshouse would be an unmerited hardship. They insist that the private associations are more economical, and more discriminating, and since their treasuries are not replenished from the proceeds of taxation, but from free-will offerings, the poor cannot make demands upon them as of right. The experience of Chalmers is constantly pointed to as showing that public relief can be swept away entirely, and private benevolence take its place. While those who would imitate him would not go as far as he did, they do ask for the substitution of private for public out-door relief. For the present, under existing conditions, in the United States, their case apparently is well made out. It is undoubtedly true that private associations are best fitted to deal with incipient dependency. But it should not be forgotten that private charities are just as open to abuse as public ones, though not to exactly the same abuses. In places where the State has relegated much of the work of relieving the poor to private benevolence, and especially to the church, abuses have grown up of as great magnitude as those that preceded the reform of the English poor-law in 1834. In Italy, where, until recently, the church administered vast relief-funds, those who wish to reform the system of relieving the poor are said to look with envy upon the English system of out-door relief as forming a rational and modifiable basis for charities. At Elberfeld also the present excellent public system originated in a break-down of the private system. There is a possibility of success or failure by either method; but experience seems to indicate that in the United States, at the present time, private is much safer and more helpful than public out-door relief, and indeed that the latter should usually be discontinued.

# CHAPTER VIII

## THE UNEMPLOYED AND THE HOMELESS POOR

**The Unemployed and Their Relief.** Until there is more discrimination between the different classes of the unemployed, all statistics regarding them must be somewhat ambiguous. The Labour Department of the English Board of Trade has published a report on "Agencies and Methods for Dealing with the Unemployed" which specifies four tolerably distinct classes, composing what is usually thought of as a single class. First, there are those who, being engaged for short periods only, have finished one job and not yet entered on another. Their loss of time is spoken of as mere "leakage." Second, there are those who belong to trades in which the volume of work fluctuates, because of seasonal changes, most commonly during a year, but sometimes during longer periods, as in the shipbuilding trades, and sometimes during periods of less than a year. Third, there are members of various trades who are economically superfluous. This may come from too many learning such trades, from changes in trade processes, from local shifting of industries, etc. Fourth, there are those who cannot get work because they are below the standard of efficiency usual in their trades.[1]

"One of the most serious features of the situation is the fact that want of employment and casual employment have themselves a powerful tendency to produce inefficiency, both by the physical deterioration due to insufficient nourishment, and the moral deterioration which often results from want of regular work." [2] The best 1,000 unemployed members of a given group of trades at any given time are less efficient, whether from physical, moral, or intellectual defects, than the worst 1,000 who

[1] Report, 1893, pp. 9-11.

[2] Labour Department of the English Board of Trade on Agencies and Methods for Dealing with Unemployed, Report, 1893, p. 12.

are in actual employment at the same time. To a very large extent, manifestly, the problem is an industrial and not a charitable one. It is only when non-employment results in destitution that its treatment is germane to our present purposes.

The most difficult problem in the whole realm of poor-relief is this of providing for the unemployed. England has worked at it intermittently from the time of Elizabeth, when one of the primitive acts of the English poor-law provided for "setting the poor on work," and authorized the collection of rates for that purpose. So far as it concerns the relief of the resident poor, it was indirectly treated under the head of out-door relief. This present chapter passes from my hand in March, 1894, when special relief-work for the unemployed is being carried forward on a scale never before known or needed in this country. It is therefore not possible to give the results of this emergency work. The general principles which have been worked out elsewhere through a long series of similar experiences may be summarized as follows: 1. Relief in work should be given by substantially the same methods as other relief, that is, after careful investigation of individual cases. Indiscriminate giving of relief in work by public authorities not connected with the poor-law administration is demoralizing. 2. The work should be real work, and as productive as possible. So far as it is used as a test, it is better if it can be continuous for each individual for a considerable time. 3. Whenever public authorities or private persons see an opportunity to do at unusually low rates, because of the hard times, work that needs doing, they ought to push such work on business and not relief principles, and in the general following of this policy is to be found a radical remedy for trade depression.

**"Passing On."** The present chapter is concerned especially with the problem of the homeless poor as a constant factor in the administration of charities. The question of how to deal with the tramp is said to be of especial urgency in every locality in the United States with which I am at all acquainted. From Boston to San Francisco, and from St. Paul to New Orleans, complaints come of a number of tramps which is alleged to be "especially" large in each case.

There are four tolerably distinct ways in which various communities in the United States have tried to deal with the homeless and wandering poor. The first and favorite way is to get rid of them as promptly as possible by sending them on. Nearly every large town makes an appropriation for the transportation of paupers, and the poor-law officers of rural communities also devote some money to the same purpose. Such funds are frequently spent without any adequate investigation. The officials having authority simply consider whether it will be cheaper to ship a given person to a place where he says he wishes to go, or to take care of him. Formerly there was in Baltimore a fund, which was disbursed under the authority of the mayor's private secretary, who was bound by the rule that transportation could be furnished only to the next large city. If a person wished to go to New York, Baltimore gave him a ticket to Philadelphia, and expected him to be forwarded from there by the mayor of Philadelphia. A large number were sent in the same way to Washington. The excuse for this was that Washington sent a large number to Baltimore, and it was only fair to get even.

The conditions in the smaller cities as regards wandering mendicants are very well reflected by the discussion of the matter which took place at the First Indiana State Conference of Charities. The superintendents of the county asylums met and discussed a paper on travelling mendicants, and compared their experience in dealing with this class. It transpired that most of the county asylums or poor-houses fitted up a room or rooms where tramps were lodged, and that they were given shelter and food with, or more commonly without, a work-test, but that, above all things, the effort was made to induce them to move on. The trustees' office at Fort Wayne reported $231.65 spent for railroad fares, or an average of 69½ cents per person railroaded out of that place. Trustees from other districts admitted that they did the same thing. When they met in this conference and compared notes, it was apparent that they were making a mistake, and a reform was begun forthwith. Unfortunately, in most of the States such conferences have not been held.

The obvious objection to this manner of providing for the homeless poor is that it does not provide for them; it is simply a way of shifting burdens from one community to another. But each community, while recognizing this fact, thinks itself bound to keep up the foolish work, so that it may not serve as the dumping-ground for the poor of all the adjacent communities.

**Imprisonment.** The second way of dealing with the homeless poor is to punish them as misdemeanants—"vag 'em," as the police say; that is, arrest them as vagrants, and commit them to the jail and workhouse. This is the old English method of dealing with what were called "sturdy beggars." But in the early days it was not a comfortable jail to which tramps were committed, and wanderers who could give no account of themselves were flogged out of the boundaries of the parish in which they were apprehended. They were also liable to be branded, have their ears cut off, or be treated in some similar fashion which would now be regarded as barbarous.

In 1879 Connecticut passed a law providing that every tramp should be punished by imprisonment in the State prison for not more than one year. Soon after this law went into effect it seemed to have been a complete success. The number of lodgers in the Hartford police-station fell off from 85 to 130 to from 3 to 5. The chief of police of New Haven said that the law had been the means of driving from the city a class of criminals who went around begging for the sake of stealing. "There is no begging from door to door as formerly," he reported. The rural authorities were equally well pleased, and for a time it seemed as though the one thing needful for the cure of trampery had been found. Latterly, however, there have been no convictions under this law, and the old order of things has returned. It gives a very good illustration of what repressive legislation can and cannot accomplish in this matter. The method, if rigidly applied, may cause tramps to disappear for a time; but there is always a doubt in the minds of the community as to whether or not many cases of honest destitution are not dealt with too harshly. Such stringent laws are very apt to become dead-letters, and the evil at which they were aimed flourishes while they are in abeyance.

**Indiscriminate Relief.** A third very common way of dealing with the homeless poor is to give them indiscriminately the relief they ask. If a man rings the door-bell, and asks for food, give him some; if he asks for the price of a night's lodging, let him have it; if men apply for lodgings at the station-house, fit up a room and let them fill it as full as they can fill it and still live; start a free lodging-house, and supplement the lodgings with free meals. If a man comes when it is cold and asks admission to the almshouse, take him in, give him comfortable shelter for the winter, and then, when spring comes, let him depart. This was the method employed in mediæval monasteries, and is still more or less practised in most of our American cities. The trouble with this method is that "we can have as many tramps as we will pay for."

A modification and improvement of this method is to give indiscriminately, but never to give at all without applying the work-test. It is substantially the method of the English Casual Ward. The Boston Wayfarers' Lodge is the best example of this plan in the United States.

**Improved Methods.** On reviewing the three methods of dealing with the homeless poor already mentioned, it is apparent that each is adapted to certain classes of applicants; some should be given direct relief, some should be punished, and some should be sent to other places. There are tramps and tramps; any method that enables us to deal with them properly must enable us to discriminate.

The machinery necessary for dealing properly with the problem of the homeless poor has been set up in comparatively few places, although it can be adapted to both large and small communities with comparative ease. It consists of an institution or place where the work-test can be rigidly applied, and where a man can earn his support pending an investigation of his case. Secondly, it includes facilities for giving meals and lodgings; thirdly, facilities for bathing and for disinfecting clothing; and fourthly, some person to investigate the case of each applicant thoroughly, and to act as circumstances require. Philadelphia was one of the first of American cities where the machinery described was operated successfully; the Society for Organizing Charity of that city established friendly inns and provident woodyards, and a special office for dealing with cases of non-residents. The station-houses were emptied, and the police referred all applicants for lodgings to the society, though by no means all went to its offices.

In Philadelphia an applicant to the agent for the care of non-residents is first asked to state his case. If he claims to have a residence, or to be able to get work somewhere else, or if he admits having relatives and friends elsewhere, or whatever may be his story, he is sent to the woodyard to earn his living while it is being investigated. No man is assisted to leave the city unless it appears on some authority, additional to his own, that he would be better off in the place to which he is sent. Many men, after telling their story and taking the card which would admit them to the lodging-house and woodyard, never present it. Some are conscious that their story would not bear investigation, and some do not care to work while it is being investigated. All cases of honest destitution, whether the applicant be a boy, a man, or a woman, are dealt with in the same kindly but thorough-going fashion; and the result is help for the deserving, and disappointment for the loafer and impostor.

In Boston there is the lodging-house and the woodyard, but no attempt at investigation; the men drift through the institution, and no one attends to their needs beyond the giving of the temporary relief. In New Haven Mr. Preston of the Organized Charities Association has improved upon the Philadelphia plan. The woodyard is open in the evening, so that a man can always work in advance of getting relief and the men work according to a certain stent, instead of by the hour as in Philadelphia. Here also the investigation is very thorough, and many cases of wanderers returned to places where they could be finally provided for might be told. In Washington the District government opened a municipal lodging-house in January, 1893. At that time there were about 150 men per night sleeping in the station-houses. It was a specially cold time; and as the municipal lodging-house could not accommodate more than fifty, it was feared that it would be over-full at once. But the woodyard was kept open for workers in the evening, the men were made to saw by the piece and not by time-work, and the institution during the whole remainder of the winter never had as many lodgers as it could accommodate, although the station-houses were completely closed to lodgers. Neither has it been full during the present winter. The same experiment was tried in Baltimore during the winter of 1893-94 with exactly similar results.

Many, especially those engaged in the agitation for the establishment of municipal lodging-houses such as those described, have thought that the whole tramp problem would be solved by their institution; but there are certain difficulties attendant upon their management, not usually reckoned with. In the first place, it is almost impossible to find anything that is really profitable for the men to do. If they saw wood, they come in competition with steam-saws, and if they break stone, with steam stone-crushers. In Washington it was found that it cost eighty cents more per cord to supply the District with sawed wood from the yard in connection with the municipal lodging-house than it did to get sawed wood direct from the contractor. This was in part because of the nature of laws regarding the letting of contracts in the District, but in no place is it possible to have men earn much by hand-sawing. The Philadelphia society finds continual difficulty in disposing of its wood supply in competition with the regular dealers; and in New Haven the wood-sawing department only pays the running expenses of the yard, and for the meal and lodging tickets which the men are given. No careful calculation has been made in Boston to ascertain what profit, if any, is made in the woodyard. Where, as in Washington, every stick of wood that a man saws costs the District a little more than if the man did nothing at all, we have manifestly not reached any real solution of the difficulty. It is just this impossibility of finding remunerative work for labor which is on the whole incompetent that has induced the English workhouses to give pure task-work to the inmates of their casual wards. But work which is avowedly task-work is not only unprofitable, but it is almost as degrading to the man who does it as to receive relief for which he makes no return. Its only justification is its deterrent influence. It is profitable because it reduces the number of applicants. Where woodyards have been made to pay expenses, as with the Appleton Homes in Boston, it is because some man has donated to the work sufficient managerial ability to make up for the poor quality of the labor and methods used. But good managers are not often available.

Another reason why the lodging-house and woodyard does not solve all the difficulty, is that its management seems to have an inveterate tendency to become mechanical. Interest is lost in the individuals; and they are ground through the regular routine without any real attempt being made to get hold of the helpable, and to punish habitual and degraded vagrants. As a consequence, there comes to be a very considerable army of intermittently drunken loafers who rely upon the lodging-house and woodyard as a place where they can always get something to eat and a lodging for the night. They are not unwilling to work for a short time and in a perfunctory way. The multiplication of this class, or at least the toleration of it as it multiplies, is said to be one of the serious evils connected with the Naturalverpflegungsstatsionen in Germany.[3] Where small account is taken of individuals, men can come repeatedly to the lodging-house in spite of a rule limiting their residence there to not more than three days at any one time.

The chief advantage of the woodyard and lodging-house arrangement is that it gives the citizens of the locality an opportunity to refuse all unknown applicants for relief, and to send them to the lodging-house. More than that, if there be but one

[3] Labor Colonies in Germany and Holland: German and Dutch experiments in the matter of relieving the unemployed are too instructive to be passed by with only the brief reference proper to them in the text.

Experiments on behalf of the unemployed group themselves roughly in three or possibly four classes. First, those based on the assumption that the unemployed are efficient workmen whom circumstances have deprived of work; they are designed to tide over the temporary difficulty by relief or relief in work, and the finding of regular work for the man. Second, those based on the assumption that the unemployed are many of them not efficient, but may be trained back into efficiency, and providing for this attempt. Third, those based on the assumption that many of the unemployed are incurably inefficient as far as ordinary industry is concerned, but may be so organized on a farm colony as to be self-supporting. These three classes of benevolent effort develop one after the other as experience accumulates in a given locality. Each succeeds in curing dependency in some cases; but finally there is a residuum of persons who cannot be made self-supporting by any education or organization, and these call for a fourth class of institution—the farm colony which does not pretend to be self-supporting. This, however, is virtually an almshouse. Most American experiments are of the first class, the German Labor Colonies are of the second, and the Dutch Free Home Labor Colonies are of the third, while the Dutch Beggar Colonies are of the fourth.

of these lodging-houses in a city, or if those that exist co-operate one with another, it is possible to stop that drifting about from one place to another in the same town, which enables a vagrant to stay there through the whole winter. This centralization was one of the very best things resulting from the establishment of the municipal lodging-house in Washington.

The machinery described is necessary machinery; but it will not run itself, and it will not solve the tramp problem. It gives the basis for proper action, but does not insure it. As already suggested, proper action can come only after there has been a thorough discrimination between cases. Proper dealing with the tramp problem in the United States is for the most part impossible until we have reformed our infamous system of county jails. The basis of all charitable work for the homeless poor should be a carefully drawn statute providing for the commitment of all the habitual vagrants and drunkards under indeterminate sentence to houses of correction. In the houses of correction they should be put at hard labor, and not let out until some evidence of reformation is given. At present, a man who is sentenced for vagrancy is usually sent for from ten to ninety days to a warm and pleasant jail, where he can play cards, chew tobacco, discuss crime, and tell indecent stories with his peers. To threaten a vagabond with arrest under such circumstances, is merely to promise to do him a favor.

If there were the proper punitive machinery for removing these worthless vagabonds from the consideration of the charitable, it would next be necessary to have properly organized institutions to care for the young, the sick, the aged, and the otherwise incapable. This would very greatly reduce the number with whom the superintendent of the lodging-house would have to deal, and if he were a man of sound sympathies and sound judgment, and were put in a position where the time at his disposal was adequate for the work, he could then discriminate intelligently between the different applicants and do the right thing by each. It is quite certain that there are resources sufficient in almost any American community to deal with the problem of the homeless poor efficiently and completely, if they could only be organized so as to meet the genuine needs. The trouble has been that here, as in England, we have vacillated between excessive severity and excessive leniency, oftener erring on the latter side than on the former, until the tramp has become an institution, and appears to think that he has an inalienable right to life, liberty, and the pursuit of vagabondage.

# CHAPTER IX

## DEPENDENT CHILDREN

At the Denver Conference of Charities, Mr. Hart of the Minnesota State Board of Charities and Corrections estimated the number of dependent children in the United States to be 74,000. The expenditures for buildings and "plant" used in taking care of these children he put at $40,000,000, and the annual expenditure for maintenance in all forms at $9,500,000. About 9,000 persons were supposed to be employed as caretakers.[1] Unless the Eleventh Census secures more reliable returns than were obtained in 1880, this estimate by a careful man is more trustworthy than the formal tabulation of incomplete or careless reports. In this department of charitable activity, it is not wise to leave wholly out of view the nominally correctional work; and so mention should be made of Mr. Hart's further estimate that there were 15,000[2] inmates of juvenile reformatories costing $10,000,000, and entailing an annual average charge for maintenance of $2,000,000.

The work for dependent children is the most hopeful branch of charitable endeavor in that it affords more possibilities of constructive work than any other line. When Charles L. Brace, the elder, was a young man, his first association with benevolent undertakings was in work for the adult vagabonds and loafers whom he found in the lower districts of New York. A little experience with these persons was enough to discourage him thoroughly, and it was not until he turned to the work of caring for neglected children that he felt sure of the helpfulness of his efforts. In work for the aged, the sick, the defective, even for the unemployed, one is conscious that for the indi-

[1] *N. C. C.*, 1892, p. 193.

[2] This was probably taken from Census Bulletin No. 72 (published May 27, 1891) where the exact number is given as 14,846. As reformatories are public institutions the census figures are approximately correct.

viduals dealt with there is no possibility of any high measure of success. There is little else possible than to make the best of unfortunate circumstances, to deal with palliatives, to brighten the individual lives, and to prevent misfortune from spreading. With children, on the other hand, especially for the quite young and tolerably healthy, there is a possibility of more positive results. The young life contains within itself the principle of growth, and may be enabled to expand into something actively useful. But if the work for children has thus its specially hopeful side, it has also its corresponding dangers, and imposes upon those who would undertake it a responsibility such as has no exact counterpart in other departments.

**Saving Destitute Infants.** The care of destitute infants (children under two years of age) is sharply distinguished from the care of older dependent children. Among the former the death-rate is the principal index of success or failure, while among the latter the death-rate is always low and the attention must be given to evidences of right or wrong development afforded by the character and subsequent careers of the children.

In a great majority of cases, it can matter but little to the individual infant whether it is murdered outright or is placed in a foundling hospital—death comes only a little sooner in one case than in the other. This fact, that foundling hospitals are, for the most part, places where infants die, is not sufficiently appreciated by the public. A death-rate of 97 per cent per annum for children under three years of age is not uncommon.[3] The printed reports of institutions for infants usually do not give the number of deaths. In an institution where no exact death-rate was computed, a study of the books brought out the following facts: Between July 1 and December 1, 1891, twenty-three children had been admitted; up to July 1, 1892, four of these children had been given in adoption, one was still in the institution, and eighteen had died.[4] Twenty-eight infants were consigned one after another by a public official to a private institution administered by a religious order, and they all died.

[3] *N. C. C.*, 1889, p. 1, gives an instance.

[4] The best way of computing a death-rate for institutions for children, as in the case of hospitals for the sick, is to find the ratio of deaths to the whole number disposed of, or perhaps to find of the whole number received how many attain the age of three years.

Of course this high death-rate comes in part from the bad condition of the children when received. They are often marasmic, rachitic, syphilitic, half dead from drugging or neglect, or from ante-natal or post-natal abuse. Yet this does not explain entirely the high death-rate common to institutions, as is shown by the fact that strong, thriving babies droop and die in them, and by the further fact that improved methods of caring for these same children bring down the death-rate to almost that of the average population for corresponding ages.[5] The high death-rate where children are cared for in institutions often results from positive neglect. A baby, if not attended to, gets into a very bad condition in a very short time. A woman who has from four to eight babies to take care of is apt to become neglectful. It is possible to clean them up for visiting day, or the inspection of directors or supervisors, but to keep them all clean and comfortable through twenty-four hours of the day, seven days in the week, and fifty-two weeks in the year, is another matter. Frequently they are left to lie in their cribs scalded by urine and in a miserable plight generally. The attendants, being assigned more work than they can do, settle into the conviction that it does not much matter whether they do anything at all or not. If attendants are hired, it is difficult to get the best class of help for such work. If they are members of a religious order the chances of self-devotion are better; but the Sisters are often ignorant and tolerably selfish women, and are usually overworked. Even when the infants are not neglected, and when, apparently, the attendants do everything possible for their comfort, the death-rate is still high. It is not possible to raise babies by wholesale. The institution baby lacks, and must lack, that affectionate handling which gives exercise to the baby muscles, and the zest to infant existence which makes it worth while for the child to live. Though the ward of an asylum be flooded with sunlight, as it frequently is not, and though the bed be clean and dry, as it generally is not, yet there still is lacking the light and warmth of affection and the comforts of personal attention.

Feeding the children is another difficulty. The doctors do their best in recommending sterilized foods of all kinds and

[5] *N. C. C.*, 1889, p. 1.

descriptions, but the infants still insist on dying. One institution in a Southern State, under the care of Sisters of Charity, undertook as a last resort to keep goats for the children to nurse, but with no good results. Many institutions admit a woman with a baby on condition that she shall nurse that and another. This is usually hard on the other baby, and the presence of a large number of these mothers under one roof makes administration very difficult. Others board the infants out with wet nurses. This is the method in the New York Hospital for Foundlings under Sister Irene. Where there is a large and healthy laboring-class this plan works very well. It is the method pursued in Paris, where the infants are sent out into the country, chiefly with the wives of peasants. In the Southern States suitable wet nurses can often only be found among the colored people. The Massachusetts State Board of Lunacy and Charity, following the example of the Massachusetts Infant Asylum, boards out infants in the country villages about Boston, placing them with women who bring them up by artificial feeding. About ten dollars per month is paid for the board of each child, and clothing is furnished by the officials. By carefully selecting the families, by subsequent visitation and frequent calls, at both stated and unexpected times, and by keeping constantly subject to summons a physician working on a salary paid by the State, it has been found possible to bring the death-rate among these children to about the same figure as that of children of similar age in the ordinary population, demonstrating the possibilities of this system.

One who has had considerable experience with the placing out of infants in this way, gives it as his opinion that a foundling hospital is the most useless institution in the world. He says that an efficient children's aid society, or an efficient public official, would always know of homes in which infants could be received temporarily, and from which they could be placed in families that would care for them indefinitely, if properly paid. He maintains that even as a place of reception the "institution" is needless.

**Reception of Dependent Children.** Next to the actual preservation of the life of the child the most important question in connection with the care of destitute infants is upon what conditions they shall be received. The mediæval device long used in France, and perhaps still used there in some parts of the country, consisted of a double cradle. When the child had been placed in the cradle on the outside of the building, the contrivance was revolved, ringing a bell as it turned. By this process the child was placed in the institution, and another cradle was waiting at once for the next comer. The purpose of these *"tours"* was to make it so easy to get rid of babies that there might be no temptation to infanticide.

The Foundling Asylum of the Sisters of Charity in the city of New York (now the New York Foundling Hospital), under Sister Irene, affords the best known American example of facilities offered for the abandonment of infants. A cradle was formerly placed in the vestibule, in which infants could be placed without observation from those inside. At last, however, they began to come two or three in a single night; [6] so now the cradle is put inside the door, and an applicant must ring the bell. If a mother brings her child, she is asked to stay and nurse her child and another. If she refuses, she is allowed to depart without further question, leaving the infant. Perhaps a majority of foundling hospitals in the United States make no adequate investigation and keep no adequate record of the parentage of children received. There are some cases where any investigation must be fruitless; but the experience of the Pennsylvania Children's Aid Society and the Massachusetts State Board of Lunacy and Charity proves that if trouble enough is taken, thorough investigations usually bring out some helpful facts, and that such a course is not only wise but kindly. It has a bad effect upon all concerned, for a woman or a man to be able to dispose of a baby "and no questions asked." [7]

Many infant asylums are also maternity hospitals. If not, the mother passes quite quickly from the institution where the child is born to the institution where she gives it up. She either deserts it at once, or promises and intends to do something for its

[6] The first year 1,399 babies were placed in the crib. Mrs. Bouvier, *New York Conference on Child-Caring,* pp. 71-2.

[7] Massachusetts, within the last few years, has passed very radical legislation designed to suppress "baby-farming." Persons making a business of boarding infants for pay are required to report to the State Board of Lunacy and Charity, and to submit to its supervision.

support. This promise it is usually not possible for her to keep, and very commonly she loses her desire to keep it.

In most cases it is quite certain that to enable a mother to leave her infant is a gratuitous mistake. Even if the child be illegitimate, her maternal instincts are the best thing about her. She is salvable through these, or probably not at all. To give her facilities for deadening these instincts is to do her final harm. I call it a gratuitous blunder, because experience has shown that with a little kindly aid she can be enabled to keep the child and support herself and it. At the worst she can enter an institution for a time, and nurse her child and another. But experiments in the cities of Boston and Philadelphia have shown that suitable service places in the country can be found to which destitute mothers may go, taking their children with them. "The demand for this class of help usually exceeds the supply," and in Philadelphia between four and five hundred mothers with their children are yearly sent to situations in the country.[8] If judiciously placed, a majority of these women give satisfaction to their employers, and are satisfied themselves. It is said that they do as well as those who take situations without children, and in many instances they are more reliable for help in the country. Of course a destitute woman with no one to help her support her child has not an easy life before her; but, on the whole, life will be happier and healthier in every way if she is aided in keeping her child, than if she is aided in getting rid of it.

Children over two years of age live quite persistently. Therefore, as regards these, we do not need to examine so closely the death-rate, for they may be very improperly cared for and the death-rate still be low. The first question of importance regarding them is upon what terms they shall be received and supported as dependents.

The rules of private institutions for receiving children are very various, and often very erratic. Sometimes illegitimacy is a prerequisite. One endowed institution required that a child should be the legitimate offspring of parents both of whom had been members of the Presbyterian Church, and one or both

[8] *State Charities Record*, March, 1892; also, *New York Conference on the Care of Dependent and Delinquent Children*, Nov., 1893, pp. 77-82.

of whom were dead. In some institutions children are received temporarily, and in others they are not admitted unless the natural parents give up all title to them. The rules of admission to private institutions are usually lax in practice if not in form; but they are nowhere so lax as in those States where the managers admit the child, and the State or city government is then constrained by law to pay for its maintenance without question. The financial aspects of this system will be considered later, but here must be noted its extreme perniciousness as regards the children. New York and California are the States most notorious for their recklessness in this matter.

Two things are necessary in order that agencies for the care of children may avoid the evil of encouraging the temporary or permanent abandonment of children. The first is, that the case of every child received must be thoroughly investigated by some competent agent; and the second is, that when relatives give up a child to be a dependent, they must give up all title to it. Guardianship should be vested completely in the agency that takes care of the child.

As to the first point, most private institutions for children are unduly negligent. It frequently happens that children are received through the influence of some member of the board of managers, or by a sympathetic matron, until the institution is overcrowded, and cases far more deserving of care then go unprovided for. Even where the matron or a member of the board of managers tries to make an investigation, it is work in which such a person is not an expert, and it is too often ill done. The business of deciding when children ought to be taken from parents, or received from parents, is becoming a specialty by itself; and the societies for the protection of children and children's aid societies ought to be asked to investigate all doubtful cases.

**Guardianship.** The second rule, namely, that when parents or relatives leave a child to be supported by charitable agency, they should lose all title to it, seems a hard one, yet in the great majority of cases it is thoroughly salutary. Perhaps the rule of the Children's Home of Cincinnati, which refuses to receive a child for more than two weeks without having the guardianship of the child vested in the Home, affords as much latitude as ought to be given. It is urged that parents are after all the best guardians of their children, and if the time ever comes when they can take care of their own it is better that the children be returned. But experience shows that it has a bad effect on parents as parents to get rid of the care of their children for a time, and that they spoil the life of a child by selfishly taking it home when they think it is old enough to be of service.[9] Parents who cannot support their children usually have not the capacity required to bring up a child in a healthful way and in a healthful environment. Besides this, the privilege of temporarily disposing of a child is frequently the means of bringing about its permanent abandonment.[10]

In the early 'seventies, two States awoke to the fact that they were disgraced by the presence of a large number of children in the county poor-houses. One State, Michigan, had about 600 persons under sixteen years of age in such institutions;[11] and New York, the other State referred to, had 2,179 in poor-houses.[12] Both State legislatures received reports showing the degrading influence of almshouse life upon the children, and giving pitiful instances of resulting disease and degeneration.[13]

In 1874 Michigan established a State Public School at Coldwater, and provided, first, that children adjudged dependent should be sent there, and subsequently placed in private families as soon as possible; second, that after an order is made to commit a child to the State Public School, "the parents of said child shall be released from all parental duties toward and responsibility for such child, and shall thereafter have no right over or to the custody, services, or earnings of such child, except in cases where the said Board has, as herein provided for, restored the child to its parents." The result of this system in Michigan has been that, whereas in 1874 she had 600 dependent children supported by public authorities, or one dependent

[9] Miss Davenport-Hill lays especial stress upon the evil of allowing the natural parents to claim their children after something has been done for their betterment in a charitable institution.

[10] *N. C. C.*, 1881, p. 282.

[11] *History of Child Saving*, p. 205.

[12] Tenth Annual Report N. Y. Board of Charities, p. 102.

[13] "In one of the county houses, three small children were found in a desolate room, one perishing with fever-sore, and the other two taking care of the sick one." Report Michigan Board of Charities and Corrections, 1874, p. 132. See also, Letchworth, *History of Child Saving*, p. 178.

child for each 2,223 inhabitants, she now has 300, or one in each 7,256 inhabitants. While the population increased sixty per cent, the number of dependent children decreased fifty per cent. Not only is this true, but the children that have passed under her care to Dec. 31, 1892 (3,317), have been well cared for, and, as a rule, restored to the normal population of the State.[14]

New York took a different course. In 1875 she passed the so-called "Children's Law," which forbade the keeping of children between the ages of two and sixteen years in the almshouses. It further provided that a dependent child should be committed, if possible, to an institution controlled by the same religious faith as that of its parents, and that the county should pay the child's board. The legal guardianship of the child was not mentioned, and so remained with the parents, if it had any. In addition to this, special acts were subsequently passed enabling certain large institutions in New York City to receive children at will, and collect from the county two dollars per week for the care of each. It only remains to contrast present conditions in New York with those in Michigan. On Oct. 31, 1892, there were in the city and county almshouses of the State of New York, 963 children, many of these, however, being crippled, diseased, or under two years of age. Besides this, there were in the private institutions of the State, but supported chiefly by the cities and counties, an army of 24,074 children. In these private institutions alone, there was one dependent child to each 270 persons in the State. If we include the almshouse children, the proportion of dependent children to the population is one to 260.

**Classification.** After the question of receiving children and their guardianship, the next most important question concerns their classification. This matter should precede the decision as to the method of care, as it will often modify it. In the first place, we are compelled to set apart those who are distinctly unsound in body or mind. The sick must be remanded to hospital care or homes for incurables; cripples pref-

[14] See *History of Child Saving*, pp. 213-14. The Michigan system has been repeatedly described at the National Conference of Charities. See "Ten Years of Child Saving Work in Michigan," by J. N. Foster, superintendent of the State Public School, *N. C. C.*, 1884, pp. 132-42.

erably to special institutions, and the feeble-minded and epileptic to institutions designed for them. There ought to be this separation of the unsound from the sound, but it is easier to say that classification is needed than to do the classifying. Every children's hospital has inmates that are well enough to be discharged, but within a month after discharge are likely to be sick enough to be readmitted.

While it is necessary not only to separate the sound from the unsound, to further classify those adjudged healthy is similarly important and difficult. First are the depraved, subdivided into criminals, misdemeanants, and unmanagables. These are usually spoken of as "delinquents," and the reform school is prescribed. As a rule, they must be so classed, and cannot be considered here, though their proper care is one of the most important problems in applied sociology. On the average, they probably have more vitality in them than the other classes of dependent children, and frequently the overt act that brings them before the court is the result of an accident. The child that has actually committed arson, theft, or assault may be not essentially different from a playmate that has not done these particular things. It has consequently come to be the rule in progressive States to give the courts wide discretion in the commitment of juvenile delinquents. They may be sent to reform schools, to charitable institutions, or consigned to the care of children's aid societies or boards of guardians. In many cases it has been found possible to board actual delinquents in private families with good results.[15]

After the delinquents, come the dependent children proper, made up of the neglected, abused, abandoned, and otherwise parentless, and the children of utterly destitute parents. While a few delinquent children are placed in the care of charitable agencies with good results, it is far commoner for simply destitute children to be sent to correctional institutions with very dubious results. The laws of most States provide a definition for vagrancy that is broad enough to include almost any neglected child, and further provide that vagrants or children that wander about and beg from door to door may be sent to reform schools. Another elastic provision is that regarding

[15] *N. C. C.*, 1891, pp. 136-45.

"incorrigibles." If the parent sees fit to swear that the child is incorrigible, the court has very little option in many States, but must commit such child to the reform school. In several institutions visited, fully half the children seem to be neglected and abandoned, rather than juvenile delinquents. Mixed with the more depraved who properly belong to the school, the chances for these boys and girls to come to the best that they were capable of is not good. The classification at exactly this point—the separation of the depraved from the merely destitute—is an essential element in the wise handling of the neglected and destitute children of any State or locality, even though it may be difficult to put into effect.

In the classification of destitute children, it will be noticed that orphans and half-orphans have not been included, a distinction which is more commonly made, perhaps, than any other; and yet for purposes of care it has very little significance. The child that must be taken from its parents is parentless, and it is of very little significance so far as the child itself is concerned whether its parents are dead or not. The distinction between orphans and half-orphans, which is recognized by the laws of California and other States in providing money for private institutions, and which is usually recognized in the administration of private institutions, is simply a device by which the managers of an institution save themselves the trouble of examining into individual cases. The distinction is made because it is easy to make, and they feel that they must draw the line somewhere. It is, however, of comparatively little consequence for our present purposes, and can only be of use in studying causes of dependency among children.

What has been said regarding classification shows the great importance of the work of the children's aid societies and the societies for the protection of children from cruelty and immorality. They are, or should be, specialists in exactly this work of classification. It is their business to understand the character of the children and the possibilities of the situation; and wherever their work is done with conscientious intelligence, the courts cannot do better than to take their advice in disposing of destitute or delinquent children. In many cases it may be found that institution life of any sort is unnecessary; and where it is necessary, the institution should be chosen with distinct reference to the individual child.

**Institutional Care.** After the matters of reception, guardianship, and classification are disposed of, the final matter of importance is the method of providing for dependent children. Broadly speaking, there are two systems: the first is the institution plan, and the second is the plan of placing out.

Without the figures of the Eleventh Census at hand, it is impossible to tell how large a proportion of the dependent children of the country is in institutions; but it is a comparatively large number. To build institutions for children has been the common and obvious thing to do in providing for them. The institution is preferred by parents, because they know where the child is, and can usually visit it, and frequently can retain the right to take it back again when they will. Institutions are also in favor with the benevolent, because the work done is so manifest. A hundred or more children, prepared for the occasion, make an attractive sight to the board of directors or to visitors. Buildings are obvious, and the money that goes into them takes a concrete form gratifying to the contributors. The churches prefer such life for the children dependent upon them, because the children can be so easily isolated from teachings other than their own. There is opportunity for catechetical instruction. In New York City all the institutions having more than a thousand children are of a distinctly religious character.

On the whole, institutions are preferred by the children themselves, at least after they have been in them for some time. They do not feel at home outside of the sheltering walls, and shrink from the rough contact of ordinary life. In many institutions former inmates keep returning again and again, either seeking work or begging to be taken back, because it is the life they are used to, and the only one for which they are fitted. I have known matrons to suggest that after orphan asylums there ought to be other custodial institutions to take adults of either sex and give them shelter for the remainder of their lives.

The institution, commending itself in interest to these various parties, has necessarily had a greater development than the placing-out system. Besides, there are many things to be said in its favor by those who have a really disinterested wish to benefit the dependents. The children receive many negative benefits. They are not cold, nor dirty, nor neglected, nor hungry, nor abused—that is, if the management is good. The grosser forms of profanity and vice can be restrained; their attendance on school exercises is entirely regular, as are also their hours of sleep and eating. But admitting these advantages, we have said about all that is favorable to institution life for children. The congregating of them together, which we found in the case of infants to result in high mortality, results in the case of older children in a low vitality. Even a small institution is different from a large family. In the latter the children are of different ages; they have different opportunities for amusement—one imitates the other. In even a small institution, one with only eight or ten children, they are apt to be of about the same age, none of them especially ambitious, and with their opportunities for self-education very limited. In the large caravansaries, where hundreds or even thousands of children are congregated, their non-development is very apparent. The fundamental fault is, perhaps, that life is made too easy. A child ought to have more opportunities of hurting himself, or getting dirty, or being insubordinate, than can possibly be accorded to him here.

A great part of the evils of institution life come from the mingling of individuals, none of whom have a very good heredity behind them, and some of whom have inherited weak constitutions and bad moral tendencies. It is a continual fight on the part of matrons to repress skin diseases and sore eyes; and these contagious diseases are but typical of the contagious vices which are not so obvious, but more to be dreaded.

It should be said that institution life has been greatly improved by the introduction of kindergarten work for the smaller children, and industrial training for those of maturer years. But the trouble is, that in the great majority of cases, the expense of giving such work properly leads to the mere pretence of giving it—going through the motions of industrial training without the spirit of it, or managing a kindergarten in a way that makes the child completely dependent upon somebody else for all its possibilities of play and enjoyment. It is not sufficiently understood that a poor kindergarten stultifies the child, and that manual training which is not well conducted has no virtues in it.

Another way in which institution life is improved is by sending the children out to the public schools. In relatively small institutions this is possible, and very desirable. It gives the child that contact with others which he needs. It is a common practice among Hebrews, unknown among the Catholics, and only practiced occasionally by Protestant and "non-sectarian" managers.

**Placing Out.** Over against the institution plan of caring for dependent children is the plan of placing them in private families, with or without the payment of board. There are two tolerably distinct methods of procedure in this work. By one, the children are sent to a great distance, and given but little subsequent supervision—that is the so-called "emigration plan"; and by the other they are placed within easy reach of the agency having them in charge, and subsequent supervision is systematic and constant.

In the United States the greatest agency for emigrating children to the West is the Children's Aid Society of New York, founded by Charles L. Brace in 1853. Up to 1892, they had emigrated 84,318 children, of whom 51,427 were boys, and 32,891 were girls. Some of these were not sent to a great distance, nearly 39,000 of them being placed in the State of New York, 4,149 in New Jersey, etc. The Western States receiving the largest number were Illinois, to which 7,366 were sent; Iowa, 4,852; Missouri, 4,835; Indiana, 3,782; Kansas, 3,310; Michigan, 2,900; Minnesota, 2,448.[16] The work of this society very well illustrates the advantages and the limitations of the emigration plan. Its great number of children were placed out at an average expense of about ten dollars per child, and much less care was taken in placing and supervising in the early years than has since been found necessary in order to reconcile the States to the reception of the children.

Hastings H. Hart of the Minnesota State Board of Corrections and Charities has investigated the results of the children

[16] *History of Child Saving,* p. 30. See also pamphlet published by the Society, 1893, *The Children's Aid Society of New York, Its History, Plan, and Results.*

placed in Minnesota by the Children's Aid Society of New York, and finds that the methods of placing were frequently too inexpensive and incautious; and while for the most part the society took care of children that did not turn out well, this was not true in all cases. In some cases they were placed in families so destitute as to be receiving public assistance, and other unsatisfactory placements were made. "From our experience," says Mr. Hart, "we are positive in the opinion that children above the age of twelve years ought not to be sent West by the Children's Aid Society. In this opinion I understand that the officers of the society concur. Secretary Brace says: 'The emigration plan must be conducted with careful judgment, and be applied so far as practicable to children under say fourteen years of age.' If the society would adhere to the wise rule laid down, we should have little cause for complaint. Our examination shows," concludes Mr. Hart, "with reference to children under thirteen years of age, that nine-tenths remain, four-fifths are doing well, and all incorrigibles are cared for by the society. If properly placed, faithfully supervised, we are willing to take our full share of these younger children in Minnesota." [17]

The placing-out system, properly so called—that is, the placing of children where they are easily accessible to the agency responsible for them—has been practised for a long time by the officers of the Poor Law Unions of England and of American towns and counties. Children were simply kept in the almshouses until old enough so that somebody would take them. Mr. Folks, in writing of this system of disposing of pauper children in Pennsylvania, says that in many cases the directors of the poor of the different counties do not know how many children they are responsible for, and their records hardly show how many have been placed out. One record simply showed that a certain child had been given to "Mr. Jones, who lives just over the hill." This, of course, is placing-out at its worst, especially if it be not resorted to until the children have been spoiled by almshouse or asylum life. Institutions must

[17] *N. C. C.*, 1884, pp. 149, 150. In the article referred to, Mr. Hart gives very complete tables of results, and an uncolored and interesting account of the methods used in placing children.

find some way to dispose of their children when the time comes for them to leave; and frequently a matron or manager of an institution is prejudiced against the placing-out system because he finds it so difficult to provide places for them. He forgets that he is not an expert in this branch of his work; that he does it during some slack season in a hurried way, and without the skill that comes from practice. Such placers-out of children frequently say that the older the children are, the better; and it is doubtless true that the older ones are less likely to be foisted back upon the institution; but it is because they are more likely to wander away and bring up in a reform school, house of correction, or prison. It is one of the things to be especially charged against institutions for children, that their methods of sociological bookkeeping are so limited that they cannot tell how the children with whose lives they have tinkered turn out; yet this, as Mr. Folks well urges, is the only real test of the results.

Placing-out as a specialty has been carried to its most satisfactory results by such public institutions as the State Board of Lunacy and Charity in Massachusetts, and the State School for Dependent Children at Coldwater, Mich., and by such private associations as the Children's Aid Society of Massachusetts, and the Children's Aid Society of Pennsylvania. With these agencies "the setting of the solitary in families" is a business. The following description, taken not literally, but in substance, from Mr. Folks's article on "Child Saving Work in Pennsylvania," [18] will give the best idea of how this system operates. The Children's Aid Society of Pennsylvania consists of a central society, with county committees in each county of the State, or in as many of them as efficient committees can be maintained, who have received from the directors of the poor or others, dependent children, whom they place at once in families. Usually they are placed in the county where they become dependent; but when the children are particularly troublesome, or relatives interfere, or the family name is unfavorably known in the locality, the main office often removes the child to a distant part of the State. A large proportion of the children are placed in Pennsylvania, but a considerable number also in

[18] *History of Child Saving*, pp. 146, 147.

adjoining States. The work of the main office is conducted under the supervision of the managers by a corps of eight salaried officials, two of whom are men. One assistant gives her whole time to the problem of homeless mothers with young children, providing for them service places to which they can take their children. Four workers are travelling almost constantly, investigating families who have applied for children, visiting children who have been placed out, or taking children to and from their homes. Having relied so largely upon the family plan, the society has given much attention to the elaboration of the details of its administration, and has thrown around it every possible safeguard. Its investigation of a family is systematic and exhaustive, and is carefully recorded. The applicant fills out a blank containing twenty-six questions relating to the various phases of the family life, as church relations, distance from school, size of farm, occupation, number of members of family, with their ages, etc. A study of this return usually reveals the real motive of the application, and gives the data for an opinion as to the *material* fitness of the family. Their moral fitness is ascertained by sending a list of questions to six of the neighbors, stating that their replies are confidential, and that the appeal to them is not known to the applicant. A personal visit completes the investigation. After the child is placed out, his welfare is ascertained and protected by from one to five personal and unannounced visits each year, by a monthly report from the teacher of the public schools, and a quarterly report from the pastor. The society uses neither indenture nor written agreement, the terms being perfectly flexible, and subject to change from year to year to suit the circumstances of each individual case. This society considers institutions for normal children needless, and has even had good success in boarding out juvenile delinquents received from the courts. A similar work has been done by the Massachusetts Children's Aid Society, which has one or two home-like institutions where abnormal children are placed until they can be fitted into a proper home.

Michigan and Massachusetts are the two States whose public officials have done most notable work in placing out. The results in Michigan have already been referred to in contrast with the results of another system in the State of New York. From the State School at Coldwater the children are sent to homes in various parts of the State, where the visitors look after their interests, and where they are visited by the representative of the State School from time to time. It has been found possible to reincorporate all normal children with the population very speedily. The number at the State School is not as large now as formerly. This system was to have been copied in Wisconsin; but there the influence of the private institutions has compelled a compromise between the system of State placing-out and the New York system of child storage. The same unfortunate condition of contending systems obtains in the District of Columbia; but in Minnesota, the Michigan system has been completely introduced, and is completely successful.

In Ohio there is a system of county homes, from which children are placed out; and the one criticism which advocates of placing out might pass upon that work is, that there is a slight tendency for the children to accumulate in the homes, instead of being promptly reincorporated with the general population. The commissioners serve without compensation. The almshouses have there been emptied of children, and a large number of unsalaried officials fill the honor offices by which the institutions are managed. A detailed statement of the Ohio county homes for dependent children will be found in Mr. Hathaway's article in the "History of Child Saving."

On the whole, the placing-out system deserves the commendation it has received from the most advanced specialists. If administered "with an adequate supply of eternal vigilance," it is economical, kindly, and efficient. If badly administered, it leads to very obvious abuses; but at its best it is the best system. In the conclusion of this chapter, attention should be again called to the fact that it is less in child-caring than in child-saving work that really helpful results are to be found. Newsboys' lodging-houses, industrial schools, reading-rooms, home libraries, and the countless agencies for benefiting the street Arab and making a man of him, carried on by the New York Children's Aid Society and the Massachusetts Children's Aid Society, and similar organizations, are doing a work which we commend, but neglect—the work of prevention. The same is true of the societies for the protection of children from cruelty and immorality; and, as we noted under the head of classification, it is necessary that these specialist organizations should be called in to classify and assign to the proper child-caring agency the children that are to be dependent. It is to these two classes of organizations also that we must look for help in the proper discharge of children from dependency; and it is especially to them that we look for a system of sociological bookkeeping that will enable us to tell with definiteness what is being accomplished—how the children "turn out." There is no better fund of raw material for sociological study than the great records of the children's aid societies and other advanced child-caring agencies of the United States. From such records we may expect some time to draw a partial answer to the question, "Whither is philanthropy leading us?"

# CHAPTER X

## THE DESTITUTE SICK

At the present time there is no way of estimating accurately the number of the destitute sick provided for in the United States. It is simply known that within the last twenty years the hospitals of the country have had a very rapid development, coming in part from the influx of the foreign population accustomed to seek hospital service, in part from the increasing density of population, but very largely, without doubt, from the increased efficiency of the hospitals. Formerly a hospital was regarded as a place that every one would stay away from if he could. It was a place where the shattered wrecks of armies must be taken, where the homeless stranger must seek refuge if overtaken by sickness, and where the abjectly destitute must necessarily be cared for. But of late the improvements in medical art, and especially in surgical processes, have enabled hospitals to render better service than can be given even in the homes of the well-to-do; and, as a consequence, there has been a greatly increased demand for accommodations for pay patients, and with the growth of every hospital has come also the growth of free wards. The increase in the number of free beds, and the increase in efficiency, have rendered the poorer classes less disinclined to seek refuge in the hospital, and especially to resort for free consultation and medicine to the dispensaries. Even if we knew how many patients had been sheltered by the hospitals of the United States, it would be a task of great difficulty to find out how many of the beds were really free to those filling them. There are those who believe that eventually hospital service will be free to all willing to accept of it at public expense, just as for the insane, hospital service or asylum care is now free to all willing to accept of it in Minnesota, and ostensibly in some other States; or as education, including support, is free in many States to all defectives.

As indicating the extent of the burden which is now imposed upon tax-payers for the maintenance of medical charities, the author has collated with some care from the official reports, verified in some instances by correspondence and personal visitation, the public expenditure for medical charities in ten American cities.

It will be seen that during the year to which the figures refer for the different cities, the expense has been from a little less than 11 to a little more than 63 cents per capita for medical charities, the average being 31.09 cents; but in any one of the cities named the amount stated in no wise represents the total expenditure for the relief of the destitute sick. The proceeds of endowments and private contributions are not taken into view at all.

TABLE XVI.

PUBLIC EXPENDITURES FOR MEDICAL CHARITIES IN TEN AMERICAN CITIES.

| *City* | *Population (Census of 1890)* | *Fiscal Year* | *Amount* | *Per Capita* |
|---|---|---|---|---|
| Brooklyn ......... | 806,343 | 1889–90 | $196,115.61 | $0.2432 |
| St. Louis ......... | 451,770 | 1889–90 | 140,773.43 | .3116 |
| Boston [1] .......... | 448,477 | 1890 | 188,177.88 | .4195 |
| Baltimore ........ | 434,439 | 1891 | 111,790.00 | .2573 |
| Cincinnati ........ | 296,908 | 1890 or '91 | 110,162.92 | .3710 |
| Buffalo ........... | 255,664 | 1891 | 67,650.00 | .2646 |
| Minneapolis ....... | 164,738 | 1890 | 17,842.64 | .1083 |
| St. Paul .......... | 133,156 | 1890 | 27,269.02 | .2074 |
| Indianapolis ...... | 105,436 | 1891 | 29,170.00 | .2767 |
| Washington ....... | 230,392 | 1890–91 | 145,625.00 | .6320 |
| All ten cities .... | 3,327,323 | .... | $1,034,576.50 | $0.31093 |

**Hospital Care.** The care of the sick, especially in the wards of a great hospital, is something that appeals very directly to the sympathies and a large amount of voluntary contributions can usually be relied upon to support such institutions. Besides

[1] The figures for Boston cover the expenditures for the City Hospital only. Since the table has passed from under my hands I learn that there are expenditures on the part of the State for medical charities which serve the poor of Boston, and the per capita might possibly be as high as that of Washington if all the items could be included. However, the service is of a much higher grade than that given in Washington, costing nearly twice as much per patient per week.

this, they usually serve a purpose in the education of medical students and young physicians, and almost invariably a purpose in building up the reputation of the physicians and surgeons in charge of them. There are cases, indeed, where the gratuitous treatment of all applicants has in it no element of charity, the clinic being worth more to the school than it costs. Advertisements are frequently kept in the dailies of a large city, announcing free dentistry to all who care to receive it. The person responding to such an advertisement will be attended to by a probably skilful student, under the guidance of the professor in a school of dentistry; and the opportunity of educating the student is fully equivalent to the services rendered. A lecturer or manager of a clinic of a medical school frequently pays a patient a considerable amount for the privilege of showing some operation or disease to the class. This is not only free treatment, but pay was given for the privilege of treating.

Not less than three strong motives, therefore, contribute to the development of medical charities—the desire to aid the destitute, the desire to educate students and build up medical reputations, and the desire to protect the public health. The latter has often been the leading cause of public appropriations for medical charities. A few hospitals decline to admit students to their advantages; but the uniform testimony of medical experts seems to be that the teaching hospitals render better service than the non-teaching institutions.

In order that there may be no clash between the officers in charge, each medical school usually desires to control its own hospital, and the officers in charge of a given hospital usually wish to be connected with some one medical school. The great public hospitals arrange as well as they can to give the facilities of their wards to the medical schools of the locality in which they operate.

The qualification for admission to a hospital as such is disease. For admission to a free bed, there should be the additional qualification of destitution; but this latter point is usually not insisted upon. The competition of medical schools, or schools of medicine, and of individual institutions, is usually so great that no one willing to put up with the inconvenience, and to take the risks of free hospital treatment, is refused. People enter hospitals as pay-patients only if they wish some special advantages or privileges. That people are admitted to free beds without investigation is especially true in those places where the private institutions admit patients for whom the municipality or county pays the bills. This is the system in vogue in Baltimore and Brooklyn, and other large cities where the subsidy system obtains. In Buffalo there has been a much more careful arrangement, by which it is required that anyone admitted to a free bed at the expense of the State must secure a permit either from the Health Department or the poor-law officers. An agent of the Health Department goes through the hospital wards weekly or semi-monthly, to see what patients paid for by the public can be properly discharged, or if chronic cases can properly be remanded to the almshouse. The city of Buffalo or the county pays a certain rate per week for the care of patients which it sends to the various hospitals. The per capita expenditure in Buffalo for medical charities is about 26.5 cents; while in Washington, where the looser system prevails, it is 63.2 cents.

Within the hospital the lines of authority should be as distinctly traceable as possible. The various departments of administration are: first, the purely business side, the getting of supplies, keeping of books, etc.; second, the housekeeping; third, the nursing; and fourth, the medical work. All of these should be under the care of a single superintendent, who may or may not be a physician. In public institutions the great problem of management is to keep out politics.

The question of politics brings us to the question of private *versus* public control of hospitals. American cities have done comparatively little in establishing municipal hospitals as compared with their activity in other lines of development. In the smaller towns the cheapest way is to subsidize private hospitals; and this is the system which has been resorted to, and which has fastened itself upon even large cities like Brooklyn and Baltimore. About the only public hospital that is maintained in many of our large cities is that in connection with the almshouse, where chronic cases are received on the general principle of almshouse management, that all who cannot go anywhere else can go there. These almshouse infirmaries frequently develop into what are really large general hospitals. There is needed in all the cities better co-ordination of all the medical charities; and yet it is one of the most difficult things to bring about, because of individual, medical, and religious rivalries. The best method seems to be for the city itself to establish a large general hospital, which shall be as well managed as the character of the municipality or county will allow, and to which the various medical schools shall be admitted as may be compatible with good service to the inmates. This hospital should be kept as large as is necessary to provide for the destitute sick. Then, if medical schools, or churches, or individuals desire to establish special additional hospitals, they should do so at their own expense.

**Dispensaries.** The dispensary is the most efficient engine of hospital extension; and therefore, where we have competing institutions, it is a department that develops first and fastest, and is the most complained about by rivals. Among those rivals must be classed the junior members of the medical profession. Dr. Savage estimated that in the city of New York there are between 300,000 and 350,000 patients treated gratis at the dispensaries annually, or one in four persons of the tenement-house population.

All statistics on this subject, however, are difficult to make definite, because there are so many duplications between different institutions and in the same institution. Some dispensaries count their patients over again every month, so that one man attending the dispensary all the year would be counted as twelve patients. One woman has been known to be attending four different clinics in the same dispensary, so she would count as four different cases.

Wherever a considerable number of dispensary cases are investigated to ascertain whether or not the patients are destitute, a tolerably high abuse-rate is found.

Dr. Savage gives the following account of certain investigations in New York City: "In the most attractive dispensary of the city, possessing an elegant building, a complete equipment, and high-grade physicians, the patients are largely of a class one might judge able to compensate a physician. The

Charity Organization investigated 1,500 cases selected out of 35,000 applicants. The answer was that about one-fourth were able to pay, another fourth had given a wrong address (possibly from an aversion to its being known that they had applied for dispensary aid, or because they resided out of the city), and the remaining half were recommended as worthy of medical charity by reason of poverty. For another dispensary the same society made investigation of 212 cases, and returned answer that 55 were able to pay, 58 were not found at the address given, 18 information not conclusive, and 81 unable to pay. These referred cases were deemed questionable out of nearly 30,000 patients." [2]

Dr. Savage doubts, however, whether the abuse has a sufficiently bad effect so that any very severe measure should be taken to correct it. This is a matter on which physicians differ widely. Charity experts usually consider that this free medical service has a very bad effect upon the applicants. The Charity Organization Society of London has waged a long and apparently losing fight against it. The Charity Organization Societies of the United States have investigated cases whenever referred to them; but, for the most part, hospitals do not want the cases investigated—they are glad to take all that come. Sir Morell Mackenzie gave it as his opinion that the out-patient department of a great hospital was the greatest pauperizing agency existing in England. Lord Cathcart, who served on the Lords' Committee on Hospitals, thinks the effect has not been nearly as bad as supposed, and that the matter had better be left to limit itself. "The out-patient department, however well managed," he says, "is a social test in itself—the crowds, long waits, unpleasant neighbors, crying and irritable children. There is also some little risk of looking in with one complaint and coming out with another." [3]

[2] *Hospitals,* note, p. 644.

[3] At the Joshua Hopkins Hospital a small charge is made for medicines, and patients usually wish to pay. One who had inquired carefully about this institution, says he thinks the abuse-rate very small. One physician who had had experience in both classes of dispensaries, stated that where the patients paid for the medicines, the medicines did them a great deal more good than where they got them free. This at first sight seems absurd; but on further consideration it appears that the patients take more care to follow directions, and in other ways to put themselves in a position to profit by their outlay. Where the medicines are given absolutely free

In England provident dispensaries have been organized to a considerable extent, at which, in consideration of the deposit of a weekly or monthly sum, medical attendance and medicine are provided. There has not been very much done in the line of provident dispensaries in this country; but the various mutual benevolent orders, and the relief associations of the railroads and some other corporations, provide medical attendance in consequence of stated contributions per month.

American municipalities vary widely in the public provision which they make for sending medical relief to the destitute sick in their own homes. In some cities there are ward physicians, or district physicians, or, as they are usually called by the beneficiaries, "poor-doctors," who are paid from $10 to $50 per month to respond to all calls for gratuitous treatment. These positions are eagerly sought after by certain junior members of the medical profession, and apparently would be if no salary were paid at all. In cities like New York, where there are no public physicians to the poor, the gap is filled by private benevolence, the large dispensaries, and the gratuitous services of the medical profession.

**Nursing** as a form of medical and charitable service existed before many of the other branches of these arts. Within the last two or three decades it has had a new access of usefulness through the advances in medicine and surgery, and from the knowledge that has been obtained of the sources of disease and the methods of antiseptic and aseptic treatment, as well as in consequence of the cultivation of nursing as a specialty.

There are substantially three types of hospitals as far as regards nursing: first, those with paid or "professional" nurses; second, those where the nursing is done by pupils under trained supervision; and third, those where the nursing is done by members of the religious orders. In certain hospitals, usually those under public management, the nursing is done by persons who are paid a small amount and keep their positions from year to year, or as long as politics allow. This, on the whole, is the cheaper form of getting the service; but the service is not nearly so good. The class of persons that will

they are sometimes thrown away outright, if the taste does not suit, or the person happens to choose to go to another dispensary.

work at this occupation continuously for a small salary is distinctly poor; and usually a hospital relying upon this system drifts into the policy of employing inmates to do the nursing. The nursing in an almshouse hospital is usually of this kind, more or less capable inmates being paid small amounts to assume the responsibility and work of nurses.

The second method of securing the necessary service is by pupil nurses, serving a novitiate usually of two years, and receiving only enough to support them. The nurses may come in from an outside training-school, or the training-school may be a branch of the hospital administration. In either case, the special work of nursing must be under one experienced person, who has full control of the *personnel* of the nursing-force, and is distinctly responsible for this branch of the work.

The system of pupil-nursing secures a much higher grade of applicants for positions; and while the necessity of continually dealing with new nurses causes the medical officials to grumble from time to time, yet most efficient service can be got by this method if there is a sufficient force of trained head nurses.

In the third class of hospitals the nursing is done by members of the religious orders. Such institutions are usually owned by the orders themselves, and the Sister Superior is at the head of the administration. Such hospitals are frequently subsidized by the municipalities; but it is rare with us, though common in Europe, for a religious order to be given charge of the nursing in a public institution.

Physicians and surgeons, according to individual experience, vary in their estimates of the relative efficiency of Sisters or others as nurses. One surgeon of wide experience tells the author that Sisters were never properly trained as nurses; and another, that none but those animated by religious zeal ever had enough devotion to make the best nurses. Both statements, as made, may be taken to be false. Some of the orders take great pains in the training of their novices. It will be interesting to see, as time goes on, whether persons of sufficient intelligence and education to make the best modern nurses will continue to enter the religious orders; and, on the other hand, whether "cash payment" and simple devotion to duty will give the entire reliability which is needed in the nurse at all times and places.

Standing between the religious orders of the Catholic Church and the paid nurses of the training-schools are the orders of deaconesses of the Protestant denominations. Their work is particularly for the poor. In this country these orders have not as yet taken up hospital work to any notable extent. They differ from the Catholic orders in that the vows are taken for only a limited period of years, whereas, after the novitiate of four or five years, a member of a Catholic order takes the vows for life. Members of the deaconess orders also retain the title to private property, and do not cut themselves off from their relatives, if they have any.

This mention of the orders of deaconesses brings us to a late development in nursing-work for the poor, namely, the so-called "district nursing," which is simply the gratuitous nursing of the sick poor in their homes. Such care of the poor has long been given by the Sisters of Charity and the *Sœurs de Bon Secours* of the Catholic Church, who have attended to it with a devotion and an amount of personal sympathy that is hardly paralleled. In the United States salaried nurses to the poor were first employed, at least to any considerable extent, by a religious society—the Woman's Branch of the New York City Mission and Tract Society. The first experiments were made in 1877. The nurse receives from $40 to $50 per month. She passes from home to home, doing what is necessary for the sick; and the influence of her example of cleanliness, order, and wise-doing is frequently contagious. "Almost every day," says Miss Summerville, "I find some former patient carrying out many of the simple directions that have been given during some former sickness."

The public authorities in this country have not, as a rule, introduced gratuitous nursing as an adjunct to the work of gratuitous medical service to the poor, rendered through the physicians in the pay of the municipality; but this is an advance that will probably come, as it has in Paris and other European cities.

In nursing, more distinctly than in almost any other line of benevolent work, is seen the sacrifice of capable people to the incapable. Nurses, especially pupil and paid nurses, are frequently overworked, and the members of religious orders also break down at an early age. The death-rate among all classes of nurses is very high. It should be seen by those in authority that strong, capable women are not killed off gratuitously by overwork which could be avoided. The conditions of their lives must be as health-giving and as health-preserving as possible; and whether they are members of a religious order or the salaried servants of a society, they must have opportunities of recruiting their strength, and so of preserving their usefulness.

# CHAPTER XI

## THE INSANE

**Scope of the Problem.** According to Census Bulletin No. 62 there were, during the year 1889, in public and private institutions for the insane of the United States, 97,535 inmates, showing an increase during the nine years from 1881 of 41,330, or 73.53 per cent. The population during the decade had increased but 24.53 per cent. In 1889 there were 1.56 insane persons in each thousand of the population. The figures do not indicate an increase of insanity in the country, but rather that institution treatment had come to be accepted by a much larger number of the insane, or by their guardians on their behalf. Further than this, each succeeding census comes more nearly to getting all the figures regarding the special classes investigated, and the increase is therefore statistical, but not actual.

Even in the case of a single State where the methods of collecting statistics have been tolerably uniform, a large part of the increase is accounted for by the fact that the definition of insanity has broadened, and many who are now classified as insane would some years ago have simply attracted attention as being queer or perverse. For comparison as between two countries, it is very important to know whether idiots and feeble-minded are classed among the insane; but, in fact, comparison between different countries are full of statistical quicksands, in which none but an expert can find footing.

Much lurid poetry and fiction have been produced having for their basis the unjust commitment of sane persons as insane; and, on the other hand, many papers have been written by physicians and others showing the danger of allowing insane persons to be too long without asylum restraint, and of the injustice that comes from making it too difficult to secure judgment of insanity and subsequent commitment and detention. Probably the danger of the commitment of sane persons has been greatly over-estimated.

**Commitment, Detention, and Transportation.** In most instances there are two things to be decided: first, whether a person is legally insane and in need of asylum treatment, or the control of a guardian, and, second, whether or not he or his relatives should be compelled to support him. The first of these decisions, that as to sanity, is primarily a medical question; the old method was to treat it as a legal one. The person "charged" with insanity was brought personally into court and tried before a jury. In the District of Columbia, Illinois, and Colorado, jury trial is obligatory in all cases, and the presence of the patient at the trial is demanded. This system is properly characterized by Dr. Riggs as barbarous. At the same time, there is a judicial element in the matter which requires that the cases should be passed upon by a court; and the more progressive States provide that all commitments shall be recorded in the Court of Records, but that the testimony upon which the action is based shall for the most part be that of medical experts. It is simply necessary that adequate publicity should be provided for, and that an adequate amount of expert testimony should determine the question.

The detention of the insane is another matter when it is necessary to protect the interests at once of the community and of the inmates. It is a matter on which the inmates will usually differ in opinion from the superintendent of the institution, and it has not been found easy to work out rules that guarantee against all abuses. In the main, the right of correspondence should remain with the patients, the letters that they write being read by the superintendent or his representative, and any which are not forwarded being filed for the inspection of directors or other supervisors of the institution.

Where the insane who are committed and detained are classified according as they or their relatives can or cannot pay for their support, the adjudication of this matter must usually rest with the overseers of the poor. There is likely to be a good deal of care exercised where the expense of maintenance is left to the towns and counties. Where the State maintains both the acute and the chronic insane, the drift is in the direction of giving free support to all insane persons, whether of the well-to-do classes or not. This is the avowed policy of Minnesota, and is practically the outcome of loose legislation in California.

Under the head of commitment and detention, must be mentioned the matter of proper escort of the insane from the place of family residence to the hospital or asylum to which they are committed. In most States this matter is left to the sheriff, a relic of the time when only the legal aspects of the matter were considered by the courts. In other States the asylums are expected to send proper attendants to take the inmates to the institution, and a few States, as for instance Michigan, provide that the county shall send a female attendant with every female patient, unless accompanied by her husband, father, brother, or son. The recent State Care Act of New York provides for female escort for females, and attaches a penalty for its non-observance.

**Institutional Care.** The history of the treatment of the insane is ordinarily divided into three periods: the first, that of neglect, when the insane were only dealt with in case they were dangerous, and when they were treated as witches or wild animals; the second, the era of detention, when they were treated under such laws as the English Vagrancy Act; and third, the present era, when insanity is recognized as "a disease and not a doom." In this country, during the early part of the present century, the English precedents were followed, and the precedents rather of the earlier than of the passing period. In New York, the law provided for the detention of the insane by chains if necessary. Dorothea Lynde Dix, who, in the middle of this century, visited a large number of places for the care of the insane, was compelled to tell a most grievous tale of abuse and barbarity. Even with the establishment of the State Boards of Charity in the more progressive States in the middle of the 'sixties and early 'seventies, the condition of things was hardly better. The reports of the early 'seventies, describing the condition of the insane in the town and county almshouses, give accounts of barbarities as hideous as any unearthed fifty years earlier in England, or described by Miss Dix in this country. The thing that had been accomplished by her agitation had been the establishment of many rather large asylums, in some of which the treatment was decidedly good; but a great proportion of the insane remained under the mistreatment of the local poor-houses.

However, it was found that the very large institutions were not answering their purposes, because their size made the individualization of cases difficult or impossible, and there was a sort of contagion of insanity resulting from the presence of such large number of lunatics on a small area. Later there has come a tendency to build cottages grouped about a central administrative and hospital building, where families of the insane in the care of proper housekeepers and attendants can live in relative seclusion. Kankakee, Ill., is probably the best illustration of this system of construction. To save expense, however, the legislature has insisted on making the "cottages" much larger than was desired by those having an interest in this new development.

The colony plan consists in making the cottages small and scattering them over a large estate. This is being tried at Kalamazoo, Mich. The great difficulty is to provide cheap and adequate facilities for water, drainage, and heat. This difficulty can probably be overcome with the advance of the mechanical arts, just as the disadvantages of scattered buildings on the cottage plan have been very largely overcome at the present time. For both systems, of course, pneumatic tubes, telephones, and electric lighting give great facility for centralizing the administration.

With this modification in the methods of building large institutions for the care of the insane, the tendency to remand all this class of dependents to the State has been greatly strengthened; and New York has finally accomplished what its State Board of Charities and State Charities Aid Association had agitated for during many years—the transfer of all insane from county to State care, except in the two counties of Kings and New York. This brings better treatment and larger expense, and has been the system adopted by the Western States almost without exception.

Wisconsin prides herself on having devised a method of county care under State supervision. Whenever cure or improvement is considered possible, the patients are sent to a

State hospital under the charge of specialists. Chronic cases not needing special restraint or care are sent back to the county after hospital treatment can benefit them no farther; but no county is allowed to care for its own insane unless the plans of its almshouse buildings and the management of that institution are approved by the State Board of Charities. If so approved, there is a small weekly per capita allowance from the State treasury to the county that cares for its own insane. If not approved, at any time the State Board has the power to transfer all the insane belonging to the county to State institutions or the almshouse asylums of other counties, and collect the bill for their maintenance from the county to which they belong. Thus it is to the interest of the county to care for its own insane and to care for them properly.

The idea of segregation and of special provision for the harmless chronic insane has been carried to the point of boarding selected cases of the insane in families. This has been experimented upon in Massachusetts. The amount paid for the board, together with the cost of the necessary visiting, makes it not much more economical than asylum care, although it is much more satisfactory for selected cases. There are those who hope that, as with children the placing-out system may supplant the institution system, so with the insane it may be possible to board larger numbers of them, and incorporate them thus in the ordinary population. In Scotland this system has been developed much farther than in this country. The advancement along this line seems to be very nearly at a standstill in Massachusetts; and other States have not followed her example, as other States have not followed the example of Wisconsin in county care under State supervision.

The cost of county or township care for the insane ranges all the way from nearly nothing to about $150 per annum, while under State care the expense ranges from about $150 per annum to $300.

Patients are probably cared for to a decreasing extent in private institutions. Some of the gravest abuses, as in Pennsylvania, have grown up in these private homes or retreats. In several medical schools lecturers on mental diseases say that, as a rule, commitment to a public institution is safer than to a private institution, unless the character of the man in charge is very well known.

**Classification.** After the classification by sex, and in the South by color, the next great line of division among the insane which specialists have attempted to make has been between acute, or possibly curable, and the chronic, or probably incurable cases. As one superintendent remarks, "You cannot do too much for a man if you can thereby cure him." In order to make cure as likely as possible, it is desirable that institutions should be small, the number of attendants large and of good character, and all the conditions of life as nearly like those of a normal home as possible. To provide such facilities as these with the purpose of curative treatment is expensive; while, on the other hand, to take adequate care of the chronic or probably incurable insane requires a comparatively small per capita expenditure, and experts have constantly agitated for the separation of the two classes. But there has hardly been a proposal to establish an asylum for the chronic insane, or the matter has hardly ever come up in the National Conferences of Charities, without some would-be orator objecting to the erection of any institution over the door of which must be written, "Farewell to hope, all ye who enter here." For this reason the asylum at Agnews, California, intended and planned by the architect for the care of the chronic insane, has been compelled to depart from this intention, and to care for all classes of the insane in large wards, and under conditions not most favorable to cure. Each asylum in the State of California receives all classes without regard to their character as curable or incurable. The compromise results in proper treatment for neither class. In the States where this classification between institutions has been measurably maintained, it results in very considerable saving, and in considerably better treatment for the curable insane. At the same time insanity is not usually a curable disease. Even in the best managed institutions, and those receiving the likeliest class of patients, less than thirty per cent permanently recover.

After the separation of the curable from the incurable, in order to provide for the proper care of each, the next most important classification is, perhaps, into the criminal and the non-criminal insane; that is, those having dangerous or criminal instincts and those who do not have them. Some States have treated the criminal insane as criminals, and provided for them in branch penitentiaries. Others have treated them as insane, and put them into the same institution with other persons of that class, sometimes to the danger and often to the disgust of such other patients and their friends and relatives. The best policy, and the one adopted by the progressive States, is to have a separate asylum for the criminal insane.

Another essential to the proper classification is the separation from the insane of those who are epileptics, and also the distinctly feeble-minded. The class of epileptics, especially, is a great annoyance both to the inmates and managers of institutions for the insane, as they require special treatment which they can properly have only in a special institution. Beyond these distinctions which obtain as between institutions, there must further be a classification of the insane in any given institution to bring together those that do not vex or excite one another, and to segregate the filthy and the unmanageable. It is one of the defects of very large institutions that have been erected in some States, that the wards are too large to make possible proper classification, and consequent individualization of cases.

No mention can here be made of the improvement in the treatment of the insane which comes only through an improvement in the personnel of the institution, through freedom from spoils politics, through the introduction of civil service reform, through the activity of clubs of men connected with each institution organized for their mutual improvement, and through the development of training-schools for attendants upon the insane. It is by these and other agencies that the present great advancement is being made along the lines of greater wisdom in treatment, greater kindness in control, and greater freedom within the bounds of safety for the insane.

# CHAPTER XII

## THE FEEBLE-MINDED AND ANALOGOUSLY DEGENERATE CLASSES

**The Problem of the Feeble-minded.** The term feeble-minded is now used to cover all grades of idiocy and imbecility, from the child that is simply dull and incapable of profiting by the ordinary school, to the gelatinous mass that simply eats and lives. If it is difficult to give an exact definition of insanity, it is manifestly even more difficult to give an exact definition of feeble-mindedness. Some have been hardy enough to say that we are all more or less insane, and it would be still easier to assert that we are all more or less feeble-minded. The class to which the technical term is applied may be expected to increase as specialists improve their acquaintance with the different symptoms of feeble-mindedness. For this reason, as in the case of the insane, the census figures bearing upon the subject indicate a rate of increase out of all proportion, probably, to any actual increase of the condition of feeble-mindedness in the population. The census of 1890 shows a total of 95,571 idiotic and feeble-minded persons in the United States. It is certain that this enumeration does not include nearly all. Of the whole number, but 6,315 were in special institutions for feeble-minded.

The buildings and grounds for these institutions alone required an outlay of about four millions, and an annual expenditure for these classes of defectives amounting to over one million.[1] It will thus be seen that the feeble-minded are next to the insane in the number to be provided for, but that provision for them has only begun.

As to the classes of the population in which they are found, in 1848 in Massachusetts, out of 574 idiots examined by Dr. S. G. Howe or his assistants, 220 were supported by the town or State, 20 had property of their own, and 26 belonged to

[1] Dr. Fernald, *N. C. C.*, 1893, p. 215.

wealthy families.[2] In Pennsylvania, in 1871, there were about 3,500 feeble-minded children. Of these, 717 were in families of ample ability to furnish support; 604 in families of moderate circumstances (they could hardly pay the rates usually charged at private institutions); 1,619 were in poor families, who would be unable to pay for their support away from home, yet would be unwilling to relieve themselves of a painful burden by casting their children on the county; 560 were in homes of the most degraded character, or at public expense in almshouses.[3]

In this particular class, which is commonly of very degenerate stock, or made up of degenerate individuals, a study of the cases of feeble-mindedness or idiocy will give much help in the appreciation of the general causes of pauperism .It therefore seems advisable to inquire what has been ascertained in this matter, although we have not considered the causes of dependency in other groups. The report of Dr. S. G. Howe already quoted was concerned especially with the causes of idiocy in Massachusetts; and as it was made at a time precedent to the large foreign immigration, which in Dr. Kerlin's opinion increased the number of feeble-minded in Pennsylvania, the causes of idiocy then found are such as might be considered indigenous. Dr. Howe had a feeling that idiocy could not have been in the plan of nature, or, as he says, "It was hard to believe it to be in the order of Providence that the earth should always be cumbered with so many creatures in human shape but without the light of human reason. . . . Where there was so much suffering there must have been sin." Entering upon the investigation with this bias, we may presume that he emphasized as fully as the facts warranted, but assuredly not more than he considered them to warrant, personal and moral causes of idiocy. "Out of 420 cases of congenital idiocy examined, some information was obtained respecting the progenitors of 359. In all these cases save only four, it is found that one or both of the immediate progenitors of the unfortunate sufferers had in some way widely departed from the normal condition of health, and violated natural laws; that is to say, one or the other or both of them were very

[2] Report on Idiocy, 1884, p. 23. [3] Dr. Kerlin, *N. C. C.*, 1884, p. 247.

unhealthy or scrofulous, or they were hereditarily disposed to affections of the brain, causing occasional insanity, or they had intermarried with blood relatives, or they had been intemperate, or had been guilty of sexual excesses which impaired their constitutions."

The origin of the work of training the feeble-minded has two sources: one the school, and one the hospital; it lies between the department of education and the department of medicine. The schools for the deaf and blind found themselves asked to educate children that were also feeble-minded, and hospitals for the insane were asked to treat a large number of imbeciles. The educational element was at first most strongly developed. Hopes were entertained of making 50 or 75 per cent of the feeble-minded self-supporting; but that optimistic view had to be modified, and it is now seen that not more than 10 or 15 per cent can be made self-supporting in the sense that they can return to an independent life in the ordinary population.[4] The educational side was well illustrated by the exhibit made at Chicago and Nashville of the work done by inmates of institutions for the feeble-minded.

The medical side of the work has been especially considered by the Association of Medical Officers of American Institutions for Idiotic and Feeble-minded Persons, which held its first meeting during the centennial year, 1876, at the institution for the feeble-minded at Elwyn. At the annual meetings different medical aspects of the matter are discussed, and surgical remedies for feeble-mindedness proposed.

On the side of philanthropy the matter has been discussed at most of the national conferences since 1884. At that conference Dr. Kerlin mildly rebuked the conference for its preceding neglect of this branch of work, and it was there introduced by a paper that showed conclusively that it must receive a progressively large share of attention from a body concerned with general philanthropy.

**Classification.** The classification of feeble-minded persons, and the treatment possible for them, can best be described by an extended extract from Dr. Kerlin's paper, read to the Conference of Charities at St. Louis.[5]

[4] Dr. Fernald, *N. C. C.*, 1893, p. 217. [5] *N. C. C.*, 1884, pp. 248-251.

It has been convenient to group the chief varieties or grades of idiocy under the following syllabus:

GROUPS
- 1. *Idiocy.*
  - (*a*) Apathetic.
  - (*b*) Excitable.
- 2. *Idio-imbeciles.*
- 3. *Imbeciles.*
  - (*a*) Lower grade.
  - (*b*) Middle grade.
  - (*c*) High grade.
- 4. *Juvenile insanity.*

To aid description, imagine that you walk through a considerable range of separated buildings, allowing me to select the types of the seven or eight grades we shall encounter in as many localities.

Here, in a large, airy, sunny room, lying on couches or advanced to rocking-chairs, is the saddest and lowest group. You are likely to stop before its type, a helpless, gelatinoid creature, ten years of age, so limp and structureless that, in the language of the nurse, "he doubles in three like a clothes-horse when lifted from his bed." The only noise that interests him is that of a bell. The only object he ever seems to look at is his hand. He cries when he is hungry. He enjoys being held and rocked, and shows actual delight when bathed. With his great, luminous, soft jet eyes, he reminds one of a seal. Perhaps his intelligence is rather below that of a trained seal. It is certainly not that of a babe four weeks old. He is a profound idiot, with epileptic complication. Near by is another of the same age, mute, dwarfed, and helpless. She actuates nothing. Her only expression of common wants is a low moan or cry; but she rewards the faithful nurse by a smile, recognizing the epithet "baby," which has been applied to her. She sleeps well, and enjoys her bath.

Excitable idiots are not so common as the apathetic. They usually die early from exhaustion, or, less happily, sink into apathetic forms; but there is a group in every large asylum of this class, taxing the ingenuity of their present care-takers, after wasting the best life of their families.

The temptation for their extinction rises to the lips of the careless, forgetful how far such practice would be from all moral or judicial right, how revolting to every religious sentiment, and contradictory to every logical principle.

So we have them with us, although so little of us. Annie F., the saddest type, aged eight years, mute, wild, and vicious, biting any one whom she can reach, with a nervousness in the act that suggests its irresponsibility; darting to an open window to throw herself headlong below, her glittering eyes, tensely drawn lips, and sudden pallors indicating the pain and commotion of her poor and worried brain. How fittingly and terribly does this disturbed life project itself from its ante-natal unrest—an unwilling and unhappy conception, for the destruction of which the mother's stormiest passions had unceasingly but unavailingly contended! And there are a few others as sad, exciting wonder why they continue to live, and greater wonder how the home and the neighborhood tolerated for years their cries, discordant noises, and uncouthness.

Advanced beyond these apathetic and excitable idiots, we find an intermediate group, the idio-imbeciles. Many have the facial appearance, the deformed heads, the dwarfishness of body, the narrow buccal arches, the imperfect teeth, of very imperfect creatures, but there is dawning intelligence. Taken from their isolation, they feebly grasp, through their shyness and sensitiveness, for the better things about them. Expecting them to do little or nothing, the trainer is daily sustained by successes, and goes on hopefully introducing most of them to a higher grade,—that of the lowest forms of imbecility; and here we discover the strongest individuality, so that it is quite impossible to select a type. T. T., age twelve, will illustrate as well as any. He is a microcephalic paralytic imbecile of low grade; articulation quite imperfect; sense of sight and hearing good; hand well formed; imitation above the grade in which he is placed; cruel in his disposition; showing discrimination, analysis, and candor, when he says he "likes to wear heavy boots—good to kick boys with." He is the better of two similarly malformed and imbecile brothers now living. In this lowest plane of imbecility will be found many mutes who are yet possessed of perfect hearing, ready appreciation of language, and often dexterous finger and hand capacity. Under special training in articulation and the inspiring effect of concert recitation and song, they come to the partial possession of speech. They rarely become perfect in speech. As their capacity is gradually developed, they are carried forward into the higher ranks, to become our most interesting children. The idiocy or imbecility displayed by them is, as often as not, the effect of their isolation. The brighter children of the family outgrow them. They betake themselves to solitary lives and belittling occupations, until the range of their intelligence becomes very limited. They are the Kaspar Hausers of our community.

Advancing into another apartment, the fifth and sixth of the series through which you must imagine yourselves to have been led, we find the middle-grade imbeciles of a congregate family. They are orderly and neat at their school tables, because, from habit training, they have become so. They are patient under the discipline of light work, many of them becoming useful drudges and domestic servants. They crowd forward into our great laundry, where, commencing with the folding of our table napkins, they come to dispute with one another for the use of the ironing-table or power-mangle. The tone of the place being industry, they creep out of their sloth and indolence to keep lagging steps with the crowd that carries them forward.

The unfairness of applying to the highest grade, or indeed to any grade of imbecile children, the word "idiot," in any other than its generic sense, will occur to any sympathetic and thinking person, as he steps across the threshold of the class-room or calisthenium devoted to the higher grades of our defective children.

The mental deficiency or deviation is often so slight, or the imperfection is found in such a limited range, perhaps involving only the power to form a judgment of values, or a judgment of social proprieties, or a judgment of moral risk, or a judgment of the prevalent wickedness outside of asylums, that it may seem strange that several of these boys and girls should be under the care of an institution of this character.

In this first rank are often found children who have been typical cases of idiocy from deprivation, who, under the advantages of educational influences especially adapted to the infirmity, rise to the first rank, many to become self-supporting under kindly guidance, but who, left to themselves, sink lower in their enforced isolation.

From this account one gets something of the feeling that comes with a visit to a well-managed institution for the feeble-minded. Nothing is more repulsive than neglected or untrained idiots; but, on the contrary, nothing gives higher ideas of the possibilities of kindness and intelligence in training all grades of the degenerate, than a visit to an institution managed like that at Elwyn, of which some idea is given by Dr. Kerlin's description. One comes to realize the educational value to the community of such kindly care, and the truth of the statement that kindness is its own reward, to society or to the individual.

**Custodial Care.** The custodial care of the feeble-minded has thus far been undertaken by the managers of the schools for the feeble-minded, it being found that, under wise administration, the adult imbeciles could be useful in the work of the institution; and it being better, therefore, to introduce the colony plan with appropriate segregation of classes, than to establish other new institutions for the custodial care of adults. For instance, at Elwyn, it was found that many feeble-minded women had a liking for children, and that they could be distinctly serviceable in taking care of the young children in the school department, a work which made them happier, and benefited their own malady as far as anything could. "It is not," as Dr. Knight says, "legislatures to the contrary notwithstanding, because the managers of these institutions wish to build up a great institution, but because by the colony plan a larger share of service can be rendered than by splitting one institution into several new ones." New York, however, has established special custodial homes for adult idiots and a home for feeble-minded women, and New Jersey has recently followed the example. It remains to be seen whether, as in the case of the insane, specialists will conclude that classification should be maintained as between institutions, or whether it should be carried on in large institutions on the colony plan.

That custodial care for most grades of the feeble-minded will come to be increasingly demanded cannot be doubted. It has been later in coming than the custodial care of the chronic insane, because the latter are more actively and obviously mischievous to society; but whenever the importance of human selection becomes better understood, the custodial care throughout life of the feeble-minded of both sexes will be demanded.

**Epileptics, Inebriates, and Other Degenerates.** The latest differentiation in the care of the classes mentally or nervously diseased is in providing special custodial homes for epileptics. It had for a long time been found that in both homes for the feeble-minded and hospitals for the insane, the presence of epileptics was unfortunate from the standpoint of the other patients, while at the same time the special attention that they needed could not be given them. Therefore, at all the large institutions, special wards or buildings were provided where those subject to epileptic seizures might be properly provided for. This was also much more satisfactory to the epileptics themselves, as many of them in the intervals between attacks were fully conscious of their whereabouts, and had well-ordered minds. It is consequently directly in the line of further classification that institutions should be established for the care of epileptics alone, although some of the specialists in the care of the feeble-minded express their doubt as to the wisdom of this course. Ohio was the first State to establish a home for epileptics, and the example has been followed in New York.

To some it may seem improper to treat of the care of inebriates in the same chapter with the care of the feeble-minded; but there is a growing tendency to consider habitual drunkenness a disease, or at least as resulting in diseased conditions, which must have medical treatment—reducing persons to a mental condition which demands custodial care. The neuroses resulting from or in habitual drunkenness have been studied of late, and one thing at least is manifest: The system of short term commitments for drunkenness in the county jails or in the houses of correction has no curative effect whatever. The person who has been convicted ten times for drunkenness and is convicted again is sentenced by the judge with the perfect knowledge on the part of the latter that no good will result, except that the person will be kept from bothering the community during the time of the sentence, and that he will come out of jail as likely to offend against the law as before he was committed. In some cases as many as one hundred and twenty commitments have been registered against a single person. By alternating jails and almshouses in order to secure a change of diet and associates, the habitual vagabond drunkard is enabled to recuperate his shattered forces at the expense of the community, and prolong his life and evil influences indefinitely.

The first State to establish a home for the inebriate was Massachusetts. Judging from the report of the board for 1893 this is by no means a success as yet.

> This hospital was designed for the restraint of excessive drinkers during a period of time assumed to be sufficient for an attempt to bring their physical and mental condition up to a point which would enable them to resist a craving for drink, and successfully to contend with the evil influences sure to surround them on their discharge.[6]

Curiously enough the superintendent of the Foxborough Hospital has no power to compel inmates to work, though this is the best remedial agency known for the disease treated. Further than this, courts have shown great looseness in committing persons to the hospital as inebriates. The institution is not a place for the idle, disorderly, or vicious classes, but

[6] Report of Board of Lunacy and Charity, 1893, p. 85.

was planned rather for those whose lives, apart from that habit, had been decent and without scandal to the communities in which they lived.[7] Yet the courts have sent a number of inmates who, by their disorderly or criminal habits and tendencies, imperil the success of the humane venture of the State. It is recommended by the State Board of Lunacy and Charity that the officials in charge of the hospital should have the power to refuse persons committed by the courts, if they are palpably not adapted to the institution. Manifestly such an institution as this must have some way of securing the inmates for which it is intended and none others; and at least it must not be made what its enemies have called it, "a place for coddling drunkards."

Analogous to the institution for inebriates would be one where persons convicted of habitual offences against chastity might be committed for treatment and especially for detention. In case cure or reform, whichever we choose to call it, should prove to be impossible, they could then be detained during the remainder of their natural lives, working for their own support in a colony. New York has at present a custodial home for feeble-minded women. Such a place as the one just suggested has been advocated by Mrs. Lowell from the Conference of 1879 down to the present. Short commitments for this class of offences are manifestly as futile as in the case of habitual drunkards. Further than this, this class of persons is especially subject to disorders analogous to feeble-mindedness; and in all institutions for wayward girls the number verging upon feeble-mindedness is found to be especially large. The managers of reformatories and refuges for fallen women frequently complain that those who come to them need hospital treatment and prolonged detention. This the custodial home could give.

There is also need of custodial institutions for male offenders against chastity, nothing at present being done, perhaps because any treatment with the present punitive and reformatory machinery would be so manifestly futile. With proper custodial homes for persons of these classes of both sexes, we could begin to segregate and thereby sterilize a large number

[7] *Ibid.*, p. 87.

of those who have proved themselves by their conduct to belong to the class of the unfit.

**Specialization.** An inefficient police department and vulgar and corrupt police courts are the greatest "cross" that an active worker for the poor in many of our large cities has to bear. No thorough-going reforms in work for the poor can be perfected until the system of jails, reformatories, and prisons is reformed.

On reviewing what has been said regarding the dependent classes, we find that from the primitive institution, the almshouse hospital, or the hospital almshouse, there have developed a dozen or more special institutions for the care of the different classes of unfortunates. It is differentiation and intergradation analogous to that which has gone on in modern industry. This specializing and classifying, however, may result in a mechanical treatment, not as helpful as the earlier individualizing of cases and the treatment of each on its own merits. If extended classification results simply in a herding together of a large number of similarly defective persons who are treated as a class, fed as a class, drugged as a class, and buried as a class, we shall have a specialization which eliminates human sympathy, and makes charity something mechanical and uncharitable. If, on the other hand, fuller classification results in the fuller individualizing of cases and the adaptation to each of the best agencies of modern science and modern sympathy for care and cure, then the development has been one not only toward wiser sympathy, but deeper sympathy, and has prepared the way for a fuller development of the changes already in progress. In other words, our modern highly differentiated methods of treating the dependent classes bring with them a possibility, but not a guaranty, of better service.

# CHAPTER XIII

## PUBLIC AND PRIVATE CHARITIES

**Public Charities Defined.** It is asserted from time to time that public charities are not charities at all. The excuse for the assertion is that the tax-payer does not contribute his money from motives of benevolence, the hired official does not disburse it because he pities the beneficiaries, and the latter receive it with no sense of gratitude. It is not benevolence, but the motive of preserving the public health and the public peace that maintains public institutions for the relief of the destitute. The reply is that benevolence is present as a motive in supporting public charities. The tax-payers submit to an increase of burdens partly because they sympathize with distress, and are anxious to have it relieved. By "charities," as the term is used in the title of this chapter and in this volume, are meant all those institutions and agencies which give direct material aid to the poor as such. On the one hand, this leaves out of view all purely educational institutions, because the aid given is not material. According to English usage and according to legal usage in this country, an educational institution, unless supported by the fees of the pupils, is a "charity." A prominent American within the last fifteen years has asserted that a free soup-house and a free school are based upon the same principle. He is wrong, because there are dangers inherent in the gifts of free food which do not inhere in the gift of free education. Benevolence may set aside the rule that if a man will not work neither shall he eat, but not the rule that if a man will not study neither shall he learn. The beneficiary can get no advantage without personal effort from free tuition; he is, therefore, not exposed in the same way as is the recipient of material relief to the danger of degradation.

In educational institutions for the defective classes material relief, free board and lodging, is given to the pupils not able to pay, along with free tuition. This, in our opinion, makes such institutions charities to a certain extent, although they protest against being so classed, and wish to be considered purely educational. For administrative reasons, however, the supervision of them is usually given to the State Board of Charities. The educational element in their work so far overshadows the relief-giving element that they have only been incidentally referred to in this book.

By "public charities" is meant those institutions or agencies which are entirely controlled by the State in any of its branches, federal, State, county, township, or municipality. The distinction is a legal one, and is perfectly simple. A public corporation is one existing under the authority of the State, and which the State can modify or abolish at will. Frequently great private charities, as Girard College or the Johns Hopkins Hospital, are spoken of as quasi-public institutions. They serve the public indeed, and the wealth which they administer might be considered as affected by a public use in the same sense as wealth owned by a railroad company; but their charters are contracts with the State and cannot be arbitrarily modified by it. By "public funds" are meant such funds as are derived from the revenues of the State in any of its branches. They are usually the proceeds of taxation.

Scanning the history of the different countries, especially of our own, the principle that underlies the assumption of relief-work by the State seems to be this: Whenever a community has been educated up to such a point that it insists on a large amount of relief-work being done, and when the methods of doing it have been reduced to a routine, then the State has been asked to undertake the work, and relieve private benevolence of the burden. This we have seen in the care of the insane, the education of the deaf and dumb and the blind, and the education of the feeble-minded. In the matter of caring for inebriates, the experiment is now in progress under private management, and it is not yet clear that the time has come for the State to take hold. Relief work is adapted to administration by the State in proportion as it can be reduced to a routine, and in proportion as it requires very large expenditures to which all taxpayers can properly be asked to contribute. The

State is not inventive, its agencies are not adaptable and flexible; but it is capable of doing a large, expensive work when the methods for doing it are sufficiently elaborated. The administration of out-door relief is dangerous for the State to undertake, for the simple reason that it never can be reduced to a routine.

**Advantages and Disadvantages of Public Charities.** The advantages of public support for charitable institutions are briefly as follows:

1. The income can be absolutely depended upon, and may be made adequate. During an industrial depression there is no shrinking of revenue, as is sometimes the case in private charities, and an amount adequate to the work may always be reckoned upon.

2. There is greater publicity in a public institution. The records will ordinarily be fuller and more open to inspection. The press is freer to expose abuses. The checks of public opinion are consequently more easily applied. The whole aim and purpose of a public institution may be modified whenever the people of a community see that modification is desirable. While not flexible in little things—the small points of administration—a system of public charities is frequently more susceptible of large adaptation than a system supported by endowments and private contributions.

3. Under a just system of taxation all persons are compelled to contribute according to their ability. The stingy man is not allowed to thrive at the expense of his benevolent neighbor. The law is primarily an agency for bringing up the laggards in the march of progress; and when the community on the average wants benevolent work done, this is the method of pushing forward those who hang back.

The chief disadvantages of public relief are the following:

1. It is necessarily more impersonal and mechanical than that of private charities or of individual action. There is less kindness on the part of the giver, and less gratitude on the part of the receiver; and yet many cases occur where those who have received aid from the State have done so with thankfulness, and with a feeling of gratitude to the community as a whole for providing the means of relief.

2. There is possibly some tendency to claim public relief as a right, and for the indolent and incapable to throw themselves flat upon it. This feeling will always assert itself whenever it is given an opportunity to do so. In the case of public charities it can be checked, as already indicated, by leading the pauper to feel that, while he can claim relief as a right, he cannot claim as a right relief enough to make him nearly so comfortable as the man who is self-dependent.

3. In public charities officialism is even more pronounced than under private management. The degradation of character of the man on a salary set to the work of relieving the poor has been called one of the most discouraging things in connection with relief-work, and perhaps it is especially true that public officials are likely to become hard and unsympathetic.

4. It is possible to do so much relief-work, that while one set of persons is relieved, another will be taxed across the pauper line. This was palpably the case in England before the reform of the poor-law in 1834. Our own expenditures for charitable institutions have seldom reached the sums that make it possible to demonstrate the connection between the difficulties falling to the lot of the struggling, self-dependent members of the community, and the increase of taxation for the benefit of the destitute. But under our chaotic system of taxation it is usually true that the burden of supporting the State tends to diffuse itself along the lines of the least resistance; consequently, money which is raised for the relief of the poor may come out of pockets that can ill spare it.

5. The final disadvantage of public institutions for the relief of destitution is the weightiest, at least in the United States. The disadvantage referred to is that the blight of partisan politics and gratuitously awkward administration often falls upon the work. City and county politics seem to degrade public charities even more than other branches of the local administration. Charitable institutions are spoils of an insignificant character, thrown frequently to the less deserving among the henchmen of the successful political bosses. The managing boards of the hospital and almshouse are not content with appointing the superintendent, and leaving the responsibility of minor appointments to him, but make a complete list of

employees, and force the superintendent to accept them. Frequently, says Mr. Low, where a board is divided, the majority meet and apportion the appointments among themselves, and then vote them through as the nominations of a caucus. "This, more than anything else, accounts for the frequency of inharmonious boards." The benevolent of a community can usually not do a better thing than to mingle in local politics enough to see that the local charities are not treated as spoils.

**Administration of Public Charities.** State institutions have been comparatively free from this blight; although politics have exiled men like Gundry from Ohio, and Drs. Gillette, Dewey, and Wines from Illinois. Politics also abolished the Board of Charities and Reform in Wisconsin, and substituted the Board of Control, with salaries for all members. The bi-partisan board is by many not considered a remedy. The city and county of New York gives many examples of the futility of this device as a means of eliminating politics. In Indiana the political spoliation of the charitable institutions, and the resultant disgust of the intelligent part of the community, has had influence, close observers believe, in turning the tide of election at one or two critical times. The State Board of Charity there succeeded, without any positive law on the subject, in securing the introduction of civil-service methods in the selection of minor employees in many State institutions.

Both in this country and abroad the administration of charities has been very greatly improved by the extension of the system of honor offices. These are offices in which no salary is paid the incumbent. The best and most efficient of our State Boards of Charity have members holding by this tenure. The directors, where there are special boards for the local hospitals and almshouses and other institutions, are frequently of this class. The only danger is that these boards, whose principal function is to select the salaried superintendent of the institutions over which they have control, or, in the case of State boards, a salaried secretary to do the work, will degenerate into mere engines of the political boss, to be used by him in the distribution of spoils. Yet the danger of this is much less with unsalaried than with salaried boards; and their further function of supervision and advisory interference with the management are usually more developed, provided that the members receive no salary. It is frequently found possible to secure for such boards the services of some of the best men and women in the community; and, where it is possible, it is usually better that both men and women should be upon each board. Appointment seems, as a rule, to secure better members than election. The term of office should be of considerable length, the members going out in rotation.

In each commonwealth the fabric of the public charitable institutions rests upon the quicksands of the poor-law, which few study and probably none understand. It was said of the English poor-law, by the commission appointed to investigate its workings, that there was scarcely one statute connected with the administration of poor-relief which had produced the effect designed by the legislature, and that the majority of them had created new evils and aggravated those which they were intended to prevent.[1] The same is substantially true in many of our own States, and especially in the older commonwealths, such as New York and Pennsylvania, where the legislatures have not been careful to repeal existing legislation when enacting new laws. The result is a tangle of statutes which cannot be rationally interpreted because they have no rational basis. The courts construe them from time to time, because they must, and not because they know how. The fact that, after years of giving out-door relief in Brooklyn, the whole system was decided to be illegal, shows the unsubstantial nature of the foundation upon which our system of poor-relief sometimes rests.

In the Eastern States the English example has been followed, and laws regarding settlement are very complicated. The State Board of Lunacy and Charities in Massachusetts is busied to a very considerable extent in deciding where the burden of providing for particular persons should rest, whether upon the town, county, or State. In the Western States, while there may be a law defining residence, and another providing that only residents shall be relieved, these laws are almost never heeded. A dependent passes from township to township, from

[1] Nicholls, *History of Poor Laws,* vol. 2, p. 259.

county to county, and from State to State, expecting to be relieved wherever he happens to need relief. It is a loose system; but it may be doubted whether the old system of settlements, as now administered in Massachusetts, is susceptible of adaptation to times when the mobility of the population is so enormously increased by facilities for transportation.

Closely connected with the subject of settlement is the matter of adjusting public burdens as between the various political units. The economical way is to make the locality bear all the burden, because then those who pay the taxes administer the relief, and are directly interested in keeping the amount as small as possible. This is the old English system. It has broken down in the case of the special classes of defectives—the insane, etc.—because there were not enough of each class in a given township or county to enable that political unit to provide for them properly. They were therefore gathered under State control, and at first the cost of supporting them was assessed upon the county or township from which they came. The difficulty of collecting these assessments, together with the fact that the local desire to save money resulted too often in the denial of relief needed, has led to the removal of an increasing number to the support of the State at purely State expense. The county is then anxious to foist as many of its dependents upon the State as possible, since it does not feel the added burden of State taxation.

There will come a time, however, when the enormous expense arising from the system of State-administered charities will be no longer bearable, and we shall have to seek methods of economy in the administration of these institutions. In some places, where the accumulation of expenses for these purposes has been recklessly allowed to increase for years, the legislature has finally had a spasm of economy, and made a horizontal reduction to the injury of the service and the distress of many inmates. More commonly the State has undertaken to do a thing, for instance, to care for the insane, and then has not done it, the appropriations necessary for carrying out the plans not being made. Economy by either of these methods is distinctly wasteful as well as brutal; and it is to be hoped that the pressure of large expenditures for charities will eventually force attention to the prevention of pauperism, and an attempt to remove its causes, instead of forcing reversion to the policy of letting suffering go unrelieved.

**Private Charities.** By private charities we understand those that in their management are independent of the authority of the State, except that the same, as private individuals, may be subject to its general police and supervisory powers. A private charity may, or may not, receive public money in the form of a subsidy. Other funds come either from voluntary contributions, or from the proceeds of legacies or endowments. We concern ourselves here chiefly with the first-mentioned method of obtaining money.

The art of inducing men to give has been practised ever since charity began, and at all times one of its most constant features has been religious or ecclesiastical influence. The motive of the giver frequently deteriorated, and became the selfish one of securing merit for himself, instead of the unselfish one of benefiting the one to whom alms was given.

At the present time, it is still the church that is the most powerful agent in inducing people to give. Whether charities are identified with any particular denomination or not, it is usually, though of course not uniformly, the people of the churches that support them; and of all the churches the one that still induces the largest amount of giving in proportion to the means of those who give, is no doubt the Roman Catholic. This is the church which has succeeded best in inducing people to give not only money, but service. The religious orders of the Roman Catholic Church are still unequalled in the amount of this kind of contribution to the care of the poor. The orders that have had the largest development in the United States are the Sisters of Charity; certain of the teaching orders, which serve chiefly in charitable institutions; the Little Sisters of the Poor, who maintain homes for the aged; the *Sœurs de Bon Secours,* who nurse the poor in their own homes. The order best known is that of the Sisters of Charity, who conduct almost any form of work that seems to need doing, according to the needs of the locality to which they are sent. In the building up of hospitals, the nursing orders of the Catholic Church have been particularly successful; and their personal devotion leads them to render especially important service in times of pestilence.

Of Protestant denominations, there are few in the large cities, where destitution is a problem, that have not done something for the care of the poor. The preventive and educational work, in proportion to other kinds, has been more largely undertaken by the Unitarians than by any other denomination. The great hospitals are likely to be supported by whatever denomination has the largest wealthy membership in any large city. There has been a great increase in the beneficial activity of the various churches within the last ten or fifteen years.

An unfortunate feature of the work of American churches is interdenominational competition, which induces many of them to develop their charities as engines of church extension. This can be, and sometimes is, carried so far as to make their charities a nuisance. The condition of things does not, however, seem to be worse than in countries having a single church. In the latter, ecclesiastical orders within the church compete one with another.

Next after religious influence, pure and simple, the most powerful of the secondary motives that induce men to give money for charitable purposes is possibly social influence. Many of the large charities of our cities are officered, so far as boards of management are concerned, by fashionable or otherwise influential people; and to contribute to the charities of the locality is one of the means by which social advancement is secured. A long chapter, and conceivably one of some value, might be written on the methods of raising money for charities by means of balls, entertainments, oyster suppers, and other devices for inveigling money from the pockets of those who would not otherwise contribute the same amounts.

A third influence that is brought to bear in order to secure contributions for private charities is that of persistent teasing or other skilled solicitation on the part of paid collectors working on a commission.

Finally, the most powerful motive that influences contributions to private charities is that of benevolence, properly so-called. It is not more certain that there are large sums seeking investment in ordinary industry than it is that there are large sums which the holders would gladly give for the promotion of the public good, if they could find ways of bestowing such sums that they were sure would result in helpfulness. In order to obtain possession of a portion of this really large fund which is intelligently given or intelligently withheld, the managers of a charity must not only do thoroughly good work, but must contrive to let it be known that they are doing such work. The methods of philanthropic advertising, using the word advertising in a distinctly honorable sense, are various. The best introduction that a charity can have to the benevolent people of the community is the gradual diffusion from one intelligent person to another of the opinion that the charity is in fact doing something that is worth while. Beyond this, most of the non-sectarian charities and those operating under the guidance of Protestant denominations issue annual reports. As a rule, it does not pay a society to economize by a failure to publish such a report. In order to reach the most influential members of the community, it must be well prepared, well printed, and discreetly distributed. Many societies publish their own condemnation in their annual reports, and many more fail to publish anything that commends them to the intelligent part of the community. The perpetual re-using of stereotyped phrases, the filling up a report with the cant of philanthropy, and having the reports year in and year out substantially in the same form, from which the essential facts regarding efficiency are omitted, brands the society as unprogressive and unsatisfactory. In addition to the annual reports, a great many societies issue circulars, and even periodicals, explaining their work as it develops. Great use is also made of the daily and weekly press, but this is frequently not as wisely used as would be for the good of the institutions. What the daily press wants is news; and there is usually, or at least there should usually be, a considerable amount of news about the development of any large charity. To offer this in a way that makes it available for the daily press, is to offer exactly the material which will do the most good when printed. It is of no advantage to a paper, nor to an institution sending the copy, to print a "lot of gush" about some charity.

In order to commend the work of a charity to the favor of the most intelligent part of a community, it is essential that no attempt should be made to do the work too cheaply. "Cheap and nasty" is a phrase that can be applied to charities as well as to merchandise. Just as a physician cannot afford to begin practice without a proper preparation for his work, and without the facilities in the way of library, instruments, and office that are necessary in order to do his work well, so a charity will not, even from the financial side, find it wise to undertake to do for seven thousand dollars a work that can only properly be done for ten thousand. It is usually easier to manage the finances of a society that insists on having a revenue adequate to the work that it is doing—that would in fact go out of existence rather than proceed otherwise—than it is to manage the finances of a society that consents to half do its work because of an inadequate income.

The advantages of private charities over public ones are that they afford on the average a somewhat larger share of personal sympathy, that their benefits cannot logically be claimed as a right (although they often are so claimed), that they do not oppress the poor by increasing taxation, and that they are supposed to bring a somewhat smaller degree of degradation to the recipient of relief. The disadvantages of this style of support are that it sometimes leads charities to resort to sensationalism to obtain contributions, that it sometimes results in undue plutocratic influence in the administration of the funds,[2] and that in some cases the amount obtained is inadequate to the work that should be done. This last was probably what led to the break-down of private relief at Elberfeld, and compelled the substitution of public relief. It is not found, however, as a rule in this country, that the funds shrink during times of depression so as to make contributions less when the need is greatest. This is a danger often anticipated without cause. It should be said, also, that where private charities have developed to a very large extent they are as mechanical and as badly administered as public charities, and it is less easy to reform them. This was the case in France before

[2] Contributors to the English "voluntary" hospital sometimes have an undue influence in deciding who shall be admitted.

the Revolution, and in Italy before the recent secularization of charities. It is just as possible to pauperize a population through private charities as through public ones, as the example of Italy especially proves. Usually, however, when great abuses grow up in connection with charities, it is because they are heavily endowed; and this subject is to be treated in the next chapter.

In conclusion, it can only be reiterated that private charities are especially useful along lines of philanthropic experimentation. People with ideas in advance of those of the general community can find through private charities an opportunity to experiment, and, by results, to satisfy the community as a whole of the need and of the possibility of doing a certain work. Private charities are not suited to the administration of large funds, and the doing of a large volume of work, unless they are made amenable to state regulation.

## CHAPTER XIV

### ENDOWMENTS AND SUBSIDIES

**The "Dead Hand."** When those who support a charity find it difficult to raise the funds they need, and are weary with unsuccessful applications for contributions; when, further, they dislike to turn to the public treasury because of the stigma attaching to public relief, their wish is apt to be that their charity were adequately endowed. Then, they think, they could give their whole time to the administration of the funds, instead of giving so much of it to securing funds. It seems as though their hands would be free for very large usefulness, and the benefits of the institution might be indefinitely extended. It consequently happens that the annual reports of nearly every charitable association which is supported by voluntary contributions contain, in a conspicuous place, a form of bequest by means of which anyone so inclined may, without inconvenience, insert a provision in his will, leaving property to this particular charity. There is also a feeling in the community that one who leaves his wealth to charity has done a commendable thing, and there is a great tendency in the older portions of the country for endowments to accumulate rapidly. Nothing is done to discourage the movement on account of the feeling that it should be as untrammelled as possible. Yet no other country has ever permitted entire freedom in the granting of charitable bequests without finding, in the course of years, or of centuries at most, that the wealth of the country was coming to be too largely administered by the "dead hand." In the United States there are special dangers in laxness in this matter, by reason of the provision of our Federal Constitution which forbids States to pass laws impairing the obligation of contracts. This makes it especially difficult for us to modify the system that is now developing. In England, whenever Parliament sees fit to change the administration of an endowment, or even to sequester its revenue for other purposes than those of the testator, Parliament can do as it will; but that is out of the question with the State legislatures in this country. If a charitable establishment has a charter in which the State has not reserved the right to amend or repeal it, then, under the Dartmouth College decision, that charter is a contract with the State, which the latter cannot alter without the consent of the corporation.

Owners of property frequently feel as if they had a "natural right" to provide for its bestowal in perpetuity. Exactly why people should expect to be allowed to manage their property after they are dead and can no longer use it themselves, it is hard to see; at least, it is hard to see why a community should think itself bound to accord them the privilege that is to make them legislators in perpetuity, regarding the disposition of a certain amount of wealth, which they happen at the time of death to possess. One feeling may perhaps be that the person who leaves money to charity acts only from commendable motives, and that his will should therefore be respected. But even if it were true that they always acted from good motives, it would have to be remembered that "hell is paved with good intentions," or, as the Bible puts it, "There is a way which seemeth right unto a man, but the end thereof is death."

But their motives are not always commendable. Hobhouse gives the following analysis of the motives of decedents who leave money to charity.[1]

1. Love of power, ostentation, and vanity. 2. Superstition. The influence of this extends far beyond the Catholic Church, and leads people who have done little good in their lives to attempt to do a great deal by the disposition of their wealth after they can no longer control it personally. 3. Spite. "An appreciable number of men," says Hobhouse, "and perhaps more women, especially those who are childless and have been teased by expectant legatees, are on bad terms with their relatives. Now, the only way to disinherit your legal heirs is to give your property to some one else; what, then, so obvious as to give it to charity?" 4. A fourth cause, which Hobhouse

[1] Hobhouse, *The Dead Hand*, pp. 15-20.

thinks is far inferior in extent of operation to the first two mentioned, is the honest belief on the part of founders that their disposition of property is best calculated to benefit their country. This is patriotism, or philanthropy, or public spirit.

But irrespective of their motives, or the wisdom of testators, endowments are not likely to accomplish as much good as is expected of them because the character of boards of management is not all that could be desired, and because of a tendency to officialism, which develops when any society finds its economic existence assured.

The expenses of administration very frequently eat up the greater part of the income. While this is not the worst possible result, it still indicates in many cases a waste of the income consumed.[2]

**Regulation of Endowments.** Three things are necessary in the proper regulation of these endowments.

1. The restriction of endowments. Our law at present declares endowments invalid for superstitious or immoral

[2] Mr. Johnson, in the article referred to, points presumably to Girard College as an example of extravagance in the administration of a charitable trust. At this college, which is really an industrial school for boys, according to the account of it given by Mr. Alden, "History of Child Saving," pp. 70-75, about three million have been spent on the construction of buildings which are of white marble. "The central or main building is the finest specimen of pure Greek architecture in America." The endowment fund of this institution is now considerably over $15,000,000 (Johnson estimates it at $20,000,000), yielding a gross annual revenue of about $1,500,000. There are less than 1,600 boys in attendance, about 150 leaving "College" each year. By comparison of such figures as these with those of the great universities, it will be seen that an enormous amount of money is invested in the education of comparatively few boys. One of the absurdities likely to cluster about endowments is found in connection with Girard College. "No minister of any sect is *ever* to be admitted within the premises, as the founder wished to 'keep the tender minds of the orphans who are to derive advantage from this bequest free from the excitement which clashing doctrines or sectarian controversy are apt to produce.'" Johnson, in the article quoted, recalls Dickens's description of "a place for the entertainment of 'seven poor travellers'" at Rochester, England. The accommodations for the keeper had improved, and those for the travellers had gradually deteriorated; and it was in contemplation, when he visited it, to build a shed outside for the travellers, and then the keeper would have a comfortable house, and those whom the house was built for would be entirely out of it. At the time of his visit only about one-thirtieth of the annual revenue was expended on the purposes commemorated in the inscription over the door, the rest being handsomely laid out in chancery, law expenses, collectorship, receivership, poundage, and other expenses of management highly complimentary to the importance of the seven poor travellers." *Charities Review,* vol. 1, p. 156.

purposes. This is a limitation left over from the time of the Reformation. It was established especially to prevent perpetual payments for prayers for the dead. Surely we have advanced far enough at the present time so that foundations for the distribution of indiscriminate doles might also be prohibited. As the problems of poor-relief are better worked out, there should be some authority to pass upon the wisdom of endowments, and to allow them to take effect or not according as public interests would or would not be served.

2. There must be a public supervision of endowments. This is necessary to prevent abuses from which inmates or institutions may suffer, as well as to prevent the misapplication of funds, and their use by private parties. There are very few States in this country that have any provision for visitation of endowed institutions. The English law, that the founder and his heirs and assigns shall be the visitors, obtains; but this visitation is not adequate, and should be supplemented by that of some responsible public official. The State Board of Charities is the proper authority where such a board exists.

3. It is necessary to provide for the revision of endowments. Times change. An endowment providing for the ransom of the captives of the North African pirates may have benefited some individuals for a time after it was made, but to provide for a similar expenditure in perpetuity was an absurdity. An endowment for superannuated wool-carders continued to support warden and bedesmen long after wool-carding had ceased to be an occupation. An endowment of 1683 for seven poor old men of the Protestant religion in the Asylum of the County of Cork, that had been soldiers and were unable to work, is handed down to a time when sufficient Protestant soldiers cannot be found in Cork to exhaust the income of the charity, and there is at present an accumulated fund of £2,300. There is a fund in Stirling worth £5,400 a year, which was given when certain trades and crafts possessed a monopoly in the town, for the indigent members of these guilds. The income of the charity became so great that it was distributed among the members of the guild irrespective of poverty and even of residence. In 1869 it was found that of the 412 members, 369 were recipients of the charity, and some of these were soldiers in Aus-

tralia. Endowments for teaching children to card, spin, and knit are of small use at the present time, or a foundation for the supply of spinning-wheels is not of any particular value.[3] Changes in religion, politics, and knowledge, as well as in industry, leave old endowments supporting something that is useless or worse, and there must be public authority for revising them.

Limitations upon the powers of testators will not lessen the amount that is given in charity eventually. They may keep a man whose motive is vanity, who is set in his own way and wishes to perpetuate his own will, from giving money to charities. He will see that public officials may interfere with his plans or whims. But those whose aim in leaving wealth is to benefit their fellows will look upon it as an advantage that, if their ideas are found not to be sound with the passage of years, there will be public authorities having power to modify and make useful their bequests.

**Public Subsidies to Private Charities.** When contributions are hard to get, when fairs and balls no longer net large sums, and when endowments are slow to come, the managers of private charities frequently turn to the public authorities and ask for a contribution from the public revenues. On the other hand, when local or State legislatures see the annual appropriation bills increasing too rapidly, and when they see existing public institutions made political spoils, and the administration wasteful and inefficient, they are apt to think of giving a subsidy to some private institution, instead of providing for more public buildings and more public officials. The former course is cheaper at the time, and seems to promise better administration.

On Feb. 2, 1893, while the Senate of the United States was sitting as town council for the City of Washington, a member moved to amend the appropriation bill by inserting a proviso that almshouse inmates or other paupers and destitute persons who might be a charge upon the public should be turned over to any private institution that would contract to provide for them at ten per cent less than they were then cost-

[3] For the foregoing and other examples of futile or mischievous charities, see Kenny, *Endowed Charities,* pp. 160 ff.

ing the District. Senator Call, who introduced the amendment, explained that it was in lieu of one which had been rejected at the previous session of Congress, whereby he had sought to have $40,000 of public money given to the Little Sisters of the Poor, to enable them to build an addition to their Home for the Aged. He defended the original proposal on the ground that this sisterhood cared for the aged poor better and more cheaply than the almshouse, and that the existence of their institution had saved to the tax-payers of the District in the last twenty years a sum believed to be not less than $300,000. It was not a novel plea; for Congress had already appropriated, since 1874, $55,000 to aid the Home for the Aged of the Little Sisters of the Poor; and each year the District appropriation bill had included subsidies for a large number of private charitable institutions, some of them avowedly under sectarian management and others not. How far the tendency to grant public subsidies to private charities had gone in the District of Columbia is in some sort indicated by the following table:

District of Columbia Appropriations for Public as Compared with Private Charities.

| | Number of Institutions | | Appropriation for Maintenance | | |
|---|---|---|---|---|---|
| | *1880* | *1892* | *1880* | *1892* | *Increase* |
| Public ...... | 7 | 8 | $78,048.82 | $119,475.05 | 160% |
| Private ..... | 8 | 28 | 46,500.00 | 117,630.00 | 253% |
| Totals...... | .. | .. | $124,548.82 | $237,105.50 | |

Appropriations 13 years, 1880-1892.

| | *Construction* | *Maintenance* | *Construction and Maintenance* |
|---|---|---|---|
| Public ......... | $155,130.70 | $1,296,125.95 | $1,351,256.65 |
| Private ........ | 300,812.53 | 840,940.00 | 1,141,752.53 |
| Totals........ | $455,943.23 | $2,137,065.95 | $2,493,009.18 |

The government of the District of Columbia is, of course, in many respects unique; but this tendency to vote public money to private charities is by no means peculiar to it. The best known example of persistence in the policy of reckless subsidies to private institutions is that of New York. A single institution in this State, officered by a religious order, receives from the city government more than $260,000 per year. A list of over two hundred private institutions for orphan children and the friendless in New York State shows that, of their total revenue, but $1,225,104.69 was derived from legacies, donations, and private contributions, while more than twice as much, namely $2,664,614.40, came from the tax-payers of the State, the counties, and the cities. A great part of the money handed over for disbursement to private institutions goes for the support of dependent children.

According to Mrs. Josephine Shaw Lowell, the administrative results of this policy in New York City have been to build up the private eleemosynary institutions of the State at the expense of the public ones. She gives the following statement covering a series of years to show this:

| *Year* | *Population* | *For Prisoners and Public Paupers* | *For Paupers in Private Institutions* | *Total* |
|---|---|---|---|---|
| 1850 ........ | 515,547 | $421,882 | $9,863 | $431,745 |
| 1860 ........ | 813,669 | 746,549 | 128,850 | 875,399 |
| 1870 ........ | 942,292 | 1,355,615 | 334,828 | 1,690,443 |
| 1880 ........ | 1,206,577 | 1,348,383 | 1,414,257 | 2,761,640 |
| 1890 ........ | 1,600,000 | 1,949,100 | 1,845,872 | 3,794,972 |

After showing how ruthlessly the estimates for the public charities were cut by the Board of Estimate and Control, she says: "The point to which I wish to call attention is that the city continues, at the bidding of the Legislature, to pay, without protest, year by year, increasing sums for the support of public dependents under care of private persons in private institutions, many of whom, but for this provision, would probably not be dependent at all, while at the same time the public dependents under the care of public officers in public institutions are housed in buildings which are in danger of falling down and are a discredit to the city." [4]

In 1889 the Legislature of Pennsylvania appointed a special committee, which investigated very fully the management of the charitable and correctional institutions of the State, and

[4] *State Charities Record,* April, 1891.

especially the methods employed by such institutions in securing public appropriations. The constitution of Pennsylvania forbids the granting of public funds to "sectarian" institutions; but the word "sectarian" is not defined, and the report of the committee shows a strong tendency to increase the number and amount of the State subsidies granted to private charities. This tendency is characterized as an "insidious danger." The committee tabulated the expenditures during a series of years for charitable and correctional purposes, amounting to about $37,000,000 and found that nearly a third of it went to private institutions.

In Pennsylvania it is found that such institutions tend more and more to be managed by a few persons who really choose their successors, and the State which grants them millions has not even the membership vote of a private individual who pays one, two, or three dollars annually as dues. Just before the advent of a superintendent of charities in the District of Columbia, a Congressional committeeman thus described the attitude of subsidized institutions towards the government:

> There is a universal feeling that, while Congress must furnish the money, each society must have absolute control of the expenditures; and none of them are willing to submit to any visitation or control of such expenditures, or even any auditing of the accounts. The beginning and end of their connection with Congress, in their eyes, seems to be, "Give each one of us so much money, and let us do what we please with it."

This fact, that there is a clear-cut distinction between public and private charities, but none between sectarian and non-sectarian charities, is one that those who shudder at every symptom of public aid to sectarian schools would do well to recognize. Protestants are willing to tease legislators for public money on behalf of a hospital or an orphan asylum in which they are interested, urging that it is "doing good," and that it is preventing crime and pauperism, and so saving money to the tax-payers. They do not see, or will not acknowledge, that the same could be said of a parochial school, and that the claim which they set up that their own institution is "non-sectarian" is equivocal and unfair, and one which in practice the courts have never been able to make definite.

**Arguments for Subsidies.** A tendency could hardly have gone so far as has that to grant public subsidies to private charities, without there were in favor of it many considerations of great force, either apparent or real. As favoring this policy, the consideration which is first and foremost in the minds of "practical" people is the matter of economy. Especially where the number of dependents in a given class is small, it is cheaper to hire them cared for than to establish an institution for them. This is the reason that in most small towns a private hospital is subsidized instead of one being erected at public expense; but, when we find a great city like Brooklyn depending entirely on subsidized hospitals for the care of its sick poor, this argument is inapplicable. Economy, however, may result from other causes, as when the private institutions are administered by religious orders, the members of which receive no pay except their support. Even in institutions not officered by members of a religious order, the salaries are apt to be lower and all the items of expense to be more closely scrutinized than in a public institution. Add to all this the further fact that frequently private contributors aid in the support of a private institution, and we see how great may be its advantage on the side of economy. To the real economies of this method of operation should be added the apparent economies when a private institution is willing to make a very low bid, to make great temporary sacrifices, in order to get the subsidy system introduced—in order to establish connections between itself and the public treasury.

Secondly, it is urged that private institutions, especially those for dependent and delinquent children, have a better effect upon the inmates than can public institutions. For one thing, dogmatic religious instruction can be given. For another, the spirit of self-sacrifice that pervades a private institution has a good effect upon the inmates, and is contrasted with the cold and officialized administration of the public institutions. Connected with this, as also with the matter of economy, is the fact that boards of trustees and of lady managers and visitors give freely of their time and energy and sympathy in aid of private undertakings.

Thirdly, it is urged that, by subsidizing private institutions, we free them from the blight of partisan politics and the spoils system. The miserable political jobbery connected with so many almshouses and insane asylums and other public charitable institutions is pointed out, and we are asked to shield as many as possible of the State's dependents from similar evils. In the matter of educating the blind and the deaf and the dumb, the private institutions managed by close corporations or by corporations of contributing members are thought to have been more successful than public institutions for similar purposes. The specialists needed to conduct them properly prefer to work for a private corporation, as their tenure is more secure, and it is easier to map out and pursue a policy of steady development and improvement.

A fourth consideration is, that by means of subsidies we aid the poor without attaching to them the stigma of pauperism. A home for the aged is more respectable than an almshouse, and a private protectory or industrial school is supposed not to discredit the inmates as much as a public reform school.

**Arguments Against Subsidies.** But this last mentioned consideration brings us to a turning-point, for it is urged against such subsidies as well as in favor of them. It is urged that private institutions receiving public money promote pauperism by disguising it. Children who would support aged parents rather than allow them to go to the almshouse, desert them promptly when some provision is made for them that is ostensibly more honorable. Parents unload their children upon the community more recklessly when they know that such children will be provided for in private orphan asylums or protectories, where the religious training that the parents prefer will be given them. And thus we reach the first great objection to granting public subsidies to private charities. While it may be cheaper to provide thus for each dependent during a year, yet the number of dependents increases so rapidly that eventually the charge upon the public is greater than if the alternative policy were pursued. The results are most astounding, where, as in the case of dependent children in New York, the managers of each institution are free to admit children and have them charged to the community. In New York City any one of many private institutions can receive any child, either temporarily or permanently, and collect a stated amount per week from the local authorities. For a large institution, there is a profit in taking care of children at the rates fixed. The larger the institution the greater the per capita profit. "A study of the reports made by these institutions to the State Board of Charities shows that at least nine of the twenty-three institutions received more money from the public funds during the year ending Oct. 1, 1892, than was expended by them during the same period for the maintenance of all the children in the institutions (including some for whom the city does not make per capita payments, but whom, as is thus shown, it does nevertheless actually support); the excess of appropriations from the public treasury over the cost of maintenance of the children varied in different institutions from $63 in one institution to $24,300 in another; the total excess of appropriations from the public funds over the cost of maintenance being in these nine institutions $65,498."

In the second place, the argument from economy in support of the subsidy system is negatived by the fact that under this system there must be so many duplicate institutions. In Maryland, for instance, there are two reformatories for boys within a mile of each other, and two for girls, both in Baltimore. Catholics manage one pair of institutions, and private Protestant corporations the other. Besides this inevitable line of cleavage between Protestants and Catholics, there are various causes of institutional fission resulting from medical or social sectarianism. Many charitable institutions have been established less from brotherly love than from a quarrel in the board of managers in an older institution. This, together with the influence of individual ambitions, has led especially to the establishment of a great number of medical charities. When the public begins to grant such favors, it is hard to draw a line. As a United States senator once said in speaking of the situation in the District—

> The very fact that Congress makes these appropriations has caused, to a great degree, the multiplication of the organizations. A few people getting together who are desirous of doing charitable work, or who have discovered some special need, or who are

dissatisfied with some feature of some existing institution, instead of adding to or modifying such an institution, will start a new one, because they can appeal directly to Congress for the money necessary to begin it, and can base their claim on the ground that they are just as good as some other association already on the list.

A third reason for objecting to the subsidies we are considering is, that when voting upon them the legislator must resist special pressure. He has not a clear-cut question of a given service to be rendered balanced by a given expenditure, but it becomes partly a question of offending or favoring some sect or nationality. The contention that the subsidy system takes the charitable institutions out of politics seems to be unsound. On the contrary, it drags them into politics in a new and unfortunate way—in a way that is found in practice to give great scope to log-rolling and kindred expedients. Often those applicants most skilled or most personally attractive were most successful, and sometimes the committees were obliged to average their gifts. After such a policy has been entered upon, it cannot be altered without injury to great vested interests, and without giving offence to large and powerful constituencies.

A fourth objection to the subsidy system of supporting charities is that it tends to dry up the sources of private benevolence. Individual contributors dislike to have their mites lost in the abundance of a public appropriation. Almost without exception those institutions that have received public aid the longest and the most constantly receive least from private contributors. In looking up the history of a considerable number of institutions, it was found that, after the public became a contributor, private contributions fell off from year to year, not only relatively, but absolutely, and in some cases ceased altogether.

Mrs. Lowell states that, of the 18,900 children supported by charity in New York City, 2,700, or one-seventh, are supported in private institutions at private expense (14 per cent of the total expenditure), and that 1,200 are supported at public expense in public institutions. Of the total expenses for all purposes of the twenty-three institutions caring for the remaining 15,000, 8.8 per cent is contributed by private benevolence. From this it appears that 21 per cent of the expense of caring for dependent children is borne by private benevolence, while 79 per cent is borne by the city. In Philadelphia, under a different system, the proportion borne by private benevolence is 97 per cent.[5] In New York one institution, that received in 1892 $250,000 from the city, received from private sources less than $500; and in the case of twelve institutions the receipts from private sources were less than 5 per cent of the total expenditure.[6]

This brings us to a fifth reason for objecting to the granting of public subsidies to private charities. It frequently does positive harm to a charitable institution, and sometimes wholly destroys its usefulness. An institution that receives no public money is freer in all its operations, and is more highly valued by those who sustain and manage it. The beneficiaries also feel differently toward their benefactors. When visiting one subsidized institution the request was made that nothing should be said before the inmates that would inform them that the institution received any public money. One could understand the wish, and presume that the inmates would work more faithfully, be more grateful for favors received, and finally "turn out better," because they were kept in ignorance of the fact. Yet we may doubt the possibility or propriety of thus using public money, and at the same time trying to conceal the fact of doing so. By no hocus-pocus of subsidy-granting can we make taxation do the work of self-sacrifice.

It should be remarked that the several States and municipalities have entered upon this policy of subsidizing private charities without deciding to do so, and even without perceiving that a decision was called for. Each request for a subsidy has been treated as a matter of administrative detail, involving no principle, and not significant as a precedent. The resultant system, as it is applied to the care of dependent children in New York City, is about as business-like as though the city should try to get its streets paved by announcing that any regularly incorporated association that should pave a given number of square yards of street—location, time, and method to be

[5] See *Conference on Care of Dependent and Delinquent Children*, New York, 1893, pp. 164, 165. [6] *Ibid.*, p. 165.

decided by itself—should receive a given amount from the public treasury. The Washington system is theoretically looser, but practically not so bad. It is as though private associations were allowed to do paving at their own discretion, and then, on coming to Congress and teasing with sufficient skill and pertinacity, they should be given subsidies on the general theory that they were "doing good" and rendering "public service."

This is subsidy granting at its worst. At its best, the government must attend to three things: First, on behalf of the poor as well as the tax-payers, it must provide for the thorough inspection of subsidized institutions, and the systematic auditing of their accounts. This work cannot be done by grand juries, or legislative committees, or *ex-officio* inspectors, who may from time to time thrust their inexperienced noses into matters which they know nothing about. The work of inspection must be done by some thoroughly experienced and otherwise suitable administrative officer, who is definitely responsible for the thoroughness of his work. Second, the State must keep in the hands of its own officials the right of deciding what persons shall be admitted to the benefits for which it pays, and how long each person may continue to receive those benefits. If it pays for beds in a hospital, one of its own officials should have entire control of admitting and discharging the patients cared for. This is necessary in order that "there may be some gauge of indigency, and some assurance that the gauge will be used." Third, subsidies should only be granted on the principle of specific payment for specific work. When any one of these three conditions is lacking, the policy of subsidy granting is necessarily pernicious.

But even at its best, and with these safeguards, the policy of granting public subsidies to private charities is one of doubtful expediency. There is ground for thinking that, if the State is too big and awkward to do a given work, it is also too big and awkward to decide properly whom it shall subsidize in order to get the work done. All that can be said against subsidies in general can be said against this form of subsidies, and more; because here we have to deal with religious, medical, and social sectarianism, and because we are giving over the defenceless to the care of the irresponsible. As a transition policy for growing communities, or for new and developing varieties of benevolent work, it may possibly have its place; but it should never be entered on inadvertently, for while all its advantages and economies are greatest at the beginning, the disadvantages and dangers of it increase as time goes on. Those who would entirely avoid establishing any precedent whatever for the voting of public money to private schools can take properly but one course. That course is consistent opposition to any and all public subsidies to private charities.

# CHAPTER XV

## ORGANIZATION AND SUPERVISION OF CHARITIES

**State Boards of Charities.** Soon after the conclusion of the Civil War, there was a movement in some of the older and wealthier States to establish public supervisory agencies known as State Boards of Charities. This was part of the general tendency to amplify and improve the administrative machinery of our State governments. The creation of boards or commissions for the care of the public health, the collection of statistics regarding labor, and similar purposes, were inaugurated at this time. The first board for the supervision of charities was established in Massachusetts in 1863, and Ohio and New York followed with similar boards in 1867. Illinois, Pennsylvania, and Rhode Island established boards in 1869. We now have nineteen States with organizations of this character.[1] Most of the boards established in later years, for instance, since 1880, have been in the new States of the West; and the movement for their establishment seems to have come to a standstill in States that were in full operation at the close of the war. Indiana, however, established a board in 1889.

In the main, these State Boards of Charities are of two general types, one having the powers of supervision and report only, and the other having powers of control over the charitable institutions of the State. Typical boards with the latter method of organization are now found in Rhode Island, Kansas, and Wisconsin. Boards with executive powers are usually made up of salaried members, limited in number—usually not more than six—who are the trustees of the public charitable institutions which they inspect, and of which they appoint superintendents and other officers. Boards without executive power are usually composed of honor officers. The number is sometimes considerable, as in the case of New York, where one member is ap-

[1] See the list of members of the State Boards, *N. C. C.*, 1893, pp. 467-469.

pointed from each judicial district in the State. These unsalaried boards, with powers of supervision and report only, are necessarily made up of persons willing to give to the work a considerable amount of time for no other return than the possible payment of their expenses. Each board, as a rule, appoints a salaried secretary who is a permanent officer, or should be permanent, and who attends to the routine work of the office. These secretaries of State Boards of Charities have been the moving force in organizing the National Conferences of Charities, and many of them are as eminent specialists as this country has produced. It has usually been found easier to keep politics out of these unsalaried boards. The supervisory board in the case of Wisconsin has been abolished to make way for politically appointed receivers of salaries. In Illinois an eminent specialist has been removed from the position of secretary for political reasons only. As a rule, however, there is "not enough in it" to induce politicians to make much of a fight to secure control of one of these advisory boards. They consequently have a greater degree of stability, and from this fact they have a much greater influence. Where officials are changing very frequently, as is the case with our State legislators, and for the most part with our State executive officers, a group of men whose position is relatively permanent, and who from year to year accumulate experience, and clarify their ideas as to what is necessary, can carry out plans of reform that would be impossible to a rapidly rotating board, even assuming that its members were of equal ability and devotion.

This does not imply that certain executive duties, such as the removal of foreign paupers from the State, as in New York and Massachusetts, and the care of certain classes of dependents, as in the case of dependent children in Massachusetts, and the removal of the insane from hospital to hospital within the State, as in Illinois and elsewhere, may not be ingrafted upon advisory boards without changing their general character. In some States, where it seems best to centralize the executive control of certain large classes of institutions, as of those for the insane, additional commissions have been created to discharge these executive functions. This is the case in New York. But over all such executive boards, there should still obtain the power of the Board of Charities to investigate and report upon everything in the line of charities within the State. A board with powers of supervision and report only is much freer in giving its opinion as to needed changes than one having executive powers. For instance, in the matter of applying to the legislature for appropriations, an executive board must subordinate everything to securing enough money to carry the institution through the fiscal period in prospect. They will usually have occasion also to make applications for extensions, and increased appropriations for other purposes. They cannot risk these important matters by recommending reforms which might antagonize certain interests, and raise up for them opponents in the legislature or about it. A board with powers of supervision and report only, is not limited in any of these matters. If it sees a reform or co-ordination possible in the charities of the State, it can recommend an improvement, even at the risk of offending influential persons, and stand out for specific reforms without endangering current appropriations. Furthermore, an unsalaried board is more likely to stand well with successive legislatures than is a set of men who get their living out of the business; and their recommendations for increased appropriations in which they have no personal interest will have more weight with many legislators than the persistent application of those whose support comes from the appropriations that they ask for. A board with powers of supervision and report only is consequently a benefit to institutions as well as a check upon them; for it can further their growth, and stand as a guaranty of honest administration, which helps them in the opinion of the community. There are two reasons why all charitable institutions, especially public institutions, should be carefully supervised and reported upon. One is that abuses may exist in such institutions, and another is that they may not. In the first place, it is for the protection of the beneficiaries and the public that supervision is desirable; and in the second place, it is for the protection of the institutions and the managers from unfounded suspicions that supervision is useful. It enables the institutions to be above suspicion, which is out of the question unless there is some disinterested supervisory power over them.

One valuable service which has been rendered by the State Boards of Charities has been to raise the standard of service of the county and township charities. The managers of these, especially in the rural counties, are usually persons of honest intention, but with small information concerning the duties put upon them. It is therefore possible through visiting, correspondence, and suggestion to place at their disposal the hard-earned experience of other communities, and to make it possible for them, without additional expense, to do an increasingly satisfactory work. In the matter of approving plans for county jails and almshouses, which is frequently given into the hands of the State board, the very fact that the plans must be submitted to the State board will frequently lead to greater care in drawing them than would otherwise be used. Many of the State boards have published for the guidance of county officials designs of the best and most economical forms of construction to be used in caring for the various classes of dependents. Sometimes a county, as Marion County in Indiana, sends a committee of its county officials travelling over the country at public expense to see the best jails and to get ideas on the construction of such edifices before building. But besides the expense involved in this, the wandering investigators may miss the most essential points in what they should see and learn, while the State Board of Charities, having representatives from year to year in the National Conference of Charities, having available in its libraries the reports of other boards, and the reports of the various conferences, having also the experience of all the counties of the State for its own information, and a knowledge of what is done in distant cities, can frequently, by pointing to certain publications, or offering certain plans, give county officials assistance in the construction and administration of charities which it would otherwise cost them large sums to seek out.

In one important particular the powers of supervision and report with which American State Boards of Charities are endowed are as a rule defective. That is, they are not given sufficient power to supervise the administration of purely private charities, and to regulate the administration of endowments. The New York Board has powers of visitation over private charitable corporations, with power to inspect and examine officials under oath, to collect statistics, and to report to the legislature. By the Act of 1883 the certified consent of the board is required as a condition precedent to the incorporation of any further orphan asylums or institutions for the care of children.[2] A few other States give their respective boards supervision of particular species of private institutions. The power of the New York Board to "visit" purely private institutions has recently been used in preparing a Directory of the Charities of the State of New York, which is of the very greatest value in giving an idea of the charities of the State as they actually exist. The mere collection and publication of these facts gives a view of the situation not otherwise obtainable. It is to the State Boards of Charities that the power should be given, in all States having such boards, to restrict, supervise, and revise endowments for charitable purposes. Testators should be made to feel that there is an authority that can insure the public against injuries from foolish or obsolete endowments, directing the money left for charities to wise purposes according to time and place.

**Local and Voluntary Supervision.** Radiating from the State Boards of Charities are certain delegated visitorial powers bestowed upon appointees in the various counties and localities of the State. A local representative of a State board is expected to visit county institutions, and call to the attention of the board anything that seems to be amiss. In Ohio the Board of County Visitors is appointed by the Court of Common Pleas. This county board consists of six persons, three men and three women, and not more than three of each party; and they are required to visit all places of charity and correction in the county where they live. They have power to visit such institutions at least four times during the year; in fact, they make many more visits. They report to the Court of Common Pleas once a year, and they send a report also to the State Board of Charities. They have special powers regarding any child likely to be sent to reformatories through the courts. These Boards of County Visitors, and other officials interested in the administration of relief, have held two annual

[2] *N. C. C.*, 1893, p. 41.

conferences, which have done much to clarify the problems attending the work of their members. The members of the boards are appointed for two years, and two members go out each year. Judges are said to take a great interest in these matters. In States where there is an active State board, but where the law does not provide for unsalaried visitors in this formal way, a considerable number of persons are in fact interested in local charities; and their visiting is made effective in the introduction of reforms through their correspondence and intercourse with the State board. Conferences of the superintendents of the poor are also frequently held under the auspices of the State board, as in Michigan, Wisconsin, and Indiana. The value of official boards has been greatly enhanced by the large number of people they have been able to interest in the administration of the public charities.

In two States, New York and New Jersey, there have grown up associations for the voluntary unofficial supervision of public charitable institutions in co-operation with the official boards. The State Charities Aid Association of New York was organized in 1872, with the object of bringing about reforms in the poor-houses, the almshouses, and the State charitable institutions of New York, through the active interest of an organized body of voluntary visitors, acting in cooperation with and as an aid to the local administration of these institutions and the official State boards of supervision. Upon the nomination of the State Charities Aid Association, through its board of managers, district supreme courts are authorized to grant to the visitors of the association orders enabling them to visit, inspect, and examine on behalf of the association any of the public charitable institutions owned by the State, county, township, or city, the poor-houses and almshouses within the State of New York, such visitors to be responsible to the counties from which these institutions receive their inmates. The association reports annually to the State Board of Charities and the State Commission in Lunacy upon matters relative to the institutions subject respectively to the inspection and control of these two official bodies. A similar organization was created in New Jersey in 1881, and worked in a single county until 1886. In that year its activities were extended to the whole State, and ten counties of the State are now included in its organization.

The New York Association has a central board of managers, largely of New York City, and county visiting committees in all parts of the State where people of the respective localities can be got to take an interest in the work of the association. The paid secretary of the association visits these corresponding boards once a year, and if possible goes with the members to inspect the different county institutions. The association is supported entirely through voluntary contributions. The expenditures are not heavy, only about $10,000 per year. There is a salaried secretary and assistant secretary. The association declares that it will not receive any money from public sources, as it wishes to be independent of all outside influence. A considerable proportion of its expenditures are for publications. It prints quite an elaborate report each year, and various pamphlets appear from time to time bearing upon pressing problems in the administration of the relief-work of the State. Thus it couples education with supervision.

The class of public institutions that need the most supervision, and ordinarily get the least of it, are those of our large cities. Ordinarily, if there is a city department, it is an executive department, subject to the influences of politics, and not gifted with the power of supervising itself satisfactorily. In Boston, in 1892, Mayor Matthews appointed a committee of private citizens to visit and report upon charitable institutions of that city for his information and that of the public. A most valuable report was prepared, from which quotations have already been made in the course of this volume. Among other things the committee recommended that an ordinance be passed providing for the appointment by the mayor of a permanent committee of visitors, men and women, for terms varying from three to five years. The committee further recommended that these visitors should have full power to inspect institutions, but no executive powers and no salaries. This, it will be seen, is a provision for a municipal board of charities with power of supervision and report only. A second committee was appointed by Mayor Matthews the succeeding year, in accordance with an ordinance passed as recommended.

**The Charity Organization Movement.** In its widest sense the organization of charities includes work already described. It is the purpose of a State Board of Charities to organize and co-ordinate the public institutions. It is the purpose of a body like the State Charities Aid Association to see that public charities work together for good. But in its technical meaning the term "charity organization" has come to be applied to the organization of all charities of a locality, either public or private, especially the charities of our large cities. It is this particular work that has been described at the National Conferences of Charities since 1880 under the heading of "charity organization."

If the charities of a State are chaotic, the charities of a large city are still more so. When we take up a directory of charities prepared by one of the American societies, and find a table of contents classifying the various agencies in the city, the first impression that we may get is that there is something systematic about the actual charitable system of the locality. But a fairer view of the actual situation in a modern city would be given by scanning a list of the charities arranged without reference to purpose. By running through the names of one or two hundred charities thrown together helter-skelter, one would come to realize the chaotic nature of relief-work in a modern city. A poor person in need of relief does not usually have a directory of charities in his library, and may be referred from agency to agency without being able to find the relief he needs, which all the while is waiting for him. In Baltimore, for instance, it will be found that there are societies to relieve any need whatever of particular classes of persons. The Hebrew Benevolent will do this for Israelites, the German Society for Germans, the St. Andrew's Society for the Scotch, the denominational societies for those of their faith and for an undetermined number of outsiders. On the other hand, there are societies that will relieve any person whatever in some particular way. The Poor Association will give coal and groceries to any applicant it considers worthy, without regard to religion, race, or color. The dispensaries will give medicine, the sewing-societies clothing, and so on. It will be noticed that the lines of activity intersect. The classification by race overlaps that by religion, while the classification by needs overlies them both, and several agencies for the same sort of work are superimposed upon the others, while unlimited claims upon individual benevolence supplement or duplicate the whole. Suppose the case of a German Lutheran who is in need of one thing, say fuel. There are four organizations to which he may properly apply: 1, The German Society; 2, his church; 3, the Poor Association; 4, the police-station. If he is sick, the Indigent Sick Society may also aid; if a soldier, he may apply to the Confederate Relief Society or the Grand Army of the Republic; if his children go to a Methodist Sunday-school, help may be had from that source; if a Roman Catholic, he may also apply to the Society of St. Vincent de Paul; and finally, if he is just out of jail, the Prisoner's Aid Association may help. All this, of course, does not include what he may obtain from private individuals.

In the 'fifties there had been organized in nearly all large cities in the United States general relief-giving societies, usually going under the title of "Societies for the Improvement of the Condition of the Poor." The "Boston Provident" belongs to this class. As indicated by the name, these societies held before themselves the highest purposes that benevolent people could seek to accomplish. In fact, most of their announced objects agree quite closely with those of the most modern societies. It was their purpose to find work for all willing to do it, to investigate all cases thoroughly, to raise the needy above the need of relief, and incidentally to relieve directly such want as seemed to require it. But as these Societies for the Improvement of the Condition of the Poor were dispensers of material aid, this function, as Mr. Kellogg puts it, submerged all others, "and they sank into the sea of almsgiving." Their work was done more or less well; but there is a general agreement that twenty years ago private almsgiving in American cities, for the most part through organized and even incorporated societies, was profuse and chaotic, while still not meeting the demands made upon it. It was dispensed in tantalizing doles miserably inadequate for effectual succor where the need was genuine, and dealt out broadcast among criminals and impudent beggars.[3] Public relief, at the same time, was in an unsatisfactory condition, out-door relief being administered with especial recklessness, and frequently tainted by political corruption. The old movement for the betterment of charities had substantially come to a standstill. While profession was still made of doing all that was needed, the energies of the societies were absorbed in giving direct relief.

The movement for charity organization had its origin in London in 1868, and was introduced into this country about ten years later, being copied direct from London at a number of independent points, such as Buffalo, Boston, and Philadelphia. After the trial of a society with similar purposes at Germantown, Pennsylvania, and certain tentative and unsatisfactory experiments in clearing-house registration of relief work in New York and Boston, the first real Charity Organization Society was established in Buffalo, in December, 1877. The Rev. S. H. Gurteen, an English clergyman, who had been active in the London society, was the moving force in the inauguration of this enterprise. Boston, Philadelphia, and New Haven established similar societies in 1878, and Cincinnati, Brooklyn, and Indianapolis followed in 1879. The society in New York was not organized until 1882, when the initiative in the matter was taken by the State Board of Charities, which adopted the following resolutions:

*Whereas,* There are in the City of New York a large number of independent societies engaged in teaching and relieving the poor of the city in their own homes, and

*Whereas,* There is at present no system of co-operation by which these societies can receive definite mutual information in regard to the work of each other, and

*Whereas,* Without some such system it is impossible that much of their effort should not be wasted, and even do harm by encouraging pauperism and imposture, therefore,

*Resolved,* That the Commissioners of New York City are hereby appointed a committee to take such steps as they may deem wise, to inaugurate a system of MUTUAL HELP AND CO-OPERATION between such societies.

[3] Kellogg, "Charity Organization in the United States," *N. C. C.*, 1893, pp. 53, 54.

"In accordance with this resolution, the New York City members of the State Board of Charities invited citizens, representing as far as possible all portions of the community, to assist in organizing this society, under a carefully prepared constitution, and to act as a Provisional Central Council until their successors should have been chosen by the society at large, at its first annual meeting. The Society was thus formed Jan. 26, 1882."

In nearly every instance the motives leading to these organizations is declared to be "discontent with the prodigality and inefficiency of public relief, and the chaotic state of private charity." Twenty-two of the associations organized at these or later dates report that "voluntary charity was lavish, uninformed, and aimless, with no concert of action; two that it was variable, and therefore unreliable; one that it was impeded by discouragement; and one that it did not exist in the community." [4] The same impulse that established the new societies abolished out-door relief in Brooklyn and Philadelphia, and greatly reduced it in Buffalo and Indianapolis.

**Objects of Charity Organization.** In order to afford as concise a view as possible of charity organization, there is given herewith, in tabular form, a statement of the objects, methods, and machinery of the societies undertaking such work.

To accomplish the first three objects may be described as the essential or constituent functions of Charity Organization Societies. The remaining five objects are usually kept in view, but not invariably so. The several societies vary much more as to the machinery than as to purposes.

Taking up *seriatim* the objects and methods of the Charity Organization Societies of the United States, it may be seen that the fundamental thought is the cooperation of all charitable agencies of a given locality, and the best coordination of their efforts. In order to secure this, it is usually requested that the societies, so far as practicable, furnish records of the relief-work done by each, so that the accounts may be compared and the overlapping of relief prevented. The Charity Organization Society maintains at its central office an

[4] Kellogg, as above, p. 61.

The Organization of Charities.

| *Objects* | *Methods* | *Machinery* |
|---|---|---|
| 1. Co-operation between all charitable agencies of a given locality, and the best co-ordination of their efforts. | 1. Comparison of relief records of the several agencies and mutual acquaintance of workers. | 1. A card or other alphabetical catalogue of cases at a central office and frequent conferences of workers. |
| 2. Accurate knowledge of all cases treated. | 2. Thorough investigation, followed by careful registration. | 2. Paid agents assisted by volunteer visitors, and elaborate case records either at central or branch offices. |
| 3. To find prompt and adequate relief for all that should have it. | 3. Bringing each case to the attention of appropriate relief agencies willing to aid. | 3. Correspondence, personal interviews, sometimes a "Golden Book," or even a relief-fund (wisdom of this last questioned). |
| 4. Exposure of imposters and prevention of wilful idleness. | 4. After investigation, notification in all cases of those likely to be deceived, and, where feasible, arrest of imposters and professional beggars. Work-test. | 4. Paid agents, sometimes (especially for this work) publication of a "cautionary list," information to all asking for it in specific cases, woodyard. |
| 5. To find work for all able and willing to do anything. | 5. To provide regular work where possible and relief-work when necessary. | 5. Employment agency, woodyard, stone-breaking, laundries, rag-sorting, etc. |
| 6. Establishment of relations of personal interest and sympathy between the poor and the well-to-do. | 6. Friendly visiting. | 6. Organization of corps of volunteer visitors who are not almsgivers, working under the guidance of paid agents. |
| 7. Prevention of pauperism. | 7. By above means and by special educational and provident schemes. | 7. Kindergarten, night-schools, industrial schools, penny provident funds, provident dispensaries, fuel funds, etc. |
| 8. Collection and diffusion of knowledge on all subjects connected with the administration of charities. | 8. Discussion, public meetings, publication. | 8. Board meetings, annual meetings, conferences, lecture courses, periodicals. |

alphabetical list of all cases that have received relief from any reporting agency whatever, or that have been investigated by itself; and this comparative catalogue of work done is a treasure-house of facts for the guidance of those engaged in the work to be done. The New York society has a register giving some account of 170,000 families, or parts of families. While this is the largest consolidated list in the country, yet the central office catalogues of Boston, Philadelphia, and Baltimore contain a very large number of cases. These are so arranged that any case can be referred to at once, and the person charitably interested in that case can get a reply regarding it from the society by return mail. This clearing-house function of the Charity Organization Society is the first and perhaps the most fundamental one, and the one most clearly stated in the name which the societies adopted. Yet efficient cooperation in this matter on the part of all relieving agencies has been one of the most difficult results to secure. In some cities it has dwindled to almost nothing, in others it is very complete. Public officials in some of the cities cooperate fully, and, as in Buffalo, submit all cases to which they give out-door relief, to the investigation of the society.

A second fundamental object of the Charity Organization Society, which is partly attained by the methods taken to secure cooperation and prevent the over-lapping of relief, is an accurate knowledge of all cases treated. Besides consulting the records of cooperating societies, this is to be gotten by thorough investigation, followed by careful registration. The old relief societies frequently depended upon the memory of the paid agent for the facts regarding different families aided; but the Charity Organization Society wishes to have records preserved with a thoroughness that can only be obtained by writing, and extending beyond the lifetime of any one individual. Investigation is not merely for the prevention of fraud, but is an essential pre-requisite of the proper treatment of cases needing relief. The giving of money or supplies is merely one form of prescribing for a case of destitution, and an investigation is as essential in dealing with the case as a diagnosis in a case of sickness with which a physician deals. The accompanying table reports the varying forms of treatment deemed desirable by the Charity Organization Societies in over 74,000 cases coming under their observation in 1892.

TREATMENT DESIRABLE IN 74,704 CASES.

| *Treatment* | *Number* | *Percentages*[5] |
|---|---|---|
| Number treated | 74,704 | |
| Continuous relief | 3,562 | 4.76 |
| Temporary relief | 18,558 | 24.84 |
| Needing work rather than alms | 11,989 | 16.05 |
| Not relieved, having relatives | 2,534 | 3.39 |
| Not relieved, having vicious habits | 7,719 | 10.33 |
| Placed in institutions | 1,182 | 1.58 |
| Placed in charge of churches or societies | 5,768 | 7.72 |
| Placed in charge of police | 572 | .76 |
| Aid procured from municipality or state | 668 | .89 |
| Aid procured from churches and societies | 8,408 | 11.13 |
| Aid procured from individuals | 4,931 | 6.60 |
| Aided by loans | 596 | .80 |
| Employment secured | 13,477 | 18.04 |
| Applicants' resources developed | 46 | .06 |
| Removed to relatives or new situations | 490 | .65 |
| Brought to self-maintenance (estimated) | 1,524 | 2.04 |
| Unclassified | | |

The third function of a Charity Organization Society is to find prompt and adequate relief for all that should have it. The society is an animated directory of charities of the locality in which it works. No one is turned away from the office of the society with the statement, "Your need is none of our business"; for the society makes it its business to see that each need is brought to the attention of the proper agency. If no agency exists, a benevolent individual (called in Boston a "B. I.") can usually be found to give the relief required; and this bringing together of the giver and the receiver under wise guidance is one of the best results of charity organization. In discharging this function of finding prompt and fitting relief for each case of need, some societies have been led to start relief-funds of their own. When the first of these organizations were formed, the antagonism of the old relief-giving societies was frequently aroused; for the latter thought they saw in the new movement a likelihood of the duplication of their own efforts, which would be mischievous in its influence on the

[5] Some of the totals in this column contain duplications of cases.

poor, and embarrassing when appeals were made to contributors. It was partly because of this position on the part of the established societies that many of the new organizations started out as non-relief-giving charitable agencies, in this matter breaking with English tradition, and making a new departure in charity work. Experience seems to have shown that this abstention from relief-giving has been the very best thing to allay the jealousy of older societies; and not only this, but that it has been the salvation of Charity Organization Societies, preserving them for the higher purposes which they had in view. A Charity Organization Society with a relief-fund must necessarily compete in its appeals to contributors with other organizations giving direct relief to the poor. These organizations are consequently jealous of it, and do not cooperate willingly, either in aiding cases it brings to their attention, or in giving to it and obtaining from it information of common advantage. It thus drifts into a condition where it is simply one of several relieving agencies.

Further than this, the public is used to organizations of the relief-giving type; and when it hears of the Charity Organization Society, it simply shrugs its shoulders and thinks, "Well, there's another one." On the contrary, when a society starts out announcing that its work is to benefit the poor, but that it does not give alms in any form, its very existence has an educational influence of great value in the community. People ask at once, "If you do not give relief, what do you do?" and then they can be induced to look over the long list of things other than relief-giving that need doing. Besides this, the older societies were continually hampered by criticisms upon them on account of the amount spent in administration. "How much does it cost to give away a dollar?" was asked again and again of their solicitors. If it was shown that twenty, thirty, or fifty per cent of the contributions went for the payment of administrative expenses, a person when approached might object, saying that he could give his money away more cheaply than that himself. Since Charity Organization Societies have no relief-fund whatever, all this comparison of expenses for administration with relief is obviated. If asked how much is spent for purposes of administration the answer is, "All," and this has a good tonic effect upon both the questioner and the representative of the society. The former begins to see that helpfulness means more than almsgiving; and the latter realizes that if he is going to win the support of the public for his work, that work must be really and demonstrably useful. Somewhat less than half the societies of the country have relief-funds of their own.

The fourth function mentioned in the tabular view, the exposure of impostors, and the prevention of wilful idleness, is frequently over-emphasized in describing the purposes of a Charity Organization Society. People look upon the society as merely an anti-mendicity league, a detective society for preventing imposition, and bringing swindlers to justice. The society is consequently regarded as bloodless, cold, and uncharitable, doing a work which may be necessary, but is certainly ungracious, and that does not appeal to the actively benevolent. As shown in Appendix G to Mr. Kellogg's report, the societies of the country suppressed nearly 1,000 street beggars and impostors during the year 1892, and detected over 100 fraudulent schemes. A society in a large city like New York or Chicago has much of this work to do, especially the detection of fraudulent charities. In smaller places there are not many fraudulent charitable enterprises, but there are always dishonest begging letter writers, and dishonest beggars from door to door. To give their contributors and cooperating agencies knowledge of these, several of the societies publish a cautionary list containing a description of dishonest applicants for relief, with their various *aliases* so far as known. The New York Society has carried farthest the special work of dealing with street beggars, employing two agents for that purpose, who aid, warn, expose, or arrest, as circumstances may seem to require in each case. This work of freeing the streets of mendicants is very much limited by the practice in most cities of giving licenses for petty peddling on the streets, or for operating musical instruments of the hand-organ type. In order to prevent wilful idleness most of the societies provide a work-test for both men and women, or one is operated by a cooperating association available for the use of the society.

Closely connected with the work of preventing wilful idleness is that of finding work for all able and willing to do anything. The woodyard and laundry may serve as work-tests, but they cannot give steady and profitable employment to all those desiring work. Each Charity Organization Society is, consequently, an employment agency, dealing for the most part and in ordinary times with the semi-capable, with those who from some perversion of character or defect of mind or body cannot fit themselves into the industries of the time, but may be able to do certain things if those things are sought out and brought to their attention.

The sixth enumerated function of the Charity Organization Society is to establish relations of personal interest and sympathy between the poor and the well-to-do. This is sought to be accomplished through what is technically known as "friendly visiting," volunteer visitors being secured who are willing to go to the poor as friends, and not as almsgivers. Preferably each friendly visitor has but one, or at most but two, cases, and the relation is made as permanent as possible. There are many instances where for years the same visitor has gone to the same family, and genuine personal attachments have been formed. Visitors should never be almsgivers; for in that case the poor look upon them as persons from whom something is to be gotten, and, on the other hand, if empowered to give relief, the visitor fails to invent methods of rendering the better service that is needed in order to cure poverty. The work of friendly visiting is declared by the most advanced societies to be the heart of the work. The motto, "Not alms, but a friend," first adopted in Boston, has come to be the motto of many of the societies.

The influence of the visiting upon the poor may be excellent, but there can be no doubt that one of its very greatest benefits is upon the visitors. It is a method by which we may hope to reach "the upper classes." In all large cities there are places which, though not far from the well-to-do geographically, are likely to be completely forgotten. Balzac said of Paris that there were streets and alleys of which the upper classes knew no more than a man knows what is going on in his pancreas. This is not as true as it was when Balzac said it; but if it is less true, it is because the great associations of volunteer workers have been looking into these different parts of the city, and taking an interest in the people that live and die there. There is no education in charitable work so good as that which comes to the friendly visitor. Becoming interested in one family, he is likely to be led out into an interest in all branches of city government, and of the county and State government as well, and may even have his attention drawn to the need of federal prevention of undesirable immigration. He who takes an interest in trying to cure poverty in a single case will soon come to find that nothing in politics or industry is foreign to him.

The seventh function of the Charity Organization Society has been enumerated as the prevention of pauperism. This is sought to be accomplished by all the means that have been indicated for the furtherance of the other specific purposes of the society. But many organizations go further and seek to establish special branches likely to assail pauperism in its causes. The Crèche, or day nursery, at which working mothers can leave their children during the day, has been established in several cities, notably in Buffalo. The kindergarten movement for poor children, or in connection with the public schools, has had the active assistance of charity organizationists. Cooking-schools, sewing-schools, trade-schools, and laundries for the education of the workers have been established, as well as different varieties of savings-funds. Several of these funds operate with a system of stamp deposits, some of them being through collections made from house to house by the friendly visitors. The New York Society has been especially active in the pushing of stamp deposit funds, having established 206 stations, with 26,732 depositors, and over $15,000 on deposit. In Boston and Baltimore provident schemes of a similar character have been established, but not under the Charity Organizations Societies, though co-operating with them. Fuel funds, by means of which summer savings can secure winter delivery of coal at summer prices, have been established by some of the societies. The rule of nearly all the societies is not to undertake these special schemes if some independent organization can be found that will push them. They are desirable things that the charity organizationist wishes to see established, but they are not undertaken by the society itself except when necessary.

Frequently such new enterprises start in connection with the society, and are then graduated into independent life.

The eighth and last function of the Charity Organization Society is the diffusion of knowledge on all subjects connected with the administration of charities. No progressive society neglects this function. Public meetings, conferences of visitors, lecture courses, and, in the case of four societies at least, the publication of periodicals which undertake to further these purposes of educating the community into wiser methods of charitable effort, are the agencies employed. In Appendix L to Mr. Kellogg's report at Chicago will be found a bibliography comprising more than a hundred titles of the pamphlets and other publications issued by the societies of the country. Their annual reports themselves are educational literature of high value, giving detailed accounts of cases, and explaining the countless things, not to be summarized, which are necessary in wisely aiding the poor.

Finally, it should be observed that the charity organizationist, properly so-called, is essentially a man who will not consent to be buried under details. Neither the work of friendly visiting, nor the pushing of penny provident schemes, nor the operation of a woodyard, and, most of all, not the giving of relief, will he allow to distract him from a survey of the whole field, and from the endeavor to improve by better co-ordination the charitable efforts of the community. He is determined that the field shall be covered with some measure of adequacy, and that charitable forces shall not be wasted in competitive and misdirected efforts. For this reason the movement, which perhaps it is no longer proper to call new, has drawn to itself some of the most active and intelligent workers for the poor in the whole country; and at the National Conference the section on charity organization has secured an amount of attention out of all proportion to the extent of the funds used by these societies, and the number of persons interested in them. It is the only section of the National Conference that has set itself with earnestness to gather statistics as to the causes of destitution. If the persons concerned are loyal to present principles, they will continue to have a part in the development of new ideals and better methods of service.

# PART III

# CONTEMPORARY SOCIAL WORK

# CHAPTER XVI

## SOCIAL MALADJUSTMENTS AND THEIR INTERPRETATION

Having reviewed American charities in their development through the 'nineties, we turn now to a study of contemporary social work in the United States. We note the changes which have occurred during the past third of a century—changes not only in techniques and agencies, but also in the underlying philosophy. We find new types of social work, new both in function and in procedure. We observe a shifting of emphasis, a redefining of tasks, a reinterpretation of causes. But along with these changes we note the persistence of attitudes, methods and organizations. We come to a new appreciation of the soundness of some interpretations and practices developed a generation ago. We realize that our own thinking and working involve many of the stupidities which seem so obvious in our predecessors.

**The Sciences and Social Work.** One of the most interesting and significant series of changes has to do with the relations between social work and the various social and biological sciences. In the 'nineties the dominant influence was clearly that of economics, although physiology and psychology were by no means overlooked. The charitable folk of that period were concerned with "the poor," the "destitute sick," "pauper idiots and lunatics." Stress was laid upon the financial burden of relieving those who did not support themselves.

Of course sickness had long been recognized as one of the principal causes of poverty, but there seems to have been no time at which the economic viewpoint yielded first place to the medical. During the early years of the twentieth century, however, there was a marked increase in the attention given to physical disorders in their relation to economic and social maladjustments. For a time social workers were inclined to attribute misconduct to tonsils and adenoids. More recently they have thought to find the source of trouble in the glands of internal secretion. As recently as 1925 a physician well known for his cooperation with social workers wrote:

> Ingenuously catalogued as sources of evil, poverty, intemperance, irresponsibility and disease are instead the gulfs whose streams retraced lead to the remote springs of mental capacity, biological balance and physical vigor. . . . From our point of view positive or concordant, as well as negative or discordant social forces all start from physical and chemical energies identical with the energies acting upon lifeless matter. . . . So long as the physico-chemical equilibrium between nerve, gland and muscle cells and their surroundings is maintained a balanced social relation exists. . . .[1]

Hardly had the attention of social workers been turned from economics to biology when two new influences were brought to bear upon them. The first was the eugenics movement coupled with the rediscovery of the Mendelian "laws" of heredity. The second was the development and application of the Binet-Simon method of mental testing. As a result the story of the "Jukes" was brought up to date and a host of new records of notorious families was published. Mental testers spread over the land and "found" that very high percentages of convicts, prostitutes, unmarried mothers, tramps, unemployed workmen, labor agitators, and other troublesome people were feebleminded. In 1917 the Psychopathic Laboratory of the Municipal Court in Chicago reported "that delinqu ncy and defectiveness are practically synonymous," and "that defectiveness is also practically at the bottom of most of our dependency, unemployability, alcoholism, asociability, wife desertion, etc." During this period of alarm about the feebleminded there was much talk about "brindle stock" outbreeding the "superior" strains; and eugenics seemed much more important than charity.

About the same time that clinical psychology was developing and sterilization laws were being passed the mental hygiene movement was getting under way. Starting as an effort to eliminate the grosser abuses in the handling of the "insane," it pressed on to improved methods of diagnosis and treatment,

[1] Dunham, Francis Lee, *An Approach to Social Medicine,* pp. 85-87.

the prevention of mental diseases, and the promotion of mental health. Something of a stir was created in the National Conference of Social Work in 1919 when Miss Jarrett read her paper on "The Psychiatric Thread Running Through All Social Case Work."

> Social case work habitually relies upon psychiatry for advice concerning the care of persons with mental disorder. This advice is indispensable and very important. But perhaps even more important is the help that psychiatry can give the social worker in understanding human nature and in dealing with the many varieties of human personality that come before the social agencies. Personalities that would be considered normal frequently present many irregularities and contradictions. When we have come to understand these peculiarities as they appear in exaggerated form in psychopathic cases, we can more readily understand them in the average person. Besides frankly psychopathic cases, the social worker deals with persons whose apparently slight peculiarities may be the result of some marked psychopathic trait, and with other persons who have very mild degrees of psychopathy, and with still other persons who are approximately normal in all mental characteristics. Whether we are dealing with pronounced psychopathic traits, or minor peculiarities, or normal mentality, the psychiatric point of view is valuable in social case-work. By the psychiatric point of view I mean the habitual recognition of mental causes of conduct together with some knowledge of the nature of the mental processes that may cause conduct disorder.[2]

In 1927 Dr. Williams found rather general assent to his statement that social, economic and legal problems can be reduced to emotional disturbances, especially anxiety, fear, and feelings of guilt and inferiority.[3] The literature of social work since the War bears striking witness to the profound influence of abnormal psychology, psychiatry, and the mental hygiene movement. Indeed, it may be said that the dominant viewpoint in social work today is not economic, nor biological, nor psychological in the ordinary sense, but psychiatric.

All through the last decade, while psychiatry has been very much in evidence, there has been a gradual infiltration of sociology. Social workers are beginning to discuss personality

[2] Jarrett, Mary, in *Proc. Nat. Conf. Soc. Work,* 1919: 590-591.
[3] Williams, Frankwood, in *Proc. Nat. Conf. Soc. Work,* 1927: 294.

as a function of social relations as well as of the nervous system. They are directing attention upon families, neighborhoods, communities, industrial, racial and other social groups. They are showing more and more interest in the relationships that obtain between persons and groups. One very interesting statement of this viewpoint was made by Frank J. Bruno, chairman of the Conference on Family Life held at Buffalo in 1927.

> We have seen poverty and sickness and disaster affect people, and they have held up their heads against fate without the slightest concession. We have seen minor reverses crumple an individual, children with apparently good advantages turn out socially unsuccessful. And the common denominator has seemed to be the family. In the first series, there has been coherence in family ties which has borne the individual over tragedy; in the latter series, family disruption or conflict laid the ground for defeat before the individual faced his test.[4]

During the War Americans became vividly aware of the presence in their midst of many new arrivals whose cultures were different from that of the older citizens. So much interest was displayed in the problems of assimiliation that the Carnegie Corporation financed a series of "Studies in Methods of Americanization." The definition formulated by the group which made these studies shows clearly the influence of sociology.

> Americanization in these studies has been considered as the union of native and foreign born in all the most fundamental relationships and activities of our national life. For Americanization is the uniting of new with native-born Americans in fuller common understanding and appreciation to secure by means of individual and collective self-direction the highest welfare of all. Such Americanization should perpetuate no unchangeable political, domestic, and economic régime delivered once for all to the fathers, but a growing and broadening national life, inclusive of the best wherever found. With all our rich heritages, Americanism will develop best through a mutual giving and taking of contributions from both newer and older Americans in the interest of the commonweal.[5]

[4] Bruno, Frank J., in *The Family*, 8: 262.
[5] Publisher's Note, Americanization Series, Harper & Bros.

Thus the various social and biological sciences have in turn exercised varying degrees of influence on social work. First it was economics, supplemented after a time by biology and medicine; then came psychology and mental testing; today psychiatry holds the center of attention; but already the influence of sociology is beginning to be felt. As might be anticipated, whenever a new note has been struck it tends to be over-emphasized and exaggerated; but after a time its dominance passes and it finds a place among those which preceded. So today social workers utilize the concepts, the techniques and the findings of all these sciences and allied professions in working out their own problems. They realize that the difficulties presented by their clients involve the industrial system (economics), heredity (biology), levels of intelligence (psychology), emotions (psychiatry), and group life (sociology).

**Methods of Studying Social Problems.** As we saw in Part II, the earlier studies of social problems were largely statistical in character. However, the procedure was often rather crude; categories were not always well defined; results were rarely presented otherwise than in simple frequency and percentage tables. Another technique for social research is known as the case-study method.

> The case-study method of sociological research is to be distinguished from the practice of social work on the one hand and from the statistical method of research on the other. It is intimately related to both, but different from either. Social case work has as its objective direct service to particular persons. Sociological research has no reference to any particular persons or types of service. It is a search for general principles. Now while the statistical technique depends upon the reduction of data to quantitative terms, in order to yield totals, averages, and correlations, the case-study technique seeks data in terms of processes, which for the most part cannot be stated numerically. The statistician selects certain specific factors involved in social situations and manipulates them so as to discover the relations between the several variables. The "case student" examines single situations, persons, groups, or institutions, as complex wholes, in order to identify types and processes.[6]

[6] Queen, Stuart A., in *Publications of the American Sociological Society*, 22: 226.

The data for case studies are secured from interviews, letters, diaries, records of social agencies, and sometimes from questionnaires and tests. They are usually presented in the form of "running accounts," narratives of events, and descriptions of personalities and situations. The great unsolved problem in this connection is how to derive legitimate generalizations from such complex bodies of data.

The social survey is a third method of studying human situations. It combines certain elements of statistical and case-study methods with journalism. It is an attempt to get a bird's eye view of the social life of a city, county, state, or other limited area, on the assumption that all the problems which appear are interrelated. Like the census and the official report, it is an effort to secure facts, so far as possible, in quantitative form. Like the case study it is an endeavor to see concretely and vividly just what is there. But unlike most forms of investigation, the survey presupposes the participation of many citizens in fact-gathering. Instead of delayed reports in "dry" public documents, it anticipates prompt and graphic portrayal. Hence the survey is a form of social control even more than it is a form of social research. Some surveys have been directed by "experts"; others have been conducted by "ordinary citizens." Some have been primarily efforts to see situations in the large; others have taken one problem and studied it in its bearings on the entire community. Some have concentrated on administrative problems, others on legislation, still others on public opinion. The conduct of a survey includes arousing popular interest, organizing committees, assembling existing information about the area and its population, preparing schedules, canvassing, tabulating data, writing descriptive accounts, securing publicity through the press, exhibits, mass meetings and other agencies.

A fourth type of study is sometimes described as "human ecology." McKenzie has defined this "as a study of the spatial and temporal relations of human beings as affected by the selective, distributive and accommodative forces of the environment." [7] It is thus related to geography, but human ecology is less concerned with location than with the processes

[7] McKenzie, R. D., in Park and Burgess, *The City*, pp. 63-64.

through which persons, groups, and institutions come to be where they are. These processes include concentration and dispersion, centralization and decentralization, segregation, invasion and succession. They are related to the mobility and fluidity of the population, and to the integration and disorganization of group life and of personality. The methods employed in ecological studies are largely those of statistics and geography. The results are displayed by means of maps, charts and statistical tables.

Culture analysis is a fifth method of studying social problems. Its significance for social workers lies in the assumption that many cases of conflict between persons or groups may be stated in terms of divergent cultures or of "lags" within a given culture. Hence we have studies of entire civilizations including folkways, mores, laws, material possessions, and institutions. Other studies deal with the changes in given cultures, that is, inventions and borrowings. Special attention is often paid to differences in the rate of change in different culture traits and complexes. Sometimes the problem is to determine what happens when peoples of diverse cultural backgrounds are thrown into close contact. The methods of cultural analysis include the use of surveys, case studies, statistical enumeration, observation and description. It should be noted, however, that this type of study, which was developed by anthropologists and sociologists, has not been widely used by social workers, although the publication of *Middletown* has brought it definitely to their attention.

As these various types of studies have been described it must be plain that they do not represent absolutely different techniques, but rather varying combinations of description, narration and enumeration. They are all efforts to view objectively the many aspects of our common life. In the paragraphs which follow this will become increasingly evident as we present samples of the different methods and of the results obtained from their use.

**Statistical Studies.** As examples of statistical studies and what they have yielded of value to social workers we may present *Social Aspects of the Business Cycle* by Dorothy Swaine Thomas, and *The Influence of Environment on the In-*

*telligence, School Achievement, and Conduct of Foster Children* by Frank N. Freeman and others.

Miss Thomas' book is an analysis of the relations which appear to exist between the business cycle and certain other events of social significance. Her data were drawn from the United States and Great Britain. In each case the business cycles were calculated separately on the basis of such figures as annual exports, production of iron and coal, railway freight receipts, bank clearings, percentage of workers unemployed and price index numbers. She first measured the long-time movement or secular trend by means of moving averages and curve-fitting and then determined year by year the percentage deviation from the trend. While the several series of business statistics did not coincide in their ups and downs, they corresponded rather closely. Hence she averaged them to secure quantitative expressions of the alternating prosperity and depression which we call the business cycle. After that Miss Thomas plotted the cycles for marriage, prostitution, crime, death rate, and other items of interest to social workers. Finally she correlated the cycles of each series of social statistics with the business cycles by the Pearsonian formula. The results of her study are summarized in the following table.

This table shows that when business conditions are good there tends to be an increase both of marriages and of divorces, of emigration and immigration, of alcoholism and deaths. At the same time there tends to be a decrease of suicide, crime, illegitimacy and pauperism. Or put the other way around, when times are hard more people ask for financial assistance, break the law, and commit suicide. About two years after the worst of the business depression there is the largest number of children born out of wedlock and the largest number of homeless persons cared for in "casual wards" of workhouses. When times are good more people get married, secure divorces, and emigrate; there seems to be a slight increase in prostitution and more alcoholic drinks are consumed. The highest birth rate comes about three years after the peak of prosperity, but, curiously, the highest death rate lags only one year. It is not at all clear to what extent changing business conditions may be regarded as causes of changing health and conduct. For

SOCIAL ASPECTS OF THE BUSINESS CYCLE [8]

| SOCIAL FACTORS | MAXIMUM COEFFICIENT OF CORRELATION WITH THE BUSINESS CYCLE | | LAGS IN YEARS | |
|---|---|---|---|---|
| | *U.S.* | *Great Britain* | *U.S.* | *Great Britain* |
| Marriage rate | .66 | .67 | 0 | 0 |
| Prostitution | | .22 | | 0 |
| Divorce rate | .70 | .00 | 0 | 0 |
| Birth rate | .33 | .30 | 1 | 3 |
| Illegitimacy | | —.39 | | 2 |
| Deaths from child birth | | .46 | | 2 |
| Death rate (general) | .57 | .30 | 0 | 1 |
| Infant mortality | .42 | .28 | 0 | 1 |
| Tuberculosis death rate | .19 | .27 | 0 | 1 |
| Suicide | —.74 | —.50 | 0 | 0 |
| Crime (all convictions) | —.35 | —.25 | 0 | 0 |
| Crime against property (without violence) | | —.25 | | 0 |
| Crime against property (with violence) | | —.44 | | 0 |
| Crime against person | | .15 | | 2 |
| Emigration | | .48 | | 0 |
| Emigration from Britain (correlated with U. S. business cycles) | | .77 | | 0 |
| Pauperism—indoor | | —.52 | | 1 |
| Pauperism—outdoor | | —.32 | | 1 |
| Pauperism—casual | | —.46 | | 2 |
| Alcoholism—consumption of beer | | .45 | | 1 |
| Alcoholism—consumption of spirits | | .60 | | 1 |
| Deaths from alcoholism | | .38 | | 1 |

example, it is hard to understand why the death rate should rise with the improvement of business conditions. But, whatever the real causal relations may be, the correlations that have been established show that social workers need to watch trends of economic conditions in order to anticipate variations in the volume of work they will be called upon to do. This study also indicates that in order to prevent certain types of social maladjustment there must be cooperation between social workers and others who are seeking to eliminate violent fluctuations from our economic life.

The other statistical study which we shall describe has an

[8] Adapted from Thomas, Dorothy S., *Social Consequences of the Business Cycle.* New York: Knopf, 1927.

even more obvious and immediate significance for social workers. Its data consist largely in mental tests and home ratings of children handled by the Illinois Children's Home and Aid Society. In all 671 children were examined to determine what effect, if any, the environment might have on their performance on the Stanford Revision of the Binet Scale and the International Test, on their achievement in school and on their conduct. One group of children was tested before placement and tested again after about four years in a foster home. The whole group showed an average improvement of 2.5 points on the Binet Scale, which, when corrected for faults in the scale itself, would mean a gain of 7.5 points. Children in the better foster homes gained on the average 5.3 points (corrected to 10.4), while those in the poorer homes gained only .1 point (corrected to 5.0). The children who had spent the years 6 to 10 in the foster homes showed a gain of 5.2 points, while those whose period of placement was from 10 to 14 showed a loss of .4. It appears from these figures that placement at an early age in a superior home is likely to produce a marked improvement in the level of intelligence.

Similar results were obtained from studying pairs of siblings (brothers and sisters) who were reared in separate homes and comparing these findings with the usual coefficient of correlation between the intelligence of brothers and sisters, which is .50. For siblings separated before either child was six years old the coefficient was found to be only .25, and when the comparison was made for those whose foster homes were of different grade the correlation was only .19. In 85 of the 125 pairs the brighter child was in the better home, and in 80 cases the brighter child was placed at an earlier age than his brother or sister.

Comparing unrelated children reared in the same home, a correlation of .34 was found between the intelligence of a foster child and an own child. The correlation between the intelligence of own children and that of their parents was .35; the corresponding coefficient for foster children and foster parents was .18. The correlation between the intelligence of two foster children in the same home was .37, which was higher than that for siblings reared in separate homes. Finally, the correlation between the intelligence of the foster child and his home rating, on a scale devised for the purpose, was .47, exactly the same as the corresponding coefficient for the own child.

In spite of the fact that the natural parents of the foster children appeared to include a large percentage of defectives, the average intelligence quotient of 484 children in the care of the society was 95.3, and only 3.7 per cent rated below 70 (the commonly accepted line between normal and feebleminded). The average I.Q. of 120 children who had one parent known to be feebleminded was 92.9; only 4 of these children rated below 70. In the case of 26 children both parents were known to be feebleminded; the average I.Q. of this group was 81.2; only 4 rated below 70, the lowest I.Q. being 63. The authors note that "it seems hardly possible that the children of such inferior parents could form a group so normal in intelligence if heredity is the only factor." [9]

The school progress of these foster children was compared with that of children in several large school systems. The wards of the Children's Aid Society showed a smaller percentage accelerated, but also a smaller percentage retarded than did the school children of Gary, Dubuque and Rockford.

In only 32 cases out of 401 children in foster homes was there misconduct of a sort considered serious. These cases included disobedience, lying, stealing, running away, masturbation, and similar conduct. Twenty-three of these 32 children had "morally defective" parents. This is 72 per cent, which is in contrast with 54 per cent for the entire group. However, of 145 children with morally defective parents only 16 per cent were themselves behavior problems, and most of these were committed to the Society after they were five years old.

In the course of this study the question was raised whether the apparent effect of good environment might not be due to the selection of bright children by superior foster parents. But a careful analysis of the circumstances surrounding the selections and placements convinced the investigators that this was not true. In most cases no tests were made until after

[9] National Society for the Study of Education, 27th Yearbook, Part I, p. 158.

placement; and young children whose intelligence would have been most difficult to estimate showed as high a correlation with home-rating as did those examined before placement.

The general conclusion, therefore, is that the environment of foster homes may be counted upon in most cases to wield a marked influence on the intelligence, school achievement and conduct of children. This position is, of course, in striking contrast with an earlier and more hopeless attitude toward children of inferior parents. Without ignoring the legal and economic tasks of segregation and financial support for certain defectives, it stresses the social tasks of transplanting and readjustment amid new surroundings.

The many other statistical studies that deserve our attention include *The Delinquent Boy* by John Slawson, *An Experimental Study of Children* by Helen Thompson Woolley, a large number of studies by the United States Children's Bureau, Women's Bureau, and Bureau of Labor Statistics, and several monographs by the National Bureau of Economic Research.

**Case Studies.** While social case work is for the most part a product of the charity organization and family welfare movements, the corresponding research technique seems to have been utilized most in studying problems of delinquency. In 1915 Dr. William Healy in his monumental work, *The Individual Delinquent,* pointed out the futility of mere speculation about causes of crime and the barrenness of mere statistical correlations. He insisted that instead of finding what circumstances might somehow, sometime enter into the production of delinquency, it would be much more profitable to study intensively the circumstances which actually did enter into the life of individual offenders. His book consists of summaries of detailed studies of 1,000 juvenile recidivists and of the conclusions which these seemed to warrant. Being a physician, Dr. Healy laid great emphasis upon the medical findings; but being also a psychologist, he stressed even more the mental life of the offender. In later works he made more of the cultural backgrounds, family, neighborhood and gang life, and other social influences. The necessity of examining all these aspects of the delinquent's life and of seeing the situation as a whole was stated with great clearness in Dr. Healy's paper at the twenty-fifth anniversary of the Cook County (Chicago) Juvenile Court.[10] The "situation" is "the particular environment of the given member of society considered together with him as active in it." But this is not merely dependent upon conditions as they are; it is also the result of previous conditions. In other words, the situation is not something fixed, but is constantly in flux; it is not a condition but a process. But perhaps the best demonstration of this method of delving into the causes of social maladjustment, which has come from Dr. Healy and his associates, is the series of case studies published by the Judge Baker Foundation of Boston. It is not feasible to reproduce even one record here, but an outline of the data covered may be presented. A sample case record includes a preliminary statement of the difficulty involved and the occasion for its being studied, backgrounds—immediate family, relatives, developmental history, home and neighborhood conditions, habits and interests, school history, etc.—, study of the individual, physical and mental, and the offender's own story. Obviously, with such a mass of data it is very difficult to devise a procedure for arriving at general conclusions. However, these studies show that the cause of trouble is not a single factor, nor merely a number of factors, but a tangled skein of influences, a long course of events subject to almost infinite variation.

Burgess has criticized Healy's work as giving too little attention to the offender's social relations, his rôle and status in the groups to which he belongs, his attitudes toward those with whom he associates.[11] Mowrer has suggested that the situations, of which Healy speaks, may be classified into *types;* and that then the *sequences* of situations or events may be classified into types. Mowrer holds that this is the method whereby the complex data produced by case studies may be reduced to order and made the basis of legitimate generalizations.[12]

[10] Healy, Wm., "The Psychology of the Situation," in *The Child, The Clinic and the Court,* pp. 37-52.

[11] Burgess, E. W., "The Study of the Delinquent as a Person." *Amer. Jour. Soc.,* 28: 657-680, 1923.

[12] Mowrer, Ernest R., *Family Disorganization,* Chaps. IX and X.

After examining one hundred cases of family disorganization, as manifested in divorce and desertion, Mowrer concluded that they could be reduced to four main types of situations or "tensions." These were (1) incompatibility in response, including what is often called "sexual incompatibility," (2) economic individualization, including vocational separation, economic independence, differences in attitude toward wife's working outside the home, and differences in standard of living, (3) cultural differentiation, including differences in religion, education and all the folkways and mores of the groups in which husband and wife grew up, (4) individuation of life patterns, including differences in those habits and opinions which are distinctive of the individual rather than of his group.

Mowrer applied these concepts to the varying situations in certain cases, but he did not succeed in establishing types of sequences. However, as a forecast of what such a typical sequence might be, if identified, he presented the following symbolic representation of the process of family disorganization in one instance—loss of respect, pattern-of-life tension, cultural tension, economic tension, loss of respect, religious tension, sex tension. Now if this should prove to be not a unique sequence of situations, but one that recurs again and again, we should have a basis for understanding and prediction in future cases.

Thomas has utilized another scheme for the analysis of data secured through case studies. He assumed that "the forces which impel to action" may be classified as (1) the wish for new experience, (2) the wish for security, (3) the wish for response or affection, and (4) the wish for recognition or status. Ordinarily the ways in which these may find satisfaction are rather well defined in the code of the group to which one belongs. However, if one becomes detached from one's group, or if the general situation in which the group lives is changed and the old rules no longer suffice, or especially if one finds oneself a member of several groups whose codes are not in harmony, the individual is likely to become confused and his conduct erratic. The satisfaction of one group of wishes may now interfere with the satisfaction of others. The conduct of one person may irritate or injure another. Under these circumstances we have an unadjusted person. If the disorganization continues long without a new "definition of the situation," a new code of behavior, the person becomes demoralized. These are the terms in which Thomas discussed the cases of 3,000 unadjusted girls whose records he studied.[13]

Other illustrations of the case-study method applied to the interpretation of the problems of individuals and families are *The Problem Child in School* by Mary B. Sayles, *Everyday Problems of the Everyday Child* by Douglas A. Thom, *Children Astray* by Drucker and Hexter, *Other People's Daughters* by Eleanor R. Wembridge, *The Adventure of Old Age* by Francis Bardwell, and *Suicide* by Ruth Shonle Cavan.

But the case-study method is not limited to the analysis of individual and family problems, it is also coming to be applied to the interpretation of larger groups, as gangs, neighborhoods and communities. In *The Gang* Thrasher presented accounts of individual groups of boys, through the study of which he identified several types of collective behavior and charted the possible stages of development which represented the "natural history" of the gang. He also worked out what he called "the conflict cycle" which he found typical of the gangs he studied. This consisted of (1) an equilibrium of conflicting interests, (2) disturbed by new conditions, and resulting in (3) unrest, whereupon (4) tensions increase and presently (5) a crisis is precipitated which is followed by (6) open conflict, and after a time (7) a tentative adjustment, and eventually (8) a final adjustment which constitutes a new equilibrium. This again represents a mode of generalizing from the complex data of case studies.

Recently there has been an increasing number of case studies of communities. Two noteworthy collections were published in 1928, *The American Community in Action* by Jesse F. Steiner and *Case Studies in Community Organization* by Walter Pettit. These studies have dealt less with "evils" and programs of reform than with the interrelations of persons and groups in a local area. They have, of course, considered the geographic and economic bases of the community life and its historical

[13] Thomas, W. I., *The Unadjusted Girl*, New York: Little, Brown, 1923.

backgrounds. But they have concentrated on such questions as these: What are the common activities, interests and traditions? What are the relations with outsiders? Is the population relatively permanent or transient? What divisions are there—political, religious, language, racial, personal? What is the quality of local leadership? In general, what influences contribute to a community of life, and what factors hinder its development?

All these case studies of persons, families, gangs and communities are closely related to the practice of social work. The latter, however, is concerned with specific situations and methods of dealing with them at once; while the former are concerned with the discovery of typical situations, and the social forces which have brought them into being, without reference to the immediate needs of particular persons or groups. But generalizations based on case studies by social scientists are making possible more effective techniques of social diagnosis and treatment.

**Social Surveys.** The first large-scale effort to see the various problems of an American city in their interrelations was the Pittsburgh Survey of 1907-08. The decade that followed witnessed many similar efforts to get a bird's eye view of some local community or larger area. One of the best examples of this type of study was the survey of Springfield, Illinois, in 1914. A group of citizens had become dissatisfied with certain conditions in their city. The occurrence of strikes made them wonder whether they were being afflicted by agitators or whether working conditions were not all they should be. While others complacently regarded Springfield as the "healthiest place in Illinois," they wondered why there were so many deaths from preventable diseases. In like manner they questioned the effectiveness of relief-giving and of the ways of handling offenders. Hence a few of those especially interested secured the assistance of the Russell Sage Foundation in making a preliminary study and report.

As a result of these initial findings a representative committee was organized to sponsor and help finance the more extensive survey. It was decided to study the public schools, the care of mental defectives, insane and alcoholics, recreation, housing, charities, industrial conditions, public health, the correctional system, city and county administration. The staff was drawn from the Russell Sage Foundation, five other national agencies, five state organizations, and the local social agencies. The various parts of the survey were directed by specialists, but much of the work was done by volunteers, who numbered over 600. Altogether the survey cost $25,000, of which $9,000 was raised by the local committee, thus guaranteeing and promoting local interest.

The steps taken, after the staff and local forces were organized, included assembling the facts, analysis and interpretation, constructive recommendations, and publicity. The field work took from March to July. It included the study of records of various organizations and institutions, visits to the agencies in operation, first-hand observations of conditions throughout the city, special tests, written inquiries and personal interviews. The analysis and interpretation called for comparison of the findings in Springfield with those in other cities. The recommendations also were based largely on what had been achieved and methods employed elsewhere. Publicity comprised daily use of the local newspapers, stories in weekly and monthly magazines, a separate paper-bound report on each of the nine parts of the survey, special pamphlets, and an exhibit in the State Armory. Sub-committees were appointed to follow-up the recommendations and see that something was done after the initial enthusiasm had waned.

In sharp contrast with the generalized survey and its whirlwind campaign of fact-gathering is the policy of making a series of surveys, taking one important social interest at a time, and following up the findings and recommendations over a period of years. Such a program was adopted by the Cleveland Foundation in 1914. The Foundation has completed three major surveys and five lesser studies. The more important surveys were of education, recreation and criminal justice. In all these much less use was made of volunteers than in the Springfield Survey. But much publicity was given to the studies in an effort to enlist the interest and cooperation of the general body of citizens.

The Recreation Survey may well illustrate the procedure

in all these specialized pieces of work. This study was divided into two main parts: first, the recreation influences, tendencies, and needs, and second, the recreation agencies of the city. Included in the first part was a study of 160 juvenile delinquents in order to determine how their use of spare time may have contributed to their waywardness. As a check on this another study covered the leisure-time activities of 100 wholesome citizens. The findings indicated that undirected and unorganized play and loafing were very frequently associated with delinquency. The second part of the survey dealt with the three general classes of recreation agencies—those supported by taxation such as parks, playgrounds and library, those maintained by private contributions such as settlements and Y. M. C. A., and those operated for profit such as movies, pool rooms, dance halls, and amusement parks. The findings showed that amid this vast conglomerate of agencies there was "overlapping of interest, neglect of some recreation needs and an over-supply for others." The follow-up work resulted in the creation of a Recreation Council whose functions were the correlation of existing agencies in Cleveland and the promotion of new activities.

Since the War there have been relatively few "blanket" surveys, but a considerable number of specialized surveys of health, education, religion, recreation and criminal justice. These all differ from the community case studies referred to earlier in that they are diagnoses of problem-situations rather than studies of the net-work of social relationships which constitute the very life of the community. Furthermore, the surveys have as their goal the achievement of some immediate practical purpose rather than the formulation of conclusions about local group life in general.

**Ecological Studies.** Studies in human ecology, which have to do with the distribution of groups and institutions and their adjustment to the environment, might perhaps be classed as one form of community case studies. But because a rather distinctive procedure has been developed it is appropriate to deal with them as a separate type.

In 1921 McKenzie published the results of his study of Columbus, Ohio, in which he displayed graphically the pattern of the city.[14] Just outside the central business district he found some areas which had once been the homes of "good" families but were then the stopping place of a miscellaneous array of transients. He found a tendency for trouble, as represented by juvenile court and associated charities cases, to be concentrated in these areas of highest physical mobility. He found in outlying parts of the city greater stability, higher economic status, less delinquency, and more consistent support of local institutions. His detailed study of a disintegrating neighborhood is especially interesting. Located on a flood plane near the center of the city, it was occupied by working-class people of American birth. Families came and went in rapid succession, except for a few of the older residents who had not yet escaped. There was little visiting back and forth. Most of the people lived there from necessity rather than from choice. Ownership of property was uncommon and there were few secondary means of communication such as telephone and automobile.

At the 1923 meeting of the American Sociological Society Burgess presented a scheme for interpreting the growth of a city. It comprised a series of concentric circles, at the center of the principal business district (Zone I), next an area in transition (Zone II), then an area of workingmen's homes (Zone III), a more expensive residential area (Zone IV), and finally the commuters' area (Zone V).

Following these leads a number of studies have been made of divorce, desertion, prostitution, juvenile delinquency, suicide, and other "indices of disorganization" to see how they may be related to the general pattern of the city. In his study of family disorganization in Chicago Mowrer identified five sorts of areas which he classified according to the type of domestic situation most common in each.[15] First were non-family areas near the center of the city where single men and some single women lived in hotels and rooming-houses. Second were "emancipated" family areas, "interstitial" (e.g., stretched along arterial highways between recognized neighborhoods and

[14] McKenzie, R. D., "The Neighborhood: A Study of Local Life in the City of Columbus, Ohio," *Amer. Jour. Soc.*, 27: 145 ff.

[15] Mowrer, E. R., *Family Disorganization*, Chap. V.

communities), where married couples without children lived in rooming houses, kitchenette apartments and residential hotels. Third were "paternal" family areas lying in Zones II and III. Here were large families of wage-earners, often of foreign birth, ruled over by the husband and father. Among these tenement dwellers divorce rarely occurred, but desertion was common. Fourth were "equalitarian" family areas in Zones III and IV. Here were small families of the business and professional classes living in apartments. The wife commonly had interests outside the home. Both desertion and divorce occurred. Finally, in Zones IV and V were the "maternal" family areas, with small families living in separate houses, the wife being the head of the house so far as neighborhood relations were concerned. Here, contrary to some expectations, both divorce and desertion were rare.

Another study of this type was made by Mrs. Cavan, also in Chicago.[16] She found significance in the spatial distribution of suicides. Dividing the city into 72 "communities," the number of suicides ranged from none at all in certain outlying districts to 87 per 100,000 in the "Loop." The areas in which the suicide rate was highest were parts of the city, in Zones I and II, in which native-born, white, single men lived in rooming houses. In these same areas were found most of the pawnshops, drug-peddling centers, and houses of prostitution. There was also a marked tendency for areas with high suicide rates to coincide with those of high rates of divorce, murder, and deaths from alcoholism. In other words, all these were found to be related to the disorganization of neighborhood and community life.

As these studies have shown, whenever business and industry invade a district that has previously been occupied by homes, families begin to leave. But because there is likely to be a temporary decline in property values with prospects of later increase, they are more ready to rent than to sell. Often they make the old house over into a converted tenement or rooming house, renting for what they can get and making as few repairs as possible until the land value is so great that they can afford to "junk" the house and sell the lot for com-

[16] Cavan, Ruth Shonle, *Suicide,* Chap. V.

mercial or industrial use. Into such an area as this drift the strangers who have limited resources. But being there because of accident or necessity, they have no stake in the district and are ready to move on short notice. As a result local institutions, such as church and school, find little support; neighborliness almost disappears. Then when misfortune overtakes an individual or family he is literally a "lost soul"; he is isolated from friends and relatives; he must turn to the organized social agencies not only for relief and professional services, but also for something that will take the place of the primary group no longer there. This area is also likely to become the "hang-out" of boot-leggers, gamblers and prostitutes, because there is no neighborhood sentiment to drive them out, and anonymity facilitates concealment.

As a result of studies such as these the social agencies of St. Louis and perhaps other cities have redistricted their work to correspond to the "natural areas" of the city. They hope thereby to deal with personal, family and other problems not merely as isolated cases of maladjustment, but in relation to the total situation in which the person or group finds itself. These studies also have a prospective influence on city planning. Hitherto emphasis has fallen chiefly on the æsthetic, economic and health interests, but in the future there seems likely to be increasing attention to provision for stable neighborhood and community life.

**Culture Analysis.** While ecological studies have stressed the relation of the person to his immediate physical and social environment, others have emphasized the significance of the culture or civilization of the larger groups to which he belongs. Developed originally by the anthropologists in their study of pre-literate peoples, the techniques of culture analysis have been applied recently to the problems of immigration and assimilation. While these later studies comprise no such detailed examination of separate traits and complexes as have been made in the case of the American Indians, for example, they do show quite clearly the significance of changing folkways and mores, of cultural lags and conflicts. Among the most important applications of culture analysis to modern social problems are *The Polish Peasant in Europe and America* by

Thomas and Znaniecki, and the *Americanization Studies* fostered by the Carnegie Corporation.

The methods of these studies included visits to peasant communities in Europe as well as to immigrant colonies in the United States, personal observation, interviews, written inquiries, attendance on meetings, utilization of newspapers, letters, diaries, and actually living with the groups in question. The more significant conclusions of these studies may be briefly summarized.

The fundamental patterns of life and behavior are everywhere the same, but each cultural group (race or nationality in ordinary parlance) attaches values to different things and different values to the same thing. The fund of attitudes and values, that is the folkways, mores, institutions, traditions, and material objects possessed by any group constitute its social heritage. Now the heritages of the immigrant groups who come to America differ in many ways from those of us who have lived longer in this country. They have different codes of morals, different systems of family discipline and control, different food, dress, language, religion perhaps. They are accustomed to a different economic and political organization. They have different conceptions of personal and family honor.

But the greatest difference lies in the substitution in America of secondary relationships and controls for the primary group life in Europe. Most European peasants live in little village communities, where everyone knows everyone else, where stability is more important than progress, where the pressure of group sentiment and opinion keeps each individual in the "straight and narrow path." But when they come to America they find no such closely knit communities. Even though they join compatriots in an immigrant colony, they are acquaintances rather than intimates; some have already acquired many American ways; the immigrant group is only a small part of a larger economic, political and social unit; the whole situation is thus utterly different. The newcomer is likely to become confused; he may behave in wild and incalculable ways, yielding to the impulse of the moment, because removed from the familiar background of the permanent community.

It is not strange, therefore, that the immigrant often gets

into trouble. The skill whereby he earned his living at home may not be in demand in America. His limited knowledge of English means that he will often misunderstand and be misunderstood. But most difficult of all is it for him to keep his balance in a country whose notions of right and wrong are so different from his own. This problem becomes particularly acute when the children become Americanized more rapidly than their parents. The youngsters are likely to regard their elders as "old fogies," or "dagoes," to rebel against the old-world type of parental authority, and perhaps later to defy all forms of social control.

When there is a family crisis, due to death, sickness, revolt of youth, desertion of breadwinner, or imprisonment, the American law or the social worker is likely to require or to advise some procedure contrary to the mores of the peasant. When he finds those who are supposed to be his friends demanding that which he has always regarded as evil, or forbidding that which he values highly, he is in greater distress than ever. Thus a cultural conflict is the key to many of the misunderstandings between well-wishing Americans and their immigrant neighbors.

Culture analysis has made another contribution to the interpretation of social problems through the hypothesis of the cultural lag. Ogburn has pointed out that while the various elements in every culture are in flux, some of them change much more rapidly than others; especially do material traits (such as tools and implements) develop faster than non-material traits (such as customs and beliefs).[17] He illustrates this by the belated provision for industrial accidents. Before the rise of the factory system most work was done by hand, accidents were few, relations between master and servant were personal. Hence when an accident did occur it could usually be handled satisfactorily on the basis of personal liability. But with the appearance of power machinery, large-scale production, and absentee ownership, the situation changed materially. The number of accidents increased, provision for the injured workman was neither certain, prompt, nor adequate. Various modifications were slowly made in the old common law, but even after

[17] Ogburn, W. F., *Social Change,* pp. 200 ff.

it had been clearly demonstrated that workmen's compensation or industrial accident insurance was essential to meet the new needs, most of the states held back and refused to enact the necessary legislation. The law-makers, and the voters behind them, were still thinking in terms of the handicraft and domestic systems of manufacture. Similar cultural lags might be shown in the realms of marital relations, taxation, representative government, collective bargaining, and international relations.[18]

Thus it is made plain to the social worker that his task involves not merely individuals, families and communities, but whole cultures as well. Some of his problems cannot be solved except by the slow process of assimilation or acculturation. Others require the harmonizing or balancing of traits and complexes within a given culture. Both processes are necessarily slow; they demand patience, tolerance and understanding.

[18] Since this chapter was written another significant study has been made in the field of culture analysis. It is *Middletown,* by Robert S. and Helen M. Lynd. This book has probably received more attention from social workers than have any of those mentioned above.

# CHAPTER XVII

## THE MENTAL HYGIENE MOVEMENT

In the preceding chapter attention was called to the various points of view that have dominated social work in various periods. Economic interpretation was the keynote of the 'nineties. By 1900 a medical and biological conception had partly replaced the economic, and the emphasis was placed on heredity, glands, and sterilization. A little later mental testing developed and intelligence levels served to explain behavior difficulties. By 1920 the voice of modern psychiatry began to be heard in every field, and mental hygiene became the dominant note in social work. Although sociology has made a number of important contributions, and its influence is steadily growing, mental hygiene is still the fashion, almost "the last word," for social workers in general, and for case workers in particular.

Since Chapters XI and XII were written a new point of view has developed with reference to the nature and treatment of mental disorders and defects. This has resulted not only in improved methods of caring for the insane and feebleminded, but also in the application of knowledge and skill thus gained to all types of personality and behavior problems. A concrete case will illustrate the type of problems dealt with and something of the technique employed.

### A SISSY

#### I. The Problem

John, a high school boy of sixteen, was referred to the mental hygiene clinic by his teachers on account of his failure in school and because they couldn't decide whether he was a "fool" or a "genius." When he appeared for his first interview with the psychiatrist he seemed an attractive boy, tall for his age, good-looking, but loose-jointed and with poorly developed musculature.

His self-assurance was obvious. He was "cocky" and conceited about himself, his family and his home. He claimed he had one of the finest and most brilliant fathers, the brightest brothers and sisters, and one of the best homes in the city.

## II. History

*Family.* According to John, his father was one of the most talented men in the city. He had planned to be a physician, but a nervous breakdown during his junior year at Harvard forced him to give up his career. John admitted, with obvious embarrassment, that his father had never been able to complete his education and was at present working in a bank. He was, however, by way of recompense for his vocational failure, a writer of genius. Unfortunately he had never had a story accepted by the publishers, since, as John explained, they were all written in a somewhat unfamiliar dialect. As a matter of fact, according to some of John's teachers, his father's writings were decidedly poor. His older sister was a very bright girl, but owing to a breakdown of some sort in high school had quit and since become a stenographer. His older brother had also been unfortunate. He too had been very bright but was struck on the head with a stone, was unable to complete high school, and became an elevator boy.

*Boy's Own Story.* John related how he had had various children's diseases before he had gained mental control over his body. Since he acquired full possession of himself he has never been sick, except once with scarlet fever, and then he had only a light attack. At this time his mother, brother and sister had also been ill and had to have doctors and nurses. His mother particularly needed medical attention because she didn't possess the powerful mind of the others. He, however, soon had control of his disease, and needed neither nurses nor physician. John said he was now in good health, and that he didn't believe in disease or germs. In fact, he said "he would be willing to drink a tumbler of so-called typhoid germs." Mind was everything, and could even control most accidents, according to his theory. He denied, however, that he was a Christian Scientist. "I am too radical," he said. He planned to be a writer, and upon finishing high school intended to enter Harvard. He would write the great American epic, "as God intended him to do." He appeared amused at his school failure and said he wasn't interested in the subjects, they were silly and unimportant. "Why should I study mathematics? If I were going to be a crook on Wall street, it might be well for me to know something about mathematics; but didn't I tell you I was going to be a writer? I don't need to know anything about mathematics and I don't want to know anything about mathematics." He was almost equally contemptuous of the other subjects despite the obvious relation of some of them to his announced vocational interests.

### III. Status at Time of Study

*Physical.* Although only sixteen years of age John was over six feet in height. He had fair, soft skin, with no beard or other secondary sex characteristics. In fact, in this respect he had the body of a boy of ten. He was loose-jointed and obviously lacked physical strength. His physical development in general was childish. It was apparent he was suffering from some form of endocrine imbalance. "His thymus gland, which should largely have completed its work some time ago and retired from the scene in favor of the pituitary, whose turn it has been to change the individual from a child to an adolescent and from an adolescent to a man, is still persisting in its activity. The other endocrine glands have been unable to bring the thymus under control and the thymus has gone along blissfully and happily, as it were, in its overactivity, not realizing that in doing so it is building for the boy a body with which it will be difficult for him to meet the problems of everyday life. What is more, a body which, because of its very difference from other bodies, will create for the boy very special additional problems. The body that is being built for the boy is an inferior body."

*Intellectual.* No psychological tests were given but the teachers reported that he had one of the highest IQ's in the school, and he was obviously superior in intelligence.

*Psychiatric.* He clearly had no special mental disease. Possibly, in the light of the family history, he had inherited some degree of nervous instability. Obviously his boastfulness and self-assurance was in the nature of overcompensation for emotions of inferiority. He was "really humility and misery itself."

*Social.* The family, in addition to John, consisted of an older brother and sister, the former being an elevator boy and the latter a stenographer, several younger children, and his father and mother. The father, as John related, was a bank clerk. The home, according to John, was considerably above the average. John had few friends, but admitted that he would like one of the right sort. He was too far ahead of most boys, according to him, to be friends with them. They believed too much in the superiority of physical over mental strength. When asked if he had a nickname, he replied, "Well, not really a nickname, but they call me sister and 'sissy.'" He maintained he didn't resent this and that he was above such things. The boys also continually tried to get him to fight. "They pick quarrels with me and then claim that I do not fight fair. They get sore because in a fight I kick, and scratch, and bite; but that's all right; any means in a fight is fair, if you reason it out correctly. Fighting itself is wrong. Therefore, there can be no right and wrong as to how one shall fight. I would not fight of my own accord, because I think it is wrong; but if they force me to fight then there can be no rules or regulations, and I am at liberty to use any means I choose. They haven't got enough brains to see that." He usually depended upon flight. "I can get away from them as I have longer legs and can run faster than any of them. What is more, I know more hiding places than all the rest of them put together, so they can't find me if I once get a start."

In school he was equally unsuccessful. At the time the study was made he was failing in all of his five subjects. Occasionally he did almost brilliant work, and the erratic nature of his performance was a puzzle to his teachers.

## IV. Diagnosis

*Etiology.* John was neither crazy nor a genius. Nor did he have any definite mental disorder. He was merely an unfortunate boy lost in the woods of social relationships, trying to find his way out and whistling to keep up his courage. His keen intelligence perceived the essential failures made by his father and older brother and sister, his sensitive emotional nature was hurt, and he sought explanations that would throw the blame on outside and unpreventable forces. He was an unstable child with retarded adolescence, who, feeling keenly his shortcomings, sought devious means of meeting the situation. He strongly desired prestige and standing among his associates, and assumed an air of superiority when these were out of his reach. They were grapes beyond his grasp, and so he termed them sour. Instead of striving for status as a student, where he might have excelled, he turned his back on this one possibility for constructive adjustment, and withdrew from competition by running away from reality and denying the value of the prize sought. "He is not inferior; he is superior. Those who torment him are his inferiors, but the brave denial does not change the situation. Again his efforts at stifling the pain only further twists and warps him, and when finally this twisted and warped personality moves out into the world, day by day, its very queerness creates new problems. . . . Higher and higher, with ever greater desperation, he builds his stockade and scuttles, like the frightened boy he is, to the top, there pitifully to continue his denials and, almost inaccessible, to hurl down defiance upon his 'inferiors.' "

*Diagnosis.* John was undoubtedly unstable emotionally, but the possibility of dementia præcox or any other definite mental disease was ruled out. "If he has such a disease at sixteen, or develops one later, it will have been made during his own lifetime and out of the materials of his own life. One need not seek to blame his grandparents."

Sociologically we may attempt a diagnosis in terms of John's reaction to social control. He has certain fundamental desires, and is attempting to realize these in accordance with standards set up by his group. He wants to conform to the social code, but is prevented by his fears and handicaps. We may picture the diagnosis schematically:

| (1) *Mental Conflict* | | (2) *Maladjustment* |
|---|---|---|
| Desire for status and for a career, as socially defined.<br>vs.<br>Social and physical inferiority and a dread of disease or accidents. | ⟶ | Accommodations of:<br>1. overcompensation<br>2. rationalization<br>3. flight. |

He has two main wishes which are being frustrated. He wants to be accepted as an equal by his companions, but his physical inferiority and delayed adolescence stand in the way. He also has ambitions for a brilliant future, but he remembers how accident and disease checked the careers of his equally brilliant father, brother and sister. He attempts to meet this situation bravely but succeeds only in making a partial, imperfect and more or less temporary adaptation which may be termed "maladjustment." He overcompensates by boasting and assuming superiority; he rationalizes both the shortcomings of his family, as due to disease and accident, and his own fear of a similar fate by denying the potency of disease itself. He refuses to face the facts of his physical inferiority and flies to the imaginary security of his assumed superiority, rationalizing his methods of defending himself when forced into a fight. Another use of rationalization is his tendency to impute inferiority to others in order to save his own self-respect.

Mental hygiene involves a number of cooperative techniques. A multiple diagnosis may be profitably made:

| | |
|---|---|
| Psychological: | superior. |
| Medical: | endocrine imbalance. |
| Psychiatric: | normal, with some instability. |
| Educational: | school failure: erratic performances. |
| Sociological: | "maladjustment" that will eventuate into an even more serious condition unless "readjustment" occurs. |

*Recommendations.* John's liabilities are apparent from the foregoing analysis. He is in a precarious condition, and must make a better adjustment shortly or his lack of adjustment will become more serious. He suffers from several types of inferiority and a dread of disease and accident. He lacks friends, and his family is apparently of little help to him. His teachers do not understand him. On the other hand, he possesses at least one important asset. His intelligence is superior. In addition, he is stimulated by a strong ambition to make something of his life. Any plan for his readjustment should be based upon specific knowledge of his condition and not on punishment, general encouragement, argument, reward, or threats. His failure in school is merely symptomatic, not important in itself, but indicative of underlying lack of adjustment and undesirable accommodations. He should, of course, be treated for his endocrine dysfunction: the thymus should be controlled and the pituitary stimulated. But even if such treatment were properly carried out he would not be "cured." His mental habits would remain. Years of rationalizing and avoiding reality must be offset by a long period of new habit formation in a new social situation, under guidance, or in the familiar situation with a new line of attack. Explanation of the mental mechanisms involved would help some, but more might be accomplished by changes in the home and school situation. Self-confidence on the basis of reality might be gained through good school work. His interest in writing might also be utilized as an aid in the process of reorganization. Thus through the modification of elements in his own make-up, in his attitudes and habits, and in the situation, readjustment may eventually be accomplished.[1]

**Mental Hygiene as a Technique.** This case illustrates a number of important points relative to the nature of mental hygiene as an art designed to aid in the analysis and treatment of behavior difficulties. The mental hygiene approach recognizes the "problem" to be usually merely symptomatic, and to demand a detailed and intensive analysis going back far into the early life of the client. John's fear of accident and disease was a result of early conditioning by the fate of other members of his family. It was found necessary to study all aspects of his personality and social environment, to note his reactions to the latter, and to view the complex situation as a whole. No mere physical or psychological examination alone would have revealed the deep-seated causes of the difficulty. His Intelligence

[1] Williams, Frankwood E., "The Mechanism of Human Behavior," in Williams, F. E., *et al, Social Aspects of Mental Hygiene,* pp. 26-36, New Haven, 1925. Re-arrangement and sociological analysis of original record. By permission of Yale University Press.

Quotient alone gave no clue to the emotional conflict, nor would a knowledge of his endocrine disorder have afforded a solution apart from a study of the social situation and of his wishes and attitudes. The mental hygiene approach is essentially a co-operative one, yet at the same time one unified by certain fundamental principles. What these conceptions are will become clearer when the history of the mental hygiene movement is reviewed.

**The History of Mental Hygiene: Early Treatment of the Insane and Feebleminded.** Among primitive peoples and even as late as the seventeenth century insanity was thought to be due to demon possession. Flogging, burning and blood-letting were among the early methods of treatment. In the eighteenth century nearly all the indigent mentally afflicted were either at large, or if dangerous, confined in jails, houses of correction, poorhouses and the like. Their plight was indeed woeful. They were frequently mixed with criminals and those afflicted with all sorts of foul diseases; usually chained, starved and flogged, in a filthy condition, and without beds to lie on.[2] Humanitarian interest in the insane began, in France, with Pinel. During the French Revolution, this well-known physician changed the traditional methods of treatment and began to experiment with a policy of kindness and decency, for the first time in history treating the insane as human beings. At the risk of his own life, he struck off their chains and placed them in hospitals under the care of sympathetic physicians. In the United States the leader of this humanitarian movement was Dorothea Dix, who traveled over the country, stirring up public interest, spreading information, and stimulating the founding of institutions.

By the end of the nineteenth century modern psychiatry was born, thanks to such men as Kraeplin, Bleuler, Krafft-Ebing, and others; and the movement began which is gradually changing insane asylums into hospitals for the mentally sick. In the United States such leaders as Adolf Meyer, William A. White, and Thomas W. Salmon began to teach that there is no sharp line between the mentally ill and the mentally well, that mental

[2] Winslow, C. E. A., "Twenty Years of Mental Hygiene." *Mental Hygiene,* 12: 504-515, 1928. *Passim.*

disease is to be regarded much as any other disease, that the patient is not to be blamed nor his family humiliated, and that much so-called insanity is preventable and curable.

At the opening of the twentieth century, however, the public had not accepted this view, nor was it understood by the profession in general. The humanitarian enthusiasm that had been aroused began to die. Hospitals failed to make good their claims and began to revert to places of mere custodial care. Some asylums were dehospitalized and standards in general fell. But between 1900 and 1920 a revolution took place in the care of the insane. Violent wards were abolished, the new psychiatry gained acceptance, prevention came to the forefront, and insanity was recognized as a form of illness, not a crime.

**The Mental Hygiene Movement.** In order to appreciate the radical changes in the care of the insane brought about by the mental hygiene movement the various stages in the history of their treatment should be recalled. According to Davie,[3] treatment has passed through three stages and is now in the fourth. The first period he terms the demonological, in which insanity was thought to be due to witchcraft and dealt with accordingly. The second period was that of dungeons and chains, during which the insane were treated as criminals. The third epoch was that of humanitarianism and empirical treatment; and the fourth, the period of scientific study and prevention ushered in by the mental hygiene movement.

Many forces contributed to the new point of view. Among them was the emphasis which psychiatrists such as Meyer and Healy began to place on environment, experience, and habit formation as causes of the psychoses. Such a conception constituted a basis for successful treatment and prevention which became the keynote of the new movement. The greatest single figure, the one usually credited with being the father of the movement, is that of Clifford Beers, whose own extraordinary experiences stimulated his "unflagging efforts to secure public interest in the inhumane and unintelligent treatment of the mentally sick." [4] He was concerned about the condition of the mentally ill because he himself had been insane and recovered.

[3] Williams, F. E., *et al., op. cit.,* "Introduction," by M. R. Davie.
[4] Williams, F. E., *et al., op. cit.,* "Foreword," by J. R. Angell.

Beers was a New Haven boy who graduated from Yale in 1897. In 1900 he became insane and for three years was confined in various public and private hospitals of Connecticut. In September 1903 he recovered—or at least his manic-depressive condition had so far improved as to permit his discharge—abandoned his business career, and decided to devote himself to improving the lot of the insane. In the elated condition characteristic of the stage of the disease in which he then was he threw himself into the fight with the zeal of a crusader. His first move was to write the story of his life, which was published in 1908 under the title, *A Mind That Found Itself*. About the same time he started the Connecticut Society for Mental Hygiene. A year later the National Committee for Mental Hygiene was founded with Beers as its secretary. By 1912 sufficient financial backing had been secured to launch a program of educational propaganda to which were later added research and the training of workers. The interests of the Committee were broadened to include care of the feebleminded, prevention of mental disorders, and problems of personality development in general. During the War the National Committee cooperated with the Medical Corps of the Army in detecting and treating mental disorders among the soldiers. After the Armistice it aided in the rehabilitation of soldiers suffering from nervous and mental diseases. Surveys were made in several states to determine approximately the number of psychopathic and feebleminded persons, the provisions for their care, and the most urgent needs. In 1921 an important and fruitful alliance was effected with the Commonwealth Fund. The united work of these organizations in the establishment of child guidance clinics and setting up visiting teacher demonstrations will be described in Chapter XXI.

In 1928 the American Foundation for Mental Hygiene was announced, having as its purpose the raising of an endowment that would guarantee the future of the movement. In May, 1930, the First International Mental Hygiene Congress is to be held in Washington, D. C.

The achievements of the mental hygiene movement from 1909 to 1923 have been summarized by Beers in a revised edition of his autobiography. During those years general knowledge about insanity increased, "asylums" became hospitals with improved institutional treatment and with out-patient clinics. The number of recoveries increased and a start was made toward prevention, through the focusing of attention upon early manifestations of abnormality. Mental hygiene societies were founded in twenty states, and bureaus in many cities. Special institutions for the feebleminded were established where there had been none. In the early days of the movement psychiatry enjoyed little recognition, but by 1923 it had been firmly established in the medical schools, and applied to the problems of delinquency, industry, education, and the behavior of children. A standard classification of nervous and mental disorders was worked out and statistics were made uniform. Popular education proceeded apace, greatly aided by the founding of the magazine, *Mental Hygiene,* in 1917. A number of mental hygiene conventions had been held and a Division of Mental Hygiene was established in the National Conference of Social Work. One of the most significant developments since 1923 is the establishment of the Yale Institute of Human Relations in 1929, in which psychiatry and mental hygiene, under the direction of Dr. William Healy, will cooperate with the other sciences dealing with human behavior in a program of professional training and research.

**Principles of Modern Psychiatry and Mental Hygiene.** Until recently the lines between general and abnormal psychology were sharply drawn. Such studies, however, as those of Charcot and Janet on dissociation in mildly hysterical patients, of Binet and Stern on suggestibility, and of Freud, Jung and Adler on psychoanalysis have changed this relationship, and are throwing a flood of light on so-called normal behavior.[5] Modern psychiatry has its roots in abnormal psychology, psychotherapy, clinical psychology and social psychology. Psychiatry is "the art of mental healing, and is a practical branch of medicine."[6] A psychiatrist is, therefore, a specialist in nervous and mental diseases and in mental hygiene. There are

[5] The reader is referred to Hart, Bernard, *Psychopathology, Its Development and Its Place in Medicine,* New York, 1927; to Dummer, E. S. (editor), *The Unconscious,* New York, 1927; and Myerson, Abraham, *The Psychology of Mental Disorders,* New York, 1927.

[6] Southard and Jarrett, *The Kingdom of Evils,* p. 371, New York, 1922.

many schools of psychiatry and numerous more or less overlapping if not contradictory basic principles. Consistency is not an outstanding characteristic of practical psychiatry. The fundamental concepts of modern psychiatry are drawn from various sources.[7] Behaviorism has contributed the theory of the mechanism of conditioning. "In the beginning certain stimuli produce certain responses. These native responses, called unconditioned, are the starting point for the building of complicated conditioned habit patterns." [8] To W. I. Thomas, a social psychologist, we owe the concept of the "four wishes" and the idea that it is the thwarting of these fundamental desires that leads to behavior problems. Adler contributed his doctrine of inferiority and over-compensation. Among the mechanisms described by Freud and the psychoanalysts, projection, transference, repression, conflict, sublimation, regression, flight from reality, rationalization, defense reactions, and wish fulfillment are perhaps the most significant for the study of conduct. Finally, to Jung we owe the definition of the extrovert and the introvert types.

The psychiatrist is perhaps primarily concerned with the treatment of emotional difficulties that hinder the adjustment of the individual to his environment. He deals with the total reaction of the person to his life-situation. His main interest, according to Lowrey,[9] is in individual reactions, i.e., in the adjustment and the maladjustment of the individual. He deals with mental conflicts, complexes, psychopathic and neurotic states, mental defect and psychoses. Although contributing much toward the understanding of commonplace behavior difficulties, it is possible that most psychiatrists will always be concerned with the grosser abnormalities. It is quite natural, therefore, that one of the major contributions of modern psychiatry should be a reinterpretation of insanity.

The newer conception of mental disorders differs in a number of respects from the ideas dominant a generation ago. To begin with, mind and body are no longer considered separate

[7] Healy, Wm., *et al., Reconstructing Behavior in Youth,* pp. 82-109, New York, 1929. [8] *Idem,* p. 83.

[9] Lowrey, L. G., "Some Trends in the Development of Relationships between Psychiatry and General Social Case Work," *Mental Hygiene,* 10: 277-284, 1926. *Passim.*

units; mental disease is regarded as involving the entire organism. As Thomas puts it,[10] mental disorder represents a failure of the organism to adapt itself to the conditions of life and especially of human society; this failure involves the functioning of the entire organism; and causation is multiple and complex, rather than simple and specific. In comparison with hereditary causes, environmental and social factors are coming to be more and more emphasized. As early as 1908, Adolf Meyer defined dementia præcox as the result of bad habit formation, thus "bringing a portion of the psychiatric material clearly into the psychological and social fields."

Ten points in the modern conception of insanity are noted in the *Mental Hygiene Bulletin* for May, 1926. These are:

1. Insanity develops gradually, not suddenly. Diagnosis should be sought at the first indications of trouble.
2. Insanity is not incurable: many are restored to health after treatment.
3. Insanity is no more a disgrace than any other disease.
4. It is not a divine visitation but a mental disease and should receive proper medical attention.
5. Asylums are no longer dreadful institutions and are rapidly becoming hospitals from which from 25 to 40% of the admissions are discharged as cured or improved.
6. Emotional shocks, loss of friends and the like, are not fundamental causes but merely releasing factors.
7. "Insanity" is merely a legal term to denote irresponsibility, and covers many forms of mental disease.
8. One can guard against insanity. There are many danger signals which should be properly dealt with.
9. We cannot say that a person is either insane or not insane; there are many degrees of mental health.
10. So-called nervous breakdown is not a disease of the nerves, but of mental and emotional condition.

The psychiatrists, along with the psychologists and other specialists, have also contributed to our changing ideas about feeblemindedness. True feeblemindedness is an actual lack of organic brain development, often an hereditary defect, and is absolutely incurable in any medical sense. In at least fifty per cent of the cases feeblemindedness is traced to accidental causes such as birth injuries, childhood diseases, and the like. Mental

[10] Thomas, W. I., and Dorothy S., *The Child in America*, p. 436.

defect resulting from such causes is, of course, not transmissible. While genuine feeblemindedness appears to be quite incurable, levels of intelligence sometimes change to a considerable degree. Hence psychometric examinations (Binet-Simon tests, for example) need to be supplemented by medical and psychiatric examinations, social histories, and observation under varied conditions.

As we have noted before, mental hygiene is much wider in scope than psychiatry and clinical psychology as these are ordinarily conceived. It is concerned not only with the treatment and prevention of mental abnormalities, but also with the promotion of mental health. "It may not be true that we are all a little insane," said Dr. Macfie Campbell;[11] "it is certainly true that we all have to face the same fundamental problems of life, and the problems before which the nervous or mental patient has broken down are only different in degree from those which each cultivated man has to face."

**Treatment of the Insane.** It is only during the past thirty years that under the influence of mental hygiene and modern psychiatry treatment has progressed from the stage of custodial care to that of scientific curative effort. While there are numerous private hospitals, the major responsibility for treatment of the insane falls upon the state institutions. These are of two types: state hospitals, for the confinement and treatment of more or less chronic cases, and "psychopathic hospitals," for preliminary examination and diagnosis. The first hospital of the latter type was established at the University of Michigan in 1906. Such institutions, together with psychopathic wards in general hospitals, meet a great social need as they facilitate the early diagnosis of mental disorder without the necessity of legal action. The hospital of the first type attempts to give the patient a wholesome environment with a minimum of restraint while his physical and mental condition receives expert treatment. Occupational and hydrotherapy, the fever treatment for syphilis, and other modern methods, including social service and parole, have greatly increased the rates of discharge and rehabilitation, while the establishment

[11] *A Present-day Conception of Mental Disorders,* Cambridge, 1925, pp. 53-54.

of out-clinics has done much in the direction of prevention. The following is a description of the social service and out-clinic departments of the Kalamazoo State Hospital:

A psychiatric social worker was placed in this hospital in September, 1921. The hospital in 1924 served 15 counties and had 2,327 resident patients, and 308 on parole at that time. The social service department consisted of only one worker at this time (one full-time and one part-time assistant were later added) to carry on both the intra- and extra-mural work. The first service rendered is that of history-taking. Information is obtained from those who bring the patient to the hospital and from a field trip to the patient's home community. The worker also informs the relatives concerning the régime of the hospital, and does as much educational work as possible in the various communities visited. In this hospital very little social work is done for patients in the institution. The other main function of the department is concerned with parole. In Michigan patients are paroled for one year before final discharge during which time they may return or be brought back to the hospital. Cases are periodically discussed at the staff conference and parole recommended whenever it is deemed advisable. The patient is then referred to the Social Service Department for re-establishment in the community. Between September 1921 and June 30, 1924, 104 placements were made. Many types are paroled, including arteriosclerosis, senile dementia, chronic alcoholic hallucinosis, dementia præcox and paranoid conditions, general paresis, involutional melancholia, epilepsy, drug addiction and constitutional psychopathic inferiority. Of those paroled during this period 72% had resided in the hospital for more than a year. Three had been residents between five and six years, and one between twenty-five and thirty years. The majority of those paroled were between the ages of thirty-five and sixty-five. The length of time on parole varied from one month to nearly three years (made possible by renewal of residence). The financial saving resulting from the above group of paroles amounted to approximately $25,000 during the period.[12]

The out-patient clinics conducted by this hospital were established in 1916 and held once a month in Kalamazoo, Jackson, Lansing and Grand Rapids. Since the beginning of this work additional clinics have been held in Holland and St. Joseph, and special clinics in other cities.

[12] Summarized from Hughes, Estella M., "An Evaluation of Social Service in the Kalamazoo State Hospital." *Hospital Social Service,* 11: 299-306, 1925.

The clinic staff consists of a psychiatrist and a psychologist. Local social workers are utilized instead of using the hospital worker. In Kalamazoo the clinic is held weekly, in the other cities, monthly. In the latter case the psychologist spends two days each month in the city where the clinic is held and the psychiatrist, one. Whenever possible complete histories are obtained from the referring agency or individual before the patient is seen. The usual procedure consists of a physical and psychometric examination followed by a psychiatric interview. Both adults and children are examined. From September, 1927, to July, 1928, a total of 357 new examinations were made by the traveling clinic in five cities visited. A total of 220 children, the majority over ten, and 137 adults were seen. Of the 357 cases, 128 were referred by social agencies, 100 by medical agencies, 55 by courts, 41 by schools, while 32 came voluntarily. The remaining one was an institutional case. 104 were diagnosed as of inferior intelligence, 97 of average mentality, 36 as psychoneurotic, and 33 psychotic.[13]

**Social Control of the Feebleminded.** Since the eighteen-nineties social programs for dealing with the feebleminded have undergone striking changes. Rediscovery of the Mendelian theories of inheritance and invention of the Binet-Simon tests lead to an optimistic belief in sterilization as a necessary and effective means of eliminating mental deficiency. Fifteen states passed laws authorizing the asexualization of certain defectives, but a storm of protest was aroused. While much of the opposition was based on purely sentimental grounds, the controversy produced some healthy skepticism as to this or any other panacea. Present-day programs for controlling the feebleminded include the following items: identification, registration, special training, social diagnosis, placement in the community, supervision, and institutional or colony care for low-grade or emotionally unstable defectives.

Identification of the feebleminded is going on in the public schools, in juvenile and criminal courts, in institutions of various sorts, and in some industrial establishments. The State of Massachusetts requires that all known mental defectives and all school children who are retarded three years or more shall be registered with the Department of Mental Diseases. (If any of them are later found not to be genuinely

[13] Annual Report of the Out-Patient Department, 1927-28.

feebleminded, they are of course removed from the list.) The purpose of this registration is to gather adequate information about the extent of the problem and to make possible some oversight of these handicapped citizens of the commonwealth. Special training is given to a slowly increasing number of defectives, not only in state institutions, but in special schools and classes of the public school system. This enables them to remain with their families and makes the tax-payers' burden less than it would be if all feebleminded children were institutionalized. In these classes emphasis is placed on personal hygiene and manual training; an effort is made to train these children in dependable performance of simple tasks which will enable them to live modestly useful and happy lives in the community.

Too often nothing further is done after the child leaves one of these special classes or schools. But in some cases a careful study is made, not only of the boy or girl, but of his family, neighborhood, opportunities for employment and recreation. Someone is found who can understand his limitations and who will help him to meet the crises, little and big, of everyday living. In other words, adequate treatment of the feebleminded includes a social diagnosis and prognosis before placement in the community. This part of the program has been especially well developed in the Walter E. Fernald School for the Feebleminded at Waverly, Mass. This institution furthermore provides supervision for its paroled and discharged inmates who are living in various parts of the state. Much use is made of informal, volunteer assistance, but the general responsibility for social adjustment rests on a professional social worker.

It is now believed that a majority of mental defectives can be enabled, by such a program as has been outlined above, to make their way in the world without being much of a burden or menace to the rest of us. But there will always be some whose low level of intelligence or emotional instability render them unfit for life outside of institutions. But even these need not be mere liabilities. At the Rome (New York) State School for Mental Defectives it has been demonstrated that many institutional cases can be trained to live in colonies where they will earn at least a goodly part of their maintenance, thus reducing taxes or extending the State's service.

**Wider Scope of the Movement.** Not only is mental hygiene concerned with mental disorders and defectiveness; during the past decade it has involved increasing attention to prevention and application of the psychiatric point of view to various social problems. Clinics have been established to which various agencies are referring their clients, and individual psychiatrists are also helping in diagnosis and treatment. The tables on page 258 summarize the results of a study of one hundred consecutive cases at the adult mental clinic of the University of Illinois School of Medicine.

Similar cooperation is developing in many cities, where social workers in family service societies, children's aid associations, juvenile courts, orphanages, prisons, and other institutions, recognize that all problems of social maladjustment have a mental aspect which frequently requires the attention of specialists. It is no longer believed that a large percentage of the persons served by social agencies are feebleminded or insane. But it is certain that many of them present emotional difficulties with which most social workers are not equipped to deal. As a result of this discovery training schools are offering courses in "social psychiatry" or mental hygiene, experienced workers are reading books on this subject, and some (known as psychiatric social workers) are specializing in this field.

The spread of this movement is by no means confined to social work. Its influence is also apparent in the field of education. In nursery school, kindergarten, grammar grades, high school, and college mental hygiene is changing the attitudes of teachers and pupils. Courses in mental hygiene are sometimes offered in colleges and universities; occasionally psychiatrists are available for consultation by students.

**Psychiatric Social Work.** In 1917 the National Conference of Social Work established a Division on Mental Hygiene. A little later the term psychiatric social worker came into current use. However, the idea was not entirely new. As early as 1905 a social worker was employed by the neurological clinic of Massachusetts General Hospital. A year later one was placed in the psychopathic wards of Bellevue Hospital

*Problems Presented*

| | |
|---|---|
| Inability to manage home | 7 |
| Friction in home | 10 |
| Sex and other delinquencies | 8 |
| Dependency | 6 |
| Failure in work | 7 |
| Mental excitement | 5 |
| Despondency | 3 |
| Fits | 6 |
| Bodily complaints | 43 |
| Special reasons | 5 |

38% referred because of difficulty in social adjustments and 8% more on account of mental symptoms which caused upsets in social environment.

*Diagnoses*

| | |
|---|---|
| Mental defectives | 26 |
| Defective delinquency | 4 |
| Inadequate personality | 1 |
| Epilepsy | 5 |
| Psychoses with organic brain disease | 4 |
| Psychoneuroses | 26 |
| Dementia præcox | 6 |
| Manic-depressive reactions | 4 |
| Neurological cases | 18 |
| General medical cases | 2 |
| Negative findings | 4 |

*Agencies by which Referred*

| | |
|---|---|
| Other departments of dispensary | 22 |
| Institute for Juvenile Research | 4 |
| Juvenile court | 3 |
| State's attorney's office | 1 |
| Jewish Social Service Bureau | 26 |
| Illinois Society for Mental Hygiene | 3 |
| Visiting Nurses Assoc. | 3 |
| Juvenile Protective Assoc. | 2 |
| United Charities | 5 |
| Immigration Industrial Commission | 1 |
| American Red Cross | 1 |
| St. Vincent's Orphanage | 1 |
| Northwestern University Settlement | 1 |
| Social Service Department Industrial Corporation | 1 |
| Voluntary application to physician | 26 |

*Treatment Recommended*

| | |
|---|---|
| Institutional | 13 |
| Social service supervision | 39 |
| Transfer to other dispensary departments | 7 |
| Treatment in clinic | 41 |

in New York. In 1911 the Manhattan State Hospital took a similar step. But it was the War that gave the greatest impetus to this development.

Psychiatric social work is the branch of social case-work that deals with cases of social maladjustment in which a mental factor or a behavior problem is of primary importance. All social cases have a psychological aspect, but psychiatric social work is concerned particularly with those in which the mental problems predominate and require attention by specially trained persons. . . .

The psychiatric social worker is a social case-worker who has had systematic instruction in the psychological factors underlying behavior and in the principles of physical and mental disease and their social aspects, and training in dealing with psychiatric cases. Her work is usually carried on in a clinic or hospital, the center from which the psychiatrist works and to which persons with mental problems come. She may also work to advantage in a social agency, a school, a court, an industrial plant, or any other institution that deals with individuals, provided that the service of a psychiatrist is available. . . .[14]

These statements seem to describe the functions and preparation of psychiatric social workers clearly enough, but in actual practice it is very difficult to know where to draw the line between them and other kinds of social case workers. Those who are anxious to make a good showing for this new field insist that it includes all visiting teachers, probation officers, and field workers attached to institutions for defectives and delinquents. Others, who are especially impressed by the influence mental hygiene has had on all social work, sometimes question the existence, or at least the need, of a special subtype of case work to be designated "psychiatric."

In addition to this problem there are some interesting questions about the relations between psychiatrists and social workers. Just how do their functions differ? How best can their services be coordinated? Perhaps the easiest way to answer the first question is to say that they differ in the point at which attention is focussed and in the background of training which they bring to the common task. The psychiatrist is a medical man who has specialized in nervous and mental disorders; his attention is concentrated on the patient himself. The social worker usually has more training in social science than in biology; his (or her) attention is concentrated on the patient's environment. To both it is apparent that patient and environment are parts or aspects of a situation whose successful handling requires both approaches. Sometimes the major responsibility is carried by the one, sometimes by the other.

The three main types of situations in which cooperative

[14] *Vocational Aspects of Psychiatric Social Work,* pp. 15-16. Published by Amer. Assn. of Social Workers.

relationships may be worked out have been described by Jessie Taft.[15] (1) Where the problem is distinctly psychiatric or neurological the case should be controlled by the psychiatrist, the social worker playing the subordinate rôle of technical assistant. (2) Where the main problem is social, on the other hand, the social worker should have control of the case. A consultation service is indicated for this type of situation. (3) Where the case requires psychiatric insight but does not involve abnormality the modern social worker, whose training has included social psychiatry, should apply his own knowledge. A larger and larger portion of everyday case work problems are seen to possess mental hygiene aspects.

[15] "Mental Hygiene and Social Work," in Williams *et al., Social Aspects of Mental Hygiene,* pp. 125-145.

# CHAPTER XVIII

## SOCIAL CASE WORK IN GENERAL

The many varieties of social work in the United States today fall rather naturally into two major divisions. When attention is concentrated upon individual persons and their adjustments we speak of case work, whether this be under the auspices of a hospital, court, industrial corporation, children's aid society, family welfare association, or board of public welfare. When attention is centered upon groups and their organization we use the term group work, whether this be done through a social settlement, neighborhood improvement league, community club, playground, Boy Scout troop, civic association, orphan asylum, home for the aged, reformatory, council of social agencies, or community chest. Obviously the distinction is relative rather than absolute, for it is impossible to help individuals make personal adjustments without being concerned with group life; likewise it is impossible to organize and promote groups without being concerned about the individuals who compose them.

Before proceeding with a general discussion of case work we shall present a concrete example, one chosen because the problems involved were relatively simple and the outcome fairly successful.

### BROWN [1]

*Introduction to the Problem.* In May 1916 a "friendly visitor" asked the Family Welfare Society in a southern city to see what it could do for an English family by the name of Brown. They had been in the city for about a year and a half during which time Mr. Brown had been working for a local jeweler. Now he had been laid off, presumably because business was slack and he was unable to do engraving as well as clock repairing. Since his discharge he had been doing odd jobs, which resulted in a very irreg-

[1] This is a summary and analysis of Red Cross Teaching Record No. 3. The full record is available in mimeographed form at the Headquarters of the American National Red Cross, Washington, D. C.

ular and uncertain income. Mr. Brown was anxious to start in business for himself and thought that a loan of $100 would be sufficient to put him on his feet. Mrs. Brown expected confinement very soon and was nervous because of the uncertain income which her husband was earning. Arrangements had been made for her care at the Metropolitan Hospital in the free ward. There seemed to be no immediate need of material relief.

*First Interview.* Two days later a visitor from the Family Welfare Society called at the home of the Browns to talk matters over with them. Both Mr. and Mrs. Brown were at home and during the interview their eight-year-old daughter came, so the case worker talked with all members of the family and saw the conditions under which they were living. Although a bit reserved they were friendly and told their story without much questioning or urging. However, they did hold back certain information about a previous business venture which proved a failure.

The story they told was briefly as follows. Mr. Brown was born in England of fairly well-to-do parents. He went through the elementary schools and had a happy childhood and youth. His father was a railroad contractor, often performing the actual labor himself. He later took an older son into partnership. As our Mr. Brown had never been very strong, he was unable to do such hard work, so was taught the jewelry business and clock repairing. After seven years of apprenticeship he held positions as salesman, bookkeeper and clock repairer in another town. There nine years before he had met and married Mrs. Brown, who also came from a fairly well-to-do family. In 1914 at the advice of friends the Browns came to the United States, expecting to be able to make more money than in England. After spending a short time in Washington, D. C., where no work seemed to be available, they moved to this southern city where, they were told, "the people were more like the English." Here Mr. Brown soon found the position which he held for sixteen months. Mrs. Brown had not made friends and now felt rather lonesome.

They felt that there was no immediate source of help except the Family Welfare Society. Mr. Brown's relatives were all dead, but Mrs. Brown's father might later send them some money. Their plan was to secure a loan, rent a small store-room near the negro district and build up a trade in clock repairing. Mrs. Brown thought that after her confinement she might take in sewing.

In the course of the interview numerous clues were given to other sources of information which might aid in better understanding this family's situation and in solving their problems. These clues included the names of former employers, prospective customers, relatives of Mrs. Brown, church, school, hospital, physician, and previous addresses. The names of the friends in Washington were not given.

The visitor left with the understanding that Mr. Brown would bring to the office an itemized estimate of probable expenditures and some samples of Mrs. Brown's sewing. Mrs. Brown's cordial invitation to return indicated that the social worker had established a friendly relationship.

*Further Inquiry.* In order to supplement the information given by the "friendly visitor" and the Browns, the case worker took advantage of nearly all the clues offered. She called on former and prospective customers, the former employer, physician, chairman of the hospital board, clergyman and school principal. She wrote two letters to England, the first to the Charity Organization Society in Mr. Brown's home town, asking for information and contacts, the second to Mrs. Brown's father, asking for suggestions and definite assistance. But an important part of the needed information was given by the clients themselves in subsequent interviews.

About a week after the first interview the visitor called again and talked with Mrs. Brown about her past life and plans for the future. In the absence of her husband she talked more freely and told among other things of her previous engagement to a young government employe. After a short acquaintance with Mr. Brown she broke this first engagement and presently married Mr. Brown. Her father was angry, since he felt his daughter was marrying beneath her social level. Because of this they had not had much to do with each other; however, her father did occasionally send them money. From her grandmother Mrs. Brown inherited $1,600, which she gave to her husband to start in the jewelry business. But he failed, losing every cent. Mrs. Brown told the visitor that she was very skeptical of her husband's plan to go into business for himself; she thought he should work for someone else. She felt that he was rather visionary, but added that he was unselfish, kind, and quick to assume responsibility.

The same day Mr. Brown came to the office to discuss his plans. He was told frankly of his wife's doubts and also that some of the people the visitor had seen told her he was a drinking man. These statements naturally did not please him, but he took them pretty well, rationalizing that his wife was nervous and that he "only took an occasional glass of beer to be sociable." In thus talking to husband and wife separately the visitor realized that she was in danger of stirring up trouble, but she seems to have handled the situation tactfully.

From other persons the case worker received rather contradictory evidence. There were several reports of intemperance and inefficiency along with others which made him out a steady, reliable workman. In his enthusiasm for the plan of going into business for himself, it appeared that Mr. Brown had counted on work from people who had never promised it. The jeweler by whom he was employed for sixteen months said that he had kept him largely out of sympathy for Mrs. Brown; that the man was a weak character, easily influenced by bad companions, and that he began to drink and squander his money until the weekly pay was turned over directly to his wife. The jeweler said further that Mr. Brown was not a good clock repairer and would not be likely to earn much at odd jobs. Letters from England reported the man as "trustworthy, steady and honest," "a smart, energetic man," who, however, "would do better under supervision than on his own account."

*Diagnosis and Planning.* As she went along it became clear to the visitor that before the affairs of the Brown family could be straightened out answers must be found to the following questions: Should the man go into business for himself or work for someone else? If the former, how should he get started? If the latter, what kind of work should he seek and where? All these questions involved the man's ability, business conditions in the city and elsewhere, possible financial resources, and the wife's attitude. Gradually the visitor came to the conclusion that the man ought to accept employment in some other line than clock repairing. But to carry out such a plan she must not only locate a suitable job; she must help Mr. Brown reach a similar conclusion himself. Hence the task involved not only employment, but also vocational guidance.

In the second place, it appeared that while the family was not in urgent need of financial assistance at the outset, there would have to be more or less material relief until the man should be settled in a steady job to which he was adapted and from which he might receive an adequate income.

With reference to Mrs. Brown it was important to discover the causes of her anxiety and loneliness and to plan how they might be removed. One specific problem had to do with her confinement. Arrangements had been made for her to enter the free ward of a local hospital, but she did not realize that this meant that she must accept the services of a staff physician. When she learned that in order to have her own physician she must go into a pay ward, Mrs. Brown was greatly distressed. She then made it known that she had saved a small sum of money and, against the advice of the visitor, she decided to use this to pay for her medical and hospital care.

*Treatment.* The major task of the visitor was apparently that of inducing Mr. Brown to change his vocation and of making it practicable for him to do so. When she first took the matter up with her "case committee" it was decided to compromise by giving the man a chance to see what he could do for himself, but with the expectation that he would probably fail. So a loan of $30 was secured, free advertising and cheap rent were arranged, one month's telephone bill was guaranteed. As a matter of fact, things did not go very well on this basis; Mr. Brown's earnings were small and irregular.

Presently the visitor began to suggest other possibilities and induced the man to inquire about other kinds of work. After some time she recommended him to a bank that needed a janitor. This job paid only $35 a month to start. Hence, because the wages were inadequate and because the work involved loss of status, she did not urge Mr. Brown to accept it. She pointed out the advantages and disadvantages and asked him to think it over and discuss it with his wife. He felt that this was "beneath his station," but decided that "it was better than nothing," and so took the place.

During the months in which Mr. Brown's wages were being gradually increased and his duties enlarged, the visitor brought material relief consisting of groceries, milk, clothing, and cash. She arranged dental care at low cost and helped the man to get a suit of clothes at reduced price. But most important of all she saw the family frequently to talk over their problems with them and to lend encouragement.

This direct personal influence began in the very first interview with Mr. and Mrs. Brown, in which they were encouraged to view their situation objectively and to consider various possible solutions of their difficulty. However, in the earlier contacts the visitor was chiefly bent on securing information; later she devoted herself to what has been called the "leadership" aspect of case work. For example, when the first plan was made—viz., to make a small loan and let Mr. Brown see what he could do for himself—Mrs. Brown was much upset and almost hysterical. Her husband thereupon became sullen and disagreeable. So they went to see the visitor in the evening at her home. She spent considerable time calming Mrs. Brown and cheering up Mr. Brown. Several times when the visitor heard things which were not to the man's credit, she frankly told him and urged him to clear them up with the persons involved.

Among the "treatment interviews," as they are sometimes called, was the occasion on which the case worker tried to induce Mrs. Brown to give up her own physician in order that she might enter the free ward of the hospital. Another was the discussion of the janitor work with the man. Still another was the home visit during which the visitor reassured the woman with reference to her husband's job and with a promise of assistance until his pay might be adequate for the needs of the family. She arranged to have Mr. Brown call at the office twice a month for the rent money and used these occasions to discuss his advancement as well as his troubles. She called at the house weekly to leave a cash allowance and to talk things over with Mrs. Brown.

*Outcome.* The most important result observed was that Mr. Brown discovered for himself that it was better to work for someone else than to try to run a business of his own. His principal unhappiness after taking the job in the bank was over delay in receiving an expected advance in wage. Here again the visitor encouraged him and talked to the banker on his behalf. Partly because of this and partly because Mr. Brown's work was well done, he was made general custodian of the building and later was given a clerical position. In twenty months his wages were increased from $35 to $125 a month. The family moved to a better neighborhood, bought furniture and then moved into a still more desirable location. They found friends and real neighbors and seemed to be happier than ever before.

**Definitions of Social Case Work.** The classic definition of social case work has been formulated by Mary Richmond. After studying many such records as the one we have just summarized, after discussing their problems and their techniques with many case workers, and after long personal experience in the field, Miss Richmond interpreted the essential function of this type of social work as follows: "Social case work consists of those processes which develop personality through adjustments consciously effected, individual by individual, between men and their social environment." [2] This definition clearly emphasizes the sociological aspects of case work. It makes development of personality the major objective, but implies that this is to be brought about through modifying the relationships between people. Put in somewhat different form, the case worker's task is one of changing attitudes—attitudes toward persons; toward groups such as family, neighborhood, gang, or race; toward institutions such as school, church, trade union, or police; toward mores such as those pertaining to self-support, recreation, or sex.

A somewhat different point of view has been presented by Father O'Grady, who says that "Social case work is the art of ministering to persons who have a great variety of needs, which, of themselves, they cannot satisfy directly or through normal agencies, through a complete understanding of those needs and through the fullest possible use of their own re-

[2] Richmond, Mary, *What Is Social Case Work?* pp. 98-99.

sources and the resources of the community."[3] This statement draws attention to the fact that the clients of a case worker present problems in the realms of health and finance as well as in personal relations. It implies that these various problems cannot be dealt with efficiently unless they are treated as parts of a single, but complex situation. One important task of the case worker is, therefore, to see that the services of physician, teacher, recreation director, employment officer, clergyman and other specialists are made available and are correlated into a common program for helping the person who is in difficulty. Conceivably any one of the others might to be the correlator or consultant on community resources, but in actual practise this function is most frequently performed by the social worker. One part of Father O'Grady's definition reflects the viewpoint of a generation ago. When he speaks of people who cannot meet their needs "directly or through normal agencies," he intimates that the persons served by case workers are unusual or peculiar, that their troubles differ from those of other people. But careful study of many situations dealt with by social case workers has convinced many that the problems of their clients differ in degree rather than in kind from those faced by people who never go near a social service agency. After all, is it very unusual to find persons who, like Mr. Brown, are struggling along in an occupation for which they are not fitted? And must we regard the bureau for vocational guidance as an "abnormal" agency? Or shall we say that those who hire a lawyer and seek in the divorce court a solution of their domestic difficulties are doing the "normal" thing, while those who secure the aid of a family welfare society to end their marital conflict are "dependent"?

Another question which has received considerable attention is whether there be any such thing as case work in general. In 1922 the American Association of Social Workers organized a group of ten persons representing family welfare work, children's aid, juvenile court, work with delinquent girls, visiting teaching, and hospital social service, who, in considering this question, recognized important differences in the details of

[3] O'Grady, John, *An Introduction to Social Work,* p. 55.

their tasks and of their techniques, but agreed that fundamentally they were carrying on the same kind of work. "In general they accepted all forms of social case work as one." [4] In October, 1923, seventeen executives and board members from six national organizations in the social case work field met for a two-day conference at Milford, Pennsylvania. Thus began the so-called Milford Conference which has held a two-day annual meeting ever since. In a report published in 1929 it was stated that perhaps the "most important result of these discussions was the emergence of a strong conviction unanimously held by members of the Conference that a fundamental conception which had come to be spoken of as 'generic social case work' was much more substantial in content and much more significant in its implications for all forms of social case work than were any of the specific emphases of the different case work fields." [5] However, an independent observer has challenged this conclusion. She is impressed with the fact that case workers have served for the most part persons with a narrow economic margin or none, and who are too ignorant to avail themselves of the community's resources. "It seems unlikely that the social worker has acquired a general technique for dealing with social problems which would enable him to function equally well as guide and counsellor to students of an undergraduate college, as personnel director in an industry, or as supervisor of delinquent boys. There appears no basis for the claim to a general technique in personality adjustments. . . ." [6] Doubtless Miss Rich's group would readily admit that no one person could serve equally well in these three capacities. But they would probably add that no one physician could treat equally well patients suffering from ulcers of the stomach, tuberculosis, and defective vision. But the diversity of medical specialties does not blind us to the essential unity of the profession as a whole. The analogy appears to be a fair one.

[4] Rich, Margaret E., "A Study of Case Work Processes," *Compass*, Nov., 1923, p. 1.

[5] *Social Case Work, Generic and Specific*. A Report of the Milford Conference, p. 3.

[6] Walker, Sydnor H., *Social Work and the Training of Social Workers*, p. 107.

**Analyses of Social Case Work.** Very likely little is to be gained by wrangling over definitions. It is much more profitable to examine in some detail the processes which enter into a case work task. Miss Richmond has given us a four-fold division of the processes and types of skill employed by social case workers. These are: "(A) insight into individuality and personal characteristics, (B) insight into the resources, dangers and influence of the social environment, (C) direct action of mind upon mind, (D) indirect action through the social environment."[7] The first type of skill involves the ability to analyze personality and determine the forces which helped to make it what it is, distinguishing, so far as may be, between "original nature" and "acquired characteristics." The second calls for an interpretation of the social situation of which the client is a part, the persons with whom he associates, the groups to which he belongs, the institutions which he utilizes, the "social atmosphere" of the area in which he lives. It also includes the discovery of "social resources," personal, institutional, or material, which might be utilized in reorganizing his scheme of life. The third process includes almost everything which may enter into the give-and-take between two persons; it is what we mean by direct personal influence. The fourth includes influencing the client's associates, changing his physical surroundings, transplanting him to other localities and groups. The first two divisions in Miss Richmond's analysis cover the first interview, investigation, diagnosis and planning, as we have illustrated them in our summary of the Brown record. They include the assembling of pertinent information and its interpretation with reference to possible treatment.

The last two divisions have been described by Porter Lee as the "leadership" and the "executive" aspects of case work. In the case of the Brown family the "executive" phase of the task included the provision of material relief, arranging loans, guaranteeing bills, putting the client in touch with possible employers. In other situations it might involve the arranging of medical care, vacation outings, removal to new living quarters, connecting the client with settlement, club, playground, or church, transferring to a different school. The "leadership"

[7] Richmond, Mary, *What Is Social Case Work?* pp. 101-102.

phase of work with the Browns included encouraging the man, calming the woman, diverting their attention from doubtful solutions to possibilities they had not considered, helping them to "see themselves as others saw them." In other cases this might include helping a foreigner to understand American folkways, stimulating and training a slovenly housekeeper in more acceptable ways, mediating between persons in conflict especially by interpreting them to each other. Mr. Lee has called the first set of activities "the executive aspect of social treatment, because it involves chiefly the discovery of a particular resource and arranges for its use." He has called the second "the leadership aspect of treatment because it involves primarily not the use of other resources but the influence of the personality of the worker." [8]

Approaching the analysis of case work processes from the standpoint of the psychologist and the juvenile court official, Miriam Van Waters makes a rather different classification. To her the four most significant phases are (1) insight, (2) transference, (3) development of personality, (4) development of new social relationships. By "insight" is meant helping the client to understand himself, "to face himself consciously as a problem," knowing "that another has shared his emotional experiences without condemning him." "Transference" may mean rapport between the social worker and his client, or it may mean attachment to any new object of warm interest and affection. By "personality development" is meant helping the client to discover unexpected resources within himself, new skills, new ways of meeting responsibility, and the joy of success. "Development of new social relationships" means not only cultivating new attitudes and new rôles in groups to which the client already belongs, but helping him to find a place in other groups both small and large.[9]

Each of these analyses aids us in gaining a clearer notion of what the social case worker is doing. Some of their differences are little more than matters of terminology, but even terminology is significant. Out of these and other interpretations we have developed the following outline which has been

[8] Lee, Porter R., "A Study of Social Treatment," *Family,* 4: 191-199, 1923.
[9] Van Waters, Miriam, *Youth in Conflict,* Chap. VIII.

helpful to us in studying the many and varied activities of social case workers.

I. Diagnosis.
  1. Initial contacts with client and his problem.
  2. Inquiry or investigation—assembling pertinent information including data from other professions.
  3. Analysis and evaluation of evidence.
  4. Organization of information into a unified picture.
  5. Prognosis—estimate of possible outcomes.
  6. Planning.

II. Treatment.
  A. Direct personal influence.
    1. Action directed upon the client himself.
      *a.* Redirection of attention—suggestion.
      *b.* Interpretation of client and his situation to himself.
      *c.* Persuasion.
      *d.* Coercion.
    2. Action directed upon client's associates—similar to that directed upon the client himself.
  B. Indirect methods.
    1. Removal of client to new social and physical environment.
    2. Change of physical conditions in the client.
    3. Change of physical conditions in the environment.
    4. Arrangement for services by members of other professions.

**Diagnosis and Prognosis.** There was a time when the tasks of a case worker, if such he might be called, were two: investigation and relief-giving. The investigation combined a sort of detective work, to uncover the "fraudulent" applicant, with harsh questioning to drive away the "unworthy." But, as has already been pointed out, investigation today is only part of the larger task of understanding the client and his situation; and the understanding itself is sought only that there may be wise planning with the client and effective measures for the overcoming of his difficulties.

What are some of the things a case worker may need to know in order to serve his client adequately? First of all, he must start with the client's statement of his immediate trouble as he sees it. But this is quite certain to be an incomplete picture of the situation; it explains nothing and may be of doubtful accuracy. As soon as possible the case worker secures complete identification, including names, addresses, ages, birthplaces, and marriages within the immediate family. Then he delves into the past, seeking to learn how the person or family came to be where it is. He will be alert not merely to physical and mental traits which might possibly be inherited biologically, but especially to influences which molded habit patterns, character, and personality. While studying the personal and family history, he will be securing more detailed information about the present situation. He will try to find out about physical and mental health, income, occupation, work habits, leisure-time activities, home life, membership and participation in various groups, personal relationships, and so on.

Where can the case worker turn for all this information? Much of it will be given by the client and his immediate family. Some will come from more distant relatives, friends, employers, tradesmen, teachers, physicians, clergymen, official records of birth, marriage, death, arrest, *et cetera,* and records of private social agencies. Some will be revealed by quiet observation as the case worker comes and goes in home, neighborhood and workshop. Interviews, letters, records, and observation are the principal methods employed in getting the desired information from these manifold sources.

There is, of course, an unlimited amount of information that might be brought together concerning any human being. Must the social case worker keep on until he has learned "everything" about his client? If not, when and where shall he stop? It so happens that the volume of his work determines the practical answer to the first question. He is usually responsible for so many persons in trouble that he cannot possibly uncover more than a small fraction of the facts which enter into each client's history. Very often, therefore, he contents himself with whatever information happens to be most accessible. But the more careful case worker does not let the accident of circumstance alone determine what data he will assemble. He plans the investigation so that it may reveal events and conditions which are relevant to the problem in hand. He organizes his facts as they appear, seeking constantly for cause-and-effect relationships. He checks his interpretations by the plans for treatment which they suggest, and he checks his plans by the results actually obtained. As Mrs. Sheffield has put it, the case worker is concerned not only about "facts," but also about their "clue-aspects." He translates the ultimate fact-items in a case history into types of situations and conduct-patterns. These he then groups according to what appear to be causal relations. If the manipulation of certain factors in a "social fact group" result in desired changes, the case worker assumes that he has discovered the clue to the trouble.[10] We may say, therefore, that the difference between a story and a diagnosis is that the former is a narrative of more or less interesting events, while the latter is an analysis. The adequacy of information available about a client may be tested by attempting to reduce it to a characteristic or typical problem-situation and a sequence of significant events. A comparison of the following outline with Jessie Taft's excellent account of a delinquent girl will make the point clearer.[11]

*Symptom of Maladjustment:* Stealing.
*Type of Maladjustment:* Mother-daughter conflict.
*Sequence of Significant Events:*

1. Mother became pregnant contrary to expectation and wish—the child was not wanted.
2. Early contacts with mother were associated with pain.
    a. Breast-feeding was painful for mother, dreaded and cut short.
    b. Constipation made bowel movements an occasion for a contest between girl and parents.
3. Father did not become object of girl's affection.
    a. He was worried over loss of job.
    b. Mother nagged, scolded and humiliated him.
    c. Girl's crying, fussing over food and defecation acted as barriers.
4. Girl steadily concentrated attention on her own bodily functions and developed increasingly antagonistic attitude toward parents.
5. Girl became jealous of her healthier and more attractive brothers and sisters.
6. Girl teased, tormented and injured other children.
7. Always wanting something new, she was never satisfied, but lost interest as soon as she got what she was after.

[10] Sheffield, Ada E., *Case-Study Possibilities,* Chaps. I and IV.
[11] Taft, Jessie, "The Effect of an Unsatisfactory Mother-Daughter Relationship Upon the Development of a Personality." *Family,* 7: 10-17, 1926. Also available in Young, Kimball, *Source Book for Social Psychology,* pp. 363-374.

8. Asked questions about sex which embarrassed her mother and brought no adequate answer.
9. Whenever mother went to hospital for confinement, girl indulged in stealing.
10. Discussion of sex matters with social worker led to gloating over parents—she had discovered what they were trying to conceal from her.
11. But after this discussion the stealing stopped.

It must be evident from the foregoing that diagnosis and treatment are intimately bound up together. But one phase of the process, planning the treatment, is still to be discussed. No one today would question the proposition that the plan of treatment should rest very definitely on the analysis of the problem-situation. But there are still some case workers who forget, if they ever realized, that a successful plan can never be worked out by themselves without the cooperation of their clients. When someone's affairs have become tangled it is easy to assume that he is incompetent and offer him a ready-made course of action. Such procedure overlooks the fact that the experience of ordering his own affairs is sought by everyone, and that no real adjustment has been effected until the given person has his own situation in hand. This does not mean that social case workers blindly endorse every scheme proposed by their clients. They point out the advantages and disadvantages of various plans for achieving the purposes sought by the clients themselves. Sometimes they help a client to try out a plan which does not offer much prospect of success, and later help him to devise a more workable plan and carry it out. This was done when the family welfare society gave Mr. Brown a chance to see what he could do at clock repairing.

**Direct Personal Influence—The Interview.** Since a large part of the case worker's activities consists in making personal contacts and exerting personal influence, no study of his techniques can be complete without special attention to the interview. In 1925 the Chicago Chapter of the American Association of Social Workers created a committee to study case work interviews. In its records and analyses the Chicago group uses substantially the following outline: (1) purpose, physical setting, and approach to the client; (2) rapport—making friendly contacts by revealing one's interest, putting client at ease, using colloquial language, and the like; (3) coping with the client's attitudes by allowing release of emotions, meeting objections, reassurance, reasoning, contrasting plans, informing, compromising, and similar acts; (4) turning point or crisis in the conversation; (5) motivation—"inciting action" by appealing to prejudices, interest, ambitions, pride, ideals, sense of humor, clinching with definite suggestions, leaving something for client to do, or other expedients.[12] A similar group in Kansas City undertook a study of interviews using the following outline: (1) background, immediate occasion and setting of the interview; (2) physical acts of the parties to the interview including (a) verbal acts, i.e., the dialogue, and (b) non-verbal acts, i.e., major bodily movements, including gestures and other expressive movements; (3) mental acts or "thought processes" including (a) inferences, (b) objectives or purposes, (c) "other conscious thinking"; (4) subsequent events which indicate the significance of the interview.[13] Following is a condensed account of one of the interviews studied by the Kansas City committee.

*Background.* Mrs. A is old and pathetic. Of her family only a son and grandson are left. The son is of low-grade mentality, but not insane, and has been alcoholic for years. Mrs. A has suffered abuse beyond description at his hands, but bore with him patiently until it became necessary to send him to the State Hospital. At first she was shamed and grieved to the point of being irrational. As time went on she became more reasonable, and finally was quite happy to know that Frank was receiving good care. He is a cleaner and presser by trade and was put in the shop at the hospital. Last week Mrs. A realized that she had reconciled herself to his absence and expressed the hope that he might remain always.

*Occasion for Interview.* Shortly after having expressed greater happiness than she had known for years, Mrs. A received a letter from the hospital superintendent telling her that Frank is to be paroled, that the Family Welfare Society has been notified and that she is to cooperate in helping Frank make his adjustment.

[12] *Interviews,* A Study of the Methods of Analysing and Recording Social Case Work Interviews, p. 23.

[13] Queen, Stuart A., "Social Interaction in the Interview," *Social Forces,* 6: 545-558, 1928.

*Setting and Opening of Interview.* Mrs. A came to the office of the Family Welfare Society to talk with one of the visitors whom she had come to know rather well. After a short wait in an open hallway she was ushered into a small room simply furnished with desk, bookcase and chairs.

Mrs. A had been helping to care for a very sick client of the Society and had grown fond of her patient who she thought was improving. But today Mrs. A was visibly nervous and upset. She began to cry and spoke of the patient's weakened condition and suffering. Sympathy was expressed and the discussion kept on the patient long enough to let Mrs. A get control of herself. She presently introduced the topic which was undoubtedly on her mind from the beginning.

*Body of the Interview.* Mrs. A (gazing directly at the visitor, tears in her eyes, her voice quick, sharp and almost shrill), "Did you hear about Frank?"

Visitor (to herself), "Tact and kindness are going to be necessary because Mrs. A is usually hard to deal with on this subject. I must be on my guard, remembering that she is both sensitive and savage when under stress. I must help her to accept this as a fact and not an emotional disturbance." (Then aloud in ordinary conversational tone, calm and deliberate), "Yes, Mrs. A, I had a letter from Dr. P."

Mrs. A (her voice lower, slow and hesitant), "He will be home in a few days. Dr. P told me he wrote you."

Visitor (to herself), "Mrs. A evidently has not resented the contents of the doctor's letter. She wants advice, although she has not asked for it. I must assure her of my thoughtful interest and encourage her by building a hopeful plan." (Then with a smile, leaning slightly forward, speaking slowly and clearly), "I'm glad you have come this morning, because I've wanted to talk to you ever since Dr. P's letter came. I answered it and asked him to keep Frank until you and I could talk things over. He told me that he felt sure Frank was cured of alcoholism, but that he could make no guarantee about whether he would return to the old habit. Now, I've thought and thought about it and I've decided that we will have to make a definite plan to help him. One of the things I thought of is to get him a job so he will lose no time at all when he comes."

Mrs. A (sitting very stiff and erect), "Oh, but he can always get work. Why, there have been several men calling for him lately."

Visitor (to herself), "Mrs. A is trying to protect Frank even at the cost of his own good. Is she going to relapse into the stubborn person she is capable of being?" (Then, still leaning forward, smiling, speaking slowly and quietly), "Yes, I'm sure he can get work, but don't you think if we had a job promised by some employer who understands, it would help keep Frank away from the places where he could get liquor?"

Mrs. A (tears springing anew, leaning suddenly forward, speaking loudly and emphatically), "But I couldn't stand for anybody to know that he's been in the asylum."

Visitor (to herself), "I must ease Mrs. A's mind, calm her, and make her feel my sympathy. Then she will respond and do away with any thought of argument." (Still sitting quietly, a smile slowly coming over her face, hand out on desk, palm upward and open), "We'll explain, Mrs. A, that he has been in the hospital and has overcome his habit, and I'm sure if we are talking to the right man, he will be glad to do anything he can to encourage Frank. Who are some of his former employers?"

Mrs. A (speaking quickly, her voice becoming louder and firmer), "Oh, I forget, but I have some cards at home."

Visitor (to herself), "Mrs. A is not convinced until she starts to answer, and then she unconsciously decides to follow my suggestion. I'll not intimate to her that she has done anything unusual in responding without argument." (Continuing in ordinary conversational tone), "Do you know any of them yourself? Would he be able to get a drink from them?"

Mrs. A (now relaxed, speaking calmly and deliberately), "I knew one place where he was paid in liquor, but I think the others are all right."

Visitor (to herself), "Mrs. A is interested in the plan and is relieved. She has ceased to be emotional and is more rational than usual in crisis. I must win her completely, if possible." (Then looking directly at Mrs. A, smiling, with a nod of the head, and speaking in louder tone), "Don't *you* think it would be best to talk to his employer and be honest about things so he can help?"

Mrs. A (clearly and almost emphatically), "Yes, I guess it would. Frank has always been so ashamed when he had to go to Leeds or General Hospital and never wanted his boss to know it, but I would ask him if he wasn't more ashamed of getting drunk."

Visitor (to herself), "Mrs. A has won a battle with herself. She has granted a point on intelligent reasoning and not on emotion. She is really taking me into her confidence. But I mustn't give her a chance to change her mind." (Then with direct gaze, speaking emphatically but not harshly), "Will you bring the cards over to Mrs. W's tomorrow so we can get them, and call at the different places? I told Dr. P we would take care of it this week."

Mrs. A (nodding her head, dropping into a low, pleading tone of voice, leans over with new tears welling up in her eyes; clasps her hands together and rests them on the desk while awaiting an answer to her question), "Yes, or I'll bring them here. But you promise, don't you, that you will say 'hospital' and not 'insane asylum'?"

Visitor (to herself), "Mrs. A is eager to help carry out the plan, but is suddenly confronted again by fear of Frank's displeasure." (Then smiling, with gentle voice, but loud and clear enough to leave no possibility of misunderstanding), "Yes, of course, because it is a hospital and Frank is not insane."

Mrs. A sat up and smiled quietly. The visitor felt that a perfect understanding had been reached and they were now ready for the next topic.

Of course, the case worker was not alone in having "asides," but since it is her account of the interview and not Mrs. A's that is available for us, we can only guess what was going on in the client's mind.

**"Executive" Aspects of Case Work.** Because this is the phase of social treatment with which most people are familiar, being mistaken by some for the whole task, we need add very little to what has been said above. The case worker always has in his head or in his card catalogue a list of community resources to which he may turn for help in solving his client's problems. Sometimes the client does not even know of their existence, at other times he is diffident about making use of them. Perhaps the client is a woman with young children and no one with whom she can leave them while she goes to a clinic or hospital; perhaps it is a crippled child who has difficulty in going to and from school; perhaps it is a stranger in the city who does not know where to look for work or where to find a suitable place to live. All these represent opportunities for service of the "executive" type, as contrasted with the direct personal influence. Such service may include providing transportation, guiding through the mazes of a large dispensary, finding someone to care for children, introducing to possible employers, arranging credit, as well as giving direct material relief.

**Case Recording.** Early in the development of social case work it was found helpful to keep memoranda of various sorts. For a long time these consisted of little more than lists of names and jottings of relief disbursed. Later there were added identifying facts about clients and something of their stories to show that the agency was helping the "worthy poor." By the 'nineties some agencies were writing fuller accounts of their clients' backgrounds and the progress of treatment. Today the better case working agencies in all fields have still more complete records, though they are not necessarily longer than those of a generation ago. There is usually a "face card" on which appear in simple, tabular form identifying facts, relatively basic, permanent data, and material for statistical summaries. Some agencies have another blank for medical reports. If they give relief, they have a budget sheet. Always there is a more or less chronological narrative. Frequently the correspondence is filed with it. Finally, there are summaries, digests of significant facts and their interpretation.

Why should busy case workers bother to write all this out? Should they not spend their time actually seeing people and doing something for them? The answer is that the busier they are, the more essential it is to keep adequate records. When a visitor is trying to help straighten out the affairs of 50 to 100 families or separate persons, he cannot possibly carry all the pertinent facts in his head. But not only are records an aid to the memory of the present case worker; they are still more important if the responsibility has to be transferred to another visitor in the same or a cooperating agency. The record further spares the client the trouble of re-telling his story and it greatly facilitates supervision of the case worker. Incidentally the preparation of systematic records stimulates the worker to more critical thinking. Beyond these immediate functions, the case record has more far-reaching values. It may be a basis for judging the work of an agency, or for standardizing the work of a group of agencies. Still more important, the facts which may be derived from a study of many records constitute an index of general social needs. That is, they are at once data for social research and guides to new legislation.

The vital place which record writing holds in modern case work has been forcefully expressed by Mrs. Sheffield. "It is not too much to say that a case work agency that keeps poor records is giving ineffective or superficial treatment to its clients." [14]

[14] Sheffield, Ada E., *The Social Case History*, p. 13.

**Varieties of Social Case Work.** Our discussion assumes that social case work represents a point of view, a fund of information, and certain skills which are equally valuable in a number of fields. In the chapters that follow we shall see how it varies, and yet how similar it is, (1) in family welfare work, whether carried on by family welfare societies, boards of public welfare, or courts of domestic relations; (2) in child welfare work, whether conducted by children's aid societies, visiting teachers, societies for the prevention of cruelty to children, or juvenile courts; (3) in hospital social service; (4) in psychiatric social work; (5) in probation and parole; and (6) in vocational guidance and placement. So far as we can see, it is as legitimate to regard these as special branches of social case work as it is to regard pediatrics, obstetrics, laryngology, and surgery as branches of medicine. The reader may form his own judgment on this question after studying these various types in turn.

# CHAPTER XIX

## FAMILY WELFARE WORK

Social case work first developed in the field of service to needy families. But even while the attention was centered upon economic problems there was growing up a program of personal service with emphasis upon the building of character and family solidarity. In its development this type of social work may be said to have passed through four stages. The first was that of indiscriminate almsgiving, with little concern about the specific needs of applicants or the results of giving them aid. The second was that of niggardly relief, in which it was made hard for anyone to secure assistance; the assumption being that the major functions of "charity agents" were to guard against pauperizing the needy and to keep expenses down. The third stage was that of relief with a plan, in which budget-making, employment service and thrift were schemes introduced with the hope of making dependent families self-supporting. The fourth stage has not yet been reached by all of the agencies that serve families in trouble. It is that of developing personality and promoting family integrity, using material relief as only one of many means for gaining these ends. Today in a growing number of family service agencies material relief plays about the same rôle that drugs do in the practise of medicine. The agency that helped the Brown family [1] had reached stage four. So too had the society that helped the Walters over a series of crises.

### WALTERS [2]

*First Contacts.* In April 1922 Mrs. Walters came to the office of a Family Welfare Society asking help in finding work for

[1] See Chap. XVIII.

[2] Summary of a record in the files of a family welfare society. This same case was summarized in 1924 by Queen and Mann in *Social Pathology*, pp. 475-479; and again in 1926 by Walter W. Whitson in *Proceedings of the National Conference of Social Work*, pp. 290-295. The present analysis was made by one of the authors in 1928.

her husband. She said that her five-year-old daughter had died the week before; they were in debt to the undertaker and landlord, but asked nothing except work for Mr. Walters.

A visit to the home revealed more about the family situation. Mr. Walters was formerly a coal miner, but since moving to the city he had been doing factory work. Not feeling well he had given this up and was canvassing, though with little success. Amy, the oldest daughter, was a stenographer earning $10.00 a week, part of which she gave her mother for household expenses. Frank, aged 14, had been helping his father, but was now working as delivery boy and contributing a little to the family income. There were three younger girls, two of them attending public school. Because the workers in the Family Welfare Society were busy and because the Walters family presently found it possible to get along without any assistance, little was done until the following December.

Then the family was reported as needing food and fuel. On visiting the home the case worker found a more complicated situation. Mr. Walters was too ill to work at all; he coughed a great deal; his wife said he was afraid to see a physician lest he be pronounced tuberculous. Amy had married and no longer contributed to the family income. Frank was attending part-time school and working in a garage; he earned $8.00 a week, $4.00 of which he turned over to his mother. Mrs. Walters was carrying out ashes for a neighbor, in return for which she was given some fine coal. The whole atmosphere of the home was one of worry and discouragement.

*Further Inquiry.* Through further interviews with members of the family, calls on various persons and special examinations, much additional information was secured. The visitor talked to neighbors, teachers, employers, a landlady, and relatives. She arranged for medical examinations of several members of the family and a psychological examination of Lucy, the twelve-year-old girl. From these various sources she was able to characterize the family as follows:

Mr. Walters, a man of 46, was a hard drinker and had tuberculosis. His teeth were bad and later were all extracted. When sober he was kind to his family, but when under the influence of liquor was disagreeable and quarrelsome. Moreover, he assumed little responsibility in the home, leaving most of the burden to his wife. At the sanatorium, to which he was later sent, he was regarded as the laziest man they ever saw,—perfectly content to sit around day after day just smoking and grumbling about things in general.

Mrs. Walters, aged 39, was a small, quiet person with a tired, worried look. Like her husband she had been reared in the rural South and had very little schooling. They had married when she was only 15. Mrs. Walters was friendly and seemed willing to work, but could not do much, for she was five months pregnant. Everyone said that she was hard-working and "very deserving." She was ambitious for her children, but too indulgent for their good. As one neighbor put it, "she made a door mat of herself for the children." Mrs. Walters also presented a number of health problems including goiter, a bad heart, and pyorrhea.

The two oldest children had married and left home. The daughter returned occasionally to help her parents. The son was an unstable person, an irregular worker and deserter, whose wife presently secured a divorce. After this he was an intermittent member of his parents' household, and when his father was killed in an accident he was helpful in many ways. Amy's marriage left at home the four younger children, to whom was added shortly a new baby girl.

Frank, aged 14, had dropped out of school and was working without an employment certificate, but he later met the legal requirements of attendance on part-time school and part-time work with a permit. He was surly in the home, disrespectful to his mother, rough and unkind to his sisters. Frank resented the very presence in the home of Emily, whose "sniffles" were a special grievance. His mother had pampered him in the effort to avoid friction. She let the younger children sleep until he left the house and gave them their supper before his return in the evening. Frank had also puzzled his teachers. Two of them said he was sullen, never voluntarily speaking or responding to their greetings.

Lucy, the twelve-year-old, was small and not very rugged, but pretty, sweet-mannered and refined, bright and ambitious. A psychological examination showed an Intelligence Quotient of 117. She was a freshman in high school taking a business course. Later Lucy had appendicitis. But her great grievance was about her clothes.

Emily, aged 10, was small and quite thin. She was later found to have tuberculosis and spent several months in a sanatorium. Like her sister, Emily was bright and stood well in her classes. Fanny, the three-year-old, was plump, active and very bright. Kathleen, the seven-months baby, was very tiny, but doubled her weight in 10 months.

In addition to their own children, the Walters had living with them at various times a niece and two nephews. Mrs. Walters had three brothers, one living in the city and willing to help as much as possible. The other two were miners, with small incomes and large families, living at some distance.

*Diagnosis.* The most pressing problem had to do with Mr. Walters' health. How was he to be induced to have a thorough medical examination and accept the treatment which this might indicate? Whatever the methods may have been, he was persuaded to go to a clinic and later to a sanatorium for tuberculosis. Other health problems included Emily's tuberculosis, Mrs. Walters' cardiac disorder, pyorrhea, and goiter, and later a number of cases of acute illness and accident.

As to mental health, no disorder was apparent and no subnormality. On the contrary, the Walters family seemed to have superior ability, though it was only in Lucy's case that this was verified.

Economic problems appeared intermittently for several years. At the outset there was need of food and fuel. As soon as Mr. Walters' condition was definitely known there was the question of how to finance the family while he was in the sanatorium. Plainly Mrs. Walters could not earn much for a long time. With only Frank working, there had to be some material relief until the others could contribute to the family income. Several times in the next six years the Walters became self-supporting, each time to be checked by some new crisis—unemployment, sickness or death.

But that which made this case peculiarly one for a family welfare society was the fact that the morale of the Walters family was seriously threatened. Mr. Walters had not been carrying his share of responsibility. He saw the family grow larger without doing anything to meet the added burden. He loafed and drank; he quarrelled with his son Frank. As a natural consequence his wife was tired, worried and discouraged. Frank had become rebellious, making excessive demands upon his mother, complaining about his sisters. The younger girls were "spoiled." All in all, the unity of the family as a group was seriously menaced. There was friction, mostly latent, but some in the open. There was lack of family pride and enthusiasm and a sense of having lost control of the situation. Baffled and discouraged by circumstances that seemed too much for them, their morale was well-nigh broken.

Also their relations with outsiders were not altogether satisfactory. No one had much use for Mr. Walters, though many felt sorry for his wife. Frank was sullen and unresponsive at school. The older children seemed to regard their marriages as a form of emancipation and thereafter accepted relatively little responsibility for the family situation.

*Cooperation Secured and Arrangements Made.* After providing emergency relief in the form of groceries and milk, the first step in treatment was to report Mr. Walters to the Anti-tuberculosis Society. A visiting nurse was able to persuade him to go to a clinic for examination and the physician who made the diagnosis of tuberculosis arranged his admission to the sanatorium. A Y. W. C. A. worker interested Lucy in the Girl Reserves, a visiting teacher secured a scholarship for her. With this and other assistance she was enabled to finish high school and secure a clerical position in a business office. City physicians and the Municipal Hospital were utilized repeatedly in time of sickness and accident. A dental college gave examinations and cared for the teeth of several members of the family. Relatives were informed of circumstances and asked to help in times of special need. They gave some money and cared for the smaller children while Mrs. Walters was in the hospital. Grocers were consulted with reference to extending credit. When Frank proposed that they buy a home on installments the visitor took a realtor out to look over the property and to advise concerning the plan of purchase. She also helped the members of the family to find employment at various times. Perhaps her most important service in this connection was performed when she persuaded the superintendent of the Tuberculosis Sanatorium to employ Mr. Walters as janitor at $50 a month and board.

The Family Welfare Society gave material relief intermittently for several years. This was mostly in the form of grocery orders, milk tickets and coal. Through a church, the Mayor's Christmas Tree, and various benevolent individuals, clothing, toys, house furnishings, and food were given.

*Direct Personal Influence.* But the visitor who gave most attention to the Walters family did not stop with the "executive" side of the task. She repeatedly brought her personal influence directly to bear upon the more intimate and difficult problems of social relationships. When Mr. Walters was well enough to work the visitor not only intervened with the superintendent on his behalf, but induced him to remain at the sanatorium as an employe in order to stay away from liquor and otherwise guard his health. When he failed to turn over a reasonable share of his earnings to the family she appealed to him to give his wife $40 a month. She both talked to him and wrote him a letter which included the following paragraph:

"I will continue to visit in the home and help Mrs. Walters plan so that she can make ends meet. You have a fine wife and lovely children, of whom I am sure you are justly proud. And now that you are getting well and will soon be strong again, you will be able to assist your family better than you have in the past, I am sure."

Mr. Walters' response was immediate and permanent. The visitor taught Mrs. Walters how to make a budget, keep accounts and organize her housework. She was glad to learn and expressed her gratitude for this help.

Frank was a more serious problem, but with the aid of teachers and his mother the visitor appealed to the boy to be more helpful about the home and avoid friction with his sisters. How she did it we are not sure, but he was induced to clean up the yard and plant a garden. Some time later when he drew his weekly pay he invited the whole family to go with him to the movies. The following year the company for which he was working transferred Frank to another city. For a time he did not send much money home and his mother had a hard time to make ends meet. The visitor wrote him a long letter complimenting him on his advancement, discussing the family situation, and offering to do anything she could for him. This brought the desired response and tided the family over the immediate crisis.

When Mrs. Walters was troubled because Lucy wanted better clothes than they could afford, the visitor talked to the girl and went with her to do her shopping. She helped Lucy to choose garments that were both attractive and durable and evidently won her confidence and gratitude.

Many times Mrs. Walters came to the visitor for advice about some problem. One time it was the question of buying a home, another time about birth control. She counted on the visitor for wise counsel, yet she was gaining in the ability to manage her own affairs.

*Results Observed.* Several times during the past six years the affairs of the Walters family have seemed to be in pretty good shape. Then some new crisis would appear and new adjustments had to be made. On the health side Mr. Walters made such gains that he was able to hold a steady job as janitor until he was struck by an automobile and killed in 1926. Emily's tuberculosis was likewise arrested. On the whole the remaining members of the family are in good health at the present time.

Economically the family has been self-supporting much of the time. Mrs. Walters and the older children have had fairly regular employment and have usually managed to pay their bills, besides starting to buy a home. At various times, however, they have had to receive assistance; for example, when the divorced son ceased paying his board, when Lucy and Frank married, and when Mrs. Walters' foot was injured.

But the greatest gains have been those of personality and family solidarity. Mrs. Walters is no longer bewildered and discouraged; she is always ready with a plan, no matter what happens. She keeps the family on a budget and organizes her work carefully. Some time ago she remarked that she had "never before been so comfortable and felt so encouraged about the future." Frank would never be recognized as the sullen, quarrelsome boy of six years ago. Until his marriage a short time ago he provided a large part of the income, helped his mother in the home and was a real brother to the other children. Lucy's ups and downs were never very serious; she is now married and has a home of her own. But Emily has recently become rebellious. She wants more money to spend on herself and goes joy-riding with doubtful companions.

The real tests of family solidarity have been such crises as Mr. Walters' death and the withdrawal of financial aid when one after another the children married and established homes of their own. Most of these difficult situations they met without asking for outside assistance or giving up their home. Sometimes the long series of troubles seems pretty hard to bear, but usually Mrs. Walters and the children who remain at home pull themselves together and face the situation with courage.

**The Philosophy of Family Social Work.** Social workers have at various times and places set forth the philosophy which underlies their efforts on behalf of the family.[3] They point to the changes in family life which have come about since the Industrial Revolution—removal from the home of such processes as laundering, baking, and sewing, outside employment of women, living in close apartments, and separate interests for the various members of the family. While others have questioned the necessity of the family and talked of its possible disappearance, social workers have usually regarded it as inevitable, fixed in the habits of the race. A few years ago they undertook to define "the normal family" in order that they might measure and treat deviations from the standard. But today they are getting away from the conception of a uniform goal and "have a growing appreciation of the fact that families are not all cast in the same mould any more than individuals are, and that a certain amount of deviation makes for progress."

One of the most interesting statements of the presuppositions of family social work has been made by Frank J. Bruno.[4] As he puts it, every social institution "has a function, or more accurately, functions; and, in addition, individuals are induced to participate in these social institutions by a variety of motives, which may or may not lead the individual to act in harmony with the function of the institution." Indeed, "one of the causes of the crises in social institutions today, and one which accounts for the rise of social work, is that the auto-

[3] See, *e.g.*, Brisley, Mary S., "Family Achievement," *Family,* 9: 167-174; Colcord, Joanna C., "The Fabric of Family Life," *Family,* 5: 172-175; de Schweinitz, Karl, "The Cultivation of Family Life," *Family,* 5: 195-199; O'Grady, John, *An Introduction to Social Work,* Chap. II; Rich, Margaret E. (editor), *Family Life Today.*

[4] Bruno, Frank J., "Family Social Work," *Family,* 6: 141-145.

matically acting motives, which the long history of the race selected into its behavior for their survival values, but without the conscious and intelligent cooperation of individuals, are gradually breaking down in the destruction of the simpler homogeneous communities of our ancestors." Applying this generalization to the family, it appears that its function is "to act as a vehicle for the transference of social heritages." "Biologically it is not necessary. Economically it has serious disadvantages—for the woman at least. . . . For the permanent monogamous family there is little need in hygiene, psychiatry or psychology." It has been "selected into our psycho-social environment because of its social survival value when tested by society's need to preserve its gains—its social heritage." But "when we compare this quite clearly defined function of the family with the motives which lead to participation in the institution, the source of much serious conflict is at once apparent. Affection, passion, economic support, economic advantage, social prestige—these and other motives lead to the formation of families. It must be apparent that some of these motives have little reference to the function of the family, and some of them are directly antagonistic." The task of social workers is, from this standpoint, one of reconciling motives and functions. More accurately, perhaps, it is the problem of finding how to reach apparently opposite goals.

A complementary statement has been made by Gertrude Vaile.[5] The family is the agency not only for passing on the cultural heritage of the race but also for training each new individual in the art of living with other people. "The family is the primary social grouping, necessary alike for the development of the well-rounded individual and the true society. It is the first, the strongest, the most intimate grouping. . . . There is the interdependence of members of varying strength and needs. There is developed the first group consciousness. There, if the family life is sound, are rooted all the qualities of mutual consideration and mutual aid that are needed to make a noble society out in the world, and practised on a scale that can teach a little child or demand the highest powers of a grown-up."

[5] Vaile, Gertrude, "Our Interpretation of the True Place of Family Life," *Family*, 4: 153-155.

With such conceptions in mind a committee of the American Association for Organizing Family Social Work has defined the content of its field as follows: "Family case work deals with the social needs of individuals as parts of family groups, and the adjustment of their relation to these groups and to society." The functions of the family are frequently threatened by such maladjustments as arise from physical and mental ills, bad habits, legal entanglements, resourcelessness, unfavorable industrial conditions, lack of decent housing facilities, and other adverse influences. Whenever such maladjustments occur there is a problem for the family welfare worker. Now "the goals of family case work are not only the elimination of the evils and resulting maladjustments threatening the family but the development of each individual member of the family to his highest possibilities, and the satisfactory functioning of the family as a group." [6]

However, since the appearance of many varieties of social case work, there are some who say that this philosophy of the family belongs as much to one type as to another. In fact, they challenge the family case workers to show that they have any particular function at all. Children's agents, probation officers, medical social workers, visiting teachers, and all the rest are interested in the family as an institution and as a social group. Each of them has a distinctive task, but all are contributing to the development of family life. What then is there left to comprise family case work? There are three possible answers to this question which Mary Richmond discussed most interestingly at the Providence meetings in 1922.[7] The first is that, after all is said and done, family case work consists merely in the odds and ends that are left over by the several specialties. The second is that the family case worker is the general practitioner of the social service field, offering an all-round service and making use of specialists as occasion demands. The third is that the family welfare society is a specialist itself, with a definite function to perform. "This function, briefly stated, is to think of the life of each family as a whole

[6] *Content of Family Social Work,* Amer. Assn. for Org. Fam. Soc. Work, Quarterly Bulletin, June, 1926.

[7] Richmond, Mary E., "Some Relations of Family Case Work to Social Progress," *Family,* 3: 99-104.

and to treat it as a whole." Perhaps there is some truth in each of these answers, for while the third statement defines the central and most characteristic aspect of family social work, it is also true that the person in this field must often be a general practitioner, and as a matter of hard necessity must often attend to the odds and ends which might well be handled by someone else.

**The Place of Relief-Giving.** Because the agencies in which family social work developed have been historically associated with the giving of material relief, and because this still constitutes an important part of their work, it is necessary to consider in more detail just what is the place of relief-giving in this field.

It is a curious paradox that during the years when there was a fairly steady decrease in the attention to economic problems and in the percentage of families receiving material aid, the total volume of relief was increasing.[8] In the 'nineties it appears that almost every family served by the charity organization societies received material relief. But in 1927 forty-two family welfare societies reported an average of 19,000 families receiving financial assistance out of an average total of 46,000 active major care cases a month. In other words, material aid was given to only two-fifths of all the families for which the organizations had accepted responsibility for carrying through the typical case work processes of diagnosis and treatment. Over against this is the fact of an increasing bill for relief. Figures for 96 family agencies show that they were spending three times as much for material relief in 1926 as they were in 1916. After allowing for increasing population and a higher cost of living we find the most significant fact to be a fifty per cent increase in the average amount given to each relief family. What has brought this about?

First of all, there have been important changes in social workers' views of relief and their methods of handling it. Formerly the policy was one of "supplying fuel when the fuel

[8] Dawson, John B., "The Significance of the Rise in Relief-Giving During the Past Five Years," *Nat. Conf. Soc. Work,* 1922: 228-236; Lynde, Edward D., "The Significance of Changing Methods in Relief Giving," *Family,* 8: 135-144, 1927; Hurlin, Ralph G., "Some Results of Two Years' Study of Family Case Work Statistics," *Nat. Conf. Soc. Work,* 1928: 245-257.

bin is empty, clothing when the family is more or less in rags, and incidentals—when we must." This era was followed by one in which family budgets came into general use. But "earlier budgets took care of food adequately and that is about all they did. Fuel most inadequately, clothing by accident, incidentals though included never analyzed and practically negligible." It is only recently that cost-of-living studies have been utilized as a basis of budget-making and of measuring the adequacy of relief. Now "an honest attempt is made in most societies to estimate, not the indispensable minimum on which subsistence can be maintained, but a budget which permits the family to function normally among other families in the community." [9] This change in policy has been questioned by some of those who help to finance social work, their minds still being bound by the old principle of "less eligibility." So a study was undertaken in Chicago to determine the relation of the Council of Social Agencies' standard budget to the actual plane of living enjoyed by unskilled wage earners. Detailed information was secured about 467 families, of whom one-half were found living below the level set by the standard budget and one-half at or above this level.[10] But in general the fact that some relief families have more food and clothing than other families which receive no relief does not worry social workers as it would have fifteen or twenty years ago. The reason is that material assistance is now regarded as one of the means of setting a family on its own feet and preparing it to meet future crises with courage and resourcefulness.

Another change of policy in some agencies has been the limitation of intake to families that require financial assistance and the dropping of cases which do not present economic distress. While this is a reversal of the trend of a quarter of a century, it has been necessitated by rising case loads and limited funds. For example, the Cleveland Associated Charities, beginning about 1924, dropped many families which did not require relief and gave more attention to those homes into which money was being put. Better case work resulted and soon a

[9] Colcord, Joanna C., "Relief," *Family*, 4: 13-17, 1923.
[10] Houghteling, Leila, *The Income and Standard of Living of Unskilled Wage Earners in Chicago.*

goodly number of the relief families ceased to need material aid.

Other reasons suggested for the increasing bill for relief are these: (1) it is not so disagreeable to ask help of a social agency as was once the case, (2) the entire population has a higher standard of living which manifests itself both in the requests made and in the willingness to grant them, (3) the community chest movement has given wide publicity to the existence of relief funds, (4) not a few persons regard their contributions to the chest as a sort of insurance against all misfortunes and a warrant for asking help in time of trouble, (5) a family welfare society in a chest city is not free to drop a client for lack of cooperation. Apparently many factors are involved in the rising cost of relief.

In days gone by social workers were often fearful lest their clients be pauperized by unnecessary extension of relief. Today they are still concerned about the possible effects of material aid, but in a somewhat different way. They are beginning to realize that many of the results previously attributed to financial assistance were really due to experiences in the client's early life, and that financial dependency is only one phase of a more inclusive dependency. Taking a cue from the psychiatrists they are coming to regard this as primarily emotional rather than economic. "There are few of us in any walk of life who are not to some degree emotionally dependent, even at the height of our adult achievement." Hence "chronic dependency is a potential in every case, but the emotional dependency from which it derives does not begin with financial dependency nor does it originate in relief." [11] Dr. Schumacher has divided those whom a previous generation would have called pauperized into three types: (1) those who have suffered a suppression or starvation chiefly of the self-regarding tendencies, (2) those who have rebelled against authority but who in that rebellion have not succeeded in establishing their own independence, and (3) those who are definitely neurotic. "It is only in the very exceptional case, if at all, that it can be said that relief is the fundamental or primary cause of the dependence the family

[11] Marcus, Grace, "Social Attitudes as They Are Affected by Financial Dependency and Relief-Giving," *Family*, 9: 135-140.

shows." [12] All this is, of course, no warrant for a return to lax administration of material aid. It is simply part of the effort to understand the possibilities and the limitations of relief in order that it may be used to the best advantage.

**Agencies Doing Family Social Work.** There are three major groups of agencies whose chief function is family welfare work. First are the private, non-sectarian agencies, including the family welfare societies which grew out of the old charity organization societies, the American Red Cross, and the International Institutes. The second group embraces a number of sectarian agencies, especially Catholic and Jewish. Third are the public, tax supported agencies, including outdoor relief departments, mothers' pension bureaus and courts of domestic relations. The American Association of Social Workers reported in 1926 that there were approximately 1,150 family service agencies in the United States distributed as follows: [13]

| | |
|---|---|
| Family welfare societies (members of the Amer. Assn. for Org. Fam. Soc. Work) | 313 |
| American Red Cross chapters | 531 |
| Catholic charities | 58 |
| Jewish organizations | 57 |
| International institutes of Y. W. C. A. | 40 |
| Public agencies | 144 |
| | 1,143 |

A family welfare society consists theoretically of a membership including all who subscribe to its principles or to its budget. Actually most of these societies have no well defined membership and control is therefore vested in a board of directors which is practically self-continuing. The board usually decides important questions of policy and chooses the executive officer who is commonly called secretary or superintendent. The executive then selects the members of the staff, subject sometimes to approval of the board. The staff includes case workers who actually deal with family problems first hand, district secretaries or supervisors, a clerical force, and some-

[12] Schumaker, Henry C., "Personality and Its Development as It Is Affected by Financial Dependency and Relief-Giving," *Family*, 9: 140-144.
[13] *Vocational Aspects of Family Social Work*, p. 25.

times special workers in the fields of dietetics or psychiatry. In large cities the area is districted, a group of workers being assigned to a definite territory. About itself the paid (and presumably trained) staff gathers a number of unpaid volunteers who render various types of service under the direction of the regular workers. Each district usually has a conference or committee that meets weekly, bi-weekly, or monthly, to consider specific cases and general problems which aries in connection with the work. About 250 of these societies have united in maintaining a national office to coordinate their efforts and raise their standards. The American Association for Organizing Family Social Work serves its constituent agencies by field visits, local and national conferences, personnel service, a four weeks' institute each year, committees, special studies and publications. Of its publications the most important are probably *The Family,* a magazine which appears ten times a year, and the annual *Directory of Family Social Work Societies in the United States and Canada.*

The Red Cross differs from the agencies just described in several respects. First, it is organized from the top down, i.e., the national office established the locals. Second, it exists primarily for relief in time of war and of major disaster, such as flood, tornado, earthquake, or fire. During the recent War a chapter was organized in nearly every county in the United States, especially for the purpose of helping families of men who had entered the army or navy. After the War was over many of the chapters continued to be active in helping ex-service men readjust themselves. Also in many small towns and rural districts, because there was no other agency available to carry on family welfare work, and because the need of such service had been demonstrated during the War, the chapters received permission from the national office to undertake a general case work program. In 1926 there were over 750 Red Cross chapters having paid secretaries and about 540 of these had been authorized to carry on family case work for the general population.

The International Institutes are branch units of the Young Women's Christian Associations. "Their aim is to aid foreign-born people and their 'second-generation' children through the many crises which beset the life of groups thrown out of their own natural social anchorage."

As we saw in the introductory chapters, the Catholic Church has long engaged in charitable activities of many kinds. In the United States until recently it has depended largely on the regular parish machinery and on such institutions as orphanages, old people's homes, and hospitals. But since 1910 various dioceses have organized central bureaus of Catholic charities "to satisfy the need for trained personnel in family service, to coordinate and improve the work of existing organizations, and to develop a unified and systematic program of social service." These diocesan agencies look for leadership to the National Conference of Catholic Charities and to the Department of Social Action of the National Catholic Welfare Conference. Their "house organ" is the *Catholic Charities Review.*

For over a century there have been organizations for social work with Jewish families. These agencies today are organized and maintained very much as are the family welfare societies described above, except that they are organizations of, by, and for Jewish people. Some of them do exclusively family welfare work, others are federations in which there is a family case work department, and a few are doing generalized or undifferentiated case work. National contacts are maintained through the National Conference of Jewish Social Service which holds annual meetings and publishes the *Jewish Social Service Quarterly.*

American outdoor relief has been modelled quite directly upon the English Poor Law. Economic distress is still the chief object of attention, deterrence is emphasized, and the work is largely handled by persons without any training or other special municipalities have employed trained case workers who are qualifications for the task. However, over 100 counties and doing genuine family social work. Sometimes they are called overseers of the poor, sometimes superintendents of public welfare, sometimes county agents. In a number of states their work is supervised by a state department.

Mothers' pensions, which have spread rapidly over the United States since 1911, are variously administered, some by juvenile courts, some by county or municipal boards, some by the outdoor relief agency, and some by state departments. As the realization grows that bereaved families often need more than financial assistance, the term "mothers' aid" takes the place of "mothers' pensions," and mere cash allowances are absorbed into a larger program of family service. The American Association of Social Workers has estimated that sixty of these agencies have reached this point in their development.

Scattered jurisdiction over matters affecting the family has given rise in a number of large cities to at least a partial centralization of cases having to do with divorce, desertion, nonsupport, custody of children, and related problems. The organization of these courts of domestic relations, or family courts, differs so greatly from city to city that it is difficult to generalize concerning them. But an essential part of their make-up is a probation department with a staff of trained case workers who make investigations, undertake reconciliations, supervise the carrying out of judicial decisions, and do almost everything that goes to make up family social work.

**Inter-Agency Relations.** We have already seen how family agencies of several types work together through national organizations. One of the important results of national integration has been the development of inter-city cooperation. The mobility of the American people is becoming so great that it is rare indeed that all the sources of understanding and assistance for a client can be found in one local area. In order to serve a family wisely it is often necessary to get in touch with relatives, friends, former employers, and public officials in half a dozen localities. Hence members of the American Association for Organizing Family Social Work are pledged to answer inquiries from similar societies in other cities. When information is desired from a place in which there is no family welfare agency, use is made of a "forwarding center," one organization in each state undertaking to keep a list of correspondents in all towns which have no family society and to forward inquiries and secure replies from these correspondents.

In a great many cities, the local family welfare societies cooperate with each other and with other social agencies through a council of social agencies, a piece of social machinery described more fully in Chapter XXXI. As regards family welfare work, such a council deals with problems of division of labor, transfer of cases, and other matters of common interest. On the whole it can be safely said that no fundamental principles have yet been developed affecting the division of labor between public and private or sectarian and non-sectarian agencies. However, as a matter of common practice, Jewish families are referred to a Jewish agency wherever one exists; emergency cases are sometimes handled by private organizations, leaving the long-time work to a public department; sometimes this is reversed; tax-supported agencies usually decline to accept responsibility for non-residents.

One important device for inter-agency team-work, the social service exchange, was long ago developed by the charity organization societies. This is an office in which are kept cards showing names, addresses, other identifying data concerning clients, and the names of agencies inquiring about them, with dates. By calling the exchange a worker can quickly discover whether any other organization is dealing with a given family or has served it in the past. If another agency is involved, the essential facts of its relation to the client are secured by direct contact with the organization itself. This makes it easier to guard against working at cross purposes and enables the visitors in different societies to unite in a common plan for promoting the interests of their clients. It makes available for the worker whose contact with the case is newest a fund of information which may have been difficult to assemble. It also spares the client re-telling a story which may not be easy or pleasant to rehearse. All reputable case working agencies, whether in the family field or any other, use the social service exchange if one exists.

The social service exchange is, of course, of value chiefly to the organizations in a given locality. Another device, known as the Transportation Agreement, has as its purpose the promotion of intercity cooperation. In 1928 over 800 agencies signed an agreement to abide by the following rules pertaining to persons asking for transportation to other localities. The agency to which application is made shall satisfy itself by adequate and reliable evidence that: "(1) the prospects of the applicant in opportunities for normal living are not decreased by sending him to the proposed destination; (2) the applicant (a) will have such resources for maintenance at the point of destination as will save him from becoming dependent on relief from an agency, public or private, or (b) is a proper charge upon the agencies there, or (c) has legal residence there." The Agency shall make (3) "reasonable effort to obtain from an appropriate agency at the proposed destination a report as to the facts included in Rules 1 and 2; (4) provision for the applicant through to the ultimate destination which has been determined by the sender." It will be observed that the principles here set forth are very different from those involved in the old settlement laws, which sought to lighten the burden of the community rather than to promote the welfare of the client. The idea was first worked out by the National Conference of Jewish Social Service in 1900; it was developed by other agencies through a committee of the National Conference of Charities and Correction in 1902; and is now administered by a joint committee representing five national organizations.

# CHAPTER XX

## CHILDREN'S AID AND PROTECTIVE WORK

Social work with children, as we saw in earlier chapters, has undergone very marked changes. In colonial times orphans and the children of ne'er-do-wells were commonly apprenticed. While officials were probably more concerned with the taxpayers' budget than with the children's development, it is unlikely that many serious abuses occurred because of the intimate acquaintance of everyone with his neighbor's affairs. After the Revolution some orphanages were founded, and in the course of the nineteenth century their numbers increased rapidly. The early institutions were under the auspices of various religious denominations; later ones were controlled by fraternal orders, non-sectarian boards, and a few by counties and states.

About the time of the Civil War the State of Massachusetts developed a scheme for boarding out dependent children in private homes. A little earlier the New York Children's Aid Society started its program of "emigration as the cure for juvenile pauperism." This Society placed children from the sidewalks of New York in rural homes, taking them out in carload lots. Gradually certain orphanages assumed responsibility for finding foster homes for some of their wards. In the 'seventies humane societies became interested in children as well as animals, and presently there sprang up a number of Societies for the Prevention of Cruelty to Children. Very early in the century Houses of Refuge were established to remove children from the common jails. These institutions developed into Reform Schools and paved the way for State Industrial Schools. In the twentieth century came Juvenile Courts and probation for "dependent, neglected, and delinquent children."

In none of these agencies were children handled on the basis of detailed study and personal adjustment. But as children's agencies became familiar with the principles of case work, they began to adopt them and adapt them to their specific problems. As a consequence needy children are today cared for both as individuals and in groups.

## ROY DANIELS [1]

*First Contacts.* Just before Thanksgiving, 1921, the head of a Church Home for Boys asked a Children's Aid Society to investigate the application which he had received for the care of Roy Daniels. The boy's father was dead and he was living with his grandmother and aunt. Before the investigation could be completed the relatives withdrew the application and placed Roy in another institution. By the following spring the second institution had found him a troublesome lad and asked the Children's Aid Society to provide a boarding home for him. But because the superintendent of the orphanage changed her mind about keeping Roy and because the aunt and grandmother talked of removing him to a third institution, nothing was done for another eight months. At the end of that time the Children's Aid Society assumed responsibility for placing the boy in a foster home.

*Preliminary Study.* Before accepting this responsibility the Society made a rather careful study of the situation, including the boy's personal and family history, medical and psychological examinations. In assembling her information the social worker first inquired at the Social Service Exchange, then called on the grandmother and aunt with whom the boy had been living before going to the orphanage. There was correspondence with other relatives, consultation with workers in a number of agencies which had dealt with the family, verification of birth, parents' marriage and father's death, and arrangement of medical, psychological, and psychiatric examinations. From these varied sources the following information was drawn.

Roy's grandmother, a refined old lady, belonged to one of the "first families of Virginia." After her husband's death many years ago she came to the city in which she now lives and became manager of a boarding home for girls. She was successful in this in spite of her strong temper, a trait she shares with several members of the family. Of her four children two are getting along nicely, Roy's father is dead, and his aunt is "insane." This aunt, with whom Roy lived for a time, had "fits of temper," "heart spells," and delusions.

The father was a telegrapher, capable of earning a good living, but a heavy drinker. On this account, he was divorced from his first wife, and had a quarrel with Roy's mother, after which he

[1] Summary of a record made available through the Child Welfare League of America.

attempted suicide. He was committed five times to a State Hospital as an alcoholic. He died of pneumonia following his last spree.

On his mother's side the history is equally significant. Roy's grandfather was alcoholic and insane, but his grandmother was said to be a very fine woman. One aunt is reported to have been insane, though she has improved greatly in recent years.

The boy's mother gave birth to an illegitimate child several years before she met Mr. Daniels. During this pregnancy she suffered a great shock from the accidental death of her brother. Soon after the child was born she was committed to a State Hospital for the Insane. Her condition improved, she was discharged, and became a stenographer. She married, but was soon separated from her husband because of his cruelty. Three years later she married Mr. Daniels. While she was pregnant with Roy she was underfed, in debt, and worried about her husband's drinking. She became depressed, suspicious, and irritable, and soon after Roy's birth was again committed to a State Hospital. She was in and out of institutions for the mentally sick until her death.

Thus Roy himself had a doubtful heredity and a poor start. From the outset he led a "much disjointed life." After his mother went to the State Hospital he spent three months with his grandmother; then a friend took him for a similar period, after which he returned to his grandmother for a few weeks. He was next placed in an Institution for Babies; after that in a hospital. Then for two months he was with his aunt. By this time his mother had been released from the State Hospital, so he spent eight months with his parents. Then his mother "went to pieces" again, and Roy was in two different orphanages for about two years each.

At the beginning of this four-year period he was described as a "good-natured, fat, chubby baby." At the end he was reported to be "exceedingly troublesome," playing with his excreta, using the wash bowl for a toilet and "soiling everything near him." He had enuresis, "yelled at the top of his lungs," and "didn't get along with other children." At school he did well in kindergarten, but failed in the first grade. His teachers regarded him as neglected and "crushed by his surroundings." A medical examination revealed a discharging ear, enlarged tonsils, and contracted foreskin. A psychologist reported an I. Q. of 98. "He seemed like a perfectly normal child who has been completely starved on the emotional side and driven back upon himself for comfort and satisfaction." Some time later a psychiatrist found that Roy was worrying about his mother, afraid of the dark, masturbating, and perhaps imitating his aunt's temper outbreaks.

*Diagnosis and Plan.* From the information gathered it seemed evident that Roy could not stay with his aunt or grandmother, and that institutional life was not developing a wholesome personality. He appeared to need a quiet environment, perhaps a boarding home on a farm, with calm, sympathetic, and understanding foster parents. The Children's Aid Society decided, therefore, to accept Roy for placement, asking the Board of Public Welfare to share the cost of his care.

*Temporary Boarding Homes.* None of the foster homes which were available seemed entirely suited to Roy's needs, so he was placed temporarily with a Mrs. Roberts, who had reared three children of her own. The visitor told Mrs. Roberts quite frankly about Roy. She seemed to understand his difficulties and to be ready to undertake the mothering of this "problem" boy. There was, however, some question as to Mr. Roberts' attitude, so the venture was regarded by all concerned as something of an experiment. Roy was very happy to leave the orphanage and quickly made himself at home with the Roberts family. But before long he was flying into tantrums, screaming, swearing and calling the foster mother all sorts of vile names. He demanded to be waited on, was very slow about dressing and always wanted something different from what had been given to him.

The visitor called frequently to talk matters over with Mrs. Roberts and with Roy. She managed to quiet them both when the tension was greatest. She advised Mrs. Roberts to splash Roy with cold water and put him to bed rather than whip or spank him when he went into a tantrum. Several times when both Mr. and Mrs. Roberts insisted that the boy be removed at once she persuaded them to try it a little longer. When Roy taunted his foster mother that she did not dare to punish him lest the Society "get after her," the visitor explained to him that Mrs. Roberts "had a perfect right to punish him just as she thought best when he was a naughty boy." Along with these direct personal adjustments, the visitor arranged to have Roy taken regularly to an ear clinic, persuaded his aunt to postpone her proposed visit to him until he might become better adjusted, explained his case to the school teacher, and provided glasses.

After three months Mrs. Roberts insisted that she could not possibly keep the boy any longer, so he was taken to the clinic for a general re-examination and then placed with a Mrs. Artman, who said that "she liked to tackle rather difficult jobs." Roy seemed rather sorry to leave the Roberts, but soon appeared to be happy with the Artmans. He stopped his screaming and was honest in all his dealings. But he talked back, was rather cruel to animals and otherwise difficult to manage. Mr. Artman and some of the relatives took a strong dislike to the boy, and when a neighbor complained that Roy had engaged in some kind of sex practise with her young son, it was too much. She asked that he be removed at once.

In spite of the apparent failure of this second temporary home, Roy had made some real headway in gaining self-control. In this connection it is interesting to note the ways in which Mrs. Artman appealed to him. She told him that she was not very well and that he must help her. She urged him to share his candy with other children. When some older boys "lit into and thrashed him up a bit," she told him that "he would have to stand such treatment if he did not behave himself with other children."

After leaving the Artmans, Roy stayed two weeks in an emergency boarding home while he had a thorough neuro-psychiatric examination. The report indicated that the boy would continue to be difficult to manage, but advised further foster home care. Roy was then taken to Mrs. Smith, with whom he has lived for several years.

*Selection of Foster Home.* Each of the three temporary homes had been utilized only after careful study. Likewise much care was taken in gaining an understanding of Mrs. Smith and her home. The first contact had been made in the previous year when the Society was advertising for a boarding home for a problem girl. Mrs. Smith had answered with a well written letter, so a visitor from the home-finding department called to see the place and talk with the members of the family. Later she called on several references, some of which had been given by Mrs. Smith; others "turned up" in the course of the investigation.

Mrs. Smith was found to be a strong, vigorous woman of English birth, a member of the Episcopal Church, not altogether happy in her marriage, but devoted to her two children, both of whom were about to marry and settle nearby. Mr. Smith was not very strong; a rather silent man, and honest, he was restless and spent much time away from home. He was American-born, a Catholic, a machinist by trade, but now engaged in secret service work. The son was a teacher in the village school, the daughter a private duty nurse. Both were wholesome, attractive young people. The house was large, in good repair and substantially furnished. It was located on a fourteen-acre "farm," a mile and a half from a small village. There were several kinds of live stock, lots of trees and a brook. The family had not much money, but were "in fairly comfortable circumstances." They evidently took great pride in their home and made it the center of their recreational life.

The visitor's impression of Mrs. Smith was that "she had a good grip on life and that she had forged it out of years of hard experience, but had come through sound and whole. . . . One felt a warm, rich nature with something rugged about it that perhaps never had its desired fulfillment; and yet her craving for joy and beauty had found its goal in a realization that after all externals are not the big things; that life is what one himself makes it." The references described her as a "woman of practical idealism, a great hand to help her neighbors."

The home was approved by the Society, but for some reason the girl was placed elsewhere, so when a home of this sort seemed likely to meet Roy's needs, the visitor went out again, talked the whole matter over with Mrs. Smith and found her ready to take the boy.

*"Permanent" Placement.* It is not to be supposed that the mere transferring of Roy to another foster home solved his problems. There were many ups and downs, but on the whole the boy has gained much ground and has at last found a home in which he can remain. At school he was so troublesome that he was expelled, but when admitted to another school his behavior was much more satisfactory and he forged ahead academically. At the end of one year he said that he "loved school," and a year later he brought home an excellent report. There was a gradual release from tension, and a growing sense of belonging. Roy said to the visitor one day, "Nobody ever loved me before." How were the changes brought about?

First of all the foster mother proved to have a happy combination of sympathy and firmness. When Roy grew careless about finishing his little chores, she made him stay out after dark to complete them. She arranged for him to have music lessons, but did not drive him to practice; when he failed to keep up his practicing she simply stopped the lessons. She succeeded in interesting the boy in flowers and birds. She had some difficulty in providing suitable playmates, but this problem was finally solved by the coming into the neighborhood of a family with several children of about Roy's age.

There were times when the foster mother herself needed guidance, which the case worker undertook to provide. When a physician remarked that Roy showed signs of masturbation, Mrs. Smith was much upset, and when he became involved with some neighbor children in group sex practices she was quite excited. In both instances the visitor tried to explain to Mrs. Smith just what was involved, urged her not to take the masturbation too seriously, advised discussing the more difficult problem with the parents of the other youngsters and furnished some pamphlets on the sex problems of children.

There were also a number of adjustments involving Roy's aunt and grandmother. When the aunt wanted the boy to visit her, the case worker persuaded her to visit him instead. When the two women urged his admission to an institution, she induced them to accept the judgment of a psychiatrist as to what would be best for the boy, and in the end brought them to see the wisdom of his remaining with Mrs. Smith. When the aunt and her husband moved into a bungalow on Mrs. Smith's "farm," Roy's conduct took a slump. The aunt was inclined to be over-critical of the foster mother, and matters became rather tense for a time. However, the good offices of the visitor were again invoked and finally the situation was relieved by the aunt's going away.

Four times in as many years Roy had a "vacation" from his foster home. Once it was to enable Mrs. Smith to visit relatives in a distant city, another time Roy was brought in for thorough medical and psychiatric examinations, the third time he spent six weeks in a boys' camp. In the first of these temporary homes the boy was impudent, disobedient, fault-finding, and of a fighting disposition. In both he was eager to return to Mrs. Smith. At the camp Roy tried to dominate the other boys, but they soon "took that out of him." He seemed to enjoy the experience greatly, though he was more or less worried lest he could not go back to his foster mother.

*"Status Quo"* (1925). "Roy came to Mrs. Smith in 1922. He had been in two foster homes within a period of about six months and had proved to be an extremely difficult youngster to handle. In fact, he had seemed almost abnormal to his teacher and the two foster mothers; had frequent fits of temper, would scream and yell, curse, was revengeful and cruel to animals, intensely afraid of the dark, very babyish in many ways, masturbated, and has had sex misconduct with other boys. From the first Mrs. Smith has given herself almost entirely to the boy. She has devoted herself to him and has not spared herself in any way, and has shown a real understanding of Roy's makeup. At times her devotion to the boy has aroused a slight degree of jealousy on the part of her children, who live nearby, but it has never caused any real difficulty.

"Mrs. Smith is of a very religious, emotional makeup. She feels that Roy has been sent to her as a mission. At times conditions have been pretty tense and emotions have been pretty high, but the deepest sort of love and understanding has sprung up between the foster mother and little Roy. She has won his confidence and his love to such an extent that he feels that she is really his mother. Mrs. Smith has had her own methods of discipline, sometimes pretty strict, but has ever been on the alert to watch out for Roy's real welfare. The result is that Roy has gradually been finding himself. He no longer stands out from an average child, although he is still nervous and high-strung at times. From doing absolutely nothing in the first grade two years ago, he is now keeping up with the third grade work. His screaming fits have quite disappeared and there are no longer any signs of masturbation. There have been one or two flare-ups of sex difficulties with other children, but these have been met with understanding and help on the foster mother's part."

**Preliminary Study and Temporary Care.** Under certain circumstances this case might have been handled by a child guidance clinic, a juvenile court, or a family welfare society, but, of course, it fell to the lot of a children's aid society to deal with Roy's problems. How is a decision reached as to which agency shall assume such a responsibility?

First of all, application is made by parent, relative, or other interested person to any organization with which he happens to be familiar. Some agencies will accept or reject the case on the basis of the load they are already carrying, the attractiveness of the child, or the persistence of the applicant. But in such a society as that which cared for Roy Daniels a different procedure is followed. Speedily and painstakingly workers will set about securing answers to these questions: Why does anyone think the child requires special care? Just what are his needs, physical, mental, economic, and social? Has he a natural home? If so, to what extent is it able to meet these needs? Can its shortcomings be supplemented without removal of the child? If so, through the tapping of what community resources? If not, where can the child be placed to the best advantage? With relatives, in a foster home, or in an institution? If a foster home or institution, of what sort? In any case, can the matter be best attended to by the agency making the investigation or some other?

Now because some organizations have not the facilities for making so thorough a preliminary study there have been developed in a few cities central application bureaus to study at least those doubtful cases concerning which no decision is easily reached. Usually, however, children's aid societies make these first investigations themselves and only cases for which institutional care is anticipated are referred to the central bureau.

While the preliminary study is going forward the child may remain with parent, relative, or friend. But if there is an emergency, he may be taken to a small institution known as a receiving home or to a private boarding home subsidized by the society. While here he is under close observation, at play, at school, or in the nursery; he receives medical and often psychological or psychiatric examinations. If necessary, dental or medical care may be given and a start made toward habit training.

The actual decision to accept or reject responsibility may be made promptly on the basis of quite obvious facts or it may come only after prolonged study and consultation. A large percentage of children for whom application is made need not be taken from their natural homes. But if placement seems necessary, the agency proceeds upon the request of parent or guardian, legal surrender of the child, guardianship, or commitment by a juvenile court. Formerly a very high percentage of the children were surrendered or committed with a view to adoption. But today a larger number remain in the legal custody of parents who by reason of broken health or some other crisis are compelled to give them up for a time. For about one-third of the children accepted for placement the societies receive payment in whole or in part. This money comes from parents and relatives and from various public and private funds.

If perchance the initial study indicates that some other agency can best serve the child and his family (for he usually has one), it is not enough to reject the case. It is important to see that the situation is actually taken in hand by the organization best equipped to deal with it.

**Selection of Foster Homes.** It is coming to be generally understood that a thorough study should be made of each child for whom application is received. The importance of an equally careful study of prospective foster homes is gaining recognition more slowly. However, a number of agencies have departments devoted entirely to the discovery and evaluation of homes into which children may be placed. Foster homes are located in a number of ways. Newspaper advertisements, radio talks, and addresses before clubs and churches bring some response, but the largest and most satisfactory returns come from the recommendations of other foster parents and observation of successful placements.

The actual steps taken in the investigation and decision are these: First of all, the applicant for a child may be asked to call at the office of the agency, where he is interviewed and fills out a blank with certain routine information. Some agencies at once inquire of the social service exchange whether the family is known to any other organization either as a client or as one who has previously cared for children. If the answer from the exchange is affirmative, the other agency will be asked to furnish whatever information it possesses that may help to determine the suitability of the home for a foster child. Sometimes what is learned in the first interview and from other agencies may warrant a denial of the application, but in most cases the investigation will go on. References given by the applicant will be consulted by letter or in person or both. In addition calls may be made on other persons who know the family. But the most important part of the investigation is the visit to the proposed foster home itself. This affords an opportunity not only to see the house, its furnishings, and its setting, but to visit with the various members of the family and sense the home "atmosphere."

The attitude of the housemother toward her own home as she exhibits it is often illuminating. Extreme pride may mean a nicety of housekeeping that would keep a child constrained and unhappy; extreme apology on insufficient grounds shows self-consciousness and perhaps an over-anxiety to make a good impression; a care-free manner, also on insufficient grounds, indicates poor standards; while a quiet take-me-as-I-am attitude, where the woman is plainly conscious that her home is not up to par today, often means a fine spirit of confidence in the visitor and a dignified willingness to stand by what one is for better or worse.[2]

Having consulted references and visited the home, the social case worker attempts to make a clear analysis of the possibilities offered. The standards of judgment vary from agency to agency, but tend to approximate those described, as follows, in a publication of the Children's Bureau:

The acceptance of a home by the Boston Children's Aid Society depended very much upon the personalities of the foster father and mother, the purpose and spirit of the family, their reasons for taking a child, and their attitude toward his future education, religious training and educational needs. They must first be people of character, in good standing in their own community, and able to offer a child, besides affection, a real home atmosphere and intelligent training. These requirements being met, the following standards were required: (1) Sufficient income for family needs without board from children; (2) sufficient room to afford a separate bed for each child, if not a separate room; (3) pure water and sanitary conditions; (4) schools near, or transportation

[2] Doran, Mary S., and Reynolds, Bertha C., *The Selection of Foster Homes for Children,* pp. 29-30.

to them by supervised bus or by the family conveyance; (5) a church connection for the family with church privileges for the children; (6) a doctor's word that to his knowledge the general health of the family is good; (7) a definite understanding as to the amount of work that will be required of the children; and (8) some recreation offered.[3]

After a home has been approved some time may elapse before a child is placed, as in the case of Mrs. Smith who cared for Roy Daniels. The position taken by most social workers in this field is that they are concerned with finding homes for children rather than children for homes. The selection of a home for a particular child depends, therefore, not on the eagerness of the foster parents nor on their general merits, but on their apparent ability to meet the needs of the boy or girl in question. As a final step they are told frankly and in some detail about the child whom it is proposed to place with them, the difficulties they may expect to face, and the help the agency stands ready to give in making needed adjustments.

**Placement and Supervision.** There are four kinds of foster homes, classified according to legal and economic status. (1) In the past most children were placed with a view to adoption (adoptive homes). (2) However, there have always been families ready to take a boy or girl for a long period of time without adoption or remuneration (free homes). (3) In late years an increasing number of children have been placed for varying lengths of time with the expectation of eventual return to parents or relatives, and with some person or agency making payments to the foster family (boarding homes). (4) Finally, a small number of older children are placed in homes where they are expected to earn their "keep" (working homes).

Whatever the basis of placement, it is essential that there be a clear understanding on the part of all concerned as to just what is expected. Not only do the foster parents need to know about the child, but the child needs to be prepared for the home to which he is going. The foster parents often need advice "not to expect too much of the child all at once, not to insist on his being this or that type of child instead of the child that he naturally is, not to look for too great a demonstration

[3] U. S. Children's Bureau, Publication No. 171, p. 43.

of affection all at once, and, above all, not to look for gratitude." On the other hand, it is wise to consult the child's feelings and preferences about foster homes and then to make reasonably clear to him the character of the family and the location selected. He needs to understand the relationships that are to obtain between himself, foster parents, his own relatives, and the case worker.

As to the placement itself, the child is usually taken to his new home by a worker whom he knows. Perhaps he goes first to visit and later for the longer stay. He is neither sent alone nor turned over at the agency's office. After placement he is visited at varying intervals which depend on his age, health and conduct. These visits, often referred to as "supervision," have as their purposes the gaining of new insights into child and foster home, the effecting of adjustments between the two, training the foster parents, and checking up on the child's health, education, recreation, living arrangements, clothing, "discipline," and especially his attitudes and those of his new associates. Instead of espionage, the main objective is personal service.

As in the case of Roy Daniels, it is often necessary for the case worker to straighten out difficulties involving jealousy, interference of relatives, conflicting standards of conduct, inability of the child to live up to the demands of his foster parents, suspicion and distrust on the part of neighbors, or a sense of insecurity on the part of the child. The visitor talks with the members of the foster family separately as well as together, but there is no effort to "go over anyone's head," or "behind anyone's back." Throughout the effort is to promote mutual understanding and team work through frank discussion of each problem as it arises.

Again, as we saw in the record of Roy Daniels, there come times when adjustment seems impossible and removal of the child is the only solution of the difficulty. Too many changes bewilder a youngster; hence great care must be taken with each placement and every resource exhausted to make it a success. In sending children to new foster homes substantially the same procedure is followed as in the first placements. But when a child goes back to his own parents or relatives the situation is a little different. Presumably there has been some work done to prepare the natural home for his return and there is reasonable assurance that the family can now "make a go of it." However, it has often been found wise to continue the supervision for some time on much the same basis as in foster homes.

When adoption is contemplated there is usually an agreement that a minimum period of time must elapse before court action is taken. Few agencies of good repute now permit an adoption to be consummated within six months of the placement. But after a child has become legally as well as socially a member of the new family, the agency's official responsibility ends. Its further contacts are on an informal and friendly basis.

The question is often asked, should foster children know that they have been adopted? Practice varies in this regard, but in a large number of cases the children do know something of the matter, and on the whole this seems wise. If the foster parents do not tell them of their adoption someone else may, and then serious emotional difficulties may arise. However, circumstances alter cases and no universal rule is likely to be agreed upon in this matter.

**Preserving and Restoring Natural Homes.** In many communities suitable foster homes are not easy to provide. Even when they are available the cost of discovery, evaluation, placement, and supervision is considerable. But most important of all, the removal of a child from his own people constitutes a shock, and transfer from home to home promotes instability. From several different standpoints, therefore, it seems wise to preserve the natural home. How can this be done?

First of all, it is pretty well agreed that poverty alone is not an adequate reason for breaking up a family. Mothers' pensions, day nurseries, workmen's compensation, and insurance are some of the devices whereby limited economic resources may be supplemented. More fundamental are the efforts to provide adequate wages and protect health. When the mother of young children is dead or ill, some agencies attempt to keep the rest of the family together by providing visiting housekeepers. When parents are negligent, the threat of removing the children is sometimes a first step in reconstructing family life.

But sometimes there seems no way out except through temporary placement of the children in foster homes. The task then is not only one of safeguarding the youngsters, but of preparing the natural home for their possible return. In the Crandall family[4] it was the mother's tuberculosis and the father's unemployment that compelled a temporary separation. While the children were cared for in a foster home, the parents' health and morale were being built up until it was eventually possible to reunite the family. In the case of Clara Vansca[5] it was her alcoholism and slovenly housekeeping that necessitated removal of her children until their mother's character had been re-formed. Some of the consequences of failing to deal with the family as well as with the child are illustrated by a case reported by the Children's Bureau.

A society boarded for over a year three small children of foreign parentage. The mother was dead and the father paid what he could toward their support. They were difficult to adjust in a family home because they knew nothing of American ways and were at first regarded as "heathen" by the foster mother. The society spent much time and patience in interpreting these children to the foster parents and succeeded in arousing their interest for the special needs of the children. Then one day the children's father appeared and announced that he was remarried and wished to have the children returned to him. Investigation showed that he had a suitable home already established, and the children were returned. Several months afterwards the father reappeared, asking the society to board the children. His new wife, a foreigner unused to American ways, had struggled with the same problems that had at first daunted the foster mother, and she had been unaided in her efforts to adjust the children. Now, completely discouraged, she refused to stay at home unless the children were removed, and no amount of persuasion could change her attitude. The society again took over the care of the children, fully realizing its mistake, but too late, in not having done for the stepmother what it had done for the foster mother.[6]

**Agencies in the Field.** The needs of children deprived of parental care have always made a strong appeal to charitable folk, and their responses have been more generous than dis-

[4] Child Welfare League of America, Case No. 1.
[5] Richmond, Mary E., *What Is Social Case Work?* pp. 59-68.
[6] U. S. Children's Bureau, Publication No. 171, p. 73.

criminating. Without stopping to inquire what agencies were already in the field, each new group of philanthropists who became aware of opportunities for service to children tended to start an organization of its own. Hence we have all sorts of institutions (to be described in Chapter XXV), home-finding societies, humane societies, societies for prevention of cruelty to children, juvenile protective associations, boards of children's guardians, and juvenile courts. It requires little study to establish the fact that a classification of agencies and a classification of functions would not coincide at all. Thus some home-finding societies rescue children from abusive parents and some humane societies place children in foster homes. Some juvenile protective societies engage in case work, while others confine their activities largely to the study of conditions affecting child life, educational publicity, pressure for new legislation, and the enforcement of old laws. Moreover, in recent years there appears to have been a growing tendency to coordinate these various types of service. Hence instead of organizations that merely place children in homes for adoption, others that do merely boarding-out work, and still others that confine themselves to rescuing neglected children and prosecuting their parents, we have an increasing number of agencies that combine these functions in order to do a well-rounded piece of case work.

As in the field of family welfare work, we find both private and public, sectarian and non-sectarian agencies. Among the private non-sectarian agencies are some that work only within a limited area and others that attempt to cover entire states. The organization of the two types differs partly because of this fact and partly for certain historical reasons. The state-wide societies have used the Illinois Children's Home and Aid Society as a model. This has a central office, a receiving home, and district agents. In the earlier days each district agent was responsible for discovering children in need of placement, finding foster homes, transporting children, supervising those placed out, arranging adoptions and raising money. The last named function seems often to have consumed most of his time. Perhaps on this account most of the agents were clergymen. But today many of these societies have separated the financial and the case work jobs. The agencies whose work is more localized have developed still greater specialization. The case workers are often divided into several departments, one for the investigation of new applications for the care of children, one for the discovery and evaluation of foster homes, one for placement and supervision.

In addition to the societies that are technically or actually non-sectarian, there are a few children's aid societies under definitely religious auspices. Most of these are Catholic or Jewish. The Catholic agencies are usually conducted by the Society of St. Vincent de Paul or the diocesan charities bureau. The Jewish agencies are commonly included in federations of Jewish charities.

Along with the private organizations there are various public departments which provide foster home care, investigate complaints, assume guardianship and render other services to needy children. For example, the Massachusetts Department of Public Welfare has a Division of Child Guardianship whose staff does the actual case work. In Minnesota the Children's Bureau of the State Board of Control does its work largely through county boards of child welfare. In Wisconsin the Board of Control maintains a State Public School from which children are placed out by "indenture" (a contract between the School and the foster parents) or by adoption. In many communities in many states the care of specially needy children is regarded as a function of the juvenile court. In others it is made a responsibility of the local department of public welfare.

Some of the state departments render no direct service to children, but supervise agencies that do render such service. Others combine the two tasks. Supervision involves not only "inspection" of the institutions and officers, but careful study of the personnel, equipment, methods of work, children cared for, and results obtained. Usually the state department has power to grant and withhold licenses and to formulate rules and regulations. Sometimes it administers a fund for "state aid to children."

Just as the local societies doing family welfare work found it desirable to create a national organization to promote the coordination of their work and to raise their standards, so the child-caring agencies have established for similar purposes the Child Welfare League of America. The League holds an annual meeting in connection with the National Conference of Social Work and several regional meetings each year. It makes studies of individual agencies and of the child-caring needs and programs of entire cities and states. It offers a consultation service and publishes a monthly bulletin.

**Results of Foster Home Care.** In the earlier years it was customary to assume that a children's aid society was "doing a noble work," and let it go at that. Most people took it for granted that to remove a dirty ragamuffin from a city street to a farm home would automatically make him over into a good citizen. But of late there has been growing up a more critical attitude. Social workers, their financial backers, and the supervising agencies alike are demanding to know what results are actually achieved. One attempt to answer this question has been discussed previously.[7] Another significant study was made by the New York State Charities Aid Association from 1922 to 1924.[8]

From 1898 to 1922 this organization placed over 3300 children in foster homes. In order to test its work an effort was made to determine the present status of all those who had passed the formative stage and were mature enough to give some indication of their development. This meant a study of 910 who were eighteen years of age or older and had been under the care of the Association for at least one year. The problem was put in this form, "Has the subject shown himself capable (or incapable) of managing himself and his affairs with ordinary prudence?" Of course, many of the points considered could not be reduced to quantitative terms; moreover, there was no attempt to set up a fixed standard. But it was nevertheless possible to secure significant data about appearance, tastes, habits, "common sense," general reputation and place in the community, earning capacity and degree of self-support, school record, and sense of responsibility.

The general conclusion was that three-fourths of the subjects had shown themselves "capable." No two of them were alike,

[7] p. 226.
[8] Theis, Sophie Van Senden, *How Foster Children Turn Out.*

but they were all "reasonably at peace with themselves and with their fellow men." About sixty per cent of the children had a satisfactory relationship with their foster parents with ties that were firm and lasting. A smaller group found homes that were temporarily satisfying, while a few found only material care. As to schooling, the average grade completed was above that for the total population, with fewer bad failures and fewer brilliant successes. As to health, there seemed to be no marked incidence of any special type of disease or physical disability. Most of the subjects were working steadily, few were incapacitated, and not many serious illnesses were reported. Their occupations were widely distributed and compared very favorably with those of their foster parents.

The 182 "incapable" subjects were divided into four groups: "Harmless—Irresponsible or shiftless persons of limited capacity or inferior character or those who are incapacitated but who are not anti-social; On Trial—Persons who because of some previous offense against social standards need special supervision and whose future development is not clearly indicated; In Institutions—Inmates of custodial or correctional institutions; Harmful —Persons now in conflict with the law or with accepted standards of morality." [9]

In 1929 the Judge Baker Foundation of Boston published the results of its intensive study over an eight year period of 500 children who presented cases of delinquency or personality problems and who were placed in foster homes.[10] In generalizing from their findings the authors asked and answered the following questions: [11]

Does any special kind of misbehavior weigh heavily against the changes of success in placing? No.

If the individual has been engaged in several types of delinquency, does this indicate markedly less chance for success than if he has committed only one form of delinquency? No, only slightly less.

Does any combination, either in extent or type, of delinquency and mental abnormality offer a particularly poor prognosis under

[9] *Ibid.*, p. 24.

[10] Healy, Wm., Bronner, Augusta F., Baylor, Edith M. H., and Murphy, J. Prentice, *Reconstructing Behavior in Youth.*

[11] *Ibid.*, pp. 246-252. The questions are quoted here *verbatim*, but the answers are abbreviated. By permission of Alfred A. Knopf, Inc., publisher.

conditions of placing? Yes, the psychotic and the psychopathic personalities did extremely poorly, although the defectives did relatively well.

Does the fact that the young person has been a repeated offender militate seriously against success in placing? Not seriously.

Are delinquents less likely to be successfully treated by placing than those who present personality problems? Not if mentally normal.

Are boys less or more likely to succeed in placing than girls? No, their chances are about equal.

Does having a court record make for or against success in placing? Neither.

Are children taken at earlier ages much more likely to succeed in placing than older ones? Not if mentally normal.

Is illegitimacy a bar to success in placing? No.

Does heredity seem to play any part in the success or failure of those who are placed? No.

Since mental abnormality seems to play such a large part in failure, does any nationality group show an undue proportion of abnormality? No.

Is private rather than public agency placing more successful? In these cases the private agencies seemed to be more successful but the essential difference appeared to lie in the adequacy of facilities, funds, and technique.

Is there any outstanding cause of failure in placing? Yes, abnormal mentality or personality.

To what extent was prognosis possible in the original study? In 88 per cent of those where the prognosis was considered good there was success.

Is there any relationship between success or failure and the number of homes in which the child has been placed? No.

Is there any relationship between success or failure and the number of visitors supervising the child? No.

How well does success or failure in foster homes correlate with success or failure after discharge from agency supervision? Fairly well.

Numerous studies such as these will make it possible to carry on social case work with children with much greater confidence than at any time in the past. More than that, they will help to lay the foundations for a real profession of social work.

# CHAPTER XXI

## CHILD GUIDANCE

No phase of the modern child welfare movement combines more scientific techniques than that of child guidance, or is further removed from the program of "saving juvenile paupers and criminals," characteristic of the "nineties." The contrast between the humanitarian but unscientific handling of dependent and neglected children described in Chapter IX, of Part II, and the modern methods discussed in Chapter XX (Children's Aid and Protective Work) and XXV (Children's Institutions) is striking enough, but in child guidance the intensive study of the individual child has been carried to the highest point in the history of such work. Child guidance is a direct outgrowth of modern psychiatry and the mental hygiene movement discussed in Chapter XVII. It is essentially the application of the point of view and techniques of mental hygiene to the problems and difficulties of the normal child.

Child guidance arose as a preventive measure to remedy the situation evidenced by the increasing numbers admitted to psychopathic hospitals and brought before the courts. Apparently both the home and the school, which had taken over many of the functions of the home, were failing in many instances properly to direct the child's development. The school was too concerned with intellectual education for later life and too little with the immediate emotional problems of the child. This need, with the rapidly developing science of modern psychiatry, gave rise to the child guidance movement, the aim of which is to prevent delinquency and insanity through the scientific direction of the child's impulses, habits, and emotions, in relation to parental attitudes, the school situation, and the whole process of socialization. Child guidance is essentially an individualized educational movement for all children who present personality and developmental difficulties, however apparently slight, preventive in its purpose, and cooperative in its nature. Its technique is a composite one based upon the contributions of all the sciences and professions devoted to the study of child behavior. A case history, topically presented, will illustrate some of the problems in this field.[1]

## "CONQUERED"[2]

There are many fathers, mothers, teachers, and other grown-ups, on a high intellectual and moral plane and animated with the best intentions toward the children for whose care they are responsible, who in countless cases bring misery upon these without even being aware of the grave errors they are committing. Often enough, when it is manifest that the education is going awry, such persons, still with the best will in the world, reach out for other means which cannot fail to bring about even greater intellectual or moral aberration, emotional suffering, or additional injury. Oskar Pfister, *Love in Children and Its Aberrations.*

### I. THE PROBLEM

*Bruce MacAllister* had been a problem for the past year, both at home and at school, on account of his lying and petty stealing. So serious had the matter become that the scoutmaster, in whom Bruce had the greatest confidence, finally persuaded him to come to the clinic with him for study and advice. Mr. MacAllister rather reluctantly consented to the plan: he believed that he had already "straightened him around," and was afraid going to the clinic would give the boy the idea he couldn't manage him. Bruce was interviewed at the clinic and seemed to be a quiet, unassuming, sensitive and rather shy boy. He looked fatigued, but cooperated well with the psychiatrist and didn't attempt to put the blame for his misdeeds on anyone else. Additional information about him was secured from his father, step-mother, older brother, and the scoutmaster who referred him. It was impossible to obtain access to the school records, as it was then summer, but information as to his school behavior and work was secured from two of his teachers who knew him well.

[1] The case of "John," summarized in Chap. XVII, should also be reviewed in this connection.

[2] Sayles, Mary B., *The Problem Child at Home,* pp. 242-261. Commonwealth Fund, Division of Publications, 1928. The book contains narrative accounts of twelve cases, one of which is summarized here. Miss Sayles and Mr. Graham R. Taylor cooperated in the preparation of this résumé, but the writer of this chapter assumes full responsibility for the form employed, particularly in the "Diagnostic Summary."

## II. HISTORY[3]

*Family.* Both parents were of American birth and parentage. The *father* was a college graduate, who after teaching a number of years, became an insurance agent in addition, but was still able to make only a bare living for the family. He described himself as having been a leader in various communities in which he had lived. He had always been an ardent church worker, acted as superintendent as well as teacher in the Sunday school. He had never used alcohol or tobacco. His main interest, apart from the church, was in reading, particularly works on sociology, education and phrenology. He admitted having had a temper but insisted that he controlled it and only punished Bruce after careful deliberation. His plan had been to make the boy humble and repentant in order to reform him. *Bruce's mother,* who died of pneumonia when he was six, had been a quiet, sweet and gentle woman. The present *Mrs. MacAllister,* whom Mr. MacAllister had married one year after the death of his first wife, was twenty years his junior. She and Mr. MacAllister had two children, and she had apparently left the management of Bruce to his father. Mr. MacAllister's oldest daughter, *Amy,* was almost the same age as her step-mother and they were good friends. She had never displayed any particular interest in Bruce. Her father had "conquered her will," when she was four, and she had been quiet and amiable ever since. Just previous to the opening of the case she had married and moved away from the city. *Luther,* the oldest boy, two years younger than Amy, had left home between sixteen and seventeen, and had supported himself ever since. According to Mr. MacAllister, he left purely for economic reasons; but Luther himself maintained he had been forced to leave on account of his father's sternness and severity. The only condition on which he would have been allowed to remain was one of absolute obedience to his father's will. He secured a position and had lived ever since in another part of the city with a family who treated him as one of their own members.

*Personal.* Bruce's birth and *early developmental history* were normal. He had the usual children's diseases, and in school had complained of headaches, which were thought by the school nurse to have been imaginary. Since the age of four he had been addicted to the spinning of rather wild stories. His mother's death when he was six made a great impression on him. He was eight when he stole for the first time, taking on this occasion a quarter belonging to his brother. For this act he was severely punished. When he was about twelve small sums began to disappear at home and Bruce was caught red-handed. About the same time

[3] Includes all facts relative to the case previous to the first interview.

he was suspected of taking money from the school club fund. Again he was punished. Once he stayed away from home all night to avoid punishment. His father thought his treatment of the boy had been effective since for the past three months he had not been caught again. During this time he continued to tell yarns at home and at school. During one Christmas vacation he left home early every morning, telling his father he had a job, which upon investigation proved non-existent. At school he related a yarn about his mother being a half-breed Indian and enjoyed the sensation thus created. Relative to his *habits and interests,* it was discovered that at one time he had masturbated to some extent, but having been severely warned of the evil consequences of such a habit by his father and a minister, who was a friend of his father's, he apparently abandoned it.

Six months before the case opened he joined the Boy Scouts. In *school* his work had only been fair. He had skipped the first two grades, but failed of promotion in the lower seventh. His teachers reported that he wrote very well, displaying imagination and originality. His manual training grades were also good. His deportment, on the other hand, was poor. He was inattentive, whispered in class, was unstable and given to day-dreaming. He was not, however, difficult to manage. There is nothing in the nature of a *vocational* history except for a short period of selling papers, terminated by his failing to turn in the money he had collected. For the past few months he had been doing outdoor chores for Mr. Morrison, the scoutmaster, on the latter's farm. For this work he was receiving $1.50 a day, which his father insisted was too much. This money was used largely to pay his Scout dues and purchase equipment. He had always wanted to become a missionary. Information received from Luther, the older brother, led the visitor to believe that this ambition had been instilled by his father who wanted one of the boys to enter religious work of some sort. Bruce's *own story* was to the effect that his father had severely punished him but that it was "all over now." He said he had stolen in order to get spending money such as the other boys had. Some of the boys he had associated with stole also, but he no longer went with these particular boys. At one time he constantly thought about stealing and couldn't do his work. He lied in self-defense and to make the fellows think he had things which he didn't. He got along fairly well in school, he said; arithmetic was easy for him but English very difficult.

## III. STATUS AT TIME STUDY WAS MADE

*Physical.* Bruce slept well and had a good appetite, but was small and fourteen pounds underweight. In addition to being poorly nourished his posture was bad and he suffered from chronic pharyngitis. His teeth also were in bad condition.

*Psychiatric.* He was obviously unhappy, cried when he talked of his own mother, and craved affection. He had, however, apparently made up his mind to comply with his father's will, and follow the latter's plans for him.

*Psychological.* Bruce was thirteen years of age when he studied and possessed superior intelligence. On the educational achievement tests he was considerably ahead of his age. His performance in the visual-motor and mechanical fields was high. In comprehension, rote memory and reasoning he was superior. His initiative, originality and persistence were also marked. He was now in the eighth grade, having just been promoted.

*Social.* The MacAllister *family* consisted of the following members:

Mr. MacAllister: about 45.
Mrs. MacAllister, Bruce's step-mother: about 25.
Amy, now married and living in another city: 23.
Luther, living in another part of the city: 21.
Bruce: 13.
2 half-sisters, both apparently healthy and normal.

Mr. MacAllister had a firm mouth and a strong, serious face. He was bombastic and a profound egoist, but interested in his own way in Bruce, whose difficulties he really failed to understand. According to Mr. Morrison, he was extremely narrow-minded and bigoted and determined to have his own way in everything. Since Bruce had begun to comply with his wishes he was anxious for him to know that he would stand by him, and once when the latter was falsely accused of stealing a bicycle he had defended and cleared him. The present Mrs. MacAllister was an alert, intelligent and attractive young woman, who did not, however, understand Bruce, whose management she left entirely to his father. The *home,* though rather shabby and in a poor neighborhood, was fair-sized and comfortable, and the step-mother was a good housekeeper. There were a piano and a library of several hundred volumes, mainly on sociology, psychology, education, philosophy and religious subjects. The case worker was impressed with the dominating influence of Mr. MacAllister, and the lax, inconsistent discipline of Mrs. MacAllister with her own children. There was a lack of harmony in dealing with them. She expressed admiration for her husband's superior intelligence and education and indicated that she deferred to his ideas. He was stern but apparently not harsh with the two little girls. The disparity in the ages of Mr. and Mrs. MacAllister was obviously unfortunate. He frequently compared the second Mrs. MacAllister unfavorably with the first, who had always agreed with him. There had been an even more marked disagreement during the first year of their marriage. Mr. MacAllister insisted that his wife had a bad temper. Bruce's teachers were certain that this home situation was one of the causes of his difficulties. One of them remarked that "there was something pathetic about the boy." It is important, too, that Bruce received no allowance or spending money. Bruce had plenty of *companions*, apparently associating with all the boys, but according to one of the teachers, was not a leader or enthusiastic about games or athletics.

*Personal.* Bruce seemed to be a boy of normal habits and interests, who, however, craved sympathy. According to his parents his main interest was in reading and in mechanical things. He made a great many contrivances himself. At home he was not a reliable worker about the house. Mr. Morrison, the scout leader, was his ideal, and his one source of income. Bruce said he liked shows, athletics, fishing, hunting and swimming. He insisted he liked his school and teachers and got along all right with the boys, and had once been pitcher on his baseball team. He said he liked his step-mother "pretty well," though she sometimes scolded and beat him, but he liked his father best of all, because he was the only parent he had since his mother died (crying). There was no one now to whom he felt he could give his affection, as his father was too busy for this sort of thing.

## IV. DIAGNOSTIC SUMMARY [2]

*Problem.* Petty stealing and lying at home and at school. School performance below level of ability; unhappy.

*Status.* Physically underweight and undernourished. Mentally superior.

*Etiology.* 1. Mother's death when client was six. 2. Father's egoistic and dominant attitude. 3. Suppression at home. 4. Failure to secure status to which his abilities entitled him. 5. Example of some of his companions. 6. Unsatisfied desire for response and sympathy. 7. *The family situation;* dynamic associations between ideas of stealing and his unsatisfied desires for response and status. 8. Habit formations.

*Diagnosis.* Bruce seems to have been adjusted until after the death of his mother. Shortly after this he apparently began to undergo a mental conflict between his desires for status, affection and individuality on the one hand, and loyalty to his father and general wish for social approval on the other. This conflict led to a condition of imperfect and more or less temporary adaptation, which may be termed "maladjustment," evidenced by the accommodations of stealing (to gain status among his fellows), defensive lying and fantasy (day dreaming). After a trial of strength with his father he made up his mind to conform to the former's wishes, and thus, about three months before seen at the clinic, had become adjusted again. It is interesting to note that his older brother, Luther, on the other hand, had openly rebelled and left the paternal roof ("Unadjustment"). At the time the study was made we find Bruce humbled and repentant in spirit, evidencing complete conformity. He would be a missionary, even, if his father wanted him to, and teach the Africans "to not do the things that he had done." By a process of "identification" he was apparently more or less unconsciously attempting to effect a reconciliation with his father and find again the love he had lost when his mother died. This state of adjustment was not, however, satisfactory; he was still unhappy. A multiple diagnosis might then be made as follows:

| | | | |
|---|---|---|---|
| psychological: | superior | psychiatric: | normal |
| medical: | normal, but under-nourished | sociological: | maladjustment |

*Recommendations.* The older brother Luther was interviewed and agreed to help by taking a greater interest in Bruce. It was suggested that he "pal around" with him, take him to shows, games and the like. The danger of crushing out all individuality in Bruce was recognized, and it was decided to try to get his father to take a different attitude toward him. The step-mother should also be urged to take more interest in the boy and show some affection toward him. Finally, it was recommended that proper medical attention be given him; that his teeth and diet be looked after and a regimen of exercise and rest set up under supervision.[4]

## V. TREATMENT AND RESULTS

Luther devoted considerable time and interest to his younger brother. He took him out with him on various trips and even made him a weekly allowance. Luther also began to cooperate with Mrs. MacAllister in a joint attempt to remake the situation for Bruce. The effort to re-educate Mr. MacAllister was a failure. His "egotism proved unassailable." There was little, he intimated, that anybody could teach him about children. His wife, however, was open-minded and received the suggestions of the clinic staff sympathetically. She admitted that she gave her own children more love and attention than she did Bruce, but her interest in him was obviously stimulated by the study and she promised to modify her behavior, and try to be more of a mother

[4] Although not suggested in the original record, it would seem that some effort might have been made to utilize Bruce's mechanical ability, and thus give him an opportunity to secure status in a legitimate way.

to him. A successful effort was also made to secure a favorable attitude on the part of Bruce's new teacher. Through her it was arranged for him to receive a hot noon meal at school each day.

VI. FOLLOW-UP REPORT

Six months after the last clinic contact it was learned from the scoutmaster that Bruce had been in no fresh difficulties, and that he seemed much happier.

**Discussion of the Case.** Several points should be noted in the account of this case. In the first place, the so-called problems, stealing and lying, turned out, as is usually the case, to be merely symptoms of an underlying and more fundamental difficulty. They represented simply Bruce's ill-advised way of meeting the situation. Furthermore, no acute problem was in evidence at the time the case was referred to the clinic: his lying and stealing had ceased. The fact that a real difficulty was unearthed shows the importance of having all such cases studied. That Bruce's school work was hampered by his emotional maladjustment is worth noting, as is also the causal significance of parental attitudes and the home situation in children's behavior difficulties. Parental guidance becomes, therefore, one of the important phases of the work of the child clinics. The manner in which such a study is made, the ways in which information is obtained, the rôles played by the various specialists, and the methods of diagnosis are also illustrated. The following diagram presents the several stages as

(1)
*"Adjustment"*
Lasting until the mother's death.

(2)
*"Mental Conflict"*
Desire for social approval and loyalty to father
vs.
wish for status and for freedom.

(3)
*"Maladjustment"*
Accommodations:
stealing
lying
day-dreaming

(4)
*"Adjustment"*
Conformity under compulsion.

(5)
*"Readjustment"*
Change in family situation. More opportunities for expression. Bruce becomes happier, and both he and the family (with the possible exception of the father) are more satisfied.

revealed by a sociological diagnosis. It should be noted that stage (2) involves both suppression by the father and repression by Bruce himself of certain of his desires.

**Types of Child Guidance Problems.** Many varieties of problems are brought to the child guidance clinics but so far no adequate classification of them has been worked out. In many cases the so-called problem is merely a "symptom" of some far more important underlying condition discovered only after a detailed study. The following table shows the distribution of such "symptom-problems" in a group of twenty-three delinquent children:

PROBLEMS PRESENTED BY TWENTY-THREE CHILDREN[5]

| *Problem* | *Frequency* |
|---|---|
| 1. Stealing, larceny, etc. | found in 20 cases |
| 2. Running away | 10 |
| 3. Sex delinquencies, masturbation, etc. | 8 |
| 4. Truancy | 7 |
| 5. Lying | 5 |
| 6. Disobedience and troublesomeness in home and school.. | 3 |
| 7. Begging | 2 |
| 8. Fighting | 2 |
| 9. Drinking | 2 |
| 10. Staying out at night | 2 |
| 11. Arson | 1 |

The "forty most common complaints of those referring patients" to the New York Institute for Child Guidance are noted below:

COMPLAINTS CONCERNING CHILDREN REFERRED TO NEW YORK INSTITUTE FOR CHILD GUIDANCE[6]

| *Problem* | *No. of Cases* |
|---|---|
| Disobedience, uncontrollable, etc. | 42 |
| Stealing | 32 |
| Temper | 29 |
| "Nervousness" | 28 |
| Lying | 24 |
| Disturbing behavior in school | 20 |
| Truancy, school | 20 |
| Truancy, home | 20 |

[5] Harper, Ernest B., "Individualizing Sin and the Sinner," *Journal of Religion,* 5: 255-276, 1925.

[6] Report of the Director of the Institute for Child Guidance, June 30th, 1928, p. 64.

| *Problem* | *No. of Cases* |
|---|---|
| Retarded in school | 17 |
| School failure | 15 |
| Enuresis | 15 |
| Masturbation | 15 |
| Quarrelsome | 14 |
| Destructive | 9 |
| Fighting with other children | 9 |
| Reading defect | 9 |
| Shy | 9 |
| Sleep disturbances | 9 |
| Stays out late | 9 |
| Fears | 8 |
| Does not get along with other children | 8 |
| Restless | 8 |
| Sensitiveness | 8 |
| Undesirable companions | 7 |
| Excess fantasy | 7 |
| Impudent | 7 |
| Mother protective | 7 |
| Overdependent | 7 |
| Physical defects | 7 |
| Sex activity | 7 |
| Stubborn | 7 |
| Unhappy | 7 |
| Defective concentration | 6 |
| Cries easily | 6 |
| No friends | 6 |
| Irritable | 6 |
| Irresponsible | 6 |
| Obscene language | 6 |
| Annoys other children | 6 |
| Speech defect | 6 |

Sometimes the problems are age-period difficulties, such as those of adolescence.[7] Again, the problems may be classified on the basis of the predominant reaction, or general field of behavior. Thus Wile [8] divides his fifty cases into four groups:

| | | | |
|---|---|---|---|
| Physical problems | 9 | Social problems | 13 |
| Emotional problems | 13 | Intellectual problems | 15 |

Many problems have to do with the development of fundamental habits both mental and physical. Among these are those pertaining to feeding, sleep, enuresis, thumbsucking, discipline, anger, fear, jealousy, destructiveness, convulsions, sex, speech,

[7] Taft, Jessie, "Mental Hygiene Problems of Normal Adolescence," *Mental Hygiene*, 5: 741-751, 1921.

[8] Wile, Ira S., *Challenge of Childhood,* Thomas Seltzer, 1925.

elimination, masturbation, left-handedness, temper tantrums, walking, and the like. Strictly speaking these are problems for the habit clinic rather than the child guidance clinic. Child guidance problems may also be classified according to their social aspects. Such a grouping is suggested by Drucker and Hexter's classification: [9]

1. Truants
2. Weaklings
3. Wanderers
4. Pilferers
5. Characterally defective
6. Precocious
7. Sex problems
8. Intractables

Finally, child guidance problems may be classified professionally as psychological, medical, psychiatric, or social, depending upon the field into which they most obviously fall. Since a number of techniques are always involved in practice, a multiple classification from the standpoint of each major technique is advisable when cases are handled by a social worker. In a multifold diagnosis, the social or sociological classification (see below under "Methods") may serve as a single unifying concept, since, in the last analysis, all the problems of child behavior, however individual they may seem, have social implications, and are thus social problems.

**Historical Development of Child Guidance.** Before discussing the methods employed in child guidance, the history of the movement should be reviewed. Although the first psychological clinic for research purposes was established by Wittmer at the University of Pennsylvania in 1896, the child guidance clinics proper did not develop until 1910. Child guidance is essentially an outgrowth of modern psychiatry and mental hygiene, as has already been indicated. In 1909 Healy began his work with delinquents in Chicago. Even at this early date the work was not purely of a psychiatric nature. Healy and Bronner have always emphasized the social as well as the individual factors. The movement thus originated with clinics established to serve juvenile courts, but it was not long before the advisability of extending such service to the entire community was recognized. Discussions of the mental hygiene of children are reported in the Proceedings of the National Con-

[9] Drucker, Saul, and Hexter, M. B., *Children Astray,* Cambridge, 1923.

ference of Social Work as early as 1921, but it was not until 1924 that the terms "habit clinic" and "children's guidance" appeared in the index of the Proceedings.[10]

The financial backing necessary to the promotion of child guidance came largely from the Commonwealth Fund.[10] About 1920 this foundation adopted child welfare as its major field. After a preliminary study the directors decided to lay emphasis upon prevention by assisting promising agencies already in the field. They were moved by three considerations: the necessity for understanding the child (psychiatry), the advisability of utilizing school contacts, and the need of increasing the number of trained social workers. The program as adopted in November, 1921, and put into operation for a five-year period in 1922, called for "community demonstrations and training of workers in the field of mental hygiene of childhood." [11] The "limited objectives" were stated as follows: [12]

> To develop the psychiatric study of difficult, pre-delinquent, and delinquent children in the schools and juvenile courts; to develop sound methods of treatment based on such study; and to provide courses of training along sound lines for those qualified and desiring to work in this field.
>
> To demonstrate in a number of widely scattered cities the value of such psychiatric study and treatment applied to children of this sort referred from juvenile courts, schools, and other agencies.
>
> To develop the work of the visiting teacher whereby the invaluable early contacts that our school systems make possible with every child may be utilized for the understanding and development of the child.
>
> To extend by various educational efforts the knowledge and use of these methods.

Three agencies, already in existence, and two new national committees, specially created for the purpose, were entrusted with the carrying out of the program. These were the New York School of Social Work, the National Committee on

[10] An article on the Commonwealth Fund Program, describing the Institute for Children's Guidance, was published in 1922 *Proceedings*, but the term is not listed in the index. See Smith, Barry C., "The Community Fund Program for the Prevention of Delinquency," *Proceedings*, 1922, pp. 168-174.

[11] *Progress Report,* Commonwealth Fund for the Prevention of Delinquency, 1926, p. 7.

[12] *Idem,* p. 8.

Visiting Teachers, the Public Education Association, the Division on the Prevention of Delinquency of the National Committee for Mental Hygiene, and the Joint Committee on Methods of Preventing Delinquency.

Four "divisions" were created. The New York School of Social Work became the Division on the Training of Workers, strengthened its department of mental hygiene, and established a psychiatric clinic and training center known as the Bureau of Children's Guidance. This Bureau, under the direction of Dr. Marion E. Kenworthy, remained in existence until 1927. Division II, on child guidance clinics, was administered by the National Committee for Mental Hygiene through its newly created department. Two traveling clinics and a permanent one were set up. The former were expected to operate from three to six months in a city, demonstrating the value of such services, and encouraging the community to establish permanent clinics of its own. In one case, at least, the demonstration clinic continued for two years. The first of the clinics was located in St. Louis. By October 1926, demonstration clinics had been operated and permanent ones established in St. Louis, Dallas, Los Angeles, and at the University of Minnesota. Consultant services were given and temporary demonstrations made in a large number of other centers. Division III, on Visiting Teachers, placed trained workers in thirty communities, each for a period of three years. At the end of this period the local community was expected to assume responsibility. By June 1926, twenty-two of these demonstrations were closed. In twenty of these communities the work was continued on a permanent basis. Division IV, known as the Joint Committee, was established to coordinate the work of the other divisions, and to interpret the program to the public through various publications.

Several subsequent developments of the program are important. In July 1927 the Child Guidance Institute was established in New York under the directorship of Dr. Lawson G. Lowrey. Its purpose is fourfold: (1) research in the mental hygiene of children and in behavior problems, (2) training students for psychiatric social work through the New York School of Social Work and Smith College, (3) provision of facilities for training of psychiatrists and graduate psychologists, and (4) diagnosis and treatment of problem children by parents, schools, and social agencies. The Commonwealth Fund Program ended July 1927 and the Bureau of Children's Guidance was discontinued. The demonstration clinics were also discontinued at this time, although advisory relations with the six permanent community clinics were continued as well as a general consultant service. With the closing of the visiting teacher demonstrations consultant service was maintained by the National Committee on Visiting Teachers to those communities that had permanently established such work as well as other communities that might desire to do so. In December 1927 the Joint Committee was discontinued. Its publication work was taken over by a new Division of Publications, organized at that time. Two Child Guidance Conferences were held during the five-year period, and in February 1928 a third was held at the Institute for Child Guidance, thus indicating that the work developed between 1922 and 1927 was to be continued, although the program itself had come to a close.

**Child Guidance Agencies: Clinics.** Most of the child guidance work today is done by special clinics or in connection with the schools. Before discussing the work of child guidance clinics proper a word should be said about another outgrowth of the mental hygiene movement, the habit clinics, also developed since 1920. The first well-known agency of this type was started by Dr. Douglas A. Thom in 1921 in Boston.[13] Typical problems presented at the habit clinic for solution are described by Dr. Thom: [14]

L.S. Age five and a half. Refuses food unless fed by mother. When left alone with food, hides it, and then tells fanciful tales of what happened to it.

X. Age three. Very shy; always sits back and watches the other children at play, taking no active part.

C.F. Age six. For the past two years has presented very marked sex interests. Takes her little sister to the park some miles away and leaves her. Goes out in the morning for school and does not

[13] Thom, Douglas A., "Results and Future Opportunities in the Field of Clinics, Social Service and Parole," *Mental Hygiene,* 6: 714-728; and *Habit Clinics for the Child of Preschool Age,* Children's Bureau Publication, No. 135, 1924.

[14] *Loc. cit., Mental Hygiene,* 6: 727-8.

return until late at night. Frequently picked up by policemen. Hangs around the moving picture shows, lies and steals.

The main distinction between the habit clinic and the child guidance clinic is that the former specializes on problems of pre-school children, more of which are primarily physical than is the case with older children. Although physical habits play an important part in the life of the child at this time, it is with their social implications that the clinic is chiefly concerned. For example, a study of one thousand children in the habit clinics of Massachusetts showed definitely that many of their bad habits were simply natural responses to stimuli in the home and family situation.[15]

The child guidance clinic is essentially a cooperative effort to make mental hygiene available to the more or less normal child as well as to the "problem child." It is a community agency for the treatment of the whole child, particularly the child that manifests "troublesome personality traits," these being regarded merely as symptoms of unsatisfactory attempts at social adjustment, in the home, at school, or in the community. Children between three and seventeen are studied;[16] these being referred in approximately equal numbers by teachers, parents, health and social agencies. A large number of these clinics now exist in the United States. Four hundred and seventy in thirty-one states are described in a recent directory.[17] Of these, more than 300 have been founded since 1922. During 1928 more than 40,000 children were studied by such agencies. Although not designated as such, the Judge Baker Foundation in Boston is one of the best known of these psychiatric clinics for children in the United States. In 1923 Healy and Bronner published a collection of twenty-seven case studies made at this clinic, which are still perhaps the most detailed and scientific available.[18]

[15] Foster, Sybil, "Personality Deviations and Their Relation to the Home," *Mental Hygiene,* 9: 735-743, 1925.

[16] There is some overlapping at the lower age levels with the habit clinics, although these may be regarded as child guidance clinics, specialized for work with pre-school children.

[17] *Directory of Psychiatric Clinics for Children in the United States*, Commonwealth Fund Division of Publications, New York, rev. ed. 1928. See also "List of Psychiatric Clinics for Children in the United States," Children's Bureau Pub. No. 191, 1929.

[18] Judge Baker Foundation Case Studies, Series 1, Boston, 1922-23.

According to Lowrey, the child guidance clinic should render two general types of services.[19] (1) "Slight services," including the mental health study of dependent children, consultation service to case workers, advice to parents, and partial examination, for purposes of discovering the presence of serious defects or abnormalities. (2) "Major clinical service," involving the "complete study and evaluation of a situation, its interpretation in terms of the dynamic stresses and strains involved in causation, and particularly the carrying out of treatment measures designed to remedy the fundamental difficulties in the situation." The functions of such clinics, as seen by another writer, are four-fold: [20]

1. Education of the community in mental health and in the mobilization of its resources.
2. To provide the community with case-work service of a co-operative type.
3. To make surveys and discover the causes of mental illnesses.
4. To educate parents, not directly but through the professional people in the community.

Clinics find their field of work in connection with the schools, the courts, social agencies and parents who bring their children for study. Probably forty to fifty of every thousand elementary school children are seriously maladjusted and may become delinquents or problems in other ways. Possibly three-fourths of this number can be handled by the visiting teachers; for the other one-fourth the child guidance clinic is needed. Child guidance clinics in connection with the juvenile courts, or else available to them, offer invaluable contributions to the prevention and scientific treatment of delinquency.

**Child Guidance in the Schools: The Visiting Teacher:** Much child guidance work may be done by the regular teacher in the school, particularly in the kindergarten and nursery school. Gesell recommends the employment of trained "special

[19] Lowrey, Lawson G., "A Program for Meeting Mental Hygiene Needs in a City," in Truitt, Ralph P., *et al., Child Guidance Clinic and the Community,* Commonwealth Fund, Division of Publications, New York, 1928, pp. 22-41.

[20] Stevenson, Geo. S., "When Is a Community Ready for a Child Guidance Clinic?" *Mental Hygiene,* 12: 492-503. Summary.

guidance" teachers for every ten exceptional children.[21] This suggests an interesting field of social work for those interested in both pre-school and case work. The great bulk of such work is at present in the grades and high schools, however, and is done by the visiting teacher. The visiting teacher is an older institution than the child guidance clinic, but since its development, she uses it, as indicated above, in the more serious cases with which she comes in contact. The visiting teacher movement came about as the direct result of the contraction of the field of influence over the child on the part of the home and the expansion of the opportunities and functions of the school. The latter has now become a habit-training as well as an information-giving institution. Thus the demand for teachers specially trained in case work arose.

The movement began in the school year 1906-1907, and developed simultaneously in New York, Boston and Hartford, Conn.[22] Three different types of organizations have contributed to the development of the movement.[23] (1) One of these is illustrated by the White-Williams Foundation, whose "counsellors," following a revision of its charter and constitution in 1920, became substantially visiting teachers. (2) In Rochester, N. Y., visiting teacher work has grown up in connection with the public school system.[24] The first visiting teacher was appointed in 1913; more workers were added in 1920, and by 1927 there were sixteen functioning in the schools. (3) Finally, a private organization, the Public Education Association (later affiliated with the Commonwealth Fund) has been of great importance in stimulating the movement by conducting demonstrations in various communities. Twenty-eight of the thirty demonstrations were closed by the end of 1927, but twenty-four of the communities concerned have continued the work on their own initiative.

The visiting teacher is expected to have had one or two years'

[21] Gesell, Arnold, "The Kindergartens as a Mental Hygiene Agency," *Mental Hygiene,* 10: 20-37, 1926.

[22] *The Visiting Teacher in the United States,* pp. 11-13. Public Education Association, New York (2d ed. 1923).

[23] Thomas, W. I., and Thomas, Dorothy S., *The Child in America,* Chap. V, "Maladjustment in the Schools," Knopf, 1928.

[24] Ellis, Mabel B., *The Visiting Teacher in Rochester.* New York: Joint Committee on Methods of Preventing Delinquency, 1925.

experience in teaching, and in addition, training in social case work ("psychiatric"). Her job is to study and treat the problems of school children arising from maladjustments in the home and in the school. Her function has been well stated by Howard W. Nudd:[25]

The visiting teacher's treatment of problem children is based upon the fact that useful citizenship and right living are the normal outgrowth of sound training and wholesome behavior in childhood, and that the attainment of these ends is vitally affected by environmental influences and by the child's attitude toward himself, toward others and toward the opportunities and obstacles he may encounter. His scholastic progress and deportment in school, his heredity, his emotional nature, his interests, ambitions, and dislikes, and the experiences which evoke the reactions that shape his character thus become the subjects of the visiting teacher's inquiry and take her into the home, the classroom, or wherever a situation exists that may help to reveal and explain the causes of his difficulties.

The reasons given for referring a child to the visiting teacher, as indicated by data obtained from fifty-seven visiting teachers, are shown below:[26]

REASONS GIVEN FOR REFERRING CHILDREN TO VISITING TEACHER

| | *Number of Visiting Teachers Naming the Given Condition as Occurring Among Their Cases* |
|---|---|
| 1. Maladjustments in scholarship | 57 |
| 2. Adverse home conditions | 57 |
| 3. Irregular attendance | 56 |
| 4. Misconduct | 53 |
| 5. Lateness | 49 |
| 6. Physical condition | 45 |

Treatment employed by the visiting teacher may involve an attempt to modify the home, school, or community situation, to effect a change of attitude toward, or on the part of, the

[25] *The Problem Child in School,* p. 254. Joint Committee, 1925.
[26] *The Visiting Teacher in the United States.* New York: Public Education Association, 1923, p. 23.

child, or both. The following table of measures applied is based upon reports from sixty visiting teachers.[27]

SUMMARY OF MEASURES USED

| *Measures* | *Number Using* |
|---|---|
| 1. Personal influence | 60 |
| 2. Information brought back to the teacher | 60 |
| 3. Co-operation of outside agencies | 56 |
| 4. Physical examination | 56 |
| 5. Mental examination | 50 |
| 6. Financial relief | 50 |
| 7. Recreation | 45 |
| 8. Change of school recommended | 44 |
| 9. Change of interests | 42 |
| 10. Change of class recommended | 41 |
| 11. Change of environment | 41 |
| 12. Referring to Society for Prevention of Cruelty to Children | 40 |
| 13. Change to a special class recommended | 37 |
| 14. Promotion recommended | 36 |
| 15. Demotion recommended | 30 |

In addition to child guidance by clinics and visiting teachers the more elaborate research work of the so-called institutes should be mentioned. Among these are the University of Minnesota Institute of Child Welfare, the Teachers' College Institute of Child Welfare Research, the Iowa Child Welfare Research Station, and the New York Institute for Child Guidance. The first three of these operate nursery schools as a part of their work.

**Methods Employed by Child Guidance Clinics.** The typical child guidance clinic consists of a psychiatrist, a psychologist, one or more social workers, and a secretary or clerk. The cycle of clinical procedure falls naturally into three divisions: the examination or study, the staff conference leading to a diagnosis, and the treatment. The entire procedure is of a cooperative nature, the psychiatrist, since he is usually the most thoroughly trained member of the staff, generally acting as director. The general aim of the investigation is, of course, the discovery of causal and particularly the modifiable factors in the individual and his environment. The first step, after the

[27] *Ibid.*, p. 49.

child is registered and accepted as a patient, is that of securing the history and data on the present social situation. This study is the function of the social worker. She attempts to collect detailed information about the patient's heredity, ancestry, social history, conflicts, adjustments, habits, companions, recreation, interests, school record and health history. In addition she secures an account of all delinquencies, difficulties, and cases of misconduct. The child is then returned to the clinic and examined by the psychologist, who attempts not only to ascertain the general level of his intelligence, by means of psychometric tests, but his special abilities and disabilities, as well as his performance on standardized educational examinations. The child is next examined by the physician and pediatrician, or by the psychiatrist, if the staff does not include a physician. After the physical and medical examination the patient is next given a psychiatric interview, in which the attempt is made to discover the child's attitudes, wishes, and complexes, and to learn what he thinks about his environment and his problems or difficulties.[28] Coming last the psychiatrist has at his disposal the data collected by the other members of the staff as a basis for his interview.

Preliminary to the staff conference the data are summarized and put into shape for discussion. In conference the first procedure is to determine the etiology (causation) of the difficulty in question, tracing it as far back into the earlier life of the child as possible, Adolescence, mental instability, personality deviations, early conditionings, physical abnormalities and the like are frequently found to be causal, but perhaps secondary to such social factors as parental attitudes, social control of the wishes, companions, family conflicts and the situational forces in general. We have passed the period when mental abnormalities were considered the major causes of delinquency or similar difficulties. Healy and Bronner, for instance, in their study of four thousand cases of delinquents, found that 72.5 per cent of them were "normal."

On the basis of the etiology discovered a diagnosis is made

[28] See "Psychiatric Examination of a Child," National Committee for Mental Hygiene. Reprint No. 222, 1926; or *Mental Hygiene,* 10: 300-306, 1926.

in psychological, medical, social [29] and psychiatric terms, and a plan of cooperative treatment is outlined. For example, in the case of Bruce, given at the beginning of this chapter, it is relatively easy to see what ought to be done, once the causal factors are laid bare. In carrying out this plan the social worker has the major responsibility. She has to reeducate the parents or teacher, see that the physical recommendations are carried out, and in the months or years subsequent to the examination, follow through the details of the plan. The psychiatrist aids, when necessary, with the attempt to change the attitudes of the child or even of the parents, if they are willing to come to the clinic for an interview. The sample "log" here presented will give a concrete picture of the social worker's activities in a child guidance clinic.

[29] For the student who may be interested in a scheme of sociological diagnosis the following provisional classification is suggested. It is based upon a fundamental sociological phenomenon, *i.e.*, the nature of the individual's reaction to social control in his attempt to realize his wishes:

1. *adjustment:* the child, motivated by a strong desire for social approval, accepts the social definition of the situation and conforms, or finds a substitute way satisfactory both to himself and the group.
2. *unadjustability:* due to mental defect or psychopathic condition the individual is unable to conform to the social standard. Calls for institutional treatment or a simplified environment.
3. *unadjustment:* involves overt conflict with social control. The child rebels against social standards and seeks to realize his desires in his own way. *Cf.* the habitual delinquent, adolescent rebel, "spoiled" child, the runaway.
4. *maladjustment: cf.* cases given in this and in Chap. XVII. Involves mental conflict. The child is torn between two sets of desires, or his loyalty to one group or pattern conflicts with that to another. Results in various "symptoms," delinquency, compensation, defensive lying, fantasy, and the like which represent incomplete and ineffective attempts at adaptation. Unconscious factors may complicate the reaction as in the case of the inferiority complex.
5. *non-adjustment:* here the child, although desirous of conforming to socially approved standards, is unable to do so on account of some temporary handicap.
6. *pre-adjustment:* a condition sometimes found in the case of very young children who have not yet developed adequate habits mechanisms of adjustment. Covers many cases dealt with in the "habit clinics."
7. *re-adjustment:* following the various types of maladaptation noted above the individual may eventually affect readjustment through conversion, sublimation, or modification of the social situation itself.

See also, Harper, Ernest B., "Personality Types: A Note on Sociological Classification." *Social Science,* 1: 26-29, 1925.

## A DAY WITH A PSYCHIATRIC SOCIAL WORKER IN A CHILD GUIDANCE CLINIC [30]

Write-up of treatment interview and analysis of case for staff conference .......................................... 1 hour

Six-year-old boy, only child, 1st grade, referred by mother at suggestion of a public demonstration school, because of daydreaming and occasional truancy. Investigation revealed that boy is expected to respond to an adult standard of behavior, due possibly to mother's feeling of social, family and personal insecurity.

History taken in clinic on new case................ 2 hours

Nine-year-old boy, only child, referred by parents at insistence of a private school. School and family recognize a reading disability; the school alone recognizes difficulty, due to boy's inability to get along with his contemporaries.

Interview out of clinic with a "source of information" on new case ........................................ ¾ hour

Pediatrician who has treated the above patient for three years and who knows the family socially as well as professionally.

Treatment interview in clinic with a parent......... ⅓ hour

Mother of a twelve-year-old Italian boy referred to the clinic one year ago because of stealing, truancy and stubbornness. The purpose of this interview was to permit worker who is new on the case to meet mother, who had appointment with psychiatrist, and arrange for appointment at home.

Time on street car.......................... 1⅓ hours

Telephone arranging appointments, 3 treatment letters..... 1¼ hours

Reported clinic findings and recommendation to school (one principal and two teachers)........................ 1 hour

Twelve-year-old boy in third grade parochial school, who was referred by the mother, at the advice of Catholic Children's Bureau, because of school retardation, disobedience at home, and because of parents' desire as to advice concerning placement possibilities. Problem appears to be that of a dull normal boy who feels displaced in the family by a younger sibling, whose mother holds him responsible for her ill health and unhappiness.

Treatment conferences with a psychiatrist.......... ⅓ hour

Twelve-year-old boy in a parochial school, referred by

[30] Odencrantz, Louise C., *The Social Worker,* pp. 328-9. By permission of Harper and Bros., 1929.

mother at the advice of a University Department, because of stealing connected with gang activities, school truancy and disobedience. Conference was devoted to a discussion of the extent to which the clinic was justified, and is equipped to handle the community phases of the case, in which unwholesome gang activity seems to have resulted from a dearth of recreational outlets.

Total ........................................8 hours

The desirability of a professionally autonomous status in the clinic for the social worker has already been mentioned, as well as for a cooperative relationship between the outside worker or agency and the clinic (Chapter XVII). The same policy should obtain in connection with the child guidance clinics, and does to a large extent. The advantage of this system is shown by the plan of the Institute for Child Guidance,[31] where, as shown below, a large percentage of the cases are handled on a purely consultant and advisory basis. Of the 479 cases accepted during the year ending June 1928 (not including those transferred from the Bureau of Children's Guidance) 50% were referred by schools, 26% by social and health agencies, 19% by parents and relatives, and 4% from other sources. The Institute accepts cases for treatment complete (clinic) or partial (cooperative), or for consultation service. Of the cases referred by the schools, 70% were for the consultation service; of the 125 cases (26% of the total accepted cases) referred by the agencies, 111 were for treatment (complete or cooperative) and 14, or 11.2%, for routine or special study only (consultation service). Of the total, 479 cases, 47% were referred for consultation.

**Results.** Porter Lee, Director of the New York School of Social Work, has made an analysis of the results of the work of the Bureau of Children's Guidance which came to an end in 1927.[32] During the five-year period 822 children were accepted at the Bureau. Of these only 591 were carried long enough to "permit reasonably adequate treatment." A special study was then made by the entire staff of the Bureau of 196 of these cases, representing work done in both the earlier and

[31] Report for the Year Ending June 30th, 1928, pp. 25-26; 61.

[32] Lee, Porter R., "An Experiment in the Evaluation of Social Case Work," *Journal of the American Statistical Association*, 23: 168-171, 1928.

later stages of the experiment. The staff appraisal of the results of treatment in these cases was:

| | | |
|---|---|---|
| Success | 93 cases | 48% |
| Partial success | 61 | 31% |
| Failure | 42 | 21% |
| Total | 196 | 100% |

It should be pointed out, of course, that since there was no "control group" it is impossible to know conclusively how many of those successfully adjusted owed their "recovery" to the Bureau's methods and not to other factors. By way of comparison, the following table shows the results obtained by the Institute for Child Guidance during the year June 1927 to June 1928:

RESULTS OF TREATMENT.[33]

Closed Cases from Treatment Service Only.

| *Duration of Contact* | *Satisfactory Adjustment* | *Partial Adjustment* | *Unimproved* | *Total* |
|---|---|---|---|---|
| 1. Less than 1 month | 3 | 4 | 0 | 7 |
| 2. 1 to 6 months | 9 | 22 | 1 | 32 |
| 3. 6 months to 1 year | 8 | 18 | 6 | 32 |
| 4. Over 1 year | 0 | 0 | 0 | 0 |
| Total | 20 (28%) | 44 (62%) | 7 (9%) | 71 |

One of the most valuable results of this work has been the accumulation of a large number of detailed and scientific case records. These are and will continue to be an important source of data for the student of case work. Some of the earlier over-optimistic assumptions of the psychiatrists, however, have been shattered. "Certainly the psychiatric approach in its present form," says Thomas,[34] "is far from being the panacea that its more ardent and less objective advocates have claimed." The psychiatrists themselves have come to see that the field is very complex, not concerned exclusively with mental abnormality, and that personality is inextricably tied up with the social situation. Hence such leaders as Dr. Ralph P. Truitt and Dr.

[33] Report for the Year Ending June 30th, 1928, p. 62.
[34] Thomas and Thomas, *The Child in America*, p. 149.

Lawson G. Lowrey are urging the necessity for cooperation with sociologists and other students of social phenomena.

Child Guidance is one of the most scientific and hopeful fields of case work, preventive in its nature, and dealing more and more with the "normal" individual. It has an important rôle in child placing, as described in the preceding chapter, and in connection with probation and the treatment of children in institutions discussed in subsequent chapters.

# CHAPTER XXII

## MEDICAL SOCIAL WORK

In retracing the history of medical charities it would be necessary for us to go back at least as far as the medieval hospital and monastery. Neither of these would be classed today as a medical institution, nor would their activities bear a close resemblance to present-day social work. But in their generous, though crude, efforts on behalf of the sick, injured, aged, and other needy folk, the monks and hospitallers were laying the foundations for both professions. The connection between medicine and social work for centuries consisted largely in the fact that certain institutions received only persons who were both physically incapacitated and financially destitute. This special interest in the "sick poor" or the "indigent sick," as they were sometimes called, was displayed not only in charity hospitals, but from the seventeenth century on in dispensaries. These newer institutions were regarded as "medical soup-kitchens" from which drugs and medical advice were offered as "doles to the needy."

From medical charities to the modern public health movement is a long jump involving a number of new developments. The first is improved medical service for the sick, based on discoveries in the physical and biological sciences and the development of genuine professional schools. The second is preventive medicine, involving quarantine, sanitation, vaccination, periodic examinations, and health education. As a matter of fact these measures not only prevent disease, but promote health and general well-being. The third significant change is in the source of financial support and control. While much health service is still on the basis of public poor relief or middle-class humanitarianism, we find more and more health centers, well-baby stations, visiting nursing, and other agencies operated by insurance companies for their policyholders, by trade unions for their members, by corporations for their employes, and by school systems for their pupils. The fourth new development has been the integration of social case work with medical service in the effort to meet all the needs of patients in hospitals and dispensaries.

> The tendency in medicine to place increasing emphasis on such values as good hygiene, adequate and proper diet, recreation, a job suitable to one's strength, a constructive attitude toward life, has created new types of medical recommendation. The physician who years ago might have prescribed medicine for a patient will today for a similar condition advise convalescent care, or a change of job. The taking of pills and powders is simple. To carry out a recommendation that a mother leave her family for several weeks' convalescent care, or that a factory worker change to an out-of-door job, may require the rearrangement of a whole scheme of life. Here begins the task of the social worker.[1]

Miss Cannon has described the immediate backgrounds of hospital social service.[2] About 1880 an organization was founded in England known as the Society for After Care of Poor Persons Discharged Recovered from Insane Asylums. Its purpose was to arrange for the care of discharged patients, especially those who had no homes, and to guide them through the process of readjustment to the community. A second contribution to hospital social work came through the "lady almoners" connected with London hospitals in the 'nineties. Their tasks were to prevent abuse of medical charities by inquiring into the financial status of patients and to refer needy persons to the appropriate social agencies. A third factor was the work of visiting nurses who early found themselves forced to undertake many responsibilities not ordinarily associated with their work. In 1904 the Presbyterian Hospital in New York sent student nurses into the homes of patients where they were "taught to give nursing care, to improve hygienic conditions, and to aid and encourage the patients by kindliness and helpful advice." The fourth significant contribution to the idea of hospital social work came through the training given to medical students at Johns Hopkins University. Dr. Emerson "recognized that truly effective medical training must include an

[1] *Vocational Aspects of Medical Social Work,* p. 16.
[2] Cannon, Ida M., *Social Work in Hospitals,* Chap. II.

understanding by a physician of the background and the standards of living of his patients." At his instigation there was organized a student board of the Charity Organization Society of Baltimore to carry on friendly visiting among the poor. The final step came with the establishment of a social service department in Massachusetts General Hospital in 1906. By 1925 there were about 500 hospitals and dispensaries with social service departments, and in 1927 the American Association of Hospital Social Workers had over 1500 members.

## ANNA SZWYDKY [3]

On July 23, 1925, Anna Szwydky, a non-English-speaking Ukrainian woman thirty years of age and without adequate funds for treatment, registered at the Mayo Clinic. She was alone and frightened and wholly incapacitated by a disease diagnosed as "an old infectious arthritis with ankylosis of both elbows and wrist joints and of the right hip and knee joint." She had been an invalid for five years. She had come from Saskatchewan, where her aged parents had lived since they immigrated, when Anna was five years old. . . . A friend, Mrs. Grabko, had come with the patient to Rochester. . . . As she was lonely and frightened the social worker was called in July 31.

*Social Investigation.* Medical examination soon revealed the condition described above and indicated that months of treatment would be needed. At best the outlook was considered poor. However, it was decided to operate on the right arm to see what could be accomplished.

The social investigation proceeded much more slowly because of the language difficulty, the patient's unresponsiveness, and the separation from friends and relatives. Mrs. Grabko gave some information, letters from Saskatchewan supplemented this, and gradually Anna herself told bits of her story, first through an interpreter and then in broken English.

The Szwydky family with about forty other Ukrainians left the old country in 1900 because it was so hard to make a living, and finally settled in Saskatchewan forming a little Slavic community. They worked very hard and were not able to save much. Anna's parents were now old and feeble. Her brother and sister, both married, lived near by and helped in various ways. All were very religious; the children attended a church school, and all made the Greek Catholic Church the center of their social life.

[3] Summary of record published in *Medical Social Case Records,* edited by Sophonisba P. Breckinridge, also in *Social Service Review,* 1: 443-469, 1927; by permission of The University of Chicago Press.

Anna had little schooling; at fourteen she dropped out to help her father with the farm work. She was devoted to her family and the church, but apparently had few other social contacts. "At first patient had a very passive and resigned attitude toward her illness. She had been helpless so long that she had lost all initiative and desire to be a normal person. As she began to get motion in her hands and feet, her initiative returned; she showed a new interest in her surroundings; she developed self-confidence, and finally quite a cheerful attitude toward life in general." She was worried because the money for this trip was taken from funds her father had saved for his old age. She told her story very excitedly. She wept much and seemed terrified by the strange surroundings and notions of what the doctors might do to her.

*Social Diagnosis and Plans.* The patient's social situation can be stated largely in terms of isolation, poverty and fear. She was cut off from most social contacts not only by her physical condition (she could not move in bed without assistance), but by separation from friends, relatives, and others who might speak her language. Also it was hard for her to fit into the life of an American hospital, because all her life had been spent in a rural community of Slavic immigrants. That is, her isolation was physical, geographic, and cultural. Poverty was the second serious element in the situation. Anna needed a long period of hospital care while she had a series of expensive operations, but she herself was without funds and her people could give but little assistance. It was natural that the patient was filled with fear and worry, so that she offered little response to the friendly approaches of physicians, nurses and social worker.

The medical prognosis was poor. Because of Anna's frail physical condition and low morale, the surgeon proposed to operate only on her right arm, keep her in the hospital for a month, and then find a home for chronic invalids in Canada to which she might be admitted. Meantime it was necessary to break down some of the barriers, encourage the patient, and discover financial resources.

*Medical Treatment.* The services of surgeon, nurse, occupational and physiotherapists, social worker, and friendly visitors are so bound together that it is difficult to separate them. However, following the medical examination, there was a series of six operations. After months in bed the patient was able to sit up in a wheel chair and eventually to take a few steps. Massage, simple exercises, and later the weaving of mats and baskets contributed to the recovery of muscular functions. But our concern here is mainly with the social service.

*Social Treatment.* Most of the social worker's service was rendered indirectly. On the financial side she secured funds from the municipality, in which Anna's home was located, and from her family. When this money was exhausted and it seemed unwise to press for more, she arranged to have some bills cancelled and paid others out of her own department's budget. She attended to the extension of Anna's bond given to the Immigration Commissioner when she entered the United States. Although it later proved unnecessary, the social worker gathered information about homes for chronic invalids. Perhaps her most important service was the discovery of two men of Anna's own nationality, who were not only able to serve as interpreters, but who also became her very good friends and contributed much to her change of attitude. The help of others was secured to take Anna about in her wheel chair, to assist her in purchasing needed clothing, to go with her to the movies, and finally to accompany her on the trip back to her home.

All along the social worker was attempting to explain Anna's condition and needs to various other persons. She told Mrs. Grabko what the physicians expected to accomplish and asked her to explain it to Mr. and Mrs. Szwydky. She wrote several letters to the secretary-treasurer of the municipality telling of Anna's progress and needs. In September with the help of an interpreter, she wrote to Mr. Szwydky that Anna "has suffered a good deal of pain, but she is very patient and does not complain. Her arm is rubbed every day to make it easier for her to move it. She appreciates letters from home more than anything else. I hope you will tell all her friends to write her as often as possible." Both before and after Anna returned to Saskatchewan letters were written to her home physician, relatives and others, telling them just what to expect, advising continued treatment, and pointing out the necessity of keeping her encouraged.

It took some time for the social worker to gain *rapport* with Anna, but she did not try to rush her. She went with the patient to the operating room, visited her in the ward, took little gifts, and for some days did not attempt to carry on a conversation. Bit by bit she won Anna's confidence and heartened her for the long struggle back to health. But most of the personal influence, which was so important in this case, was brought to bear through other persons. As soon as she was called in, the case worker asked John Ohab, a dishwasher at the hospital, to talk with Anna. Immediately she seemed relieved and reassured, partly because John spoke her language, and partly because he explained what different members of the staff were trying to do. He convinced her that there was nothing to fear. From this time on John wrote letters for Anna, read to her, and talked to her many times. For a long time he was the only one who seemed able to get any response from her. In September the case worker found another fellow countryman, a patient working in occupational therapy. This man contributed much to Anna's improvement by his cheerful disposition and by reading aloud an Ukrainian newspaper to which he subscribed. Then there was an American woman patient who brought little presents and talked with Anna. Through all these and other persons the case worker kept stimulating Anna to do the many things essential to recovery.

*Patient's Response.* It is most interesting to trace through the record the slowly accumulating results of the medical social work as indicated by the patient's responses. We saw how hopeless and frightened she seemed on arriving at the clinic. The first steps in changing these attitudes included the case worker's quiet approach and the reassuring talk with John Ohab. On September 4, the record reads, "Although it hurts her to bend her arm, she smiles faintly at what she can do." On October 19, Anna used a spoon for the first time. "It took five minutes for her hand to get from the plate to her mouth. She needed a great deal of encouragement, but when it was accomplished she smiled broadly for the first time." By December she had learned enough English words to carry on a short conversation without an interpreter. Joe and John were very faithful, and Anna sometimes laughed out loud when they were with her. In January she started to make a wicker tray under the direction of occupational therapy. The record notes that "It seems to please her very much to be able to do the same things other patients are doing." January 15 Anna wrote her first letter home. Other bits from the record show her continued progress, not only in physical strength and muscular function, but in attitudes and social contacts.

January 15. "Patient is immensely pleased with things she is beginning to do for herself."

February 21. "Patient is able to be up in a wheel chair. . . . She asked for sauerkraut and pickles and sausage."

February 25. "Patient stands alone today for the first time. She is very timid, but well pleased with herself."

March 13. "Patient is developing some initiative; she frequently asks for things she would like to have or do, and seems to take great satisfaction in doing the same things for herself which other patients in the ward do for themselves. She was seen very shyly looking at herself in the mirror the other day."

April 12. "She takes a childlike interest in everything that goes by."

April 20. "Patient has been walking a little each day in the walker. . . . She was very timid at first and sometimes quite stubborn about refusing to try. It takes a good deal of persuading and cajoling to get her to make the effort. She is very proud of what she can do now, but very loath to try anything new. Worker has been talking to her for some time about going home. She wants to go, and yet has been in the hospital so long she dreads the thought of a change and fears she will not be able to get along at home."

May 10. "Patient of her own accord arranges with Joe to take her in the wheelchair to buy a new spring hat."

June 5. "Patient asks to have her hair marcelled before she starts home."

In September, after three months at home, Anna wrote of walking a quarter of a mile across the fields. She was helping her mother at home and apparently was quite happy. A local Ukrainian newspaper had an article about her "cure," which brought many visitors from the surrounding country. This evidently encouraged her to do her best and led her to attempt new activities.

**Functions of Medical Social Work.** In the case of Anna Szwydky the main problems presented were her chronic disease, poverty, social isolation, and her attitudes of fear and discouragement. The treatment of the physical condition as such was a task for physician, surgeon, nurse, occupational and physiotherapist. The offsetting of her poverty, the breaking down of her isolation, and the modification of her attitudes were primarily tasks for the social worker. However, it is well to bear in mind the fact that all these specialists worked closely together and their success depended upon their full cooperation.

Many other types of social adjustments must be made by and for patients who come to hospitals and dispensaries. It may be an injured workman who needs help in securing compensation, a crippled child who requires special provision for his education, an unmarried mother who is uncertain what to do with her baby, a tuberculous wife whose children must be cared for while she is in the sanitarium, or a syphilitic husband whose family must be told of his condition and advised how to avoid infection. All these are tasks which may come to a hospital social worker. All are handled by techniques of general case work, adapted, however, to the necessities of medical institutions.

One interesting classification of patients who come to a dispensary divides them into these four types: (1) those whose social problems are evident and acute, as in the case of Anna Szwydky; (2) those whose social problem is not acute, but whose disease is dangerous to others—e.g., a man in the second stage of tuberculosis with young children living in crowded quarters; (3) those who present no acute social or economic problem, but who need to return several times for treatment—e.g., patients with rheumatism, indigestion or bad teeth; (4) those who have no acute social problem and whose medical treatment can be completed at the first visit—e.g., patient with toothache requiring extraction.[4] The fourth type clearly does not require the services of a social case worker. The only non-medical problem likely to be considered pertains to the patient's ability to pay, and that can probably be handled by a skilled clerk at the admission desk. The third type may call forth the efforts of a social worker to persuade the patient to return for needed treatments. In such a case it may be necessary to visit the home and learn why the patient is unwilling or unable to keep his appointments at the clinic. Ordinarily, however, this type does not need much attention from the social service department. The second group may be handled successfully by the medical staff, but if there is ignorance, fear, or unwillingness to take the precautions necessary to guard against infection, the social worker may be called in to discover the source of these attitudes, and to modify them if possible. Patients of the first type obviously need the services of a social worker quite as much as those of a physician.

In general the tasks of social workers in medical institutions may be divided into three classes: (1) direct assistance in the cure and prevention of disease in individual cases, (2) participation in administrative work, (3) sharing the community relations of the hospital or dispensary. The first group of duties includes discovering facts about the patient's personality or circumstances which relate to his physical condition, overcoming obstacles to successful treatment such as may arise in his home or work, arranging for supplementary care when required, and educating the patient and his family that they may cooperate with the physician to the best advantage. The second set of duties includes assisting in the admission of patients, providing information on which admission fees and hospital rates may be based, interpreting for non-English-speaking pa-

[4] Cannon, Ida M., *Social Work in Hospitals,* pp. 171-2.

tients, and aiding in the management of separate clinics in the dispensary or out-patient department. The third group of tasks includes furnishing medical information and advice concerning medical resources to outside individuals and to social agencies, arranging suitable care for patients not admitted, reporting unsanitary conditions discovered in the course of regular work, and carrying on educational publicity concerning health needs and facilities.

Perhaps it would be well, before examining each of these functions in detail and the methods by which they are performed, to point out that there are several types of workers in the general field of medical social work. In addition to hospital social workers, who are really social case workers attached to medical institutions, there are public health nurses, nutrition workers, household economists, sanitary engineers, and health officers. The public health nurses visit homes to care for sick persons, arrange for further treatment, and give instruction in nutrition, hygiene, and care of the sick. Nutrition workers give instruction with demonstrations in the selection and preparation of foods and in food and other health habits. The household economists, sometimes called visiting housekeepers, give instruction with demonstrations in foods, budgets, clothing, house furnishing, and sanitation. The sanitary engineers plan and supervise water supplies and sewage disposal. The health officers make inspections, enforce quarantine and other legal requirements and give publicity to matters affecting the public health. All these specialists are concerned both with physical well-being and with social relations; their methods are those of education rather than of medication; hence they may all be called medical social workers. Perhaps that is why the case workers in medical institutions take pains to use the more specific title of hospital social workers.

**Technique of Hospital Social Service.** A very clear analysis of the technique of hospital social service has been prepared by a committee of the Associated Out-Patient Clinics of the City of New York. A portion of its report is presented here.[5]

[5] *Technique of Hospital Social Service,* pp. 9-13.

I. Service to Patients Through Contributing to Medical Care.

1. Securing the information which enables her to place before the physician all the factors in that patient's personality and environment which may affect his diagnosis and treatment. . . .

   This information is usually obtained through such sources as the patient himself, the physician and the medical record, consultation with the social agencies, and home visits. The Social Service Exchange should be consulted to learn what other agencies, if any, are interested. Many cases will indicate need of other special investigation, such as consulting relatives, the employer, previous medical records, and schools. The study of the patient's personality and environment should be based on the individual treatment of the individual patient. . . .

2. Analyzing all the evidence in the light of all knowledge available on such a problem in order to
3. Make a social analysis by defining
   a. Obstacles to effective medical treatment.
   b. Underlying social causes of physical disability.
   c. The available social and economic resources, such as employer and family.
4. Determining upon a plan of social treatment; this must be related to the conditions found by the physician and what he directs for their relief and must be worked out in coöperation with the physician and the patient.
5. Following through the case with constant alertness for new evidence which may modify diagnosis or treatment, medical or social. After the initial conference with the physician, this work usually falls under the following headings:
   a. Work with the patient himself; making sure that the patient understands the treatment recommended, that he realizes the importance of carrying out such treatment, and that his will to do his share is enlisted. . . . Sometimes it is necessary to persuade the patient to change his whole method of living and the habits of a lifetime. . . .
   b. Work with the family and others in immediate environment of patient. It is necessary often to influence relatives, employers, and others to a different attitude, or to seek assistance in carrying out a plan from church, teacher, lodge, insurance agent, club, or landlord. . . .
   c. Work with cooperating agencies in the community. . . .
   d. Regular conferences with the physician in charge of the patient. . . .

II. Service to Patients Through Certain Administrative Duties.

1. In admissions
    a. Patients in wards. Ward patients are often emergency or accident cases and require immediate social service work, such as getting in touch with relatives and friends and providing for the emergency in the home.
    b. Making sure that the patient understands the conditions of admission to the institution, such as fees and hours, and is prepared to meet them.
    c. Securing information which may contribute to the treatment of the case . . . and passing on this information to the workers who will deal with the patient in clinic or ward.
    d. Fulfilling the administrative requirements of the institution in regard to assignment of patients and their eligibility. It is usually the responsibility of the worker, under rules laid down by the institution, to direct rejected patients to the appropriate agency through which the needed care can be obtained instead of merely refusing admission.
2. In clinic management
    a. Routing the patient through the clinic and through the various procedures recommended. Routing is here used to mean not only directing the patient through the various parts of the building, but explaining preparation required for tests or special treatments ordered, and their cost, and making arrangements to have them done.
    b. Interviewing each patient to see that he understands the physician's plan of treatment, and going over his plan for following this treatment; if he cannot carry out treatment arranging for some adjustment or for further social service to work out some plan. . . .
    c. Carrying on the administration of an appointment system to promote regular attendance of patients as directed by the physician.
    d. Following those patients who break their appointments and helping them to overcome the obstacles which interfered with their continued treatment. . . .
    e. Supervising the transfer or refer of patients to other departments within the out-patient department or hospital or to other institutions, and checking up not only to see if the patient has followed the instructions but also to obtain for the physician any necessary reports.
    f. Keeping a record of medical intake and disposition of cases for each clinic.

g. Gaining from patients or their parents, the consents necessary for surgical and other out-of-routine work, necessary for the progress of the patient. . . .
**h.** In teaching institutions, assisting in collecting material suitable for teaching cases; also persuading the patients who are needed as teaching material to consent to make this contribution to medical knowledge.

In addition to their studies within the medical institution, social workers usually share in the outside contacts. One of their problems in this conection is to determine when to accept responsibility for social treatment. The social service exchange is, of course, used to discover whether any other agency is interested in the patient and if so what are its relations to him. Then in consultation with the physician an effort is made to determine what significance the patient's illness and his social situation have for each other. "Only if they bear a relation of cause or effect is the medical social worker justified in undertaking responsibility for planning social adjustment." If there is some problem which requires the services of another social agency, the case is referred to that organization and a plan of joint supervision is devised. If the social need is likely to outlast the medical connection, contact is soon made with an agency which can continue to serve the patient throughout the period of his unadjustment.

Another duty of the hospital social worker in his or her outside contacts is explaining to non-medical social workers the significance of medical conditions and of service rendered or required. Sometimes it is the administrative routine of the hospital or dispensary which needs explanation. The hospital social worker may also perform a valuable service in helping to interpret health problems and agencies to the community through addresses, newspaper stories, and various personal contacts. He may point out unmet needs which call for higher standards or expansion of programs in existing agencies or possibly for the establishment of new organizations. Preceding such recommendations there is often a careful analysis and interpretation of data included in the case records. Indeed research into medical social problems is one of the important functions of a hospital social service department. Closely related to this is participation in the teaching of students in the three fields of medicine, nursing, and social work.

**Organization and Personnel.** There are four general types of organization of social service departments in medical institutions: (1) those established and controlled by the hospital board, (2) those established by hospital authority and affiliated with the training school for nurses, (3) those initiated by an individual or group and supervised by a self-appointed committee recognized by the hospital or dispensary, and (4) those established and supervised by an outside agency such as the Red Cross.[6]

While the start may of necessity be made in various ways, it is pretty generally agreed that social service should be organized as a department of the hospital or other institution in order that its work may be completely integrated with that of the medical and nursing staffs. This means, of course, direct responsibility of the head worker to the chief executive of the institution. Often there is an advisory committee with representatives from the board of trustees, medical staff, social workers in outside agencies, and interested citizens. Such a group may act as a case committee or it may deal with general problems of policy. Its chief function is often to promote interest and understanding on the part of the public.

As in other case-working agencies, systematic record keeping is exceedingly important, both as an aid to serving the individual patients and as a guide to policy making. This means that the files will contain detailed case records and statistical summaries.

The fundamental training of hospital social workers has a great deal in common with that of other case workers. In fact, they take many of the same courses in the professional schools. However, a larger percentage of hospital social workers has been recruited from the nursing field rather than from other forms of social work or from the professional schools. A committee of the American Hospital Association has set forth what in its opinion are the most important qualifications for

[6] Cannon, Ida M., *Social Work in Hospitals*, pp. 157-8.

hospital social service. These include some traits which are obviously needed in any form of social work and some which are fairly distinctive of this particular field.[7]

Some of the more evident characteristics which are required in medical social workers are: interest in people resulting in an understanding of the points of view of patients, physicians, and others, and in tact in dealing with people; a broad educational background; freedom from fear of disease and dirt; sense of values in life; ability to face facts and think clearly; powers of persuasion; a sense of humor; good health and mental balance.

It is believed that the elements which should be derived from training and experience are five in number.

1. Knowledge of the chief diseases, groups of diseases, and health problems, primarily in their social implications.
2. Understanding of the social, industrial, and economic problems as they affect family life.
3. Knowledge of the purposes and activities of the chief public and private health and social agencies and of legal and community conditions which affect health.
4. Understanding of the traditions and customs of the medical profession and of medical institutions.
5. Ability to utilize both knowledge and personal qualities in attaining understanding of people and practical results in co-operation, guidance and leadership.

[7] American Hospital Association, Bulletin No. 23, pp. 9-10.

# CHAPTER XXIII

## PROBATION AND PAROLE

The techniques of social case work which were developed first in the field of family welfare have thus been taken over and modified by agencies dealing with homeless children, youngsters maladjusted at home or at school, and the sick. Much the same thing has happened in the handling of delinquents. A hundred years ago most peoples dealt harshly with those who broke their laws. Offenders were pilloried, or whipped, or thrust into prison, or banished, or put to death, all in a spirit of vengeance, though with some hope of deterring others from committing crime, and with vague notions of reforming those who had already gone wrong. During the nineteenth century this harshness was gradually mitigated by the efforts of earnest humanitarians who were interested in the reformation of offenders. Their work in turn has been followed by the study of delinquents by physicians, psychologists, psychiatrists, and sociologists. So today we find a mixture of motives and viewpoints with, however, a fairly well defined trend. The first of the following excerpts represents the attitude of "treat 'em rough," the second that of sentimental humanitarianism, the third that of modern psychiatry.

The Day's Question: What can be done to reduce crime in Chicago? and some answers. (1) Build a gallows in Grant Park and use it every day for a week. Ever notice how yellow these guys get after a hanging at the county jail? (2) Let the federal government put 5,000 Great Lake sailors or Camp Grant soldiers in the city for patrol duty. Give them all rifles and orders to "shoot to kill." (3) Increase the police force, taking on young men; put them in plain clothes and have two to every block where crime is running high. Throw these extra men into any district where there is trouble, and crime will decrease immediately.[1]

[1] *Chicago Tribune,* April 10, 1919.

To the earnest worker, the delinquent once was the "evil doer" who has "fallen from grace," the "outcast from society" who has "ruined his life" unless he can be brought to "repentance" and "reform." He was a "black sheep" who might be "redeemed" from the "way of transgression" if he could be "made to see the light" and be "convinced of the error of his ways." His sinning sister who began life as "pure and innocent" had "fallen" and must be "saved from sin." Perhaps she had been admitted as a "penitent" within the portals of a "rescue home for fallen girls" (always spoken of by the layman with a lowered voice). At best she was "wayward" or "ungovernable" and needed the "uplifting influence" of a "healer of broken souls." [2]

We have steered away from this sentimental and semi-religious phraseology based on the old approach to conduct problems, which reveals the sympathetic but unscientific attitude of a time not so long gone by. Now we see the "individual delinquent" with a "behavior pattern" which we must first "diagnose" and then "treat." We "analyze" all of the "contributing factors," personal and environmental, entering into the problem. We see "sex irregularity" as "symptomatic" of some underlying condition of "maladjustment." We "prescribe treatment" according to a carefully formulated plan and we even venture to make a "prognosis." Our "unstable delinquent" may be "defective," "subnormal" or "abnormal," he may be an "extrovert" or an "introvert," and his "antisocial conduct" may be traced to a "defense mechanism" or may be the outcome of an "inferiority complex." [3]

From the era of harshness we have inherited capital punishment, prisons, deportation, a spirit of vengeance, and a myth about balancing the scales of justice. Nineteenth century humanitarianism introduced cleanliness, religious and educational activities, industrial employment, the indeterminate sentence, parole, and probation. Only since the opening of the twentieth century have the findings of modern science and the methods of social case work been applied to the handling of delinquents.

Parole was introduced from Australia in the 'seventies of the last century. It represents an intermediate stage between imprisonment and discharge during which the prisoner is under control of the institutional authorities and is helped in the making of his adjustments. Probation, which also appeared in the 'seventies, seems to have been an American invention. It is

[2] Bulletin of the National Probation Association, Oct., 1928. p. 1.
[3] *Ibid.*

a substitute for imprisonment, offered to convicted persons who are believed able, with guidance, to become law-abiding citizens without removal from the community. In the beginning neither parole nor probation was based on a careful study of the individual offender. Even today they are often administered as matters of routine or as forms of leniency. Hence it is natural that they should be generally misunderstood and that under dishonest or inefficient administration they should often degenerate. But at their best they are applications of social case work to the reformation of delinquent attitudes and habits.

## GEORGE WOOD [4]

In February, 1926, George Wood stole $190 from a clock in which his landlord kept his savings. Suspecting George, Mr. Albright notified the police, who secured his confession to the theft. In court the boy pled guilty, but before passing sentence the judge ordered the probation officer to investigate and report "on the circumstances of the offense, criminal record and social history of the defendant."

*Preliminary Study of Offender.* The probation officer found that George was 18 years old, and had lived all his life in the city. He had been left an orphan at the age of 7 and spent about nine years in an orphanage. He finished the eighth grade and obtained some training in the plumber's trade. His scholastic and conduct records were good. In 1924, the boy went to live with his aunt, a coarse, unsympathetic woman, who alternated between ruthless discipline and neglect. After a year and a half the friction became so great that George went to live in a furnished room with the Albrights. They found him a quiet, well-mannered youth, but noticed that he began to draw away from the family and to keep late hours. His employer said that he worked steadily, but he suspected him of having stolen some bolts of silk from the truck on which he worked. The city prison psychiatrist reported that George seemed to be in good health and of normal mentality. He had been arrested once before and fined for gambling. He seemed to have an insatiable desire for expensive amusements, spending most of his money on shows, gambling, and good clothes. He also drank moderately. The Albrights were very friendly and offered to take him back into their home provided he would make restitution. Upon the officer's recommendation, therefore, the

[4] Summary of a case record presented by Edwin J. Cooley to the National Probation Association and published in its Proceedings for 1928, pp. 255-295.

court placed George Wood on probation for one year, with the requirement that he pay back the money he had stolen.

*Probation.* To this point the work of the probation officer had been confined to the securing of information and interpreting it to the court. After sentence was passed the officer's duties included the making and revising of plans, securing additional information, various executive tasks, direct personal influence on the boy, and influencing others who were in touch with him, thus supplementing investigation with treatment.

At the very outset the problem was formulated in terms of the probationer's habits and attitudes. He was described as sullen and suspicious, deeply hurt by this experience, resenting authority, feeling the hand of society to be against him, self-conscious and diffident, with no helpful friends or understanding relatives, craving novel experience and exciting pleasures. The explanation was felt to lie in the five stages of his personal-social development: (1) "His early childhood, passed under the incubus of poverty, disease and involuntary neglect, was followed by (2) confinement during the entire period of puberty and adolescence in a large orphan asylum . . . (where) being a naturally sensitive youngster, his emotional development took an introverted direction. (3) Upon his release from the institution he came under the guardianship of an aunt, who . . . treated him with harshness and indifference. (4) He escaped from this tyranny only to succumb to the pitfalls of unrestrained liberty. . . . (5) The blow that has now fallen on him has bewildered and somewhat embittered him."

In the face of this situation the probation officer set up two main objectives: "(1) The probationer must be assisted to acquire the economic and educational means to a useful and satisfying life in the community, the lack of which has contributed in large measure to his delinquency. (2) His emotional life must be reconditioned by overcoming his suspicious and rebellious attitude towards law and order." To realize these objectives a plan was made which included: (1) physical and mental examinations to determine his abilities and limitations, (2) educational and vocational guidance based on the findings of the examinations, (3) progressive employment to earn his living, to make restitution for the theft, and to encourage through advancement, (4) discipline and supervision close enough to have a steadying influence but not so rigorous as to confirm his present antagonism, (5) instruction in thrift, (6) diversion into new channels of recreation, (7) contact with personalities who might establish in him a sense of security and worth, (8) convincing him that the probation officer is really his friend, and finally (9) bringing together the scattered members of the family in order to build a stable foundation for the boy's future. In the main this plan was carried out, though some changes were made as the treatment progressed.

The executive part of the officer's work included such items as receiving the boy's weekly reports, helping to secure employment, arranging medical and psychiatric examinations, visiting the home in which George lived and calling on his employers to make sure that matters were proceeding satisfactorily, handling the money paid in as restitution, taking the boy to see his younger brother in an orphanage, permitting him to visit his sister in another state, going with him to call on his pastor, and finally recommending his discharge from probation.

The personal influence of the officer began with thorough instruction in the requirements of probation. "The imperative need for procuring employment at once was impressed upon him as well as the obligation on his part to institute promptly regular and substantial payments as ordered by the court. The assistance of the probation officer in finding suitable employment was promised him, but he was instructed to accept whatever offered for the present, and to keep in constant contact with this department until he had secured a steady position." The probation officer discussed with George the importance and the possibilities of securing vocational training, insurance, savings, personal hygiene, use of the public library, joining the Y. M. C. A., and so on. Apparently a good deal of pressure was put on the boy, but he was not scolded or reproached for his delinquency. Rather he was urged forward; new possibilities were set before him; and with opportunity to succeed, he was encouraged to assume direction of his own affairs.

Much of the personal influence on George Wood was exercised through third parties such as the Albrights with whom he lived, his employers, his pastor, and friends he made at the Y. M. C. A. During the first home visit the officer explained to Mrs. Albright the aims and methods of probation and invited her cooperation in carrying out the program of treatment. She responded with genuine interest and intelligence, always avoiding reference to George's offense, and striving to make him a real member of their family circle. The officer later discussed with the Albrights the wisdom of keeping their savings in a bank both for safety and for the removing of temptation from George and others who might be in their household. Through the library George became much interested in good reading, and at a Y. M. C. A. party he became acquainted with a girl who worked in a book store. Her friendship seems to have been a wholesome stimulus to the boy's development. The contacts with his brother and sister made George increasingly eager to establish a home for the scattered members of his family, though this was not accomplished during the time of his probation.

*Response of Probationer.* To all these and other efforts that were made on his behalf, the probationer responded quite positively. As noted, in the beginning he was sullen, suspicious, resentful of authority, and hostile toward the probation officer. But when a job was secured for him at $20 a week he immediately felt encouraged, for this was more than he had ever earned before. His employer said that he went to work with enthusiasm and was rapidly becoming competent to do it without direction. Within a month he volunteered to increase his weekly payments of restitution from $4 to $5, and later he gradually brought the amount up to $10 a week until the whole sum had been repaid. Mrs. Albright reported that George seemed appreciative and anxious to do well. He made himself helpful about the house, although he was under no obligation except to pay for his board and room. When urged to change from night work to a job which would enable him to attend an electrical school, he expressed interest but wanted to be very sure that he would not lose out financially until he had paid all he owed the Albrights. When the necessary arrangements were made he seemed to find new zest in life and soon outstripped all the others in his class. He attended church regularly, joined the Y. M. C. A., made good use of the public library, and came to have a friendly attitude toward the probation officer. When his restitution was completed, he started a savings account. On the basis of these changes in habits and attitudes, the court discharged George Wood from probation at the end of one year.

**Preliminary Study of Offenders.** Not everyone found guilty is a good subject for probation; or, put the other way around, probation is not the proper treatment for all convicted offenders. How then shall the court decide between imprisonment and probation? Unfortunately there is no short and easy way to make this decision. It is necessary first of all to discover the causal factors underlying the delinquency, and then to estimate the possibility of bringing these under control by various means. The particular crime committed is of relatively little consequence, but the character of the offender is of very great importance. Since character is the product of a long series of events, it is usually necessary to search far back in the individual and family history as well as in the life of the community to identify the process through which the prisoner became delinquent. In this respect the investigation and diagnosis made by a probation officer differ only in detail from those made by other social case workers. Several different outlines of study have been devised.[5] The one offered here is an adaptation and abbreviation of these.

1. Circumstances immediately attending delinquent act.
   a. Were there associates? Casual or permanent?
   b. What was the purpose or objective? Was it socially acceptable?
   c. Was the crime a repetition of previous acts?
   d. Was it preceded by other forms of delinquency?
   e. In general, what seems to account for the particular act at the given time and place?
2. Character (habits and attitudes) as to:
   a. Work—occupation, regularity, efficiency, associates.
   b. Recreation—kinds, amount, time, associates.
   c. Group life—family, neighborhood, gang, church, etc.—loyalty, leadership, intimacy, etc.
   d. Authority—parental, legal, mores—acceptance or rejection.
   e. Planning and organizing own activities vs. drifting and depending on stimulus of the moment.
3. Mental Traits.
   a. Intelligence level.
   b. Special abilities and disabilities.
   c. Emotional balance.
   d. Dominant interests.
4. Physical Traits.
   a. Appearance.
   b. General vigor.
   c. Specific diseases.
   d. Chronic disabilities.
5. Personal History.
   a. Physical health and development.
   b. Mental health and development.
   c. Home life.
   d. Neighborhood and community life.
   e. Other associates—church, lodge, gang.
   f. Schooling.
   g. Employment.
   h. Institutional experiences.
   i. Previous clashes with the law.
6. Family History.
   a. Brothers and sisters.

[5] Cooley, E. J., *Probation and Delinquency*, pp. 55-90. Van Waters, Miriam, *Youth in Conflict*, pp. 201-202. U. S. Children's Bureau, Publication No. 141, pp. 88-102. Burgess, E. W., "Study of the Delinquent as a Person," *Amer. Jour. Soc.*, 28: 657-680, 1923.

b. Parents.
c. Grandparents and other relatives.
d. Crises in family life.
e. Trends in family life.

7. Environment in General.
   a. District in which offender resides—homogeneity, mobility, and trends of population, rates of delinquency, poverty, and other pathological conditions, recreational facilities, physical characteristics.
   b. Districts of former residence.
   c. House—privacy, crowding, state of repair, furnishing.

Obviously not all of these items will be equally significant for every case. Selection will be made among them according to indications of their contribution to the delinquency. In the course of assembling the relevant data there will be interviews with the prisoner, home visits, contacts with teachers, employers, and other associates, consultation of social service exchange and bureau of identification. The conclusion will be based on a composite picture of all these facts and the light they shed on the offender's character and the opportunity he may have to "make good." The data are assembled and interpreted by probation officers; the decision is made by the judge. If it is adverse, the prisoner will be committed to an institution. If it is favorable, he will be placed on probation.

**Executive Tasks of the Probation Officer.** In adult cases the probation officer's first contact with an offender is often made in the court room, but in juvenile work he more frequently sees the boy or girl and makes a preliminary investigation before the court hearing. But in both criminal and juvenile courts the probation officer is required to be on hand to receive instructions and to furnish information. Besides attending court he must keep certain office hours for hearing reports and interviewing probationers. In all too many instances this involves a routine procedure that accomplishes little beyond the assurance that the offender is still about and letting him know that some kind of check is being kept on his activities. But in such cases as that of George Wood these required interviews are occasions for talking over the probationer's problems, making arrangements for supplementary services, offering suggestions and advice, and sometimes giving definite orders.

As in the case described, the probation officer often helps in finding employment and makes adjustments concerning wages, hours, and relations to superiors and fellow workmen. He suggests the use of recreational facilities and sees that they are actually available. He secures the interest of clergyman or school teacher, paving the way for reentrance into the church or classroom. Sometimes he helps the probationer find a suitable place to live and makes arrangements about payment for board and room. Often he refers the delinquent to health agencies for examination or treatment. Officers connected with juvenile courts often do many of these things without any judicial action being taken at all. This is sometimes known as "informal treatment." Juvenile court officers are also frequently responsible for the safekeeping of youngsters concerning whom petitions have been filed or complaints made.

**Personal Contacts Between Officer and Probationer.** But the really important part of probation consists in the personal give-and-take between officer and probationer. It must be described in terms of those elusive aspects of conduct which we call attitudes, rather than in terms of formal procedure. Because no legal authority or other external pressure can prescribe the subtle influence of one personality on another, the choice of probation officers is a matter of very great importance.

> Many lay people and some judges still believe that children can be adjusted by the widow of a ward captain; or an old maid suffering from repressions; or the patronizing type who calls a child "you dear little thing"; or the wealthy society leader whose cases serve as after-dinner stories; or the broken-down politician too tired to serve his party except as a probation officer; or the unsuccessful man or woman who complacently "takes up" social work because it seems easy; or the religious fanatic who sermonizes; or the woman "prayer" who believes in much prayer and little action; or the sensationalist, thrilled over the colorful sex stories of her wards. . . .
>
> Go into many juvenile courts over the country and as you walk down the halls you will hear "tell me the truth—do you hear? Come clean, now, or I'll send you away. Come across or you'll go to the Reformatory"—and other confidence-inspiring threats. Imagine the psychological effect upon the sensitive mind of a child, up against the law, when confronted by an ignorant adult bliss-

fully unconscious of the fact that nothing is so fundamentally important as the effect of the first interview. This blundering officer fails to appreciate the fact that the child's ideas of justice, his sense of responsibility to the laws of social conduct and morality are being molded as he sits there, impressionistic and susceptible. . . .

And now, let's consider the probation officer's attitude of mind toward her work and the child. So many complex factors contribute to attitude—education, training, standards of conduct taught when a child, the capacity for reading and observation and the subsequent realization that adolescence is not a mood, but a condition; age is important, and no mental old maid should handle a girl delinquent. Chronological age is of no consequence. She may be sixty and love youth—she may be thirty and fail to understand the ecstatic thrills of adolescence. Other contributions to attitude of mind are the officer's ideas of God and her power to appeal religiously to the child; her ability to ignore the non-essentials, such as plucked eye-brows, carrying a new curve each day, cheeks that register a high temperature, lips colored to fit each mood. . . .

. . . Our sex delinquent needs the services of a woman who believes that after all sex is a beautiful and not an abhorrent thing; who realizes that a sermon to Mary at 10 A. M. about sex indulgence will not control her physical urge at 9 P. M.; and who refrains from lectures and sentimentalism but immediately seeks a substitution. One of my girls, after listening to me nonchalantly, shrugged her shoulders expressively and drawled out, "Well, what have you to offer as a substitute?" Impertinently as it was said, this girl sounded the keynote of social service—substitution for the sex urge and its indulgence. . . .

. . . Ten years ago we knew little of the effect of one personality on another. The judges, in appointing their probation officers, never discussed in solemn conference, as we do now, the various types of personality—the inferiority complex type, harmful to the child; the puritanical soul saver, humorous to the boy or girl; the ego-centric, interested in her own effect upon the child; the paranoid type, antagonizing her ward by suspicion; the inadequate type, colorless and ineffective.

Our ideal probation officer is emotionally poised, bridging the age gap between herself and the child, understanding adolescent impulses and weaknesses even while detachedly analyzing them. . . .[6]

While Miss McChristie's discussion is primarily of the woman probation officer attached to a juvenile court, it applies

[6] McChristie, Mary E., "The Probation Officer of 1915 and 1925," *Proceedings, National Probation Association,* 1925: 14-23.

equally well, with a few obvious changes, to men officers and to those of both sexes connected with adult criminal courts.[7] Thus we see that probation is not merely "giving the offender another chance," nor that plus supervision. Far more important than either are interpretation of the delinquent to himself, redirection of his interests, transference of his group loyalties, and provision of opportunities to succeed in tasks that will both satisfy his fundamental desires and bring social approval. Hence probation is neither a form of leniency nor of espionage. It is a type of social treatment involving both understanding and guidance in the development of wholesome attitudes and social relations.

**Organization of Probation.** The idea of probation developed gradually out of the common practise of suspending sentence, at first temporarily and then indefinitely with certain conditions implying good behavior. But the first statutory provision for probation officers was a Massachusetts law of 1878 applying to the municipal court in Boston. Two years later this was extended to other cities of the commonwealth, but for twenty years no other state made any such provision. In 1899 the establishment of juvenile courts in Illinois and Missouri started a movement which quickly became very popular and carried the idea of probation throughout the United States. In the main, however, it was limited to juvenile offenders and it was often administered by part-time officers who were otherwise occupied as policemen, janitors, or ward politicians. Gradually probation was extended to adults convicted in various criminal courts. Its use in juvenile courts is little hampered by statutory restrictions, but in the criminal courts there are frequently limitations denying probation to those who have committed certain offenses or who have been previously convicted of a felony.

Probation officers are generally appointed by the judge of the court to which they are attached. In a few instances they must be chosen from a civil service list, but usually there is no restriction upon the judge's choice, and appointments are not

[7] In this connection it is well to note again the discussion of direct personal influence in Chapter XVII. See also, Van Waters, Miriam, *Youth in Conflict,* Chapter VIII; Van Waters, Miriam, "The Juvenile Court from the Child's Viewpoint," in *The Child, the Clinic and the Court,* pp. 217-237.

infrequently payments of political debts. State laws commonly fix the salaries which are usually so low that competent people are not attracted to this work. In large cities the probation departments are organized under chief probation officers, and members of the staff are assigned to districts, to racial or national types, to age groups, or persons found guilty of particular offenses. Women officers are commonly employed to handle the cases of women and girls; in juvenile courts they often attend to small boys as well. Because the number of probation officers is rarely adequate to do all the work that comes before them, they make considerable use of private agencies. Sometimes the probationer is placed in the custody of the agency as such, sometimes he is legally in charge of a regular officer, sometimes members of the staff of the private society are appointed probation officers without salary.

In order to extend the use of probation, to guide judges in the choice of officers, to raise the standards of work done, and to facilitate cooperation between various localities there have been created a number of state supervisory bodies. Massachusetts and New York, for example, have unpaid state commissions with paid officers who stimulate the development of probation work by providing manuals of instructions and record forms, by consultations with courts, conferences of probation officers, and other services. In Ohio the State Department of Public Welfare performs similar functions. In Wisconsin the State Probation Department actually handles probationers over the age of twenty-one, although juveniles are left to the care of local officers.

Being on probation does not necessarily mean that one has violated a law. Children are frequently made wards of the juvenile court and placed on probation for their protection rather than for correction. Husbands and wives whose marital conflicts have brought them to a court of domestic relations are also frequently dealt with by probation officers either with or without court action. Hence probation is distinguished from other forms of social case work by the auspices under which it is administered rather than by the problems faced or the methods employed.

**How Parole Differs from Probation.** Another application of social case work to the handling of delinquents is known as parole. While in many respects very similar to probation, it presents certain important legal and sociological differences. In the first place, it is granted by a parole board after the offender has served part of his sentence in an institution, instead of by a court in lieu of imprisonment. In the second place, parole officers are appointed by and responsible to the institution head or governing board, rather than the court. Sociologically, parole represents restoration of broken contacts and re-establishment in community life after a period of separation, while probation involves readjustment within an existing social situation.

Like probation, parole has developed gradually out of preexisting practises. Long ago some prisoners were indentured; then philanthropic societies interested themselves in after-care of discharged convicts; in 1845 Massachusetts appointed a state agent to look after ex-prisoners; but genuine parole in the United States dates from 1869 and the law which authorized its use in connection with the new reformatory at Elmira, New York. As stated at the beginning of the chapter, the idea was borrowed from English convict colonies in Australia, where something akin to parole appeared under the name "ticket-of-leave" as early as 1820. Today the practise has spread until all but two states have some form of parole for both juveniles and adults.

In many states this system is correlated with more or less indefinite sentences. Usually a prisoner is required to have served a certain minimum period of time or fraction of a definite sentence. In some states life prisoners, recidivists, and those convicted of specified offenses are not eligible for parole. The authority to grant and administer paroles is variously vested in the governor, special parole board, department of public welfare, or some other agency. In some states the law requires consultation with the committing judge, district attorney, and warden. There must usually be assurance of employment, and sometimes of "suitable home," "first friend and advisor," or other conditions before parole may be granted.

The laws sometimes specify certain rules governing the paroled prisoner; these may include written reports, regular employment, avoidance of bad company, abstention from gambling, drinking, or other specified violations of the mores.

One might easily justify the application of parole to every delinquent who has been institutionalized and who is going to be returned to a life of freedom, the argument being that change from the restricted and directed life of a prison, reformatory, or industrial school to the relatively independent life of the outside world involves difficult adjustments, in making which the offender usually needs help. Since the great majority of prisoners are eventually released, this means that practically all of them might better be paroled than discharged directly from the institution to the community. Incidentally, this does not necessarily mean a shortening of the time spent inside the walls; as a matter of fact, the introduction of parole has often been followed by a longer average stay.

An analysis of parole displays steps or phases very similar to those identified in the study of probation. There is first a preliminary study of the offender, then his preparation for parole, preparation of the community for his reception, various specific arrangements, and direct personal influence.

Theoretically we might expect the preliminary study to be easier than when probation is being considered; and, moreover, if the most significant facts about the delinquent have been discovered and recorded by the court and the institution, the task of the parole officer and board is greatly simplified. It is important to have at hand all the information that would be needed by a judge and probation officer, plus an account of the offender's development in the institution and a study of the outside situations into which he might fit. Hence, if these data are not readily accessible, someone must assemble them, if an intelligent decision is to be made concerning the prisoner's application and if he is to be guided wisely when on parole. Since investigation of the delinquent's general background has been considered in relation to probation, our present discussion may be confined to the evaluation of his prison record and the possible adjustments outside. Sutherland has emphasized the fact that behavior in the institution is not a suitable test of fitness for release. There are three types that may behave well in an institution: those who really desire to profit by the experience and training, those who attempt to secure an early release by good behavior in order to return more quickly to crime, and those who reach their highest level under the careful control of others. The good behavior of the first group alone indicates fitness for parole. On the other hand some prisoners who behave very badly while under the constant guidance of prison guards get along satisfactorily in the general community.[8]

Also it is important to realize that no matter what development may have taken place in the offender while in the institution, parole is likely to be disastrous, unless there is reasonable prospect of his finding promptly a suitable job, a wholesome place to live, and a set of associates who are either unaware of his delinquency or are willing to aid him in re-establishing himself as a "good citizen." Hence the parole officer has the task of studying the situations outside and of preparing, accordingly, for the coming of the prisoner.

The assumption—unfortunately not always valid—is that institutional life has been making the offender ready for a place in the outside world. But even if this be true, there are many problems to be discussed before he is ready in body and mind for the change. Instead of finding a job for the prisoner, many parole officers guide him in finding a place for himself. They explain to him just what he will "be up against" when he goes out, what handicaps he will have, what opportunities will be his, and of course the parole regulations.

When at last the offender has been paroled and has gone out to a home, a job, and a place in the community, there are some very delicate problems involved in maintaining contact between him and the parole officer. The latter obviously must know how his ward is getting along and must be ready to help him meet new difficulties as they arise; but at the same time he must guard against humiliating the paroled person. Different officers meet this situation in different ways. Some have established such relationships with employers, for example, that they can tell them very frankly about the offender's past. These employers use the information discreetly in helping the delin-

[8] Sutherland, E. H., *Criminology*, p. 534.

quent get a new start. In other cases the officer is not known as such to the employer and may even avoid him entirely. Probably the most serious failures are made by those untrained parole officers who regard themselves essentially as detectives whose duty is to "check up" on their wards, or those "kind-hearted" officers who leave the parolees so completely to themselves that they might as well be completely discharged.

**Results of Probation and Parole.** Administrative boards and officers frequently make extravagant claims for the success of probation and parole. Others seeking to discover the facts are handicapped by lack of facilities for following up discharged offenders to determine the degree of their adjustment to the larger community. The New York State Probation Commission made the following estimate of outcomes of probation in that state over a fourteen-year period.

RESULTS OF PROBATION IN NEW YORK STATE, 1907–1921.[9]

| | *Adults* (%) | *Juveniles* (%) |
|---|---|---|
| Discharged with improvement | 77.0 | 81.7 |
| Discharged without improvement | 6.5 | 4.0 |
| Committed to institutions | 9.7 | 13.7 |
| Absconded and lost from oversight | 6.8 | 0.6 |

A careful study by the Massachusetts State Commission on Probation uncovered less encouraging results. Of about 400 men guilty of "general offenses" 35 per cent had another court record within eight years; and of 200 cases involving drunkenness 40 per cent were known to have a subsequent court record.[10] Even when probationers make successful adjustments and "turn out well" it is difficult to estimate the extent to which this is due to probation and the extent to which they might have succeeded anyway. Commenting on the wide divergence in methods coupled with apparently similar results in the juvenile work in Cincinnati and Boston, Thomas remarks "that we have idealized the juvenile court as an institution and that its successes, where it has successes, are not closely correlated with the procedure but due to unknown

[9] Johnson, Fred R., *Probation for Juveniles and Adults,* p. 77.
[10] *Ibid.,* p. 80.

causes." [11] Perhaps the same might be said of all probation work.

When we turn to parole we have much the same difficulty in evaluating results. "Several states report a surprisingly low percentage of violations. The figure in Vermont is 3 per cent; in West Virginia 4 per cent; in Maine, Nevada and North Carolina 5 per cent. . . ." [12] Over against these probable exaggerations we have lurid editorials and articles in newspapers and magazines under such titles as "turning criminals loose," "a debauch of leniency," and the like. To displace boasts, accusations, and wild guesses with a measure of fact-finding several special studies have been made. One of the most notable has recently been published as *The Workings of the Indeterminate-Sentence Law and the Parole Systems in Illinois*. The investigators found that something over one-fourth of 3000 paroled men were known to have violated the conditions of their parole. But perhaps the most significant part of their study was an analysis of factors making for success or failure on parole.[13]

Twenty-two points were considered in their relation to the outcome in the 3000 cases examined. (1) As to nature of offense, it was discovered that men convicted of sex offenses, murder and manslaughter did relatively well on parole, while those convicted of fraud, forgery and burglary showed high rates of violation. (2) Those who had three or more associates in their crime did surprisingly well, while those who worked alone had a high rate of violations. (3) As to nationality of prisoner's father, the recent immigrant groups made a better showing than the older groups. (4) Among men coming from broken homes the percentage of violations was higher than the average. (5) Single men violated parole more frequently than those who were married. (6) First offenders were clearly a "better risk" than habitual or professional criminals. (7) As to "social type," farm boys and newly arrived immigrants did much better than hoboes, urban ne'er-do-wells, and drug addicts. (8) The county from which a man was com-

[11] Thomas, W. I. and D. S., *The Child in America*, p. 143.

[12] Report of the Pennsylvania State Parole Commission, 1927, vol. 2, p. 195.

[13] Chapter XXVIII of the above-mentioned report, by Ernest W. Burgess.

mitted did not seem especially significant. (9) There was a uniformly low violation rate for those who lived in the open country. (10) In the city violations were more frequent among men who lived in rooming house districts, hobohemia, or the criminal underworld. (11) Curiously, transients showed a lower rate of defaulting than did actual residents of the communities from which they were committed. (12) Cases recommended for parole by the trial judge or state's attorney did better than those protested. (13) There seemed to be no relation between change of pleas and success on parole. (14) Men who were given flat sentences and heavier indeterminate sentences violated parole less frequently than men with light sentences. (15) Men who served short periods in the institutions made a better showing on parole than did those who stayed longer. (16) Men with previous reformatory or penitentiary records showed high rates of violation. (17) Those with records of regular employment seldom violated parole. (18) Prisoners punished by solitary confinement or demerits or demotions in the institutions had high rates of violation. (19) The youngest and the oldest made a better showing than did those between 25 and 50. (20) Mental age and intelligence quotient seemed not significant for success on parole. (21) But personality types seemed very important, the egocentric facing the greatest difficulties in making new adjustments. (22) Finally the psychiatric prognosis showed a very high correlation with success on parole.

On the basis of these results a system of scoring was devised and an expectancy table worked out. This should be useful in future work of parole boards, though it will doubtless be modified in the light of further studies. Obviously parole and probation have both grown up empirically and are taken or rejected largely on faith. Yet such studies as have been made indicate that they have real value and that with more enlightened direction they will yield increasing returns in the control of delinquency.

# CHAPTER XXIV.

## SOCIAL WORK IN INDUSTRY

### A GENERALIZED WELFARE DEPARTMENT

The Kalamazoo Stationery Company is a branch of the Western Tablet and Stationery Corporation which is a manufacturing concern with headquarters in Dayton, Ohio. The company now has seven branches. Social work in the Kalamazoo branch began about three and one-half years ago with the coming of the present welfare worker. She had been trained as a nurse, and was employed originally to do general health work. The scope of her activities expanded almost immediately, however, and soon involved three general types of service; nursing and first aid, employment and personnel, and general welfare work.

The health and first-aid work is well organized. Employees have been trained to seek treatment for even slight injuries. Safety and accident prevention campaigns are held periodically. Up to the present time the company has required no general physical examination upon employment although such a procedure is favored by the worker.

Employment is given on the basis of an interview and the filling out of an "employment card." There are no psychological tests or examinations, but the mere ability to answer the questions on this form correctly gives some indication of the applicant's status. Furthermore, a majority of those seeking employment are known to the worker either directly or indirectly. The Company employs some 600 people, about half of whom are women. Only nineteen of these employees are under the age of eighteen, and there are no foreigners or Negroes. Consequently the factory is practically a homogeneous, face-to-face group. The worker makes a trip through the plant daily and is in constant personal touch with all the operatives. After being given a job the new employee is "followed up" by the worker for three months and his production rate and adaptability to the particular operation at which he works checked. A definite attempt is made to shift the workers around in order to find the type of work for which they are best suited. Aptitudes are ascertained by actual trial on different jobs. The employees are not organized and have no participation in the management of the factory. The work of the factory is to a slight extent seasonal; additional employees being hired in the fall in order to increase the production of Christmas cards. A fairly large number of married women are taken on at this time for several months' employment. Although nothing approaching industrial democracy exists a close relationship between the management and the workers is maintained. There is a foremen-and-superintendent conference monthly.

The welfare work involves a number of miscellaneous activities. There is a mutual sick benefit association to which each employee pays fifty cents a month and from which he draws $12 a week when ill. Membership is voluntary but practically all the workers belong. Premiums are deducted from the wages by the company which also makes up all deficits. The company carries a group life insurance policy for the employees who pay a premium of 50 cents a month, which entitles them to a policy of $1,000. Employees are eligible for this insurance after one year's service, but it is on a voluntary basis. In all but a very few cases the insurance costs considerably more than the employee pays, the company paying the additional cost. A "welfare fund" has been built up from fines paid for being late to work, and is used for loans, relief and recreation. The employees manage their recreational activities themselves although the welfare worker administers the finances. The company belongs to the "twilight industrial league" of the city, and has a creditable baseball team. Another duty of the worker is the management of the cafeteria, which is quite successful. Formerly the company issued a house organ but this has been discontinued. There is little need for family case-work as employees in need of relief are referred to the city family welfare association. Only three or four families a year are handled directly by the company worker. Finally, and in addition to these rather numerous duties, the welfare worker cooperates with the industrial department of the Y. W. C. A. in its club work, investigates and follows up all accident compensation claims, and handles all garnishees, court orders, suits against employees and any other matters affecting the welfare of the worker.[1]

This case illustrates the type of social work found perhaps in the majority of small manufacturing concerns that attempt anything in this direction. Its general non-technical nature is apparent; it involves case, group and administrative work as well as health supervision and duties of a semi-legal nature. The social worker, while efficient as far as the demands of her job are concerned, was really trained for only one phase of her

[1] Interview with Miss Myrtle Hooven, Welfare Worker, Kalamazoo Stationery Co.

present rather complicated duties. The work is largely paternalistic in nature, although recognized as "good business." Some employee participation is seen in the benefit association and the athletic league. Finally, the administration of this work as a personnel department, directly under the general manager, is in line with present tendencies.

In contrast with other kinds of social work, the industrial variety does not fall under any one of the four main types previously distinguished. Indeed, as illustrated above, it may involve all four types. Next to institutional work it is the most general of all forms, which is to say, simply, that social work in this field has developed less than in any other, and that, except in rare cases, is relatively unspecialized. Another distinguishing characteristic of industrial social work is the fact that in general practise, it has not progressed as far away, as have other varieties, from the paternalistic and humanitarian motivation dominant in Warner's day. These two characteristics are, of course, closely related. Social work in industry arises from the fundamental need for dealing with the human factor. From the standpoint of the management, it should result in decreased turnover and labor friction and in increased production. It may be defined as the "effort of the employer to establish and maintain certain standards in respect to hours, wages, working and living conditions of his employees, which are neither required by law, nor by the conditions of the market." [2] This statement is in line with the characterization by the Bureau of Labor Statistics in their report of 1919,[3] where industrial welfare work is described as "anything for the comfort and improvement, intellectual and social, of the employees over and above wages paid, which is not a necessity of the industry or required by law." Such a definition, although general, is satisfactory if modified to read, "not an *immediate* necessity of the industry, or required by law *or custom*."

Attempts on the part of the employer to deal with the human factor in industry started with paternalistic and philanthropic efforts of an untechnical and unskilled nature, usually

[2] Boettiger, L. A., *Employee Welfare Work*, p. 19. Ronald Press, 1923.
[3] "Welfare Work for Employees in Industrial Establishments in the United States," U. S. Bureau of Labor Statistics, Bul. No. 250.

referred to as "welfare" work, but have progressed in recent years to a more democratic and professional stage. Today, the state imposes certain requirements, far-sighted business management dictates a comprehensive personnel policy, mental hygiene argues for an adjustment of working conditions to meet the basic instinctive needs of the worker, and industrial democracy demands justice and mutual respect in the relations between employer and employee. The change that has taken place in theory, if not altogether in actual practise, is essentially one from benevolent and unskilled work with employees to a non-paternalistic and professional interest in the human element in the production process. The discussion that follows will indicate first the historical factors involved in the transition from "welfare" work to the more modern schemes for accomplishing the same fundamental objectives, and then briefly the various aspects of present programs whatever the particular plan may be.

**Historical Background.** Industrial welfare work in a general sense is very ancient. Evidences of it are to be found in the history of the Middle Ages, in activities of the gilds, and in the experiments of various individual employers. In a strict sense, however, it started with the industrial revolution and the development of the factory system in England. The first great experiment in the social organization of an industrial community was made by Robert Owen, at New Lanark, a Scottish textile town of 2,000 population, in which deplorable conditions prevailed. About 1813, so impressed was he with the problems incident to the factory system, that Owen withdrew from the company with which he was connected, and in 1813 started a new one with a comprehensive welfare program, including a "company store" and various types of schools for the children. Industrial welfare work did not start in the United States until some 50 or 60 years later. Housing was one of the first problems to receive the attention of the manufacturers. One of the earliest experiments of this sort was made in 1848. In 1865 the Waltham Watch Company erected a boarding house which is still in use.[4] Recreation was first

[4] Queen, S. A., *Social Work in the Light of History,* Chap. V. Lippincott, Philadelphia, 1922.

provided by the Conant Thread Company, in Rhode Island, in 1870. In 1889 the Illinois Steel Company built a "Steel Works Club" for the benefit of its employees. All such work at its best involved a recognition of the individual in industry, a desire to reestablish the old personal relations between employer and employee, and a hope of improving production. At its worst it represented an indirect attempt at exploitation. In any case it was paternalistic and humanitarian, not democratic. In addition to housing and recreation this early welfare work included, or came to include, such activities as home visiting, nursing, first aid, the establishment of lunch rooms, rest rooms, clubs, and benefit societies. The welfare worker of this period had little to do with employment or training; this was left to the superintendent. Such was the situation in Warner's time.

One of the outstanding attempts to organize an industrial community that eventually failed was the establishment of the town of Pullman, Illinois, in 1880. This town was planned by the Pullman Car Company as the "model" industrial community of that day, with great attention paid to the health, housing, recreation and education of the employees. Every house was supplied with water and gas. There was a central park around which the various civic institutions were grouped. The whole town was company owned and controlled, which made possible its rapid growth. This centralized control was, however, resented by the people, who opposed the invasions by the company of what they considered their private rights. Discontent reached a climax in the strike of 1894. In 1889 Pullman was annexed to Chicago and its unique character lost. The late Professor Albion Small, commenting on the situation during the strike, said: "It would be contrary to the evidence to doubt that in motive, George M. Pullman was a conscientious philanthropist. His mistake was in principle that of all the genuinely benevolent despots. He confounded philanthropy with patronage. He had not found out that the best way for men to help men is not to do things for them, but do things with them, and perhaps better still to remove removable hindrances to their doing things for themselves." [5]

Organized labor has always been suspicious of this sort of

[5] "Americans and the World Crisis," *Amer. Jour. Soc.*, 23: 164.

welfare work—"hell-fare work," Samuel Gompers called it. Ordway Tead has pointed out that the worst strikes have often occurred where the most welfare work has been done. Labor has felt that such work might be simply a means of exploitation, or a poor substitute for industrial justice.

Welfare work of this paternalistic kind has not disappeared from the industrial stage. It still thrives, for example, in the Southern cotton mills, the industry in which it originated. Harriet Herring has recently investigated welfare programs in the mills of North Carolina, and her findings corroborate this statement.[6] One of the first special workers in the mills was employed in 1895. The World War gave an impetus to welfare work in the mill towns, but a reaction followed. At the time the study was made (1926) only 88 of the 322 mills investigated had some sort of a special paid worker. Some of these were nurses and physicians and did no general welfare or community work, such work being found in only 68 plants. Only 16 of the 322 mills had paid community workers before 1914. During the war 80 more mills added workers, forty-seven of which were discontinued after the war. As most of the mills in North Carolina are small there are few community houses, such being found by Miss Herring in only 48 cases. Much of the community work is on a personal and volunteer basis, but is encouraged by the employers. The mills are also interested in education, as they are in the churches, and in many cases give financial aid in the establishment of better schools. It was found that the children of all but 2,000 of the 66,000 employees involved had something better in the way of education than a county 6 months term. Preventive and educational health work dates from the influenza epidemic in 1918, but little is done now. The mills quite generally established company stores, which are now being driven out by the greater accessibility of neighboring city stores. Forty plants were found to have group insurance policies. Saving plans, industrial democracy, personnel departments, plant papers and the like are "recent and rare." Housing, which was originally a necessity, and led to the building of the mill villages, has now become a

[6] *Welfare Work in Mill Villages.* Chapel Hill: Univ. of No. Carolina Press, 1929.

welfare activity. About 70% of the workers were housed by the mills in the cases studied, and the quarters are more comfortable than they formerly were. Miss Herring concludes that welfare work in the cotton mills is still in the formative stages, but that "a belief in (it) . . . is common and continuous in the great majority of North Carolina plants." [7] The objects have been: (1) to increase the efficiency of the employee; (2) to anticipate legislation, and (3) to bring harmony in industrial relations, and also to help keep out the unions.

In contrast with the small mills of North Carolina is the welfare work of some of the larger concerns, which is more elaborate but equally paternalistic. Across the state line, near Danville, Virginia, is the mill village of Schoolfield. The "Riverside Cotton Mills" here employ some 5000 "hands" and have an extensive system of welfare activities, including elaborate club and recreational center, clinics, kindergartens, grade schools, a company department store, a Y. M. C. A., and athletic organizations.

**The General Nature of Modern Industrial Welfare Work.** The motives for early welfare work were paternalism, philanthropy, the desire to get more out of the worker and, in some cases, to restore the old personal relations. These motives still exist but the emphasis has been changed. Philanthropy cannot explain the modern equivalent of welfare work in industry. Instead it is an outgrowth of the relatively recent efficiency methods in labor management plus the development of a somewhat more democratic spirit. Of the "four M's" in labor management—men, materials, machinery and methods, the first has come to be recognized as of paramount importance. It is hard to fix any definite date for the transition to the new type of work, but no great evidence of it appeared before 1915. The new "welfare work" came to be known under different names in different parts of the country and in different industries. But whether the title used was "employees' service department," "labor service department," "personnel department," "personnel service" or "labor department," the purpose was the same in all cases, and fundamentally identical with that of the older welfare work, i.e., to look after the human factor

[7] *Ibid.*, p. 31.

in the industrial process. The organization of the Hood Rubber Company's Employees' Service Department about 1919, for example, provided for employment, health, safety and sanitation, education, and general service. The Personnel Department of the Plimpton Press has five divisions: employment, maintenance, training, research, and community relations. The same general divisions are to be found in the Personnel Service Department of the Thomas A. Edison plant at Orange, N. J., namely, employment, adjustment, betterment, safety and health. All such departments operate more or less directly under the general manager of the plant.

In 1919 the U. S. Bureau of Labor Statistics published a report of a study of welfare work in 400 establishments.[8] Three hundred seventy-five were found to have some form of medical service, 200 had rest or recreation rooms, and 100 had club rooms or houses. Libraries, classes, night schools, family service, disability funds, insurance and pensions were also found. From this report, however, it is evident that such work was still very largely on the old humanitarian basis. Boettiger [9] describes three stages in the evolution of welfare work: (1) indefinite and spasmodic efforts of the employer of an avowedly paternalistic nature; (2) the employment of trained specialists, "social secretaries" or "welfare agents," with little authority, and responsible directly to the management, to establish and maintain personal relations between employer and employees; (3) the coordination of all work dealing with the human element in industry as a "major staff function" under specialists with considerable authority, called variously "employment managers," "welfare directors," or "personnel administrators." He estimated that in 1923 about one-half of all the industrial welfare work in the country was still in the first stage, one-third in the second, and the balance in the third stage which is limited, in the main, to the larger establishments. In 1926 Epstein [10] examined some 1500 of the larger concerns in the

[8] U. S. Bureau of Labor Statistics, Bul. No. 250, "Welfare Work for Employees in Industrial Establishments in the United States," 1919.

[9] Boettiger, L. A., *Employee Welfare Work,* pp. 122 ff. Ronald Press, 1923.

[10] Epstein, A., "Industrial Welfare Movement Sapping American Trade Unions," *Current History,* 24: 516, 1926.

United States and found that more than 80%, with 4,000,000 workers, were doing welfare and social work of some sort, and that one-half of these had elaborate schemes. From a study of 189 Ohio industrial firms representing various sizes and types, now being conducted by the Bureau of Business Research of Ohio State University, the following facts relative to their welfare work have been ascertained:[11]

| *Type of Service* | *No. of Firms Performing Designated Service* |
|---|---|
| Medical examinations | 36 |
| Hospital service | 39 |
| Visiting nurse | 24 |
| Absence investigation | 42 |
| Cafeteria | 43 |
| Company store | 12 |
| Employee mutual benefit association | 22 |
| Building and loan service | 4 |
| Old age pensions | 11 |
| Group insurance | 59 |
| Employee magazine | 15 |
| Employee library | 14 |
| Vacation plans | 81 |

In contrast with the earlier welfare activities there are today three general types of work with individuals and groups based upon three principles representing modern changes in viewpoint. These are: democracy and mutual service, legal compulsion, and efficient business management. From these principles there have developed three schemes for securing and improving the conditions of industrial employees: (1) mutual benefit associations, (2) industrial legislation, and (3) personnel work. Since a great deal of the old type of welfare work persists this makes a fourth scheme. And, since also, in actual practise, these benefits and plans are often combined we may add another or combination scheme, making five general types of industrial welfare work found in operation today.

Mutual benefit associations represent the first step taken by employers to meet the risks of sickness among their employees.

[11] *Ohio Sociologist,* Bulletin of Ohio Sociological Society, Columbus, Ohio, 3: 10-11, May, 1929.

The aims of such an association are "to foster a fraternal spirit among its members, to give relief for disability through sickness or accident, to provide death benefits, and to assume general supervision over the activities which concern the welfare and progress of the workers." Mutual benefit associations constitute a step toward industrial democracy, when they are voluntary and cooperatively administered. Most authorities agree that the workers should pay the costs of the actual benefits, while the company bears the overhead expense. In many instances, however, the company contributes to the benefit fund directly. There are usually fixed weekly dues. Ten cents per week will provide a benefit of $1.00 a day for a period of 13 weeks.[12] One of the outstanding examples of such industrial cooperation is found in the Philadelphia Rapid Transit Employes Cooperative Association. According to the 1928 report the cooperative wage fund now totals $14,000,000 which is administered by trustees elected by the employees. It is invested in company stock. The association has a membership of 11,200, including all the eligible employees. The dues are $1.50 per month per member, the company adding dollar for dollar. Sick benefits, pensions and life insurance are provided under the plan.[13]

In relatively recent years there has grown up a greater and greater feeling of public responsibility for the conditions under which men and women work. The result has been a body of social and industrial legislation, which represents another advance over the laissez-faire doctrines which held sway in industry in Warner's day. The first statutory regulation of hours of labor was in behalf of children, and similar protection was later extended to women. Such legislation has spread rapidly since 1908. Similar legislation for men developed more slowly and has never been extensive. In 1912 a ten-hour law applying to men employed in factories was enacted in Mississippi, and the following year a similar law was enacted in Oregon. The most significant legislative efforts in behalf of the industrial worker have been the accident compensation laws.

[12] For cases and decisions in legal controversies over the payment of such benefits, see *Harvard Business Reports,* vol. 4, pp. 490, 498, 510 and 518.

[13] "Service Talks," Mitten Management, Inc., Philadelphia, Pa., Dec. 20, 1928.

By 1912 sixteen states had such laws, and by 1925 the number had increased to 43 states and 3 territories.

Personnel work is the answer of business and industrial experts to the old problem of the human factor in industry. A modern personnel department is concerned not only with the welfare functions and activities of the older sort but with employment problems as well. In fact, a well organized personnel department is a complete system for handling all the various problems that might come under the headings of welfare, employment, training, health, recreation, mutual benefit associations and the like. It is not a branch of welfare work, but on the contrary, as found in many modern organizations at least, includes this among all the other functions related to employees both as human beings and as workers. "Personnel Administration," according to Tead and Metcalf, "is the direction and coordination of the human relations of any organization with a view to getting the maximum necessary production with a minimum of effort and friction, and with proper regard for the genuine well-being of the workers." [14] A properly qualified personnel director is trained in scientific business management, applied psychology and social work. He or she might indeed be a social worker with special training and experience in psychological measurements and business administration. The personnel department of a large concern may, in fact, include one or more case and community workers in its staff. In the last analysis the personnel worker is or should be a social psychologist.

Industrial personnel work is an outgrowth of (1) a developing art of the selection and training of employees, and (2) vocational psychology. Vocational psychology began with the pioneer studies of motormen on the Boston Elevated Railroad made by Münsterberg in 1911. The work developed rapidly and at the opening of the World War a considerable amount of important data on the subject had been compiled by such men as W. D. Scott, and at such centers as the Carnegie Institute of Technology. The War gave a great impetus to the testing movement in general. One million seven hundred thousand sol-

[14] Tead, Ordway and Metcalf, Henry C., *Personal Administration*, p. 2. McGraw-Hill Co., 1920.

diers were tested and the attempt made to fit them to various positions in the military establishment on the basis of the results, particularly of the trade and vocational tests. Rating scales, qualification cards and other devices were developed by a group of psychologists cooperating with the National Research Council. Eventually army personnel work reached a fair degree of efficiency—as great as could be expected perhaps under the emergency conditions. Since the War vocational psychology and personnel work as a whole has made considerable progress, both "on the job" and in research.[15] Cooperative work has developed on a large scale, stimulated by such organizations as the Psychological Corporation, founded in 1921, and the Personnel Research Federation and the Bureau of Public Personnel Administration, established one year later.

According to Watkins,[16] the purposes of personnel work are to increase the length of service of the employee, reduce the turnover, increase the efficiency of the organization as a whole, eliminate waste and promote industrial good-will. A typical personnel department consists of six divisions.[17] (1) Employment. The function of this division is the selection of employees, utilizing personal histories, questionnaires, intelligence and vocational tests, rating scales, interviews and other similar devices. It makes and maintains contact with sources of labor supply, follows up all workers employed, controls tardiness, absenteeism, turnover, transfers and promotions. (2) Health, Safety and Sanitation. This division includes the medical and nursing staff, and is concerned with physical examinations, first-aid, promotion of personal hygiene, diagnosis in case of disease, and supervision of the safety program. (3) Education and Training. Job instruction, education for promotion, and cooperation with public night schools are among the functions of this division. (4) Employees' Service Division. This division handles the "welfare work," including the administration of loans and benefit funds, supervision of housing, organization of recreation, legal aid, and cooperation with the social

[15] Rossi, Wm. H., and Diana, I. P., *Personnel Administration: A Bibliography,* Baltimore, 1925.

[16] Watkins, Gordon S., *Labor Management,* p. 647. A. W. Shaw Co., 1928.

[17] *Ibid.* See Chap. VI for a good general description.

work agencies of the city. Such a division may frequently be under the direction of a social worker, responsible to the personnel manager. (5) Research. The duties of the research division involve the making of job analyses (descriptions of occupations), devising trade and other tests, labor and plant analyses, wage studies, and statistical service. (6) The Joint Representations Division exists to facilitate cooperation between the various divisions of the plant as well as of the personnel department in relation to common problems.

The adjustment of personal difficulties and the handling of the problem employee is another function of the personnel worker. This will be discussed below in connection with mental hygiene in industry. Personnel work offers an interesting field to the student considering social work as a profession, particularly if he is interested in industrial problems and psychology. There are fewer fields of social work open to men than to women, and personnel administration is one of the most attractive of these.

**Unit Activities in Industrial Social Work: Vocational Guidance.** Irrespective of which of the five general schemes outlined above is in operation there are certain fundamental or unit divisions of industrial social work. These will be briefly discussed. Vocational guidance is closely connected with industrial social work for a number of reasons. In the first place, it was started in this country in settlement houses and by social workers. Again, it preceded personnel work and had an important influence upon developments in this field. In the third place, industrial personnel problems, such as turnover, are immediately affected by the kind of vocational guidance done in the community, or by its absence. Furthermore, the industrial social worker or personnel officer is called upon to assist in the vocational guidance program of his community, and should be familiar with its techniques. It falls to him largely to make the job analyses upon which intelligent guidance is partly based. Finally, the problem of promotion and transfer in industry itself is essentially one of vocational guidance.

Vocational guidance has grown up on account of the increasing complexity of our occupational life, the necessity of early training in line with the vocation later chosen, and as a means of decreasing the costs of excessive turnover. The movement in this country originated at the Civic Service House in Boston.[18] It was here that Dr. Frank Parsons began his work in 1908 with the organization of the "Vocation Bureau," of which he later became the director. The first public school system of vocational guidance was put into operation in Boston in 1909. In 1914 Boston University established the first university department specializing in this subject. Now several graduate departments exist, which offer work leading to the doctor's degree.

As defined by the National Vocational Guidance Association, "vocational guidance is the giving of information, experience and advice in regard to choosing an occupation, preparing for it, entering into it, and progressing in it." [19] Three main processes are involved in vocational guidance and counseling. (1) The analysis of the individual. This is accomplished by the use of tests of "general intelligence" and of aptitudes, interviews and other diagnostic devices. (2) Study of occupations—"job analysis"—as a basis for preparing tests and for information to be used in counseling pupils. (3) Establishing contact between the individual and the job. This involves, first an intelligent choice of a vocation for the individual; second, preparation for it, and third, placement in it. It may involve, further, follow-up and supervision work with the individual placed. Many college and university personnel departments are now following their graduates into business, industrial and professional life until satisfactory adjustment is made.

The passing of compulsory school attendance laws, and granting to boards of education the right to issue employment certificates gave a decided impetus to the vocational guidance movement in the schools. How such guidance operates in a city's school is seen in the case of Cincinnati, for example.[20] The work in this city was begun in 1911. For four years the bureau was occupied with the administration of the employ-

[18] See Payne, A. F., *Organization of Vocational Guidance,* McGraw-Hill, 1925, and Brewer, John M., *The Vocational Guidance Movement,* Macmillan, 1918.

[19] Edgerton, Alanson H., *Vocational Guidance and Counseling,* p. 17, footnote. Macmillan Company, 1926.

[20] "Vocational Guidance and Junior Placement," *Children's Bureau* Pub. 149, 1925, Washington, D. C., pp. 191-222.

ment-certificate provision of the child labor law and in carrying on an intensive study of a group of working children. In 1915 a placement department was organized, and in 1916 a psychological department. The bureau did not attempt to initiate vocational counseling in the schools, but as early as 1919 instituted conferences between the director and the teachers to explain the function of the bureau and encourage its use. In 1921 began a series of pamphlets on various occupations for the use of the teachers. By contrast, the vocational guidance department of the Boston Public Schools carries on four main activities.[21] (1) promoting school counseling, (2) placement, (3) following up and supervising all persons registered with the department, and (4) collecting information on vocational opportunities and industrial openings and the like.

**Employment** is of course one of the most important functions of the personnel department. Scientific methods of selection on the basis of psychological examinations and job analyses have already been referred to. But not all employees are hired at the door of the factory. Most concerns draw from private and public employment agencies to a greater or less extent. There has been a great deal of criticism of the practices of the private, fee-charging agencies. The New York State Industrial Survey Commission recently called attention to the exploitation of applicants by such agencies, and recommended that such bureaus be required to post a surety bond of $3000, and pay a license fee of $100. The Consumers' League of Cincinnati also made a careful study of the same problem and recommended a central clearing house through which employers and employees might be brought together. Many agencies are grossly inefficient. One reported that of some 96,000 applicants during the year it had placed only 5%. The League recommended that private agencies be controlled by city ordinance, and that the state-city employment bureau be developed to the utmost. The consensus of opinion seems to be in favor of state-city agencies affiliated with a Federal Employment Service as the best solution of the problem. Modern personnel methods may be expected to develop in the public city-state-Federal agencies of the future, furnishing a thorough place-

[21] *Ibid.*, 90 ff.

ment service on the basis of a modified form of social case work.

**Education and training** includes preparation for the immediate job, for promotion or transfer, or for "general improvement." Training departments are conducted by many industrial establishments, which also cooperate through their personnel departments with evening vocational classes in the public schools. One of the most interesting recent developments in this field has been the summer schools for industrial girls, which started at Bryn Mawr and are now held also at the University of Wisconsin, Sweet Briar College (Virginia) and in a number of other places.

**Unemployment relief** is another vital problem with which the social worker in industry must deal. Unemployment reached large proportions in 1928 and a tremendous extra burden was thrown upon the established case-working agencies. They had to deal not only with the tangible loss of family income, but with the intangible attitudes of discouragement and despair in the men thrown out of work. As most agencies operate on a limited budget this additional strain meant inevitably the neglect of other phases of their work. It is obviously unfair that such costs of the pathological conditions in industry should be borne by private agencies. Instead unemployment relief is primarily a responsibility of the public and of industry itself. Private agencies may be expected to handle a portion of the cases, but the brunt of the burden should probably be borne by public relief organizations and by the industries themselves until employment insurance becomes general. One of the primary duties, therefore, of the industrial personnel department should be the attempt to regularize employment and to decrease in every possible way the extent of unemployment.

**Mental hygiene** has made some significant contributions to the study of unemployment. Many individuals out of work are really psychopathic, unstable, or abnormal in some way, and therefore more or less unemployable. Hence the advisability of psychiatric training for the personnel or social worker in industry. An increasing number of concerns have added a psychiatrist to their personnel staff, and such a specialist attached to the health division should be of considerable service not only with psychopathic but with normal employees as well. The mental hygienists have emphasized also the importance of the study of the emotional make-up of the applicant for a job as well as his I. Q. An individual's attitudes, emotions and type of interests have perhaps even more to do with his success than his level of intelligence. Dr. E. E. Southard was one of the first psychiatrists to study the mental hygiene aspects of industry and to urge the introduction of such a service. 1920 may be taken as the approximate date for the beginning of this movement, following an investigation made by Dr. Southard for the Engineering Foundation. In recent years the so-called psychiatric social worker (see Chap. XVII) has found a place in industry. She not only deals with the relatively small number of actually insane employees, but the more valuable phase of her work has to do with normal individuals with mild personality difficulties. Her primary aim is to keep the employee adjusted to his work—to the total situation. "It is the business of the total situation psychology in industry to investigate and eliminate conditions which lead to disharmony in the individual's mental background, and to promote that orientation which alone makes reasoned adjustment to the job possible." [22]

As an illustration of the economic waste involved the following case of a definitely psychopathic employee is given: [23]

At the time of his examination the patient was a young man of thirty, of Irish-American parentage. His condition was diagnosed as paranoid dementia præcox. His family had been known for a long time to the charity organization society of the large city where his father formerly owned a good business. Later his father became first a saloon keeper, then a doorman at a public building; the later job being a reward for service to the political machine of which he had been a hanger-on for many years. He had been a heavy drinker and during the later years of his life developed tabes. He finally committed suicide, due, according to his son, to Tammany's going back on him. His mother also killed herself, cutting her throat on the day of her husband's funeral.

The patient graduated from grammar school at the age of fourteen, and then went to work in a lawyer's office. His ambition

[22] "Mental Hygiene of Industry," *Bulletin of the Amer. Assoc. of Hospital Social Workers,* March, 1925.

[23] Powers, Margaret J., "The Industrial Cost of the Psychopathic Employee," *Nat. Conf. Soc. Work,* 1920: 342-46. Summarized by permission of the University of Chicago Press.

was to go into politics; his ideal Charles F. Murphy. After his father's death in 1910 the patient began a life of wandering from one job to another. He had lived in nearly every city in the northern states. He recalled his home as one of conflict between his father and mother who differed in both politics and religion. He lived on political gossip and the doings of those in high places. He believed that all his trouble was due to the revengeful hand of Tammany, many of whose secrets he possessed and had threatened to reveal. He justifies his continued failures by throwing the blame on the political machine of his native city which makes every job impossible for him. He believed that this gang would eventually smash such organizations as the National Committee for Mental Hygiene for trying to help him. He kept an elaborate work record from 1910 to 1919, showing evidence of 123 different jobs, the year he held each, the city where he was, the type of work, the name of his employer and various other data. Most of these facts were verified, and it was found that the 123 jobs represented 103 different firms for which he had worked, and 33 different occupations he had followed. His longest period at any one job had been eight months; the shortest one day. The average for all positions was 12½ days. He had worked a total of 1,545 days for the period covered, or about one day out of every two. He was discharged 80 times, resigned 20 times, and filled temporary positions 19 times. His total earnings for the ten years were $3,316.21.

The kinds of work which this patient had done might be grouped under three main headings: labor, clerical, and semi-skilled work. The number of jobs of each kind was approximately the same. Using a scale considered conservative, as a basis for computing the cost of the labor turnover for this single individual, his cost of hiring might be estimated as $47.50; of training at $960; of wear and tear, $392; of reduced production, $1,879; making a total of $3,608.50, a sum which exceeds his earnings by about $300. If the normal earnings of a man of this class are estimated at $1,200 per year, then the total wages which he should have received for his time, or $12,000, must be added to the foregoing in calculating his cost to society.

To find situations in which psychopathic workmen may function with some success, to "steady" them, and sometimes to eliminate them from the competitive struggle are tasks for the mental hygienist and the social worker in industry.

**Compensation laws** have been fairly successful in meeting another great problem of industrial life, that of accident. The cost of industrial accident is enormous, approximately $1,000,-

000,000 annually for the United States, according to a number of estimates. The principle that such cost should be borne by industry and ultimately the public at large has now come to be generally recognized. Under the common law the employer was liable, but was protected by the doctrines of negligence on the part of the employee, assumed risks, and the fellow-servant principle. The first attempt on the part of organized labor to improve the situation was aimed at the regulation of the employer's liability. When this failed, workman's compensation laws were urged. As a result of such agitation sixteen compensation laws were enacted before the close of 1912. Such legislation represented an extension of the police power and an expansion of the principle of collective responsibility.[24] By 1929 only four states, and those in the southern part of the country, had failed to pass compensation laws.

Compensation acts or systems vary greatly among the states but are of three general types. (1) Under the compulsory system the employer must come under the act. (2) In the elective plan he may accept or reject the act, but in case he rejects it his common-law defenses are abrogated. This is the most common system, thirty-one states having such acts. (3) In the voluntary scheme, which is found in only a few states, the employer does not lose his common-law defense if he fails to come under the act. Workman's compensation has several great advantages over other systems of handling industrial accidents. It greatly reduces litigation, makes awards relatively certain, and charges the bill to industry as a whole. But many compensation laws are quite limited in their benefits. They still leave the injured employee to bear an undue share of the loss. Rarely do they provide anything except medical attention and a small cash allowance. However, in New York the State Department of Labor has a staff of social case workers who assist in making various supplementary adjustments.

One of the good results of the War was the development of rehabilitation schemes to supplement the compensation acts. Massachusetts adopted the first industrial rehabilitation act in

[24] See Downey, E. H., *Workman's Compensation,* Macmillan, 1924, and Bossard, J., *Problems of Social Well Being,* Chaps. XIX-XX, Harper and Bros., 1927.

1918. In 1920 a federal statute was enacted providing for subsidies to those states that accepted the dollar-for-dollar cooperative plan laid down in the law. In New Jersey, out of 10,700 accident cases in one year, 1,865 were unable to return to their previous employment and were given rehabilitation service.[25] A "rehabilitation clinic" handles the cases of many men whose needs would not have been completely taken care of under the compensation law.

**Miscellaneous services** constitute a large phase of any plan of industrial social work. Such services include group and community work, recreation, company stores, restaurants, housing, accident prevention and health work. Many plants with no other form of service have medical, nursing or first-aid work. In many cases such work is very elaborate, medical service being given not only to the employee himself but to his family also. The Postum Cereal Company, for instance, has a staff of several full-time physicians and nurses who serve the employees and the members of their families free of charge. The Endicott-Johnson Shoe Company, whose 16,000 employees are a large percentage of the population of one city and two towns in New York State, has a well-equipped medical center at which both employees and their families are given complete medical attention except for the most elaborate surgical and dental work. The company has found that this service is profitable in the long run.

Labor leaders, who are naturally suspicious of welfare workers, sometimes assert that the adoption of their program—trade union, socialist, or other—would render social service unnecessary. Indeed, it is practically certain that higher wages, shorter hours, healthier work-places, careful placement of individuals at suitable tasks, adequate insurance schemes, and participation in management would eliminate the need for some things industrial welfare workers now attempt. But it is hard to conceive of any economic system in which individuals would not run amuck and need the skilled services of social case workers. Neither is it likely that even fundamental economic changes would eliminate the need of organized recreation and

[25] McBride, Andrew F., "Rehabilitation as an Aid to Compensation," *Rehabilitation Rev.*, 2: 203-7, 1928.

of various devices for maintaining group morale. Hence social workers will have definite and important functions, whether they operate under capitalism or under socialism, whether their salaries come from a corporation, a trade union, a cooperative association, or the State.

# CHAPTER XXV

## CHILDREN'S INSTITUTIONS

As already intimated, social work might well be divided into four main types: case work, group work, institutional work, and administration. Case work, discussed in the chapters immediately preceding, involves diagnosis and treatment of personal relationships between individuals or families and their social environment. In group work to which Chapters XXVIII and XXIX will be devoted, less attention is paid to the individual than to the social matrix of which he is or may become a part. Institutional work, treated in this and the two following chapters, is really a combination of the other two types. However, it differs from them both in at least one important respect. Most case work and most group work deal with people in their "natural" setting. Institutional work involves removing folks from ordinary neighborhood and community life, segregating them for a longer or shorter period, and subjecting them to external control. Because of this fact the managers of an institution must supply many goods and services for which other social workers look to the community. Among these are shelter, food, clothing, education, recreation, medical care, and religious services. Often the institution is a little world apart, though sometimes close contact is maintained with outside activities. In any case, the patient, ward, or prisoner must make two important adjustments. First, he must become used to a rather definite routine, fairly obvious external control, and usually little privacy. Then after a time, unless he spends the rest of his days in the institution, he must again learn to shift for himself in the ordinary world of families, workshops, and communities. The distinctively social side of institutional work consists largely in helping people to make these two rather difficult adjustments. In so far as each "inmate" is individualized he is dealt with on a case work basis. In so far as he is absorbed into cottage family, athletic team, work detail, scout troop, or military company, group work is being done.

## HOMEWOOD TERRACE [1]

In 1871 the Jewish people of San Francisco established the Pacific Hebrew Orphan Asylum. For a long time this was housed in a large frame structure near the heart of the city. But in 1921 the institution was moved out to a new location west of Twin Peaks, in a new and attractive residential section. At the same time the name was changed to Homewood Terrace.

The grounds comprise thirteen acres of land, three-fourths of which are occupied by buildings, playgrounds, and approaches, leaving nearly four acres for scouting and other recreational activities, as well as for additional accommodations that may be required. The plot plan sets the playground on the street front, framed by the main road on which all the service buildings are located—gymnasium, administration building, laundry, power house, and superintendent's residence. The reasons for this plan are that children of the vicinity may use the playground and that visitors may come and go without intruding upon the cottages and gardens.

In addition to the buildings already named, there are a health center, technical training school, a home for the assistant superintendent, and nine cottages for children. While there is harmony in the appearance of the buildings, each is different from all the others. Moreover, each cottage has a number, so that the children may have "regular" street addresses. Thus when asked where he lives, a boy or girl may answer, "Number 7 Homewood Terrace," instead of "Pacific Hebrew Orphan Asylum."

Each cottage has living rooms, dining room, kitchen, six bedrooms with lavatories and baths for children, and a suite of rooms for the house mother. These accommodations are similar but not identical in all nine cottages. The floor plans differ; interior decorations vary—some living rooms are furnished in leather, others in wicker, still others in Chinese rattan, fumed oak, etc. Each cottage is expected to be the home of ten boys and ten girls of varying ages. Each child has his own locker, wardrobe, toys, and shelf of books.

The gymnasium is well equipped for physical training and various sports. It also has a stage and dressing rooms for dramatics. The health center is planned not only for examination of incoming children, attention to minor ailments, and care of the seriously ill, but for a well-rounded program of health educa-

[1] This account is a summary of data made available through the courtesy of Dr. Samuel Langer, Superintendent of Homewood Terrace, and Dr. Jessica Peixotto of the University of California.

tion as well. There is an attractive play room for small children; a reference library for both staff and children; and a chapel with an air of dignity and peace, where also the comfort of the worshippers has been considered in such details as height of the benches and arrangement of lights.

The regular staff includes some twenty people in addition to which there is a large corps of volunteer workers. The superintendent, as in all well managed children's institutions, combines the functions of social worker, educator, and business manager. In this case he happens also to have planned the new establishment, both plant and program. There is an assistant superintendent who has special oversight of the boys, a dietitian, an assistant in charge of clothing, another for recreation, a registered nurse, a house mother for each cottage, a man who cares for the grounds, and an office staff.

While salaries cannot be large, they are higher than in most children's institutions. However, it is the spirit of the place, the attractive surroundings, and the privilege of living a "normal" life that make it possible to secure and retain high grade assistants. For example, house mothers are not buried in institutional routine, but each one is off duty one entire day, one evening, and either Saturday or Sunday afternoon every week. She is encouraged to continue her activities in the larger community, on the assumption that this is not only her due, but will make her a more valuable member of the staff. When the house mother is away her place is taken by a volunteer worker known as a "relief mother." Each cottage also has a group of six to ten unpaid helpers called "sewing mothers," who come every week to sew with and for the children. Both among the paid and the volunteer workers there is a relatively small turnover. This has obvious advantages from an administrative standpoint, and it helps to give the children a sense of security and "homeiness." Another interesting fact is the tendency of volunteer helpers to graduate into full-time, paid assistants. The "lure" seems to be the same as that which leads women to become house mothers for fraternities and sororities.

Since there are limits only on the age of admission, but none on the length of stay, the children range in age from four to twenty. Some are in kindergarten and some attend college, but the majority are going to public elementary and high schools. Applications for admission are handled through a cooperative bureau established in 1917. "The Children's Welfare Bureau has carefully refrained from formulating any set rules for the disposition of children, preferring to decide each case by itself. The general policy, however, has been based firmly on the principle of keeping families together. . . . Brothers and sisters, who in previous years were scattered among different boarding homes, are being united in one of them or in Homewood Terrace. Problem cases which would be dangerous or disgusting to others in close association are boarded out in specially selected homes for which adequate subsidies are provided." (54th Annual Report.)

Homewood Terrace was planned primarily as a home-making project rather than an educational project. Its characteristics, in so far as they differ from other child caring institutions, are traceable to this decisive condition. It is not claimed that ideal home conditions exist, or can exist in this or any other institution. There are numerous circumstances which prevent institution groups from corresponding in every detail to ordinary family groups. Diverse inheritances must be associated in the same group units, and the children have not inherited from those who stand to them in place of parents. Continued intercourse is maintained between children and surviving parents in addition to the relationship between child and guardian. Frequently this means unavoidable exposure to conflicting standards if ties of kinship are to be preserved. Yet mutual loyalty and understanding between the children and their relatives should be conserved, or built up if it does not already exist, despite the difficulties thereby superimposed on institution managers. These are only a few examples of the kind of thing which hampers the home builder. Nevertheless, considering the defects of the environments from which the children are drawn and the limitations of other substitutes for the natural home—in many respects the same as with institutional homes—it seemed possible to work out a worth-while scheme, one which will give the human relationships and emotional life, the social experiences and poise, the responsibilities and sacrificial spirit which are usually developed in a home of small means and high standards, as well as giving the housekeeping dexterities which are to be acquired there.

The groups in which the children live are so constituted that all normal relationships can be normally, unconstrainedly developed. There are twenty children in each, ten boys and ten girls, each sex with children from youngest to oldest. So each one can know intimately every other member of his own group and make acquaintances and friends in other families with whom he is less constantly and closely in contact. Every one in each family must make some contribution for all the rest. The little ones contribute their helplessness and themselves to be loved and taken care of. The bigger ones give their growing powers and derive a double satisfaction—the egotistic pleasure of using abilities which others have not yet developed and the unselfish pleasure of making others happy by personal exertions. The little ones have opportunity for developing hero-worship, the bigger ones for becoming the object of such worship. Not only the relationships of younger to older, of weaker to stronger, of slower to brighter are adjusted, but also of boy to girl and of handy man to home-maker. Every cottage has at least one family with real brothers and sisters, which fact serves to fix a wholesome attitude between the sexes for all the children. Each cottage is headed by a House-mother to guide and teach and love and work with her children, so that her children may work heartily and lovingly with and for her. Since there is no set age of discharge, but every child once admitted, is retained until self-supporting or otherwise properly cared for, the range of ages in each cottage is from four to eighteen or more, for both boys and girls. So there is no help problem in these households, for there are hands enough to carry on all the work under the guidance of the mother. Thus each child gets the same group of experiences which he would have in a home of small means and high standards.

There are certain matters which are taken for granted in good homes yet which by no means are innate or come by chance. The decencies of life and personal reserves are such. So are property rights. So also the right to privacy and solitude. These are social rights in any civilized community. These are the things which add dignity to efficiency and culture to education. This has been well remembered at Homewood Terrace. Each child has shelf space in the cottage library all to himself. Instead of dormitories there are rooms for three and rooms for four children. In these rooms each child has a built-in wardrobe, amply provided with shelf space, hanging space and drawers, all to himself. His own books, his own toys, his own clothes, his own toilet articles, and his own private place for each, sacred to himself to enable him to play or read or think by himself, away from the milling mass. With this provision a child ought to grow up knowing how to work and how to sport with others, and yet able to stand alone and work out his own private problems individually and staunchly.

This is bounteous opportunity. But it is only opportunity. It means comfort and happiness only as a result of personal effort. There can be no sitting idly by to enjoy the fruits of another's exertions. The children must keep their homes beautiful and comfortable by their own labor. When someone visits and admires the home, the excellence of the cooking, the happiness of the family, then the glow of pride warms the heart of every child in the household, for each one has a share in this sweet praise. The ideals of home life, with the knowledge and habit of participation, should go through life with these children, back into the habitations of their kin, if they return thither, and into their own homes when they establish them.

It is now seven years since the change was made from the congregate institution to Homewood Terrace. There has been time to estimate the effect of the changed environment on the children while they are in the institution and results are beginning to show from them in their maturity and on their citizenship. Of the latter, however, no more will be said here.

The improvement in manner and initiative and responsibility is remarkable. The children have experience both as hosts and as guests, and these social adventures are by no means limited to Homewood Terrace homes and people. Not only parties and dances and other special occasions are here referred to, but ordinary visits and meals and normal social interchanges.

Sex problems have never been any more prominent than before the mixed cottage families were organized. Actually there is less bother from such matters than before. The dangers of propinquity were grossly exaggerated. Expectations of wholesome effects from closer cooperation between girls and boys in family life, have been amply justified in these years of experience.

The opportunities for leadership are multiplied by the number of cottages. Opportunities for success are vastly more numerous and varied, both because there are more and different things for the children to do and because groupings among the children are smaller and more fluid. The extremes of docility and forwardness are less in evidence than formerly, but, surprisingly enough, there is less of the old-time gallantry and chivalrous consideration. The vast amount of service rendered to home and foster brothers and sisters seems to have heightened the attraction which babies exert, and visiting little ones are always besieged by adoring groups.

Housekeeping arts are, of course, well developed, and both boys and girls take on the management of the household quite naturally when illness or other causes interrupt the activities of the House-mother. The children have progressed much farther in the management of materials than in the appreciation of money values. Economic education is most difficult to give when so many relatives and friends give so many unearned coins and clothes and treats of food. The Children's Bank, The Store at which they must buy and pay cash for toilet articles and school supplies, the shopping fund which enables the older girls to select and pay cash for food supplies within a limited amount each month,—these are helpful palliatives, but they are not cures. Even budgeting a household leaves the iron hand of a limited fixed income out of the velvet glove of assured provision. It is much, however, that the youngsters know good things from bad, and know how to do with things when they have them—and that they know what they ought to have for a good life.

It seems futile to try to squeeze a few more details into an account necessarily so brief as this one. It is not possible here to describe in detail to what extent or how the emotional as well as the mental and physical needs of the children are fulfilled. What has been set down above may serve to show how background and organization have been moulded to meet both material and non-material needs. It is devoutly to be hoped that the vision which provided bounteous opportunity was large enough and keen enough to provide adequate administration too. (Child Welfare League of America, Bulletin, March, 1928.)

**The Place of Institutions for Children.** In simple communities, such as those of colonial America, children whose natural homes failed for any reason were usually taken in by relatives or neighbors. When no kinsman or friend was ready to step into the breach, local officials indentured the child to someone who was supposed to provide the necessities of life and teach him a trade. Sometimes they took him to the almshouse or poor farm. But as towns increased and the factory system developed the numbers of such needy children outgrew these simple provisions. One after another religious denominations, fraternal orders, municipalities and states established special institutions for orphans and other children deprived of parental care. The numbers of these orphanages and children's homes grew from six in 1800 to 1400 in 1925, some 400 being founded between 1890 and 1903.[2] In 1923 there were in the care of various agencies in the United States 405,000 children of whom 205,000 were in institutions.[3] For a time it was quite generally assumed that an institution was the proper place for every child who was "neglected, dependent, or delinquent." However, with the coming of child-placing societies and boards of children's guardians this tradition was challenged, and for a time there was a lively struggle between the advocates of institutional and of foster home care (the latter discussed in Chapter IX). Today it is commonly assumed that agencies of both types are needed, although there is not complete agreement as to just what functions each should perform.

On the whole it has been found that infants do better in boarding homes than in institutions. However, the experience of St. Ann's Infant Asylum in Cleveland indicates that "infants under one year of age receiving hospital type of care in an institution receive better medical supervision, better nurs-

[2] Reeder, R. R., in *Survey*, 54: 284.

[3] *Children Under Institutional Care, 1923*, U. S. Bureau of the Census, p. 14.

ing care, better dietetic watchfulness, and better mental hygiene than infants in the homes of even the well-to-do."[4] But unfortunately most institutions for infants do not provide the hospital care Dr. Thompson has specified as essential to good results. Two other groups of children have until recently been considered proper subjects for institutionalization, the feebleminded and the delinquent. But in the last quarter of a century it has been demonstrated conclusively that many morons and some imbeciles may be trained in special classes to support themselves and take an humble part in community life.[5] Also it has been shown that many delinquents make good adjustments on probation and need never be committed to prison, reformatory, or industrial school.[6] One statement of the place of institutional care and training for the general run of children has been made by Dr. Reeder.[7]

(a) If the children of a family are full orphans of school age, and placement in family homes cannot be made without separation and estrangement, they should by all means be placed in an institution for care and training. The most important thing in the world for such unfortunate children is to keep them together, nurture their family ties, and permit them to grow up with a common background of mutual experience and helpfulness. Placing them in two or more foster families or in separate communities is certain to stress their loneliness and deprive them of a life-long family feeling and association. The deepest yearning of the child heart is for family kinship. The greatest shock to the child is loss of parents, but the remnant that is left of the family relation expressed in terms of "my brother" or "my sister" becomes all the more precious. A few years of life together in an institution may preserve this cherished feeling.

(b) If an unattached orphan or otherwise dependent child requires special training or educational opportunities which the foster family cannot provide, the institution should open its doors.

(c) If there is a surviving parent or a close relative unable to provide for the child, but standing in affectionate relation to him, both the child and his relatives may be kept closer together and all made happier by placing the child in an institution rather

[4] Thompson, J. R., in *Survey*, 54:621. *Cf.* Chapin, H. D., in *Survey*, 55: 485-488.

[5] Davies, S. P., *Social Control of the Feebleminded.*

[6] See Chap. XXIII. See also Healy, Wm., *et al., Reconstructing Behavior in Youth.*

[7] Reeder, R. R., in *Survey*, 61: 483-4. Dr. Reeder's position has been challenged by several writers in *Survey*, 61: 824-5.

than in a family home, however suitable the latter may be. Again the human relation should be the determining factor. Reunion and the rebuilding of a broken home may take place after the institution has prepared the children for self-support.

(d) Following the careful social investigation of a dependent child, an interval for study and treatment before placement in a family home is frequently necessary. If the institution is adequately staffed and equipped for such expert work, it may thus serve a most useful purpose as a clearing house for determining what is best to be done.

(e) If a child has been a repeated misfit in family placing, necessitating several changes from one foster home to another, the institution should be able to do a better job than successive family homes.

(f) Probably the largest field of usefulness for institutions is in the care of motherless children when there are no relatives available to help the father maintain his home. Widows' pensions have been provided for fatherless families, but no provision has been made in any state for maintaining intact the families of widowers of limited incomes. They present almost a helpless family situation, and on account of the mutual relations of father and children, foster-home placing is not likely to prove satisfactory. Care in an institution, with father and children kept in as close touch as possible with each other, seems to offer practically the only solution. . . . A housekeeper, unless a relative of the widower's family, is usually too expensive for the limited income of a working father, and even when this is not the case, the housekeeper solution is not likely to be satisfactory. Institutional care is usually preferable.

In contrast to these motherless children it may be said that children whose mothers are living and unable to provide for them by reason of poverty only should not be admitted to institutions. To do so relieves the state of its legally assumed obligations, retards progress in establishing adequate widows' pensions, and deprives the children of their most precious heritage—mother-love and care. The children of widows who are physically, mentally and morally able to function as mothers should not be admitted to an institution. This is a limitation upon institution work that should be universally observed.

(g) Finally, there is still another function in child-welfare work that at least some of our institutions may assume. They may provide free maintenance and school training for children of two special groups: those of special educational promise and those too far below average mentality to profit by public-school training, all from families of widows, widowers, or with both parents living, but under such economic stress or poverty of environment that they do not have a fair chance for development.

There have been numerous criticisms of Dr. Reeder's criteria. With reference to item (a) it may be pointed out that institutions often fail to provide for entire family groups, while foster homes sometimes meet this need. (b) After all it is the school rather than the home which provides the special training Dr. Reeder mentions. Acceptance or rejection of this criterion depends on whether one conceives of the institution as a boarding school or as a home. (e) The child who has been a repeated misfit in foster homes—or in institutions, so far as that is concerned—clearly needs further study; it is by no means clear that an institution can solve his problems. (g) Children of superior ability and promise are precisely the ones who may be expected to make good adjustments in homes and communities. For them scholarships and loans seem much more appropriate than placement in institutions. Items (c) and (d) are rather generally accepted, while item (f) is one on which social workers disagree.

Miss Taylor has suggested institutional care for several groups of children not mentioned by Dr. Reeder.[8] First, there are children "who need especial protection from their own parents or from publicity or notoriety in a court or other case." Sometimes there is a child "whose emotional problem or make-up is such that he is helped to adjust by group life and institution régime and discipline." There are others with chronic physical disabilities which demand special training difficult to provide outside an institution. Fourth, there are certain delinquent children "who after repeated trials in the community fail to conform," or "who prove a definite menace at school or at play." Miss Taylor would also recommend institutional care for those with marked mental abnormalities and those with certain physical ailments.

Part of the confusion in such discussions as this arises from the fact that the various writers are not thinking in the same terms. Dr. Langer, for example, conceived Homewood Terrace as a home for "normal" children; Dr. Reeder evidently thinks of institutions as combining the functions of home and school; while Miss Taylor has in mind specialized institutions serving children who deviate in various ways from the "normal."

[8] *Nat. Conf. Soc. Work,* 1924: 126.

Doubtless there is need for all these types, but obviously each must have a different basis of admission.

**Admissions and Dismissals.** The day is not far past when some institutions accepted almost all children who were brought to the door or left on the step. Some even went out and hunted up children to fill their dormitories. But today an increasing number of institutions are scrutinizing all applications carefully to determine first the needs of the particular child and then the ability of the institution to meet these needs. This means that admission or refusal is based on a social diagnosis made by someone skilled in case work. Obviously such a diagnosis must rest on facts pertaining to the child's health, mental development, habits, family situation, and general background. This study of the child in his social setting may be made by a member of the institution's own staff or, as in the case of Roy Daniels,[8a] by a children's aid society, or, in a few cities, by a central application bureau. The details of organization are less important than the principle of thorough analysis of each case. In addition to the usual reasons for social diagnosis we have here the additional fact that "empty space in an orphan asylum is a brick-and-mortar appeal to move in."

The results that followed the employment of a social case worker by a southern denominational orphanage are indicated in the following table. In fourteen months 362 applications were received, but only 101 children were accepted. However, the other 261 were not merely rejected, they were transferred to other agencies or adjustments were made within their own family circles.

After the decision has been made to admit a child to an institution the next steps are quarantine and introduction to the people and the routine of the house.

Every child, upon entrance to an institution, should be isolated long enough to protect the other children and the adults from danger of contagious and infectious diseases. The new arrival may come from a dirty, insanitary home. He may bear in his clothing or upon his person malignant germs. He may be about to "come down" himself with measles, mumps, diphtheria, or some other "catching" disease. Upon arrival at the institution he should receive a hot bath, his clothing should be removed and be either

[8a] See Chapter XIX.

DISPOSITION OF APPLICATIONS FOR ADMISSION TO THE PRESBYTERIAN ORPHANS' HOME, BARIUM SPRINGS, NORTH CAROLINA.[9]

| | *Number of Children* |
|---|---|
| Applications withdrawn when applicants had a clearer understanding of orphanage work | 38 |
| Relatives able and willing to support | 92 |
| Other agencies and institutions better suited to relieve the dependency | 95 |
| Refused because children were sub-normal | 7 |
| Refused because children were over-age | 7 |
| Investigations not completed | 22 |
| Total not received | 261 |
| Admitted or placed on waiting list | 101 |
| Total applications | 362 |

burnt or disinfected as its condition warrants, and after clean clothing has been substituted he should be taken at once to the quarantine quarters to await the physician's examination. He should remain in quarantine at least two weeks and leave only upon the order of the physician.[10]

The following suggestions are offered to cottage mothers in the institution maintained by the Hebrew Sheltering Guardian Society of New York.

When the child enters the cottage on the first day, it is very important that the cottage mother should greet him very warmly and cheerfully, call him by his full name, and introduce the child to each of the other members of the cottage family group, and that then he be assigned his definite place in the dormitory, in the dining room and other places of the cottage so that he may know that he is immediately considered a full fledged member of the family with definite responsibilities, duties, obligations, and privileges. It will be well for the cottage mother to have a personal and confidential talk with the child as early as possible and to keep close to the child until he becomes convinced that his welfare will be considered at all times.

Acquaint the child with the general physical routine of the cottage life, and let him learn as quickly as possible what will be expected of him in the matters of neatness, cleanliness, order-

[9] Child Welfare League of America, Bulletin, Jan. 15, 1928.

[10] Richardson, C. S., *Physical Care of Dependent Children in Institutions*, p. 5.

liness, physical care of his body, care of individual articles of personal property, personal appearance, regularity in matters of diet, bathing, sleep and the prompt obedience of the simple but necessary rules and regulations of the cottage.

Acquaint the child with the important and essential rules of the institution so that he may learn as quickly as possible, how, when and where to attend to certain specific duties required of him, and thus avoid any friction or misunderstanding with the heads of any of the departments of the Society at large.

Encourage the child to keep up his warm contacts with parents, relatives or friends in the City. No matter what the causes were which led to the breaking up of the child's normal home, it should be our duty to help to maintain those natural ties which existed before the child came to us, and to do everything in our power to assist in rehabilitating the natural home of the child, wherever possible. Cottage mothers should therefore advise children under their care to write letters to the folks at home as frequently as possible. Visits by parents or other relatives and friends to our children, and visits by our children to their relatives should be encouraged.[11]

While the child is being adjusted to life in the institution its staff or that of some cooperating agency has the task of preparing a place for him after he leaves. Usually this means case work with his family, for "in two thirds of the cases the children in most institutions are returned to the same family group from which they came after an average residence of two or three years in the institution." [12] That is, the child is institutionalized because something has gone wrong at home. In correcting the difficulty attention may have to be concentrated on the child himself or on the family as a whole, or more frequently on both. When the child is ready—in health, habits, and attitudes—to go home, and when the home is ready—in equipment, support, harmony, and understanding—to receive him, it is time for the second great adjustment. However, instead of relinquishing all interest in the child when he leaves its gates, the staff of many an institution will follow him for some time to see how he is getting along, to help him meet difficulties which arise, and to bring him back to the institution if need be. If legal custody is involved, this becomes essen-

[11] Hebrew Sheltering Guardian Society, *Manual for Cottage Mothers*, pp. 88-89.

[12] Peixotto, Jessica B., in *What Dependent Children Need*, p. 13.

tially a period of parole. But even if there is no question of authority, it is the part of wisdom to keep in close touch with children who have recently left the institution. If circumstances are such that the natural home cannot be used, it is the responsibility of the institution or some cooperating agency to find a suitable foster home in accordance with the procedure outlined in Chapter XX, and to help in making necessary adjustments until the child is adopted, married or of age.

**Types of Children's Institutions.** So far children's institutions have been discussed as though they were all alike; and so, indeed, they are in many respects. But still they vary sufficiently to warrant their classification into a number of distinct types. First of all, they may be divided according to the auspices under which they operate. There are public, or tax-supported, institutions maintained by cities, counties, and states. Then there are semi-private institutions controlled by churches, lodges, and other groups. This division also suggests the sources of financial support, although many private institutions receive public funds either as a direct subsidy or as payment for the care and training of particular children, and both types collect board, whenever possible, from parents or guardians.

A second classification has reference to physical equipment. Most of the older institutions had large dormitories, dining rooms, and assembly halls, in great buildings which were monuments to architects and philanthropists of bygone days. Children were handled *en masse* with little individualization or small-group life. Over against these "congregate" institutions there has grown up an increasing number of "homes" and "schools" "on the cottage plan," like Homewood Terrace.

Finally, we may classify institutions according to their functions as orphanages, receiving or detention homes, day nurseries, nursery schools, industrial schools, and institutions for handicapped children.

The word "orphanage" is really a misnomer, because most of the children in such institutions have one or both parents living. However, the term does specify a place where children live for months or years in fairly large groups. They come because of some disturbance in the home situation; usually death, divorce, desertion, illness, or imprisonment, of one or both parents. An "orphanage" or "children's home" may accept children of only one sex, of certain ages, of specific religious or fraternal groups, and so on. It may or may not demand legal custody. But in general, it tends to be a home and school for two or three years for children who will later return to their parents or other relatives.

A receiving or detention home is a place where a child may stay a few days or weeks while information is being secured about him and a plan is being formulated. Here he may be given medical and psychological examinations; he may be observed at play, at work, and in the school room; he may be protected against interference by relatives or others; his presence in court may be guaranteed. Such institutions as this are commonly maintained in connection with juvenile courts and children's aid societies.

A day nursery is a small institution for the care of young children while their mothers work. The youngsters are brought by their mothers in the morning and taken home at night. All sorts of people make use of day nurseries, but in general they seem to be most helpful to strong, healthy mothers of one or two children of pre-school age, who for some reason must earn their own living. Many of these institutions stop with mere physical care of the children; others offer kindergarten training; and some undertake to teach the mothers various aspects of child care.

The nursery school is much less a "parking place" for youngsters. It combines habit training, especially for "problem children," with education for parenthood, and with research. Children come from families on all economic levels, and there are student assistants who are being prepared for their own future parenthood. The number of genuine nursery schools is still small, although the name is spreading rather rapidly.

The industrial schools are mainly tax-supported institutions which receive children by commitment from juvenile courts. Presumably these children are "delinquent" and in need of "reformation"; but, as a matter of fact, every sort of child may be found here. These institutions differ from the others we have named in laying greater emphasis on safekeeping and "discipline." They have more locks and bars, and sometimes look very much like prisons.

Finally, there is a considerable number of specialized institutions for children handicapped in mind or body—homes and schools for the feebleminded, blind, deaf, or crippled. All of these are educational institutions, except a few which offer little more than custodial care.

**Plant and Equipment.** The physical equipment of these institutions varies greatly. Receiving homes, detention homes, day nurseries, and nursery schools usually occupy modest buildings planned to accommodate a small number of children and their attendants. Day nurseries are often conducted in social settlements or neighborhood centers, but the others usually have independent establishments. At their best they are simple, but attractive, fire-proof buildings, with facilities for examinations, simple medical and dental treatment, elementary school work, play both indoor and outdoor, feeding, and resting.

Because the children stay longer and in greater numbers the equipment of "orphanages" and industrial schools is usually more extensive. A relatively large tract of land is needed for the various buildings, gardens and playgrounds. In a "modern" institution the children are housed in separate dwellings with living room, playroom, dining room, kitchen, lavatories, bedrooms for three or four children each, and a small suite for the house "father" and "mother." Furnishings are in good taste, but not expensive. Books, toys, victrola, radio, and pictures are provided as in the home of an artisan or small business man. Each child has definite places for his own toilet articles, clothing, toys, and other personal possessions. Besides the cottages there are service buildings for administration, hospital and isolation, gymnasium, perhaps school, garage or barns, heating plant, and laundry. Somewhere places for pets are provided. The whole establishment is so designed as to surround the child with comfort, convenience, and beauty, without creating a taste for things which he will be unable to have in later life.

**Life in a Children's Institution.** Every household must have a measure of routine in order to reduce friction, misunderstanding, and wasted energy. When from 25 to 200 people live together the necessity for fairly definite programs of work, rest, and play is greatly increased. However, even here this can easily be overdone. With fixed hours for rising, meals, school, work, and retiring, the rest of the program may be left rather flexible.

Some members of the staff must spend most of their time looking after the children's physical welfare. There are menus to plan, baths to supervise, clothing to wash and mend, periodic examinations to arrange, sick children to nurse, and health habits to teach. Someone must assign the tasks whereby boys and girls help with the institution housekeeping and learn to sweep, wash, cook, make beds, and acquire a sense of responsibility. Someone must be responsible for playtime, planning games, encouraging shy children, settling disputes, seeing that toys and apparatus are in order, leading group singing, directing pageants, and many other services. Another set of tasks pertains to economic training, the management of earnings, allowances, savings, and purchases. Then there are the problems of "discipline," correcting conduct which interferes with other people, creating new interests and ideals, developing group loyalty. Often it is possible and wise to develop a considerable degree of self-government.

In the matter of schooling there is diversity both of opinion and of practice. Some institutions maintain their own schools, others send all children out; some have school for younger children, but send out those who are ready for higher grades; others have public school teachers sent to them. On the ground that many children are in institutions because of their need for special care and training it may seem wise to have a school on the grounds. But in view of the facts that children suffer from isolation and that later they will return to the larger community, there is much to be said for the public school. As a matter of fact, circumstances alter cases, but if the problems which the children present are not too serious, if they can go out to school without being a marked group, and if the equipment and personnel of the school system are adequate, the advantage appears to lie with schooling away from the institution.

But, after all, the purpose of all these "arrangements" is to aid in redirecting behavior, developing character, and promoting a wholesome balance of interests and activities for each child in his particular social setting. This means that personal influence is more significant than any detail of equipment or routine. The most important part of the institution's work is done through the informal daily contacts between the adults on the staff and the children who are their wards. But its results are not secured through sermonizing, fault-finding, threatening, or punishing. They are brought about rather by understanding, suggestion, encouragement, and wholesome living together. In all this members of the staff often make use of older boys and girls in the institution who act as "big brothers" and "big sisters"; they utilize such organizations as Boy Scouts; they cooperate with relatives and friends outside, they encourage the keeping of pets.[12]

In some institutions great stress is laid on religious instruction and worship. Under wise direction and leadership this undoubtedly contributes greatly to the changing of ideals and habits. The religious ceremonies and teachings may aid in the development of courage, ambition, stability, unselfishness, loyalty, and appreciation of beauty. But the ritual and the sermon may actually hinder the child's personal growth if they are uninteresting and poorly presented. It is exceedingly important that his religious leaders be understanding adults who offer religion at its best, free from superstition, dogma, and insistence upon non-essentials.

**Personnel and Administration.** Most institutions have boards of trustees who hold title to the property, determine general policies, select the superintendent, raise money, and perform a variety of other functions. Sometimes they have committees or individual members who undertake to handle details of hiring employees, purchasing supplies, repairing clothing, and other items of institutional housekeeping. Not infrequently their activity takes the form of espionage or meddling. At the other extreme, they rarely visit the place and scarcely

[12] It is obviously impossible to give in brief space anything like an adequate picture of the lively give-and-take between adults and children which constitutes the most important part of institutional life and work. For such a picture the reader is referred to Drucker and Hexter, *Children Astray.*

know its general policies, much less the details of its administration. A more wholesome situation is one in which ultimate responsibility rests with the board, whose members are intelligent advisers of the staff, but who wisely leave the actual administration to the superintendent and his associates.

Within the institution selection of helpers, division of labor, and delegation of authority are among the superintendent's most important and most difficult tasks. Because salaries are usually low, hours on duty long, vacations short, and responsibilities great, it is not easy to build up a staff of high-grade persons. The employees of some institutions might well be described as "misplaced policemen and washwomen." "After a superintendent has done his best in the choice of associates," one institution head says, "I believe that the great and important step of the chief executive of an institution is to grade and classify his vested authority among his assistants in such a manner that to all appearances he, the superintendent, is exercising no authority at all."

Among the functions to be performed by members of the staff are those of "house mother," and "house father," dietician, nurse, recreation leader, gardener, liaison officer, record clerk, purchasing agent, and teacher. These duties may be variously combined, depending on personal abilities and the number of employees. But each person on the staff, no matter what his official position, is primarily chosen to help in the personal development of boys and girls. Hence his character, poise, refinement, and professional spirit are no less important than his technical skill.

# CHAPTER XXVI

## HOMES FOR THE AGED

In Chapter VI it was shown that in the 'nineties the almshouse was the main provision for unfortunate old people in the United States. It was an institution that rarely reflected credit on the community that maintained it. It was usually the county or town dumping ground for all sorts of maladjusted folk—crippled, insane, feebleminded, vagrants, unmarried mothers, homeless children, and poverty-stricken old people. It was ordinarily run by a political appointee who might be a fairly good farmer, but who seldom knew anything about institutional management; often he was a "hard boiled" office holder, interested in little besides drawing his own salary. The buildings were either dilapidated farmhouses or unattractive brick barracks, located with little reference to convenience. There was a minimum of provision for medical care, recreation, or suitable occupation. Of course, "inmates" who were able to be about were expected to help with the chores and odd jobs about the house, but there was no systematic effort to provide interesting and profitable tasks for the old people. Unfortunately these conditions still obtain in many localities at the present time, but elsewhere the tide is turning. As a sample of changing conditions we present the following excerpt from a recent report by the California State Department of Social Welfare.[1]

### HOW CALIFORNIA COUNTIES CARE FOR THE NEEDY AGED

California, fortunately, is so young a state that it has escaped many of the unhappy names and conditions which older communities have attached to county institutions and housing for the aged poor. The terms, "workhouse," "poorhouse" and "poor-

[1] "Old Age Dependency," pp. 20-23, California State Printing Office, 1928.

farm" never have been applied to these California institutions; in some districts the name "almshouse" was used in early days but that, too, is now obsolete. In a new community which had the opportunity to begin where older civilization had just arrived after years of weary struggle, there were no disgraceful buildings or traditions to clear away. California had no public institutions until some of the old pioneers of the gold rush days began to break down; the first buildings for shelter of these unfortunates were called "county hospitals" and it is by this name that they have always been known. They are really old people's homes with medical supervision. It is only within the last twenty years that the county institutions have become medical hospitals in the modern meaning of the word. There are now in California some of the finest and best equipped modern hospitals in the country, maintained as county institutions for the medical and surgical treatment of those who are unable to pay for care in a private hospital. The development of public health education, health centers, diagnostic clinics, treatment clinics and training schools for nurses under public control is closely connected with the higher standards in county hospitals. One result of this spirit of growth has been the tendency to separate the sick from the aged in county institutions, much to the advantage of the aged. Even in counties where there is not actual division of administration, there is usually provision for segregation in wards or floors, so that the old people may come and go without being depressed by the sights and sounds of sick patients.

No children are supposed to be in the county hospital except for observation or medical treatment; county detention homes are provided for temporary housing of homeless children. Criminals are not sent to county hospitals except for medical care; insane and feebleminded are not detained in the quarters occupied by the old people. In the newer institutions, there is separate housing of the senile aged; this, however, is not done in every county. The mingling of senile dementia patients with normal old people is one of the unsatisfactory features still to be corrected.

Many of the county homes compare very favorably with private homes for the aged. In what private home could an inmate receiving free care go away for the summer months and have his room reserved until his return? This is done in some of the rural county hospitals in the mountains of California. Old prospectors are restive in the spring and the doors of the county institution swing both ways; a weatherbeaten old "burro" is driven up, the pick and pan loaded on his patient back, and with many wavings of farewell to the old men left behind the old mountaineer goes off to "earn his keep" till the autumn rains drive him back to the shelter of the "winter boarding house"—the county hospital. There are vacant beds in some institutions of the mountain counties. The population of these counties is not increasing and the old men are passing.

In the San Joaquin and Sacramento valleys, on the contrary, the county homes and hospitals are filled to overflowing. In two of the central counties, on the day of visit, there were beds on the porches and the county officers were considering a plan for "boarding out" some of the applicants who could not gain admission. In most of the large counties there is such a demand for beds that only the sick or disabled can be admitted. The result is a tendency to give out relief to an increasing number of old people outside the institutions.

Los Angeles County maintains an extensive and well equipped institution for the aged out at the County Farm, while the county hospital in the city is crowded with patients and anxiously awaiting the completion of the new 1600-bed hospital now in the course of construction. The farm really is a combination of three institutions and is an instance of remarkably good management and efficient personal service. The segregation of the old people, by their needs, into (1) the infirmary, (2) the psychopathic department and (3) the general home, makes for the best interests of all. The population on the day of visit was 1800, with very few vacant beds.

San Francisco County has just erected a new building for the homeless aged poor, which carries over its imposing entrance the name "Laguna Honda Home." In the same grounds is the hospital building for aged chronic patients. This whole institution is entirely separate from the downtown county hospital for medical and surgical patients. The modern conveniences of the home as well as its spacious comfort and beautiful location make it a desirable shelter for those who have no other home. Occupation is one of the features stressed by the superintendent of the institution and the advantages of this system both to the institution and to the old people themselves are apparent. The population of Laguna Honda Home on the day of visit was 1560.

Alameda County two years ago opened a magnificent new medical hospital in the city of Oakland, leaving its former county hospital buildings at San Leandro for the housing of chronic patients and homeless old people. Both institutions are now filled. The home at San Leandro, now known as Fairmont Hospital, is so crowded that it has a waiting list of aged applicants for admission. One of the unique features of this institution is the "industrial department" where the old men make toys, baskets and other articles which are sold on orders; and where workers are busy in the cobbler shop, the tailor shop, the mattress shop, the machine shop, the canteen where special comforts may be purchased, the laundry and other activities. The workers there could not earn a living on the outside because they are partially disabled by age or sickness and unable to work full time. But they are so eager to be busy and earning something that the shops have therapeutic as well as business value. The average daily population of the institution is 720. Only 280 are able to take any part in the industrial activities. The rest are bed patients or too feeble to be allowed any exertion.

San Diego County is one of the progressive counties which have separated the care of the aged from the care of the sick. Edgemoor Farm houses all the homeless old people except about fifty who are bed patients in the chronic ward at the General Hospital. The senile aged are in special quarters quite apart from the other old people. The farm is attractive and well managed; the care and food are excellent. The population of the farm is 217 aged persons.

Fresno County was one of the first in the state to furnish a separate building for the care of its old people as distinct from the sick in the hospital. A county building which had been used previously as an orphanage was remodeled for the housing of the homeless aged and is now known as the Old Peoples Home. It is not too far from the hospital for ready transfer in case of sickness. While the building is well kept and has some attractive features, it is not satisfactory for its present use; the stairs that were climbed so nimbly by children's feet are somewhat steep for feet that have trod three score years and ten, and the large dormitories are not as well suited to the broken slumbers of the aged as smaller rooms would be. All the institutionally housed aged are at the Old Peoples Home except those who are bed patients at the General Hospital. The General Hospital is so crowded that beds are set on the porches. The Old Peoples Home is filled to capacity and unable to accommodate all applicants for admission. An effort is made to have the county welfare department find boarding places for some of the aged applicants and to put others on the outrelief list. Fresno County is giving excellent service to its sick and aged poor but in sadly inadequate buildings. The population of the Old Peoples Home was 110 [at the last report].

Forty-seven county institutions combine the care of the sick and aged under one administration. San Joaquin County has perhaps the best provision for the care of aged in the group of combined institutions. Here the buildings for the aged are new and well planned with small wards, a number of private rooms, easy inclines instead of stairs, separate dining rooms and large reading rooms as well as an assembly hall for entertainments.

Mariposa County, which has but five institutional patients, boards them in the hospital of a neighboring county at an agreed payment for their care. The cost of administration for an institution to care for five old people would not be justified; in this county it would involve also the cost of building, as there is no suitable county hospital building in Mariposa.

Owing to the growing tendency in counties to extend outrelief to the old people who are physically able to care for themselves in their own homes or who have relatives or friends to look after them, the institutional group is becoming more and more a selected body of persons who are physically, mentally or socially incapable of living away from institutional or nursing care. From personal observations, during this survey and from information given by doctors, nurses and superintendents it is estimated that not more than 5 per cent at the most and in some institutions not more than 1 per cent of the inmates could live comfortably outside the county hospital on an income of $30 per month. This income will not provide nursing care. It is difficult to find a private boarding place for old people at $30 per month.

The greatest increase in the population of the county hospitals, at the present time, is in the medical and surgical wards and in the newer psychopathic wards which are being added to all the institutions in all the large counties.

If present indications continue, the "county hospital" in California will soon be a hospital in fact as well as in name, caring only for physically and mentally sick patients; with a separate and distinct "Home" department for old people who are homeless or suffering from chronic ailments and who cannot be cared for adequately outside of the institution.

In addition to public institutions many old people's homes are maintained by churches, fraternal orders, and other groups. While some of these are for the penniless aged, most of them are relatively expensive. A good example of a moderately priced private institution is the Home for the Aged in Kalamazoo, Michigan.[2]

The single building which constitutes the Home was constructed and opened in 1925, and accommodates fifty people. It is a pleasant, three-story brick structure with sun porches and airy living rooms situated near the edge of the city in a good residential neighborhood and on a main street that leads into one of the important state highways. The institution is a semi-charitable one, controlled by the Reformed Church, but although it depends almost entirely upon Hollanders for support it has no restrictions relative to nationality, religion, or place of residence. During the four and one-half years the Home has been in operation not more than fifty per cent of the inmates have been Dutch.

[2] Description based upon personal observation and interviews with the acting matron and the President of the Board, Mr. Ralph Kooi.

The rooms are fair-sized and well furnished and lighted—much like modern hotel rooms. Most of them are single, but there are a few double rooms for married couples, and occasionally it has been necessary for two of the old people to share a room for a short period. The minimum age for entrance is sixty-five. Only in one instance has a member left at the end of the three months' probationary period, and that was at the request of the Board.

There is a common dining room for all the residents. The food is well cooked and served on clean, oilcloth covered tables in thick white china. An attempt is made to have the food and service as nearly as possible like that to which the old people have been accustomed. The women who are so inclined help in the dining room and all residents look after their own rooms except when they are ill. The institution provides medical care in case of illness and reserves the right to send members to the hospital if the physician in attendance advises it. All hospital expenses are borne by the Home, which also pays funeral costs.

The financial arrangements are agreed upon by the Board and the applicant in each individual case after conference, and the attempt is made to have every one bear as large a proportion of his cost to the institution as he is able. The minimum price, however, is three hundred dollars annually, or a thousand dollars cash settlement, to cover all expenses from admission to death. The difference between the amounts paid by the members of the Home and the cost of operation is raised by private subscription, appropriations from the churches, income from socials, and the like. The original capital investment for the construction of the building was made by the Reformed churches and certain individuals. On the whole, the Home for the Aged seems a very pleasant and satisfactory retreat for old people of the community who for some reason cannot be cared for by their children or relatives.

The daily routine in the Home is simple enough. The old people are awakened by a gong at 6:30. They dress, and at 7 o'clock breakfast is served. After breakfast the old men smoke their pipes and take their "constitutionals" out-of-doors, if the weather permits, or on the sun porch if it is inclement. The old women help with the bed making and the dishwashing. During the morning the men play games, read, "swap" stories, dig in the garden a little or go walking as they wish. The old ladies sew, knit and gossip. After lunch comes a lull when naps are the general order of the day. Visitors usually drop in, and the matron is free for chats or to be sociable in other ways. The "help" are middle-aged women of the same general class and background as the old folks of the Home and the preparation of supper is therefore a social affair. Afterwards comes a little more smoking, a little more reading and chatting, and bed. Each day is like every other, varied only by the weather, an occasional visit or entertainment, and the weekly religious service, which is held by ministers from all the evangelical churches in rotation.

**The Problem.** These two types of institutions represent the main provisions made for the care of the dependent aged in this country. The almshouse or public home takes care of the vast majority. Approximately half the "inmates" of the almshouses are more or less infirm and helpless old people. Despite other methods employed to care for this group of the population, institutionalization remains the principal one. Where the aged person has no relatives and boarding out in a private family is not feasible, life in a public or private home is necessary to prevent isolation and demoralization. But it need not carry too great a stigma, particularly if combined with some form of old age insurance or pensions. When, too, on account of infirmities or disabilities special care is needed it may best be provided in an institution. The scientific care of the aged under such conditions is one form of institutional social work as defined in the preceding chapter. The case work job with such clients is not usually rehabilitation and placement as with defectives, children, and delinquents, but rather their permanent adjustment to large-group life so that they may be happy and contented.

**Extent, Causes, and Nature of Old Age Dependency.** Statistics on old age dependency in the United States are not very accurate or complete, although in recent years, due to an increased interest in the problem, a number of important and thorough investigations have been made in several states. The number of the aged in the general population has steadily increased as is seen by the following table:

INCREASE IN THE NUMBER OF THE AGED.

Sixty-five and over.

| *Year* | *Percentage of the Total Population* |
|---|---|
| 1880 | 3.5 |
| 1890 | 3.9 |
| 1900 | 4.2 |
| 1910 | 4.3 |
| 1920 | 4.7 |
| 1926 | 5.0 estimated |

Most persons, on attaining this age, have given the country some forty-five years of service. Their number has been increasing by approximately 100,000 each year, until it reached the estimated total of five and one-half million on January 1, 1926. About 27% of this group are foreign-born. Approximately one-half are women. As the average person of sixty-five may still expect twelve or more years of life, the problem of his support is a serious one.

For the United States as a whole approximately one out of three or from 1,800,000 to 2,000,000 persons reaching sixty-five are dependent upon relatives or strangers. According to Lucile Eaves,[3] nearly one in every four Massachusetts citizens when he becomes sixty-five requires aid, as almost one-half have incomes of less than $300 annually. About 15% receive support from public or private agencies. The low earning power and consequent need of the aged of Pennsylvania was shown in the Report of the Pennsylvania Commission on Old Age Assistance in 1925. According to this report approximately 80% of the aged were receiving under $1,100 per year; 29% earning between $14 and $20 a week; 14% less than $12 a week; while 37% earned nothing.[4]

Traditionally idleness and thriftlessness during the earlier years of life were considered the main causes of the poverty of old age. Numerous studies of incomes in recent years, however, have shown conclusively that no such simple ethical explanation is valid. Investigations such as those cited below indicate that for the average man or woman in industry saving for old age is well-nigh impossible. The explanation of old age dependency is largely economic: low wages, unemployment, strikes, and business failures are mainly responsible. Physical and mental disability, and the decreasing size and solidarity of the American family are two other important causes. But the mere financial dependency of the aged is not the only aspect of the problem. Due to a lack of normal family connections, isolation, insecurity, loss of former occupational contacts, and a feeling of futility engendered by inactivity, they tend to be-

[3] Eaves, Lucile, "The Aged Citizens of Massachusetts," *Survey,* 55: 554-555, 1926.

[4] Epstein, A., "Challenge of the Aged Poor," *Nat. Conf. Soc. Work,* 1925; 328-334.

come maladjusted emotionally. Any program for the proper care of the old must take the total situation into account.

The problem is far more serious than the small amount of discussion (until very recently) would indicate. Increasing numbers in the upper age groups of the population, due to the immigration of adults and a lowered death-rate, a rising standard of living which makes saving difficult if not impossible, and the increasing tendency on the part of industry to scrap its workers at fifty or even forty-five because of greater demands for speed and specialization, have made the problem one of the first magnitude socially. Remunerative work for the old is daily more difficult to secure. Employers are apparently unwilling to face the responsibility of providing for aged workers when the time for retirement comes, and hence get rid of them before this time or avoid employing them. Thus the aging worker faces a triple problem; to prepare for an old age whose length medical science has increased, with saving made well-nigh impossible by the standard of living, and with the prospect of being laid off long before he has reached the limit of his productivity. The following case of "Nora Brown," a widow, age fifty-five years, illustrates several phases of the problem. She has worked as a machine operator since she was sixteen, likes the people in the factory, and is welcomed by her married children as long as she can support herself.

> She is discharged, kindly, but finally, because of a change of supervision bringing in the idea that workers over fifty are not efficient at such work. She has enough saved to last through if she is extremely careful, but she wants to work. Her social life has gone with her industrial life. She was a strong, capable, interested, happy worker. She is, overnight as it were, changed into a disappointed, indifferent, unhappy old woman with nothing to do.[5]

**Types of Institutions for the Aged.** Institutions for the aged may be classified as public and private. Under the former are included the almshouse and poorfarm, military and naval homes, the county hospital for the aged sick such as those in California, and state institutions. Private homes are religious, fraternal, occupational, racial and the like. Some of these are

[5] Gilbreth, Lillian M., "Scrapped at Forty," *Survey,* 62: 400, 1929.

excellent, but most of them are closed except to a small percentage of the aged who can afford to purchase a place in one of them.

The poorhouse is pretty much what it was in Warner's day. The percentage of the aged in such institutions is steadily increasing, although the absolute number is not large. According to the census report [6] there were on January 1, 1923, less than 42,000 persons sixty-five years of age and over in almshouses, who were being maintained at a *per capita* cost to the county of from $400 to $500 a year. The reconstruction of the almshouse has been long delayed, but at last the problem is receiving the attention of professional students and social workers. A number of valuable suggestions have been made and some significant experiments are in progress. The main reforms needed include expert and efficient administration, classification and segregation, modification of physical structure, limitation of admission to the aged and infirm, location nearer population centers, enlargement of the area served by the almshouse to include a number of counties, close supervision by a state board of control, correlation with other agencies and institutions, improvement of the general tone or atmosphere, and skilled attention to individual physical and emotional needs.

The cottage system has been tried successfully in a number of places. For example, the District of Columbia almshouse and the Cleveland poorhouse are both constructed with detached wings, or buildings. Such an arrangement facilitates the classification and segregation of inmates for the purpose of specialized treatment. This plan can be followed, of course, only where the institution is relatively large and serves a number of counties. Another tendency is toward converting the almshouse into a hospital for the infirm or chronically sick aged. Recent Boston studies of old age dependency and sickness have shown the inadequacy of the present hospitals to care for chronic aged cases. More institutions similar to the one described below are needed. Preferably such almshouse-hospitals should be relatively large and under direct state control or supervision.

[6] *Paupers in Almshouses;* 1923. Bureau of the Census, 1925.

BRIDGEPORT[7]

Almshouse is owned by the city and is situated . . . about ten minutes' walk from the East Main Street line of electric cars. One hundred and sixty-two acres of land are included in the property. . . . Superintendent, Angus P. Thorne, who is also superintendent of the City Charities Department. Daily average number of inmates 245. . . . A considerable staff of paid employees is maintained, including 16 nurses and attendants, resident doctor, druggist, and paid help in the kitchen and laundry.

The Bridgeport Almshouse is run entirely along hospital lines, there being three wards for sick women, two wards for sick men, and a psychopathic ward each for men and women. In addition to the adults in the main building an average of about twenty children are cared for in the Margaret Ford Cottage which is situated on the same grounds. The group of buildings erected for the almshouse was first occupied July 1, 1916, and is called the Hillside Home. The institution is a model of its kind, arranged on the group plan, with separate pavilions for the different classes of inmates, connected with enclosed corridors. The buildings are two stories in height, of brick and stone, fireproof in construction, and all departments are equipped with the best modern apparatus and furnishings.

A dietitian is employed in connection with the institution and as a result, a greater variety of food is provided for the inmates at a lower cost. All of the bread and milk used in the institution are provided from its own bakery and dairy and in addition, a large quantity of milk is distributed to other city departments.

In other states some of the almshouses have been made over into boarding homes, where under certain conditions the applicant for admission pays a nominal charge. The very appropriate suggestion has been made that the large, district, state supervised almshouses of the future should have social service departments analogous to those of the state hospitals for the insane. One of the duties of the social worker of such a department would be that of securing histories of all applicants for admission. On the basis of the facts thus available the applicant might be accepted and properly classified, or referred to another institution in case special treatment were needed. Still another function of the social worker might be to assist those aged persons who after a period in the institution might

[7] *Report of the Department of Public Welfare, State of Connecticut,* 1927, p. 128.

be turned over to relatives who had been discovered and had consented to receive them. Or, others might be boarded out when a satisfactory home for them could be found. Either of these plans would articulate nicely with a pension or insurance scheme.

**Admission Policies and Practices.** Very few old people really want to live in institutions, whether public or private, and most of those who finally go to a county farm or old people's home do so only after having shunned it as long as possible. This means that application is usually made by aged persons who turn to the institution as a last resort, or by relatives who want to "get rid of them." Of course, there are some elderly people who have no relatives, others whose kinsmen are really unable to care for them, and still others whose physical or mental condition makes them unfit for life outside an institution. These facts make the problem of admission very different from that in a children's institution.

In most cases applications for admission to a county farm or almshouse are made directly to the county commissioners or supervisors. They, of course, make no real study of the situation, but take action on a "common sense" basis, or, all too often, in accordance with prejudice, "pull," or demands for economy. However, in an increasing number of localities a genuine case study is made by a trained social worker employed by the county or by a cooperating private agency. An effort is made to determine the physical and mental health of the applicant, personal habits, economic status, the ability and willingness of relatives to help, and general relationships to other people. In the light of this information the following questions are answered: Is it wise for this person to live alone? With relatives? In a private boarding home? In an institution? What boarding homes or institutions are available? How can the plan be financed? In this way public institutional care of the aged becomes an integral part of a larger program.

Most of the private homes for old people limit their "inmates" or "residents" to persons of specific religious or fraternal affiliations, to persons who have lived a long time in a particular community, or to members of one sex or of a given racial group. In addition, as noted above, there are usually financial conditions to be met. Frequently a flat payment of several hundred or even several thousand dollars is required, and all property must be turned over to the institution; or certain monthly payments must be guaranteed. But in a growing number of instances arbitrary restrictions have been abandoned and homes for the aged are linked up with case work agencies, which make such studies of applicants as were indicated above.

Because the change from home to institution means inevitably an upsetting of long-established habits, and because a stigma attaches to most institutions, it seems appropriate that the institution should be frankly a place of last resort. (This does not mean, however, that it should be devoid of physical comfort or of kindly personal ministrations.) But there seems little likelihood that old people's homes can be eliminated. There are many elderly persons whose physical or mental condition, whose personal habits or general "cantankerousness" render them unfit for life in any domestic situation which is available. The social work task in these cases is to induce "patients" to accept institutional care and to help them adjust to large-group life. Because the old folks are more often coerced than persuaded, a difficult problem confronts the Home to which they go.

One superintendent of a large county farm met the situation in this fashion. He made it a practice always to meet the bus which brought new "guests" out from the county-seat town. Most of them were old men who needed a shave and a bath; so, after greeting them cordially, the superintendent personally shaved them and supervised their cleaning up, all the time "jollying them along" and telling them some of the things they needed to know in order to be comfortable and happy.

**Old People Who Come to Institutions.** This task of making the old folks comfortable and happy is not always easy; it can be performed successfully only if the staff have some appreciation of their guests' backgrounds and personalities. These naturally vary to an almost infinite degree, but certain characteristics occur with sufficient frequency to deserve special mention.

Probably the majority of old people hate to "let go." Not

only have they formed habits which involve certain activities and relationships, but their sense of usefulness, their pride, and self-respect rest on their occupation and their place in the life of family and community. When to this natural disinclination to "give up" is added the necessity of accepting charity and entering an institution they are likely to become resentful or morose. Even when this hardship does not come to them "they are usually quite set in their ways, decidedly opinionated, free to criticize, jealous of their rights." [8]

Francis Bardwell, who has been for twenty years inspector of almshouses in Massachusetts, has set forth in a discerning way those personal traits which staff members of an institution for the aged should expect to encounter. First of all, old people love little children and the necessary separation from their companionship is likely to be a real hardship. Old folks are usually independent. "To them the younger generation is still a generation of infants; suggestions from it are not solicited and advice is seldom willingly followed." Old people crave attention. "They resent the least slight, strive for selective recognition; want to become known because of some characteristic, or some incident in a past life that sets them apart from others." Naturally these folks are interested in the past. Usually they are devout; they desire peace. Many of them dread mental decadence. "Almost invariably people who attain great age seem reconciled to passing."

Even in a county poorhouse the "inmates" do not come from any single element in the population. Here you will find a former judge alongside a village ne'er-do-well, an unmarried woman whose life has been devoted to the care of her failing parents next door to a wandering prostitute. What they all share is loneliness and poverty. In the private institution poverty is not always present, but there is usually a separation from friends and kinsmen through death or alienation.

**Life in a Home for the Aged.** Daily activities in homes for old folks are apt to be pretty much alike whether the home is public or private. Single rooms enable the resident to main-

[8] Bardwell, Francis, *The Adventure of Old Age,* p. 12, Houghton, Mifflin Co., 1926. The remainder of this section is based largely on Bardwell's discussion.

tain some privacy and to store his few possessions and souvenirs of the past. Where old couples can be kept together their life is far more satisfactory and happy. Since old people are anxious to "keep going," worth-while activities should be provided. Illustrations of occupations provided by various institutions have been given in the cases described in this chapter. The women will naturally assist in the house work. The old men, while incapable of full-time work, should be given interesting, industrial or agricultural employment, which not only increases the revenues of the home but makes for the mental health of the residents. Various types of recreation are possible: radio, occasional entertainments and socials, reading, walking, gardening, conversation with visitors, including members of the families of the old people, attending church, knitting, making baskets, and similar light occupations. In such homes rules and regulations should normally be relaxed and a maximum of individual freedom permitted. Informality and friendliness should characterize the relationships between the staff and the residents and give the institution the atmosphere of a real home.

**Housing and Physical Equipment.** Modern developments here have involved two departures, as already indicated: (1) the cottage system is being substituted for the large single building in many places, and (2) those old people who are more or less normal and active are being housed separately from those who are medical and surgical cases. Special hospital buildings or wings should be provided for the latter.

Housing of the dependent aged, however, is on the whole woefully inadequate, even in the case of private institutions. A recent report of the New York City Welfare Council showed 13,000 aged in 82 homes in the city with a waiting list of 6000. In attempting to meet this situation the New York Association for Improving the Condition of the Poor is planning to spend $67,500 for the care of the aged in their own homes.

In addition the Association has established four interesting institutions for this group. (1) The Crawford Shops provide work for ninety old people who found they could not "keep up" in modern industry. (2) Sunset Lodge is an attractive summer vacation home for the old. (3) Ward Manor is an 800 acre estate which serves as a home for seventy aged workers who have retired. (4) The newest project is an apartment house for decent old people who are still working. It is to be a building of six stories with accommodations for sixty-five, and a roof to be utilized for recreation. Couples as well as individuals will be admitted. The first floor is to have a sitting room, cafeteria, and quarters for the house mother and the nurse. It is not to be considered an "old people's home," but rather the residence of a congenial group who will live their own lives in their own way.

**Alternatives to Institutional Care.** Other methods of relieving the dependent aged include individual saving, outdoor relief, care by relatives, boarding out, and the various forms of pensions and insurance. In addition, reforms in industry, including increase in real wages, prevention of accident, and regularization of employment; public health services, and case work with families and individuals in danger of disorganization, will go far toward prevention. Saving, formerly urged as the most desirable and obvious method of avoiding poverty in old age, seems to be out of the question, at least as far as most industrial workers are concerned. In a study made in 1921 of women shoe workers in Lynn, Massachusetts, it was found that of the 257 who were unmarried or divorced one-half had saved nothing, one-quarter had no more than $500, and of the 15% who had accumulated more than $1,000, only six, obviously exceptional women, had managed to save over $3,000. Almost one-half (44%) had no insurance. The explanation lies primarily in the small earnings received. Of 403 women who reported earnings for the year 1920, 91% earned less than $1000.[9] Other factors were irregularity of employment, dependent relatives, business depression, and labor disputes. Later studies in various states yielded much the same conclusions. In Hamilton, Ohio, for example, it was discovered that only 36.5% of the aged owned homes free of debt. In Cincinnati the percentage was even smaller (23.5). Still more recently an investigation of 13,785 aged persons living in eleven repre-

[9] Channing, Alice, "Savings for Old Age of Women Shoe Workers," *Survey*, 47: 680-682, 1921.

sentative communities in Massachusetts revealed the fact that three in ten had no property at all. On the basis of this and other similar studies Lucile Eaves estimates that only 20 or 25% of the people of the United States have incomes sufficiently large to enable them to save.[10]

In his recent exhaustive work Abraham Epstein compares the annual earnings of a representative group of workers year by year, from 1920 to 1927, with the income necessary to maintain a minimum of health and decency during each of these years. He concludes that "not even during the last few years of unprecedented national prosperity did the wages of the great masses of American workers permit them to live upon the standard generally set by students and government authorities as necessary for a minimum of health and decency." [11] For example, the average earnings of New York State factory employees for 1927 were $1,465. The estimated minimum family budget for that year was $1500, $35 above the average earnings of this class of workers. Commenting on the increase in wages that has taken place during the past ten years, he says: "Despite the actual increase in wages of the past decade, only a negligible number of workers manage to earn a wage commensurate with the American standard of health and decency.[12] It should be pointed out that Epstein bases his conclusions upon the needs of the so-called average family of five, dependent upon the income of one wage-earner. As a matter of fact, according to the census figures for 1920, there were in that year, not 5, but 4.3 persons per family in the United States. Furthermore, in an increasingly large percentage of families the income is supplemented by other members of the family. Despite this criticism his conclusion is substantially valid. Even if the average family were able to come up to the minimum decency standard, saving for old age would still be impossible or undesirable. For as he says: "It may be infinitely more economic to buy high-grade milk for the babies, warmer and better clothes, give a better education to the children, or send the family to a good physician than to put the

[10] Eaves, Lucile, "Pensions or Poorhouses?" *Survey*, 59: 613-15, 1928.
[11] Epstein, A., *The Challenge of the Aged*, p. 108. Vanguard Press, 1928.
[12] *Idem*, p. 111.

money in the savings bank." [13] We are, therefore, forced to conclude that the old cannot depend upon their savings for support.

A considerable number of old people are assisted in their own homes by private organizations or public officials. Such outdoor relief may provide for those who have some sort of a home until they come to demand personal care. Support by relatives is the oldest solution, but with the decreasing solidarity of the family, the rising standard of living, and greater mobility, fewer and fewer among the lower economic classes can be looked after in this way. Theoretically it is, of course, a highly desirable solution of the problem. Boarding out as a solution has the advantage over outdoor relief that in carefully selected homes the aged person who cannot look after himself could be cared for in a far more pleasant way than in the almshouse. It has not been tried to any great extent in the United States. Combined with a state pension system it might be a very satisfactory plan in many cases.

Private insurance in the shape of endowment or annuity policies, while an excellent method of providing for the necessities of the old, is possible for only a small percentage of the population. To attempt to carry such insurance frequently means depriving one's family of the necessities of life. Hence this plan cannot be considered as a universal solution. Industrial pensions, i.e. an allowance for life given in consideration for past services, meet the need of a few. In 1928 approximately 400 firms, employing 4,000,000 workers, had adopted some pension scheme, providing for the retirement of those employees who at sixty or sixty-five had been with the company for twenty or thirty years. Most of the pension plans have been put into operation since 1910, and the total number now receiving payments would not exceed 90,000, or only from 5 to 6% of all the dependent aged in the country. In addition to this fact, so many other objections are pointed out by Epstein on the basis of his exhaustive study of the plans of 370 establishments that this method cannot be considered a satisfactory solution of the problem of old age dependency in general.[14] Public service

[13] *Idem*, p. 109.
[14] *Idem.*, pp. 161-166.

pensions, such as those for military or naval service, help the situation, but are of course limited to certain classes of the aged.

**State Pensions and Old Age Insurance.** About 1923 a new era in the history of the care of the dependent aged began. A number of pension laws were enacted and several commissions were created to study the problem. In 1927 the American Association for Old Age Security was organized. According to Abraham Epstein, the executive secretary, "The sole and specific purpose of this Association is to promote adequate protection for the dependent aged through either state old age pensions or contributory government insurance plans." [15] The following year the first national conference of the Association was held in New York. Despite these important advances the United States remains in the class with China and India, among the populous countries, in failing to provide constructive care for the aged, according to the recent report of the Pennsylvania Old Age Commission. This Commission concluded (1) that the present system of poor relief and almshouse care is antiquated and costly; (2) that insurance and pension plans of private employers cover only a very small percentage of workers; (3) that public opinion in Pennsylvania indicated that state action was necessary; (4) that some plan of contributory pensions should be introduced. Other commissions have reached similar conclusions.

State insurance and pensions are of three general kinds: (1) voluntary and subsidized old age insurance, (2) compulsory, contributory old age insurance, and (3) straight, or non-contributory old age pensions. The 1925-1927 Pennsylvania Commission on Old Age Pensions, created by the State Legislature to report on the "advisability and practicability of a contributory system as against the straight pension idea," presented a plan involving payments by the worker, the industry and the state. Under this scheme all persons thirty-two years of age at the time the plan was put into operation would accumulate, through their contributions and those of their employers, sufficient capital for an annuity at the age of sixty-

[15] Epstein, A., *The Challenge of the Aged,* p. 29. The Vanguard Press, 1928.

five without any outside assistance. A pension of $365 a year in the case of a male worker commencing payments at thirty-two would cost him and his employer thirty-five cents a week. In the case of persons above thirty-two the state would make a contribution sufficient to keep the individual premiums the same whatever the age.[16]

In California the State Department of Public Welfare recently recommended a bill to provide for the aged based on the contributory insurance principle. In accordance with this plan the administration of the scheme will be in the hands of the counties and cities which adopt it. The amount of aid is determined by the needs of the individual applicant, but should not bring his total to more than $1 per day. An interesting feature of this plan is its provision for supervision by experienced social workers. Advice on health, housing and other matters would be given the individual, who would be able to remain in his own home if capable of taking care of himself.[17]

The criticism of such volunteer contributory plans, as found in actual operation, is that relatively few workers take advantage of them. This fact has led to the suggestion of compulsory insurance which, however, is open to a great many objections. In the United States straight old age pensions are the preferred plan. Epstein, for example, presents eight arguments in its favor.[18] (1) It is simple to administer. (2) It is just, because it is the duty of the state to take care of its aged poor. (3) Although nominally non-contributory, such pensions are in reality paid by everyone in the shape of taxes. (4) They would stimulate loyalty, hope, ambition and independence. (5) They would encourage thrift and saving. (6) The cost has not in the United States or abroad proved burdensome. (7) They would help to keep families intact. And (8), such a plan by providing security for old age would prolong life. If such scheme were made universal, that is, applied to all or practically all above a certain age, not merely to the destitute,

[16] *Idem.*, 245-56.

[17] This law passed in 1929 but in a form that makes it simply modified poor relief. Its chief advantage over previous legislation in California is that it provides state subsidy and state supervision of local relief.

[18] *Op. cit.*, 217-221.

it would have the further advantage of escaping the stigma which attaches to "poor relief."

**Conclusion.** Non-contributory state old age pensions, although perhaps theoretically the best single way of providing against old age dependency, will not solve the entire problem or meet the needs of all the aged poor, as has already been pointed out. We shall probably always need institutions of some sort, which when articulated with a pension or insurance plan will come nearer than anything else in the past to solving this problem adequately.

In its development, institutional work with the aged has lagged behind other branches of social work. There is no reason, however, why it should not reach the same degree of development that has been attained by children's institutions and hospitals for the care of the mentally ill. The following chapter will deal with another type of institutional work that has also been slow to develop, that in correctional schools.

# CHAPTER XXVII

## SOCIAL WORK IN PRISONS AND REFORMATORIES

The attention of the entire country was riveted upon the situation in our prisons as a result of four outbreaks that occurred in the months of July and August, 1929. Two of these, those at Leavenworth and Lansing, Kansas, were of minor significance, being a mere "blowing off of steam" in the first case, and a desperate dash for liberty on the part of a group of six prisoners in the second. The disturbance at Dannemora, New York, on July 22, and the riot at Auburn, on the 28th, however, were indicative of deep-seated dissatisfaction and despair, due partly to crowded and disgraceful living conditions, but primarily, as Winthrop D. Lane pointed out in a recent number of the *Survey*,[1] to a tightening of parole and the passage of such bills as the Baumes law and the "fourth offense" statutes, increasing sentences and decreasing hope. But this would seem to have been only the releasing or exciting cause of the outbreaks. In a deeper sense they might be ascribed to a growing feeling of hopelessness engendered by the realization on the part of the convicts that nothing was to be gained by continuing to submit to a prison regime that was not only almost unbearable, but which accomplished little or nothing in the way of constructive preparation for rehabilitation. In short, these disturbances in the New York institutions, at least, suggest the need for a prison administration that conforms with the principles of social work.

The administration of prisons and reformatories is a form of institutional social work more or less analogous to that of children's institutions and homes for the aged, described in the two preceding chapters. Since the purpose of correctional institutions is social re-education and the eventual reconstruction of social attitudes and relationships, their administration to this

[1] "Prisons at the Breaking Point," *Survey*, 62: 557-8; 849, 1929.

end is essentially a form of social work, although physical, psychiatric, educational, and vocational techniques, as well as case and group work, are also employed and are of great importance. The treatment of delinquents takes into account individual differences, recognizing the social nature and needs of the person, and utilizing the factors of active choice and group participation.[2] In this chapter, therefore, the different procedures involved in the administration of institutions for criminals and delinquents will be discussed as a branch of institutional social work. In order to indicate the nature of the problems involved in various types of institutions a number of short descriptions, mainly of institutions of the better type, are given below.

## CONNECTICUT STATE PRISON

The Connecticut State Prison is located at Wethersfield. The property consists of about fifty acres of land and a group of structures, of which the original part was erected in 1827 and to which extensive additions and alterations have since been made from time to time.

The main group of buildings contains two large cell blocks, congregate dining room for male prisoners, kitchen, chapel and library, and the offices, guard-rooms and officers' quarters. At the east end of the group is the women's department, with a block of twenty cells and a large, well-lighted laundry, in which female prisoners are employed, while at the west end are the hospital and a special ward for insane male prisoners. In the yard is situated a large three-storied building which contains six work shops, where the principal industry of the prison, shirt making, is carried on under contract with an outside concern.

Not including the hospital and the insane ward, the prison contains a total of six hundred and forty-eight cells. The buildings are heated by steam, are well lighted and ventilated and are kept scrupulously clean. The food supplied to the prisoners is plain but wholesome, and a different bill of fare is provided each week.

Three classes are recognized in the system of grading prisoners at Wethersfield, all newcomers being enrolled upon arrival in the first grade. Promotion and reduction are determined by a system of marks, which are given on conduct, work and mental advancement. All convicts upon entering the prison receive a thorough physical and mental examination. Prisoners who are

[2] Queen, Stuart A., "Social Work in Prisons and Reformatories," Boston: Wright and Potter, 1922.

reported for petty violations of rules are warned in the first instance, but on successive repetitions are, according to circumstances, placed in solitary confinement, or are docked a portion of their time allowance for good behavior, or are reduced from a higher to a lower grade. No officer is allowed to strike a prisoner except in self-defense.

With the exception of the sick prisoners, all of the inmates are engaged in some form of work, while a few trusty men are engaged in raising farm produce on a part of the land outside the walls. Religious services, both Protestant and Roman Catholic, are held in the chapel every Sunday morning. In the school room on Monday, Tuesday and Wednesday evenings during the winter instruction is given under the direction of the chaplain, assisted by two civilian and several inmate teachers, to a number of classes, including about one hundred and fifty men, in elementary subjects, such as reading, writing and arithmetic. Attendance is obligatory for all illiterate prisoners. The library contains about five thousand volumes, and twice a week the men are allowed to select books from it. A small printing office is conducted, also, where, under the direction of the chaplain a monthly paper is published, to which the prisoners contribute a considerable portion of the contents. On Saturday afternoons general recreation in the prison yard is permitted for all members of the first and second grades, a series of inter-team ball games being the chief form of exercise. There are also contests with teams from outside the prison. Members of the first and second grades have the privilege of quiet recreation in the yard on Sunday afternoons. During the winter a number of entertainments, consisting of musicals, readings, lectures, stereopticon exhibitions, etc., are given voluntarily by clubs, societies and individuals for the improvement and amusement of the prisoners. Radio concerts in the chapel and cell blocks are provided by the prison management.[3]

Here we have a description of an old line prison of a somewhat better type. Cell blocks are in use, but are kept clean and well heated, and the food is apparently satisfactory. Employment is provided, but on the undesirable contract plan, and with no mention of remuneration. Physical and mental examinations are given new admissions and the medical care of the convicts on the whole seems to be adequate. Discipline, however, is of the repressive type, formal education of the most rudimentary kind, and recreation limited and practically unplanned and unsupervised. Except for the radio concerts,

[3] Adapted from the Report of the Department of Public Welfare of the State of Connecticut, 1927 and 1928, pp. 37-40.

entertainments are furnished by benevolently inclined outsiders. The prison paper and the athletic teams seem to be the only evidences of spontaneous group activities. Finally, the chaplain is the official "welfare" worker. In contrast, the prison at Wilmington, Delaware, attempts the social reconstruction of the individual by means of well developed group life and a system of "self-government." "Here . . . the organization of the prison as a community based upon a system of inmate cooperation has been realized to a greater extent than anywhere else in the United States." [4] This institution is inappropriately termed a "workhouse."

## NEW CASTLE COUNTY WORKHOUSE

The warden of this Delaware prison, M. S. Plummer, startled the board in 1920 by his request to try an experiment. Instead of the twenty-seven guards then employed for the 400 prisoners, he proposed to have only three. Under the present system the prisoners themselves are responsible for discipline. Liepmann at the time of his visit found an excellent spirit of activity and orderliness in the workshop which was supervised by nine elected inmate guards. In the farm barracks the men are entirely free from official control, and some are even employed on farms in the neighborhood. The demand for such laborers increases from year to year. A special "honor court" which deals with problems of disorder and violations of discipline, is elected by the inmates. One of the functions of this court is the making of rules for the conduct of the prisoners. The directors of the institution report that 90% of the men behave themselves. There has been but one escape during a number of years, and the inmates themselves raised several hundred dollars to apprehend the traitor to their system! The convicts are paid for their work, receiving about 20% of the profits from the workshops. An excellent spirit of cooperation and mutual respect exists between the prisoners and the officials, and the "graduates" are proud of the institution.

The best institutions from the social work standpoint are the training schools for juveniles. Descriptions of two of these will convey some notion of their work.

[4] Liepmann, M., "American Prisons and Reformatory Institutions; A Report," *Mental Hygiene,* 12:225-315, 1928. The two descriptions here given are based upon this report.

## THE WHITTIER STATE SCHOOL

This school is located near Los Angeles, California, and is maintained for neglected or delinquent children. Follow-up studies show that 75% of those discharged do well for several years at least after leaving. Upon admission a careful study, both physical and psychological, is made of the child, and his social history is secured. Newcomers are admitted to the hospital first and it is here that the mental tests are given. They then pass to a receiving cottage where they remain for from six weeks to three months. During this time a detailed plan is made for each individual, including physical, educational, vocational and social régimes. The California Bureau of Juvenile Research cooperates with the institution in this study of individual cases, and its Journal of Delinquency is printed at the School. After the probationary and investigation period the boy is assigned to a selected group in one of the cottages which is equipped with playgrounds and under the direction of a house supervisor. Not more than thirty boys are assigned to a single house. The daily schedule includes four hours of formal education in the morning, followed by an equal period of vocational training in the afternoon. Nine teachers, mainly women, are employed, and work through the senior high school grade is given. Two hours a day are given to recreation, the School being provided with a swimming pool, athletic grounds, theater and other necessary equipment. Competitive games are held with neighboring schools. Within the institution a natural and friendly relationship prevails between the inmates and the officials and no corporal punishment is used. In each cottage there is a common dormitory for all newcomers and others who need supervision. The advanced boys are given single bedrooms and permitted the greatest freedom. The highest grade students are eligible for the Boy Scouts who have a cottage of their own, wear their uniforms and insignia, and enjoy many privileges. There are no physical walls around the school but a strong esprit de corps effectually prevents escapes. [Success is facilitated by a separate institution for older boys.]

The Whittier State School is in the class with the Children's Village, at Dobbs Ferry, New York, and a few other equally excellent institutions. These training schools are characterized by careful individual study, a homelike and friendly atmosphere, organized recreation, responsible group life and excellent formal and vocational education. Many of these schools are run on military lines, as in the case of the Boys' Vocational School at Lansing, Michigan.

## THE BOYS' VOCATIONAL SCHOOL, LANSING, MICHIGAN

When the boys are received at this institution, we endeavor to make them feel from the first that we are interested in them and want to help them rather than to "reform" them. For the most part, they seem willing to tell us all about their past and their home life.

Upon the boy's arrival he is placed in the Reception Cottage for at least twenty-one days. During this time he is given a mental examination and a complete history of his case is taken by the School Psychologist. This information gives us an opportunity to place the boy intelligently in both his school and his industrial work. It is our problem to give him a new point of view and to supplant wrong ideals with right ones.

Another important feature of our work with a boy when he is still in the Reception Cottage is to give a thorough physical examination to determine whether or not his delinquency has been due to any physical defect. After a boy remains in the Reception Cottage until all danger of contagion is past he is regularly assigned to a cottage and becomes in fact a member in full standing. At six o'clock in the morning he will awake at the sound of a bell, will arise, find himself only one of about thirty other boys similarly disturbed, don his clothing and march down to the basement where his toilet is made. Military drill and calisthenics are given for twenty or thirty minutes and at seven o'clock he is ready for breakfast. The boys eat in their cottages, which makes it much more homelike than the old method of a central dining room. After breakfast the work around the cottage, cleaning, dusting, etc., is taken care of and at 8:30 the bell sounds again for "detail," where the various squads are formed for school and work, and marched away to the activities of the day. "Recall" sounds at 11:30 and all are again marching away to detail hall, companies are formed and, upon arrival at their cottages, toilet is completed, and mess is sounded at 12:00. The dinner over, some necessary work is done in washing dishes and cleaning up around the cottage and at 1:30 all are assembled at detail for the afternoon's work. "Recall" again at 4:30 and supper at 5:00. After supper the boys read, play games and spend their time in various ways. Games of various sorts have been provided for each cottage to help pass the long winter evenings, and also a phonograph and a radio, made by the boys in our own radio department. At 8:30 taps sounded completes the daily routine of life at the Boys' Vocational School.

The Cottage system consists of a cottage manager and his wife who have about thirty or more boys under their care. The cottage manager is head of the family, the one held responsible for the good conduct, safety and health of the boys under him, and the proper care of property in his immediate charge. He must be a man of intelligence and good character and of a disposition adapted to the direction of a lively set of boys.

The Matron of the cottage is in fact the housekeeper. The best matron comes near supplying the place of a mother in looking after and sympathizing with the boys in their troubles and helping them over a period of homesickness.

Various occupations are taught the boys who come to us, including printing, baking, smithing, green house work, machine shop, radio, band and orchestra training. Our school system we feel is doing efficient work. We are organized under the supervision of the State Department of Public Instruction. Our work is carried on much as it is in the public schools, with a principal in charge of a corps of twelve trained teachers. Two ungraded rooms have been established to handle the very backward boys.

During the summer, the boys have all kinds of outdoor sports. In the winter, the gymnasium is constantly in use, under the supervision of an athletic director. High class motion pictures also furnish a great deal of amusement. The religious life of the boys is not neglected.

When a boy leaves the institution, on parole, a card giving his name and address is sent to the Scout Executive in his district. Boys who have continually failed are now making good because upon their return home they were immediately invited by the Scout Executive to join with them, instead of being neglected and allowed to renew their old associations.[5]

**Historical Background.** The traditional method of handling the offender was the infliction of punishment, which varied with the enormity of the crime. Punishment satisfies the attitude of hostility against the malefactor, but fails to reform him or deter others. The modern method aims at the protection of society by the attempt to reconstruct the attitudes of the criminal in accordance with a plan based upon detailed, individual study. It substitutes "treatment," especially in a social sense, for punishment and revenge. It is scientific in contrast with previous sentimental theories of reform, and utilizes all available techniques to effect the social rehabilitation of the offender.

The first state prison in this country was established in Connecticut in 1773. The early prisons existed merely as insti-

[5] Adapted from Bulletin of the Boys' Vocational School, Lansing, Michigan, 1929.

tutions for custody and segregation. A second stage is represented by the development of the penitentiary and the growth of the "reform" idea. At the end of the eighteenth and the beginning of the nineteenth centuries a wave of humanitarianism radically affected prison administration in this country. The so-called Pennsylvania System was introduced in that state as an attempt at reform based upon solitary confinement in place of the old custom of promiscuous association between all kinds of prisoners. It was hoped that this plan would prevent the contamination of young delinquents. But the system failed for obvious reasons, and in 1824 New York state introduced the "Auburn System," which involved industrial work on the part of the prisoners, carried on, however, under the "rule of silence." The first reformatory in the United States was established at Elmira in 1869. A deliberate attempt was made to change the personality of the prisoner by educational, vocational and physical training, and the establishment of the grading or merit system through which the convict progressed to final parole. The Elmira institution has since lost its distinctive character, but the reform idea has been adopted to a greater or less degree by the majority of prisons so that the term possesses little significance today.

The third stage in the history of prison administration may be considered as commencing with the founding of the George Junior Republic, in 1895. Various degrees of inmate self-government and community organization within the prison had been tried long before that date, but since most of the recent experiments have followed this model it may be looked upon as initiating a new period. The honor, or "trusty" system, "self-government," and the "mutual welfare league" are all forms of group participation and democracy in the prison. Thomas Mott Osborne, who for fifteen years was a member of the board of trustees of the George Junior Republic, introduced the Mutual Welfare League at Auburn and Sing Sing, in 1914, and at the Naval Prison at Portsmouth, in 1917. Under this system the inmates of the prison elected representatives to various committees, such as those on athletics, organization, entertainment, education, employment, and the like, which cooperated with the administration and looked after the interests of the inmates. The values of such participation in the government of the institution in terms of training for later responsible social life are obvious. Self-government systems on the whole, however, have not been successful, due largely to their indiscriminate introduction into institutions under conditions which made success almost impossible. There is nothing inherently fallacious about the plan as such.

Prisons for adults are condemned by the best criminological thought of the present time. They fail to deter or reform in any effective way and, according to Sutherland [7] among others, should eventually be abolished—except for those cases judged to be "hopeless"—in favor of the more effective and scientific non-institutional methods that are gradually developing. In the meanwhile, however, attempts to improve the reformative procedures carried on in the prison should be continued. The remainder of this chapter is devoted to a description of these procedures, especially as they have developed in institutions for juveniles. Before taking up the problems of administration and discussing the various activities in the modern correctional institution let us note briefly the various types of prisons and the number of their inmates.

**The Number of Prisoners in Various State Institutions.** State institutions for criminals and delinquents are of three main types. (1) Prisons or penitentiaries are intended for adult offenders and are sometimes graded for different types of lawbreakers. In 1926 there were 65 state prisons in the United States. (2) State Reformatories, of which there were 27 in the same year, are institutions for first offenders usually, or for juveniles for whom a more repressive regime than that afforded by the third class is deemed advisable. The inmates of reformatories range in age from about sixteen to about thirty. (3) Vocational, industrial or training schools for juvenile delinquents constitute the third type of state institution. As a rule they are the most scientifically administered of the three types. According to the Census report,[8] on January 1, 1923, there were 81,080 adult convicts in the state and federal prisons,

[7] Sutherland, E. H., *Criminology,* pp. 442-4. Philadelphia: Lippincott Company, 1924.

[8] "Prisoners—1923," and "Children Under Institutional Care—1923," U. S. Bureau of the Census, 1926 and 1927.

chain gangs, reformatories, state farms and houses of correction, not including those in the military and naval prisons, the insane and mentally defective, nor the 1,650 juveniles in these adult institutions on that date. On the same day there were in state institutions for juvenile delinquents 23,003 individuals. If we add to this number the 1,650 in institutions primarily for adults, we get a total of 24,653 children between 10 and 17 confined in correctional institutions in that year. These statistics are based upon returns from approximately 100 state schools, and it is in these almost entirely that modern scientific institutional social work with delinquents is done.

**The Administration of Correctional Institutions: Physical Equipment.** The administration of a prison, reformatory or training school is itself a social work job, but its discussion is beyond the scope of this chapter. The discussion will be limited very largely to the case and group work aspects, with brief reference to other questions of interest to the institutional administrator. We may begin with a brief consideration of housing and physical equipment in general.

In harmony with their dominant purpose of securing the persons of the inmates, prisons of the traditional type have been monumental structures of steel and concrete. One of the newest and most perfect examples of this type is the prison being constructed by the state of Illinois near Joliet, which consists of multiple tiers of cell blocks in circular buildings. A guard in the center tower is supposed to be able to see into every cell, and thus maintain constant surveillance of every prisoner. As the purpose of the penitentiary has come to be conceived as educational and therapeutic the style of architecture has begun to change. Such modifications are absolutely necessary to secure privacy, segregation by classes, and other arrangements essential to the work of a modern warden. The tendency is toward buildings of a more temporary nature. Kirchwey, for example, has suggested that no permanent building be built, but that instead the prisoners be housed in barracks on farm and industrial colonies. The District of Columbia prison, at Lorton, Virginia, consists of unbarred cottages with provision for the confinement of a small percentage of the men of a desperate character in barred cells. The new Federal institution for women at Alderson, West Virginia, is built in the Colonial style with fifteen cottages, a receiving building, workshops and hospital.

In the juvenile institutions the cottage system is rapidly becoming general. The Pennsylvania Training School, near Morganza, consists of ten unusually pleasant cottages situated on a plot of seven hundred acres and surrounded by gardens. Each cottage houses not more than thirty children. In the Children's Village, at Dobbs Ferry, New York, the cottages are organized on a self-governing basis. An intermediate stage is found in such reformatories as that at Ionia, Michigan, where the inmates are housed in large halls, or "dormitories," off the main building. Each dormitory contains forty or fifty men and boys. The cottage system seems to be the best form of architecture so far devised for correctional institutions and lends itself readily to individual and social treatment and the development of community and group consciousness.

**Reception and Admission Procedure.** Another essential element in the modern scientific and professional administration of correctional institutions is the provision for individual study and case work, beginning with the admission of the prisoner. The present day use of psychiatric and psychological methods developed out of the work of the prison physician and the giving of physical examinations. In 1916 Warden Osborne established a clinic at Sing Sing for the purpose of eliminating those defectives among the inmates that would hamper the successful working of the Mutual Welfare League. Dr. Bernard Glueck became the director of this work, which in 1926 had developed into a "reception and classification clinic" with a budget of $40,000 for a psychiatric staff and equipment. In accordance with the New York plan all convicted persons should pass through the observation prison, where they would be carefully examined, physically and psychologically, and a study made of their educational and vocational possibilities. Normal prisoners would then be sent to one of the two industrial prisons, or, if suited for agriculture, to the farm institution. There will be, if the plan finally goes into effect, a separate hospital-prison for the criminal insane and another for the mentally defective. All sentences would be indefinite, depending upon the progress toward reconstruction made by the individual.

The use of psychiatrists and psychologists in correctional institutions seems to be increasing at a satisfactory rate to judge from a report of a recent study.[9] In this survey replies were received from 259 institutions. Of these, 35.9% employed psychiatrists on full or part time, and 32.8% had psychologists. Fifty per cent of the institutions favored this practice, which was less frequent in the South and far West than in the North and East. Reformatories used such service more than other types of institutions. Juvenile institutions had fewer psychiatrists but ranked next to the top in the use of psychologists. All the army disciplinary barracks had full time psychiatrists.

Admission and examination procedure in the juvenile institutions involves the following stages. (1) Quarantine in the reception building or hospital. During this period the newcomer is given physical, psychiatric and psychological examinations. (2) Classification is then made on the basis of the results of the tests. The kind of group in which the individual would be best located is determined and he is assigned to a cottage. (3) A plan involving educational, vocational, social, and physical training is made for each individual. Of course, few institutions have such a complete program, but the following cases show that much is actually being done. At the Sleighton Farm school for girls in Pennsylvania, for example, the new girl is first admitted to the receiving cottage, and remains there for three months. During this period physical and mental examinations are carried on, and the girl is given work on the farm or in the school. This term of three months is considered a probationary period, and after its conclusion a conference of the staff is held in which her "case" is studied from every angle and it is decided to which of the honor system cottages she is to be sent.

At the Children's Village, Dobbs Ferry, New York, there is a "classification committee" consisting of the psychologist, the physician, the head of the school, the director of the welfare

[9] Overholser, Winfred, "Psychiatric Service in Penal and Reformatory Institutions and Criminal Courts in the United States," *Mental Hygiene*, 12: 801-838, 1928.

department, and a representative of the social workers, which makes a detailed study of each new admission and plans the treatment. The California Bureau of Juvenile Research co-operates with the staff of the Whittier School in making physical and psychological examinations of boys committed to that institution. The newcomer is admitted first to the hospital where the tests are given. He then goes to the receiving cottage where he remains for from six weeks to three months while a plan for his training is made.

Not only should an individual study of the newcomer to a correctional institution be made at the time of admission but a process of continuous case study and case work should be carried on. This is actually done in some of the better institutions. At Dobbs Ferry, for instance, the "Classification Committee" meets weekly and periodically plans treatment for each student inmate for several weeks ahead. In this regime of individual treatment mental hygiene should play an important part. Considerable research has been done utilizing the psychological and psychiatric data secured by surveys in institutions for delinquents, and as a result scientific programs for guiding the mental and emotional life of the inmates of prisons and reformatories are being constructed. In the chapter on Mental Hygiene some of these questions were discussed, and the danger of assuming mental and emotional abnormality as causes of crime should now be pointed out. We have no adequate surveys of the psychiatric condition of the general population against which to check the rather high incidence of more or less abnormal conditions among the inmates of correctional institutions, hence we cannot yet conclude that such abnormality is in itself a cause of delinquency.

**Discipline.** On account of the supposed desperate character of prisoners discipline in penitentiaries has customarily been very severe. Arbitrary, cruel, unjust, and repressive measures have been employed in the past and are still to be found in many prisons. Discipline must, of course, be maintained in such institutions but it should be just, deliberate, based on fact, individualized and socially sanctioned in order to be effective and constructive. Complete self-government is probably impossible and undesirable, considering the prison population, but some measure of inmate participation and cooperation is essential. Such modified self-government appears to work satisfactorily in many institutions. The Children's Village at Dobbs Ferry and the Pennsylvania girls' institution of Sleighton Farm both have a scheme of self-government in the cottages. At the latter school the members of the cottage elect a "council," which has charge of order and discipline at meals, at work and at recreation. There is also a disciplinary court in each house. Liepmann, who visited this institution, describes a session of this court which he attended: [10]

The chairman of the court quietly formulated the accusation. Then the "sinner" was asked what she had to say in her own defense; as it happened, no defendant on this particular occasion denied the accusation. The defendant was then sent out and the court deliberated on what was to be done, carrying on the discussion with great seriousness, with the obvious desire not to be too harsh; the various possibilities were debated frankly and quietly. The teacher of the cottage . . . as well as the woman disciplinary officer (of the whole institution) helped occasionally with suggestions and advice, without, however, voting officially. There was no suggestion of "play" about it all; the whole procedure struck one with its earnestness, composure, and just weighing of facts.

**Activities.** Activity, the keynote of modern correctional institutions, was first introduced by William Penn, in 1615. Today the whole regime is one of varied activities, and on such a program depends the hope of regeneration. Miriam Van Waters says that this program should be built around the playground, the gymnasium, the swimming pool, the dining room, the sleeping porch, work, and education.[11] The aim is, of course, personality adjustment. Education, formal and informal, is the immediate aim of the training school. According to Stutsman,[12] there are five lines of reformatory training: (1) physical education, (2) intellectual education, (3) disciplinary training, (4) vocational education, and (5) religious training. As a mat-

[10] Liepmann, M., "American Prisons and Reformatories; A Report." Reprint, National Com. for Men. Hyg., 1928, p. 59. From *Mental Hygiene,* 12: 225-315, 1928.

[11] *Youth in Conflict,* Chap. IX, Republic Pub. Co., 1925.

[12] Stutsman, Jesse O., *Curing the Criminal,* Chap. IX. Macmillan Co., 1926.

ter of fact, practically the entire reformatory program may be included under the term "education." In the formal sense education in the prison originated with the attempt of the Quakers in the United States to teach the inmates to read in order that they might study the Bible and be reformed thereby. The first organized educational work was started at the New York House of Refuge, and shortly afterwards, in 1826, classes were organized at Auburn. In 1918 a survey of state prisons showed that 20% of them had no school work of any kind. The typical prison today offers about two and one-half hours of education per day, in the evenings, for three days a week and seven months a year. More work of course is given in the reformatories and training schools. As Sutherland [13] points out, prison education in the broad sense is essentially a problem of socialization. The aim is to transfer allegiance to the general social group and its values. Prisoners therefore must be put in contact with social ideals. A real conversion is required which is produced by (1) immersion in descriptions of social values, (2) building up new habits, attitudes and social interests, and sublimating the wishes. Hence not only the formal schooling given in classes and through correspondence courses, but the vocational training, use of the library, entertainments, military training and experience in self-government are all contributory to this end.

In a prison described by Joseph Frederick in a recent number of the *Survey*,[14] the formal education offered the inmates consisted only of elementary work. The classes were supervised by a teacher from one of the city schools, and met for one hour, three times a week. Only about 8% of the prison population attended the school. Those who wished more advanced work were able to get it through the extension department of the state university. Some 400 correspondence courses were offered, and students were enrolled by a representative of the university once a month. At the time the article was written 86 men were enrolled. English, mathematics, mechanics, and engineering were the subjects most frequently elected. Each convict paid a fee for the privilege of taking a course. Rebecca

[13] Sutherland, E. H., *Criminology*, Chap. XX. J. B. Lippincott Co., 1924.
[14] "Education in Prison," *Survey*, 57: 490-92, 1927.

Porter, in another *Survey* article,[15] says the convicts in the San Quentin prison take the courses offered by the University of California for the following reasons: to become writers, on account of general interest, for their vocational value, and to master language. Courses given by inmates are not usually successful, she adds, since the men have little respect for such teachers and they fail to give any contact with the outside world. Courses in fiction writing possess mental hygiene value as they offer a channel for the release of repressions.

The better training schools emphasize both general and vocational education. At the Whittier State School, which has already been described, the program calls for four hours of formal schooling in the forenoon, and four hours of vocational education in the afternoon. A definite attempt is made in a number of institutions to build up the educational program for each student on the basis of individual, mental and vocational testing. Miss Van Waters summarizes the values of correctional education under the following six heads.[16] (1) Health and physical well being. (2) Emotional readjustment. (3) "The restoration of confidence and the respect of the individual for his own personality. This is best accomplished by the discovery of tasks within the strength and capacity of the young person, tasks, the performance of which win merited approval from the group." (4) Loyalty, developed by "means of participation in the actual conduct of affairs within the student-group." (5) "New outlets . . . formed for the creative energy of youth." (6) The restoration of the social status of the individual. "He must be absorbed into the community, which in its turn must be educated to recognition that the young person has been returned to full citizenship in our common humanity."

Work activities in prison or reform school should be constructive, interesting, and instructive. It is generally conceded that they ought also, in prisons for adults, at least, be remunerative. Furthermore, the selection of work should be based upon a vocational study of the individual, both of his abilities and of his probable future needs and activities. Thus the pris-

[15] Porter, Rebecca N., "The World of Forgotten Men," *Survey,* 61: 738-740; 752, 754-75, 1929.

[16] *Youth in Conflict,* pp. 221-22. New Republic Pub. Co., 1925.

ons may eventually become industrial and agricultural re-training centers, and the training schools really vocational institutions fitting the boy or girl for a self-supporting and productive life in the larger community on "the outside." Both boys and girls are sent to the Pennsylvania Training School, and a varied program of vocational activities combines productive work with training. The girls do all kinds of housework and in addition are given instruction in domestic science. The boys engage in fifteen different lines of work, and the actual work is accompanied by technical and theoretical instruction. The various occupations include baking, blacksmithing, bricklaying, carpentry, cooking, dairy farming, engineering, music, painting, paperhanging, plastering, printing, shoemaking, tailoring, and agriculture. All the work connected with the institution is done by the boys. The shops are clean and provided with modern equipment. Inmates particularly excel in agricultural and garden work and have taken many medals and ribbons in farm products contests.

Certain phases of group and community life within the institution have been discussed under the head of self-government. Other opportunities for social experience are found in the athletic activities, in connection with the school band, and on teams of various kinds. Such regulated group participation is absolutely essential for the development of self-control and the attitudes required for effective and satisfactory community life in the larger society to which the individual will one day be returned. The utilization of the small amount of leisure permitted is perhaps chiefly valuable for these social by-products. Music and drama are also important from the mental hygiene point of view. At the National Conference of Social Work in 1922, Atkinson pointed out how the change in the theory of delinquency has made recreation in the correctional institutions possible.[17] There is also the need for promoting the physical development of the inmates. Today the athletic program in a large training school rivals that of a college or university. Atkinson suggests three reasons why recreation is now accepted as a legitimate phase of the life of correctional institu-

[17] Atkinson, R. K., "Recreational Activities in Institutions," *Nat. Conf. Soc. Work,* 160-163, 1922.

tions. (1) Health. The prison pallor has disappeared as a result of the athletic programs, and mental health is also improved for the same reason. (2) Training. Education in the proper use of leisure time is a valuable addition to the equipment of the "graduate" of the reform school. (3) Discipline and social adjustment. This is accomplished through team play, and recreational units offer one of the best opportunities for the introduction of some form of self-government or honor system.

Recreational programs were included in the descriptions of the various institutions with which the chapter began, but the place of music in the recreation of the boys of the Pennsylvania Training School deserves special mention. This institution, where the military system is in vogue, has an excellent cadet band, which gives concerts in the neighborhood. The boys also provide music for church services and at games, and valuable training as well as recreation is thus secured. A number of "graduates" have secured good positions in orchestras after leaving the school. Some theatrical and operetta work is also done. Occasionally, too, a concert is given outside the institution: one at the Capitol Theater, in Washington, Pennsylvania, was attended by an enthusiastic audience of 1700 people.

The religious life of the inmate should not be neglected. If properly guided it may be a powerful force in his reconstruction. Finally, the informal, personal contacts with the staff and officials of the institution are an important factor both in discipline and in the creation of desirable social attitudes. The cottage system with its resident house "mothers" and "fathers" offers an effective and natural way of providing such contact.

**Preparation for Discharge.** The whole program of the correctional institution is directed toward the moment when the inmate is to be returned to the community. Having been carefully studied and properly classified at the beginning of his term, he should progress through the different "grades" or "classes," each higher grade more nearly approximating conditions in the outside world, until in the judgment of the staff he is ready for the experiment of normal community life. His rehabilitation is greatly facilitated if the institution employs a parole officer who makes an investigation of the inmate's home and neighborhood before he is returned to them, and assists him in his attempt at readjustment. At the Pennsylvania Training School near Morganza, the work of the parole officer begins as soon as possible after the admission of the boy or girl.

> The child's home has to be investigated, and if it proves to be unsuitable, a "good home" must be found through the parole bureau. The average age on discharge . . . is sixteen years and four months for boys, and seventeen years and five months for girls. Each child discharged is kept under close supervision. According to the report, about 75% of those discharged do well.[18]

**Conclusion.** On the basis of the material presented in this chapter we may summarize the administrative procedures of a correctional institution under three headings. 1. *Admission.* This process should include physical, mental and psychiatric study of the newcomer, securing an adequate history, particularly of his social life, quarantine, and the setting up of an individualized plan for his life in the institution, on the basis of a case study such as that indicated, and specifying the vocational, educational, physical, and social experiences that seem best adapted to effecting his readjustment. 2. *Guidance and Training.* The education given the student should be equal to that he would receive on the "outside," his vocational experiences should be arranged primarily from the educative standpoint, recreation should make for physical and mental health, and his social life should include opportunity for wider community contacts which would eventually fit him for independent non-institutional life. During his time of training his case should be periodically studied and reviewed by the staff and revisions in the plan adopted for him made as the circumstances may indicate. 3. *Discharge.* He should be "graduated" from the school when, in the judgment of the staff, he has become capable of leading an efficient and socialized existence in a normal community. His readjustment and rehabilitation should be facilitated by the parole officer of the institution, and "follow-up" investigations of his progress should be made until his adjustment seems complete.

Success in work of this sort involves the building up of a scientific technique of reform. The main elements in such a

[18] Liepmann, M., *loc. cit.*, p. 50.

technique, from a sociological standpoint, according to Sutherland, are the following.[19] (1) Reformation may be accomplished in two ways: first, by stimulating desirable tendencies, or removing stimuli to undesirable ones; second, by the sublimation of the tendencies in question. (2) Both processes involve the reconstruction of *habit*. (3) Reformation is assisted by helping the offender to understand the situation: insight into his own mental mechanisms possesses great therapeutic value. (4) The process of repressing and sublimating the tendencies of the delinquent is a problem in the direction of his fundamental wishes for security, new experience, social status, and intimate response from persons for whom he possesses affection. (5) The plan of treatment must be continually readjusted to the changing attitudes of the subject. (6) The individual must be given an active share in effecting his own reform. (7) Finally, the process should be based upon a knowledge of all physical, mental or emotional defects or abnormalities. Removing these will not necessarily overcome the delinquency, but no plan that disregards them can be completely successful.

Professional social work with delinquents confined in institutions is a stimulating occupation and demands a specially adapted personality. Miss Van Waters warns against two types of workers:[20] those who wish to dominate the delinquents with whom they deal in institutions where their power over them is very great, and those who are too sentimental and over inclined to pity. A successful worker should himself have an adjusted, normal personality that includes a real interest in human beings, and a balancing sense of humor. Adequate preparation involves professional school training and experience. One institution specialized for this type of worker merits especial mention, namely, the "National Training School for Institutional Executives," connected with the Children's Village, at Dobbs Ferry, New York.

This chapter completes the group of three devoted to institutional social work. The two following chapters deal with group work and recreation in neighborhood and community.

[19] Sutherland, E. H., *op. cit.* The foregoing summary is based upon pp. 595-598.

[20] *Op. cit.,* Chap. XI.

# CHAPTER XXVIII

## NEIGHBORHOOD AND COMMUNITY WORK

So far the chapters in Part III have dealt with case and institutional work. There are two other major types of social service: group work and administration. Chapter XXIV (Social Work in Industry) was concerned to some extent with group work, but the main discussion of this phase of social work is found in this and the following chapter; one dealing with community organization and the other with recreation. In this field the attention is focused on the social situations which influence the individual rather than on his own make-up. After all, case workers can effect readjustments only for a relatively small number of clients, and furthermore they very quickly come to see the importance of controlling the social environment as well as the individual. Social and individual disorganization are closely bound up together, thus necessitating two complementary approaches to social problems. The case worker is very largely dependent upon the social resources of the community in his attempts to reorganize the life of his client, hence his interest in this broader phase of social work. Furthermore, one of the best possible approaches to social legislation and reform on a large scale is through case studies: experience in the solution of particular problems suggesting often a basis for a community or state program.

What is meant by "community" and "community organization"? "A community," according to one definition, "is a local grouping of people who share a number of important interests and activities, and who are more concerned about those things they have in common than those things wherein they differ." [1]

[1] Queen, S. A., "What is a Community?" *Social Forces*, 1: 382, 1923. *Cf.* also: "A community is a local area over which people are using the same language, conforming to the same mores, feeling more or less the same sentiments, and acting upon the same attitudes." Harvey W. Zor-

Although frequently used interchangeably, the term "neighborhood" may be considered as referring to a smaller, more informal, face-to-face subdivision of a community. As Professor Arthur Evans Wood says, a neighborhood is simply "where neighboring takes place." The neighborhood becomes a community when the centers of common life are organized and made more formal. "Community organization" is the rather indefinite term applied to a number of movements of the last twenty-five or thirty years all aimed at the revival, expansion, reconstruction, and integration of neighborhood or community life. The need for community organization arose ultimately out of the industrial revolution and the subsequent growth of cities. As these centers of population became larger and larger people came to realize their dangers. Genuine parliamentary government does not function in the city; there is poverty, vice, and congestion in the urban center; and class lines set up barriers between different elements of the population. As such conditions became more and more apparent various movements arose to restore the village type of life in the cities; to build up neighborhoods and local communities within the larger structure where life would be more like that of the small town.[2] But it seems as though this movement had come a generation too late. As Steiner[3] has pointed out, this community movement is the direct product of the conflict between the old village type of culture and the forces that are undermining this culture and building up in its place the complex pattern of modern city life. Indeed, the radio, the automobile, and other modern means of communication and transportation seem likely to urbanize the countryside. However, not even these changing conditions necessarily destroy the validity of a community movement, though they may compel some remodelling. The whole issue will perhaps be clarified by consideration of a specific local situation.

baugh, in *The Gold Coast and the Slum*, p. 223. Univ. of Chicago Press, 1929.

[2] Another need that give rise to the community organization movement, of course, was the desire to bring some order out of the chaos produced by the existence of so many competing and uncorrelated community activities and agencies.

[3] Steiner, Jesse F., "Whither the Community Movement?" *Survey*, 62: 130-131, 1929.

## *ROXBURY:*

## FROM VILLAGE HOMOGENEITY TO URBAN HETEROGENEITY [4]

### I. THE PROBLEM

The explanation of Roxbury's problem is to be found in the history of its transition from a colonial village to a congested industrial center. "For about two hundred years this suburb of Boston maintained its unique and sharply defined character as a primary village community centering about common religious interest." About the middle of the last century its growth was suddenly accelerated and the village assumed an urban character. The coming of immigrants and industries, the increase in mobility and absorption into the adjoining metropolis destroyed the old homogeneous neighborhoods and primary group organization, setting up larger groups and secondary relations. The social controls of the old régime broke down and disorganization appeared in various forms. To the older inhabitants, whose traditions center around the Congregational Church, the situation seems unendurable.

### II. HISTORY

The colony of Rocksborough was settled in 1630 by sturdy farmers from Essex. They survived the hazards of the severe winters and the Indian wars and did their full share in the Revolution. At the end of the war the town was still a country village chiefly dependent upon husbandry. Road building, the stage, and in 1834 the Providence Railroad brought some expansion. Primary group relations persisted, however, until the middle of the nineteenth century. The Congregational Church, the Town Hall, and the Masons served as unifying forces. About 1830 there was a marked interest in civic improvements. A board of health, fire department and newspaper were established, and the school system was greatly improved. Wealth increased; many private mansions were built and the first public library, founded in 1805, was followed in 1872 by the Fellowes Athenæum. In 1841 Brook Farm, a socialistic experiment, was established, but although it persisted for six years it had little influence upon the community.

With increasing prosperity the first evidences of disorganization began to appear. There was a sharp increase in land values and some conflict arose in connection with real estate deals. But the

[4] Steiner, Jesse F., *The American Community in Action,* H. Holt, 1928. A collection of twenty community case studies made by graduate students of their home communities, pp. 107-33. Summarized and reanalyzed by permission of the publishers.

first real evidence of the breakdown of social control was in the church life of the community. At the beginning of the nineteenth century the support of the church had been put on a voluntary basis and attendance was no longer required. Additional churches, including those of several new denominations, were built, but interest in church, particularly on the part of the younger people, began to wane. Between 1840 and 1850 the population doubled, and in 1846 the City was chartered. In 1867, when Roxbury was annexed to Boston, it had pretty nearly lost its suburban character. Immigration and industrial development completed the disorganization of the old community. The Irish, who were the first immigrants, came in 1818, followed by the Scotch and Germans. The Irish, being Catholic, resisted efforts at assimilation. "By the end of the century the congestion already apparent was increased by pressure from South Boston which was reaching the saturation point of population and industry." Then came the Jews, Negroes, Letts, Poles, Italians, Greeks, Albanians, and Armenians. "The torrent of immigration flowed in so fast that there could be no satisfactory solution of the housing problem, and no orderly racial grouping." The public schools and the churches came into conflict with each other in their uncoordinated attempts at assimilation of these new groups, and disorganization was complete.

## III. PRESENT SITUATION

No racial lines are drawn in Roxbury today with the exception of a tendency toward the segregation of Jews and Negroes. The churches have been the main "centers of uplift" in the community, but today a number of social agencies exist. The Family Welfare Society, with a history of fifty years, is an effective institution. There have been boys' clubs, and even a Workingmen's institute but they have exerted little influence. The Boston Y. M. C. A. is near the border and the churches have encouraged their young men to join. There is also the Roxbury Neighborhood House which serves the immediate district as a settlement. The most effective nonsectarian force, however, is the Norfolk House Center, with a total membership in 1925 of 1,744, a staff of five full-time and fifty part-time workers, almost as many volunteer assistants and a complete, diversified program. According to the report of 1926: "The most striking addition to the work has been the admission . . . of groups of Lettish-Americans who seemed ten years ago to be a markedly separate and alien factor in the community life." An attempt at a community council (Roxbury Improvement Society) was made about 1905, which not only failed in its purpose but created new difficulties in the community.

Deterioration has affected the whole district; even the former aristocratic section is as shabby as the rest of the town today. "Many streets present the picture of close-packed buildings at various angles, some having about them shreds of beauty and dignity, others patently cheap and flimsy structures of no known type of architecture, in several stages of disrepair." Many of the older families have become extinct, and the descendants of others have moved away. Indicative too of the change in culture is the fact that the Latin School, once famous, has been moved. It is interesting that the old residents, although they have left Roxbury, continue to contribute to its churches and social agencies and to serve on the boards of these institutions. [Perhaps they thus perpetuate a cultural lag.]

The constructive efforts of the churches and the social agencies are nearly offset by the demoralizing influences of the so-called athletic clubs, whose forerunners were local gangs, where dancing, drinking, gambling and vice flourished. Another factor in the demoralization of the district is the extent of cheap commercial recreational facilities. The churches, weakened by the influx of different racial stocks, are now making their stand against new conditions in the old community. But they have no resident sources of strength. Their most influential and wealthy supporters no longer live near at hand. The young people have become a serious problem to the churches. "In one year 50% of a class of teen-age girls had a record of illegitimacy as a result of relaxed vigilance and control during the summer months." There are five strong Roman Catholic churches and a good many other denominations in addition to the original Congregational forces. They are well disposed toward each other and toward the social agencies, but there is little coordinated effort. "Thus . . . in the midst of an overabundance of churches, religious belief is not today the guiding principle of Roxbury."

## IV. DIAGNOSTIC SUMMARY

*Causes.* The chief factors in the present maladapted, disorganized and demoralized district of Roxbury seem to have been:

1. Sudden increased growth due to immigration and industrial expansion.
2. Resultant destruction of primary group relationships.
3. Extreme mobility.
4. Overshadowing influence of the larger city of Boston.
5. Migration of the older and abler members of the community.
6. Their loyal but absentee control over the machinery of reorganization, i.e., the churches and the social agencies.
7. The absence of any real neighborhood or "natural" communities, due to economic, industrial, social and political factors.

8. The absence of any thoroughgoing and comprehensive plan, based upon careful study of the district as it now is, and articulating Roxbury with the Boston situation.

*Diagnosis.* Roxbury represents a state of serious community disorganization caused by the destruction of the older system of primary group control through a sudden increase in population and the failure of the social forces of the district to reorganize adequately in the face of the new conditions.

*Recommendations.* (1) A thorough and scientific study of present conditions, forces and needs, and (2) a community organization program that will provide for Roxbury as a district of Greater Boston.

This "life-history" of Roxbury illustrates the sort of information needed today for satisfactory community organization. It shows the necessity for understanding the historical, social, economic and political forces which affect a situation before attempting a community plan. Finally, it makes it very clear that community organization is more than the coordination of social agencies, the cooperation of churches, or the integration of any one or two sets of forces, agencies or institutions. Before dealing with community organization systematically, a brief reference to the history of the movement since Warner's day will serve to indicate the origin of the various social agencies and organizations that faced the Roxbury situation.

**Historical Background.** The most important new social institution of the latter part of the nineteenth century uplift and reform period was the settlement. The social settlement originated in England, in a spirit of religious service and philanthropy and as a reaction against the suffering caused by the industrial revolution. Ruskin, Carlyle and Kingsley pictured the conditions in city slums so vividly that numbers of university students became interested in the plight of the working class. Philanthropy proving ineffectual, the experiment of living among the slum dwellers was tried, in the hope of raising the tone of the communities through neighborly service and friendship. Toynbee Hall, founded in 1884, was the first recognized settlement. As the result of the visits of Jane Addams and Robert Woods to England three pioneer American settlements were established about 1889: Hull House in Chicago, South End House in Boston, and the Neighborhood Guild in New York. By 1894 there were four settlements in Chicago and these first four are still dominant. Although the original motivation was religious the settlements soon became nonsectarian. They have aimed at the restoration of neighborhood life, interpreting one class to another, and stimulating the "normal" agencies of the city to function in behalf of "the poor" in the congested districts. Recreation was from the first one of the predominant activities of the settlement, but various other programs have been promoted, including health work, clubs, forums, and adult education. Some of these have since been taken over by specialized agencies and organizations. The settlements are really inter-period institutions: they are post-Warner, but still for the most part, pre-professional. Although strictly nineteenth-century products their influence today is considerable. They will be dealt with below in connection with present-day community organizations.

About 1900 we enter a new period in the history of community organization, which might be called the modern professional stage.[5] The literature of exposure and muckraking, characteristic of the late nineties and the early years of the new century, was replaced gradually by fact-finding studies as the social survey developed. One of the first great surveys was that of Pittsburgh, begun in 1907 and completed the following year. Another characteristic of this period was the gradual diminution of sentimentality and uncritical optimism. Finally, in contrast with the preceding period, it may be described as democratic rather than paternalistic; professional rather than humanitarian. The entire period from about 1900 to the present falls readily into two divisions: the stage before the World War, and that during and following it. In the early years of the present century many of those interested in community organization turned from the settlement, which had suffered from a spirit of patronage, to the public school building as a center of neighborhood activity of a more democratic nature. The Rochester demonstration of 1906-7 showed the possibilities of the

[5] In 1902 the National Conference of Charities and Corrections had a section on neighborhood work for the first time.

wider use of the schools as centers around which to organize the leisure time and recreational activities of the community. In October 1911 the first National Conference on Civic and Social Center Development was held at Madison, Wisconsin, and this date marks the beginning of the movement on a large scale. This first conference was characterized by an almost religious enthusiasm. A woman from the "Gold Coast" of Chicago, who attended the meeting, writes of it as follows:

> It was the deepest and most inspiring experience I have ever had with a group of people. . . . Some of us had caught the vision from the South Park Field House; others were fired by the experience of Edward Ward in the Rochester School centers. . . . Woodrow Wilson spoke at one meeting. He said that the idea of the conference, if put into practice, would make America a true democracy. . . . William Allen White spoke at the closing banquet. It was not like most closing banquets. It was a crusade consecration, and that not in any spirit of duty but a joyful conviction that we had found the way into a new world. Trembling we stood on our feet and sang a Hymn to Brotherhood.[6]

During the decade between 1911 and 1921 a remarkable development of both school and non-school community centers took place. In small towns and rural districts some three hundred community buildings were erected. The activities of the social or community centers, as they came to be called, included recreation, which was foremost, adult education, neighborhood forums, and such "community services" as libraries, health work, vocational bureaus and the like. The community center movement was promoted by the increasing hospitality of the school and municipal authorities toward the wider use of school and city buildings for various purposes, and by the services of trained leaders furnished by such national organizations as the Playground and Recreation Association of America. Certain difficulties arose, however, in the period immediately preceding our entrance into the World War. Dangers of municipal and school board control began to be recognized. There was too strong a tendency toward regimentation—always a weakness of the public schools—and sometimes a conflict of author-

[6] Zorbaugh, Harvey W., *The Gold Coast and the Slum*, p. 202, Univ. of Chicago Press, 1929.

ity, since school districts do not necessarily coincide with natural community areas. In the larger cities the old neighborhoods were breaking down and the population of foreign districts evinced no great interest in the new centers. Referring to those established on the Near North Side as a part of the Chicago School Center Movement, Zorbaugh says:[7]

> Within a year all but one of these community centers on the Near North Side had failed. It was not enough to open doors. There was no response from the community. Children came to the playgrounds. A few mothers came to the movies. But the men did not come. There was no evidence that people wanted to come together to discuss politics or local affairs. Neighborhoods did not support the centers. The doors were closed. [This happened before the War.]

One of the boldest attempts at community organization ever made in the United States was the Cincinnati Social Unit experiment. The principal objective of the project was to bring about a combination of democratic control and professional services. To this end the 15,000 people who occupied the 31 blocks of the Mohawk-Brighton district were organized along two lines. Each adult residing or working in the district was suposed to participate in groups through which he would be represented, first, as resident and consumer and, second, as producer and practitioner of some special skill. The first part of the organization was based on block councils which were supposed to be elected by all persons over eighteen years of age living in each block. Each council was then to choose a member to represent it on the Citizens' (district) Council. These representatives also had some executive duties and received a small stipend. The second part of the organization was based on occupational councils of teachers, artisans, physicians, merchants, social case workers, and other vocational groups. One member of each of these bodies was its representative in the central Occupational Council. Finally, the Citizens' Council and the Occupational Council meeting together constituted the General Council. Numerous obstacles were encountered, among them the influenza epidemic of 1918, the general ex-

[7] *Ibid.*, p. 203.

citement of war time, and the opposition of certain politicians at the city hall.

In spite of these handicaps most of the projected organizational machinery was actually set up and made to function. The development of a health service for small children will illustrate its method of operation. Some outsiders first suggested such a program. The matter was discussed in the Citizens' Council. Then each member talked it over with the residents of her block. She reported the results of her conferences back to the Citizens' Council which finally decided to undertake the general plan. But for details of procedure they turned to the Occupational Council and particularly to the physicians' and nurses' councils. The latter made very definite proposals which were discussed by the Citizens' Council, referred to the separate blocks, and again considered by the central group before adoption. When the program was completely outlined its actual inauguration was relatively easy; it was a sound plan from the medical standpoint; and it was understood by the whole population.

This "experiment" was continued for three years, 1917-1920, with financial support partly from the local community and partly from a national organization. The period was too short to yield conclusive results, although there were numerous achievements. On the other hand, its discontinuance when outside support was withdrawn is not convincing evidence of failure, because of the unusual obstacles previously discussed.

The World War caused first a rapid expansion of the community movement and then a serious reaction when the attempt was made to carry over the ambitious programs of war-time to the post-war period. Due to the emotional appeals, increased mobility and communication, and the pressure of national organizations, most of the population centers of the country were "organized." Localism and neighborhood integration were sometimes destroyed due to the organization of interest groupings allied with similar groups outside the community.

Under the War Camp Community Service cities provided centers for social and recreational activities of the soldiers stationed nearby. Nearly everyone was involved in some sort of war-time activity or organization. Immediately following the war the various national organizations attempted to continue their programs, modifying them somewhat to fit post-war community needs. Fayetteville, N. C., for example, with a population of only 7,000, bonded itself for $115,000 to erect a community center as a war memorial. In Grand Rapids a Council for "after war service" was formed. But there were many disappointments. About this time the Interchurch World Movement failed, although it had a world-wide appeal. Community Service, Inc., also failed, and the American Red Cross gradually contracted its community work to disaster relief, home service for ex-soldiers, and some public health work.

The failure of various organizations developed during the war to survive afterwards, particularly in the larger cities, is well illustrated by the history of the "Lower North Community Council" in Chicago.[9] During the war the Twenty-first and Twenty-second ward organizations of the Chicago unit of the Council of National Defense were particularly active. After the war, when it was suggested that the local units of the National Council continue as community councils, these two ward organizations which roughly corresponded with the Near North Side, combined and formed the Lower North Community Council. A trained secretary was secured in 1919 and a democratic plan of organization intended for a membership of 5,000 was set up. "The work of the community council was to consist in the coordination of agencies and efforts devoted to the amelioration of conditions of the Near North Side, to the securing of needed improvements for the Near North Side, and, above all, to the building up of a spirit of neighborliness and of community interests among the varied groups living on the Near North Side." Committees on health, sanitation, recreation, housing, music, and membership set to work. Some attempt was made to organize the blocks after the social unit plan, a civic forum was opened, and the office on Clark Street was transformed into an information and advice center, "the visible symbol of the new neighborliness that was to weld the Near North Side into a community." But the task was impossible—there were now too many cross-currents of interest and culture; the temporary and emergency neighborliness gen-

[9] *Ibid.*, Chap. X.

erated by the war had vanished. First, the volunteers, on whom the Council had depended, drifted into other activities, the professional men lost interest, and the "community" itself failed to respond. The membership drive recruited less than one thousand, funds were exhausted, the "social block" experiment went to pieces, and interest in the forum waned. A crisis was reached in 1921, the secretary was allowed to resign, and the policy of the Council changed. Efforts at creating neighborliness ceased, and under a part-time secretary the organization tried to discover its place in the district. Finally, in 1922, after two controversies, the Council surrendered its idealized program of community life, became realistic, studied the forces in the life of the district and eventually became a social agency with limited functions rather than a democratic community organization.

**Community and Neighborhood Work Today.** Despite the failure of the roseate dreams of war camp community organizers to materialize, and the difficulties now more clearly recognized, a great deal of neighborhood and community work is being done in this country today. Among the agencies most prominent in this field are the settlements, school centers, playgrounds, and clubs of various kinds.

The settlement faces many difficulties today.[10] Industry is encroaching more and more and the old neighborhoods are disappearing. The original population of the districts has in many cases moved out and the newcomers are not always sympathetic with the aims of the settlement. Criticism of the settlement as a neighborhood institution comes from a number of quarters. It is pointed out that they appeal mainly to adolescents and women, and are usually run by women also. They seem to have lost contact with their clients in many cases. "It is unquestionably true," says Tibbitts,[11] "that, in the main, the settlement is not conversant with the underlying forces of community activity." Their lack of democracy in many instances and their tendency toward patronage are objected to as un-American, and it is pointed out that even the English settlement is becoming a democratic center of community life rather than

[10] Tibbitts, Clark, "A Study of Chicago Settlements and Their Districts," *Social Forces,* 6: 430-437, 1928. [11] *Ibid.,* p. 435.

a place of residence for benevolently inclined outsiders. On the side of social research, too, the universities have to a large extent succeeded the settlements, and the latter on the whole have not even availed themselves of the findings of the former.

On the other hand the modern settlements find many supporters. But they are committed to a modification of the traditional program and are developing new methods of work. Some settlements meet the changing conditions of their vicinity by a complete shifting of emphasis in their work. If a new nationality has "invaded" the district, the social workers seek to interest the newcomers in the "house" and its services. Then they have the task of teaching the old and the new inhabitants to respect each other and to cooperate for the common good. Occasionally a settlement follows its departing clientele to another location. When the area is invaded by business and industry, instead of by a new race or nationality, the settlement is often faced with a more difficult problem. Such a change in the use of land commonly sounds the death knell of neighborhood life. The social workers must therefore decide whether to abandon the district or to continue the house as a "service station" for the dwindling and transient population.

Similar to the settlements in many ways are the school social centers. They carry on many of the same activities, but the school centers have no resident staffs, they maintain no household of "professional neighbors." Typical of this kind of agency is the East Boston School Center.[12]

East Boston, situated on two islands, has a population of 63,000, two-thirds of which are native born. Italians constitute about one-half the foreign-born residents. The "community" is divided into four sections: the first and second border on the water front and have most of the manufacturing and mercantile establishments. The third district is residential, and the fourth suburban. The "community" has one real park, four school playgrounds and a municipal gymnasium. There are a number of commercial recreational institutions, including four moving picture houses and seven dance halls. East Boston is predominantly Roman Catholic; the four synagogues and the fifteen Protestant churches are weak and poorly attended. Relief is administered by the Jewish Charities, the Family Welfare Society and the Society of St.

[12] Remer, Alice W., "The East Boston School Center," *Social Forces,* 5: 97-102, 1926. A summary.

Vincent de Paul. Other agencies include the Boston Health League, three settlement houses, a public library and a dispensary.

The School Center is located in the High School which is in the residential district. It has very little space, few facilities, and is neither beautiful nor new. There is a staff of twenty connected with the work of the Center, all being paid workers except the leader of the Girl Scout troop. All but three are residents. "With all these people, the center work is a subsidiary occupation and several of them are in the Center as much if not more from interest in the community than for the money they receive." All but two workers are or soon will be on the city payroll. "The Center gets what it can from the city for the full time term, and raises the rest of the money required for its activities in the district." Regular activities include: (1) the Women's Club, (2) the Center Melodic Society, (3) the basketry class, (4) the Community Center Social Dance, (5) free moving pictures, (6) the Beatrice Club for older Italian girls, (7) an orchestra, (8) Junior City Council, (9) Girl Scouts, (10) dressmaking class, (11) millinery class, (12) boys' and girls' athletics.

The district is not a real community, and the Center is handicapped by an attitude of passivity on the part of the inhabitants, but the writer points out that the Center is the only institution viewing the district as a whole, and concludes that for the effort and money put into it "there has been excellent return."

A recent study by the U. S. Bureau of Education revealed the fact that thirty-two states and the District of Columbia have laws providing for the community use of school buildings. Between 1919 and 1924 there was a definite increase in the number of school centers, this increase being as great as 55% in cities over 5,000.[13] The distribution of the two hundred and twelve clubs in the seventeen community centers of Washington, D. C., in 1925 is shown in the following table:[14]

| | |
|---|---|
| Miscellaneous: musical, parliamentary law, public speaking, etc. | 65 |
| Athletic | 53 |
| Industrial arts, home economics, etc. | 42 |
| Social | 17 |
| Rhythm | 13 |
| Dramatic | 11 |
| Language | 11 |
| Total | 212 |

[13] The National Community Center Association attempts to promote this type of community organization throughout the country.

[14] Bowman, Le Roy E., "Community Progress: Developments in Community Organization," *Social Forces,* 5: 91-94, 1926.

In addition to the settlements and social centers[15] any thorough study of community organization should take into consideration many other types of association. Often a chamber of commerce seeks to coordinate the civic as well as the business interests of a local area. Sometimes a federation of women's clubs, a city club, an improvement association, a council of churches, or a welfare federation may provide the leadership and the mechanism for community action.

Most of the discussion so far has been concerned with urban conditions. But community organization is probably as well developed in the country as in the city. Even before the coming of professional social work to rural districts, important contributions to neighborhood and community life were made by the Grange, the Farm Bureau, and the consolidated school. Each of these brought people into closer cooperation for economic, educational, and recreational purposes. The rural Y. M. C. A. has achieved something toward breaking down religious barriers. During the War nearly every county in the United States had a Red Cross chapter. People worked together to make bandages, sweaters, and other supplies for the soldiers; they looked after the needy families of men in service; they promoted friendly feeling between various ethnic, religious, economic, and "social" groups in the county; they introduced the idea of professional social work. About the same time several states were experimenting with county welfare departments.[16] These have frequently resulted in the coordination of social work activities and have made possible the employment of persons with professional training. However, this movement has not spread very widely. Social work in the conventionally limited sense is rare in rural regions, but the promotion of neighborhood and community life is going forward no less actively and successfully than in cities.

[15] The settlement today is more devoted to the adjustment of immigrants than anything else, and to the effort to bring to the underprivileged generally all the benefits of the city. The community center now aims not merely to hand down traditions, but to form a matrix in which new values can be worked out by neighbors facing a new social situation. It is "to be judged by its efficiency in adapting groups of people to changing civic and social life."

Summary of discussion at the 1928 National Conference of Social Work, reported in *Social Forces,* 7: 97, September, 1928.

[16] The North Carolina plan is outlined in Chap. XXXI.

Work for the Negro is also relatively undeveloped. North Carolina, however, has recently undertaken such work on rather a large scale, the experiment involving the organization of twenty-six counties.[17] Community work in the South generally received a tremendous impetus as a result of the War, and the movement has continued. In 1919, for example, Richmond, Va., had a recreational system costing $7,000. In 1920 the budget increased to $27,500, but the business men of the city felt that even this was insufficient for the needs of the community and raised $35,000 in addition. From other similar evidence it is apparent that the South has now discovered that it is not as poor as it thought and that it has sufficient wealth for the support of needed social and community work.

The various forms of organization for coordinating community activities and social work will be discussed in Chapter XXXI; there remains only the question of the evaluation of community work. Robert W. Kelso, at the 1927 meeting of the National Conference of Social Work, proposed the following tests of progress:[18]

## TESTS OF PROGRESS

"The purpose of all community efforts is to advance the community welfare by protecting society from anti-social forces, by rendering favorable forces more effective, and by developing a program of service conducive to such advancement." This involves the union of groups and individuals into a cooperative organization, the efficiency of which may be determined by the following tests:

1. How thoroughly and adequately is the whole field of need covered?
2. Are methods efficiently coordinated? Is the community willing to pay for expert leaders?
3. What of the "soundness of the principles of action which lie beneath the methods used?" Apply this test to the care of the aged, of children, and similar classes.
4. What is the degree to which competition is disappearing and cooperation increasing?

[17] Oxley, Lawrence, A., "Organizing the North Carolina Negro Community," *Southern Workman,* 58: 3-11, 1929.

[18] "Tests of Progress in Community Organization." *Proceedings,* 1927, pp. 478-81. Summary.

5. What is the "degree to which community consciousness is developed by educational interpretation of problems and methods?"

**Sociological Criticism of the Community Movement.** In recent years there has been a gradually increasing amount of sociological criticism of the community movement culminating about 1925 in a new type of approach to the study of the community and the problems of community organization. In marked contrast to the books published around 1920, are those of Professor Jesse F. Steiner, for example, which suggest a far more scientific approach to the subject. A few of these sociological studies will be referred to briefly, an analysis made of their implications, and some general conclusions presented.

Scientific methods for the study of neighborhoods and cities include (1) surveys, (2) ecological investigations, (3) community case studies, and life-histories which may or may not be ecological, and which are usually more general, less exhaustive and more concerned with history, and (4) culture analysis. Surveys and ecological studies have already been described in Chapter XVI. One of the first examples of ecological approach to the study of a city was R. D. McKenzie's "The Neighborhood: A Study of Local Life in the City of Columbus, Ohio." [19] "Human Ecology," as seen by Professor Arthur E. Wood, is the study of the "adaptation of the community to its economic, geographical, and cultural environment; the differentiation and segregation of areas, groups and institutions within the community; and the process of structural and social change undergone by the community as a whole and within its component parts." [20] Another such study of particular interest to students of community organization is Zorbaugh's *The Gold Coast and the Slum,*[21] an investigation of the Lower North Side of Chicago. This region is one mile wide and a mile and a half long, bounded by the Chicago River on the south and west, by the Lake on the east, and North Avenue and Lincoln Park on the north. It contains a population of 90,000

[19] *American Journal of Sociology,* 27: 145-169; 344-364; 486-510; 588-611; 780-800, September and November, 1921, and January, March and May, 1922.
[20] *Community Problems,* p. 11, Century, 1928.
[21] Zorbaugh, H. W., University of Chicago Press, 1929.

Americans, Italians, Irish, Greeks, Persians, Poles, Hungarians, Sicilians, and Negroes. Some twenty-eight nationalities are represented. The area is divided north and south into three districts: the "Gold Coast" on the lake front, a rooming house section in the middle, and "Little Italy" on the west. The region is in process of disintegration. Expansion, succession, physical changes, the rise of occupational and other divisive interests, the breakdown of local culture and public opinion, increase in social distance, mobility, and centralization have destroyed the homogeneity of the area until it can no longer properly be termed a community. Such studies show the futility of attempting to restore the old neighborhood life in the large cities at least.[22]

There are two good collections of community case studies and life-histories: Pettit's *Case Studies in Community Organization*,[23] and Steiner's *The American Community in Action*.[24] The first consists of five long studies of communities in which organizers were definitely trying to secure community coordination along certain specific lines. The second is a collection of twenty studies by graduate students of their home communities in all their various aspects; history, conflict, disorganization, demoralization and readjustment. It was from this book that the case given at the beginning of the chapter was taken.

The best recent example of a "culture analysis" is the Lynds' *Middletown*.[25] This book of over five hundred pages embodies the results of an exhaustive study of a typical American com-

[22] *Cf.* Thomas, W. I., *The Unadjusted Girl,* p. 44. Little, Brown Co., 1923. "The typical community is vanishing and it would be neither possible nor desirable to restore it to its old form. It does not correspond to the present direction of social evolution, and it would now be a distressing condition in which to live. But in the immediacy of relationships, and the participation of everybody in everything, it represents an element which we have lost, and which we shall probably have to restore in some form of co-operation in order to secure a balanced and normal society—some arrangement corresponding with human nature."

[23] Pettit, Walter W., Century Co., 1928.

[24] Steiner, Jesse F., Henry Holt Co., 1928. Case-studies of individuals are also a valuable index to community organization or disorganization. For example, Case No. 5 in the Judge Baker Foundation Series gives a very clear "inside" picture of community conditions in this particular town.

[25] Lynd, Robert S. and Helen M., *Middletown: A Study in Contemporary American Culture,* Harcourt, Brace and Company, 1929.

munity (Muncie, Indiana) made after the anthropological manner. As a study of the life and activities of the average adjusted American it is unparalleled. The "cultural lag," i.e., the failure of the educational and religious institutions and the ideas of the population to keep pace with the advancing industrial and technical development, is clearly shown. As one reviewer put it: "Here, as never before, is proof, and plenty of it, that a man with stone-age ideas can drive around in a high-priced automobile." [26]

Such studies as those cited attempt to unearth all the social forces, ecological, cultural, and political, that make for integregation as well as disorganization. They have shown that increased mobility, improved communication and wider contacts are breaking down the old segregated communities and that the development of the city as a whole affects that of the neighborhoods, which are thus, as localistic units, rapidly disappearing. We may regret the passing of the old village type of life in urban communities, but, as Steiner says, "We are not willing to obtain the old neighborhood values at the price of isolation." [27] They have shown too the importance of the "natural areas" of the city, which community organizers cannot afford to disregard, and the value of the historical study of the community, of its traditions, and the course of development of its institutions. Steiner, again, has pointed out that disorganization in itself is not deplorable; it is a necessary condition that precedes reorganization. Finally, community disorganization is coming to be interpreted generally as a failure on the part of the local social forces and institutions to adapt themselves to changing conditions in the community life.

**Conclusion.** The "way out" in community organization will come, if it all, through the appreciation of four principles: first, a recognition of the importance of regional and inter-community relationships; second, a recognition of the passing of the neighborhood as a basis for organization, and the necessity for association on a selective basis, articulating with larger interest groupings, rather than geographically; third, a recog-

[26] Grattan, C. Hartley, "A Typical American City," *New Republic,* Feb. 27, 1929, pp. 48-9.

[27] Steiner, Jesse F., "Whither the Community Movement?" *Survey,* 62: 130, 1929.

nition of the necessity for basing programs of community organization on realistic and scientific social psychological studies; and fourth, a recognition of the fact that community programs must involve more than the correlation of social agencies; that in addition they should attempt to promote general community solidarity by building up varied activities in which all participate.[28]

Community and neighborhood work should not be thought of as contrasting or conflicting with case work with individuals, but rather as complementary to it. In successive periods in the history of social work the emphasis has been placed first on one, and then on the other. But both are needed. Social problems seem to possess both individual and social aspects. There is maladjustment of the individual as well as maladjustment of the community, institutions, or organizations; individual disorganization and demoralization as well as social. The individual may be out of adjustment with his environment, or his social environment may be maladjusted as a means of satisfying the needs and wishes of the individual. Social and personal disorganization are two sides of the same shield. Furthermore, community agencies and institutions are important in the adjustment of the individual. Hence the case worker finds it necessary to be familiar with the social resources of the community.[29] Such knowledge is an integral part of his professional equipment. Every case worker, therefore, should also be a student of community organization.

There is a great need for professionally and scientifically trained leaders in the field of community and neighborhood work. So far such training has been largely on an experimental or apprenticeship basis. The place of community study and training in the curriculum of the school of social work has not yet been determined satisfactorily. Courses in community organization are apt to be somewhat vague and general in attempting to be as comprehensive as the subject requires. But

[28] *Cf.* Pettit's definition of community organization: "Assisting a group of people to recognize their common needs, and help them to meet these needs." Pettit, Walter W., "Some Prognostications in the Field of Community Work," *Nat. Conf. Social Work,* 1925: 681-685.

[29] Byington, Margaret F., *What Social Workers Should Know About Their Own Communities.* Russell Sage Foundation, 1924.

there are signs, such as the existence of case books, to which reference has already been made, that this will not always be true.[30]

In the next two chapters, to which this one has served as a general introduction, we shall deal with two particular aspects of the general field of community organization, namely, recreation and group work, and promotion and publicity.

[30] Steiner, Jesse F., *Community Organization,* Century, 1925, Chap. XXV.

# CHAPTER XXIX

## RECREATION AND GROUP WORK

There seems always to have been a close relationship between community organization and the playground and recreation movement. Settlements and other social centers have provided facilities for play and leadership for small groups of various kinds. Athletic managers and playground directors have regarded their work as inseparable from the development of local group loyalty. In the minds of some people the promotion and supervision of leisure time activities are identical with community organization. We have already shown how much broader is the real scope of neighborhood and community work. It remains to demonstrate the place of recreation in this larger field. Briefly the "logic" of the situation is this: people who play well together are likely to work together successfully; and the integration of communities can be achieved best through the development of team work in small groups.

The techniques of group work and of the direction of leisure time have not been as thoroughly analyzed as have those of case work. There is a great deal of trial and error and following of "hunches," but by no means everything is left to "inspiration." The following history of a women's club will display some of the functions of such a small group and some of the methods used by the social worker who sponsored it.

### A WOMEN'S CLUB [1]

Near the heart of a large city in the Middle West is a small Neighborhood House which fosters numerous social and civic activities. It is located in a district of small homes owned or rented for the most part by artisans of native white stock.

[1] Prepared with the cooperation of two social workers who were in close touch with this club for five years.

Several years ago a nurse and a social worker on the Neighborhood House staff felt that there was need of some organization to provide instruction in homemaking and to develop outside interests for mothers who were attending the Baby Welfare Station. The first invitation went out to women who were not active in other groups such as parent-teachers' associations or churches. Advantage was taken of their expressed desire to renew the experiences of war time, when women of the district gathered in the name of Red Cross to make various articles for soldiers and to perform other services. These gatherings had afforded opportunities not only for useful activities but for wholesome good times as well. In the four years since the War the women had missed these busy, friendly groups, but no one had taken the initiative to revive them or to provide a satisfactory substitute. This was the situation when the social worker and the nurse launched their project of a woman's club. The expressed purposes of the proposed organization were to help specially needy mothers by sewing and to study various aspects of child care. Other activities were also suggested.

The club was started in 1922 with most of the initiative coming from the residents of Neighborhood House. The women met weekly to sew and to play games. There were talks by outsiders on child training. Once a month there was an evening party to which husbands were invited. During the year some new members were added who were not primarily interested in children. Perhaps that was one reason why enthusiasm never rose very high. The women felt that the new club did not equal the Red Cross which had provided the only other organized group experience most of them had known.

During the second year the program was again planned by the social worker, but now in conference with the club officers. There was a series of talks on homemaking subjects, and service was stressed at the expense of recreation. Evening parties were continued, but they were less frequent. Some members of the club were themselves beneficiaries of work done by the group. This proved to be a policy of dubious merit. It seemed to promote mutual sympathy and group solidarity, but it attracted new members interested in material benefits.

Presently there were two factions in the club. One felt that all recreation was a waste of time for busy women like themselves. The other had a very indefinite idea of what it wanted to do, except that it did not want to work so hard. The president happened to belong to the latter group. When she could not win over the members of the other faction she became disgusted with the dispute and withdrew from the club. Her example was followed by a number of her personal friends. However, this did not break up the club entirely. The membership had increased and the places of those who resigned were presently taken by new members.

In 1924 the program was planned largely by a committee with only a few suggestions from the social worker. There were "know-your-city" trips; speakers were invited to tell of the work of other social agencies; millinery classes were held; special days were set aside for social events, chief of which was a monthly pot-luck luncheon; evening parties were held occasionally; sewing was done for particular families whose identity was not disclosed, and some sewing was done as a money-making project for the club. The new leaders seemed to be more competent, and the spirit of the club was much improved.

In 1925 the Neighborhood House moved into a new and attractive building. The new quarters seemed to improve the spirit and dignity of the club. Also there was much work to be done to put the new house in order. From working for Neighborhood House to working for other social agencies was but a step. Before the year was out the women were sewing for a hospital.

In 1926 the formal program consisted of educational talks and music, both provided from the outside. Various services were undertaken for the Needlework Guild, Boy Scouts, and Girl Reserves, in addition to work done for Neighborhood House. There was recreation after the work hour. Special parties were planned for the families. There was marked growth during this year. Business meetings were conducted with more dignity; a constitution was written; the name was changed from Mothers' Club to Women's Club; the group became a member of the city-wide Council of Clubs. A new group of young mothers was sponsored; a joint contribution was made to the Community Fund and individuals took part in the annual campaign; influence was exerted to have a near-by park improved.

The following year the program committee met with the social worker and made its plans month by month. There were two meetings a month for service. At one meeting there was a formal program and a tea for prospective members. The fourth meeting was devoted to business and a pot-luck luncheon. Group consciousness and loyalty seemed to keep on growing, and there was increased interest in civic affairs of the larger community.

In looking back over the five years' history of this club several points seem significant. Membership has changed, of course, but not rapidly. Losses have been due principally to change of residence and to acceptance of responsibility in other groups. There has been only one factional split, and recovery from that was fairly prompt. New members have been chosen from friends of those already in the group, from women living in the immediate vicinity, and from lists of persons suggested by nurses or social workers. There is no formal initiation.

The rôles of the various members now in the club have been characterized by the social worker as follows: four constitute a sort of inner circle, seventeen make up the rank and file, while eight are "on the fringe." The president is an accepted leader, as are two other members. There are two or three "would-be" leaders, a "scatterbrain," a "bonehead," a "slattern," a chronic complainer and disloyal idler, a grateful recipient, a clown, an incessant talker who takes herself very seriously, and a bragging quilter.

While the social worker has always been at hand to make suggestions and to take a hand when conflict threatens, the members of the group have developed a great deal of initiative and executive ability among themselves. The esprit de corps of the group is manifested in enthusiasm for various projects and in a spirit of mutual aid. The success with which the withdrawal of several prominent members was met indicates that on the whole the club has developed good morale. There is an unwritten law against gossip. There is a tradition that every new baby shall be provided with a blanket. There is genuine interest and participation in several civic enterprises.

The social worker who organized this club and guided its destinies seems to have been successful in steering a middle course between the two extremes of domination and neglect. She neither did too much for the group nor did she leave it to flounder when difficulties appeared. The club itself has come to mean a great deal to its members. It provides an escape from the routine of everyday life and work, training in team work, wholesome play, and a connecting link between the individual and the larger community.

Similar group experiences are provided for boys and girls through the Y. M. C. A., Y. W. C. A., Boy Scouts, Campfire Girls, Girl Scouts, Pioneers, 4-H Clubs, and a host of other agencies. Play facilities and leadership are also made available in many places through the public schools, parks, and playgrounds. Two plans for the administration of public recreation are illustrated by the following summaries.

## KALAMAZOO, MICHIGAN [2]

Recreation in Kalamazoo, which is a city of about 60,000 population, involves two city departments and the Board of Education.

[2] Based on interviews with Mr. Lawrence P. Mosher, Director of the Recreation Department, and Mr. Curtis Davis, formerly of the Department.

The Park Department is responsible for the upkeep and improvement of the city parks, three of which are used as playgrounds. The Recreation Department employs, trains, and supervises the playground leaders, provides equipment and supplies, and directs activities. The Board of Education permits the use of six school playgrounds and contributes half of the recreation budget. The Director is directly responsible to the Recreation Commission, which is composed of six members, three appointed by the city and three by the Board of Education. The Commission employs eighteen playground leaders, nine men and nine women, and three special swimming instructors during the playground season. The Director, and his assistant, who is on part time, are employed on a year-round basis. Applicants for positions as playground supervisors are generally chosen from the graduates of the ten weeks' Spring Institute, and are commonly students or graduates of one of the two local colleges.

In the summer recreation for children of the community centers around the nine playgrounds. Each is directed by two leaders, a man and a woman, and is open from one in the afternoon until dark, for a period of eight weeks. Eight of the grounds are open five days a week; the ninth, which is in the poorer district, operates six days. Games and activities of various kinds furnish recreation for the attendants. During the summer of 1929 there were twenty-four playground teams, organized into six leagues. The total attendance for the eight weeks was approximately 100,000.

Kalamazoo has a year-round recreation program for both adults and children. During the winter months the schools are responsible for the athletic and amusement activities of the school children. The Recreation Department provides ice-skating rinks for both children and adults and utilizes the school gymnasiums for the non-school group winter program.

In addition to the work of the Recreation Department the Park Department maintains and improves the numerous parks, which include a large recreation park, a tourist camp, and a well-equipped park for children provided with a merry-go-round, wading pools and a menagerie. Several years ago a municipal golf course was started by the Park and Recreation Departments but was later turned over to a separate organization.

Special recreational facilities are provided for the Negroes of the city by the Douglas Community House. Its program is supervised by the Playground and Recreation Association of America. The City Recreation Department is not affiliated with that organization. City playgrounds in districts where Negroes reside are of course open to them.

## CLEVELAND, OHIO

Cleveland has one of the best playground systems in the country but due to the fact that it is administered by two separate departments some duplication and overlapping have resulted. The Recreation Department of the city conducts a number of playgrounds of its own with little reference to those conducted under the Board of Education. The latter board maintains forty-nine playgrounds. These school grounds are open during the summer from nine in the morning until dark, and each field is supervised by three or four leaders. These leaders have usually been selected on the basis of competitive examinations given in various colleges and universities in Ohio and neighboring states by a representative of the Board of Education. During the playground season they attend a training class, and their work on the playgrounds is carefully supervised by field workers who thus maintain liaison between the leaders and the administration. The activities include games of all kinds, shows, folk dancing, sewing, woodwork, track meets, dramatics, inter-playground baseball for both girls and boys, swimming, boxing, harmonica bands, pageantry, and other forms of recreation. Many of the special activities are supervised by expert instructors who cooperate with the leaders on the various grounds.

The first case illustrates a cooperative plan involving the schools and the city departments of parks and recreation, operating under a representative board with a joint official. Excellent results are secured, harmony on the whole is maintained, and duplication avoided. In Cleveland, on the other hand, with its two separate departments, overlapping is unavoidable. The activities on the separate playgrounds are varied and interesting, and the work is carried on under excellent supervision. The weakness lies in the administration of recreation for the city as a whole, which lacks unification due to the existence of two autonomous departments. In Los Angeles the overlapping is carried even further. Here three distinct departments conduct recreational activities with little reference to each other, and no adequate division of labor. Eventually the Board of Education hopes to conduct all the recreational activities involving school children. At Oxnard, California, the city, the county, and a private organization have combined to "put on" a county-wide program that is probably as good as any in the country for a community of this size. Recreation in Baltimore, Maryland, is still more complexly organized, and involves a combination of city, county, state, and private enterprise. Unification is secured by means of a director who represents all four interests, but this centering of responsibility in a single individual involves a serious danger.

**Need for a Recreational Program.** For ordinary purposes we may define play as activities which are engaged in for their own sake, and define work as activities which are directed at some more remote objective. Play is therefore relatively spontaneous; participation is to a certain extent under one's own control. Work is performed more frequently as a necessary evil; often it involves subjection to another person or to an impersonal corporation. For the man with an interesting job or for the football player play and work tend to merge. But in general they are not difficult to distinguish.

There are still a few people who look upon play as a waste of time. There are many more who regard it as a legitimate activity, but assume that it will "take care of itself," and can see no reason for a program of organized play and recreation. But to an increasing number it is clear that play is a necessity for which definite plans must be made.

The development of machine production with minute subdivision of labor has brought increasing monotony of work. The man whose grandfather made sheets of leather into shoes may be performing just one of 200 operations involved in the manufacture of shoes. His grandfather was something of an artist; he is a little better than a machine. On the other hand, the factory system has made possible a great increase in the amount of leisure time. In 1909 eleven-twelfths of the industrial workers in the United States were occupied more than eight hours a day; at the present time it is estimated that three-fourths of them are employed on an eight-hour basis.[3] There is thus more time to play and more need of recreation than there was a generation ago, but there is reason to believe that most people do not know how to play.

In the first place, many persons engage in spare-time activities that are very much like their work. Bookkeepers and other

[3] Nash, Jay B., *The Organization and Administration of Playgrounds and Recreation,* p. 54 ff.

sedentary employees play cards while day laborers pitch horseshoes. But more serious is the substitution of passive enjoyment of movies or radio for participation in group activities through which one may find self-expression and social recognition. For those who seek action in dancing, pool, or bowling, there are too few inexpensive establishments with wholesome surroundings.

Both in small towns and in great cities there is a great deal of loafing, especially on the part of boys and young men. The experience of juvenile court judges and probation officers indicates that the old adage about Satan and idle hands still holds good. When the use of spare time is not planned, there is not only individual idleness but also the development of gangs. "The boy with time on his hands, especially in a crowded or slum environment, is almost predestined to the life of the gang. . . . Once a boy has tasted the thrilling street life of the gang, he finds the programs of constructive agencies insipid and unsatisfying." [4]

So far our discussion has referred primarily to people on the lower economic levels. But professional and business folk also need systematic recreation. With them work is often so interesting that it is absorbing. The game of getting ahead becomes too thrilling; they take themselves too seriously; nerves get wrought up; and irritability ensues which bodes ill for industrial relations, family life, and the whole social fabric. For these and many other reasons it has been found necessary to make definite provision for systematic and directed recreation for people of all ages and incomes.

A closely related function is the regulation of commercial recreation. Theaters, pool halls, bowling alleys, amusement parks, dance halls, excursion steamers, and road houses cater to the popular demand for escape from drab routine. But their proprietors are not primarily interested in furnishing wholesome amusement. They are immediately and often exclusively concerned with making money. Hence they are often disposed to wink at irregular and illegal practises when they do not actually encourage them.

Thus there is need in every community for a well-rounded

[4] Thrasher, Frederic M., *The Gang,* p. 79.

program of spare-time activities which will contribute to the development of healthy personalities and friendly social relations.

**Playground and Recreation Movement.** Credit for originating the recreational movement is generally given to the settlements whose history was described in the preceding chapter. The first period of the play movement was that roughly between 1885 and 1893.[5] During this time the first sand gardens and play areas were established in crowded sections of large cities under direction of settlements and churches. These were the earliest provisions for free recreation made in this country for the poor of the cities. They were prompted by the humanitarian spirit characteristic of the age. The second period, from 1894 to 1900, was that of small playgrounds. By this time there were four settlements in Chicago, and to one of these, Hull House, we owe the first "model" playground. This was the period, too, of the early city parks. After 1900 programs demanding more elaborate equipment, trained leaders, year-round activities, and public support began to appear in a few cities. Unfortunately the uplift motive which characterized both these early periods has not entirely disappeared; evidences of it are still found in the recreational systems of many communities today.

During the period 1900 to 1905 many of the cities reclaimed the smaller parks for public use and equipped them for play at municipal expense. The period 1905 to 1912 was characterized by the expansion of the park system and of municipal recreation. In 1906 the Playground and Recreation Association of America was formed and for nearly a quarter of a century now this organization has taken the lead in the fight for public, city-wide recreation. Chicago was the first great city to undertake organized municipal recreation on a large scale. In the summer of 1905 the South Park Commission opened ten elaborately equipped parks to the public. During this same period a movement which goes back to the settlements began to develop rapidly, namely, the attempt to organize recreation

[5] See Rainwater, C. E., *The Play Movement in the United States,* Chicago: University of Chicago Press, 1922, for excellent historical discussion. The division into periods here used is roughly that made by Rainwater.

on a neighborhood or community basis. In Chicago parks well equipped field houses were built, containing usually an assembly hall, gymnasium, swimming pool, club rooms, and a branch of the public library. In order to secure the interest and co-operation of the surrounding districts neighborhood associations and community councils were formed in connection with each park. Simultaneously a movement to utilize the schools as neighborhood centers developed. In this scheme Rochester, New York, led the way in 1907.

The period 1912-14 is termed that of "civic art and welfare" by Rainwater. Municipal orchestras, dances, dramatics, pageants and the like became popular. Some research was also carried out during these years. Recreational surveys were made in Detroit and Cleveland, and considerable legislation, both state and local, having to do mainly with the use of school buildings for community and recreation purposes, was enacted. During the war years of 1914 to 1918 recreation became more and more an affair of the local communities, under neighborhood associations and councils. In 1917 the War Camp Community Service was established by the Playground and Recreation Association of America in order to organize the social and recreational resources of the communities in the neighborhood of the army camps. In carrying out this program the work of numerous national and local agencies was correlated. Councils were established in six hundred communities.

The post-war period of 1918 to 1920 witnessed a slump in recreational activities according to figures reported by Abbie Condit.[6] These are based upon a study made by the Playground and Recreation Association of America. Forty-one cities discontinued recreation work in 1918, and 172 of 277 others reported unfavorable effects of the War on their work. One hundred and five reported that the War had no effect on their activities.

One result of the war-time activities was the rise of the idea of organizing communities on the basis of recreation. In 1919 Community Service, Inc., was established under the direction of the Playground and Recreation Association of America. Community organizers, as they were called, established local

[6] "Recreation Facts," *Playground,* October, 1919.

service associations throughout the country to assist the various localities to "organize." The separate existence of this agency was discontinued after about three years and it became a department of the parent organization. This fact was symptomatic of the decay of community recreational organization on a semi-private or voluntary basis and of the rise of the belief in municipal support.

Since 1920 progress on this new basis has been rapid, not only in actual municipal playgrounds and equipment but in the philosophy of the movement as well. According to Dr. Rainwater, there has been a series of progressive transitions. Thus provision is now made for all ages, not merely for children. Programs calling for a few months of activities are giving way to year-round schedules. Outdoor work is being supplemented by indoor. Recreation is no longer a movement of the slums, but is being promoted in all types of communities. It has spread from the city to the country. It has progressed from private to public support, from free play to organized recreation, and from the objective of individual well-being to that of group integration. Nash sees four stages in this development.[7] (1) The charity period, from 1890 to 1900. (2) The park stage, from 1900 to 1910. During this period taxes began to be used for recreational purposes. (3) The playground and recreation commission stage, from 1910 to 1920. (4) The school stage, from 1920 to the present. It was during the fourth period that the school came to assume a greater and greater degree of responsibility for the full out-of-school play time of the child.

The steady growth of the recreation movement during this last period is shown in the following figures compiled from the reports of the Playground and Recreation Association of America, *The Recreation Yearbook,* and other sources. They indicate the status of recreation in 1925. The number of cities with organized recreation had grown by this year to 700 as contrasted with 10 in 1900. In 1907 public expenditures for recreation totaled one million dollars; in 1925 $18,816,000. There were only a few score of paid workers in 1907; in 1925 there were 17,177. The use of school buildings had greatly increased in 1925 as compared with 1919. Two hundred and

[7] *Op. cit.,* 20 ff.

nineteen cities reported 1,389 schools used as evening recreation centers. By 1925, too, specialists and experts in the field had appeared. As Weaver Pangburn says, the transition had been made from untrained matrons presiding over sand gardens in Boston and Chicago to skilled leaders.[8] Houston, Texas, for example, by this time had a staff of specialists in dramatics, athletics, music, and the like, in charge of its recreational program. In this year 107 cities reported they were conducting training classes for their paid workers. Much new equipment had appeared: pools, beaches, fields and courts of various kinds; picnic grounds, skating rinks, dance pavilions, community houses, summer camp facilities, wading pools, parks, forests, lakes, gymnasiums, auditoriums, and churches were added, or, if they already existed, utilized. Recreation expanded beyond the city limits. Counties and states developed facilities. Highland Park, Michigan, for example, has one of its two camps 400 miles away. In 1925 eighty-three cities reported 123 summer camps. Among these geographical expansions, as Weaver Pangburn calls them, the national forests should not be omitted. In a sense they represent the climax of the play movement in this country.

In this development the South has been retarded, but considerable progress has been made in very recent years. About 1921 the Playground and Recreation Association began to center more of its efforts in the Southern states and succeeded in starting a number of private recreation organizations.[9] In 1923 an enabling act was passed in Alabama for the establishment of municipal park and recreation boards. Similar laws were enacted by the Florida and Georgia legislatures in 1925. In 1927, Southern cities reported a total of $1,750,018 spent for recreational purposes. There are now about 80 cities in which recreation programs are carried on as a municipal function. Developments in this section of the country are a matter of the last seven years only, but the recently awakened interest of various social and civic groups indicates that growth will be rapid. Thus, what twenty-nine years ago, for the country

[8] "Trends in Public Recreation," *Social Forces,* 4: 109-12, 1925.

[9] Williams, Jane B., "Progress in Community Recreation in the South," *Nat. Conf. of Soc. Work,* 1928: 316-19.

as a whole, was a summer playground movement for the children has now become a broad leisure time, year-round program for all ages and classes, and involving all types of activities.

**Recreational and Group Activities: In Community Centers.** Although many modernized settlements are supplying numerous forms of recreation, they are in their traditional form, at least, contrary to the modern American democratic spirit, in that they represent the activities of benevolently inclined individuals who come in from the outside to "uplift" a depressed neighborhood. In so far as this is not the case and they have become democratically organized institutions they are really a type of community center. Such centers are variously called social, recreation or community, depending largely upon who owns the building, but the nature of their work is essentially the same. They are not generally places of residence for people who come from the outside of the community, and they are usually supported in whole or in part from public funds. According to the leaders, the school center was not intended to replace any existing institutions, or to do relief work. Neither was it to be a reform organization, or new type of evening school, or a substitute for the church, or the local improvement association. On the contrary,

> It was just to be the restoration to its true place in social life of that most American of all institutions, the Public School Center, in order that through this extended use of the school building, might be developed, in the midst of our complex life, the community interests, the neighborly spirit, the democracy that we knew before we came to the city.[10]

The establishment of recreation centers in field houses in Chicago parks has already been noted. The activities of these early centers included five forms of recreation. (1) Physical exercise, involving indoor gymnasium work for all ages during the winter months, and track and field events during the outdoor season. Many baseball and other teams were also formed. (2) Manual work, including kite making, modeling and the like. (3) Social activities, comprising dances, banquets and club meetings. (4) Æsthetic interests, including concerts, the-

[10] Quoted by Clarence E. Rainwater, *op. cit.*, 115.

atricals, and interpretative dancing. (5) Citizenship activities, involving lectures, exhibits, and women's club meetings. By 1922 the South Park Commission had fifteen of these field houses under its control, and the example of Chicago had been followed by a number of other large cities in various parts of the country.

A recent study of the Bureau of Education reveals the fact that thirty-two states and the District of Columbia had laws permitting the community use of schools in 1927.[11] Control over 1,569 school centers in 722 places rests with the Board of Education in 61% of the cases; with an official Recreation Commission in 12%; it is shared with a private organization in 16% of the centers; and in 12% the control is entirely in the hands of such groups. A tendency toward control by municipal boards in cities over 5,000 is evident. In 41% of the centers the leaders are paid; in 42% they are voluntary; and in 17% there is a combination arrangement. Forty-one percent of the centers are supported by taxation; 21% by private funds; and the balance in both ways. The following table shows the nature of the activities of these centers:

DISTRIBUTION OF ACTIVITIES IN 1,569 SCHOOL CENTERS[12]

| *Activity* | *Percentage of Cases in Which Found* |
|---|---|
| Athletics | 70 |
| Clubs | 50 |
| Entertainments | 45 |
| Social meetings (informal groups) | 44 |
| Lectures | 27 |
| Social occasions (parties, etc.) | 27 |
| Civic occasions | 23 |
| Dancing | 21 |
| Night school | 18 etc. |

Not all the school and community centers have been successful; in fact many have been forced to close. An analysis of such failures suggests several conclusions. In the first place, success will depend to a large extent upon a careful sociological

[11] Bowman, Leroy E., "Group and Community Organization," *Amer. Jour. Soc.*, 34: 130-9, 1928.

[12] Compiled from *The Recreation Yearbook*, 1927.

study of the neighborhood and community served; a recreation center's program must be based upon a realistic knowledge of community needs and resources. Again, such centers should strive to build up not only neighborhood self-consciousness—increasingly more difficult and not altogether desirable—but also inter-community and even regional relationships. Finally, community centers will probably eventually become one phase, namely, the indoor, of the comprehensive playground and recreational program either of the school, in the case of children, or of the city, in the case of adults, while their control remains in the hands of local self-governing groups. According to Nash,[13] these centers will be located in schools, churches, settlements, field houses or libraries, and will be of two general kinds: the "Community Council" type, presided over by a resident director and controlled by the neighborhood council, and the "Permit" type, where individuals or groups obtain permission to use the facilities administered by a private or public organization.[14]

**Clubs and Organized Groups.** The work of recreation centers is closely related to club activities of various kinds. In fact "clubs" appeared as the second most frequent activity in 1,569 school centers as shown in the preceding table. The history of clubs is older and not directly related to that of community and school centers until recently, when the latter have promoted the organization of more or less formal groups as a phase of their program. As life in the cities has departed more and more from the informality and directness of the village and neighborhood and become more and more complex, organized and interest groups have replaced the spatially determined associations of the primary groups, and clubs of all types have rapidly increased in number.

Adult clubs and organizations have of course existed since the beginning of time but it is only since 1900 or thereabouts that the movement for the development of boys' and girls' clubs, particularly for those in the adolescent period, has de-

[13] *Op. cit.*, Chap. XXV.

[14] For a detailed case study of the reorganization of a community center showing some of the professional problems involved, see Pettit, Walter *Case Studies in Community Organization,* New York: Century Co., 1928 201-345, "Woodland."

veloped. First came the boys' department of the Y.M.C.A. and the girls' department of the Y.W.C.A. These were followed by the Federated Boys' Club. In 1910 the Boy Scouts of America was incorporated, and somewhat later the Girl Scouts, Camp Fire Girls, Big Sister and Big Brother movement. Still later, as a result of a process of "constrained adaptation," to use a phrase of Professor Ross', the Y.M.H.A. and Y.W.H.A. were formed.

The Lynds, in their intensive study of Muncie, Indiana, selected as a typical American community, found an extensive club organization.[15] They discovered 458 active clubs, probably about four-fifths the number in the city in 1924, the time the canvass was made. This would represent one club for every 80 people. In 1890 there were only 92 clubs, or one for every 125 persons. Of the total of 458 clubs, 95 were juvenile organizations. These groups represented all sorts and conditions of people and interests, educational, religious, "psychological," cultural, social, dancing, athletic and civic, but they seem to have exerted little really constructive influence on the community. "Certainly it is true," the authors conclude, "that a wide gap exists between the activities of the civic clubs and the major maladjustments of which Middletown complains." [16] They found also that with greater and greater organization of the social activities of the community there had come an increasing standardization of leisure-time pursuits, that men seem to have adopted more rapidly than women the new leisure-time inventions, and finally, that some informal social activity has managed to persist despite the high degree of formality and organization.

Space will permit only a brief description of some of the most important boys' and girls' clubs. The Boys' Club Federation should be noted on account of its work in promoting the formation of clubs. This organization reported for 1927 a total membership of 227,201 boys in 278 clubs. An interesting attempt to decrease delinquency in Chicago by reorganizing the boys' gangs into a club under trained direction was made

[15] Lynd, Robert S. and Helen M., *Middletown: A Study in Contemporary American Culture,* pp. 285-312. Harcourt, Brace and Co., 1929.
[16] *Ibid.,* 305.

by the Union League. This Union League Boys' Club is described by Thrasher in *The Gang*.[17]

The Boy and Girl Scouts are so-called "character education" organizations, which utilize the child's interest in nature, pioneer life and adventure. In 1927 the membership was reported as 346,000. There are 110,000 adult scout workers in the United States but less than 500 are paid workers. The "turn-over" in membership, of course, is very great, about 20% of the boys, and 35% of the scout masters retiring annually. The Girl Scouts is a rapidly growing organization, modeled with necessary modifications, after the Boy Scouts. The Big Brother and Big Sister organizations attempt to enlist the interest of adult men and women in problems of boys and girls. Their national federation reports 502 local Big Brother organizations serving 460 communities. Finally, luncheon clubs, which exist primarily for social and business purposes, also undertake a certain amount of work with underprivileged children among other forms of "service," and should be mentioned in any list of organized groups.

These various boys' and girls' clubs have been subjected to a certain amount of criticism. W. I. Thomas, for example, points out the probable bad effects of such self-conscious and competitive virtue as that engendered by the Scout organizations. "In general," he says, "we seem to have here a good influence with bizarre features. The most serious limitations of the program are that it is not adapted to the under-privileged boy, does not appeal to nor receive the boy who is a behavior problem, and practically does not touch the great mass of gang life." [18] The good boys are amenable and the bad inaccessible. Furthermore, these movements do not reach the child until his behavior patterns are already set. Leroy Bowman [19] also points out that recent studies having to do with the formation of habit traits have thrown a great deal of doubt on the former assumptions of "character building" agencies that traits formed in one type of situation "carry over" into

[17] Thrasher, Frederic M., *The Gang*, pp. 520-23, University of Chicago Press, 1927.

[18] *The Child in America*, p. 174, Alfred A. Knopf, 1928.

[19] "Group and Community Organization," *Amer. Jour. Soc.*, 34: 130-39, 1928.

situations of an altogether different nature. Nash believes that both the child and adult groups will ultimately become a part of the school or public playground and recreation program of the community and be tax-supported.

**Parks and Playgrounds.** In 1925-6 approximately 1,680 cities possessed some 250,000 acres of park land and recreation spaces. The area in the three largest, New York, Chicago and Philadelphia, was greater in proportion to the population than in any other group of cities from 25,000 upward. The most significant trend now seems to be the utilization of parks for active recreation and play purposes. Over $1,000,000,000, it is estimated, is invested in parks in this country today, the upkeep and maintenance of which costs more than $100,000,000 annually.

Playgrounds are of two general types: school and community. The latter may be either publicly or privately supported. Playground authorities aim ideally to provide opportunities for varied and wholesome play for every child and adult in the community. The greatest stimulating agency nationally is the Playground and Recreation Association of America, whose purpose is "to bring to every boy and girl and citizen of America an adequate opportunity for wholesome, happy play and recreation. Playgrounds, community centers, swimming pools, athletics, music, drama, camping, home play, are all means to this end." The trend since 1925, at least, has been in the direction of year-round recreation of both physical and cultural types, for all ages and for all social, racial and economic groups. Municipalization is being extended, and more trained leaders and adequate equipment are being furnished. The following table, based upon the 1927 *Park Manual and Recreation Yearbook,* shows the increase in the number of athletic leagues of various kinds in 1927 over 1926.

PLAYGROUND LEAGUES IN 1926 AND 1927

| *League* | *No. in 1927* | *No. of Cities* | *No. in 1926* | *No. of Cities* |
|---|---|---|---|---|
| Baseball | 2,060 | 536 | 1,425 | 420 |
| Playground ball | 2,054 | 357 | 1,610 | 274 |
| Basket ball | 1,690 | 345 | 1,302 | 289 |
| Volley ball | 1,115 | 350 | 861 | 285 |

Financial comparison of these two years is also interesting as measuring the expansion of recreational activity. The total expenditure for playgrounds and recreation in 1926 was $19,-202,123.25; in 1927, $32,191,736.32.

The various games and other activities to be found on the playground include athletics, pageants, camping, theatricals, golf, swimming, music, dancing and many others.[20] All these require a great deal of room. There has been considerable discussion relative to the amount of space a city or school should devote to playgrounds. A rough standard for all parks and playgrounds is 10% of the total area of the city. In addition to the out-of-town park, or "reservation," the large recreation park near the city limits, and the small in-town parks, specific provision is needed for the schools and neighborhoods of the city. Estimates of the square footage required for play purposes for each school child range from 25 to 300. A minimum space is necessary, however, for any playground. A fair minimum standard for each elementary school would seem to be 4 acres; for each junior high school, 10; and for each senior high school, 20. In addition there should be district playgrounds for both children and adults of from 10 to 24 acres for every 8,000 to 12,000 of the population. For children under twelve there should be a play-yard within a radius of one-quarter mile; for those under six sand lots should be provided in each block. Older children should not have to travel more than one-half mile to a playground.[21]

Leadership is the most important single factor in the success of the playground. Fortunately trained persons are more and more available and are being more generally utilized every year. In 1926, 790 cities reported community recreation programs under leadership, and the number of such cities is increasing every year. The technique of leadership and the psychology of play are discussed in the two manuals just cited, and in other publications listed in the bibliography.

[20] The reader interested in the organization of playground activities is referred to the following manuals: Nash, Jay B., *The Organization and Administration of Playgrounds and Recreation*, New York, A. S. Barnes Co., 1927, and Elsom, James C., *Community Recreation*, New York: Century Co., 1929.

[21] For somewhat different estimates see Eldridge and Clark, *Major Problems of Democracy*, pp. 331-2.

The administration of parks and playgrounds may be private or public. If it is in the hands of some public board or commission the tendency seems to be in favor of a separate department. Of 696 cities reporting in 1925, 310 had private playground and recreation associations. The following table shows the nature of the administration in the municipally operated systems for 1925 and 1926.

PUBLIC PLAYGROUND ADMINISTRATION

| | *Number of Cities* | |
|---|---|---|
| *Managing Authorities* | *1925* | *1926* |
| Playground and recreation commission or department | 135 | 197 |
| Boards of education | 122 | 124 |
| Park boards | ... | 127 |
| Park boards, or park and recreation commission | 93 | ... |
| City councils | 21 | 10 |
| Other municipal departments | 15 | ... |
| Combined control: e.g., board of education and park commission | ... | 17 |
| Totals | 386 | 475 |

Playgrounds—private, school or municipal—are usually free, in contrast with recreation and amusement parks. There are several instances, however, of publicly owned amusement parks operated for profit. The best case of this sort is probably that of "Playland," one unit in the Westchester County (New York) park and recreation system.[22]

**Recreation and the City Community.** The trend of opinion and of practice is in favor of a unified and comprehensive city-wide administration of recreation. Two typical systems were described at the beginning of this chapter. In the opinion of the experts there should be two distinct though cooperating administrative systems: the School Board assuming responsibility for the play and recreational activities of the school children, and a Recreation Department (a combination of the formerly separate park and playground and recreation departments) providing facilities and supervision for the remainder of the community. Until the schools are able to do their full share they should be assisted by the recreation department, according to Nash, who suggests that the latter

[22] Darling, Frank W., "Playland—How it Pays," *Survey,* 62: 396-99, 1929.

department might furnish leadership and heavy equipment in so far as these are required by the schools. Legal provision would have to be made for such cooperation, but the schools should retain full control over the play activities of the child. The following diagram indicates the nature of the inter-relation:

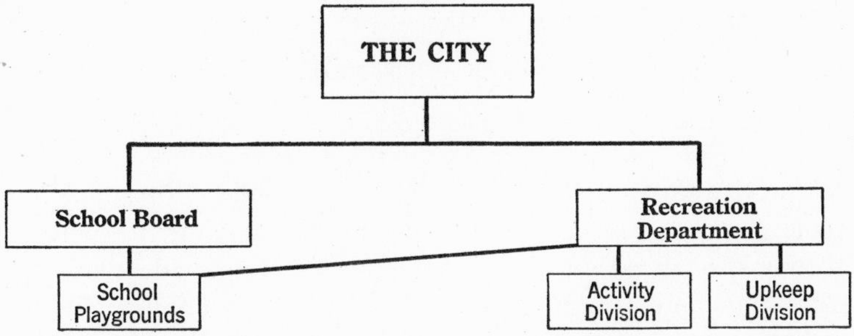


*Approved form of organization, showing cooperation between the Recreation Department and the School Board until the latter is able to provide independently for the needs of the children of school age.*

Preliminary to inaugurating a recreational system a city should preferably undertake a survey of the needs and existing resources. The Cleveland Recreation Survey in 1917 was described in Chapter XVI. In 1922 Buffalo made a study of its recreational facilities and needs which was published jointly by the Department of Parks and Public Buildings, the City Planning Committee of the Council, and the Buffalo City Planning Association, Incorporated. The most extensive study is that now being made of New York and its environs, a part of which has already been published under the title of *Public Recreation: A Study of Parks, Playgrounds and Other Outdoor Recreation Facilities.*[23] The services of the Playground and Recreation Association of America are available for community surveys.

In such a study of community facilities and resources attention must be paid to the important question of the relative rôles to be played in the system as finally set up, by public and private agencies. A large number of private organizations were discovered in Buffalo as shown in the following table:

[23] New York: *Regional Plan of New York and Its Environs,* 1928.

PRIVATE RECREATIONAL AGENCIES IN BUFFALO, 1924–25 [24]

| | |
|---|---|
| Churches with recreational facilities | 114 |
| Organizations promoting sport and recreation | 65 |
| Masonic lodges | 44 |
| Clubs for adults | 34 |
| Dramatic clubs and organizations | 23 |
| Choral clubs | 16 |
| Settlements and neighborhood organizations | 10 |
| City-wide organizations for young people | 9 |
| Total private organizations | 315 |

The city should probably assume responsibility for supplying generally recognized recreational needs, leaving to private groups specialized and localized activities. To be adequate, the recreation and play program of any large community should include provision for racial groups, especially the Negro, industrial districts, and any other special group or need that may demand attention. Rural recreational organization will normally be in the hands of the county government.

The problem of commercialized recreation in any community is a serious one. The extent of this form of recreation is enormous. New York, for example, has 208 theaters and 580 movies, with a total of 858,973 seats. Taking the leading cities as a whole it has been found that they possess sufficient theaters and movies to seat one out of every nine of their total population. Dance halls in New York earned $8,000,000 in 1920. The effect of the conflict between community and commercial recreation is well stated by Ethel Gardner, after a recent study of dance halls for the Children's Bureau. She says:

> The provision of community recreation and training in recreational activities will not eliminate the commercial dance halls, but they should assist in greatly modifying the character of the commercial amusements as well as developing the play interests of the whole population, providing types of amusement not commercially profitable, and developing latent leadership in the provision of a wholesome neighborhood social life.[25]

[24] Anderson, Nels, and Lindeman, E. C., *Urban Sociology,* p. 173. Alfred A. Knopf, 1928. Adapted.

[25] *Public Dance Halls:* Their Regulation and Place in the Recreation of Adolescents, Children's Bureau Pub. No. 189, 1929, 52.

The good results of a wholesome and varied play and recreation program on the city are seen in improved health, decreased number of accidents, heightened morale, civic consciousness and loyalty, increase in value of land, the incoming of desirable citizens and industries, the socialization of aliens, the integration of the community, the stabilization of the family, and the decrease in juvenile delinquency. While there is some doubt that the organization of boys' clubs in a lawless neighborhood will decrease delinquency, it is undeniably true that the provision of adequate recreation for all ages tends to do so. Even if play does not reform it does result in keeping non-delinquent children good.[26]

**Recreation as a Form of Social Work.** The demand for trained recreation leaders is steadily increasing and the field is an attractive one for both men and women interested in the profession of social work. Positions include those of playground and recreation director, Boy or Girl Scout executive, secretary of the Boys' Department of the Y.M.C.A. or of the Girls' Department of the Y.W.C.A., boys' club director, settlement worker, community center director, specialized work as that of the community dramatic coach or music director. The Playground and Recreation Association has a little brochure entitled "What Recreation Executives Do," [27] listing forty-nine functions from that of securing the largest possible use of all regular playgrounds and athletic fields to arranging a special welcome for new citizens! Adequate training involves an undergraduate course in college followed by a specialized course at one of the three or four good professional schools Among these are the former Recreation Training School of Chicago, absorbed by Northwestern University in 1927, and the National Recreation School, maintained by the Playground and Recreation Association of America.

Recreation as a type of group social work is intimately related to the other phases of the profession, particularly to case work, and should accomplish more than simply to consume

[26] For an excellent case illustrating the demoralizing effects of the lack of proper recreational facilities on the young, see Steiner, J. F., *The American Community in Action*, 1928, pp. 226-246, "Stuart-Harmon."

[27] Playground and Recreation Association of America, 315 Fourth Avenue, New York, Pamphlet No. 212.

leisure time. Recreation is frequently employed as a method of treatment in individual cases, and proper "recreational placement" requires a careful analysis of the needs and abilities of the child or adult, and a study of his play history. Hence the recreation leader should know something of case work, and the case-worker, on the other hand, should at least be familiar with the play facilities of the local community. The recreation leader also has many administrative problems, particularly those of promotion and publicity, which are discussed in the following chapter.

# CHAPTER XXX

## PROMOTION AND PUBLICITY

This is the first of three chapters dealing with various aspects of the organization and administration of social work, the fourth type of social work as described in Chapter XXXIII. It deals with the general techniques of publicity and promotion. The two following chapters discuss the problems of coordination and financing. Details of the administration of separate agencies have been included in the description of each important field of social work already given. Deliberate promotional and publicity methods have developed largely since Warner's day when the consolidation of relief societies, the establishment of settlements, and attempts to secure housing and prison reform legislation, represented practically the only cases of promotion. One of the most interesting fields for promotion today, intermediate between national movements and the programs of local societies, is to be found in the activities of the various state conferences of social work. Of these, the Wisconsin Conference stands out for the variety and efficiency of its undertakings. The following summary of the "Wisconsin Better Cities Contest," staged in 1924 and 1925, is a good illustration of the type of promotion carried on in this state.

### THE WISCONSIN BETTER CITIES CONTEST [1]

In 1924 the suggestion of a better cities contest was made and the State Conference of Social Work assumed responsibility for the project. Eight organizations cooperated with the Conference, including the university and a number of state departments. The feeling of the board of directors of the Conference relative to the Contest was expressed in the introductory announcement.

[1] Account based upon publications of the Wisconsin State Conference of Social Work and communications from the Secretary, Mr. Aubrey W. Williams.

For a critical evaluation of the Contest, see Boettiger, L. A., "The Wisconsin Better Cities Contest," *Social Forces,* 5: 436-46, 1927.

"It is too frequently the custom to measure a city's worth and progressiveness by its bank deposits, the volume of business done, the number of industries which it has, and the general material prosperity, with but a minor emphasis upon those things which are not of a material nature. It is with a view to emphasizing these human values and to bringing them into relief that the Wisconsin Conference of Social Work has organized and is conducting the Wisconsin Better Cities Contest. Such a contest becomes an inventory time for the cities interested. It affords an opportunity for self-examination and paves the way for a constructive program of improvement. The object of the contest is to determine the one best place in the state in which to rear a child." The primary purpose of the Contest, as stated in the foreword of the handbook sent to the competing cities, was "To stimulate interest and pride in those aspects of city life affecting child welfare, family life, and community well-being, and to promote activity among the municipalities of the State in improving conditions of morals, health, recreation, education and various other projects related to the human side of community life . . . and in addition to stimulating interest in community well-being, it is hoped that the standards of education, health and physical development, industry, public library, public administration, recreation, religion, social welfare, town planning and zoning and city beautiful, and town and country relations, will provide a basis for making an inventory of the community and will make possible the measuring of the effectiveness of institutions and the effect upon citizens of educational, religious, recreation forces, and it is hoped that with this knowledge gained from such a study a permanent basis of planning and growth will be provided."

The first step was to devise standards and a method of scoring for the ten general fields to be considered. These fields were education, health, industry, social welfare, religion, library, town and country relations, city planning, municipal government and recreation. With this purpose in mind ten committees were appointed, one for each of the general divisions. These committees began their work in 1923, and finally devised standards in the various fields. Cities were grouped into two classes: those with a population from 3,000 to 10,000 and those from 11,000 to 50,000. Somewhat different standards were set up for each class. It was discovered later that this rough division on the basis of size involved limits that were too wide, and that the cities should have been grouped more carefully.

Considerable promotion and publicity were recognized as necessary in order to interest the cities of the state, for this was the first time that such a state-wide better cities campaign on a scientific basis had ever been staged. There was a natural lack of confidence on the part of the cities in the project and an understandable reticence about revealing facts concerning the community. With some misgivings, but in recognition of basic human impulses, it was determined to organize the movement in the form of a contest. Accordingly two prizes were offered: $1,000 for the city between 11,000 and 50,000 population judged to be the best place in which to raise a child, and $500 for the town with a population between 3,000 and 10,000 judged to be the best in its class. Sixteen cities entered the contest and fourteen completed it, including Appleton, Ashland, Chippewa Falls, Eau Claire, Fond du Lac, Janesville, Kenosha, Ladysmith, Oshkosh, Sheboygan, Sparta, Waukesha, Waupun and Wausau.

In each of the communities entering the contest a local city-wide Better Cities Committee was organized and also ten joint inventory committees, one for each of the ten fields. The next step was that of collecting the multitude of facts required. Eventually some 2,000 citizens in the various localities were enlisted in this work. The office of the State Conference furnished supervision, encouragement and aid of various kinds to all the committees involved. Nine national authorities were secured to act as judges and a committee made up of clergymen, educators and social workers undertook to pass on the degree of development in the field of religion. After twelve months of work the towns and cities forwarded their committees' findings to the office of the Conference. These reports were then turned over to the judges, who selected five cities in the larger group and three in the smaller. A personal visit was then made by the judges to the eight cities thus selected and the winner determined. The award was made on the night of October 28, 1925, with every city in the contest represented. Kenosha was rated first by a wide margin; Oshkosh ranked second, and Appleton, third. Of the cities under 10,000 population, first place was awarded to Chippewa Falls and second place to Ladysmith.

Follow-up work was carried on by the Director of the State Conference, and the cities which had been involved cooperated in their attempts to remedy some of the community short-comings indicated by the contest. One of the values of the contest was that of acquainting the citizen with his community. In the second place, the contest standards gave the average citizen some idea of what is generally held to be desirable in community life, and discouraged exclusive attention to any one or two of the ten general fields of appraisal and possible improvement. A number of objections to the contest have been pointed out by critics and their importance freely admitted by the State Conference committee. They recognize, for instance, the danger of trying to standardize community development, the fallacy of appraisal of resources and activities by laymen, and the crudity of the methods employed in general. Despite these and other pertinent criticisms, however, the Wisconsin Better Cities Contest is on record as an excellent piece of state-wide promotion and publicity in the field of social work.

**Does Social Work Need Publicity?** In the foregoing case considerable publicity and a definite technique of promotion were needed to make the Better Cities Contest successful. The scheme involved an element of competition and an appeal to local pride, newspaper publicity, public addresses, bulletins, meetings and the judgment of nationally known authorities. It was more or less scientifically conceived and educational in its wider significance. The results seem to have been more than transitory. In a bulletin issued by the conference about a year later it was pointed out that every one of the cities concerned had reorganized its efforts for civic improvement along the ten lines covered by the contest and was striving to realize the standards set up as the basis of the competition.

Social work needs publicity today for the same reason that every other activity and profession does—to attain its objectives and to recruit desirable and capable people for its personnel. Social work campaigns demand publicity because the public understanding of aims and methods lags far behind social work practice. Intelligent advertising is necessary not only to secure support but to secure it for the professionally most approved causes and scientifically sound methods from a public that is willing to respond to old appeals but is suspicious of "new-fangled" projects. Intelligent publicity must, therefore, bridge the gap between new ideals and the uninformed benevolence of the public.

There are three main aims of social work publicity. (1) To obtain the necessary financial support. This is placed first since it is the *sine qua non* of social work, but the raising of money should not be considered the primary aim of social work promotion; it is merely instrumental to the program of social work. (2) To effect changes in personal conduct, especially in the field of health and safety. (3) To precipitate social action—inaugurate movements, secure new social legislation or promote the enforcement of old laws. In order to realize these purposes social work publicity must attract attention, hold the interest and eventually bring about action on the part of the individual or the group. Such response should be secured not through an appeal to superficial and temporary emotional attitudes, not by the use of some of the sensational advertising methods employed today by commercial concerns (there is a real danger in social work attempting to employ the methods of the modern "high-powered" salesman), but rather on the basis of accurate and interesting information about the program of social work yielded by scientific study. This means, as we shall see later, an analysis of the processes of social work and of the various legitimate bases of appeal to the public.

Practically all types of social work need to employ deliberate promotional and publicity measures. Thus the family welfare society lays its "problem cases" before the "case committee," explains its technique and elicits the interest and support of the members and, through them, of the community. Human interest stories are given the press by such agencies also, particularly just before the annual "drive." Industries utilize numerous publicity schemes in their accident prevention campaigns. This necessity for "pushing a good thing" is seen also in "clean-up" and other "weeks," better babies and better families campaigns and contests, and similar activities. The community chest movement is perhaps the most outstanding example in the whole field of the use of intensive and expert promotional and advertising methods. Fifty-five million dollars were raised through chest campaigns in 1925. In 1927, 300 cities in the United States had community funds. The programs of such national organizations as The American Federation of Organizations for the Hard of Hearing, The American Foundation for the Blind, The American Social Hygiene Association, The American Society for the Control of Cancer, The National Society for the Prevention of Blindness, and a host of others illustrate the need and use of publicity methods on a country-wide scale.

Chapters XXXI and XXXII will deal with two important aspects of promotion, namely, coordination and financing; this chapter is limited to a consideration of publicity methods and media as essential aids in social work promotion. The point of view is that the methods which social work finds advisable and even necessary to employ today should be scientific, educational and professional, not sentimental or sensational. Some of the means that have been employed in the past will be discussed first; next the attempts to raise the standard of social work advertising will be noted; and finally, the various mediums of publicity and types of promotion programs in use today will be described.

**Publicity and Promotion in the Past.** Self-conscious and deliberate attempts at social work publicity as such hardly antedate the year 1900. The first efforts centered in the survey. In 1905 the *Charities and Commons,* later the *Survey,* made a study of Washington, D. C., the first of its kind ever attempted, and pointed out the evils that existed under the very shadow of the capitol. The staff of this same magazine began a similar but more ambitious investigation of Pittsburgh in 1907. This study was completed in 1908, and marked the beginning of the survey movement. A third survey was made under the same auspices in 1909, of Birmingham, Alabama, as perhaps the most important industrial city of the South. In 1914 the famous Springfield survey was made, under the direction of the Department of Surveys and Exhibits, established by the Russell Sage Foundation in 1912. The survey, although there are many criticisms of it today, and particularly of these earlier examples, does represent a thoroughgoing attempt to get at the facts of community life, and to use these as a basis for publicity and improvement. The various purposes to which the survey may be put in connection with publicity are illustrated by the topics listed in one of the sections of the National Conference of Social Work. In 1924, for example, the question "How Much Use Can or Should Be Made of the Survey Method?" was discussed under the following headings: "For General Education of the Community," "For the Discovery of Needs Not Met," and "For the Revamping of Existing Organizations." [2] The survey still has a place in publicity work today, though its methods have been changed and its importance somewhat diminished.

The great bulk of social work publicity in the local community up to very recently has consisted of sentimental, exaggerated or typical "sob stories." The evil results of such an

[2] *Nat. Conf. Soc. Work,* 1924: 492-504.

emotional appeal are well illustrated by the famous picture of "Wlad of the Beets" which an over-zealous publicist, seeking human interest material, painted in 1923 on behalf of the National Child Labor Committee, which had just published an excellent report of conditions that existed in the sugar beet fields of Michigan.[3] "Wlad" was admittedly a fictitious boy, but "real" in that he was typical (according to the publicist, not the Report) of the numerous children who suffered the loss of fingers or other injuries in topping beets. The appeal was sentimental rather than intelligent.

The following illustrates a somewhat different type of "sob story," one that might have attracted attention, but which, as a mere anecdote, certainly failed to interpret child welfare to the reader. It appeared in a great city daily several years ago.[4]

A pretty young German woman sat on the floor playing with two small children. It was her afternoon "off" and every precious minute of the time was for her two babies in the Life Line Orphans Home.

The two-year-old boy was investigating the mechanism of a new ten-cent toy; the three-year-old girl was licking the inside of a paper sack which had contained the weekly treat of cookies and candy. Mrs. Coe, the matron, paused at the door with a visitor. The young woman stood up and smiled shyly.

"How do you think the babies are looking?" asked the matron.

"Oh, Mrs. Coe," and the shyness was all gone now, "They look wonderful, I think they have grown a pound since Sunday. And here's this week's money. Is it all right?" She handed Mrs. Coe a dollar and three dimes.

"It's all right if you have kept something for yourself."

"Yes, Ma'am, I have. I paid $2.00 on my shoes, paid my board, and put away the dollar like you said to. I spent 40 cents for the children's toys and candy and 15 cents for Pettie."

Mrs. Coe and the visitor passed on down the hall. "She was a war bride," the matron said. "Married an American soldier while our boys were in the Rhine country. He abandoned her after she had been in America about six months. She couldn't go back to Germany; she had no friends in the United States. I really don't know what might have become of her if someone hadn't been able to take care of the babies and give her a chance to go to work."

[3] See Williams, Frances B., *New Republic,* 35: 284-6, Aug. 8th, 1923.

[4] *Kansas City Kansan,* Nov. 9, 1924. Quoted by Queen, S. A., in "Non-statistical Studies of Social Work," *Nat. Conf. Soc. Work,* 1927: 459-466.

Such emotional appeal, as Stillman points out,[5] "is justifiable to the degree that the play on the emotions is not inconsistent with, or is not building barriers in front of, progress in the appreciation by the public of the underlying purpose of social work."

Propaganda, in the undesirable sense of the word, has been freely used, and is another form of social work publicity the use of which should be discontinued.

> Propaganda in social work has been taken over from the commercial world and is based almost entirely on the promoter's and the salesman's appeal. The purpose of propaganda is not to form judgments but to create emotions; not to make clear the reasons for certain kinds of social treatment, but to pass over those reasons into a wholesale acceptance of a method which the general public must receive and endorse as a whole. The right kind of publicity, on the other hand, invites discrimination.[6]

Still another undesirable form of publicity has been used, particularly in connection with local agencies and chest campaigns. This consists of crude tables of figures showing the number of old and new cases, visits made, "contacts" established, tons of coal delivered, and the like. Such an attempt to portray social work is inadequate, misleading and ambiguous. It is a mere enumeration, frequently of unimportant details and activities, and fails to give the public a realistic picture of the nature and extent of the services of the given organization.

The prevalence of such emotional, sensational, propagandistic and inadequate methods of publicity in social work promotion has suggested the need for a scientific study of publicity methods in general by those interested in the professional development of social work. Since 1920 several groups and organizations have beeen working on this problem with the result that considerable interest has been aroused in methods of a higher and more efficient type.

**Development of Professional Standards.** The earliest attempts at more scientific publicity came with the establishment

[5] Stillman, Charles C., *Social Work Publicity: Its Message and Its Method,* New York, Century Co., 1927, p. 60.

[6] Stillman, Charles C., *Social Work Publicity,* New York: Century Co., 1927, p. 60. Quoted from "Publicity Versus Propaganda in Family Work," by John R. Brown, *The Family,* May, 1926.

in 1912 of the Russell Sage Foundation Department of Surveys and Exhibits. In recent years this department, under the leadership of the Routzahns, has become the center of information on social work publicity for the United States. At the 1920 meeting of the National Conference of Social Work, an informal organization of individuals engaged in, or responsible for, publicity in social and public health work, was effected. Mary Swain Routzahn of the Sage Foundation became the secretary of this new "Committee on Publicity Methods in Social Work." The committee meets annually with the National Conference, at which time "publicity clinics" are held. It also issues a news bulletin from the executive offices at 130 East 22nd Street, New York. In 1929 the name of the organization was changed to the "Social Work Publicity Council." A number of other groups and agencies in closely related fields have aided the movement. Among these should be mentioned the "Section on Public Health Education," of the American Public Health Association, the department on "Education and Publicity" in the monthly *American Journal of Public Health,* the publicity bureau of the National Congress of Parents and Teachers, and the publicity work of the National Tuberculosis Association, the American Social Hygiene Association, and the United States Public Health Service.

One of the methods adopted to stimulate interest in this problem has been the publicity contest. In 1926 a contest was held in Richmond, Virginia, in connection with the community fund campaign. For several years the "Committee on Publicity Methods in Social Work" has made awards for publicity of unusual merit, and the prize-winning material has been displayed at the meetings of the National Conference of Social Work. In 1928 the Harmon Foundation, in cooperation with the Social Work Publicity Council, announced two series of prizes. The first consisted of awards, ranging from $50 to $300, for unpublished articles about social work. The purpose was "to encourage writers to prepare saleable articles which will increase the general reader's appreciation of the important part social work plays in the life of America." [7] This contest

[7] Announcement, Harmon Foundation, 140 Nassau St., New York City, 1928-30.

closed September 15, 1929. The second series of $100 awards was offered for "a complete record of a well planned and executed program covering a year's work in publicity carried on by a public or private agency engaged in social or health work." The closing date for this contest is February 1, 1930.

As a result of this increased interest in publicity and promotion on the part of various professional bodies there has gradually grown up a more scientific conception of the methods involved. Social workers have come to see (1) that programs of promotion and publicity must be based upon facts that truly represent the processes of their profession, and that such facts must be secured in scientific ways, and (2) that skill and a definite technique must be acquired in successfully presenting these facts to the public. One of the first pieces of genuine statistical work in this field was the American Association for Community Organization's *Study of the Volume and Cost of Social Work.* Healy and Bronner's study of 4,000 delinquents in Chicago and Boston is another illustration of a scientific attempt to get at the facts relative to the causes and treatment of crime.[8] In an interesting paper read at a recent meeting of the National Conference of Social Work, Miss Deardorff [9] pointed out the numerous research organizations and institutes that are supplying scientific information about social work today and urged that programs and publicity be based upon such factual material. Needless to say, intensive individual case studies are equally as important in getting at the actual problems and processes involved as quantitative and statistical investigations.

From the standpoint of presentation to the public much has been learned from the psychology of propaganda and advertising as worked out in other fields. Much more may still be learned if the danger of wholesale and indiscriminate borrowing is avoided. For example, a careful study must be made in any publicity campaign of the attitudes to which an appeal may be made. Among these attitudes, sympathy and pity, the desire for divine approval, the wish to satisfy the expectations

[8] Healy, W., and Bronner, A., *Delinquents and Criminals,* New York: Macmillan, 1926.

[9] Deardorff, Neva R., "Fact Finding and Research as a Basis of Program Making in Social Work," *Nat. Conf. Soc. Work,* 1928: 415-424.

of one's friends, actual interest in the activity itself, loyalty, the pleasure of doing good, and the like are particularly important in social work publicity. But other group forces, tradition, habit, prejudice, imitation, social pressure, collective ideas, and sentiments must be taken into account if the program is to be based upon an intelligent analysis of social work services instead of a general appeal to do the generous and expected thing. As was pointed out several years ago at the National Conference of Social Work, there are three kinds of skills involved in preparing social work publicity.[10] These are: (1) "Accuracy in making and recording observations of problem situations and social work processes"; (2) "ingenuity in classifying situations and processes"; and (3) "facility in giving the public vivid pictures (in words, tables, or photographs) based on accurate and typical data." Both statistical and non-statistical data should be employed. To quote again from the same paper: "People want to know that what they are getting is really a sample and not an exception (essentially a statistical problem), but they also want the sample presented in such shape that they can tell what it really is and compare it with other samples. This requires an accurate and objective statement . . . which can be offered only if one has first made a painstaking analysis, accurate in detail, and objective in point of view." Whether the publicity material presented be statistical or case material, or both, the three skills enumerated above are involved. "Only when they are developed will it be possible to educate the public instead of merely selling social work."

But something more is needed than accurate, interesting, and typical data. The method of presentation must be adapted to the particular audience, attention must be attracted and held, and good will and the desired response obtained. A discussion of the details of a technique for accomplishing these ends would exceed the scope of this chapter. For an excellent presentation the reader is referred to the recent book on the subject by the Routzahns.[11] The sort of publicity for social work here described has come to be termed "educational." Two definitions

[10] Queen, S. A., "Non-statistical Studies of Social Work," *Nat. Conf. Soc. Work*, 1927: 459-466.

[11] Routzahn, Mary Swain, and Evart G., *Publicity for Social Work*, New York: Russell Sage Foundation, 1928.

of educational publicity are given below in order to make clear the position of representative leaders in the field of social work. According to Kelso:

> Educational publicity as applied to social work is the interpretation to the general public of social problems and their remedies, both those in use, and others proposed, and is for the purpose of developing sound public opinion based upon knowledge of the facts of social ills and the reasoning of attempted and possible remedies, which understanding and opinion may form a sanction and a moral support for professional social work and may guarantee also a more stable financial backing for the social work program.[12]

As defined by Stillman, educational publicity is:

> Sustained effort by all appropriate means, to lead the entire public, or any part of it, to register progress in intellectual appreciation of the facts or underlying philosophy of any sound movement, thus affording a background of understanding which may be depended upon for continuous moral and financial support.[13]

The term "appropriate means" in this definition raises a question of professional ethics. Just what are the appropriate and honest means that social work may use to indicate to the public the value of its services? A recent writer discusses the three main ways that have been employed.[14] (1) The results and value of social work may be stated in terms of costs. Despite the lack of sufficient scientific studies, it is true in general that the cost of social work has not risen as fast nor as high as the average income. This fact may be used as a plea for financial support. (2) Statistics of problems and services may be given. Unfortunately most agency reports are unsatisfactory for this purpose, as noted above. (3) Or, the results accomplished may be given to the public in terms of an expert evaluation. Not being able to "make heads or tails" out of the average statistical report, the ordinary citizen would be satisfied, and legitimately so, with a simple statement, in terms of the per-

[12] Kelso, Robert W., "The Need of Educational Publicity in Social Work," *Nat. Conf. Soc. Work,* 1926: 637-641.

[13] Stillman, Charles C., *Social Work Publicity,* New York: Century Co., 1927, p. 12.

[14] White, R. Clyde, "Integrity in Social Work Publicity: A Platform of Facts and a Platform of Ethics." *Nat. Conf. Soc. Work,* 1928: 596-608.

centage of successes and failures, made by a reliable specialist on the basis of a careful evaluation of the reports of the social work organization. Integrity in publicity demands that the public be given as adequate, typical, and understandable report of the services rendered by social work as it is possible to supply.

**Publicity Mediums.** The newspaper is ranked as the most important avenue of public information despite the fact that, according to several studies, the average man spends only about fifteen minutes per day reading morning and afternoon papers. A considerable amount of social work news gets into the papers, especially in connection with chest campaigns. In 1926 a special committee of the American Association for Community Organization measured the amount of newspaper publicity in eight community chest cities, having a combined population of over 3,500,000. They took the calendar year of 1925, and found a total of 92,555 inches, divided as follows:[15]

| | | | |
|---|---|---|---|
| Straight news | 44,815 | inches | 48% |
| Community chest publicity | 31,253 | " | 34% |
| Educational publicity | 14,578 | " | 16% |
| Editorial comment | 1,909 | " | 2% |

Getting into print is not, however, sufficient. Items of social work importance compete for the reader's attention with far more interesting news in most cases. Hence the necessity for securing a better position in the make-up for social work publicity items, more attractive headlines, and a style that will hold the reader's interest. The Routzahns point out three requisites of successful newspaper publicity.[16] These are (1) "an understanding of what editors are likely to want and how they like to have it prepared"; (2) "the ability to find in the field from which the information is drawn material which meets their requirements"; (3) "a familiarity with the methods of getting news articles into print." Indirect methods are best. Supplying items of real news value, when asked to do so, is far more effective than inducing the editor on the grounds of personal acquaintance or civic duty to print articles of dubious news value.

[15] Stillman, Charles C., *op. cit.,* 218. [16] *Op. cit.,* 66-67.

Printed matter—leaflets, circulars, pamphlets and the like, is perhaps next in importance as a medium of publicity. An enormous quantity of such material is issued by the national and state organizations. The American Social Hygiene Association, for example, reports that in one ten-year period it distributed 2,000,000 copies of its bulletins and pamphlets. The American Society for the Control of Cancer in a single "Cancer Week" estimated that some 6,000,000 pieces of literature were distributed throughout the country. State and large local organizations distribute in the aggregate far more even than do the national agencies. Most of this "literature" is naturally of an inferior quality, but the recognition of a few simple principles would do much to improve its effectiveness. The Routzahns have collected samples from a multitude of sources, and on the basis of a study of these have arrived at certain conclusions relative to the physical make-up, decoration and illustration, copy, and methods of distribution that should be of great value to anyone charged with the responsibility of publicity.[17]

The channels of publicity are almost countless. Whatever people will read, listen to, look at, or attend to may serve as a medium of publicity for social work. Among the media that have been used are the radio, the movies, talks and addresses, letters, house organs (for example, the Detroit Community Fund News), statements and appeals, posters, graphs, exhibits and window displays, drama, contests, paid advertisements, billboards and stunts of various kinds. Even the homely annual report may be a potent agent of publicity if conceived and executed with some imagination as to its effect upon an audience.

**Publicity Programs and Promotion Campaigns.** Haphazard and spasmodic efforts are not sufficient. Publicity is an integral part of social work and should be planned as such. Although the advertising of special projects and the promotion of campaigns are necessary and important they should be subordinated to a carefully worked out year-round publicity schedule. In such a publicity program the objectives, immediate and remote, should be clearly defined, the nature of the information to be used, its timeliness and soundness consid-

[17] *Op. cit.,* Chaps. VIII, IX, X, XI, XII.

ered, the particular audience to be reached "sized up," the types and combinations of publicity methods to be employed thoughtfully worked out, and the times for the release of the various elements of the program carefully determined. Finally, results obtained should be checked as far as possible and plans modified accordingly.

The programs of the various national associations and societies contain much of interest to the student of publicity methods. For example, the movement for the prevention of blindness has a long history of promotion. It developed out of the work of a group of people in New York State interested in lessening or preventing the damage from infections of the eyes of newborn babies. The earliest activities of this group date back to 1908. In 1915 the National Committee for the Prevention of Blindness was formed which later became the National Society. Some 400 agencies are now cooperating with the Society. It has a ten-point program of publicity.[18] (1) Preparing bulletins of information at nominal cost. (2) Making available the latest authentic discoveries. (3) Collecting for general use a library of literature, photographs, slides and the like. (4) Arranging courses of lectures. (5) Arranging for research. (6) Assisting in the formation of societies and associations for the prevention of blindness. (7) Cooperating with medical and educational authorities. (8) Cooperating with illuminating and safety engineers. (9) Promoting legislation. (10) Publishing news of the movement.

Social work promotion has reached its most intensive development in the field of community chest campaigns. Certain phases of this topic will be discussed in Chapter XXXII, so that a brief consideration here will suffice. According to Harry P. Wareheim, Manager of the Community Chest in Rochester in 1922,[19] there are four main factors in the conduct of a successful campaign. These are (1) "the selection of competent and aggressive leadership"; (2) "careful planning and developing of an adequate soliciting organization"; (3) "systematic and careful preparation of prospect cards"; and (4) "intelligent and adequate publicity." Twelve campaign divisions

[18] From the literature of the Society, 370 Seventh Ave., New York City.
[19] "The Campaign," *Nat. Conf. Soc. Work,* 1922: 410-415.

were organized in Rochester, which is a city of approximately 300,000 population. Eight of these divisions were soliciting and four non-soliciting. The latter included the speakers', publicity, complaint, and auditing divisions. The actual soliciting was done over a period of seven days, but months of preparation were required. The Rochester plan calls for year-round publicity with a special campaign just before the drive.

Four years later at the National Conference of Social Work, Ellwood Street also insisted upon a year-round program of publicity for the community fund.[20] He advocated an "internal organization," consisting of a publicity secretary, assisted by a good stenographer and record keeper, and an "external organization" involving a committee representing the constituent agencies, an annual meeting of the users of publicity (the newspaper editors and others), and an advisory committee of experts from the local advertisers' club. As a result of such organized publicity he found that in St. Louis from three to five times as much space in the newspapers was secured as had been without such an organization, and that twice as many agencies received publicity.

Many changes have taken place in the technique of community chest campaigns in the last few years. The introduction of mechanical bookkeeping devices, for example, has greatly increased the efficiency of chest offices and made it possible to handle a great amount of work with a relatively small force. The general conclusion of observers seems to be that the chest idea is an essentially sound one, but that publicity should be really educational and should extend throughout the year, and that the community fund should be continuously directed by a professional social worker, with perhaps some expert outside assistance during the annual campaign, instead of the campaign being a periodic upheaval, engineered by a high-priced, high-powered specialist from a national publicity and promotion bureau. The mechanics of publicity, financing and promotion should not be permitted to submerge the activities which they exist to support. In the words of Charles C. Stillman, formerly Secretary of the Grand Rapids Welfare Union:

[20] "The Proper Form of Organization for Federation Publicity," *Nat. Conf. Soc. Work,* 1926· 648-655.

"Educational publicity, on behalf of a sound cause, must seek out mediums and methods. But the cause is the thing. The method of social work publicity should be subordinate to its message." [21]

**Publicity and Promotion as a Professional Field.** According to the Routzahns, social work publicity is employed for three main purposes.[22] (1) It is used to influence the behavior of individuals; for example, to bring about an improvement in their health habits. (2) It may be employed to alter social conditions. Thus legislation may be an objective. (3) Finally, it may be used to inform the public about the nature of the work of a case agency, or any other organization that deals with individuals or small groups. This use would tend to build up a friendly feeling toward the agency on the part of clients and make the work of its visitors easier, as well as to secure greater financial and moral support from the community. Publicity, however, should promise no more than the organization is equipped to give.

Such important uses for publicity would seem to demand a large number of trained individuals, but up to very recently there have been few persons or organizations prepared to do either publicity work or promotion except in the field of money raising. In the last few years, however, an increasing number of national, state and large city agencies have employed full-time publicity directors. It is logical to expect, therefore, that in the next decade a considerable demand for persons trained in this work will develop. Positions of this sort would include that of publicity director for national societies and associations, state and federal departments and bureaus, large city agencies, and for community chests and welfare unions. Many community fund organizations require a special publicity secretary in addition to the campaign director, who has a combined publicity and promotion job.

At the present time there are no established sources of supply for organizations wishing publicity and promotion experts except the commercial chest campaign organizations. There are no training schools. An increasing number of conferences, institutes, "clinics," and courses are being organized and undoubt-

[21] *Op. cit.,* 207.

[22] *Op. cit.,* 369 ff.

edly it will not be long before this educational demand will be adequately met. Already Columbia University is giving an extension course on "Methods of Health Publicity"; the Routzahns are also offering a course in the New York School of Social Work on "Social Work Publicity"; and "publicity methods and the mobilization of community resources . . . both from the standpoint of intensive campaigns and all year round publicity" constitute a phase of a course on "Public Relations" given at the Fordham School of Social Service, in New York City. Other similar courses might be mentioned.

Of the positions in this general field, that of community chest campaign director is perhaps the most highly developed. In the last few years it has reached the status of a profession. A. C. Marts, in a recent number of the *Survey,* points out that this occupation developed along with the "rise of the modern short-term campaign method for financing philanthropy." He urges that it be kept professional and not commercial. He offers seven suggestions for a code of ethics aimed at this objective.[23]

1. The philanthropic campaign should be directed on a salary or fee basis; never on a percentage basis.
2. The high pressure type of director should be kept out of this profession.
3. A campaign corporation should not assign a man to direct a campaign unless he is fully experienced and seasoned.
4. A campaign should not be directed for an organization which is not thoroughly worthy of the money it seeks.
5. Charges and costs should be kept low.
6. A thoroughly experienced campaign director can generally tell, after a brief study, what the probable results of the campaign will be. He should give his professional opinion candidly to his prospective client.
7. The "outside" campaign director should be brought in only—as a general rule—to direct capital fund campaigns.

[23] "A Campaign Director Looks at His Profession," *Survey,* 61:818-19, March 15, 1929.

# CHAPTER XXXI

## COORDINATION AND SUPERVISION

In the slum section of one of our large eastern cities lives an immigrant family. The husband was taken ill about a year ago and has been practically bedridden ever since. The mother is illiterate, a bad housekeeper and entirely ignorant of American customs. Anna, the oldest child, a girl of sixteen, had become troublesome, largely because of the mother's lack of understanding and the poor home environment. George, a boy of twelve, had played truant repeatedly. Rose, seven years old, is bright for her age, but gives evidence of abnormal cruelty in her behavior to playmates and to dumb animals. There are two younger children, a girl of three and a baby of nine months. The family is entirely dependent.

There is a wealth of facilities in the community, and the problems of this family are apparently being handled well. Assistance is furnished by the Relief Society, and a case worker from that organization calls at least once in two weeks. The Home Economics Association sends a housekeeper at frequent intervals to instruct the mother in the proper management of her household. A neighborhood worker from the local settlement visits with more or less regularity to maintain a personal contact for that organization. A nurse from the Visiting Nurses' Association calls once a week to care for the man; another nurse from the Infant Welfare Station visits to help the mother carry out the instructions of the pediatrist. The Big Sisters Association became interested in the older girl, and assigned a worker. Similarly, to cope with the boy's delinquent tendencies, a big brother was appointed by the Big Brothers Association. The unusual behavior of Rose brought her to the attention of the Psychiatric Clinic, and a psychiatric worker was detailed to this problem. . . . Eight workers in all are visiting the home and dividing up the problem.[1]

Obviously with so many social workers and nurses attempting to serve one family the opportunities for misunderstanding, friction, and working at cross-purposes are very great. Even if each worker is aware of what the others are doing and all are proceeding in accordance with a common plan, the clients

[1] Kaplan, Hyman, in *Survey,* 51 : 681.

may be confused. But if the various specialists are not in touch with one another, the result is likely to be nothing short of chaos. This is the problem of coordination as viewed by case worker and client. Let us see how it appears from the standpoint of the community.

Sioux Falls, South Dakota, has a population of approximately 25,000. The city has no great wealth, but a number of families are well-to-do. There is an active Chamber of Commerce, and an unusually large number of intelligent socially-minded men and women who are taking an active interest in the social work of the community.

Previous to the War there was little contact with outside organizations, but in 1917 national agencies began to find their way into this little city.

1917— 1. An American Red Cross Chapter was organized and Home Service work for disabled, ex-service men still continues.

2. The Salvation Army established a headquarters and organized family welfare and religious work.

1919— 3. The Y. M. C. A. began a campaign for the erection of a $450,000 building. Thus far, work has been limited chiefly to younger boys.

4. The American Association for Organizing Family Social Work, at the request of the Chamber of Commerce, made a survey of the community and established a family welfare society, which maintains an executive secretary, social worker, and nurse.

5. The National Association for the Advancement of Colored People organized a branch.

6. The Child Welfare League of America admitted the South Dakota Children's Home Society (headquarters in Sioux Falls) to membership.

1921— 7. The Y. W. C. A. established a local unit and organized educational and recreational activities.

8. The National Council of Catholic Women appointed a Sioux Falls representative to organize a unit in this territory.

9. The National Congress of Mothers and Parent-Teacher Associations received one of the local Parent-Teacher Associations in an affiliated membership.

1922—10. The National Tuberculosis Association sent a representative to Sioux Falls to assist the State Association in uniting in one League the four groups in this county which had previously been selling Christmas seals and undertaking separate activities.

11. The American Society for the Control of Cancer organized a committee of physicians to secure publicity on the prevention of cancer.
12. The National Committee on Visiting Teachers financed a visiting teacher to work in Sioux Falls.

Thus in five years ten local units of national organizations were formed and two other national affiliations were established. With one exception, these national agencies made their respective approaches to Sioux Falls independently of each other and the city responded. But in 1922 a county nurse who had been employed for two years was released for lack of funds. There was a strong sentiment in favor of discontinuing the work of the County Demonstration Agent. The Y. M. C. A. had to float a bond issue to complete its building and there was nothing left for equipment. The Y. W. C. A. found itself in competition with the Women's Alliance which had for twelve years maintained a boarding home for girls and organized classes and recreational groups. The budget of the health department was cut from $12,000 to $8,000. Clearly all was not well with Sioux Falls.[2]

There are thus a number of conditions which indicate a serious need for the coordination of social work efforts. (1) There is often failure to develop cooperation needed in specific tasks. (2) This easily leads to working at cross-purposes. (3) There is much overlapping—several agencies doing the same kind of work in the same city, the same neighborhood, and even the same family. (4) But still more serious is the "overlooking" of unmet needs due to lack of perspective. (5) Under such circumstances it is easy for all sorts of irresponsible folk to initiate enterprises which meet no real need, or have no adequate budget, or exploit their patrons. (6) Even well intentioned persons fail to learn from the mistakes and achievements of others simply because they are cut off from professional contacts.

**Development of Coordination.** One of the simplest mechanisms for promoting coordination is the conference. Starting in 1874 the National Conference of Charities and Correction (now National Conference of Social Work) has played an important part in bringing together social workers and interested citizens to discuss their problems, their methods, and their

[2] Lee, Porter R., Pettit, Walter W., and Hoey, Jane M., *Report of a Study of the Interrelation of the Work of National Social Agencies in Fourteen American Communities.* Adapted from pp. 95-98.

philosophies. It has unquestionably done much to break down the barriers between workers in different fields and to overcome provincialism. But it was early recognized that many persons could not afford to attend national meetings and that many more would not take the trouble. Hence state conferences have been organized in most parts of the country. Some of them merely bring together a handful of the faithful once a year; others maintain a year-round service of information and advice besides assembling hundreds of delegates to hear stimulating addresses and confer with national leaders. Other organizations whose major function is the holding of an annual meeting are the American Prison Association, International Association of Policewomen, Intercity Conference on Illegitimacy, National Children's Home and Welfare Association, American Country Life Association, National Housing Conference, National Conference of Catholic Charities, National Conference of Jewish Social Service, National Federation of Settlements. Corresponding to some of these are state and local conferences which bring together limited numbers of workers in special fields.

Another type of correlation is represented by the charity organization movement.[3] This was one of the earliest efforts to unite separate agencies in cooperative service to their clients. While the charity organization societies never succeeded in combining many of the little relief and service agencies, they did make them aware of each other's existence and established contacts which have led to a slowly increasing amount of teamwork. Moreover, they invented two very useful pieces of social machinery, the district conference and the social service exchange.[4] Closely akin to the Charity Organization Society in spirit and organization is the joint application bureau, such as may be found in Cleveland, Chicago, and other cities. This type of agency has been especially useful in promoting an intelligent division of labor among children's institutions. Another device for coordinating the work of case working agencies is the Transportation Agreement which has been signed by some 800 local organizations.[5]

[3] See Chaps. I, II, XV, and XIX.
[4] See Chap. XIX.
[5] See Chap. XIX.

Occasionally two or more agencies recognize the overlapping of their work and enter into a definite agreement as to division of labor and exchange of services. Such a policy was adopted by the Family Welfare Association and the Juvenile Protective Association of Milwaukee in 1925.

It is recognized that the Juvenile Protective Association and Family Welfare Association are both essentially case working agencies. . . . In general the Family Welfare Association cares for families in their own homes. . . . New applications to place children in boarding homes will be handled by the Family Welfare Association when there appears to be a possibility that a family home may be maintained or re-established. This will include cases in which parents are living together; parents are separated but not divorced; father is dead and mother living; parents are divorced and mother has custody of children. New applications will be handled by the Juvenile Protective Association when there seems no possibility of maintaining or re-establishing the home; for example, when the mother is dead or institutionalized, or when the custody of the children has been granted to the father in divorce court.[6]

Another type of coordination is seen in the federations of special groups of local agencies. Sometimes these are the societies and institutions maintained by a religious denomination. Thus the Catholic Charities of the Archdiocese of New York was established in 1920 "for the purpose of unifying the aims, improving the quality of service rendered by the existing agencies and extending this service to meet existing and new needs." Sometimes these federations unite agencies doing a particular kind of work. A committee of New York social workers reported 30 such federations in their city in 1924.[7] These included the Association of Day Nurseries, Associated Out-Patient Clinics, Child Welfare Federation, Council on Immigrant Education, and United Neighborhood Houses. The federations based on locality rather than on function included the Chelsea Neighborhood Association, East Harlem Health Center, Lower East Side Association, and Yorkville Community Association. One of the most interesting of this last group is the East Harlem Health Center which was established

[6] Clow, Lucia, and Halverson, Jeanette, in *Family,* 7: 242.

[7] *Better Times,* May 12, 1924, p. 24. Four of these federations were denominational and seven were based on locality.

in 1921 by the New York County Chapter of the American Red Cross in cooperation with the City Health Department and 19 other organizations. To coordinate the work of the various agencies and integrate it with that of schools, churches, and other established institutions a council was created consisting of 15 representatives from the cooperating agencies, 15 from the district, and 15 from the Red Cross.[8]

A variation of this general type of coordination is the "Iowa plan" for combining public and private case working agencies in rural counties. This scheme involves the creation of a central organization frequently known as the County Social Service League, with a board of directors including the county supervisors, representatives of the county medical society, board of education, farm bureau, and chamber of commerce, and a group of eight or ten contributors. The board employs a social case worker who becomes secretary of the league and overseer of the poor. Funds are raised partly from taxes and partly from private sources. The plan is purely voluntary, but it has been continued for over fifteen years in some counties.

Occasionally we find complete amalgamation in which several previously independent agencies merge into one large and comprehensive organization. This happened in Houston when the old family welfare society, visiting nurses' association, settlements and day nurseries were united in the Social Service Bureau. Another example of amalgamation is the Kansas City Health Conservation Association which combines the Tuberculosis Society, Consumers' League, Social Hygiene Society, Mental Hygiene Society, Dental Hygiene, Cancer Control, and Heart Committees.

A fifth type of coordination is represented by national agencies with local branches or affiliated societies. These are of two general classes: (1) those which are organized from the top down, like the Red Cross, Salvation Army, and Y. M. C. A., and (2) those which are really national federations of local agencies, like the American Association for Organizing Family Social Work, Child Welfare League of America, National Desertion Bureau, National Urban League, and Association of Community Chests and Councils. The American Red Cross,

[8] Bowman, Leroy E., in *Social Forces,* 4: 339-345.

based on European models, was first organized nationally and chartered by Congress. Not until the World War did it establish local chapters in any considerable number. In 1917 fourteen geographical divisions were created; and from the headquarters of each division organizers went out to establish county chapters. Since the War the divisions have been abandoned and many of the chapters have ceased to function, but there are still several hundred local branches of the Red Cross carrying on work for ex-service men, public health nursing, and family case work, under instructions sent out from national headquarters. Through handbooks, bulletins, and conferences the work is standardized and unified. Of course, local initiative is not stifled, but on the whole control is centralized.

In contrast with the highly centralized national agencies are a number of associations which have been built "from the bottom up." Control is vested in the local societies which are the members of the national organization. If standards are set, this is done by a more democratic procedure, and enforcement is through education rather than through compulsion. In the last resort each local society makes its own program and sets its own standards, but through the national association it receives information and suggestions which are invaluable guides.

Finally there is a group of national agencies, usually with individual memberships, which hold conferences, make surveys, issue bulletins, and offer advisory service, but have few, if any, local branches. Examples are the National Probation Association, National Child Labor Committee, Playground and Recreation Association of America, National Committee on Visiting Teachers, and National Committee for Mental Hygiene.

**Councils of Social Agencies.** By the time we entered the World War the importance of coordination in social work was pretty generally recognized; but there were real differences of opinion as to how this should be accomplished. An especially sharp controversy was carried on between the advocates of "functional" and of "financial" federations. Both terms were misnomers, but by "functional" federation was meant an overhead organization created by the existing agencies to promote team-work in service to their clients, while the term "financial" federation was applied to two quite different arrangements: one was essentially a council of social agencies with the added function of joint financing, the other was an organization of contributors who wished to escape the burden of repeated calls for money and who sometimes assumed a dictatorial attitude toward the agencies concerned. Today there is a marked tendency for the "functional" and the "financial" types of organization to be combined or at least closely affiliated. Leaving the discussion of financial problems to the next chapter, we may consider here the coordination brought about through councils and federations of various sorts.

A council of social agencies is usually built "from the bottom up." It consists in the main of elected or appointed representatives of various private societies. But in addition certain public officials are usually *ex officio* members of the council and a few outstanding citizens may be chosen to represent the community as a whole. The following excerpts indicate something of the philosophy, functions and methods of such an organization.

There is no big stick philosophy in it. Representatives of agencies, working together, find the true way ahead, and then, having agreed on a program, go back to their individual boards and induce them to approve the program so far as it concerns their particular societies.[9]

Things will be worked out in committees, not apparently but literally. The committees are melting pots of the ideas and experiences of their members. Issues are fought out hotly, plans are devised, and agreement is arrived at as to the best instruments for carrying out their plans. Thus the agencies discover and use their own powers. This kind of council obtains practical results, and avoids the dangers assumed to be inherent in federation. It does not decide, for example, that a hospital or a settlement must be located here or not located there, but it ensures that the subject shall be talked out until it becomes evident that only one answer to the question as to where it shall be located is sound enough to be defended.[10]

A Welfare Council would serve the community and the member social agencies in these ways:

1. As a forum for the discussion and determination of common welfare aims, interests and problems.

[9] McLean, Francis H., *The Central Council of Social Agencies*, p. 26.
[10] Devine, Edward T., in *Survey*, 47: 624.

2. By developing a city welfare plan, assisting member agencies to take their appropriate place in the plan, and by anticipating some of the problems and requirements of the future.
3. By certifying or endorsing to the public the work of responsible, efficient welfare agencies, and by discouraging the establishment or support of irresponsible or needless agencies.
4. As an advisory unit in financial campaigns, budget making and accounting. (If developments justify, the Council might properly establish a department for the central financing of member agencies.)
5. As a publicity and information bureau to inform the public of the needs, problems and achievements of the several fields of welfare effort.
6. By stimulating sound methods on the part of member agencies.
7. By reporting on pending legislative measures.
8. By performing for its constituents other common services, as for example, research and surveys, purchasing of supplies, recruiting of paid and volunteer personnel, and operating a confidential exchange.[11]

The various councils of social agencies have done much to educate the public of their cities concerning social needs and ways of meeting them. They have done this through newspaper stories, special reports, public addresses, and personal contacts. They have headed off ill-advised ventures and stimulated the development of new activities in both public and private agencies. They have brought about the reorganization, combination and abandonment of old agencies. They have raised standards of work and have established channels of intercourse and cooperation which are actually being used.

In addition to the local councils of social agencies there have been a few attempts to work out the same sort of thing on a state-wide basis. The first was the Ohio Council of Social Agencies established in 1919. "The purpose of the council is to enable each of the associating organizations to discuss its program and policies with other agencies of the council, to prevent overlapping and duplication of social work, to enable the associating societies to co-ordinate their state work and work in local communities, and to enable them to act jointly in promoting social work in local communities." [12] The move-

[11] *Better Times,* May 12, 1924, p. 16.
[12] Croxton, Fred C., in *Nat. Conf. Soc. Work,* 1921: 439.

ment spread to Texas, Georgia, Kansas, and other states, and great things were hoped for. But lack of funds and the consequent lack of full-time executives have been responsible for the relative failure of these state councils. In contrast with their brief and disappointing history is the successful working out of the National Social Work Council established in 1923 by a group of organizations such as the American Red Cross, Boy Scouts of America, National Health Council, American Association for Organizing Family Social Work, Playground and Recreation Association of America, and the National Consumers' League.

Similarity of problems and the need for a closer coordination of their work stimulated the executives of twelve leading national social work organizations in 1920 to begin regular monthly meetings for conference. Formal organization of the National Council occurred in 1923, two delegates being chosen from each of sixteen national agencies. (The number has since increased to twenty-two.)

In spirit and method the Council has remained the same throughout the eight years of its history. Its purpose is to help existing organizations better to fulfill their functions. It does not undertake new activities of its own. It has no administrative staff, but seeks rather to accomplish its purpose through the service of board and agency staff members and other volunteers.

It has sought first of all to develop an atmosphere of mutual confidence and understanding among all concerned as a basis for continuing full and free consideration of the work needing to be done, the most appropriate organization for its accomplishment and the most economical plans for its adequate support.

It is endeavoring to face frankly the fundamental questions being raised about the place of national social work organizations in the whole social work field.

It is exploring the general field of relationships in an effort to ascertain where more intensive studies of specific problems may well be made.

It is helping to locate key people whose interest, experience and influence are needed.[13]

A problem which has occupied the attention of the Council for some time is the proper relationship between national and local programs for the coordination of social work, or, more specifically, the relation between national agencies and com-

[13] Mimeographed memorandum dated August, 1928.

munity chests. In its study of this question the Council has held meetings with persons in local communities and with the Association of Community Chests and Councils. Other problems dealt with are: How can national agencies sufficiently understand each other to be able to take their part intelligently, community by community? How can they work together for the common good in a particular community? How can they develop wider public sympathy for their purposes so that while each works on its own special problems it may also help and receive benefit from the work of other members? It is the experience of the Council that the most effective way of working at these questions is what it calls the "Bridgeport plan." This is similar to the case committee of the family welfare society, except that the "case" now is the situation obtaining in a community instead of that in a single family. Representatives of both national and local agencies meet together to discuss community needs which may be served by national agencies.

As an aid to more effective cooperation in field work, advance itineraries for field workers from seven national organizations were being circulated in 1928. Similar itineraries from ten organizations in the health field were also on file. Notices of new surveys and field reports which are connected with these itineraries may constitute the beginning of a central exchange of information about communities. On request the office of the Council has gathered information on special topics such as experience with moving picture films, joint field service between national and state agencies, by-laws of organizations, salary schedules, and the like. One meeting each year is devoted to a consideration of the greatest achievement, the greatest failure, and the greatest present need of each national organization. At the present time (1929) the Council is considering the advisability of a study of local endorsement experience, the development of an advisory service on local survey and community council problems, and a study of the community chest movement over a ten-year period.

**Development of Supervision.** In Chapter XV was traced the history of supervision as carried on by state boards of charity. The theory was that an unpaid board of informed and interested citizens could perform a valuable service by checking up and advising those who were engaged in the actual administration of social agencies. Hence they were first charged with the duty of inspecting and reporting on state institutions for delinquents and for the mentally and physically handicapped. To these were presently added county and municipal institutions. Still later the state boards of charities were made responsible for licensing and regulating certain private agencies, especially orphanages, child-placing societies, and maternity homes. In some states this authority has been effectively used to eliminate useless, inefficient, and fraudulent institutions. But very often lack of appropriations and incompetence of the staff have made such regulation a farce. Since 1900 supervision by state boards has fallen into the background. The boards themselves have either taken on many executive functions or have given way to boards of administration. In part, at least, this has been compensated for by the development of endorsement committees, councils of social agencies, community chests, and national organizations.

Curiously little has been done to control legally the establishment of new social agencies. In most states the granting of a charter is a mere formality. But in Massachusetts the Secretary of the Commonwealth is required to "send a rescript of the application to the Department of Public Welfare, which shall make an investigation of the petitioners, their probable ability to conduct the charter prayed for, the *bona fides* of the claim, and all other matters pertinent to the issue." [14] The Commissioner of Public Welfare must hold a public hearing, but cannot make official recommendations to the Secretary of the Commonwealth. In actual practice, however, the latter has been guided by the findings and judgment of the Department of Public Welfare. This is in marked contrast with the situation in most states where "the running of a peanut stand is sanctioned with as much ceremony and as much, or more, guarantee of public security as the undertaking of an enterprise which goes among the homes of the poor, separating brothers and sisters, breaking up family groups and taking physical control of helpless children." [15]

[14] Kelso, Robert W., *The Science of Public Welfare*, p. 83. [15] *Ibid.*

Between 1900 and the War a number of cities experimented with private supervisory agencies usually known as endorsement committees. The Cleveland committee was created by the Chamber of Commerce, one in San Francisco had representatives both of contributors and of organizations soliciting from the public. In New York the Charity Organization Society established a Bureau of Advice and Information which later became the National Information Bureau. In Kansas City "charities endorsement" was made a function of the Board of Public Welfare. All of these were attempts to protect givers against fraudulent appeals and assure them that the agencies to which they contributed had attained at least a minimum standard of efficiency. They were also efforts to educate the public to withhold their gifts from organizations not on the "white list." For a time these committees seem to have performed a useful service, but since the development of councils of social agencies and community chests most of them have passed out of existence.

**Boards of Public Welfare.** All the time that private agencies have been increasing in number and variety there has been a corresponding development of social work in governmental bureaus, departments, and institutions. For centuries we have had prisons, almshouses, hospitals, and "outdoor relief" administered by public officials. The nineteenth century added children's institutions, parole and probation. The twentieth has given us mothers' pensions, juvenile courts, workmen's compensation, employment bureaus, housing commissions, public playgrounds and social centers, psychiatric clinics, and visiting teachers. Thus have the volume and scope of "public welfare work" expanded. But this growth of tax-supported agencies has presented problems very similar to those involved in the multiplication of private organizations. By the turn of the century the need of coordination was widely recognized and by the end of the War central administrative boards and departments had become quite general. These new agencies are called boards of control or administration, departments of public welfare, or departments of institutions and agencies. They have been created by cities, counties, and states.

The first municipal board of public welfare was established

in Kansas City, Missouri, in 1910. It developed out of the Board of Pardons and Paroles which was made responsible in 1909 for administering the workhouse. The next year it was given "broad powers to devise and execute plans to fulfil the duties of the city toward all the poor, the delinquent, the unemployed, the deserted and unfortunate classes in the community, and to supervise the private agencies which solicited money from the public for these purposes." [16] This new department not only brought together a lot of activities previously carried on by separate officials, but it initiated new types of social work and developed very close cooperation with private agencies. One of its first acts was to move the workhouse to the country and develop a municipal farm. It paid wages to prisoners and their families. It set up an endorsement bureau which issued a "white list" of approved private agencies. It established a public employment bureau, municipal quarry, free legal aid, and remedial loan agency—the last being privately financed but supervised by the Board of Public Welfare. It maintained a social service exchange, department of factory inspection, supervision of commercialized recreation, training course for social workers, and research bureau. Its departments for homeless men and for family welfare work were consolidated with existing private agencies. Everything seemed to go forward smoothly until War time, when the politicians had their innings, and the staff of experienced social workers was displaced by automobile salesmen, mechanics, and milkmen. Since then several changes have occurred, but there continues to be a considerable degree of coordination of social work activities carried on by the city. The cooperation with private agencies is not so close, and at no time, either before or after the War, has there been a satisfactory "tie up" with the county departments.

In 1917 the State of North Carolina launched an interesting experiment in the coordination of social work activities under county governments supervised by a state department. A law enacted in that year required the State Board of Charities and Public Welfare to appoint a local board of three unpaid members for each county, "whose duty shall be to advise with and

[16] Halbert, L. A., in *Nat. Conf. Soc. Work,* 1918: 220-221.

assist the state board in the work in the county . . . and to act in a general advisory capacity to the county and municipal authorities in dealing with questions of dependency and delinquency, distribution of poor funds, and social conditions generally." [17] The law also provided that counties with a population of over 25,000 (32,000 since 1921) must have a superintendent of public welfare appointed by the county board of education and the board of county commissioners. However, the person so appointed was not allowed to enter upon his duties until he received a "certificate of approval of his fitness" from the state board. But when so qualified he became *ex officio* secretary of the county board of public welfare. In the smaller counties the superintendent of public instruction might be superintendent of public welfare as well. But in spite of the fact that only 29 counties were required to have a separate person for this position, 55 counties had appointed superintendents of public welfare by 1926.[18] The comprehensive list of duties specified in the law indicates how thoroughly this plan was intended to consolidate social work activities in North Carolina counties.

The county superintendent of public welfare shall be chief school attendance officer of the county, and shall have other duties and powers as follows:

1. To have, under control of the county commissioners, the care and supervision of the poor and to administer the poor funds.
2. To act as agent of the state board in relation to any work to be done by the state board within the county.
3. Under the direction of the state board, to look after and keep up with the condition of persons discharged from hospitals for the insane and from other state institutions.
4. To have oversight of prisoners in the county on parole from penitentiaries, reformatories, and all paroled prisoners in the county.
5. To have oversight of dependent and delinquent children, and especially those on parole or probation.
6. To have oversight of all prisoners in the county on probation.
7. To promote wholesome recreation in the county and to enforce such laws as regulate commercial recreation.
8. Under the direction of the state board, to have oversight over dependent children placed in the county by the state board.

[17] Sec. 5014, *Consolidated Statutes of North Carolina.*
[18] Odum, Howard W., in *Nat. Conf. Soc. Work,* 1926: 462.

9. To assist the state board in finding employment for the unemployed.

10. To investigate into the cause of distress, under the direction of the state board, and to make such other investigations in the interest of social welfare as the state board may direct.[19]

This law further provided for the consolidation of municipal and county departments, thus making possible a degree of integration impossible under the Kansas City plan. The State University established a School of Public Welfare primarily to train people for these new positions. So far, however, its main contribution to the problems of personnel has probably been made through summer institutes which are attended by the county superintendents. Unquestionably this is one of the most important attempts that has been made to unite the various types of social work under governmental auspices in a local area. Naturally it has not functioned with 100 per cent efficiency; some superintendents have not been well trained, funds have not been adequate, town and country folk do not always cooperate, and the whole thing has not been satisfactorily integrated with the work of farm demonstration and home demonstration agents or public health nurses. Nevertheless, real headway has been made.

Coordination of state agencies doing social work started, as we saw before, with supervision by state boards of charities and corrections. As these supervisory boards took on administrative functions or gave way to central boards of control, several different types of organization appeared. In some states, as in Illinois and New Jersey, consolidation is almost complete; while in others, as in Massachusetts and New York, social work is done in several different departments.

The law creating the New Jersey Department of Institutions and Agencies provides that the governor shall appoint an unpaid board of eight persons who shall choose an executive officer known as commissioner. The board is authorized to create divisions of education, medicine and psychiatry, labor and agriculture, statistics, parole, food and dietetics, and others as need may arise. It appoints boards of managers for each state institution and non-institutional agency caring for the

[19] Sec. 5017, *Consolidated Statutes of North Carolina.*

insane, feebleminded, epileptic, disabled soldiers, blind, delinquents, and dependent children. The state board has supervision over all county, municipal, and private agencies to which state funds are paid for the care of needy persons. It also has power of visitation and inspection of all jails, detention homes, county hospitals, almshouses, and private agencies for care of any of the groups named above.

In Massachusetts the work which would be under one board in New Jersey is divided between three departments—Public Welfare, Mental Diseases, and Corrections—and the Commission on Probation. At the head of each department is a commissioner appointed by the governor; there is also an advisory board. The duties of the Department of Public Welfare include supervision of five state institutions, infirmary, hospital school, and three industrial schools, direction of relief to persons who have no legal residence in any town or city, supervision of mothers' aid given by cities and towns, care of children who become wards of the Department by court commitment or otherwise, care of children on parole from the industrial schools, supervision of city planning boards, inspection of private incorporated agencies, investigation of petitions for incorporation, inspection of county and municipal institutions, investigating legal settlement, licensing infant boarding homes and maternity hospitals.

Thus we find on every hand evidence of the acceptance of the principle of coordination, but considerable difference of opinion as to how far it should be carried and as to the best methods of putting it into effect.

# CHAPTER XXXII

## FINANCING SOCIAL WORK

The precise scope and cost of social work in the United States cannot be determined with any accuracy, but we have a number of indications that the total is enormous. In his presidential address before the National Conference of Social Work in 1927 Dr. Lapp estimated "From four to five million people actually recipients of material relief; a million and a quarter in institutions for defectives, dependents, and delinquents; nine millions at the free dispensaries for medical aid; five hundred thousand dependent children in the care of public or private benevolences. Twelve million people in the United States suffer at this moment from the calamity of destitution or its near approach." [1] Of course, it is true that by no means all of these unfortunate folk are receiving the benefits of social work, as we have defined the term. But on the other hand, many persons who are not below the poverty line are helped by social workers in the making of personal adjustments. Hence without any pretence of exactness we can safely say that the clients of social work agencies each year number several millions.

What does it cost to provide for the needs of these maladjusted folk? Norton estimated in 1923 that the cost of operating private social agencies in the United States is about three-quarters of a billion dollars a year.[2] The expenses of public agencies would easily add another $250,000,000, so that the total is probably not far from one billion dollars. Of course, this sum includes material relief as well as professional services, and it includes the expenses of agencies that are primarily medical or psychiatric rather than social work. Therefore even if all the figures were in, their classification would depend on

[1] Lapp, John A., Justice First, *Nat. Conf. Soc. Work,* 1927, p. 10.
[2] Norton, Wm. J., in *Survey,* 51 : 184.

one's definition of social work. Hence we must again content ourselves with a generalization, albeit a safe one, that social work in the United States costs several hundred millions of dollars each year. Where does all this money come from?

**Sources of Financial Support.** From time immemorial charitable agencies have received casual gifts and have made sporadic efforts to collect additional funds. Even today there are institutions whose staffs depend upon "the ravens" to feed them and provide the other costs of maintenance. Another ancient and honorable source of revenue has been legacies and endowments ranging all the way from a few dollars for some specific purpose up to millions to be dispensed at the discretion of a board of trustees. The amount of such permanent funds is steadily increasing, but it is impossible at present to determine the total. A hint of its size is given by the fact that a few years ago the private philanthropies of Philadelphia, Boston, and Chicago received $7,236,000 annually from endowment earnings. A third means of supporting social work ever since the colonial period has been taxation. Data concerning public funds devoted to this purpose should be easily accessible, but unfortunately they are not. "An approximate estimate of New York State appropriations during 1926-1927 for various welfare activities (including institutions, state prisons, and parks, hospitals, playgrounds, reformatories) is about $130,000,000." [3] Until relatively recently both public and private funds were raised and expended on a basis of guess and hope. But today most of the larger agencies have budgets and more or less systematic ways of securing the needed funds. The specific devices used include tag days, charity balls, letter solicitation, pulpit appeals, newspaper stories, and many others, some new, some old. But while these still represent random efforts in some agencies, they are parts of definite plans in a growing majority of organizations.

Probably nothing has given more of an impetus to the budgeting of income and expenses than the community chest movement. Beginning with a few experiments in the 'eighties and 'nineties of the last century, this movement gained strength

[3] Walker, Sydnor H., *Social Work and the Training of Social Workers*, p. 51.

during the War and now includes over 300 chests in as many different American cities, raising about $70,000,000 a year. During the same period there have been established a number of foundations and trusts, some national, some local, differing from ordinary endowments in that definite machinery has been set up to receive and administer legacies and other funds from any number of persons. Also the charters of these foundations usually allow the trustees considerable discretion in determining the uses to which their incomes may be put.

Certain types of agencies depend for a large part of their income on earnings or payments for services rendered. Sometimes these payments are made directly by the individual client, sometimes indirectly through insurance, union, or lodge dues. Hospitals (which should be classified as health agencies rather than social work) are, of course, notably large earners. So too are the Christian Associations (whose classification is rather more doubtful). But homes for the aged, children's institutions, and children's aid societies also receive from their clients varying amounts which sometimes constitute as much as one-third of their total income.[4] Club dues in settlements and the sale of products from workshops for the handicapped are likewise significant sources of revenue. Since one of the purposes of social work is to preserve or restore self-maintenance, it is interesting to watch the earnings of social agencies grow.

One of the most careful studies of the financing of social work was made by Raymond Clapp under the joint auspices of the American Association for Community Organization (now Association of Community Chests and Councils) and the Welfare Federation of Cleveland. In his unpublished report Mr. Clapp has tabulated data concerning the income of social agencies in nineteen representative cities. From this we have our first reliable indication of the relative importance of various sources of revenue.

It is especially noteworthy that in all but three cities earnings constituted the greatest single source of income. In Detroit, Buffalo, and Rochester somewhat larger amounts were secured through taxation. In no cities did contributions exceed earnings, and in only seven of the nineteen did they exceed

[4] Norton, Wm. J., "What the Client Pays," *Survey,* 51: 507-509, 1923.

SOURCES OF INCOME FOR SOCIAL AGENCIES IN 19 AMERICAN CITIES, 1924[5]

| *Source* | *Amount* | *Per Cent* |
|---|---|---|
| Earnings | $47,872,544 | 43 |
| Taxes | 34,975,702 | 31 |
| Contributions | 25,339,150 | 22 |
| Endowment | 4,593,128 | 4 |
| Total | $112,780,524 | 100 |

taxes. Endowment was a relatively small item in all of these cities. Among the purposes for which the money was spent "health" bulked largest in every city studied, with the exception of Dayton, where "character building" ranked first. In general, "dependency" was second and "character building" third in the amount of money absorbed. "Health" and "dependency" took about equal amounts of the unearned income, but the earnings of the health agencies were greater than those of any other group.

All of the cities studied by Clapp had community chests, Chicago alone excepted. However, his data do not indicate any important differences between Chicago and the other eighteen cities. We may turn to a report of the Boston Chamber of Commerce for a more adequate picture of the situation in an "unfederated" city.[6] Data from 255 private agencies showed that of a total income amounting to $16,000,000, 53 per cent came from earnings, 28 per cent from contributions and 18 per cent from investments. Earnings were highest in educational and recreational agencies, lowest in homes for the aged. The percentage of income from investments was exactly reversed, being highest in homes for the aged. Contributions bulked largest in neighborhood work and lowest in health promotion. Nearly 44,000 contributors were reported, of whom 50 provided 20 per cent of all the money given. One-third of all givers contributed together one per cent of the total collected. On the average each person gave to 2 1-3 agencies a total of $60.26. Nearly three-fourths of the contributors gave to one agency only, but 3,300 persons each gave to six or more

[5] Clapp, Raymond, *Study of Volume and Cost, Social Work, 1924.* Mimeographed report, p. 3.

[6] *Final Report of the Special Committee on Financing of Social Agencies,* Boston Chamber of Commerce, 1925.

agencies. Six organizations received less than 50 contributions apiece, while one society received over 5,000. The average number of individual contributions per agency was 760. Over a ten-year period the income of these agencies grew fairly steadily, by far the greatest increase being in earnings. However, there were two groups of agencies whose income showed little change, those engaged in relief and those caring for the aged. Methods of raising money included mail solicitation, personal calls, newspaper appeals, entertainments, sales, street collections, and in a few instances the employment of outside money raisers.

**Community Chests.** In many cities, it was found that a handful of well-to-do and generous folk were being solicited over and over again by a host of organizations of every description. Many people quite able to contribute were giving little or nothing to any social agency. Still others confined their donations to their own "pet" charity. Hence the idea of joint financing was early conceived, though it yielded little fruit until 1913. As long ago as 1873, in Liverpool, England, a number of agencies were induced to make their appeals through one office and on a common pledge sheet. A central committee circulated a list of societies which it was sponsoring, and every subscriber put down the amount he was willing to give to each organization. The first American experiment of this sort was made in Denver in 1888. This was under the auspices of the Associated Charities, which combined a number of functions. Besides undertaking to finance twenty-three separate societies, the Denver Associated Charities itself dispensed relief, promoted friendly visiting, provided employment, and sought to suppress begging. Many difficulties arose out of the attempt to make one organization serve the dual purpose of direct service to clients and centralization of policy and finance for other agencies. Eventually this program had to be given up. So far as we know, the only other American ventures in joint financing of social agencies before 1900 were the federations of Jewish charities in Boston and Cincinnati. In both of these the plan of organization seems to have been very much like that adopted in Denver, except, of course, that it was restricted to agencies serving Jewish clients.

One of the first financial federations to achieve real success was established in Cleveland in 1913. Because it has been so widely studied and imitated, its history and organization deserve more than passing comment. In 1900 the Cleveland Chamber of Commerce created a Committee on Benevolent Associations to carry on the work of charities endorsement. In addition to its routine duties this committee made two careful studies of the whole of the city's giving in the years 1907 and 1909. It found, in round numbers, 75 agencies spending $1,500,000 a year of which $650,000 was secured through direct contributions from 5,500 givers, about one per cent of the population. It found that six people were giving over forty per cent of the total amount and that the number of givers was steadily decreasing. It advised the adoption of some system of joint financing. After much discussion of the committee's findings and recommendations the Cleveland Federation for Charity and Philanthropy was established in 1913. Originally the Chamber of Commerce had intended to make the raising of money for philanthropic purposes a subsidiary function of its own, but it abandoned this idea in favor of a new plan, which was in effect a trusteeship of thirty persons, ten selected by the organizations to be financed, ten by the givers, and ten by the Chamber of Commerce. A full-time executive with experience in money-raising was employed and a quiet but vigorous campaign was set in motion. Instead of the "charity week" with which we are so familiar today, this was a program of letter writing, telephone canvassing, personal calls, and advertising, carried on throughout the year. Moreover, individual agencies were encouraged to continue their own soliciting, givers being promised immunity only if they gave as much as they had contributed the previous year and gave it through the federation. At first most of the money was raised by the separate agencies, but in four years the amount that came through the federation rose from 32 per cent to 71 per cent. Both the amount of money and the number of givers steadily increased. But there was no general budget, and this together with other sources of friction led to the formation in 1914 of the Cleveland Welfare Council, a council of social agencies such as was described in the preceding chapter. In 1917 the federation and the council were merged into a new body known as the Welfare Federation of Cleveland.

Before the new organization was well launched everything was upset by the War and the appeals of Red Cross, Y. M. C. A., and similar agencies for immense sums of money. The local federation was hard put to it to make ends meet until it joined with these national organizations in a War Chest. After the signing of the armistice the War Chest Board became the Community Fund, which undertook to finance the Welfare Federation with its constituent agencies, the Y. M. C. A. and the Jewish federation which had previously kept aloof, together with local quotas for state, national, and foreign organizations. It thus became in effect a federation of federations. As such it has continued, though with much overlapping of board membership, staff, and budget-making machinery. Elsewhere the initiative, the organization, and the policies have differed, sometimes very much, but the whole community chest movement has been greatly influenced by the Cleveland federation.

After the War the idea of joint financing spread rapidly until in 1929 there were known to be about 330 community chests in the United States and Canada. A variety of motives has animated their founders and a corresponding variety of plans has been followed in their organization. Some were intended to protect givers against excessive and annoying solicitation, some were expected to increase the money-raising power of the agencies, some were aimed at elimination of waste, others emphasized the integration and improved quality of work along with the centralization of financing. Norton has listed seven plans that have been tried in the establishment of financial federations or community chests.[7] (1) The Liverpool plan was essentially an association of givers created largely for their own convenience. (2) The first Denver plan was a cross between a charity organization society and a community chest, a rather unsuccessful hybrid. (3) The first Cleveland plan provided for joint control by givers, agencies, and Chamber of Commerce. With all its advantages, certain weaknesses appeared. Norton

[7] Norton, Wm. J., *The Cooperative Movement in Social Work,* Chap. VIII.

points out that "it relieved the agencies both of money raising and of responsibility for an equitable distribution of appropriations"; it did not enlist full and whole-hearted support of the "financial brains" of the city; and because it excluded most of the influential social work executives from participation it failed "to generate harmony." (4) In Cincinnati a council of social agencies created a financial federation within itself. This department of the council functioned through a budget committee composed of representatives of the agencies sharing in the joint financing. After a time the list of agencies in the chest came to be almost identical with the whole membership of the council. It is important to note that instead of the financiers bringing the social agencies together, it was the agencies that brought about joint financing; or as some would put it, functional correlation preceded financial federation. This procedure is generally regarded as wiser than its opposite. (5) Under the Kansas City plan a department of the Chamber of Commerce undertakes to raise and distribute the money for most of the private social work organizations. In this particular city there is also a council of social agencies through which budgets are presented to the chest, but final control is vested in the Chamber of Commerce rather than in the agencies or in the public as a whole. While this form of community chest seems to have been successful in raising money, it offers unusual danger of domination by a group that may not always be sympathetic with social work programs. (6) The sixth type of experiment was the war chest, which has been described as "a limited corporation of a few men who set out to raise money from the public and to distribute that money on a basis of their own best judgment to organizations applying for it." (7) The community fund, as it functions in Detroit, for example, is essentially the war chest renamed. It is an exclusive, self-perpetuating board of trustees, who raise and distribute money for the agencies. Sometimes the budgets are actually made by the agencies, separately or through a council, but in any case the real power is in the hands of the community fund board.

While the actual organization and procedure vary greatly from city to city, a number of principles or policies have found rather general acceptance. (1) One of these is budgetary control, which means that each agency prepares in advance a detailed budget, which, when approved by the chest or federation, is not to be exceeded without permission of the controlling body. Living on a budget is certainly a great improvement over depending on chance, but the placement of control is open to question. (2) The whirlwind campaign has been quite generally adopted as the principal, if not the only, means of raising money. Large numbers of solicitors cover the city systematically within a week or ten days, during which time there is much publicity from newspapers, movies, placards, billboards, and parades. "Pep" meetings of the workers are held daily with a climax in the "wind up" dinner. "High pressure salesmanship" is used to induce or compel the largest possible number of persons to give the largest possible amount of money. Employees in industrial establishments are pressed to "give one day's wage" in order that the plan may be "100%." Large givers are sometimes solicited beforehand by a special committee. Divisions and teams vie with one another to "go over the top," raising their quotas by canvassing business and residential districts. (3) In many cities "the immunity rule" has been adopted. This means that persons who contribute to the community chest are promised freedom from further solicitation during the year by agencies within the federation. This rule is often modified so as to permit special campaigns for building funds, appeals for emergency or disaster relief, sale of Christmas seals by the Tuberculosis Association, membership campaigns, and certain special appeals for individual clients. (4) A less general policy is that of providing for designated gifts. Many givers object to certain organizations, while others are anxious to throw their whole support behind agencies in which they are especially interested. Hence opportunity is frequently given for the contributor to specify how he wishes his donation to be distributed. However, most givers do not bother to designate, hence the practice appears to be falling into disuse. Other fiscal policies which seem to be gaining rapidly are (5) centralized accounting, and (6) centralized purchasing. Among the non-financial principles that have won widest acceptance are (7) centralized, continuous, educational publicity, and (8) the coordination of social work programs. These last have been taken over from the councils of social agencies rather than developed by the community chests.

Certain results of joint financing are pretty plain. The community chests have increased both the amount of contributions and the number of givers. However, these gains are in all cases most marked in the early years of federation and may possibly cease after a time. Hence no very definite conclusions on this point are justified except for the decade since the War.[8] Eleven cities which started community chests during or after 1920 raised $3,800,000 in the last year before federation, and $5,800,000 in the first year of joint financing. Forty-four cities raised in the first year of federation $27,438,500 out of the $28,149,000 set as their goal. For 1927 the combined goal of 40 cities was $35,390,000, of which they raised $33,550,000. If it were not for the fairly steady increase both in the amount sought and in the amount raised this might be regarded as a sign of weakness. It is more likely that without goals a little beyond any sum previously raised the giving of a city might slump. The persistence of community chest gains is shown by the following table.

MONEY RAISED BY COMMUNITY CHESTS IN 10 REPRESENTATIVE CITIES, 1922-1929[9]

Reported in thousands of dollars.

| | *1922* | *1923* | *1924* | *1925* | *1926* | *1927* | *1928* | *1929* |
|---|---|---|---|---|---|---|---|---|
| Philadelphia | 1,955 | 2,579 | 2,890 | 2,920 | 3,120 | 3,138 | 3,270 | 3,200 |
| Detroit .... | 2,310 | 2,304 | 2,519 | 2,679 | 3,050 | 2,975 | 3,400 | 3,426 |
| Cleveland .. | 3,820 | 4,250 | 4,175 | 4,286 | 4,430 | 4,445 | 4,525 | 4,605 |
| Los Angeles | .... | .... | .... | 2,492 | 2,702 | 2,500 | 2,573 | 2,573 |
| Toronto ... | 387 | 445 | 400 | 377 | 408 | 440 | 425 | 432 |
| Milwaukee . | 392 | 482 | 690 | 763 | 842 | 908 | 985 | 1,010 |
| Minneapolis | 1,048 | 1,011 | 1,053 | 1,042 | 1,130 | 1,112 | 1,204 | 1,252 |
| Kansas City | 772 | 842 | 920 | 926 | 966 | 1,061 | 1,063 | 1,075 |
| Seattle .... | 637 | 596 | 671 | 688 | 685 | 713 | 605 | 658[10] |
| Atlanta .... | .... | .... | 485 | 465 | 410 | 446 | 397 | 375[10] |

[8] Data on which this paragraph is based are taken from bulletins of the Association of Community Chests and Councils, a report to the Chicago Council of Social Agencies published in 1924, and Norton, W. J., *The Cooperative Movement in Social Work.*

[9] Data from bulletins of the Association of Community Chests and Councils.

[10] Incomplete.

Even more striking is the increased number of contributors. In the last year before federation 37 cities had 117,000 givers; in the first year of the community chest these same cities had 972,000 givers. Thirty-six cities, including some in the previous group, had 749,000 contributors in 1920, 916,000 in 1921, and 1,040,000 in 1922. When more recent figures are available we will undoubtedly find a continued, though much smaller increase in the number of persons supporting community chests. Another criterion of success is the decrease in the cost of money raising. In 18 cities before federation the average cost of separate appeals was about 15 per cent of the amount raised. In these same cities after federation the campaign expenses ranged from 1.5 per cent to 8.7 per cent, and the total cost of the community chest machinery ranged from 4.2 per cent to 12.8 per cent. However, as Edward T. Devine has pointed out, "The ultimate test of a welfare federation is not in the amount of money which it collects, nor in the number of its contributors, nor in the degree of immunity which it may give from annoying drives; but in the number of well informed and well disposed citizens whom it discovers and associates for the purpose of doing what they can to secure a good life for themselves and their neighbors." [11]

**Problems Raised by Joint Financing.** In spite of its apparent success, the community chest movement has left a good many problems unsolved and has raised others whose solution is no less difficult. First among these is the question of what agencies should be included in a financial federation. What agencies will be more successful outside than in? What agencies can a chest not afford to accept? These questions pertain especially to such civic organizations as voters' leagues, law enforcement associations, and societies promoting economic reform. In general, such groups are omitted from schemes of joint financing on the ground that the chest must limit itself to agencies acceptable to a majority of the population. This may be a sound criterion, but one is inclined to suspect that often it is a mere rationalization, and that the real reason is that those in control of the chest represent the conservative elements and are unwilling to lend aid and comfort to "reform" or

[11] Devine, Edward T., *Welfare Federations*, p. 53.

"radical" movements. On the other hand, it may be much better for propaganda organizations to have to make their own way independently, to win financial and moral support together, and to be free from obligations to the conservative majority. The question of admission or exclusion has been raised also with respect to sectarian, "character building," and cultural agencies. In so far as a line can be draw between strictly religious work and social work conducted by a church, it seems wise to exclude the first and include the second. But this is not an easy line to draw. Some contributors object to including the Y. M. C. A., Knights of Columbus, Y. M. H. A., Boy Scouts, Campfire Girls, and similar organizations, on the ground that they are not "charitable" but "character building" agencies. This distinction seems rather absurd. A sounder criterion would be one based on their sectarian affiliations and their capacity for self-support. Orchestras, art museums, and drama leagues are usually omitted, apparently on the ground that they are "luxuries." Whether they would fare better in a financial federation than outside is hard to tell.

Another unanswered question is this: will a community chest work in small cities? It is here that the annoyance of constant appeals for money is probably greatest. It is here that the number of persons competent to manage a financial campaign is smallest. On the surface it would seem that here, if anywhere, joint financing is needed. But limited resources mean difficulty in securing a competent executive, and community chests do not run themselves. Data collected by the Association of Community Chests and Councils indicate that small city chests frequently fail to reach their goals, and are often abandoned altogether. Out of 64 cities with less than 50,000 population, 37 raised less for 1927 than they did in 1926, and incomplete figures for 1928 seem to indicate the same tendency.

Assuming the establishment of a financial federation, what shall be its attitude toward national agencies? Where local branches of national organizations belong to the federation, as is commonly true of the Red Cross, their quota for the national office is usually included in the budget. Such agencies as the Near East Relief are sometimes given appropriations from a general fund, and sometimes admitted on the same terms as local organizations. A good many national and state-wide agencies are simply ignored, whether for better or for worse is hard to say.

Another problem confronts societies that depend on memberships both for raising money and for developing popular understanding and support. Sometimes the fiction is maintained that the "first dollar" of one's contribution to the chest constitutes membership dues in a particular constituent agency. But this does not select those persons whose interest is genuine, and, as a matter of fact, the constituency of some agencies dwindles away after joint financing is adopted. Annual meetings become farcical and control falls into the hands of a small, self-perpetuating board of directors.

Then there is the problem of how to provide capital funds for new buildings and equipment. Shall the chest include such items in its regular budget? Shall it arrange special campaigns? Or shall it ignore the problem and leave each organization to go its own way? Apparently the last course is the one most frequently followed, although in many cities it is understood that any participating agency which contemplates a building or endowment campaign shall consult the federation before going ahead and shall abide by the federation's decision.

A problem more frequently faced is what to do when the regular campaign falls short of the goal. Sometimes the budgets of all participating agencies are cut proportionately. In some cases a deficit is carried by the chest. Sometimes the curtailment of expansions makes it possible to balance the books. In other instances the entire chest budget is revised with a view to eliminating or reducing the least important or least popular items.

But perhaps the most important and difficult problem of all pertains to control. Before the days of joint financing, every agency was presumably the creature of its members, who elected their governing board and officers, adopted and raised their budget, hired and fired their staff. But when someone else holds the purse strings, this independence disappears, if indeed it really existed before. As a matter of fact, most of the contributors and members never took much interest in the actual conduct of "their" organizations. However, in the majority of cases each agency had at least a small group of loyal supporters, genuinely interested in the purposes of the organization, and more or less informed concerning its field of work. The directors and budget committee of a community chest may, on the one hand, acquaint themselves sympathetically with the agency viewpoint and add to it a wider outlook; or they may, and sometimes do, undertake to dominate and dictate. In the latter case the future of both the individual agency and of the federation is threatened. An extreme instance of such conflict occurred in 1925 at Columbus, Ohio, when the arbitrary methods of the community chest wrecked the family welfare society.[12]

Superficially viewed, the chest with its many contributors and varied interests is more democratic than any other system of financing private agencies. But, as Joseph Lee has pointed out,[13] these added numbers come largely from industrial employees who give from fear of losing their jobs rather than because of interest in social work. The pressure on street-car conductors, department store clerks, school teachers and others of modest means increases the fund for social work, but it often brings a feeling of resentment, which, rather unfairly, is expressed against social workers more than against financiers.

But the real mockery of this alleged democracy is shown in the almost total absence of provision for participation by the clients of social agencies and the condescending or hostile attitudes of business men toward social workers. A leader in one community chest is quoted as having said, "Too many social workers are radical, and all social workers are queer." Whenever that spirit dominates the board of a financial federation, the results are pretty clearly forecast. But often the attitude of those on the boards of individual agencies is very similar. Whatever the form of financial organization, social work is largely dominated by persons with aggressive personalities and large bank accounts.

**Endowed Trusts and Foundations.** The city of Cleveland, which has contributed so much to the community chest movement, has also given the chief impetus to another form

[12] "What Happened in Columbus," *Survey*, 56: 261-263.
[13] Lee, Joseph, "The Chest and Social Work," *Survey*, 59: 749.

of joint financing known as the community trust or foundation. This is essentially an arrangement by one or more trust companies to accept money or property in trust "for the welfare of the community." The intention is that gifts shall be undesignated in order that as social conditions change the income from the endowment may be put to new uses. However, designated funds are usually accepted along with those whose use is practically unrestricted. In their enthusiasm the early promoters of this idea hoped to create "the possibility of making a fool-proof bequest—one which will be as flexible as human need, as safe as a trust company, as broad as the community, as intelligent as the advancing public sentiment, reflected in a representative distributing agency." [14] However, it was perhaps inevitable that the trustees and distributing committees, being drawn from the most conservative elements in the population, should confine their activities largely to subsidizing established agencies and programs rather than launching new and untried schemes. As a striking exception to this general rule, the Cleveland Foundation has conducted a series of thorough-going surveys to discover outstanding needs, and has promoted several new ventures in the fields of recreation, health and education.

Notwithstanding the high hopes entertained for the community trust idea, it has, during the thirteen years which have elapsed since it was launched in Cleveland, yielded only meagre results. A recent compilation shows that of fifty existing community trusts, thirty have received no gifts or legacies whatever. The combined endowment of the other twenty amounts to less than $10,000,000, and the income expended during 1925 did not exceed $600,000. Much of this income, moreover, appears to have been specifically designated by the donors.[15]

In addition to these local community trusts there are a number of endowed foundations whose interests and activities extend in some cases throughout the world. Seven of these foundations have a combined endowment of $500,000,000 and an aggregate annual income of $28,000,000. They are the

[14] Devine, Edward T., in *Survey,* 44: 694, 1921.

[15] Williams, Pierce, "Could Community Trusts Work?" *Survey,* 58: 223-4, 1927.

Rockefeller Foundation, Laura Spelman Rockefeller Memorial, General Education Board, Carnegie Corporation, Milbank Memorial Fund, Commonwealth Fund, and Russell Sage Foundation.[16]

The Rockefeller Foundation has from the beginning concentrated on public health. It has made grants to medical schools, nurses' training schools, and academic departments of biology, psychology, chemistry and physics. It has offered fellowships to enable gifted students and scientists to pursue their studies and carry on research. It has conducted public health demonstrations in cooperation with county and state departments. It has itself carried on extensive campaigns against yellow fever, malaria, and hookworm.

The Laura Spelman Rockefeller Memorial was at first chiefly interested in the so-called "character building" agencies. It also contributed toward emergency aid for Chinese famine and Japanese earthquake sufferers and for post-war relief in Europe. But at present the trend is away from grants to miscellaneous organizations for general operations and in the direction of special support for research in the social sciences.

The General Education Board and the Carnegie Corporation are not primarily concerned with social work. The Milbank Memorial Fund is supporting three public health demonstrations in cooperation with local health and social work organizations.

The Commonwealth Fund has made as its major objectives the promotion of child health and the prevention of juvenile delinquency. The child health program was at first confided to the American Child Health Association, but it has since been taken over directly by the foundation, under the direction of a staff specially employed for that purpose. The other program included psychiatric study of "difficult" children, promotion of the visiting teacher movement, training courses for psychiatric social workers, visiting teachers and probation officers, and educational publicity. A Joint Committee on Methods of Preventing Delinquency correlated the various activities carried on in cooperation with the New York School of Social Work, the

[16] Assn. Com. Chests and Councils, Special Information Bulletin, Aug. 12, 1927.

National Committee for Mental Hygiene, and the National Committee on Visiting Teachers.

The Russell Sage Foundation differs from the others described in that most of its work is done through its own departments rather than through other agencies. "The staff of the Foundation study social conditions and methods of social work, interpret the findings, make the information available by publications, conferences and other means of public education." Its departments are charity organization, recreation, delinquency and penology, industrial studies, remedial loans, statistics, surveys and exhibits, and library. The Foundation has published over 100 books and 500 pamphlets presenting the results of its various studies.

These large foundations are playing an important rôle in the development of social work through their research, demonstrations, and publications. Incidentally they render service to individuals in need, but this is not their primary function. They are experimenting and pioneering in the fields of public health, recreation, education, and social case work, but they are not devoting much attention to the economic basis of social maladjustment.

**Taxation for Social Work.** Ever since the days of Queen Elizabeth an increasing amount of social work has been financed through taxation; and ever since the enactment of the first Poor Law there have been discussions and debates as to the proper division of labor between public and private agencies. In Chapters XIII and XIV we saw how the matter stood in the United States at the end of the nineteenth century. One of the most recent statements of this issue has been made by Robert W. Kelso.[17] He holds that the public agency should handle "those problems fully demonstrated as equitable, practicable and appropriate for the whole people to deal with," with special responsibility for cases requiring long continued help, problems involving custody or control of the person, and other cases involving court action. He would leave to private agencies experimental undertakings and demonstrations, responsibilities with which public departments are charged but which they fail to meet, and "research efforts not connected with the actual re-

[17] Kelso, Robert W., *The Science of Public Welfare,* Chap. VIII.

lief of individuals." As Kelso himself says, "Obviously the field of operations is not divisible." There is nothing to do but to proceed opportunistically. Moreover, with the development of community chests the flexibility of private agencies may be quite as limited as that of public departments. Domination from chambers of commerce may be no more helpful to social work than domination from ward politicians. While taxation seems to be the "logical" thing, he would be bold indeed who would undertake to forecast the future of the financing of social work.

# CHAPTER XXXIII

## SOCIAL WORK AS A PROFESSION

In the first chapter it was stated that social work had become a profession during the past third of a century. Now that its development has been studied in some detail, it should be of interest to review the evidence bearing on the status of social work among the various occupations and to ask again certain questions. First of all, is social work one or many? Is it a single vocation, or is it a collection of fairly distinct though related fields of work? Second, is it, or are they, on a basis that may legitimately be called professional? Third, what is involved in the actual or potential professionalizing of social work?

**What Is Social Work?** The many varieties of social service discussed in previous chapters may be classified into four main groups: case work, institutional work, group work, organization and administration. Each of these in turn includes a number of sub-varieties indicated in the following outline.

TYPES OF SOCIAL WORK.

| | |
|---|---|
| Case work | Family welfare work. |
| | Children's aid and protection. |
| | Visiting teaching. |
| | Hospital social service. |
| | Psychiatric social work. |
| | Probation and parole. |
| | Vocational guidance and personnel work. |
| Institutional work | For children. |
| | For the aged. |
| | For delinquents. |
| Group work | Direction of leisure time. |
| | Club work with small groups. |
| | Neighborhood work. |
| | Community organization. |
| Organization and administration | Administration of social agencies. |
| | Publicity. |
| | Coordination and supervision. |
| | Financing. |
| | Promotion of new social programs. |

What elements are common to the types of social service in each of these groups? What elements are common to all four groups? We have found fairly general agreement that the various forms of social case work are closely related and constitute a single vocational type. All have to do with persons out of adjustment with their social environment; all make use of personal influence and modifications of environment to effect readjustments; in all of them success depends largely on skill in interviewing. Institutional work, on the other hand, takes persons completely away from their customary surroundings and places them into controlled situations where most of them are supposed to be prepared gradually for return to life in families and communities. In a sense the institutional worker is also a group worker, but the latter term is more commonly applied to one who deals with people in their ordinary associations, stimulates new affiliations, and promotes joint activities on the part of club, neighborhood, community, and other groups. Organizers and executives establish and maintain social machinery through which other types of social workers accomplish their purposes. Preceding discussion would appear to justify the proposition that each of these four main types involves a rather well defined field of human endeavor. How much do they have in common?

Again and again case workers have found that they cannot effect satisfactory adjustments for individual persons because of conditions obtaining in the community. In the development of their clients' personalities they frequently have recourse to organized groups and sometimes to institutions. While concentrating their attention on persons and on families, they cannot help dealing with the religious, economic, local, and other groups to which these persons and families belong. Group workers, in turn, have discovered that they cannot deal exclusively with clubs, neighborhoods, and communities as such, but must pay attention to the persons of whom these groups are composed. They have to single out individuals for special consideration. Institutional workers are no longer concerned merely with providing food, shelter, and other physical needs of their wards; they find it necessary to combine these functions with the practise of both case work and group work. More and more they are studying each separate personality, and developing programs which unite individualization with socialization. The executives, organizers, promoters, and publicity agents also share many functions with other kinds of social workers. Even case work, as we have seen, involves "executive" tasks; certainly this is true of group and institutional work. Every social worker, no matter what his main duty, is likely to have a part in policy making, internal administration, money raising, and interpreting his work to the public. Differences, therefore, seem to be largely matters of emphasis, of major responsibility, and of auspices under which one works. This does not mean that the various types of social workers may be interchanged without difficulty, but it does mean that they all have much in common. It is probably safe to say that practitioners in the fields of case work, group work, institutional work, and social service administration share as much of philosophy, information, and technique as do specialists in surgery, pediatrics, internal medicine, and eye-ear-nose-and-throat. Indeed the analogy seems quite appropriate.

How then may we define social work as a whole? Miss Cheyney makes it include "all voluntary attempts to extend benefits which are made in response to a need, are concerned with social relationships, and avail themselves of scientific knowledge and methods." [1] One of the training schools announces that "social work is immediately concerned (1) with the development or rehabilitation of those individuals, families, and institutions which for whatever reason are not adjusted to the communities of which they are a part, and (2) with the development or reorganization of communities as a whole. It seeks to increase personal, institutional, and communal efficiency wherever it finds the opportunity." [2] In the opening chapter we offered as a tentative definition, "the adjusting of personal relationships and the reorganization of social groups." Perhaps the three might be combined into some such definition as this: The development of personality and of group life through adjustments systematically effected between persons or groups and their social environment.

[1] Cheyney, Alice S., *The Nature and Scope of Social Work*, p. 24.
[2] University of Southern California, Bulletin, October, 1928, p. 11.

**Is Social Work a Profession?** Nothing is more obvious than that many personal and group conflicts are "ironed out" without the intervention of anyone who would be recognized as a social worker. Parents and children straighten out their own difficulties, employers and employees settle disputes, native and foreign born learn to live peacefully together, sometimes without any orderly planning, and usually by dint of their own efforts. These obvious facts raise certain questions. Is there, after all, a real difference between the social adjustments of the "professional" and of the "amateur"? Is there any need of professional social workers? Can their vocation be put on a professional level anyway? Before answering these questions we must agree on what we mean by the term profession.

At the 1915 meeting of the National Conference of Charities and Correction Abraham Flexner presented seven criteria by which a profession may be distinguished from amateur activities on the one hand and from business and trades on the other.[3] The first mark of a profession is that the activities involved are essentially intellectual in character. This implies individual responsibility for making important decisions rather than the routine application of thought-out techniques. Second, the raw materials of a profession are drawn from science and learning. This distinguishes it from a trade, which may be developed by trial and error and passed on by apprenticeship. Third, however much the various professions may overlap, each has a well defined nucleus of functions for which it is clearly responsible. These functions, moreover, involve the achievement of certain concrete, practical results, which differentiate a profession from a science or a philosophy. The fourth criterion is possession of an "educationally communicable technique." That is, the methods used by members of each profession have been analyzed and formulated, so they can be passed on systematically to competent persons desirous of entering the field. Fifth, a profession tends toward self-organization. Flexner spoke of it as a brotherhood, whose members are watchful of ethical standards, critical of methods, and devoted to the advancement of professional interests. Sixth,

[3] Flexner, Abraham, "Is Social Work a Profession?" *Nat. Conf. Char. & Corr.*, 1915: 576-590.

the interests of the public take precedence over those of the vocational group and of the individual practitioner. By implication Flexner added a seventh criterion, that of having a literature recording the development, achievements, methods and underlying philosophy of the vocation.

Viewing social work of 1915 in the light of these criteria, Flexner found it wanting in at least three important points. He felt that the social worker did not bear the sole, or the major, responsibility for making needed adjustments. "The very variety of the situations he encounters compels him to be not a professional agent so much as the mediator invoking this or that professional agency." Furthermore, he found social work lacking a definite and concrete aim. "It appears not so much a definite field as an aspect of work in many fields." Also "the occupations of social workers are so numerous and diverse that no compact, purposefully organized educational discipline is feasible." Finally, social work in 1915 possessed almost no professional literature.

Reviewing the whole field in 1925, William Hodson found evidence that social work had traveled far toward the achievement of professional status.[4] He saw many social workers still serving as helpers to physicians, teachers, ministers, and members of other professions, but he found an increasing number assuming the major responsibility for solving their clients' problems. Still more noticeable was the increasing clearness with which the central tasks of social workers were being defined. Instead of charitable odd jobs and the steering of people to appropriate agencies, emphasis was being laid on the adjustment of personal relations and the organization of social groups. The intervening decade has also seen the rise of several professional schools and the beginning of a professional literature. But probably the most important development of all was the founding of a professional organization, the American Association of Social Workers. Nevertheless, Hodson found this new vocation failing to meet one essential test. "A profession is only in actual existence when it is accepted as such by people generally." "The public thinks of the social worker's client as

[4] Hodson, William, "Is Social Work Professional?" *Nat. Conf. Soc. Work,* 1925: 629-636.

a mendicant seeking alms, forced to do as he is told, unable to express intelligent criticism, and without influence if he could do so." Many people still regard social workers as kind-hearted, but rather inferior persons, who are doing a "noble work," but one which is not very important. "Real folks" are out making money, getting elected to office, and displaying themselves in "Society."

These popular attitudes are in part heritages from the past, when almsgiving was a passport to heaven and conspicuous charities yielded entrée to the "four hundred." In those days the actual giving of relief was often left to servants, and the administration of philanthropic institutions to persons themselves in need of assistance. Even yet the majority of those who hold social work positions are mere time-servers, "lame-duck" politicians, broken-down clergymen, and misfits from various other vocations. The 20,000 incompetents almost obscure the 5,000 trained and experienced social workers.[5] The situation is further complicated by the activities of many thousands of "volunteers." Some of these unpaid and usually part-time folk are well equipped for the duties they assume, but the majority are without training or experience. Unquestionably there are and will continue to be many tasks which they can perform in conjunction with and under the direction of professional workers. Moreover, they can help to interpret social work to their friends and associates. Still there is serious ground for wondering whether they do not hamper the development of social work as a profession. But "while the real services of social work are gradually becoming more widely understood, so that professional recognition may ultimately be accorded, there is nothing to prevent social workers from setting up for themselves the rigorous standards, the exacting discipline, the faith in their tasks, and the humility in the performance of them which characterize a true profession." [6]

**Professional Spirit in Social Work.** In other words, the making of a profession depends not merely on technical achievements, but on the spirit or attitudes of the practitioners

[5] These figures are based on estimates presented by Ralph Hurlin at the 1926 meeting of the National Conference of Social Work (See Proceedings p. 589) and on membership of the American Association of Social Workers.
[6] Hodson, *loc. cit.*, p. 635.

as well. What then is a professional spirit? Perhaps we can define it best by means of contrast. The helpful relationships between people can be reduced to four types—friendly, benevolent, commercial and professional. Friendliness is, of course, intimate and mutual. When we help a member of our own primary group we act spontaneously and generously. When we accept aid from our friends we do it without humiliation. It is all a matter of "natural" give-and-take. Benevolence, however, implies social distance. Our charities are for people outside our primary groups, for whom we feel sorry. We get personal satisfaction out of giving them a "lift," and the only compensation we expect is some expression of gratitude. With our real friends we visit back and forth quite freely, but if one on whom we call as a "friendly visitor" should come to our house we would be quite dumbfounded. Commercial relationships differ very sharply from both friendliness and benevolence. In business we bargain for the exchange of goods and services, seeking a maximum return for a minimum outlay, but assuming that "the other fellow" is doing the same thing. Hence the world of commerce and industry is frequently described as hard, cold, and impersonal. Professional relationships are still different. The lawyer, physician, or other professional man whom we consult is usually not a personal friend at all; indeed, he may be a total stranger. But neither is he a philanthropist of whom we ask some boon, or whose charity we shamefacedly accept. We go to him because he possesses some knowledge and skill of which we desire to take advantage and for which we usually pay. Yet this is not like a commercial transaction. We do not offer to buy so many dollars worth of medical diagnosis or of legal advise. We place ourselves in the hands of the lawyer or doctor and ask him what we need. He in turn is under some obligation to serve us, to tell us the truth, even though it be unpleasant to hear, and to advise programs of action which may be very hard to carry out.

In which of these categories does social work belong? In the past it has been predominantly a matter of benevolence. Today it is increasingly a matter of professional service. This means a number of important changes in viewpoint. Social work interprets human trouble in terms of natural processes, that is, "laws" of cause and effect. It rests on relative rather than absolute standards of conduct. As means of control it looks to "insight" and manipulation of natural processes, rather than "ordering and forbidding" and exhortation. Its motives for service are neither the "religious merit of almsgiving" nor "love of mankind," but rather a "sporting interest" in a thrilling and important "game."

It is believed that by displacing theological concepts with scientific, *i.e.,* "supernatural" with "natural," the prospects of understanding, prediction and control are considerably enhanced. Instead of praying for rain, we study the weather map, investigate possibilities of irrigation, dry farming, or substitution of other crops for wheat. Instead of praying for jobs and prosperity, we go in for business forecasting, consider ten-year programs of public works, solicit non-seasonal orders with long delivery time, and experiment with unemployment insurance. Instead of attributing the poverty of hookworm sufferers to laziness and shiftlessness, we verify the presence of the parasite, employ medication for its removal, and outline a program of sanitation which will prevent its reappearance. Instead of laying the erratic and annoying behavior of some person to a wicked heart and urging him to repent, we make a careful study of his personal history and present conditions to see when and how the trouble started, and by what medical, surgical, hygienic, domestic, or other means it may be controlled.

In other words, we are not looking for mysterious origins of human ills to be corrected by magical devices. Neither are we concerned with finding fault or assessing blame. In a certain sense, our approach is no more moral than it is theological. We do not set out with a set of norms or ideals to which we hope to make individuals or groups conform. We do not often use the words "should," "ought," "right," "just," "betterment," "progress." Instead, we seek first to discover what the facts are, then "how they got that way," and third "what of it." That is, when an individual or group comes to us asking for help in straightening out a situation that is unsatisfactory to the person or group in question, we try to see and aid them to see just what the situation really is. Together with them we try to find how the trouble came about. Then we consider with them various ways out of the tangle, trying to forecast what are likely to be the further consequences of each available line of conduct, and ask them to make their own choice. Thus we do not say, "You ought to do so and so." We say, "If you want to achieve such and such a result, this is what you will probably have to do in order to get it. If you insist on having or doing this or that, you will also have to put up with so and so.

What do you really want to have or do? Are you willing to pay the price?"

Someone has called attention to the fact that this represents an apparent return to the "free-will" position. Certainly it is not in accord with the crude statements of determinism. It differs from the latter in stressing the action of the client as well as the influences brought to bear upon him. It differs from the former in calling attention to the fact that this action occurs in a social setting and as one of a series of connected events. All this means that we identify conduct as "belonging" to some person or group, but inextricably bound up with antecedents and consequences. As a result we hold the person or group "responsible" for what he does, but do not sit in judgment, saying "this is good," and "that is bad."

All this means that we come to the problems of persons out of adjustment with their social environment in much the same spirit that a physician approaches his patient or a lawyer his client. The professional man usually does not love the persons he serves. Neither is he hunting for people whom he may uplift. He simply puts his specialized knowledge and skill at the disposal of persons who want to take advantage of them in overcoming difficulties which they cannot handle themselves. Not only does the professional person usually not love his individual patients or clients; neither is he conscious of any particular love for mankind in general, or even for all sick people, all criminals, all unemployed, etc. He has chosen his calling because it appeals to him as a sporting proposition. It is an interesting game; one that he believes to be "worth while"; one through which he can win recognition and earn a living, and have a good time doing it. Of course he is concerned about those whom he serves, but he doesn't need to love them. In fact, he finds it advantageous to maintain a certain reserve, and to deal with his clients on the basis of secondary rather than of primary relationships. He needs to keep a certain distance in order to have perspective for viewing his clients' problems. He tries not only to see things from the clients' viewpoint, but also from many other viewpoints, and this can be done only if he refrains from identifying himself too closely with the persons to be served.

There is, of course, one set of circumstances under which the professional person approaches his client or patient, not at the latter's request, but in the name of the community or the state. Thus, if the patient has smallpox but does not wish to see a physician, he is likely to receive some medical attention whether he wants it or not. The larger group has discovered that smallpox involves certain consequences, and it has decided not to stand for these if they can be avoided. Hence use is made of the police power to enforce quarantine at least. The same principle applies to certain kinds of conduct such as family desertion, stealing, prostitution, etc. None of these cases is in conflict with the principle formulated before. Only now the client is the group rather than the individual. The professional person is responding to the appeal of the group to help solve some problem which can not be successfully dealt with by informal methods of social control.[7]

**Schools of Social Work.** As in the case of every other vocation, social work was carried on for many years before there was any semblance of formal training. Each newcomer in the field struck out for himself, picking up a few "tricks of the trade" from his predecessors and associates. It was all largely a matter of good intentions plus trial and error. There was little indeed for one generation of workers to pass on to the next. But gradually there grew up a body of knowledge and of crudely tested methods which the beginner could hardly acquire except from experienced social workers. There was no systematic instruction, but by watching older visitors, by talking to executives, and by attending conferences the neophyte learned something of "the art of helping people out of trouble."

In 1898 the New York Charity Organization Society held a summer institute which was probably the first attempt at organized training. Various societies began to arrange lectures and plan reading for their new workers. In time these schemes developed into apprenticeships whereby beginners were initiated gradually and systematically into the practise of social work. At the present time a limited number of agencies maintain such training programs. They select candidates carefully on the basis of alertness, tact, poise, health, and education. They plan a course of study, which may include extension classes conducted by some professional school or university. The workers-in-training do assigned reading, have regular conferences with supervisors, receive systematic instruction in the function, organization, and administration of the agency, visit other societies and institutions, and through practise gradually acquire the skills deemed most necessary. The period of apprenticeship varies from one to two years, during which time the trainees receive a salary ranging from $50 to $100 per

[7] Queen, Stuart A., *Contrasted Approaches to Social Problems,* Proceedings, Seventh National Conference on Social Service of the Protestant Episcopal Church, 1927.

month. A very large number of agencies take on new workers who must learn "on the job," but very few have well planned training programs. A genuine apprenticeship built on a good foundation with social science as its cornerstone may produce an excellent social worker. But the more common procedure, in which the beginner is chosen by "guess" or by "pull," and in which he must shift pretty much for himself, learning by trial and error—this is full of hazards. It continues because board members are unconvinced as to the value of formal preparation for social work, and executives are satisfied with their ability to give whatever training may be needed.

In 1904 the New York institute developed into a nine months' course and the New York School of Philanthropy was launched. Gradually the scope of work was enlarged, the program was extended to cover two years, and the name was changed to School of Social Work. Since 1904 thirty-five such training schools have been established, of which all but five are integral parts of some college or university. The New York school, which is one of the five "independents," continues, however, to be the largest and probably the best equipped of these institutions. It is still "conducted by the Charity Organization Society of the City of New York," although it has a separate board of trustees and a separate endowment. Its bulletin of April, 1928, announces a faculty of twenty-three, most of whom give full time to the school. The admission requirement is "(1) an undergraduate degree from a college of recognized standard, or (2) a minimum of two full years of college work plus one of the following: (a) four years of social work of substantial character, (b) the completion of a nurses' training course, (c) other experiences or types of training to be determined in individual cases." Candidates for admission are passed on by a committee which considers not only their academic and vocational history, including training in social science, but also their physical and mental health, interest in equipping themselves for professional service; and asks whether each one has "a personality adapted to the interrelationships that social work must undertake." The curriculum of this school is best described in the annual report of the director.[8]

[8] Bulletin of the New York School of Social Work, Oct., 1928.

For the past two years the Faculty of the School . . . has undertaken, through its Committee on Instruction, a protracted study of changes in social work and our own experience in the training of social workers as a basis for further curriculum development. The result of this study thus far has been the acceptance of the unity of social work rather than its specialized aspect as the focal point of instruction. We have, therefore, begun the reorganization of the curriculum for the purpose of providing students with professional education which will be as nearly adequate as possible for the practise of social work within a specialized field on a substantial foundation of education and training in the things that are essential to every form of social work.

We have divided the subject matter of social work as it appears in the curriculum of the professional school under four headings: (1) The Fundamental Techniques of Social Work; (2) Scientific Material and Formulations of Human Experience Adapted to the Requirements of Social Work; (3) the Practise of Social Work; (4) the Orientation of the Social Worker. . . .

The courses in the School curriculum as given or planned would be classified under these four headings as follows:

1. The Fundamental Techniques of Social Work: Social Case Work; Recording; Methods of Community Organization; Methods of Administration; Social Surveys and Community Studies; Social Investigation; Interviewing; Institutional Management; Technique of Group Work.

2. Scientific Material and Formulations of Human Experience Adapted to the Requirements of Social Work: Health and Nutrition; Problems of Disease; Labor Problems; Problems of Industry; Labor Legislation; The Nature and Varieties of Human Behavior; Psychopathology; Statistics; Crime and Punishment; Criminal Justice; The Social Worker and the Law; Social Education; Leisure Time Problems; The Immigrant; Clinical Psychiatry: Social Implications of Mental Testing.

3. Practise of Social Work: Social Work with Families; Delinquent and Neglected Children; The Social Worker and the Handicapped Child; Visiting Teaching; Community Organization; Rural Social Work; State Wide Views of Child Welfare; Medical Social Work; Psychiatric Social Work; The Administration of Public Welfare; The Work of Chests and Councils; Settlement and Neighborhood Work.

4. Orientation of the Social Worker: Social Work and Social Philosophy; Orientation of the Social Sciences and Social Work; The Philosophy of Community; The Family; Professional Ethics; The History of Social Work; Seminar in Social Work.

We have given special attention to the New York School of Social Work, not only because it was the first one established, but because it continues to lead the field in many ways. However, there are some significant developments in other professional schools which should not be overlooked. The University of Chicago maintains a Graduate School of Social Service Administration in which more emphasis is laid on research and less on the other techniques. The general point of view is legal and economic rather than psychiatric and sociological. Students spend less time in the field and more in the class room than in some of the other schools. There is no specified period of training, but many students complete the requirements for a master's degree, and a few receive the doctorate of philosophy. This school has made an especially important contribution of teaching materials, having published several books and established a quarterly magazine, *The Social Service Review.*

Western Reserve University has a still different type of graduate professional training for social work. Its School of Applied Social Sciences has working agreements with several Cleveland agencies whereby students are put on the payroll while they combine actual practice with academic work. Heretofore students have had only five hours a week of class work, but in the future beginners are to divide their time more nearly equally between the agency and the university. Certain persons are on the staff of a social agency and of the professional school at the same time. This provides a close "tie up," but can hardly obviate difficulties due to the winter rush and other "emergencies" of the cooperative agencies. Unquestionably students get a more adequate notion of the day-by-day work, but it hardly seems possible for them to become as well grounded in "fundamentals" as at the New York and Chicago schools. The Cleveland program extends through twenty-one months, or two academic years and the intervening summer, during which time the student's stipend increases from $75 a month to $105. Those who complete all the requirements receive the degree of Master of Science in Social Administration.

Yet another plan is presented by Smith College. The course covers a period of fourteen months divided into three sessions. The first and third are held in successive summers on the college campus. The second is spent with cooperating social agencies in various cities. Those who complete the program receive the degree of Master of Social Science. In the Smith school special emphasis is laid upon the psychiatric approach to social problems. Seven other schools offer professional training on a graduate basis, but the four we have described display the principal variations.

Ten schools of social work are distinctly undergraduate in character while fourteen more are predominantly so. At Ohio State University, the University of Minnesota, Washington University, Carnegie Institute of Technology, and several other institutions, students may in their sophomore or junior year elect the social work curriculum. As they advance the courses become increasingly professional in character and more time is spent in the field. At the University of Oregon and at Simmons College undergraduate students spend three years on the campus and a fourth year at a down-town professional school. There is much debate as to the relative merit of graduate and undergraduate schools without much prospect of a decision. Those who finish an undergraduate curriculum with a "major" in social science and then go on to a graduate professional school are undoubtedly better equipped for social work than those who combine their liberal arts and vocational courses. But the expense of an additional year and the meager salaries paid to beginners will for some time to come limit the number of those who are trained in a graduate school.

In addition to the general schools of social work are several that cater to special groups, religious, racial, or vocational. The most important of these is probably the Training School for Jewish Social Work. Its founders had in mind five principles: first, that successful work with Jewish people requires an intimate knowledge and sympathetic appreciation of their background; second, that the Jewish community is but part of the general community; third, that there are distinctively Jewish problems which require either special methods or modifications of general methods; fourth, that Jewish life in America and elsewhere is undergoing important changes; and fifth, that the large turnover of Jewish social workers presents serious dangers. The program involves close cooperation between this school and the New York School of Social Work. Students attend a summer session at the Jewish Training School, spend nine months at the New York school, and return to the Jewish school for a second summer. In this way they are specially equipped to deal with a particular ethnic group, but do not lose their contact with the profession as a whole.[9]

In contrast to the Jewish school is the National Catholic School of Social Service. This was founded as a counterpoise to schools that are secularist in tendency by stressing not only the religious aspect of social work, but in particular the Catholic point of view. While some of the field work is done in non-sectarian agencies, students do not have the range of contacts made possible by the Jewish plan. On the other hand, their living together, and their daily religious services, must contribute much to the esprit de corps and morale of the group.

There are other special training schemes, such as the National Recreation School, summer courses for community chest executives, and institutes for workers in various fields. Each of them has some merit and meets a genuine need, but nothing seems to be an adequate substitute for a well-rounded course in an established professional school.

**Professional Organization and Recognition.** The older professions, such as of law, medicine, and engineering, have their organizations to promote various group interests. But until quite recently there was nothing of this sort in the field of social work. But in 1921 the American Association of Social Workers was launched with the hope of doing for this new profession what the American Bar Association and the American Medical Association have done for their respective vocations. So far the Association of Social Workers has been occupied with the formulation of professional ethical standards and membership requirements, job analysis, study of personnel practises, interpretation of social work to the public, recruiting, and promotion of professional training. The Association has forty local chapters in which face-to-face discussion supplements the information and inspiration derived from bulletins, *The Compass* (a monthly "house organ"), and an annual meeting. General policies are worked out by the National Council in which each chapter has one or more representatives; the

[9] Beginning with the fall of 1929 this program is being extended to cover two academic years.

actual business of the Association is conducted mainly by the Executive Committee which is elected at the annual meeting. A national office is maintained with a paid staff, which together with all other regular expenses is supported by membership dues. Grants have been received from large foundations for special studies. The membership requirements as revised in 1929 are as follows:[10]

Applicants for Junior Membership shall after January 1st, 1930, have the following qualifications for Junior Membership in the Association:

(1) Minimum age of 21 years.
(2) Completion of at least two years' work in an approved college.
(3) Three additional years of general education, technical training, or employment in an approved agency. This requirement may be satisfied in either one of the two following ways:
  (a) Completion of two additional years' work in an approved college plus one year's work in an approved school of social work.
  (b) Three years spent in some combination of: attendance at an approved college, attendance at an approved school of social work, or employment in an approved agency, provided however that the applicant has satisfactorily completed:
    Fifteen semester hours of social or biological science in an approved college or school of social work.
    Ten semester hours of approved technical social work courses.
    Three hundred hours of supervised field work in connection with technical social work courses.
(4) Employment at the time of application in an approved agency.

Applicants for Membership shall, after July 1st, 1933, have the following qualifications for admission to Membership in the Association:

(1) Completion of at least two years' work in an approved college.
(2) Five additional years of general education, technical training, or employment in an approved agency. This requirement may be satisfied in either one of the two following ways:

[10] *Compass*, August, 1929.

(a) Graduation from an approved college, plus one year in an approved school of social work, plus two years of employment in an approved agency.

(b) Five years spent in some combination of: attendance at an approved college, attendance at an approved school of social work, or employment in an approved agency, provided however that the applicant has satisfactorily completed:

Twenty semester hours of social and biological science in an approved college or school of social work.

Twenty-four semester hours of approved technical social work courses.

Three hundred hours of supervised field work in connection with the technical social work courses.

Two years of employment in an approved agency.

(3) (Substitute for requirements 1 and 2.) Graduation from a four year college plus completion of a two year graduate course in an approved school of social work shall be regarded as fulfilling requirements 1 and 2.

In other fields there is not only professional organization, but also some form of recognition and control by the state. So far nothing of this sort has appeared in social work, but a bill now pending before the California legislature (Spring, 1929) provides for the registration of social case workers. Group workers, institutional employees and executives were deliberately omitted in order that the test might be made first with a fairly homogeneous and well-defined group. The provisions of this bill are very similar to those which involve registration of nurses.[11]

All in all, it seems fair to say that social work is going through stages of development very much like those already transversed by other professions. Even now it is probably no exaggeration to say that the ethical and technical standards of those who belong to the American Association of Social Workers are as high as the standards of those who belong to the American Bar Association, the National Organization for Public Health Nursing, or the National Education Association.

The central field of social work has been pretty well defined, and its immediate future seems clear; but what will happen in

[11] This bill failed to become a law.

the borderlands where social work touches education, law, medicine, psychiatry, and religion no one may yet predict. The relation of social work to government seems unlikely to undergo any sudden or radical change; perhaps a growing volume and portion of social work will gradually be taken over by public departments. Social work and the labor movement have never been very close to each other. The supporters of social work have in general been hostile to organized labor and to left-wing political parties, and the wage-earning group has consequently been very suspicious of social work. Perhaps as social work lives down its reputation of being the alms of the rich and wins recognition as a special type of skilled service, there may be a drawing together. But in the main this profession and its relationships with other fields of human endeavor are still in the making.[12]

[12] An excellent discussion of the political significance of social work is to be found in Chap. VI of *The New Citizenship* by Seba Eldridge. Whereas other writers have regarded social work as an important means of training citizens and enabling them to participate in public affairs, Eldridge points out certain very serious limitations. The educational phases of social work "do not affect, except indirectly and remotely, the great mass of citizens. . . ." "This is partly because their prime interest in their supporters concerns their financial cooperation, not their civic development. . . ." "Partly because of these deficiencies in educational procedures, and partly because the social worker is so dependent on well-to-do persons for financial support, agencies attempting to deal with the underlying factors in unsatisfactory social conditions are generally unable to secure adequate funds for their work, while agencies whose work carries a simple, sentimental appeal are apt to be generously supported."

# APPENDIX A

## SUGGESTED OBSERVATION TRIPS AND FIELD WORK

As stated in the Preface, the purpose of this book is to introduce students and others to social work. For the most fruitful study of this new profession concrete material is quite essential. Most of the chapters in Part III are introduced by case studies or equivalent material: additional original data should be collected by the student in observation trips, interviews, and field work. The text itself is intended primarily to orient the student and aid him in interpreting concrete data, and arriving at generalizations which should be tested out on local situations.

Suggestions for field studies here presented will be classified according to the major types of social work distinguished in the text—case work, institution work, group work, and administration.

**Case Work Agencies.** Very often teachers, community chest executives and others initiate field study by trips to institutions But this seems inadvisable for several reasons. In the first place the visitors are likely to give most of their attention to physical equipment. This is so easy to display that guides and staff alike often fail to discuss the social work processes involved. In the second place, there are fewer trained social workers connected with institutions than with case work agencies. Hence there is less real social work to describe as well as a lack of ability to interpret.

Other things being equal, the first visit should preferably be to a family welfare society or one doing undifferentiated case work. However, the ablest interpreters of social case work are sometimes found in a children's agency, a travelers' aid society, a medical social department, or a Red Cross chapter. If the American Association of Social Workers has a chapter in the vicinity, it will probably have a Vocational Committee through which observation trips and other contacts can be planned to the best advantage. If there is a council of social agencies or a community chest, helpful advice is usually available there. In any case, the choice of agencies to visit should be made on the basis of the scope and quality of work and the interpretative skill of the staff. Also, students should visit at least two or three different types of case work agencies in order to appreciate both their differences and their similarities. Before the trip students should be prepared through reading and discussion to listen intelligently and to ask discriminating questions. The chapters in the text indicate the general ground to be covered. Wherever possible, an organization chart and routing chart should be shown. The staff members should make clear the principal functions of the agency, *i.e.,* the types of clients, the occasions of their coming to the agency, and the services rendered. They should also explain the nature of the organization, auspices under which maintained, sources of support, distribution of responsibility and division of labor. It is usually unwise to allow students to read records, but they can be shown the record forms and the filing system. Sometimes staff members can "stage" an interview for the benefit of their guests. Case work agencies worth visiting may be any of the following:

Family Welfare Society (formerly usually called Associated Charities).
Children's Aid Society.
Mother's Pension Bureau.
Probation Department.
Catholic Charities Bureau.
Jewish Social Service Bureau.
International Institute.
Travelers Aid Society.
Hospital Social Service Department.
Department of Public Welfare.

**Institutions.** Because so many visitors to institutions wax sentimental about the "dear children" or the "poor old ladies," it is necessary to discuss very carefully beforehand the purposes of the institution to be visited and the general type to which it belongs. Attention will naturally be fixed first on the buildings, grounds, and furnishings. These should be discussed in terms of their specific functions and the adequacy with which they are fulfilled. The staff especially should be observed, noting attitudes toward "inmates," conception of the tasks to be performed, background, and specific training. The "naturalness" or "artificiality" of conditions at the time of the visit merit attention. The arrival of visitors inevitably disrupts the institutional regime more or less; but sometimes the personnel will try to "carry on" about as usual, while in other cases they are obviously "on parade." Students and other visitors are always interested in the patients, wards, or residents. They need discriminating advice as to when and how they may wisely talk with or about these folk. By no means should the visitors treat them like "specimens" in a museum or a zoo. They should either pass them by most casually or chat with them quite "naturally." Old people usually like to talk. Prisoners are more likely to resent groups of visitors. Patients in hospitals should be disturbed as little as possible, especially in hospitals for mental cases. Children make quite varied responses. Sometimes they like to show off, sometimes they are shy. But always and in all types of institutions there is danger of making the "inmates" painfully aware of their situation. Every effort should be made to avoid this.

In discussing the institution with its staff it is important to cover not only such matters as diet, clothing, recreation, medical service, discipline, and the like, but also the policies and procedures relative to admissions and dismissals, the relation to other social agencies, and what is known about the "graduates." Some institution heads boast that their wards "like it and want to come back." This, when true, is not so much evidence of a well managed institution as it is of unfortunate experiences before admission. Whether visiting an institution or any other kind of social agency one should beware of those who claim to be "doing a wonderful work." The range of institutions that may be profitably visited include:

Children's Home ("orphanage").
Old People's Home.
County Farm ("almshouse").
Day Nursery.
Detention Home.
Industrial School (for juvenile delinquents).
Reformatory.
Prison.
School for Feebleminded.
School for Blind or Deaf.

**Group Work Agencies.** Many of the suggestions offered under the two preceding heads apply equally well to group work. Here, however, it is profitable to spend considerable time inquiring about the area in which the agency operates. If it is a neighborhood house or a social settlement, who are the "neighbors"? Is the population stable or transient? Is it homogeneous or mixed? What is the reputation of the area? How did the house come to be located there? Is it rendering the services most needed? Is it failing to serve any of the important groups in the area?

In the case of such organizations as Boy Scouts and Campfire Girls it will be interesting to make a spot map of the city and see whether certain areas are being neglected. If so, try to find out why? Also a study of "turn-over" or changing membership is worth while. Relations to other social work, civic, and religious organizations may also be profitably studied. Do the staff members regard themselves as social workers or not? Just what is their conception of their task?

In group work, as in the other fields, the most important things are the intangibles. Hence it is much more profitable to chat with staff and persons served, to sit quietly in a corner and watch regular activities, than it is to witness pageants. Among agencies that may well be contacted are:

Neighborhood houses and civic centers.
Social settlements.
Playgrounds.
Boy Scouts.
Campfire Girls.
Y. M. C. A. and Y. W. C. A.
Y. M. H. A. and Y. W. H. A.
Knights of Columbus.

**Administration.** In visiting any of the agencies mentioned heretofore it is possible to learn a good deal about social service administration. But certain bits of social machinery have to do with coordination, supervision, publicity, and financing, rather than with direct service to persons and groups. In studying these the annual report and the organization chart are especially important. But in addition it is well worth while to arrange interviews with staff members who can make the whole "set-up" more real and who can answer the many questions which are sure to be raised. It is interesting to collect samples of social work publicity and discuss them with reference to the variety of appeals they make. It will also be instructive to compare the viewpoints of chest executives with those of workers in service agencies. Among the offices that may well be visited are:

Council of Social Agencies.
Community Chest.
State Department of Public Welfare.
Social Service Exchange.

**Practice Work.** The suggestions offered thus far contemplate rather brief contacts and superficial acquaintance with social workers and their organizations. Sometimes, however, it is possible and profitable to initiate the beginner by an extended period of actual participation in the activities of some one agency. Of course, the student must begin with very simple tasks; but by assuming responsibility for definite duties and spending certain hours regularly in the office he will certainly gain considerable insight into the purposes and methods of the organization, its relations to other agencies, and its place in the life of the community. Usually such regular "field work" should not be attempted by college undergraduates. They have many conflicting interests; they are immature; and too often cannot be depended upon for regular service. In courses intended to introduce students to social work, therefore, arrangements should always be made for observation trips and interviews, and but rarely for practice work.

# APPENDIX B

## SELECTED READINGS

### *Note*

The selections here listed are not intended as complete bibliographies, but as samples of materials found useful in interpreting social work to undergraduate students. Starred books and articles are especially recommended. Supplementary readings for Part II have not been listed, since Warner's own presentation seems adequate for the purposes of this book.

## CHAPTER I.

### THE BEGINNINGS OF SOCIAL WORK.

Bosanquet, Helen D., *Social Work in London*. New York: Dutton, 1914.

Brandt, Lilian, *How Much Shall I Give?* New York: Frontier Press, 1921.

Breckinridge, Sophonisba P., *Public Welfare Administration in the United States*. Chicago: University of Chicago Press, 1927.

Folks, Homer, *The Care of Destitute, Neglected and Delinquent Children*. New York: Macmillan, 1902.

Herring, Harriet L., *"The Beginnings of Industrial Social Work,"* Social Forces, 5:317-324, 502-507, 1926-27.

*Kelso, Robert W., *The Science of Public Welfare*. New York, Holt, 1928.

Lallemand, Leon, *Histoire de la Charité*. 4 vols. Paris: Picard, 1902-1912.

National Conference of Charities and Correction, *Proceedings*, 1874-1916.

Nicholls, Sir George, *History of the English Poor Law*. 2 vols. London, 1854.

Picht, Werner, *Toynbee Hall and the English Settlement Movement*. London: Bell, 1914.

*Queen, Stuart A., *Social Work in the Light of History*. Philadelphia: Lippincott, 1922.

*Spalding, Henry J., *Chapters in Social History*. Boston: Heath, 1925.

Watson, Frank D., *The Charity Organization Movement in the United States*. New York: Macmillan, 1922.

Webb, Sidney, and Beatrice, *English Poor Law History.* New York: Longmans, Green, 1927.

Webb, Sidney, and Beatrice (editors), *Minority Report of the Poor Law Commission.* 2 vols. London: Longmans, Green, 1909.

Woods, R. A., and Kennedy, A. J., *The Settlement Horizon.* New York: Russell Sage Foundation, 1922.

*Young, Erle F., *History of Social Work.* Los Angeles: Western Educational Service, 1926.

## CHAPTER II.

### SOCIAL WORK FROM 1893 TO 1928.

Cannon, Ida J., *Social Work in Hospitals.* New York: Russell Sage Foundation, 1923.

Cheyney, Alice S., *The Nature and Scope of Social Work.* New York: Amer. Assn. of Social Workers, 1926.

Cooley, Edwin J., *Probation and Delinquency.* New York: Nelson, 1927.

Davies, Stanley P., *Social Control of the Feebleminded.* New York: Nat. Com. for Men. Hyg., 1923.

Dexter, Robert C., *Social Adjustment.* New York: Knopf, 1927.

Ford, James, *Social Problems and Social Policy.* Boston: Ginn, 1923.

Halbert, L. A., *What Is Professional Social Work?* Kansas City: 1923.

National Conference of Social Work, *Proceedings,* 1917-1928.

Norton, William, *The Cooperative Movement in Social Work.* New York: Macmillan, 1927.

Odencrantz, Louise C., *The Social Worker.* New York: Harper and Bros., 1929.

*O'Grady, John, *Introduction to Social Work.* New York: Century, 1928.

*Queen, Stuart A., *Social Work in the Light of History.* Philadelphia: Lippincott, 1922.

Rainwater, Clarence R., *The Play Movement in the United States.* Chicago: University of Chicago Press, 1922.

Richmond, Mary, *Social Diagnosis.* New York: Russell Sage Foundation, 1917.

Richmond, Mary, *What Is Social Case Work?* New York: Russell Sage Foundation, 1922.

*Steiner, Jesse F., *Community Organization.* New York: Century, 1925.

*Tufts, James H., *Education and Training for Social Work.* New York: Russell Sage Foundation, 1923.

Walker, Sydnor H., *Social Work and the Training of Social Workers.* Chapel Hill: University of North Carolina Press, 1928.

Wood, Arthur E., *Community Problems.* New York: Century, 1928.

Wulkop, Elsie, *The Social Worker in a Hospital Ward.* Boston: Houghton Mifflin, 1926.

Periodicals—
*The Family,* monthly, except Aug. and Sept., New York.
*Hospital Social Service,* monthly, New York.
*The Compass,* monthly, New York.
*Social Service Review,* quarterly, Chicago.
*The Survey,* semi-monthly, New York.
*Catholic Charities Review,* monthly, except July and Aug., Washington.
*Jewish Social Service Quarterly,* Philadelphia.

## CHAPTER XVI.

### Social Maladjustments and Their Interpretation.

#### *General.*

Palmer, Vivien M., *Field Studies in Sociology.* Chicago: University of Chicago Press, 1928.
Queen, Stuart A., and Mann, Delbert M., *Social Pathology.* New York: Crowell, 1925.
Thomas, W. I., and D. S., *The Child in America.* New York: Knopf, 1929.
Wile, Ira S., *The Challenge of Childhood.* New York: Seltzer, 1925.

#### *Biology and Medicine.*

Boas, Franz, Child, C. M., and Herrick, C. J., in *The Child, The Clinic, and the Court,* pp. 126-188. New York: New Republic, 1925.
Frank, L. K., *"The Management of Tensions."* Amer. Jour. Soc., 33: 705-736, 1928.
*Jennings, H. S., *Prometheus.* New York: Dutton, 1925.
Langdon-Davies, John, *The New Age of Faith.* New York: Viking Press, 1925.

#### *Economics.*

Chase, Stuart, *The Tragedy of Waste.* New York: Macmillan, 1925
Douglas, Paul H., *Wages and the Family.* Chicago: University of Chicago Press, 1925.
*Gillin, John L., *Poverty and Dependency.* New York: Century, 1926
Houghteling, Leila, *The Income and Standard of Living of Unskilled Laborers in Chicago.* Chicago: University of Chicago Press 1927.
*Kelso, Robert W., *Poverty.* New York: Longmans, Green, 1929.
National Bureau of Economic Research, various publications.
National Industrial Conference Board, various publications.
Peixotto, Jessica B., *The Control of Poverty.* Berkeley: University of California Syllabus Series, 1923.

Thomas, Dorothy S., *Social Consequences of the Business Cycle.* New York: Knopf, 1927.
United States Bureau of Labor Statistics, Bulletins.

*Psychology and Psychiatry.*

Burt, Cyril, *The Young Delinquent.* New York: Appleton, 1925.
*Davies, Stanley P., *Social Control of the Feebleminded.* New York: Nat. Com. Men. Hyg., 1923.
*Fishbein, Morris, and White, W. A., *Why Men Fail.* New York: Century, 1928.
*Healy, William, and others, *Reconstructing Behavior in Youth.* Chap. 10. New York: Knopf, 1929.
**Mental Health Primer.* New York: Nat. Com. Men. Hyg., 1926.
*Mental Hygiene.* Quarterly magazine. New York.
Morgan, J. B. B., *The Psychology of Abnormal People.* New York: Longmans, Green, 1928.
National Conference of Social Work, Division VII.
National Society for the Study of Education, *Twenty-Seventh Yearbook.* Bloomington, Ill.: Public School Publishing Co., 1928.
Thom, D. A., *Everyday Problems of the Everyday Child.* New York: Appleton, 1927.
Wembridge, Eleanor R., *Other People's Daughters.* Boston: Houghton, Mifflin, 1926.

*Sociology.*

Burgess, Ernest W., *"The Interdependence of Sociology and Social Work."* Jour. Soc. Forces, 1: 366-370, 1923.
*Cavan, Ruth Shonle, *Suicide.* Chicago: University of Chicago Press, 1928.
Karpf, M. J., *"Development of the Relations Between Sociology and Social Work."* Proceedings, Amer. Sociol. Soc., 21: 213-222, 1927.
*Lynd, Robert S., and Helen M., *Middletown.* New York: Harcourt Brace, 1929.
*Mowrer, Ernest R., *Family Disorganization.* Chicago: University of Chicago Press, 1927.
*Ogburn, W. F., *Social Change.* New York: Huebsch, 1922.
*Park, Robert E., and Miller, H. A., *Old World Traits Transplanted.* New York: Harpers, 1921.
*Steiner, Jesse F., *The American Community in Action.* New York: Holt, 1928.
*Thomas, W. I., and Znaniecki, Florian, *The Polish Peasant in Europe and America.* New York: Knopf, 1927.
*Thrasher, Frederic, *The Gang.* Chicago: University of Chicago Press, 1927.
*Zorbaugh, Harvey W., *The Gold Coast and the Slum.* Chicago: University of Chicago Press, 1929.

## CHAPTER XVII.

### THE MENTAL HYGIENE MOVEMENT.

*General.*


Bossard, James H. S., *Problems of Social Well-Being.* New York: Harper and Bros., 1927.

Burnham, W. H., *The Normal Mind.* New York: D. Appleton and Company, 1923.

Mental Hygiene (magazine), and the Mental Hygiene Bulletin.

Proceedings of the National Conference of Social Work, Division VII.

*Williams, Frankwood E., *et al., Social Aspects of Mental Hygiene.* New Haven: Yale University Press, 1925.


*History of Mental Hygiene.*


Beers, Clifford W., *The Mental Hygiene Movement.* New York: Doubleday, Page and Co., 1923. Quoted from the revised edition of *The Mind That Found Itself.*

Emerson, C. P., *"The Next Step in the Mental Hygiene Movement."* Mental Hygiene, 6: 257-262, 1922.

Hart, J. K., *"The Fortuitous Present."* Survey, 53: 535-538, 1925.

Komora, P. O., *"The History and Development of the National Committee for Mental Hygiene."* Welfare Magazine, 19: 163-168, 1928.

Stevenson, G. S., *"The Mental Hygiene Movement."* Mental Health Bulletin, Illinois Society for Mental Hygiene, 6: 1-3, October, 1927.

*Winslow, C. E. A., *"Twenty Years of Mental Hygiene."* Mental Hygiene, 12: 504-515, 1928.


*Definition and Principles of Mental Hygiene.*


Abbott, E. Stanley, *"What Is Mental Hygiene? A Definition and an Outline."* American Journal of Psychiatry, 4: 261-284, 1924.

Bossard, James H. S., *Problems of Social Well-Being.* New York: Harper and Bros., 1927. Chap. 25, "Problems of Mental Hygiene," pp. 553-580.

Burnham, W. H., *The Normal Mind.* New York: D. Appleton and Company, 1923. Chap. 20.

Burnham, W. H., *et al., A Mental Hygiene Primer.* Mass. Society for Mental Hygiene, Publication No. 42, 1925. (Out of print.)

*Campbell, Charles MacFie, *A Present Day Conception of Mental Disorders.* Cambridge: Harvard Univ. Press, 1925.

Durea, Mervin A., *"The Province and Scope of Mental Hygiene."* Journal of Abnor. and Soc. Psy., 22: 182-193, 1927.

*Hart, Bernard, *Psychopathology: Its Development and Its Place in Medicine.* New York: Macmillan Company, 1927.

MacPherson, John, "*The New Psychiatry and Influences Which Are Forming It.*" Journal of Mental Science, 74: 386-399, 1928.
*White, W. A., *Principles of Mental Hygiene*. New York: Macmillan Co., 1917.

*Insanity.*

*Beers, Clifford W., *The Mind That Found Itself*. New York: Doubleday, Page and Co. Revised edition, 1923.
Hillyer, Jane, *Reluctantly Told*. New York: 1926. Autobiography of a recovered psychopathic patient.
Jackson, J. A., and Pike, H. V., "*Community-Service Activities of the Danville (Pa.) State Hospital.*" Mental Hygiene, 10: 130-142, 1926.
Myerson, Abraham, *The Psychology of Mental Disorders*. New York: Macmillan Co., 1927.
*Pressey, S. L., and L. C., *Mental Abnormality and Deficiency*. New York: Macmillan Co., 1927.
Queen, S. A., and Mann, D. M., *Social Pathology*. New York: T. Y. Crowell, 1925. Chap. 25.
Rosanoff, A. J., *Manual of Psychiatry*. New York: John Wiley and Sons, 1920.
Southard, E. E., and Jarrett, Mary, *The Kingdom of Evils*. New York: Macmillan Co., 1922. Case studies.
*White, W. A., *Outlines of Psychiatry*. Nervous and Mental Disease Publishing Company, 1923.

*Feeblemindedness.*

Berry, Chas. S., "*The Case for the Mentally Retarded.*" Mental Hygiene, 9: 725-735, 1925.
Cornell, Ethel L., "*Function of the Special Class in the Public School.*" Mental Hygiene, 9: 556-561, 1925.
*Davies, Stanley P., *Social Control of the Feebleminded*. New York: National Committee for Mental Hygiene, 1923.
Pratt, Geo. K., "*Mental Hygiene for the Feebleminded.*" Survey, 58: 96-98, 1927.
Queen, S. A., and Mann, D. M., *Social Pathology*. New York: T. Y. Crowell, 1925. Chap. 26.
Robinson, Bruce B., "*Problems of the Community Management of the Non-institutionalized Feebleminded and Delinquent: In the Public School.*" Nat. Conference of Soc. Work, 1928, 367-372.

*Broader Applications of Mental Hygiene: Psychiatric Social Work.*

Adler, Herman M., "*Program for Meeting Psychiatric Needs in the State: Aims and Problems of the Illinois Plan.*" Nat. Confer. Soc. Work, 1926: 419-424.
Bain, Edith, "*The Psychiatric Social Worker as Consultant in a Social Agency.*" Mental Hygiene, 13: 118-122, 1929.

Blanton, Smiley, *"The Function of the Mental Hygiene Clinic in the Schools and Colleges,"* in Jane Addams, *The Child, the Clinic, and the Court,* pp. 93-102. New York: Republic Publishing Co., 1925.

Harper, Ernest B., *"Social Re-Education and Nervous Disorders."* Jour. of Religion, 3: 170-187; 290-307; 361-377.

Hopkins, C. D., *"What Can the Small City Do for Mental Hygiene?"* Survey, 52: 351-353, 1924.

*Lowrey, Lawson G., *"Some Trends in the Development of Relationships Between Psychiatry and General Social Case Work."* Mental Hygiene, 10: 277-284, 1926.

*Odencrantz, Louise C., *The Social Worker.* New York: Harper and Bros., 1929. Part III.

*Taft, Jessie, *"The Relationship of Psychiatry to Social Work."* Family, 7: 199-203, 1926.

Truitt, Ralph, *"Mental Hygiene and the Public Schools."* Mental Hygiene, 11: 261-271, 1927.

Vocational Aspects of Psychiatric Social Work. Prepared by a committee of the American Asso. of Psychiatric Social Workers. New York: American Asso. of Social Workers, 1926.

Wickman, E. K., *Children's Behavior and Teachers' Attitudes.* New York: Commonwealth Fund, Division of Publications, 1929.

Wile, Ira S., *"Mental Hygiene in the Public Schools."* Mental Hygiene, 13: 70-80, 1929.

Williams, Frankwood E., *"Mental Hygiene and the College Student."* Mental Hygiene, 5: 283-301, 1921.

## CHAPTER XVIII.

### Social Case Work in General.

Baskett, Janet D., *"Undifferentiated Case Work Through the Medium of Rural Schools."* Nat. Conf. Soc. Work, 1928: 85-89.

*Bibliography for Social Case Workers.* References to Articles Published in *The Family,* Volumes 1-9, 1920-1928.

Brisley, Mary S., *"An Attempt to Articulate Processes."* Family, 5: 157-161, 1924.

*De Schweinitz, Karl, *The Art of Helping People Out of Trouble.* Boston: Houghton Mifflin, 1924.

Lee, Porter R., *"A Study of Social Treatment."* Family, 4: 191-199, 1923.

Lucas, Jean M., *"The Interview of Persuasion."* Family, 5: 128-132, 1924.

Mowrer, Ernest R., *Domestic Discord.* Chicago: University of Chicago Press, 1929.

*Myrick, Helen L., and others, *Interviews.* New York: Amer. Assn. Social Workers, 1928.

Odencrantz, Louise C., *The Social Worker.* New York: Harper and Bros., 1929.

Queen, Stuart A., *"Social Interaction in the Interview."* Social Forces, 6: 545-558, 1928.
Reynolds, Bertha C., *"Treatment Processes as Developed by the Social Worker."* Nat. Conf. Soc. Work, 1926: 400-407.
Rich, Margaret E., *"A Study of Case Work Processes."* Compass, Nov. and Dec., 1923.
Richmond, Mary E., *Social Diagnosis.* New York: Russell Sage Foundation, 1917.
*Richmond, Mary E., *What Is Social Case Work?* New York: Russell Sage Foundation, 1922.
Sheffield, Ada E., *Case-Study Possibilities.* Boston: Research Bureau on Social Case Work, 1922.
Sheffield, Ada E., *The Social Case History.* New York: Russell Sage Foundation, 1920.
Sheffield, Ada E., and Myrick, Helen L., *"Reflective By-Products of a Social Treatment Interview."* Jour. Soc. Forces, 3: 657-665, 1925.
Taft, Jessie, *"The Social Worker's Opportunity."* Nat. Conf. Soc. Work, 1922: 371-375.
**Social Case Work, Generic and Specific.* A Report of the Milford Conference. New York: Amer. Assn. Soc. Workers, 1929.

## CHAPTER XIX.

### Family Welfare Work.

Almy, Frederic, and others, *Fifty Years of Family Social Work.* Buffalo: Charity Organization Society, 1927.
American Association for Organizing Family Social Work.
*Quarterly Bulletins.*
*Directory* (annual).
*The Family* (monthly).
*Bibliography for Social Case Workers.*
Bogue, Mary F., *Administration of Mothers' Aid in Ten Localities.* U. S. Children's Bureau, Pub. No. 184, 1928.
Breckinridge, Sophonisba P., *Family Welfare Work in a Metropolitan Community.* Chicago: University of Chicago Press, 1924.
*De Schweinitz, Karl, *The Art of Helping People Out of Trouble.* Boston: Houghton Mifflin, 1924.
Gillin, John L., *Poverty and Dependency.* New York: Century, 1926.
Karpf, M. J., *A Social Audit of a Social Service Agency.* Chicago: Jewish Social Service Bureau, 1925.
Kelso, Robert W., *The Science of Public Welfare.* Chaps. 8-14. New York: Holt, 1928.
Lundberg, Emma O., *"Progress of Mothers' Aid Legislation."* Soc. Serv. Rev., 2: 435-458, 1928.
McLean, F. H., *The Family Society: Joint Responsibility of Board, Staff, and Membership.* New York: Amer. Assn. Org. Fam. Soc. Work, 1927.

McLean, F. H., *The Organization of Family Social Work Societies in Smaller Cities.* New York: Amer. Assn. Org. Fam. Soc. Work, 1921.
Mowrer, Ernest R., *Domestic Discord.* Chicago: University of Chicago Press, 1928.
National Conference of Catholic Charities.
*Proceedings* (annual).
*Catholic Charities Review* (monthly).
National Conference of International Institutes.
*Proceedings* (annual).
National Conference of Jewish Social Work.
*Proceedings* (annual).
*Jewish Social Service Quarterly.*
National Conference of Social Work.
*Proceedings,* Division IV (annual).
National Probation Association.
*Proceedings,* Reports of Committee on Domestic Relations (annual).
*Odencrantz, Louise C., *The Social Worker.* Part I. New York: Harper and Bros., 1929.
*O'Grady, John, *Introduction to Social Work.* Chaps. 2-4. New York: Century, 1928.
Richmond, Mary E., *Social Diagnosis.* New York: Russell Sage Foundation, 1917.
*Richmond, Mary E., *What Is Social Case Work?* New York: Russell Sage Foundation, 1922.
*Sixty-Six Years of Service.* Chicago: United Charities, 1922.
Steiner, Jesse F., *Community Organization.* Chap. 14. New York: Century, 1925.
Townsend, Harriet, *Social Work, a Family Builder.* Philadelphia: Saunders, 1926.
**Vocational Aspects of Family Social Work.* New York: Amer. Assn. Social Workers, 1926.
*Watson, Frank D., *The Charity Organization Movement in the United States.* New York: Macmillan, 1922.

## CHAPTER XX.

### CHILDREN'S AID AND PROTECTIVE WORK.

Bernstein, Salome, *"Mothers by Proxy."* Survey, 56:81-83, 1926.
Child Welfare League of America.
*Bulletins* (monthly and special).
*Case Studies.*
*Directory* (annual).
Crutcher, Hester B., *"Some Misplaced Children."* Survey, 56:83-84, 1926.
Doran, Mary S., and Reynolds, Bertha C., *The Selection of Foster Homes for Children.* New York: School of Social Work, 1919.

Guibord, Alberta S. B., *"Educating the Dependent Child."* Men. Hyg., 10: 318-344, 1926.
*Healy, William, and others, *Reconstructing Behavior in Youth.* New York: Knopf, 1929.
Kelso, Robert W., *History of Public Poor Relief in Massachusetts.* Chap. 8. Boston: Houghton Mifflin, 1922.
Merrill, Laura, *Where Shall Children Be Brought Up?* Family, 5: 224-227, 1925.
National Conference of Social Work.
*Proceedings,* Division I (annual).
Parker, Ida R., *"Fit and Proper?"* Boston: Church Home Society, 1927.
Slingerland, W. H., *Child Placing in Families.* New York: Russell Sage Foundation, 1919.
Taft, Jessie, *"The Placing of Children Who Are Difficult to Adjust."* Family, 4: 39-46.
Richards, Esther L., *"Formulating the Problem in Social Work with Children."* Men. Hyg., 11: 688-702, 1927.
*Theis, Sophie van Senden, *How Foster Children Turn Out.* New York: State Charities Aid Assn., 1924.
*Theis, Sophie, and Goodrich, Constance, *The Child in the Foster Home.* New York: School of Social Work, 1921.
Towle, Charlotte, *"The Evaluation of Homes in Preparation for Child Placements."* Men. Hyg., 11: 460-481, 1927.
United States Children's Bureau, Publications.
No. 148, *Adoption Laws in the United States,* 1925.
No. 150, *Children Indentured by the Wisconsin Public School,* 1925.
No. 169, *The County as a Unit,* 1926.
*No. 171, *The Work of Child-Placing Agencies,* 1927.
No. 173, *Public Child-Caring Work,* 1927.
Nos. 174, 175, 180, *Child Welfare in New Jersey,* 1927.
No. 176, *Child Welfare in Seven Pennsylvania Counties,* 1927.
No. 177, *The Children's Bureau of Cleveland,* 1927.

## CHAPTER XXI.

### Child Guidance.

Anderson, V. V., *"Child Guidance Clinics Planned for Problem Children."* Nation's Health, 6: 684-689, 1924.
Basch, Goldie, *"Some Phases of Cooperative Case Work."* Mental Hygiene, 13: 108-117, 1929.
Blanton, Smiley, and Margaret G., *Child Guidance.* New York: Century, 1927.
Ellis, Mabel Brown, *The Visiting Teacher in Rochester.* New York: Joint Committee on Methods of Preventing Delinquency, Pub. No. 6, 1925.

Emery, E. van Norman, *The Child Guidance Clinic.* New York: National Committee for Mental Hygiene, 1926.
Foster, Sybil, "*Personality Deviations and Their Relation to the Home.*" Mental Hygiene, 9: 735-743, 1925.
Kenworthy, Marion, "*Mental Health in Childhood.*" Mental Hygiene, 10: 242-252, 1926.
List of Psychiatric Clinics for Children in the United States. Children's Bureau, Publication No. 191, 1929.
Lowrey, Lawson G., *A Child-Guidance Clinic: Its Purposes and Methods of Service.* New York: National Committee for Mental Hygiene, 1924.
Neumann, Frederick, "*The Effects on the Child of an Unstable Home Situation.*" Mental Hygiene, 12: 742-750, 1928.
*Oppenheimer, J. J., *The Visiting Teacher Movement.* New York: Joint Committee on Methods of Preventing Delinquency. Pub. No. 5, 1925.
Progress Report, Commonwealth Fund Program for the Prevention of Delinquency. New York, 1926.
Reynolds, Bertha C., "*Environmental Handicaps of 400 Habit Clinic Children.*" Hospital Social Service, 12: 329-336, 1925.
Robinson, Bruce B., "*Types of Clinical Service Available to Children's Agencies.*" Nat. Conference of Social Work, 1926, 407-412.
*Three Problem Children.* Pub. No. 2, Joint Committee, New York, 1924.
*Sayles, Mary B., *The Problem Child in School,* Pub. No. 4. 1925.
*The Problem Child at Home.* New York: Commonwealth Fund, Division of Publications, 1928.
The above three volumes are collections of case studies.
Schaffner, Halle, "*New Candles of Understanding.*" Survey, 61: 674-675, 1929.
*Smith, Barry C., "*The Commonwealth Fund Program for the Prevention of Delinquency.*" Nat. Conference of Social Work, 1922: 168-174.
Stevenson, George S., "*When Is a Community Ready for a Child Guidance Clinic?*" Mental Hygiene, 12: 492-503, 1928.
*Thom, Douglas A., *The Practical Application of Mental Hygiene to the Welfare of the Child.* U. S. Children's Bur., Pub. No. 157, 1926.
*Everyday Problems of the Everyday Child.* New York: D. Appleton and Company, 1927.
*Habit Clinics for the Child of Preschool Age.* U. S. Children's Bureau, Pub. No. 135, 1924.
*Thomas, William I., and Dorothy Swaine, *The Child in America.* New York: A. A. Knopf, 1928.
*Truitt, Ralph P., *et al., The Child Guidance Clinic and the Community.* New York: Commonwealth Fund, Division of Publications, 1928.
Wile, Ira S., *The Challenge of Childhood.* New York: Thomas Seltzer, 1925.
*Williams, Frankwood E., *et al., Social Aspects of Mental Hygiene.* New Haven: Yale University Press, 1925.

## CHAPTER XXII.

### MEDICAL SOCIAL WORK.

American Hospital Association, Bulletins.
No. 23, *Survey of Hospital Social Service,* 1920.
No. 55, *Training for Hospital Social Work,* 1923.
Baker, Edith M., *"Fundamentals of Hospital Social Service and Its Relation to Other Agencies."* Family, 6: 244-248, 1925.
*Breckinridge, Sophonisba P. (editor), *Medical Social Case Records.* Chicago: University of Chicago Press, 1928.
Brogden, Margaret S., *Handbook of Organization and Method in Hospital Social Service.* Baltimore: Norman Remington, 1922.
Bryant, Louise Stevens, *"Statistical Report of One Thousand Social Cases Classified and Interpreted."* Hosp. Soc. Serv., 17: 446-500, 1928.
Cabot, Richard C., *"Hospital and Dispensary Social Work."* Hosp. Soc. Serv., 18: 269-320, 1928.
*Cannon, Ida M., *Social Work in Hospitals.* New York: Russell Sage Foundation, 1923.
Cannon, M. Antoinette, *"History and Development of Hospital Social Work."* Family, 4: 250-255, 1924.
Catlin, Lucy C., *The Hospital as a Social Agency in the Community.* Philadelphia: Saunders, 1918.
Davis, Michael M., *Clinics, Hospitals, and Health Centers.* New York: Harper and Bros., 1927.
Farmer, Gertrude L., *Form of Record for Hospital Social Work.* Philadelphia: Lippincott, 1921.
Hamilton, Gordon, *A Medical Social Terminology.* New York: Committee on Dispensary Development, 1927.
Henry, Edna G., *The Theory and Practise of Medical Social Work.* Ann Arbor: Edwards, 1924.
*Hospital Social Service,* monthly magazine.
Moore, Harry H., *Public Health in the United States.* New York: Harper and Bros., 1923.
Odencrantz, Louise C., *The Social Worker,* Part II. New York: Harper and Bros., 1929.
Schroeder, Agnes, *"Prize Medical Social Case Record: Charles Roque."* Soc. Serv. Rev., 2: 304-322, 487-496, 626-636, 1928.
*Selected Bibliography on Social Work in Hospitals and Dispensaries.* Baltimore: Amer. Assn. Hosp. Soc. Workers, 1923.
*Technique of Hospital Social Service.* New York: Associated Outpatient Clinics, 1926.
**Vocational Aspects of Medical Social Work.* New York: Amer. Assn. Social Workers, 1927.
*Wulkop, Elsie, *The Social Worker in a Hospital Ward.* Boston: Houghton Mifflin, 1926.

## CHAPTER XXIII.

### Probation and Parole.

American Prison Association.
*Proceedings* (annual).
Bramer, John P., *Parole*. New York: 1927.
*Bruce, A. A., Burgess, E. W., and Harno, A. J., *"The Workings of the Indeterminate Sentence Law and the Parole System in Illinois."* Jour. Crim. Law, May, 1928, Part II.
Burleigh, Edith N., and Harris, Frances R., *The Delinquent Girl.* New York: School of Social Work, 1923.
*Cooley, Edwin J., *Probation and Delinquency.* New York: Nelson, 1927.
Gillin, John L., *Criminology and Penology.* Chaps. 29, 34, 35. New York: Century, 1926.
Healy, William, and others, *Reconstructing Behavior in Youth.* New York: Knopf, 1929.
Hiller, F. H., *Probation in Wisconsin.* New York: Nat. Prob. Assn., 1926.
Johnson, Fred R., *Probation for Juveniles and Adults.* New York: Century, 1928.
*Journal of the American Institute of Criminal Law and Criminology,* quarterly.
Kuhlmann, A. F., *Guide to Material on Crime and Criminal Justice.* New York: Wilson, 1929.
Lenroot, Katharine F., and Lundberg, Emma O., *Juvenile Courts at Work.* U. S. Children's Bureau, Pub. No. 141, 1925.
*List of References on Juvenile Courts and Probation.* U. S. Children's Bureau, Pub. No. 124, 1923.
Lou, H. H., *Juvenile Courts in the United States.* Chapel Hill: University of North Carolina Press, 1927.
Massachusetts Commission on Probation, *Report on an Inquiry into the Permanent Results of Probation.* Mass. Senate Document No. 431, 1924.
Missouri Crime Survey, Part XI, *Pardons, Paroles and Commutation.* New York: Macmillan, 1926.
National Conference of Juvenile Agencies.
*Proceedings* (annual).
National Conference of Social Work.
*Proceedings,* Division II (annual).
National Probation Association.
*Proceedings* (annual).
*Bulletins* (monthly and special).
*Bibliography.*
Pennsylvania State Parole Commission, *Report,* 1927.
*Probation in New York State:* A Review of the Development and Use of Probation from 1907 to 1921. Albany: State Probation Commission, 1922.

*Sutherland, Edwin H., *Criminology*. Chaps. 13, 22, 23. Philadelphia: Lippincott, 1924.

*The Child, The Clinic, and The Court*. New York: New Republic, 1925.

Thomas, William I., and Dorothy S., *The Child in America*. New York: Knopf, 1928.

*Van Waters, Miriam, *Youth in Conflict*. New York: New Republic, 1925.

## CHAPTER XXIV.

### Social Work in Industry.

Anderson, V. V., *Psychiatry in Industry*. New York: Harper and Bros., 1929.

*Bingham, Walter, and Freyd, Max, *Procedures in Employment Psychology*. Chicago: A. W. Shaw Co., 1926.

*Bloomfield, Daniel, ed., *Problems in Personnel Management*. New York: Ronald Press, 1923.

*Labor Maintenance*. New York: Ronald Press, 1920.

*Boettiger, L. E., *Employee Welfare Work*. New York: Ronald Press, 1923.

Burtt, Harold E., *Principles of Employment Psychology*. New York: Houghton Mifflin, 1926.

Commons, John R., *Industrial Government*. New York: Macmillan, 1921.

*Downey, E. H., *Workman's Compensation*. New York: Macmillan, 1924.

Edgerton, Alanson H., *Vocational Guidance and Counseling*. New York: Macmillan, 1926.

Harvard Business Reports, Volume IV.

Herring, Harriet L., *Welfare Work in Mill Villages*. Chapel Hill, N. C.: Univ. of North Carolina Press, 1929.

*"Beginnings of Industrial Social Work."* Jour. Soc. Forces, 5:317-324, 1926, and 5:502-507, 1927.

*Myers, James, *Representative Government in Industry*. New York: Doran, 1924.

Payne, Arthur F., *The Organization of Vocational Guidance*. New York: McGraw-Hill, 1925.

Personnel Journal. Baltimore: Williams and Wilkins. Formerly the Journal of Personnel Research.

Queen, Stuart A., *Social Work in the Light of History*. Philadelphia: J. B. Lippincott, 1922. Chap. 5. "Industrial Welfare Work." 90-103.

*Queen, S. A., and Mann, Delbert, *Social Pathology*. New York: Crowell, 1925.

Southard, E. E., *"The Movement for a Mental Hygiene of Industry."* Mental Hygiene, January 1920.

*Tead, Ordway, and Metcalf, Henry C., *Personnel Administration*. New York: McGraw-Hill, 1920.

Todd, A. J., *"Social Work and Industry."* Applied Sociology, 8: 325-328, 1924.
*Watkins, Gordon S., *Labor Management.* Chicago: A. W. Shaw, 1928.

## CHAPTER XXV.

### CHILDREN'S INSTITUTIONS.

Chapin, Henry Dwight, *"Family vs. Institution."* Survey, 55: 484-488, 1926.
Child Welfare League of America.
  *Bulletins* (monthly and special).
  *Case Studies.*
  *Directory* (annual).
*Children Under Institutional Care, 1923.* U. S. Bureau of the Census, 1927.
Clifton, Eleanor, *"The Rôle of Personalities in the Treatment of Problem Children in an Institution."* Nat. Conf. Soc. Work, 1926: 442-448.
*Deardorff, Neva R., *"The New Pied Pipers."* Survey, 52: 31-47, 56-61, 1924.
*Drucker, Saul, and Hexter, Maurice B., *Children Astray.* Cambridge: Harvard University Press, 1923.
Goldrich, Leon W., *A Manual of Directions, Suggestions and Guidance for Cottage Mothers and Supervisors.* Pleasantville, N. Y.: Hebrew Sheltering Guardian Society, 1925.
Hincks, Anne P., *"The Place of Institutional Care."* Family, 5: 243-246, 1925.
National Conference of Juvenile Agencies.
  *Proceedings* (annual).
National Conference of Social Work.
  *Proceedings,* Division I (annual).
Queen, Stuart A., *"Are Orphan Asylums Necessary?"* Jour. Soc. Forces, 2: 384-388, 1924.
*Reeder, R. R., *How Two Hundred Children Live and Learn.* New York: Russell Sage Foundation, 1909.
Reeder, R. R., *"Our Orphaned Asylums."* Survey, 54: 283-287, 1925. (See replies, Survey, 54: 623-625, 1925.)
Reeder, R. R., *"The Place of Children's Institutions."* Survey, 61: 482-484, 1929.
Richardson, C. S., *Round Table Plan for Trustees of Institutions for Dependent Children.* Five monographs. New York: Russell Sage Foundation, 1916.
Thompson, J. R., *"Health and Happiness in an Institution."* Survey, 54: 621-623, 1925.
Tyson, Helen Glenn, *Day Nurseries in Pennsylvania.* Pennsylvania Dep't of Welfare, Bul. No. 17, 1924.
Tyson, Helen Glenn, *The Day Nursery in Its Community Relations.* Philadelphia: Assn. of Day Nurseries, 1919.

Ueland, Elsa, "*The Care of Children in Institutions.*" Nat. Conf. Social Work, 1924: 128-130.
Wahl, Spencer A., "*Keeping Children Well in Institutions.*" Survey, 53: 461-462, 1925.
Wile, Ira S., "*The Changing I. Q. in Children's Institutions.*" Survey, 61: 89-91, 1928.
Wile, Ira S., "*Child Care or Child Development?*" Survey, 61: 370-372, 1928.
Williams, C. V. (editor), *What Dependent Children Ought to Have.* New York: Child Welfare League of America, 1922.
Williams, R. R., "*The Effects on Personality and Social Attitudes of Institutional Placement.*" Nat. Conf. Soc. Work, 1928: 231-238.

## CHAPTER XXVI.

### Homes for the Aged.

*Bardwell, Francis, *The Adventure of Old Age.* Boston: Houghton Mifflin, 1926.
Chesley, Annie L., *Who Are the Benefactors?*" Boston: Beacon Press, 1924.
Clapp, Raymond, "*The Aged in Institutions.*" Survey, 59: 632-634, 1928.
Connecticut, *Report of the Department of Public Welfare.* Pub. Doc. No. 28, 1927.
Dublin, Louis I., "*Old Age: An Increasing Problem.*" Survey, 56: 545-546, 1926.
Dutcher, Elizabeth, "*Care of the Aged from the Point of View of the Private Society.*" Family, 7: 146-151, 1926.
Eaves, Lucile, "*Almshouse Care for Chronic Patients.*" Survey, 61: 807-808, 1929.
Eaves, Lucile, "*Pensions or Poorhouses?*" Survey, 59: 613-615, 1928.
Eaves, Lucile, "*The Aged Citizens of Massachusetts.*" Survey, 55: 554-556, 1926.
*Eaves, Lucile, *Aged Clients of Boston Social Agencies.* Boston: Women's Educational and Industrial Union, 1925.
*Epstein, Abraham, *The Challenge of the Aged.* New York: Macy-Masius, 1929.
Epstein, Abraham, "*Challenge of the Aged Poor.*" Nat. Conf. Soc. Work, 1925, 328-334.
*Evans, Harry C., *The American Poor Farm and Its Inhabitants.* Des Moines: The Yeoman Shield, 1926.
Folks, Homer, "*Home Life for the Aged.*" Survey, 53:71-72, 1924.
Frankel, Emil, *Poor Relief in Pennsylvania.* Harrisburg: State Dept. of Welfare, Bul. 21. 1925. Chapter 4.
Gillin, John L., *Poverty and Dependency.* New York: Century Company, 2d Ed. 1926. Chapters 14 and 18.
Indiana *Bulletin of Charities and Corrections,* July 1928. *County Poor Asylums and Their Administration,* 345-362.

Johnson, Alexander, *The Almshouse*. New York: Russell Sage Foundation, 1911.
Johnson, Alexander, "*The Care of the Aged Poor.*" Family, 9:19-24, 1928.
Massachusetts Commission on Pensions, *Report on Old Age Pensions*. Senate Documents, No. 5, 1925.
National Conference of Social Work, 1926: 519-532.
*Paupers in Almshouses, 1923*, U. S. Bureau of the Census, 1925.
Pretzer, Clarence A., "*The Care of the Homeless in Cleveland.*" Family, 7: 42-44, 1926.
*Some American Almshouses*. New York: Nat. Civic Fed., Women's Dept., 1928. XXVI.
Stewart, Estelle M., *The Cost of American Almshouses*. U. S. Bur. Lab. Statistics, Bul. No. 386, 1925.
*Sweeney, Ed., *Poorhouse Sweeney: Life in a Country Almshouse*. New York: Boni and Liveright, 1927. Autobiographical.

## CHAPTER XXVII.

### Social Work in Prisons and Reformatories.

Barnes, Harry Elmer, "*Scientic Treatment of Crime.*" Current History, 27: 309-314, 1927.
Breckinridge, Sophonisba Preston, *Public Welfare Administration in the United States*. Chicago: University of Chicago Press, 1927.
Connecticut, *Report of the Department of Public Welfare*, 1927-1928.
Doll, E. A., "*Some Principles of Correctional Treatment.*" Crim. Law and Criminol., 18: 197-206, 1927.
*Drucker, Saul, and Hexter, Maurice B., *Children Astray*. Cambridge: Harvard University Press, 1923. Case Studies.
Frederick, Joseph, "*Education in Prison.*" Survey, 57: 490-491, 1927.
Garrett, P. W., and MacCormick, A. H., *Handbook of American Prisons*. New York: G. P. Putnam's Sons, 1925.
Harper, Ernest B., "*Individualizing Sin and the Sinner.*" Jour. of Religion, 5: 255-276, 397-418, 1925.
Hart, Hastings H., "*The Rural Jail.*" Nat. Conf. Soc. Work, 1927, 152-157.
Kirchwey, George W., "*Why We Send Folks to Prison.*" World Tomorrow, 8: 131-133, 1925.
*Liepmann, M., "*American Prisons and Reformatory Institutions: A Report.*" Nat. Committee for Men. Hygiene, 1928. See also Mental Hygiene, 12: 225-315, 1928.
MacCormick, Austin H., "*Send Them Up—To What?*" Survey, 8: 598-601, 634, 1926.
Martin, Walter B., "*Development of Psychoses in Prison.*" Crim. Law and Criminol., 18: 404-415, 1927.
Osborne, Thomas Mott, *Within Prison Walls*. New York, 1914.
Overholser, Winfred, "*Psychiatric Service in Penal and Reformatory Institutions and Criminal Courts in the United States,*" Mental Hygiene, 12: 801-838, 1928.

Parsons, Philip A., *Crime and the Criminal.* New York: Alfred A. Knopf, 1926.
Porter, Rebecca N., *"The World of Forgotten Men."* Survey, 61: 738-740; 52: 54-55, 1929.
Queen, Stuart A., *The Passing of the County Jail.* Menasha, Wis.: Geo. Banta Co., 1920.
*Reeves, Margaret, *Training Schools for Delinquent Girls.* New York: Russell Sage Fdn., 1929.
*Stutsman, Jesse O., *Curing the Criminal.* New York: Macmillan Co., 1926.
*Sutherland, Edwin H., *Criminology,* Philadelphia: Lippincott Co., 1924.
United States Bureau of the Census, *"Prisoners—1923."* Washington, D. C., 1926.
United States Bureau of the Census, *"Children Under Institutional Care—1923."* Washington, D. C., 1927.
Van Waters, Miriam, *"What is the Test of Success?"* Nat. Confer. Soc. Work, 1925, 117-120.

## CHAPTER XXVIII.

### Neighborhood and Community Work.

*Case Studies and Concrete Material.*

de S. Brunner, Edmund, *Village Communities.* New York: Institute of Social and Religious Research, 1927.
Franklin, S. P., *"A Community Study: Berea, Ohio."* Journal of Religious Education, 24: 308-313, 1929.
Glueck, Eleanor T., *"Description and Analysis of Dorchester School Center, Boston."* Jour. of Social Forces, 3: 468-473, 1925.
Jackson, Thorstina, *"Icelandic Communities in North Dakota."* Jour. of Social Forces, 4: 355-360, 1925.
Krout, Maurice H., *"A Community in Flux. The Chicago Ghetto Resurveyed."* Jour. of Social Forces, 5: 273-282, 1926.
*Lynd, Robert S. and Helen M., *Middletown: A Study in Contemporary American Culture.* New York: Harcourt, Brace and Co., 1929.
Perry, C. A., *"School Center History in Chicago."* Jour. of Social Forces, 3: 291-4, 1925.
*Pettit, Walter W., *Case Studies in Community Organization.* New York: Century Company, 1928.
Reid, Ira De A., *"Mirrors of Harlem—Investigations and Problems of America's Largest Colored Community."* Jour. of Social Forces, 5: 628-634, 1927.
Remer, Alice W., *"The East Boston School Center."* Jour. of Social Forces, 5: 97-102, 1926.
*Steiner, Jesse F., *The American Community in Action.* New York: Henry Holt, 1928.
Street, Elwood, *"Community Organization in Greater St. Louis."* Journal of Social Forces, 6: 248-252, 1927.

Whitehouse, W. W., *"Principles of Community Organization."* School and Society, 28: 467-472, 1928.

*General*

Addams, Jane, *"How Much Social Work Can a Community Afford?"* Survey 57: 199-201, 1926.

*Bowman, Leroy E., *"Group and Community Organization."* Amer. Journal of Sociology, 34: 1081-8, 1929.

*Community Conflict.* New York: The Inquiry, 1929.

Earle, Genevieve B., *"The Meaning of the Community Center Movement."* Jour. of Social Forces, 3: 294, 1925.

Eldridge, Seba, *"Community Organization and Citizenship."* Jour. of Social Forces, 7: 132-140, 1928.

Gillette, J. M., *"Community Concepts."* Jour. of Social Forces, 4: 677-690, 1926.

Glueck, Eleanor T., *The Community Use of Schools.* Baltimore: Williams and Wilkins, 1927.

Groves, Ernest R., *The Rural Mind and Social Welfare.* Chicago: Univ. of Chicago Press, 1922.

Guild, June P., *"An Institute on Community Planning."* Jour. of Social Forces, 7: 261-262, 1928.

Harris, E. P. and Hooke, F. H., *The Community Newspaper.* New York: Appleton Co., 1923.

Jordan, Orvis F., *"The Community Church as a Community Builder."* Jour. of Social Forces, 5: 282-8, 1926.

Kellogg, Paul U., *"Our Hidden Cities and American Zest for Discovery."* Survey, 60: 391-2; 409-411; 416, 1928.

Kellogg, Paul U. and Deardorf, Neva R., *"Tools for Applying Social Research to Community Progress."* Survey, 60: 478, 1928.

McClenahan, B. A., *Organizing the Community.* New York: Century, 1922.

Park, Robert E., *"Community Organization and the Romantic Temper."* Jour. of Social Forces, 3: 673-7, 1925.

Queen, Stuart A., *Social Work in the Light of History.* Philadelphia: J. B. Lippincott, 1922.

Queen, C. N., and S. A., *"Obstacles to Community Organization."* Applied Sociol., May-June, 1924, 283-8.

Snedden, David, *"Neighborhoods and Neighborliness."* Jour. of Social Forces, 5: 231-37, 1926.

*Steiner, Jesse F., *Community Organization.* New York: Century, 1925.

*Wood, Arthur Evans, *Community Problems.* New York: Century, 1928.

Woods, Robert A., *The Neighborhood in Nation Building: The Running Comment of Thirty Years at South End House.* New York: Houghton Mifflin, 1923.

*Zorbaugh, Harvey W., *The Gold Coast and the Slum.* Chicago: Univ. of Chicago Press, 1929.

## CHAPTER XXIX.

### Recreation and Group Work.

Anderson, Nels and Lindeman, E. C., *Urban Sociology*. New York: Alfred A. Knopf, 1928.

Bowman, Leroy E., *"Group and Community Organization."* Amer. Jour. Soc., 34: 130-9, 1928.

Bowman, Leroy E., *"Group and Community Organization."* Amer. Jour. Soc., 34: 1081-8, 1929.

*"Buffalo's Recreation Survey."* Jour. of Social Forces, 4: 566-575, 1926.

Butterworth, W. S., *"Case Values of Recreation."* Survey, 61: 229-230, 1928.

Curtis, H. S., *"Scope and Tendencies of the Play Movement,"* Jour. of Social Forces, 5: 430-435, 1927.

Elsom, James Claude, *Community Recreation*. New York: Century, 1929.

Hanmer, Lee F., *et al.*, *Public Recreation: A Study of Parks, Playgrounds and Other Outdoor Recreation Facilities*. New York: Regional Plan of New York and Its Environs, 1928.

Hanmer, Lee F., *"The Relation of Public Recreation to Delinquency."* Amer. City, 40: 119-120, 1929.

Jones, H. S., *"Recreation Trends in America."* Annals of the Amer. Academy, Jan., 1923.

Jones, Wm. H., *Recreation and Amusement among Negroes in Washington, D. C.*, Howard University Press, 1927.

Lies, Eugene T., *"Community Responsibility toward the Leisure-time Problem."* Nat. Conf. Soc. Work, 1928: 310-13.

Nash, Jay B., *The Organization and Administration of Playgrounds and Recreation*. New York: A. S. Barnes, 1927.

*Playground Magazine*. See files. Also *Yearbook* numbers.

Playground and Recreation Association of America, 315 Fourth Avenue, New York. Publications—
*Park Manual:* Survey of Parks and Playgrounds, 1927.
*Play Areas: Their Design and Equipment.*
*Community Drama.*
*Normal Course in Play.*
*Camping Out. A Manual on Organized Camping.*
*Community Music.*

*Rainwater, C. E., *The Play Movement in the United States*. Chicago: University of Chicago Press, 1922.

Seman, Philip L., *"Chicago's Program for Meeting Its Recreation Needs,"* Nat. Con. Soc. Work, 1925: 493-509.

Steiner, Jesse F., *Community Organization*. New York: Century, 1925, Chap. 8.

Street, Elwood, *"Important Elements in a Comprehensive Leisure Time Program."* Nat. Conf. Soc. Work, 1928: 313-316.

Thomas, William I., and Dorothy Swaine, *The Child in America,* New York: Alfred A. Knopf, 1928. Chap. 4. "Community Organizations."
Washington, F. B., "*Recreation Facilities for the Negro.*" Annals Amer. Academy, 140: 272-282, 1928.
Williams, J. B., "*Progress in Community Recreation in the South.*" Nat. Conf. Soc. Work, 1928: 316-319.
Williams, Marguerite P., *Sources of Information on Play and Recreation.* New York: Russell Sage Fdn., rev. ed., 1927.
Wood, Arthur Evans, *Community Problems.* New York: Century, 1928.
Wood, Mabel T., "*America Gets on the Grass.*" Survey, 60: 95 ff., 1928.

## CHAPTER XXX.

### Promotion and Publicity.

American Society for the Control of Cancer, 25 West 43d Street, New York.
Committee on Publicity Methods in Social Work, 130 East 22d Street, New York.
De Schweinitz, Karl, "*A Federation Publicity Program.*" Nat. Confer. Soc. Work, 1922: 405-9.
Eklund, Edwin G., "*Rechristened and Re-made at 65.*" Survey, 60: 603-4, 1928.
Emerson, Haven, "*A Plan for Promoters.*" Survey, 57: 221, 1926.
Graves, W. B., *Readings in Public Opinion.* New York: D. Appleton and Co., 1928.
Guild, A. A., "*A Mid-Year Publicity Contest.*" Survey, 56: 647-8, 1926.
Gwin, J. Blaine, "*The Romance of Philanthropy.* Survey, 61: 476-7, 1929.
Haynes, R., "*Necessity of Factual Basis in Planning Community Work.*" Nat. Confer. Soc. Work, 1927: 454-9.
Hodges, L. M., "*Which Way Publicity?*" Survey, 62: 457-461, 1929.
Kelso, Robert W., "*What is a Social Work Executive?*" Survey, 57: 820-822, 1927; 58: 114-115; 121, 1927; 58: 229-231, 1927.
Kelso, Robert W., "*The Need of Educational Publicity in Social Work.*" Nat. Confer. Soc. Work, 1926: 637-641.
Kinsley, Sherman C., "*Interpretive Publicity.*" Nat. Confer. Soc. Work, 1920: 263-265.
Kohn, Laura U., *A Publicity Primer.* New York: Publicity Bureau of National Congress of Parents and Teachers.
*Marts, A. C., "*A Campaign Director Looks at His Profession.*" Survey, 61: 818-819, 1929.
Matson, Carlton K., "*The Resources of the Average Community for Publicity.*" Nat. Confer. Soc. Work, 1920: 439-443.
Pettit, Walter W., *Case Studies in Community Organization.* New York: Century Co., 1928.
"*Publicity Awards.*" Survey, 61: 778, 1929.

*Queen, Stuart A., *"Non-statistical Studies of Social Work."* Nat. Confer. Soc. Work, 1927: 459-466.

*Routzahn, Mrs. M. S., and Routzahn, E. G., *Publicity for Social Work,* New York: Russell Sage Foundation, 1929.

Routzahn, Evart G., and Routzahn, Mary Swain, *The A B C of Exhibit Planning.* New York: Russell Sage Foundation, 1919.

*Stillman, Charles C., *Social Work Publicity; Its Message and Its Method.* New York: Century Co., 1927.

Street, Elwood, *"Starting from Scratch."* Survey, 62: 147-149, 1929.

Walker, Sydnor H., *Social Work and the Training of Social Workers,* Chapel Hill: University of North Carolina Press, 1928.

White, R. Clyde, *"Integrity in Social Work Publicity: A Platform of Facts and a Platform of Ethics."* Nat. Confer. Soc. Work, 1928: 596-608.

## CHAPTER XXXI.

### Coordination and Supervision.

*Better Times* (weekly magazine; see especially May 12, 1924).

Bowman, Leroy E., *"The Development of Coordination in Neighborhood Organization in New York City."* Nat. Conf. Soc. Work, 1924: 401-405.

Bowman, Leroy E., *"Tangible Results of Coordination of Health and Family Welfare Work in a Defined City Area."* Jour. of Social Forces, 4: 339-345, 1925.

*Breckinridge, Sophonisba P., *Public Welfare Administration in the United States,* Chicago: University of Chicago. Press, 1927.

Burke, W. W., *Administration of Private Social Service Agencies,* A Topical Bibliography, Chicago: University of Chicago Press, 1927.

Clow, Lucia, and Halverson, Jeanette, *"An Experimental Policy on Intake Between a Family and a Children's Agency."* Family, 7: 241-243, 1926.

Curry, H. Ida, *Public Child-Caring Work in Certain Counties of Minnesota, North Carolina, and New York.* U. S. Children's Bureau, Pub. No. 173, 1927.

Devine, Edward T., *"Central Councils of Social Agencies."* Survey, 47: 624, 626, 724, 726, 1922.

Emerson, Haven, *"The Community's General Staff."* Survey, 53: 444-445, 1925.

Halbert, L. A., *"Boards of Public Welfare."* Nat. Conf. Social Work, 1918: 220-229.

Hall, Bessie F., *"The Social Service Exchange."* Nat. Conf. Social Work, 1925: 509-515.

Kaplan, Hyman, *"Federating from the Bottom Up."* Survey, 51: 681-685, 1924.

*Kelso, Robert W., *The Science of Public Welfare,* New York: Holt, 1928.

*Lee, Porter R., Pettit, Walter W., and Hoey, Jane M., *Interrelations of the Work of National Social Agencies in Fourteen Communities,* New York: Nat. Inf. Bur., 1923.

Lundberg, Emma O., *The County as a Unit for Organizing a Program of Child-Caring and Protective Work,* U. S. Children's Bureau, Pub. No. 169, 1926.

McClenahan, Bessie A., *"County Organization of Welfare Agencies."* Nat. Conf. Social Work, 1918: 595-604.

*McLean, Francis H., *The Central Council of Social Agencies,* New York: Amer. Assn. Org. Family Social Work, 1921.

National Conference of Social Work. *Proceedings,* Divisions VIII and IX (annual).

*Norton, William J., *The Cooperative Movement in Social Work.* New York: Macmillan, 1927.

Odum, Howard W., and Willard, D. W., *Systems of Public Welfare.* Chapel Hill: University of North Carolina Press, 1925.

Queen, Stuart A., *Social Work in the Light of History,* Chap. 2, Philadelphia: Lippincott, 1922.

*Steiner, Jesse F., *Community Organization.* New York: Century, 1925.

Waldman, Morris D., *"New Issues in Federation."* Nat. Conf. Jewish Social Service, 1925: 210-222.

Wallerstein, Helen C., *The Functional Relations of Fifteen Case Working Agencies.* Philadelphia: Seybert Institution, 1919.

Watson, Frank D., *The Charity Organization Movement in the United States.* New York: Macmillan, 1922.

## CHAPTER XXXII.

### Financing Social Work.

American Association for Organizing Charity, *Financial Federations.* New York: Russell Sage Foundation, 1917.

Association of Community Chests and Councils (formerly American Association for Community Organization) *Bulletins.*

Boston Chamber of Commerce, *Final Report of the Special Committee on Financing of Social Agencies.* Boston, 1925.

Brandt, Lilian, *How Much Shall I Give?* New York: Frontier Press, 1921.

Burke, W. W., *Administration of Private Social Service Agencies,* Chicago: University of Chicago Press, 1927.

Clapp, Raymond, *Study of Volumes and Cost of Social Work, 1924,* mimeographed, Cleveland: Welfare Federation, 1926.

Cooper, Charles C., *Settlement Finance,* Boston: Nat. Fed. Settlements, 1923.

*Devine, Edward T., *"Welfare Federations."* Survey, 46: 203-5, 269-271, 401-3, 493-6, 1921.

Douglas, Paul and Dorothy, *"What Can a Man Afford?"* Amer. Econ. Rev., Dec. 1921, Supplement pp. 1-95.

*Financing of Social Agencies,* Chicago: Council of Social Agencies, 1924.
Geary, Blanch, *Association Finance,* New York: Nat. Bd. Y.W.C.A., 1915.
Goldsmith, Samuel A., *"Jewish Federations and Community Chests."* Survey, 54: 629-631, 1925.
Hart, Hastings H., *"Endowments, How to Leave Wisely $25,000 to $1,000,000."* Nat. Conf. Soc. Work, 1921: 420-427.
*King, W. I., *Trends in Philanthropy.* New York: Nat. Bur. Econ. Res., 1928.
*Lee, Joseph, *The Chest and Social Work."* Survey, 59: 749-750, 1928.
Moley, Raymond, *"The Community Trust."* Nat. Conf. Soc. Work, 1921: 427-432.
National Conference of Social Work. *Proceedings,* Division VIII (annual).
North, C. C., *"The Community Fund and the Community."* Jour. of Social Forces, 7: 90-97, 1928.
*Norton, William J., *The Cooperative Movement in Social Work.* New York: Macmillan, 1927.
Norton, William J., *"The Bill for Benevolence,"* etc. Survey, 51: 183, 374, 507, 685; 52: 86, 1923-24.
Persons W. Frank, *Central Financing of Social Agencies,* Columbus: Advisory Council, 1922.
Proctor, A. W., and Schuck, A. A., *The Financing of Social Work.* Chicago: Shaw, 1926.
Purdy, Lawson, *"How Much Social Work Can a Community Afford?"* Nat. Conf. Soc. Work, 1926: 100-107.
Street, Elwood, *Sympathy and System in Giving.* Chicago: McClurg, 1921.
Swift, Linton B., *"The Chest and the Family Society."* Family, 6: 119-124, 1925.
Walker, Sydnor H., *Social Work and the Training of Social Workers,* Chap. 3. Chapel Hill: University of North Carolina Press, 1928.
*"What Happened at Columbus?"* Survey, 56: 261-263, 1926.

## CHAPTER XXXIII.

### Social Work as a Profession.

American Association of Social Workers.
*The Compass* (monthly).
*Vocational Pamphlets.*
*Studies in the Practise of Social Work.*
Cannon, M. Antoinette, *"Underlying Principles and Common Practises in Social Work."* Nat. Conf. Soc. Work, 1928: 564-569.
Cheyney, Alice S., *The Nature and Scope of Social Work,* New York: Amer. Assn. Social Workers, 1926.
Eldridge, Seba, *The New Citizenship.* New York: Crowell, 1928. Chap. VI.

Eubank, Earle E., *"The Schools of Social Work in the United States and Canada."* Soc. Serv. Rev., 2: 263-273, 1928.

Halbert, L. A., *What Is Professional Social Work?* New York: Survey, 1923.

Jarrett, Mary C., *"Present Conditions in Education for Psychiatric Social Work."* Jour. of Social Forces, 6: 221-229, 1927.

Karpf, M. J., *"The Relation between Sociology and Social Work."* Jour. of Soc. Forces, 3: 419-427, 1925.

Kelso, Robert W., *"The Private Practise of Social Work."* Survey, 59: 767-770, 1928.

Macadam, Elizabeth, *The Equipment of the Social Worker.* New York: Holt, 1926.

National Conference of Social Work. *Proceedings,* Division XI (annual).

Odencrantz, Louise C., *The Social Worker,* New York: Harper and Bros., 1929.

O'Grady, John, *Introduction to Social Work.* New York: Century, 1928.

*Queen, Stuart A., *Social Work in the Light of History.* Chap. 1, Philadelphia: Lippincott, 1922.

Steiner, Jesse F., *Training for Social Work.* Chicago: University of Chicago Press, 1921.

Taft, Jessie, *"The Relation of Psychiatry to Social Work."* Family, 7:199-203, 1926.

*Tufts, James H., *Education and Training for Social Work.* New York: Russell Sage Foundation, 1923.

*Walker, Sydnor H., *Social Work and the Training of Social Workers,* Chapel Hill: University of North Carolina Press, 1928.

# INDEX OF SUBJECTS

W

# INDEX OF NAMES

# INDEX OF CASES

Brent House -
Dinner -
Sunday -
Scoh Hing -
Katherine -